Los Angeles

timeout.com/losangeles

Penguin Books

PENGUIN BOOKS

Published by the Penguin Group
Penguin Books Ltd, 27 Wrights Lane, London W8 5TZ, England
Penguin Books USA Inc., 375 Hudson Street, New York, New York 10014, USA
Penguin Books Australia Ltd, Ringwood, Victoria, Australia
Penguin Books Canada Ltd, 10 Alcorn Avenue, Toronto, Ontario, Canada M4V 3B2
Penguin Books (NZ) Ltd, 182-190 Wairau Road, Auckland 10, New Zealand

Penguin Books Ltd, Registered Offices: Harmondsworth, Middlesex, England

First published 1997
Second edition 1999
Third edition 2001
10 9 8 7 6 5 4 3 2 1

Copyright © Time Out Group Ltd, 1997, 1999, 2001
All rights reserved

Colour reprographics by Westside Digital Media, 9 Bridle Lane, London W1
and Precise Litho, 34-35 Great Sutton Street, London EC1
Printed and bound by Cayfosa-Quebecor, Ctra. de Caldes, Km 3 08 130 Sta, Perpètua de Mogoda, Barcelona, Spain

Edited and designed by
Time Out Guides Limited
Universal House
251 Tottenham Court Road
London W1T 7AB
Tel + 44 (0) 20 7813 3000
Fax + 44 (0) 20 7813 6001
Email guides@timeout.com
www.timeout.com

Editorial

Editor Cath Phillips
Consultant Editor Frances Anderton
Deputy Editor Ros Sales
Listings Editors Matthew Duersten, Linda Keels, Anne Kellogg, Liz Tarshis
Proofreader Marion Moisy
Indexer Julie Hurrell

Editorial Director Peter Fiennes
Series Editor Ruth Jarvis
Deputy Series Editor Jonathan Cox
Editorial Assistant Jenny Noden

Design

Art Director John Oakey
Art Editor Mandy Martin
Senior Designer Scott Moore
Designers Benjamin de Lotz, Lucy Grant
Scanning/Imaging Dan Conway
Picture Editor Kerri Miles
Deputy Picture Editor Olivia Duncan-Jones
Picture Admin Kit Burnet
Ad Make-up Glen Impey

Advertising

Group Advertisement Director Lesley Gill
Sales Director Mark Phillips
Advertisement Director, North American Guides
Liz Howell (1-808 732 4661/US only 1-888 333 5776)
Advertising in the US co-ordinated by Time Out New York
Alison Tocci (Publisher), Tom Oseau (Advertising Production Manager), Claudia Pedala (Assistant to the Publisher)

Administration

Publisher Tony Elliott
Managing Director Mike Hardwick
Financial Director Kevin Ellis
Marketing Director Christine Cort
General Manager Nichola Coulthard
Production Manager Mark Lamond
Production Controller Samantha Furniss
Accountant Sarah Bostock

This guide was written by:

History Bill Fulton. **LA Today** Mick Farren (*Let's get spiritual* Frances Anderton). **Geography & Climate** Bill Fulton. **Celebrity LA** Peter Whittle. **Car City** Frances Anderton. **Architecture** Frances Anderton. **Ethnic LA** Frances Anderton. **Accommodation** Katy Harris. **Sightseeing** Frances Anderton (Introduction, Westside: Beach Towns, East LA), Michael Datcher (South Central), Jade Chang (The Valleys), Matthew Duersten (*Street talk, Guided tours*), Dan Epstein (Westside: Inland, Downtown, Hollywood & Midtown), Peter Frank (Museums, *The Watts Towers*), Helen Franks (East of Hollywood), Vince Kowalick (*Life's a beach*), Stephen Lynch (Heading South). **Restaurants** Katy Harris. **Coffeehouses** Dee McLaughlin. **Bars** Dan Epstein. **Shops & Services** Matthew Duersten, Katy Harris (Food & drink, Health & beauty, *Global snacking, Spas & masseurs*), Coralie Langston-Jones (Fashion, *Local talent*). **By Season** Matthew Duersten. **Children** Diana Rieseman. **Film** Peter Whittle. **Galleries** Peter Frank. **Gay & Lesbian** Peter Whittle (Gay), JC Swiatek (Lesbian). **Music** Dan Epstein. **Nightlife** Dee McLaughlin. **Sport & Fitness** Vince Kowalick, Helen Franks (Cycling and mountain biking). **Theatre & Dance** Dee McLaughlin. **Trips Out of Town** Frances Anderton, Andy Bender, Katy Harris (*Palm Springs*). **Directory** Matthew Duersten, Dan Epstein (Media). **Further Reference** Matthew Duersten, Cath Phillips, Ros Sales.

The Editor would like to thank:

William Karpiak and the staff of Ramada West Hollywood, Alicia Amerson of the LACVB, Judy Gibbons of Alamo, Gary Wosk of the MTA and Lesley McCave. Special thanks to the extra listings checkers who helped out at the last minute, Amanda Edwards and Mike Harrison.

Maps by: JS Graphics 17 Beadles Lane, Old Oxted, Surrey RH8 9JG.

Photography by Amanda Edwards except: page 6, 10, 11, 12, 22 Corbis; page 9 AKG; page 20 Associated Press; page 24 AFP/PA; page 26 All Action; page 108, 205, 261, 268, 269 Cath Phillips; page 253 Allsport; page 258 Joan Marcus; page 263 Thomas Wiewandt/Telegraph Colour Library.
The following photographs were supplied by the featured establishments: pages 62, 119 and 240.

Car rental supplied by Alamo (reservations: UK 0990 994000, US 1-800 327 9633).

Contents

Introduction

'LA's the place where the hard-core is happening' was a rap anthem of the early 1990s, when riots, fires, floods, earthquakes and gang fights were tearing the city apart. Now the city may have other concerns, but the LA homeboy's words still ring true. At the start of 21st century, it is a world leader in immigration and urban expansion, in extreme wealth and extreme poverty, in obsessive dieting, exercise and plastic surgery, in passionate creativity and police corruption and religion. It's a place that's still young enough and energetic enough to do things 200 per cent. Even if, in reality, there are fewer mobile phones than in Helsinki and the subway doesn't provide a comprehensive service, LA feels like the city where the next – hard-core – thing is always happening.

But you may not sense that on arriving in the sprawling megalopolis basking between mountains and ocean, with gently swishing palm trees and a speed limit of 65mph (97kph) on the freeways. Because LA's a place that does not reveal its secrets instantly. Go exploring, and you will meet a city of multiple identities, of clashing and fusing cultures that are constantly in flux: Anglo, Latino, Jewish, gay, super-rich, Third World, black, Mexican, Asian.

See bohemian Venice by the beach; exclusive, lush Beverly Hills; hilly and hip West Hollywood, Silver Lake and Los Feliz; the suburban, scorching Valley; poor, defiant Watts and East LA; and gritty Downtown. Find the expected – theme parks, malls, movies and junk food – as well as the unexpected – the Getty Center, a superlative orchestra, countless bookshops, offbeat artists and charming farmers markets. Embrace a place that is at once as fake as the films it produces and full of its own strident character.

Los Angeles may be sunny but it is not the tropics; it emerged from semi-arid desert, and that desert gives the city a nip in the air at night and a dry edge during the day. An edge that fuels the ambition that brings people here to pursue their dreams, an edge that can turn into extreme behaviour, even aggression, by both man and nature. LA's the place – hard-core but happening. Enjoy.

Frances Anderton

ABOUT TIME OUT CITY GUIDES

This is the third edition of the *Time Out Los Angeles Guide*, one in an ever-expanding series of city guides, now numbering over 30, produced by the people behind London and New York's successful listings magazines. All the contributors to the guide are resident in Los Angeles and specialists in the subjects on which they have written.

THE LOWDOWN ON THE LISTINGS

Above all, we've tried to make this book as useful as possible. Addresses, phone numbers, websites, transport information, opening times, admission times and credit card details are all included in our listings. We've also included zip codes for hotels and other organisations that you might want to write to. As much as possible, we have also given details of facilities, services and events. Many of our chapters are subdivided into areas, so your choice of restaurant, for example, doesn't have to be a schlep away from where you are.

We've provided detailed driving directions, giving not only the address and cross street for places listed but instructions on how to reach them from the most convenient freeway or major road. (The exit given might not be the nearest, but it should be straightforward.)

All listings information and other factual details have been thoroughly checked during production of the guide. However, owners and managers can change their arrangements at any time and we strongly advise you to phone ahead to check opening times and the like. While every effort and care has been made to ensure the accuracy of the information contained in this guide, the publishers cannot accept responsibility for any errors it may contain.

CREDIT CARDS AND PRICES

The following abbreviations have been used for credit cards: American Express (AmEx); Diners' Club (DC); Discover (Disc); Mastercard (MC); and Visa (V). Virtually all shops, hotels, restaurants and attractions will accept dollar travellers' cheques issued by a major financial

There is an online version of this guide, as well as weekly event listings for over 30 international cities, at **www.timeout.com**.

institution (such as American Express). In all cases, the prices we've supplied should be treated as guidelines, not gospel. Fluctuating exchange rates and inflation can cause prices to change rapidly, particularly in shops and restaurants. Note that prices marked in shops do not include sales tax, currently 8.25 per cent in LA County. If prices vary wildly from those we've quoted, ask whether there's a good reason. If not, go elsewhere. Then please write and let us know. We aim to give the best and most up-to-date advice, so we want to know if you've been badly treated or overcharged.

TELEPHONE NUMBERS
All phone numbers in the guide are prefaced by a 1 and an area code; for example 1-310 923 1361. If you are dialling from within that area, you can drop the 1 and the area code. However, if you're calling from abroad, you still need to add a 1 before the area code: it's the code for the USA. You can dial most (but not all) 1-800 numbers from the UK, but they are not toll-free: you must pay for the call at the usual transatlantic rate.

ESSENTIAL INFORMATION
For all the practical information you might need for visiting LA – including emergency phone numbers, websites, advice on disabled facilities and access, information on the local transport system and driving, tipping and the weather, plus the location of tourist information offices – turn to the Directory chapter at the back of the guide. It starts on page 278.

MAPS
The map section at the back of the guide – starting on page 302 – includes maps to the central areas of the city most frequented by visitors, an overview map of the Los Angeles region, a map of the Metro rail system and a map relating to the Trips Out of Town chapter, plus a comprehensive street index. Map references in the listings indicate the page and square on which a central Los Angeles address will be found.

LET US KNOW WHAT YOU THINK
We hope you enjoy using the *Time Out Los Angeles Guide* as much as we enjoyed putting it together, and we'd like to know what you think of it. We welcome tips for places to include in future editions and take notice of your criticism of our choices. There's a reader's reply card for your comments at the back of the book; or alternatively, if you prefer, you can email us on losangelesguide@timeout.com.

Welcome to New York.

Now get out.

The obsessive guide to impulsive entertainment

On sale at newsstands in New York
Pick up a copy!

To get a copy of the current issue or to subscribe, call *Time Out New York* at 212-539-4444.

In Context

Hollywood Boulevard in the 1930s.

History

A city built on real-estate speculation, LA has survived boom and bust, earthquakes, scandals and riots to emerge as the mega-metropolis of today.

PRE-1888: MISSIONS AND COW TOWNS

Perhaps it shouldn't be surprising, given Los Angeles's more recent history, that human settlement here began with a series of Native American single-family suburbs scattered across the landscape in seemingly haphazard fashion. Prior to the arrival of Spanish colonists in the latter part of the 18th century, what is now metropolitan LA was populated by some 30,000 Native Americans. But they were not farmers – they relied on hunting and native plants for food – and, unlike the Iroquois and other tribes in North America, they had not organised into strong political confederations. Instead, they lived in small settlements surrounding the area's few rivers, each group adopting a separate identity (the names most of them are known by today – Gabrieleno, Juaneno, Luisenos and so on – were given to them by the Spanish).

The Spanish arrived in 1769 and established a string of Franciscan missions along the Californian coast (the first at San Diego), backed by military muscle. The San Gabriel mission was founded in 1771, marking the first Spanish foray into the Los Angeles area. The supposed purpose of the missions was to spread the Christian faith and the early Franciscan missionaries, especially their leader Father Junipéro Serra, have been glorified over the centuries. In fact, mission life was feudal and even brutal, especially for the reluctant Native American converts. They were rounded up from their small settlements and virtually enslaved by the Franciscans, and thousands died – a problem that forced the missions to expand deep into the countryside in search of more converts.

The history of Los Angeles as a city dates back to 1781 – the same year that the British surrendered to George Washington in Virginia, ending the American War of Independence – when the Spaniards decided they needed a settlement, or pueblo, in Southern California to serve as a way-station for the military. A site was selected nine miles (14 kilometres) east of the San Gabriel mission, where the Los Angeles River widened from a narrows. California's military governor, Felipe De Neve, laid out a plaza 275 by 180 feet (84 by 55 metres), with lots around it, each with a 55-foot (17-metre) wide frontage on the plaza. He commissioned his aides to recruit 24 settlers and their families from Sonora, over 300 miles (480 kilometres) away, and on 18 August 1781, after a forced march of 100 days through desert heat, what remained of this group arrived at the plaza: 12 men, 11 women and 21 children. They were immediately quarantined because of smallpox. What is left of the plaza can be viewed at El Pueblo de Los Angeles Historical Monument (more commonly known as Olvera Street), a 44-acre (18-hectare) historical area in Downtown LA, bounded by Alameda, Arcadia, Spring and Macy Streets. As many writers have observed, El Pueblo de Nuestra Señora la Reina de Los Angeles began as it has always grown – not with a hardy band of motivated settlers, but with a real estate agent looking for customers.

The new settlement remained a dusty cow town for decades – in 1800 the population was 315 people and 12,500 cows. But other missions were added in what would become the Los Angeles area, including San Buenaventura, San Fernando and San Juan Capistrano.

After Mexico declared itself independent and annexed California in 1822, Spanish-born priests were ordered out of California, the mission system broke down and powerful local families – eager to exploit mission land – received dozens of large land grants from the Mexican government. Most of these 'ranchos', typically several thousand acres in size, were recognised as valid claims of title when California entered the United States in 1850. Many remained intact into the 20th century – one of many factors that allowed large-scale, mass-production land development to occur in Los Angeles.

The Americans had been informally colonising LA throughout the era of Mexican rule, as opportunists arrived in town, married into prominent 'Spanish' families, and called themselves 'Don Otto' or 'Don Bill'. The actual transfer of the cow town into US hands occurred during the forcible annexation of California that triggered the Mexican-American war of June 1846. Two months later, on 13 August, Commodore RF Stockton landed at San Pedro with 500 marines and started his march to the pueblo. With political support from the 'Dons', he captured the settlement

without firing a shot. The US-Mexican treaty of 1848 confirmed US dominion over California and on 9 September 1850, it officially became the 31st state of the Union. (Its entry as a 'free' state – as opposed to a 'slave' state – was one of the precursor events to the American Civil War.)

Los Angeles grew steadily but unspectacularly for the next 20 years, becoming a centre of California's 'hide and tallow' trade – raising cattle and selling the hides for coats and the fat for candle tallow to trading companies from the East Coast and Europe. California's first literary masterpiece, Richard Henry Dana's *Two Years Before the Mast*, features memorable scenes of Dana himself trudging through the shallow water of San Pedro harbour with cowhides on his back. When the Gold Rush hit Northern California, however, the cattle barons of Los Angeles discovered they could sell the cows for beef at $30 a head to the goldfields, rather than $3 a head to the traders. The 1872 publication of Helen Hunt Jackson's novel *Ramona*, which romanticised rancho life at the expense of historical accuracy, sparked a period of national publicity and interest in Southern California.

In 1886, the transcontinental railroad from St Louis to LA was completed, bringing with it the long-expected – but short-lived – boom. A price war broke out among the railroads, and the cost of a one-way ticket to LA dropped from $125 to $1. In 1887, Southern Pacific Railroad transported 120,000 people to Los Angeles, then a city of about 10,000 residents. The result was LA's first real-estate boom, with more than 100 communities subdivided in a four-year period.

Paper fortunes were made overnight – and then lost when the boom shrivelled in 1889. 'I had half a million dollars wiped out in the crash,' one fictional character reported in a novel. 'And what's worse, $500 of it was cash.' The population had grown dramatically, in part because many immigrants could not afford to leave. But, despite the crash, the boom of the 1880s had permanently transformed Los Angeles from a cow town into a fast-growing hustlers' paradise.

1888-1929: BOOMS AND BUSTS

After the boom of the 1880s, the land barons and real-estate operators who came to dominate Los Angeles's growth were determined to build a more solid basis for expansion. Forming the Los Angeles Chamber of Commerce in 1888, they took the unprecedented step of embarking on a nationwide campaign, focused on the Midwest, to attract new immigrants. It was this campaign that led the journalist Morrow Mayo, writing in the 1930s, to conclude that Los Angeles was not a city but 'a commodity;

something to be advertised and sold to the people of the United States like automobiles, cigarettes and mouth washes'.

The Chamber of Commerce began sending speakers, advertisements and brochures to the Midwest; 1902 saw the launch of the Rose Bowl (a college football game held on New Year's Day) and the preceding Rose Parade (in which flower-covered floats parade through Pasadena), as a promotion for LA's sunny climate. It was not long before the advertisements had the desired effect and, as commodity prices rose in the first decade of the new century, thousands of Midwestern farmers sold out and a new boom ensued.

Encouraged by the boom, the city's land barons pulled off one of the most audacious and duplicitous schemes ever devised to ensure a city's future greatness. In 1904, a former mayor of Los Angeles named Fred Eaton went to the Owens Valley – a high-desert region 230 miles (370 kilometres) north of Los Angeles – claiming that he was working on a dam project for the federal government, and began buying land along the Owens River. Once the land was purchased, Eaton said the federal project was dead and revealed his true purpose: to divert the Owens River through an aqueduct to LA.

'LA began as it has always grown – not with a hardy band of motivated settlers, but with a real estate agent looking for customers.'

Whipped into a frenzy by trumped-up fears of a drought, LA voters approved a bond issue in 1905 to build an aqueduct from the Owens Valley to the city. LA had enough water to serve the population at the time, but not enough to grow. As William Mulholland, the city's water engineer, put it at the time: 'If we don't get it, we won't need it.' Mulholland, a self-taught Irish immigrant, then accomplished one of the great engineering feats in US history. Eighty years after its completion, his 230-mile (370-kilometre) aqueduct still operates, without electrical power, entirely on a gravity system. 'There it is,' Mulholland told the people of Los Angeles when the floodway opened in 1913. 'Take it.'

The aqueduct didn't come to Los Angeles proper, however. Instead, it went only as far as the San Fernando Valley, an adjacent farming region. In the last – and most masterful – part of the scam, Los Angeles's land barons had secretly bought the valley cheaply, annexed it to the city and then splashed Owens Valley

water on to it for irrigation, greatly increasing its value. Today, the San Fernando Valley, population 1.5 million, is the prototypical US suburb, and its people regularly chafe under the LA City controls that brought water to their valley in the first place. The past few years have seen a renewed attempt by Valley 'secessionists' to break off from Los Angeles and form their own city (*see page 13* **Independence day**).

With the water in place, Los Angeles boomed in the 1910s and 1920s as did no other US city – partly on the strength of real-estate speculation, and partly on the rise of three new industries: petroleum, aircraft and movies.

With little natural wood and almost no coal, isolated Los Angeles had always had a fuel crisis almost as severe as its water crisis. The discovery of oil throughout metropolitan Los Angeles between 1900 and 1925 changed all that. Oil fields were discovered around the La Brea Tar Pits and in Huntington Beach and Santa Fe Springs. The result was a plentiful supply of oil that enriched the region and helped to fuel the city's growing love affair with the car.

More dispersed than any other US city, Los Angeles took to the car more readily than anywhere except Detroit. Soon the city had its own thriving oil, automobile and tyre industries, each with their own monuments. In 1928, Adolph Schleicher, president of Samson Tire & Rubber Co, constructed an $8-million tyre plant modelled after a royal palace once built by the king of Assyria. The plant (at 5675 Telegraph Road, City of Commerce) has recently been reborn as a shopping mecca known as the Citadel.

Movies and aircraft came to LA during the 1910s, and for the same reasons: the area's temperate weather, low rainfall and cheap land provided the wide open spaces that both needed to operate. Donald Douglas founded his aircraft company (a predecessor to McDonnell-Douglas) at Clover Field in Santa Monica – now the Santa Monica Municipal Airport – in 1921, while the Lockheed brothers started their company in Santa Barbara in 1914 before moving it to LA. Jack Northrop, who had worked with both Douglas and the Lockheeds, started his own company in Burbank in 1928. All three firms later formed the foundation of the US's 'military-industrial' complex.

Filming began in Los Angeles around 1910, and moved to Hollywood when the Blondeau Tavern at Gower Street and Sunset Boulevard was turned into a movie studio overnight in 1911. At the time, Hollywood was being marketed as a pious and sedate suburb of large homes, and the intrusion of the film industry was resented. The movie business was never

Olympics fever.

really centred there, however; Culver City and Burbank, which also have studios, have equally strong claims as the capital of film land. Nevertheless, Hollywood became the financial and social centre of the industry, growing from a population of 4,000 in 1910 to 30,000 in 1920 to 235,000 in 1930, and the wealth of the period is still visible today in the magnificent commercial architecture along Hollywood Boulevard between Cahuenga and Highland Avenues. The early movie palaces (some still in operation today) were built not in Hollywood but downtown on Broadway, adjacent to Spring Street.

In the 1920s, when the population of Los Angeles doubled, the city was a kind of 'national suburb' where the middle class sought refuge from the teeming immigrant groups evident in other large cities. During this period, civic leaders worked hard to build the edifices and institutions they thought a big city should have, including the Biltmore Hotel and the adjacent Los Angeles Central Library, Los Angeles City Hall, the University of Southern California and adjacent Exposition Park, and Los Angeles Coliseum. LA also became the financial capital of the West Coast during this decade with the creation of the Los Angeles (now Pacific) Stock Exchange. The 'Wall Street of the West' was centred on Spring Street, between Third and Eighth Streets, where many of the original buildings remain today.

However, this same process of making Los Angeles the great 'white' city marginalised the minority groups that had always been a part of life here. The Mexican and Mexican-American population, which was growing rapidly to provide labourers for the expanding city, was pushed out of Downtown into what is now the East LA barrio. African-Americans, who had previously lived all over the city, became confined to an area south of Downtown straddling Central Avenue, which became known as South Central. Both these developments laid the foundation for later social unrest.

Still, Los Angeles in the 1920s had an irrepressible energy that even its critics loved. The boom and the arrival of so many newcomers created a rootlessness that manifested itself in a thousand different ways, many of which provided the seeds for the city's later kooky reputation. Those in need of companionship were drawn to the city's many cafeterias (invented in LA), which served as incubators of random social activity. Those in need of a restored faith had (and still have) their choice of any number of high-profile faith healers. And those with a little cash searching for a quick profit were drawn to the tantalising claims of local oil companies in search of investors.

Indeed, nothing captures a sense of the primal energy of Los Angeles during the 1920s as well as stories from the oil business. With a steady supply of gushers spouting in the suburbs (often in residential neighbourhoods), oil promoters had a ready-made promotional device with which to attract investors. With a stream of equity-rich farm refugees from the Midwest, they also had a ready-made pool of gullible investors. The promoters took out newspaper ads, held weekend barbecues at the gushers and used other strong-arm tactics to attract investment.

The most skilled oil promoter was a Canadian immigrant named CC Julian, who attracted millions of dollars to his oil company with a string of daily newspaper ads that had the narrative drive of a continuing soap opera. When it became clear that Julian couldn't deliver on his investment promises, he was elbowed out of his own firm by an array of other swindlers who continued the scam and turned it into the longest-running scandal of the 1920s. By the time it was all over, Julian Petroleum had issued millions of bogus shares and the district attorney had been indicted on a bribery charge. The end came in 1931, when a defrauded investor opened fire in a LA courtroom on a banker who had been involved in the scam. The failed investor had ten cents in his pocket when he was arrested; the crooked banker had $63,000 in his pocket when he died. The murder epitomised the disreputable state that Los Angeles was in by the time the 1920s boom ended.

1929-1965: GROWING UP

The 1930s was a more sober period for LA, as elsewhere in the US. With the boom over and the Depression settling in, the city grew more slowly, and the new arrivals were very different from their predecessors. Instead of wooing wealthy Midwestern farmers, LA now attracted poor white refugees from the so-called 'Dust Bowl' of Oklahoma and Texas – the 'Okies' made famous in John Steinbeck's novel *The Grapes of Wrath*. These unskilled workers wound up as farm labourers and hangers-on in the margins of society.

Dealing with these newcomers proved difficult for Los Angeles, and was intertwined with another problem – how to handle the equally poor and unskilled Mexican and Mexican-American population. Since farm owners chose to hire the Okies over the Mexicans, LA County was overwhelmed with the cost of public relief and resorted to forcibly 'repatriating' even those Mexicans who were born and raised in Los Angeles.

Meanwhile, the continued arrival of Okies and other 'hobos' caused a nasty public backlash. But it also built a liberal political mood among the have-nots, which culminated in the near-election of reformer and novelist Upton Sinclair as governor of California in 1934. Having moved to Pasadena in the 1910s, Sinclair wrote a diatribe called *I, Governor of California, and How I Ended Poverty*. As a result, he founded the End Poverty In California (EPIC) movement and won the Democratic gubernatorial nomination. Only a concerted effort by reactionary political forces (aided by movie-house propaganda from the film industry) defeated Sinclair's bid. Afterwards, he wrote another book, this one called *I, Governor of California, and How I Got Licked*.

The region had other problems, such as the 1933 Long Beach earthquake, the first major quake to hit the city since it became populous. But in the mid-1930s, optimism returned, heralded by the 1932 Olympic Games, which were held at the city's Coliseum. To celebrate the games, Tenth Street was expanded, spruced up, renamed Olympic Boulevard and lined with palm trees – thus setting the fashion for palms in LA. In 1939, the first local freeway was built: the Arroyo Seco Parkway, now the Pasadena Freeway. A new aqueduct bringing water from the Hoover Dam along the Colorado River opened in 1941. And then the coming of World War II caused the biggest upheaval Los

The 1942 **Zoot Suit riots** targeted Latinos.

Angeles had seen to that point, and set the stage for the modern metropolis.

Already at the forefront of aviation, LA industrialised rapidly as it became a major military manufacturing centre and staging ground for the United States fight against Japan in the Pacific Ocean. More than 5,000 new manufacturing plants were built in LA during the war, mostly in outlying locations. New dormitory communities sprang up to accommodate the workers. Many were 'model' towns sponsored by industrialists or the military, and they helped to establish the sprawling pattern of city development that came to characterise LA in the post-war period.

Los Angeles's population quickly diversified, laying more groundwork for the racial unrest that would later characterise the city. During the war, more than 200,000 African-Americans moved to the city, mostly from Texas and Louisiana, to take advantage of job opportunities. But the South Central ghetto wasn't allowed to expand geographically to accommodate them, resulting in the creation of an overcrowded district. (In 1948, the Supreme Court threw out restrictive convenants, paving the way for an exodus of middle-class blacks west into the Crenshaw district.) In need of labourers, Los Angeles again welcomed the return of the Mexicans and Mexican-Americans who had been pushed out a decade before. However, a backlash once again ensued.

After a murder at the Sleepy Lagoon swimming hole in East LA in 1942, the authorities arrested more than 300 Latino youths, putting 23 on trial for first-degree murder. Most were minors. In a trial thick with racial epithets, 17 of the defendants were convicted. The convictions were later overturned by an appeal court, but several months later, a mob, including many servicemen, attacked Latinos and others in what became known as the 'Zoot Suit' riots after the baggy suits the men often wore. Thereafter, local newspapers, stoking the fires of prejudice, stopped referring to Latinos as Mexicans and, instead, called them 'zoot suits' or pachucos.

Discrimination against LA's growing Japanese community was even more pronounced. Most Japanese-Americans on the West Coast were interned in camps by the federal government during World War II, no matter how patriotic they were (in a supreme irony, some young men were permitted to leave the internment camps to join the US armed forces; those able to make this transition did so enthusiastically). Most Japanese lost their property, then concentrated in the Little Tokyo area of LA just east of City Hall. It took decades for Little Tokyo to return to prosperity, but an infusion of Japanese capital in the 1970s and 1980s has now created a thriving district.

Many African-Americans, Latinos and Japanese from LA fought for the United States during World War II. When they returned to suffer continued housing discrimination, police brutality and the general LA attitude that they were not 'real Americans', their sense of alienation grew further. But, because Los Angeles was a highly segregated city, most whites could ignore the race problem – especially after the war, when the city reaped the benefits of industrialisation and a new suburban boom began.

The post-war era in LA is often recalled as an idyllic period of prosperity and harmony. In fact, it was an unsettled period in which the city struggled to keep up with the demands of massive growth. Taxes rose in order to build new facilities and heavily oversubscribed schools went on 'double-sessions', teaching two classes in the same classroom at different times of the day.

Most of all, the entire LA region devoted itself to building things. Freeway construction, which had been stymied by the war, exploded in 1947 when California imposed an additional petrol tax to pay for it. Virtually the entire freeway system – truly a marvel of modern

engineering – was built between 1950 and 1970. Perhaps its most important long-term effect was to open up vast tracts in outlying areas for urban development, especially in the San Fernando Valley and Orange County, which was linked to Los Angeles by the I-5 (Golden State Freeway). A seminal event in this suburbanisation was the opening, in 1955, of Disneyland. It was the first theme park ever built and helped to popularise Orange County.

Other leisure attractions also helped to establish LA as a major city during this period. In 1958, the city achieved 'major league' status by luring New York's Brooklyn Dodgers baseball team. But, as has so often been the case in LA's history, even this event was marred by the tense relationship between the races. To obtain the team, the city gave the Dodgers a spectacular site in Chavez Ravine, overlooking downtown Los Angeles. Located in a low-income Latino neighbourhood, the site had been earmarked for use as a public housing project, which was never built. However, Dodger Stadium remains one of the finest sports facilities in the US.

As suburbanisation continued in the 1950s and 1960s, more and more neglected areas were left behind as LA prospered. On a hot summer night in 1965, the pent-up frustrations of the black ghetto exploded into one of the first and most destructive of the US's urban riots. The Watts riots began when an African-American man was

The aftermath of the 1965 **Watts riots**.

Popular mayor **Tom Bradley** helped heal LA's racial wounds.

pulled over on a drink-driving charge; by the time they were over, dozens of people had been killed and hundreds of buildings had been destroyed. For many Angelenos living in their comfortable suburbs, the Watts riots were the first indication that all was not well in their metropolis.

1965-2000: THE MEGA-METROPOLIS

After the Watts riots, Los Angeles began to suffer from an image problem for the first time, and the city struggled with it for the better part of a decade. National newspapers and magazines proclaimed the end of the California Dream. The Los Angeles Police Department, under a series of hard-line chiefs, continued to treat minority neighbourhoods as if they were occupied territory. As in other US cities, the breakdown of African-American families left black teenagers with few male role models, and they began to form gangs.

In 1966, LA actor Ronald Reagan, with no previous experience in politics, was elected state governor on a law-and-order platform. Three years later, the Charles Manson cult killed actress Sharon Tate and others at a home in Benedict Canyon, disturbing the sense of tranquillity even in that high-end Beverly Hills suburb. In 1971, the city suffered its worst earthquake in 38 years. It escaped a high death toll only because the quake struck at 6am.

Out of this troubled situation, however, emerged a towering political figure capable of healing the city. Tom Bradley was an African-American police captain who had grown up in the segregated world of Central Avenue and later held his own in such white-dominated enclaves as UCLA and the LAPD. In the 1950s, Bradley was assigned to improve relations with beleaguered Jewish shopkeepers in black neighbourhoods, a task he used to create the foundation for a cross-racial political alliance that sustained him for 30 years.

After retiring from the police force, Bradley was elected to the City Council and, with strong support in South Central and the largely Jewish Westside, ran for mayor. He lost in 1969 but ran again in 1973 and won, becoming the first African-American mayor of a predominantly white city (according to the 1990 census, the black population of the City of LA is only 13 per cent and that of LA County even less, 10.5 per cent). By moving into the mayor's mansion, he helped to desegregate the Hancock Park neighbourhood, which had violently resisted the arrival of Nat 'King' Cole some years before.

A low-key man with a calming personality, Bradley successfully ruled the city for 20 years through the power of persuasion. During the 1970s, he sought to heal racial wounds, while in the early 1980s, he turned his attention to business development, reviving Downtown and courting international business; the 1984 Olympics were his greatest triumph. Bradley's efforts also benefited from a huge flow of Japanese capital into Los Angeles real estate in the 1980s. He died in 1998.

However, this period proved to be a mere respite from LA's chronic social and racial tensions. The area became more polarised in the 1970s, as affluent whites grew more conservative and found little in common with the immigrants who were turning LA into the new US melting pot. Los Angeles had traditionally drawn its immigrants from the rest of the US. From the 1960s, however, most of its newcomers came from abroad.

The decline of agriculture in Latin America made LA a magnet for immigrants – legal and

Independence day

Los Angeles has always been a reluctant metropolis, its suburban residents clearly ambivalent about being part of one of the world's great cities. So it's not surprising that LA, already divided into almost 90 separate jurisdictions, may soon divide itself once again by splitting off the San Fernando Valley into a separate city.

The greater LA region contains 16 million residents, but only four million of them live in the City of Los Angeles. Still, that's far too many for some people, especially for the white, middle-class political leaders of the Valley. Forcibly brought into the city more than 80 years ago because of its water supply, the Valley has agitated since the 1970s to get out again. Residents claim that their schools and police services suffer and that their taxes go 'over the hill' to Los Angeles, and are not seen again. And as the demographics of the older parts of LA have changed, the momentum for separation has increased.

Soon the Valley may get its chance. Perhaps as early as 2002, Los Angeles City residents will get to vote on the question of whether to split into two – one part consisting of the San Fernando Valley (population approximately 1.5 million) and the other

consisting of the remainder of Los Angeles (population approximately 2.5 million). If the vote is in favour, Los Angeles will become the first great city in world history to carve itself into smaller pieces. The consequences of such a change would be considerable. The new Valley city would contain most of the existing city's white population, while the rump City of LA would be the most overwhelmingly Latino city in the US.

LA's political leaders have sought to forestall Valley secession by adopting a new city charter that gives neighbourhoods more power. But even if secession passes, it may take years before the new city comes into being, as the terms of the 'municipal divorce' would be extremely complicated. Police officers, water systems and the city's airports and harbours would have to be separated with care – and probably with lots of litigation. Furthermore, even if the Valley were to become a separate city, secession advocates could find themselves with a hollow victory. Like the rest of LA, the Valley is becoming more diverse, and there's a good chance that a San Fernando city would soon be mostly Latino – and with a high percentage of poor residents.

illegal – from rural Mexico and elsewhere, while political strife in Central America also brought in hundreds of thousands. The city's position on the edge of the burgeoning Pacific Rim also attracted people (and capital) from Korea, the Philippines, Taiwan and Hong Kong.

The vast central areas of Los Angeles were re-energised by these newcomers. Tourism, trade and the garment industry boomed, as did the rapidly expanding Koreatown. But, as the neighbourhoods changed, friction grew. Latin American immigrants began crowding into historically black South Central, creating a culture clash with middle- and working-class homeowners. African-Americans, in particular, felt more alienated than ever.

These tensions, fuelled by a declining economy shattered by defence cutbacks at the end of the Cold War, turned Los Angeles into a social tinder-box at the beginning of the 1990s. The arrest and beating of black motorist Rodney King by four LAPD officers in 1991 (captured on tape by a home-video enthusiast) proved to be the turning point. When a jury acquitted the officers of assault in 1992, it touched off a riot far more widespread and

destructive than the Watts riots of 1965. It lasted three days, during which 50 people died and over 1,000 buildings were destroyed by fire and looting. More than 1,000 people were arrested, more of them Latino than black. It was the worst urban riot in US history.

Then, in 1995, the arrest and trial of football and TV star OJ Simpson gripped the city as it did the nation. Simpson, an African-American divorced from a white woman, was accused of killing his ex-wife and another man; his acquittal stunned white residents and reassured black residents that the legal system could be on their side, but did not lead to more violence.

Yet despite racial tensions, an economic renaissance beginning in the mid 1990s has brought new life to Los Angeles. As the aerospace industry declined, the entertainment industry expanded rapidly. Asian immigrants are helping with the current economic recovery. And, in 1997, house prices started to skyrocket again, just as they did in the 1970s and 1980s.

Meanwhile, the Latino community has grown dramatically. Latinos are now the dominant racial group in LA County, and are starting to gain representation in the political and business leadership. Many older shopping areas have been revived with Latino commerce, including Broadway in Downtown LA and Pacific Boulevard in Huntington Park. During the 1998 World Cup, Anglo LA paid little attention, but near-riots rocked Pacific Boulevard in celebration of Mexico's performance.

Most recently, the city's changing demographics have begun to shape its political character. Beginning with the mayoral election of 1997, Latinos began to vote in large numbers and became the pivotal voting group in the city. (Ironically, given the assumption that Latinos are liberal, they cast their votes overwhelmingly for Republican Mayor Richard Riordan.) In 1998, LA's Antonio Villaragoisa became California's first Latino assembly speaker in more than a century, and promptly used the position as a launching pad for a serious run at the mayor's seat in 2001.

As LA reached the millennium, it continued to face the political tumult typical of a big American city. In 2000 alone, for example, the city was confronted with a new police scandal featuring corrupt officers engaged in drug-trafficking, major protests on Downtown streets outside the Democratic National Convention, and the city's seventh bus strike in 28 years. All of which suggests that, as LA ponders the 21st century, it faces the challenge of casting aside its history as the national suburb once and for all, and finding ways to harness its multicultural strength to retain its position as one of the world's great cities.

▶ For more on the history of the **film industry**, see chapter **Film**.
▶ For information on visiting California's **Spanish missions**, see chapter **Trips**.

Key events

1771 Spanish mission established at San Gabriel.
1781 Pueblo of Los Angeles founded on present site of Olvera Street Plaza.
1822 Mexico declares independence from Spain and annexes California, freeing Los Angeles from Spanish rule.
1846 US marines land at San Pedro and take Los Angeles pueblo from the Mexican army without a fight.
1848 US-Mexican treaty confirms the dominion of the US over California.
1850 California becomes the 31st state of the Union.
1851 California recognises most large Spanish land grants in the Los Angeles area.
1868 Transcontinental railroad reaches San Franciso, opening up California to the East.
1886 Transcontinental railroad reaches Los Angeles.
1888 City experiences first real-estate boom. Chamber of Commerce is set up and begins promoting LA in the Midwest.
1889 City experiences first real-estate bust.
1902 Rose Parade is founded.
1905 Los Angeles announces plans to build aqueduct from Owens Valley.
1913 Owens Valley aqueduct opens.
1917 US enters World War I.
1923 Biltmore Hotel opens in Downtown LA.
1929 Stock market crash; Depression begins.
1932 Los Angeles hosts the Olympics for the first time.
1933 Long Beach earthquake.

1937 Auto Club of Southern California proposes freeway system.
1939 The Arroyo Seco Parkway (Pasadena Freeway) opens.
1941 US enters World War II.
1943 Zoot Suit riots.
1955 Disneyland opens in Anaheim.
1958 Brooklyn Dodgers baseball team moves to Los Angeles.
1965 Watts riots erupt.
1966 Ronald Reagan elected governor of California.
1969 Charles Manson and his followers murder Sharon Tate.
1971 Sylmar earthquake hits.
1973 Tom Bradley is elected mayor of Los Angeles.
1984 Los Angeles hosts the Olympics for the second time.
1990 Los Angeles is hit by cutbacks in the defence budget.
1991 Rodney King arrested.
1992 King verdict sparks widespread rioting.
1994 Northridge earthquake hits.
1995 OJ Simpson is acquitted of murdering his ex-wife.
1998 Rupert Murdoch buys the LA Dodgers baseball team. Former mayor Tom Bradley dies.
2000 Police scandal rocks city; Al Gore nominated for president at Democratic Convention at brand-new Staples Center.
2001 Antonio Villaragoisa and Xavier Becerra emerge as first major modern-day Latino candidates for mayor.

LA Today

Novelist and urban fabulist Mick Farren contemplates the future of Tinseltown.

A certain significance could be attached to how Los Angeles, aside from a couple of token fireworks displays and a light show on the Hollywood sign, almost completely ignored the millennium celebrations. London went wild and in New York they packed into Times Square, but LA was quiet even by the standards of an average New Year's Eve.

Of course, the Pacific Coast of the US does get a raw deal from the rotation of the earth. It always stands last in the timeline. The new millennium dawned over Japan, with Shinto ceremonies to greet the rising sun. It progressed across China, India, Eastern and Western Europe, then jumped the Atlantic to find only Cuba a non-participant because Fidel Castro stuck to the pedantic (though correct) assertion that the 21st century didn't start until January 2001. New Orleans ran a special Mardi Gras, with the same booze, beads and breasts as usual, but by the time the new century had made it all the way to Los Angeles, we appeared to have run out of steam. What was

the point of kicking off our own shindig, when the revellers everywhere else were wending their weary way home? LA doesn't work well without an audience.

LA has always suffered from being in the second-to-last time zone on the planet. It's why there's never been an effective LA stock exchange – it would operate too late in the day to compete with Tokyo, London and New York. And it's the reason why movie studio execs play golf at five in the morning and are at their desks by eight. New York is already moving towards lunchtime, and the LA suit is always the disadvantaged early bird trying to keep up with the worms in the East. In all but the most recent (and most bizarre) presidential election, the rest of the United States has always waited impatiently for the returns from the polls in California.

The time factor, however, may not be the only reason Los Angeles waxed decidedly cool on the arrival of the 21st century. In every way, LA is the paramount example of

Let's get spiritual

Southern California, and the City of Angels in particular, has always been synonymous with kooky religion and cults. Evelyn Waugh immortalised LA-style death in *The Loved One*, while Nathaniel West mocked LA spirituality in *The Day of the Locust* through his character Tod Hackett, who worshipped at different churches each night.

But religion is also a serious business in LA, generating development and sustaining millions of newcomers seeking answers, community or simply a connection to the culture they have left behind. *Time* magazine noted that LA has more places of worship per capita than any other city in the US. On one small stretch of Jefferson Boulevard, between Western Avenue and Crenshaw Boulevard, there are no less than 21 religious buildings, four of them mainstream churches, as well as a mosque, several storefront Spanish Pentecostal churches, some Nation of Islam mosques and a Rastafarian centre. Out of three major civic buildings under construction at the time of writing, two are cathedrals.

Catholic missionaries founded the city, and Catholicism is far and away the largest religion in LA, with Latinos making up almost half the city's population, although a significant number of Hispanic Catholics are converting to Protestant evangelism (preached in modest shopfront churches all over Latino LA). The Catholic church has four million members; and the mayor, Richard Riordan (who will be replaced in 2001), is a devout Catholic with a chapel in his garden, a strong friendship with the powerful Cardinal Roger Mahony and a tendency to soften his Republican fiscal conservatism with spiritually motivated calls to aid the poor and the weak. A $163-million **Catholic cathedral** in Downtown, designed by Spanish architect Rafael Moneo, is due to be completed in late 2001.

But while Catholics conceived Los Angeles, this city gave birth to Pentecostalism, now the fastest-growing movement within Christianity, claiming over 17 million followers worldwide. It was introduced by a charismatic black Texan, William Seymoure, who arrived in 1906 and shocked city fathers with his racially mixed meetings where he would work blacks and whites into a frenzy of hugging, singing, dancing and speaking in tongues.

He was followed by the infamous Aimee Semple McPherson, who personified LA's religious zeal as well as its eccentricities – she attracted thousands to her Foursquare Gospel Church (her 1923 **Angelus Temple** is at 1100 Glendale Boulevard, but church leaders have recently decided to move to a new building), then faked her own drowning in 1926. But she also paved the way for modern-day televangelism, using radio and all the theatrics of Hollywood to woo followers. Her approach was taken up and burnished by the formidable Reverend Robert Schuller, who began preaching from the roof of a refreshment stand at a drive-in cinema in the late 1940s and now broadcasts his televangelical services from the all-glass **Crystal Cathedral** (*see page 34*) on what he terms his '22-acre shopping centre for Christ' in Orange County.

For sheer nuttiness, no one beats the 39 members of the Heaven's Gate sect, who in 1997 committed mass suicide in a suburban house north of San Diego, so as to speed themselves to a rendezvous with a spaceship that they believed was following the Hale-Bopp comet. Other sinister groups that have sprung forth from this soil include Charles Manson and his followers in the 1960s and the Branch Davidians, known for their fatal showdown with the FBI in Waco, Texas.

GOD AND HOLLYWOOD

Religion has long had a relationship with Hollywood. The most prominent current manifestation is the hugely successful **Church of Scientology**, which boasts John Travolta, Tom Cruise and Nicole Kidman among its many celebrity members, and owns a growing stockpile of property. Its headquarters are housed in a former movie mogul's house in Hollywood (5930 Franklin Avenue, 1-323 960 3100/www.scientology.org); the visitor centre is open to the public from 9am to 10pm daily.

Richard Gere and Steven Segal use their star status to promote Buddhism and the plight of the Dalai Lama, while Madonna, the original Material Girl, became for a while a devotee of Kabbalah, a brand of Jewish mysticism recently much in vogue in Hollywood – other celeb followers have included Jeff Goldblum, Courtney Love and Roseanne Barr. The **Kabbalah Learning Centre** is at 1062 South Robertson Boulevard in Beverly Hills (1-310 657 5404/www.kabbalah.com).

But while unconventional sects attract the most attention, the real boom in religious devotion is in the world's oldest religions. Catholicism, Judaism, Buddhism, Islam and evangelical Protestantism are all on the rise in LA, thanks in part to the huge influx of immigrants who've brought their belief systems with them, and in part to the tendency of baby-boomers to experiment with religions other than those they grew up with, or to return to a stricter version of their own religion.

Among Jews, for example, you'll find growing numbers of both 'Bu-Jews' (Buddhist-Jews) and Orthodox Jews. The latter attribute their growth to the need for discipline and structure in a decadent society, while Bu-Jews believe people are searching for a commonsense code and path to happiness that suits real life in modern California. Buddhism was brought here by immigrant Chinese railroad workers; for immersion in the Taiwanese version, you could visit the **Hsi Li Temple**, 1203 West Puente Avenue, West Covina (1-626 913 0622), which is the largest Buddhist temple in the western hemisphere. The numbers of Baptists, Presbyterians, Episcopalians and adherents to other brands of Protestantism are kept up by Asians, especially Koreans, who have taken over the traditionally WASP churches on Wilshire Boulevard in Midtown and made them their own.

Lesser-known religions are also attracting converts: Santeria, the animist Afro-Caribbean faith, is said to be practised in private living rooms by 100,000 believers; the relatively new Church of Religious Science, or Agape, is an amalgam of different beliefs with an upbeat spirit and inter-ethnic congregation that appeals to increasing numbers (for locations and service times, call 1-310 348 1260); while Mormonism claims to be doubling in size thanks to its emphasis on family values. Its huge **Temple of the Church of Jesus Christ of Latter-day Saints** is unmissable, looming over Santa Monica Boulevard at Overland Avenue in West LA.

The visitor centre (1-310 474 1549/www.lds.org), with its Center for Genealogy – Mormons believe that even ancestors can be saved – is open 9am to 9pm daily. Non-Mormons cannot enter the church.

This new-found zeal has prompted a building boom in a variety of religious institutions, from private day-schools to church-related youth centres, as well as places of worship. For the same $50-million price tag as the Catholic cathedral (thanks in part to donations from such high-profile members as Magic Johnson and Denzel Washington) the city's other cathedral under construction is a huge new centre for the West Angeles Church of God in Christ now being built at the corner of Crenshaw and Exposition Boulevards. How ironic that seemingly secular, self-absorbed Los Angeles should mark its entry into the 21st century with new buildings that express homage to one of the oldest pursuits in the world – finding God.

WHERE TO WORSHIP

Pick up a copy of the *LA Times* on Saturday for a full listing of services, plus articles on religion. *See also page 288.*

Otherwise, highly recommended for atmosphere are: **Our Lady, Queen of the Angels**, known as La Placita, in Downtown (535 North Main Street, 1-213 629 3101), the oldest Catholic church in Los Angeles, particularly festive on Sunday mornings; the **West Angeles Church of God in Christ** in Crenshaw (3045 Crenshaw Boulevard, 1-323 733 8300/ www.westa.org), which has more than 16,000 members, an incredible choir and holds five services on Sundays; **Wat Thai Temple** in North Hollywood (8225 Coldwater Canyon Avenue, 1-818 780 4200/www.watthaila.org), where you can eat Thai vegetarian food as well as join Buddhist devotees; and the **Self-Realization Fellowship Church's Lake Shrine** in Pacific Palisades (*see page 77*), a lovely retreat for meditation with a spring-fed lake, lush gardens, swans and picturesque pathways, where anyone is welcome to quietly wander.

the 20th-century city, and whether it can adapt to the 21st is highly debatable. It hardly had a history before 1900, but was the first to build freeways and embrace car culture. The suburban sprawl of the San Fernando Valley set a pattern for big cities across the world. And as the primary manufacturer of global entertainment, it gave us *Spartacus* and Phil Spector, *Star Wars* and *The Simpsons*, while generating and popularising everything from slasher movies to the Doors.

> ## 'The most pessimistic prediction is that Los Angeles is almost certainly doomed some time in the 21st century.'

In just the past 50 years, Los Angeles has gone from the shape of things to come to a potential anachronism, and – even by the most optimistic predictions – its cultural future may well be as a museum piece. Where Venice and Florence provide echoes of the High Renaissance, LA offers the Technicolor, wide-screen pop-trash of the 20th century, preserved in distorting, fun-house aspic.

The idea that Angelenos have begun to live in a blast from the past is already evident at hamburger joints such as Johnny Rockets or the revamped Astroburger, which attempt to transport customers to a quasi-1950s, when cars had fins and Buddy Holly would never die. The souvenir stores on Hollywood Boulevard will sell you images of Britney Spears and Matt Damon, but their real stock-in-trade is the quasi-religious icons of the century past: Elvis, Marilyn, James Dean, Jayne Mansfield, Humphrey Bogart, dear departed homeboy Jim Morrison and the multiple eras of Frank Zappa. The brass and marble stars of the Walk of Fame are the grave markers of a passing pantheon. The second-hand clothing stores on Melrose, and around the hipster community in Silver Lake, stock everything from distressed World War II bomber jackets to John Waters disco polyester, while boutiques next door display retro reproductions of the same thing. Even Charles Manson glaring from a T-shirt with the logo 'Charlie Don't Surf' is detail on the LA historical tapestry.

PROPHETS OF DOOM

The most pessimistic prediction is that LA is almost certainly doomed some time in the 21st century – unless, ironically, a really major earthquake so devastates it that Angelenos are forced to rebuild from scratch. While following

its current course, it will have no choice but to become a science-fiction dystopia – but probably not *Blade Runner*; it will be more drought-stricken than humid. Much of the city's water comes from as far afield as Nevada and Northern California, and if drought and global warming convince the folks in Las Vegas, San Francisco or Silicon Valley that they need their fluids for themselves, we have a problem.

Car culture will never be abandoned in any predictable future. Fossil fuel pollution will continue to be something hardly talked about. Poverty, immigration and an exponential birthrate will choke the poorer areas with a constantly growing underclass. On a more psychological level, LA also stands as the target for a storm of denigration from people in the rest of the US who claim Keanu Reeves movies and gangsta rap are the roots of America's woes, while the religious right defines LA as Sodom and Gomorrah on the Pacific.

But in LA we've seen so many prophets of doom, we just get bored. As the Sex Pistols once remarked: 'We don't care'. Angelenos have lived in the now for a hundred years. We have learned an overwhelming sense of 'here today, and gone tomorrow' from the simple act of setting up a city in a serious earthquake zone, and while the trappings of paradise remain, so will we. The sun still shines, palms still wave, sunsets are spectacular, motels are cheap and celebrities still go to restaurants the rest of us can't afford. The Lakers dominate the NBA, scantily clad young women still rollerblade on the Venice esplanade, guitar bands still naively work the nightclubs for no pay, confident they'll soon be as big as Limp Bizkit, and the Bay isn't so polluted you can't swim and surf – although a degree of circumspection does help.

The aspiring hot and sexy from the rest of country still arrive by train, plane, Greyhound bus or beat-up Honda, hoping to be the next Brad Pitt or Reece Witherspoon. A tiny minority make it, but the majority have to settle for waiting tables, lap dancing, phonesales or pornography. (This is not to denigrate porn, or, as it likes to be called, the adult entertainment industry. Mainly centred in the San Fernando Valley, it now outgrosses rock 'n' roll, with huge multinationals indirectly bankrolling smut production via their cable TV interests.)

'We don't care', on the other hand, can create an almost self-destructive myopia. A current symptom of this shortsighted irresponsibility is the rush by everyone to follow the nationwide craze for huge sports utility vehicles (whether or not they can afford one). The SUV has become the favoured mode of transport of the urban inadequate. High and mighty, it gives great visibility in traffic and a largely illusionary invulnerability from the heavily media-promoted carjacker. Unfortunately, it also consumes massive quantities of petrol and generates as much as five times the pollution of a standard car.

The effect of these vehicles on streets, highways and parking lots is the choking near-gridlock one might expect if a couple of panzer divisions had moved into town and gone on the razzle. Inexplicably, affluent parents give SUVs as gifts to their offspring the moment they are old enough to drive, and thus many SUV drivers are young and inexperienced, but figure themselves omnipotent in command of their personal tank. It took two full decades to wean Americans off huge, gas-guzzling automobiles, but now they are back with a vengeance, and the relapse may not be reversible. The TV commercials for SUVs show them kicking up dust in a desert sunset, but the ones I see are lined up on Sunset Boulevard, overheating with drivers nearing road rage or trying to squeeze their bulk into a parking space for a compact outside Ralph's Supermarket.

(I swear the people who drive SUVs are the same ones who pushed through the ban on smoking in bars. California is so paranoid about second-hand smoke that tobacco use is now illegal in bars, restaurants and most other places; as comedian Eddie Izzard once commented: 'It won't be long before they ban drinking and talking as well.')

PARTNERS IN CRIME

Living in the now, deprived of cigarettes when we most need them, we console ourselves with a good scandal – and, currently, the Los Angeles Police Department is supplying all we could hope for. The old gag claimed that the police were the biggest and most heavily armed gang in town, but the truth of this was only revealed when one Ramparts Division narcotics officer, looking to cop a plea on a corruption beef, ratted out all his partners in crime. At the time of writing, almost 2,000 drugs convictions have been overturned, and the promise is of many more revelations to come.

Throughout the 1990s, the LAPD was a destructive embarrassment. Their beating of Rodney King triggered the 1992 riots. Their petulant pullout from South Central made the riots worse than they might have been. Their fumbling and underhand evidence work turned the OJ Simpson murder trail into a judicial farce. Their overreaction to fans celebrating the Lakers becoming NBA champions in 2000 turned an impromptu carnival into a car-burning riot. A last-stand, we-own-the-streets show of force show was staged for TV at the Democratic National Convention, held at the

Staples Center in Downtown, in June 2000. Following a free concert by Rage Against the Machine, a heavily armoured line of riot cops fired indiscriminate volleys of rubber bullets into a crowd, which, in their opinion, was not dispersing with sufficient swiftness or humility. No real disturbance was visible – unless a free show by Rage Against the Machine, in and of itself, constitutes a riot.

The scandal in the Ramparts Division has revealed LAPD narcotics officers as principal players in the Downtown cocaine, crack and heroin industry, responsible for frames, high-level buying and selling and maybe a string of murders. The nightly news now treats us to an unfolding image of narcs so out of control that one lawyers' group is attempting to charge that the LAPD constitutes a 'conspiracy to criminal enterprise'.

'Los Angeles is a city on the margins of the unknown – but then it always has been.'

Fortunately, the Ramparts scandal seems have marked a turning of the tide. District Attorney Gil Garcetti survived the taint of OJ, but was voted out of office after his attempt to downplay law enforcement gone insane. A ballot proposition making possession of a small quantity of recreational drugs a matter for medical treatment rather than jail-time may be a first quiet step to decriminalisation. We in the city laugh like drains each time a new cop corruption revelation shows up on the news, but we still sweat when a black and white pulls in behind us on Olympic.

Harlan Ellison, himself an LA resident, not to say landmark, once wrote a *Star Trek* episode called 'The City at the Edge of Time'. The phrase could equally well sum up Los Angeles today. It's certainly a city on the margins of the unknown – but in many respects it always has been. Nobody knew what would happen when they started making those films, or building the freeways. The LAPD only got into stormtrooping through an overweening sense of drama from seeing too many TV cop shows. The SoCal living would be easy if everyone wasn't so motivated to overconsume.

But wasn't that what the 20th century was all about? Consumption, contradiction, contrast and a vast unpredictability have always been hallmarks of the LA way of life. Tinseltown, like an ageing whore, may be tawdry and have no sense of permanence, but it's still here. Los Angeles abides as a continuing cheap mystery – but don't we all love a cheap mystery?

Geography & Climate

Mudslides, floods, fires and earthquakes threaten the promised land of endless summer.

In many ways, there is very little reason for Los Angeles to exist. It has none of the natural features so common to big cities elsewhere in the world. It is not located along a great river, has no natural deep-water harbour and is far from any of the raw materials necessary for urban life – especially water (an exception is oil, which has always been abundant). It is also the largest city in the world to be located so near to a geologically unstable mountain range. And even before the Europeans came, the natives complained about the smog.

The city also seems unconnected to the land on which it has been built: so many mountains have been levelled, deserts paved and rivers turned into channels, the argument goes, that Los Angeles – like New York – has become nothing more than an alienating concrete island. And Angelenos often seem to inhabit a wholly artificial environment made up of air-conditioning and cars, freeways and airports, with their biggest river little more than a storm drain.

But, in fact, the natural environment makes itself felt far more strongly in Los Angeles than in, say, the big cities of Northern Europe. Earthquakes threaten lives and fortunes, as do wildfires, floods and mudslides. And LA also owes much of its wealth to nature: to the oil fields that lie under the city and, overhead, the bright, clear sunshine of its fabulously benign climate, which drew the infant movie business here – and now draws tourists in great numbers every year.

Los Angeles has often been described as an 'island on the land' – sealed off from the rest of the world by mountains to the north and south, desert to the east and the ocean to the west. Because of this isolation, Southern California, like Australia, contains numerous plant and animal species found nowhere else in the world.

Likewise, the shape of Los Angeles has been determined by natural topography. Southern California, like most of the American West, is a series of rugged and dramatic mountain ranges interspersed by valleys of all sizes, and it is the few passes between the mountains that have set the terms for urban growth.

For example, Los Angeles is often considered a city created by the automobile, but today's freeway system simply follows the same logical routes that were used by Native Americans, pioneers' horses and early commuter railroads. British architectural historian Reyner Banham, writing almost 30 years ago in his definitive study *Los Angeles: The Architecture of Four Ecologies*, identified a 'transportation palimpsest' – a natural tablet of five transport routes written upon by each generation. Today, these most beaten of tracks form the basis of the Hollywood (Highway 170), Santa Monica/San Bernardino (I-10), Santa Ana (I-5) and Harbor (I-110) Freeways.

CLIMATE IS CRUCIAL

Mountains and valleys have played an important role in moulding the city, but the greatest natural influence on Los Angeles is its weather. Without the city's Mediterranean-like climate – quite possibly the most temperate in the world – there would be no LA. Standing at the confluence of the desert and the ocean, the Los Angeles basin basks in the mild commingling of gentle, cool ocean breezes and warm desert sun. Winters are so mild that Angelenos often forget to pack an overcoat when they fly east in February. Summer comes in April at the latest and lingers at least until October. And although temperatures can reach 100°F (38°C), it's a dry, desert-like heat: to a dripping tourist from Atlanta or Baltimore, the most humid summer day in Los Angeles will seem like an airy heaven.

'Southern California is geologically 'young' and therefore unstable, with a fragile natural environment.'

Snow is out of the question – a dusting will hit the mountain tops every decade or two – and, in Mediterranean style, rain is seasonal. The first storm will typically hit in November, and a rainy day beyond the end of March is an anomaly. At about 14 inches (36 centimetres), the city's average annual rainfall is a third of New York's and a quarter of Tokyo's.

Yet alongside the sameness and mildness that characterise Los Angeles's climate are the more subtle and often frightening habits of the natural environment. The seasons do change – just not very dramatically. Spring is often cool and overcast. In June and July, the coastal cities are swathed for most of the day in sea mist, known as 'June gloom'. The hot, dry summer

can turn sour in September and October, when the typical wind pattern is reversed and the hot, dry 'Santa Ana' winds come roaring out of the desert toward the ocean (writers as varied as Raymond Chandler and Joan Didion have relayed tales of how people get spooky and weird at Santa Ana time).

This is also prime smog time – during hot, dry periods, Los Angeles's ring of mountains creates a kind of pressure cooker in which car pollutants 'bake' into photochemical haze. (It's worth noting, however, that strict air-pollution regulation has paid off; smog episodes are less frequent and now it is Houston, not LA, that ranks as America's smoggiest city.) Once that's over, autumn and winter can feature torrential rains as Southern California gets pounded by one El Niño-like storm after another. And driving in a Los Angeles rainstorm is nightmarish: unaccustomed to wet weather, drivers treat every drizzle as if it were a blizzard.

Just as important, the climate changes dramatically from place to place. Cut off from the ocean breezes by the mountains, the San Gabriel and San Fernando Valleys can be 20-30°F (11-17°C) warmer than the beachfront communities. The foothills of Hollywood and West Hollywood, above Sunset Strip, trap heat so well they can be 10°F (6°C) hotter than the flatlands only a few blocks away. A drive in February from Venice to Mount Baldy – only 40 miles (65 kilometres) away inland – can mean a tour of several such microclimates: starting with a mild 60°F (15°C) at the beach, you will pass through valleys steaming at 90°F (32°C) to find the mountain top still snowy at 30°F (-1°C).

DROUGHTS, FIRES AND FLOODS

Probably 95 per cent of the time, LA's mild weather is harmless, even with the dramatic temperature variations. But the other five per cent of the time, you'd better get out of the way. Southern California is geographically 'young' and therefore unstable, with a fragile natural environment that's easily thrown out of whack. The weather and precipitation patterns can also vary dramatically from year to year. Earthquakes (*see page 22* **The Big One**) are the least of it. Just as frequently, Los Angeles suffers a deadly cycle of drought, fires and floods.

If you look on the mountains and hillsides around Los Angeles, you'll see a mixture of native 'chaparral' (thick scrub) and European annual grasses. Come summer, these plants are pure kindling. The annual dry season, often stretching into October or November, provides ample opportunity for them to burn, as they

The Big One

With slo-mo violence that puts Sam Peckinpah to shame, the vast slab of rock – or tectonic plate – that is the bed of the Pacific Ocean is crashing into another plate that we know as North America. As the plates grind against each other, they slip and judder. Which is where earthquakes come from.

Sitting on top of this geological crumple zone, LA is regularly rocked by ground-shaking events large and small. In fact, tiny tremors hit the city thousands of times each day, but only rarely is an earthquake large enough for people to actually notice it. The big ones, however, are hard to miss – and in recent years they seem to have been growing in frequency.

California's most important geological fault line, the San Andreas Fault, runs in a north-west/south-east direction through the Mojave desert east of Los Angeles. Dozens – or maybe even hundreds – of other, smaller faults criss-cross the region. Most are classified as 'inactive', meaning they have not erupted in the past 10,000 years. But the thing about earthquakes is that you never know when or where one will hit. Unlike a blizzard or a hurricane, a big earthquake could happen anytime, without warning.

Los Angeles lives in fear of the 'Big One' – a San Andreas quake measuring 8 or 8.5 on the Richter scale, which would undoubtedly destroy large parts of the city. Such a quake has not rocked LA since it began getting big a century ago. But the most recent 'Little One' was scary enough. The Northridge earthquake (see picture), measuring 6.8 on the Richter scale when it hit in January 1994, caused apartment buildings and shops to collapse, killed more than 20 people and left thousands homeless. As in most earthquakes, the problems were compounded by fires created by broken fuel lines. Aftershocks measuring above 5 on the Richter scale rocked the city even as President Clinton held a special meeting on the crisis. Many people lost their homes altogether, or were forced to wait a year or more until repairs could be done.

Angelenos respond to the risk of earthquakes with equal parts fear, preparation and laconic humour. A century of small quakes has led to strong building standards that lessen the likelihood of complete disaster: in comparison with the 20 deaths of the Northridge quake, the recent quake in Armenia – about the same level on the Richter scale – killed 25,000.

Most Southern Californians have water and food stashed in the garage and some cash hidden under the mattress in case the Big One hits and knocks out supermarkets and ATMs. As a visitor, you can't go to such survivalist extremes, but all the same, it's smart to carry a small torch to cope with the inevitable power failures after a big quake. And if you feel a shaking underfoot, you can participate in LA's favourite parlour game: guessing the Richter intensity of the earthquake even as it's going on. Old-timers insist they can tell the difference between a 'four' and a 'five', and they'll argue with each other as if they were trained seismologists.

WHAT TO DO IN AN EARTHQUAKE

● Get away from anything that might collapse, indoors or out: notably trees, bridges or power lines.

● If you're inside, stand under a solid door frame or sturdy piece of furniture such as a large table or desk. Hold on to it firmly until all movement has subsided.

● If you're in a car, pull over and stop where it's safe. Keep away from flyovers and power lines.

● After the quake, think twice before you do anything. Don't light a cigarette, a candle or anything else, and don't turn on lights or use any electrical appliance (not even a telephone): chances are you'll be near a gas or water leak or power line break, and you could spark an explosion or cause a shock.

American Red Cross LA

2700 Wilshire Boulevard, Los Angeles, CA 90057 (1-213 739 5200).
The Red Cross helps to co-ordinate disaster relief operations and sends out information packs on earthquake readiness. In the event of a quake, it recommends non-US citizens phone a friend or relative at home as soon as they can, to prevent the phonelines getting clogged up with enquiries from abroad (outgoing calls are more likely to get through than incoming ones).

often do – in fact, the local ecosystems rely on regular incineration for refreshment and rebalancing. And Californian wildfires move rapidly. Once they get moving, they often skip over whole streets and blocks: firefighters prefer to contain them and let them burn out rather than try to extinguish them.

But as the city has pushed up against these grassy hillsides, Angelenos have put themselves in harm's way. Hence the almost annual television footage of bomber planes dumping loads of water and chemicals on some burning hillside in Malibu, trying to pummel the fire into submission before it sweeps away a whole neighbourhood.

The pattern of incineration is bad enough by itself, but it gets even worse during the periodic droughts. In the late 1980s and early 1990s, for example, Southern California's annual rainfall dropped to as little as two inches (five centimetres) a year in some places. The result, not surprisingly, was that the entire region became a tinderbox. Devastating fires swept Santa Barbara in 1991 and Malibu and Laguna Beach two years later.

Destructive as they are, the fires themselves are not the worst of it. These conflagrations typically set off a vicious cycle of flooding as well. The fires burn the plants that bind the soil of hillsides. When the winter rains come, the hillsides turn into a muddy, unstable goo that is politely known in local circles as a 'debris flow', which barrels down the mountains into the riverbeds below, washing away everything in its path. This phenomenon is reported to most of the world as 'flooding', but this does not do it justice. A debris flow is a kind of rolling mountain that gathers momentum as it heads downhill, collecting trees, cars and houses as it goes.

It has taken all that modern engineering can offer to keep this phenomenon from wiping out Los Angeles completely. The LA County Flood Control District has spent millions of dollars building 'debris basins' – essentially, large pits in the ground at the bottom of the San Gabriel mountains – to catch the slurry and keep it from moving downstream. With the help of the federal government, the Flood Control District has also converted virtually all the rivers in LA into concrete culverts to minimise the chance of flooding. Environmental advocates have sought to restore the natural flood flow in some areas, especially along the LA River, but they are coming to understand what the flood engineers knew decades ago: that the volatility of Southern California's climate (two inches of rain one winter, 40 the next) creates an extremely volatile natural landscape that is difficult to manage alongside a massive city.

EL NINO AND LA NINA

To make matters worse, the rains that create this flooding do not come in a predictable pattern. Scientists can calculate figures for average yearly rainfall – but there is no such thing as an average year in Southern California. Once the drought cycle passed in 1992, rainfall moved progressively upward until the El Niño winter of 1997-98, when the region was battered by about 40 inches (100 centimetres) of rain. Some areas got up to eight inches (20 centimetres) – over half the 'average' annual rainfall – in a single day.

The El Niño effect has hit Los Angeles twice in the past 15 years, and each time the result has been a series of devastating storms. In a typical year, Southern California doesn't really get any rainstorms of its own: the rainfall that arrives is just the dregs of harder storms that pound the Pacific Northwest and Northern California. But with the El Niño cycle, which warms the water in the Pacific, the typical storm pattern drops much further south, so that for a few months LA feels like Seattle: gloomy, saturated, reeling from the last storm and skittish about the next one.

The most recent El Niño has been so severe that it has limited LA's famous mobility. The spectacular Pacific Coast Highway was wiped out for almost the whole winter in 1998 as a result of El Niño-driven mudslides, and other road closures cut off Santa Barbara and some remote areas. Even after El Niño vanished, however, a peculiar trailing set of weather patterns brought more storms, heatwaves and other climatic extremes. The La Niña effect, as it soon came to be known, led to a dramatic drop-off in rainfall, once again bringing the possibility of catastrophic drought.

El Niño has simply reminded the world that, while the weather is great most of the time in LA, sunny days can sometimes be deceptive. Indeed, the big unknown about Los Angeles's climate is just how stable it really is. Recent history shows a pattern of about six or seven wet years followed by six or seven dry ones. The early years of the 21st century are likely to be dry ones, following as they did the wet El Niño years. But deeper historical evidence suggests that much longer 'mood swings' have occurred in the past.

Still, the fire-and-flood cycle yields one ironic bonus: it tends to hit the rich hardest. They're the only ones who can afford to live high up on those treacherous hills.

▶ For information on **average temperatures** and **rainfall**, see page 291.

Celebrity LA

It's true, the stars really do shine brighter in Tinseltown.

It's a cliché but nonetheless absolutely true that fame in America is like fame nowhere else in the world – it's a commodity that stretches further and wider here than anywhere else. And Los Angeles is without question the headquarters of world celebritydom. Other countries ('foreign territories' in movie industry parlance) may have their own stars, but for the most part these personalities mean little outside their home nations. In LA, however, faces that are known to millions from Peru to Japan live, work and hold court rather like characters in some alternative universe where international fame is the common currency.

This makes LA a fascinating place to visit if you are at all interested in the all-consuming cult of celebrity. Stars here are treated like royalty, and proximity to them, however fleeting, is both valued and envied among ordinary Angelenos. Unlike with royalty, though, people feel that in some strange way they own their celebrities; they might be idols and icons now, but they came out of a crowd, a crowd of which you might still be a member. There is something almost refreshingly

democratic about this. And to many aspiring eyes it follows that, given the right place and the right time, you, too, could be elevated to worldwide fame. After all, didn't Hilary Swank, Oscar-winner in 2000, spend months after her arrival in Los Angeles sleeping in her car?

This sense of personal connection means that stars are talked of in very familiar terms, which would make your average cynical European wince; even those Angelenos only marginally connected to 'the business' can be heard fondly referring to Barbra's latest album, Mel's new direction or why Keanu has just made a bad career move. Angelenos enjoy gossiping about their celebs – there is a plethora of scandal rags on sale at every supermarket checkout – but tend to be less damning than the public elsewhere. After all, if the winners are tarnished, then the game gets devalued.

But just in case there is the threat of some negative coverage, celebrities are surrounded by armies of publicists (the mighty PMK being the most famous and powerful) who ensure that their clients remain completely protected. Indeed, such a stranglehold on the media do these minders have that, in this respect, Hollywood has seen a return to the tightly controlled studio era of the 1940s and '50s. Coverage of stars, whether it be in the vast numbers of celebrity mags on offer, or on old-established TV shows such as CBS's daily *Entertainment Tonight*, is at best uncritical and at worst outrageously fawning. Even the supposedly more 'edgy' E! Entertainment channel – a whole TV station given over to round-the-clock coverage of showbiz – is hardly rigorous in its approach.

Angelenos working in 'the business' – and sometimes this seems like everybody – largely accept the rules of the game and their place in the fame hierarchy. And in Hollywood, this pecking order is fairly strict. Without question, Steven Spielberg (pictured), whose films bring in millions and also lay claim to some sort of artistic cred, is undisputed King of Hollywood, his name mentioned in hushed tones. Tom and Nicole are undoubtedly its Golden Couple, with Brad and Jennifer hard on their heels.

And the prospect of becoming a star – if not in movies, then music or TV – is what still unfailingly attracts thousands to LA every year. Among these are the genuinely talented and sincere, along with the frighteningly ambitious, who will simply do whatever it takes to get what they want. Then there are the oddballs: characters such as Dennis Woodruff, who drives around town in a car emblazoned with headshots and begging slogans, or Angelyne, an absurdly busty baby-doll blonde with her own (personally paid-for) giant billboards. But these two, beloved as they are by unimaginative foreign TV crews trying to make cheap points about Hollywood, are regarded as jokes by the locals. Because the business of Making It is a deadly serious one.

It's often said of LA that the obsession with stars – and with showbiz in general – precludes any sense of the outside world. Indeed, it's certainly a bit crazy when Michael J Fox's departure from his hit TV show *Spin City* gets headline billing on the local TV news. But there's another way of looking at this: the entertainment and communications industry is arguably the biggest business of the new millennium. If this is true, then if you're in LA, you're at the centre of the new universe.

STAR-SPOTTING
Coming to Los Angeles without even a passing interest in stars and celebrity is as perverse as avoiding art and sculpture in Florence. World-class celebrities really are thick on the ground, and your chances of making a good sighting within, say, a two-week stay are high – if you're determined enough and go to the right places.

Within the space of one week, this writer sat on a neighbouring table to Sharon Stone at Orso's restaurant, queued next to Harry Hamlin in Koontz Hardware on Santa Monica Boulevard, walked past Ray Liotta on Rodeo Drive and had drinks near Drew Barrymore in Bar Marmont on Sunset. So take heart.

You could buy a **Stars' Homes Map**, on sale anywhere on the more famous parts of Sunset and Hollywood Boulevards. They are usually well out of date – but can unintentionally be a great way of getting to know LA. Brad Pitt has bought the home of TV personality Elvira, so if you see her name on a star map, you know who lives there now. Jack Nicholson has lived in the same place for years, so he's pretty much a sure thing. Or take a **Movie Stars' Homes Tour** (1-800 286 8752/ 1-323 937 3361, four departures a day). It costs $29 and takes you to the more well-known residential districts. There are the high-profile events such as the **Walk of Fame** ceremonies, when a star makes an appearance and has his/her name emblazoned on the pavement of Hollywood Boulevard. Call the Hollywood Chamber of Commerce (1-323 469 8311) to find out if there are any scheduled during your visit.

As for catching celebrities away from the press and cameras, much depends on how eagle-eyed you are – most stars dress down in order to merge with the crowd. And remember that because virtually nobody walks in LA, such chance encounters will be at specific places – a restaurant, shopping mall or even a cinema. If you need some retrospective guidance, *Movieline* magazine has a monthly column, 'Spotted', which lists sightings of stars all over the metropolis.

Shopping is always a good start. Try **Barneys New York** in Beverly Hills. It's a pleasure to promenade in, and you may catch sight of the likes of Calista Flockhart (TV's *Ally McBeal*) or latest teen hunk James Van Der Beek (*Dawson's Creek*), both recent shoppers here. Otherwise, the **Beverly Center** mall in West Hollywood is a good bet, as is the still intensely fashionable **Fred Segal** on Melrose Avenue. Also visit the small but very attractive mall known as **8000 Sunset Boulevard**, nestled at the corner of Sunset and Crescent Heights Boulevards. It houses Laemmle's Sunset 5 cinema, a haunt of Julia Roberts and Winona Ryder, and Crunch, LA's gym of the moment, which boasts the best bodies in the city. Nicholas Cage, Elizabeth Shue and Salma Hayek have all been spotted here, pounding the treadmill. Or wait in line with Faye Dunaway at Buzz Coffee, and then visit Virgin Megastore next door, a good place to catch Quentin Tarantino and *Friends*' David Schwimmer.

And the winner is…

The number of awards shows held every year in LA is now getting slightly out of hand; there are so many that the whole (already shaky) concept of prize-giving is becoming even more devalued. But from a celebrity-watching point of view, they are a must. They provide a chance to see your favourite film, music and TV personalities dressed in all their finery, waving to the crowd and photographers from the red carpet – behaving, in fact, just as stars should.

MTV now has its important Movie Awards (which move between LA and New York), VH1 has its Fashion Awards, and Latino Media and GLAAD (Gay & Lesbian Alliance Against Defamation) give out their highly publicised prizes. But for the industry mogul and star-spotter alike, these are the most important:

The Academy Awards

Without question, the Oscar remains head and shoulders above all other gongs. And it's hard to over-emphasise the importance the Academy Awards have in LA. Oscar day, usually held on a Sunday at the end of March, is like LA's own Christmas, and the atmosphere is one of feverish excitement. The ceremony is held alternate years at the Dorothy Chandler Pavilion and the Shrine Auditorium, though this will change when the much-anticipated new Oscar Theatre is completed on Hollywood Boulevard, next door to Mann's Chinese Theater. The 2002 ceremony should be the first to be held there. This will be an event of great symbolic significance to film fans – for the first time in more than 40 years, Oscar will be going 'home' to Hollywood itself.

Fans queue for days to get places in the stands overlooking the red carpet (there's no booking in advance), so it might be better to watch the show on TV. But if you're in LA during Oscar week, and star-spotting is your aim, you'll hit pay-dirt. Everybody is in town, and one of the best places to see them all is at *Vanity Fair*'s post-Oscar party at Morton's or Elton John's AIDS benefit at Spago's. Many people will have come straight from the ceremony, some clutching gold statuettes. See also page 204.

The Golden Globes

The Globes have become enormously important in recent years. Held a couple of months before the Oscars, they are treated as the most significant precursor to the Main Event. Handed out by the Hollywood Foreign Press Association – pretty much the only thing it's known for – the Globes ceremony is as star-studded as the Oscars and affords great gazing opportunities. It's traditionally held at the Beverly Hills Hilton, but check the local press first.

The Emmys

The Emmys – essentially TV's Oscars – are held in early September. As with the Oscars, the days when celebrities didn't bother to show up to such 'uncool' events are long gone – there's far too much at stake – so you'll be treated to a full raft of stars from the small screen, as well as film people acting as presenters for the evening. Check the local press for venue details.

LA has movie premières every week, and these can be great occasions to see famous faces up close. Most of the first-nights happen at a select group of movie theatres – most prominently, **Mann's Chinese Theater**, in the heart of Hollywood, or, more frequently, at the **Bruin** or **Mann's** in Westwood. Premières are usually on Monday, Tuesday or Wednesday.

Stars have to eat, drink and relax, too. **Morton's** restaurant in West Hollywood is a real hangout for the showbiz establishment, particularly on Monday nights. The relatively new **Les Deux Café**, just off the fast-reviving Hollywood Boulevard, is très chic; Madonna

and Rupert Everett have dined here. Pricey **Spago's** and **Mr Chow's**, both in Beverly Hills, will yield famous faces most nights of the week, and **Orso's**, with its air of low-key discretion, is also a good bet. **The Ivy** in West Hollywood is unconnected with its London namesake, except in that it is a hot favourite with the celebrity in-crowd (especially at lunch).

Finally, although the song goes 'Fame, I'm gonna live for ever!', nobody, unfortunately, is immortal, not even in Tinseltown. If you want to see the final resting places of many of Hollywood's biggest stars, visit the **Hollywood Forever Cemetery** (*see page 89*).

Car City

LA's suburban sprawl, dependence on freeways and drive-thru mentality means the automobile still rules supreme.

' I drive, therefore I am' should be the motto of Los Angeles, a city whose culture, urban form and image is predicated on ownership of an automobile. Not that this was always so. The vast agglomeration that is contemporary LA was in its early years a collection of small, distinct cities, such as Pasadena, Santa Monica, Venice and Los Angeles (now Downtown and surroundings), which were connected first by carriage and horse tracks, then by steam, and subsequently by the Redline electric railroad.

Downtown emerged as the commercial and transit centre, with Union Station as the hub of an efficient network of trams and rail. But by the 1940s the area had become highly congested and a burgeoning car-driving populace voted for the development of the boulevard system. The boulevards, traversing LA from west to east and criss-crossing the north-to-south avenues, were the first step towards the decentralisation of LA and the amalgamation of the separate cities into Greater Los Angeles (*see also page 68* **Street talk**).

BUILDING THE FREEWAYS

In 1939, the Pasadena Freeway (US 110), the first of its kind and now considered a classic, was built. Designed for cars travelling at 45mph (70kph), it is a charming byway that weaves its way under stone bridges and through rolling landscapes from Downtown LA to Pasadena. In the 1950s, major freeway construction began. The planning of the routes was a highly politicised process. Avoiding the wealthier districts of the Westside, the freeways gouged their way through poor, disenfranchised neighbourhoods, leaving in their wake broken communities and a network of concrete and tarmac viaducts that have become the chief arteries and defining forms of the city.

Freeway construction more or less stopped in the 1970s (though a painful 30-year battle to prevent the extension of the Pasadena Freeway into picturesque South Pasadena still rages). The last freeway to be completed, after a lengthy construction process, was US 105 (aka Century or Glenn Anderson Freeway) in 1995.

This dramatic feat of engineering (immortalised in the movie *Speed* while still under construction) supposedly heralds the freeway of the future. It comes complete with high-tech sensors and a rail system along the centre.

The latter reflects a new stage in the evolution of LA. To cater to an expanding population, a vast, federally funded public transport project, comprising overground train and subway systems and intended to wean the populace from car dependency, is under way. Administered by the Metropolitan Transit Authority (MTA), this, too, is a highly politicised undertaking, which has not only been riddled with scandal and construction problems from the start, but also ill serves the poorer neighbourhoods that need it most and neglects to improve the existing bus system.

The result is that locals have little hope of Los Angeles becoming a public transport-based city and, despite the many measures conceived to mitigate air pollution (including catalytic converters, emission-free petrol and incentives to car-pool), automobile use continues to rise.

That said, 2000 has seen the completion of the Red Line stretch of the subway, carrying passengers from Downtown to North Hollywood. Though limited in its reach, the service is extremely clean, efficient and uncrowded. It has also attempted to be a destination in itself, with stations individually designed by public artist-architect teams to reflect the neighbourhoods they are in. A more popular addition is the Rapid Bus, also launched in 2000, ferrying riders relatively speedily from Santa Monica through Beverly Hills to Downtown.

THE DRIVING EXPERIENCE

Driving in LA delivers agony and ecstasy in equal measure. The ecstasy of whizzing along a freeway towards infinity, music playing, is countered by the pain of being stuck on that same freeway in rush hour – or worse, breaking down on it, ending up huddled in a locked car on the hard shoulder, praying for the arrival of the Automobile Club of Southern California. (At around $50 a year for roadside assistance and four free pick-ups, it's the club for sensible Angelenos; *see page 280*.)

Delight in acquiring the vehicle of one's choice – be it classic, wrecked, customised or hot off the production line – and the availability of ridiculously cheap petrol is tempered by the direct and hidden costs of car use. Quite apart from the obvious expenses of insurance (the highest in the US), maintenance, registration, emission tests, parking tickets and so on, a good half of California tax revenue goes towards the construction and maintenance of the highways system and the California Highway Patrol that protects it. Driving in LA also evokes the conflicting feelings of joy at being on the open road in one of the most spectacular terrains on the planet, and guilt that such liberation is achieved at the expense of that self-same natural environment.

A CITY BUILT FOR THE CAR

Car dependence has left its mark on the city not only in the freeway network, but in the form of the city itself. Car use encouraged the typical suburban LA lifestyle, emphasising private over public. Acres of land are covered by tracts of one- and two-storey single-family housing, with wide streets and driveways, two-car garages and large front and back yards, complete with pool and barbecue. The portable barbecue, incidentally, was invented by Henry Ford, who promoted the idea of 'picnicking' as one of the joys of leisure driving.

Car use also spawned a city zoned into residential neighbourhoods (some of which do not even have pavements), and commercial boulevards – 'strips' lined with buildings designed to cater to the driver. If not actually the originator, Los Angeles popularised stores with entrances on the rear parking lot (the historic Bullocks building on Wilshire Boulevard was the first of this type), corner mini-malls and drive-in motels.

Drive-through fast-food restaurants and diners flourished on the strips. McDonald's, Jack in the Box, Taco Bell and In-n-Out Burger are ubiquitous and largely anonymous – though must-see outlets include a great new retro-style In-n-Out in Westwood Village, a sculptural Kentucky Fried Chicken on Western Avenue and one of the earliest McDonald's, in Pomona. Some classic diners, such as Bob's Big Boy on Riverside Drive in Burbank, still exist.

Most noticeable of all, however, are the signs. Since business owners realised they needed to catch the eye of a motorist skating by at 40 or more miles an hour, commercial art – huge advertising billboards, ads painted on the sides of buildings and buildings as signs in themselves – have emerged as the vernacular artform of Los Angeles.

Drive along Sunset Strip between Doheny Drive and La Cienega Boulevard for the most sensational, eye-popping sequence of huge signs. Take in the Cabazon Monster (a life-size model of a dinosaur) on the I-10 east of Los Angeles, and visit Tail-o'-the-Pup on North San Vicente Boulevard in West Hollywood or Randy's Donuts on West Manchester Boulevard in Inglewood to experience the few remaining iconic incarnations of buildings as signs. There are also the 'Giant Triplets': huge, menacing advertising icons comprising 'Golf Man' (off the I-405 in Carson), 'Lumberjack Man' (outside a hardware store on Long Beach Boulevard) and 'Gas Station Man' (on Third Street in East LA).

Los Angeles is also the city of car lots, lube shops, 'body shops', car showrooms, car washes and, most of all, parking lots, which cover huge amounts of land. To get the full flavour, visit West Hollywood's **Heritage Classics** (8980 Santa Monica Boulevard, at La Peer Drive, 1-310 657 9699) or **Sunset Carwash** (7955 Sunset Boulevard, at Hayworth Avenue, 1-323 656 2777) for a classic car wash experience.

YOU ARE WHAT YOU DRIVE

Car culture has bred a weird sense of time and space – locals measure the length of a journey by the time it takes rather than the distance covered. It has also generated a mindset in which other forms of locomotion are confined to leisure activities, such as walking or cycling (you drive to the gym to use the step machine) and a dependence on technology that spawns yet more technology; hence the ubiquitous car phone/fax/stereo and the 'intelligent' freeway, with in-built sensors supposed to alert drivers to traffic problems ahead.

'Driving in LA delivers agony and ecstasy in equal measure.'

Car culture has also created snobbery based on the car you drive, with those millions who do not drive or own a car at the bottom of the social ladder. Typically, poor Latinos, African-Americans and school children ride the buses; they are pretty much the only form of transport for the Latino maids, gardeners and nannies who often travel several hours by bus every day back and forth to their employers on the Westside from South and East LA and the Valley. This sense of a transport hierarchy is reinforced by the fact that the California driving licence is the most commonly used form of ID in the state. It is used instead of a bank card to authorise a cheque, get access to clubs and to prove you're old enough to buy alcohol.

Angelenos go to absurd extremes to keep up automobile appearances. Many cars on the road in LA are not actually owned but leased, for a night or for as long as you can keep up the payments. Some people define themselves by their car, as they define their location by the freeway exit to which it is closest. Within the hierarchy of car ownership are numerous automobile subcultures: tribes include Latino lowriders, Valley Boy hot-rodders, media trendies in Jeep Wranglers, executive Lexus

owners, proud custodians of classic American cars (still going strong because the desert dryness means that cars do not rust), wannabe macho dudes in pumped-up pick-up trucks and urban survivalist Westside mothers battling the streets in four-wheel drive Ford Explorers.

The cult of the car has bred a whole battery of gimmicks and services for car users, from bizarre personalised number plates – BRAK NEK, FAT LADY, SSTA GRL and ALI CAT are some we've spotted – to valet parking. Legions of besuited valet parkers mark the entrances to restaurants, clubs and, sometimes, even car parks. (Don't forget to tip your valet.)

You can probably hire any type of car in LA, but for a *California Dreamin'* experience, try the infamous car-wreck supplier to the studios, **Rent-A-Wreck** in West LA (12333 Pico Boulevard, 1-310 478 0676/www.rentawreck. com). And if you want to do the movie star thang, the car rental of choice has to be a stretch limousine. Limos, used to transport people in style to prom nights, the Oscars and the Grammies, or as mobile party rooms for stag nights, are available for hire in numerous makes and lengths. At **Mercedes Limousines** (9641 Sunset Boulevard, Beverly Hills, 1-310 271 8559) you can hog the road in a stretch Lincoln for $60 an hour (plus tip), a stretch Merc for $110 and, for $110-$130, a Roller.

Car culture has also bred some terrific radio – for choices, *see page 286*. On the downside, car dependence has given rise to drive-by shootings, car-jacking, impossible building codes (demanding unachievable levels of parking space to accompany a new building), acquisitiveness, smog and traffic school. This last is an only-in-LA institution dreamed up by insurance companies, whereby you pay to attend a day of traffic school instead of getting an endorsement on your driving licence. It's a total con, but has given rise to all sorts of variations, such as Comedy Traffic School and Chocoholics and Ice-cream Lovers School.

But, surprisingly, reliance on cars has also bred a generosity of sorts. With a collective sense of 'there but for the grace of God, go I – and my car', Angelenos will drive miles out of their way to give acquaintances a ride home, porter friends to and from the airport and often freely lend out cars (insurance permitting), exhibiting a casualness that results from taking the car for granted.

To find out more about the evolution of automobile culture in LA as well as see some fabulous historic cars, visit the **Petersen Automotive Museum** (*see page 124*). It offers a largely uncritical view of the car, but is great fun nonetheless. For more information on driving in LA, including car hire, *see page 279*.

The space-age **Theme Building** at LAX.

Architecture

LA's skyline may lack the soaring drama of New York's, but there are architectural gems among the low-rise sprawl.

Los Angeles was founded and repeatedly reinvented by adventurers and fortune-seekers, some of whom came laden with cultural baggage, others with 'nothing to declare but their genius', as Oscar Wilde told a US customs officer. This helps to explain why most of Los Angeles and its 170 contiguous communities are a chaotic mishmash of borrowed styles, often executed with little finesse or imagination. But originality has also flourished here, ever since the arrival of the intercontinental railroad in 1887 and the rapid transformation of a dusty cow town into a metropolis.

There are few major public buildings or landmark corporate structures, although this year two significant civic buildings are under construction in Downtown. One is the **Walt Disney Concert Hall**, on the corner of Grand and First Streets, designed by Frank Gehry, which is scheduled to be ready in late 2003. The other is a new **Catholic Cathedral** by Spanish architect Rafael Moneo, at 555 Temple Street (between Hill and Grand Streets), which should

be completed in 2001. But LA for the most part appears bewilderingly vast, featureless and horizontal from the freeways; one needs to explore the neighbourhoods to discover its extraordinary diversity and well-concealed treasures. Topography offers a clue: much of the best work is tucked away in the hills, clinging to 'unbuildable' sites that appeal to clients whose ambitions are matched by their budgets.

For organised tours that feature architecture, art and design, contact **Architours** (1-323 294 5825) and the **Los Angeles Conservancy** (*see page 71* **Guided tours**) Occasional house tours are also offered by the LA chapter of the **American Institute of Architects** (1-213 639 0777) and the **Society for Architectural Historians** (1-800 972 4722). For guides to LA's buildings, *see page 292*.

We've given details for buildings that are open to the public (admission is free unless otherwise stated). For more on many other buildings mentioned here, *see chapters* **Sightseeing**, **Accommodation**, **Film**, **Museums** and **Theatre & Dance**.

In Context

A CITY IS BORN

Only a few fragments remain of the original 18th-century settlement with the long-winded name, El Pueblo de Nuestra Señora la Reina de Los Angeles. Misty-eyed preservationists blather on about the city's roots and the adobe tradition, but the evidence is unconvincing: dull provincial buildings, rebuilt or prettified, are best forgotten. There is, however, a rich legacy of buildings from the land boom of the late 1880s, notably the houses built in the Queen Anne and Eastlake styles on the 1300 block of **Carroll Avenue**, between Douglas Street and Edgeware Road, in Echo Park, just north-west of Downtown. Also, in Downtown, at North Main and Arcadia Streets, north-east of the I-101, is the newly restored **El Pueblo** district. This is the original city centre of 19th-century LA and consists of a patchwork of buildings around a square, La Placita (now lit up at night like a Mexican plaza). Among them is the Italianate Pico House, built in 1870, LA's first hotel with indoor plumbing.

One of the Victorian offices was the **Bradbury Building**. Behind its century-old brick façade is a stunning skylit atrium surrounded by tiled galleries with polished wood balustrades and open-cage lifts. It was inspired by a science fiction novel and, fittingly, appeared in the film *Blade Runner*.

At the foot of the San Gabriel Mountains lies Pasadena, a winter resort for rich Easterners around the turn of the 19th century. Remnants of the flamboyant resort hotels survive, as do many handsome 'bungalows' in the 'Craftsman' style – an offshoot of the Victorian Arts and Crafts movement. The standout is the **Gamble House**, built by Charles and Henry Greene in 1908, a marvel of polished mahogany and Tiffany glass.

Bradbury Building

304 S Broadway, at Third Street, Downtown (1-213 626 1893). Metro Civic Center-Tom Bradley or Pershing Square/bus 1, 2, 3, 4, 10/I-10, exit Fourth Street east. **Open** *Ground floor only 9am-6pm Mon-Fri; 9am-5pm Sat, Sun.* **Map** p309 B2.

Gamble House

4 Westmoreland Place, at Walnut Street, Pasadena (1-626 793 3334). Bus 177, 267/I-10, exit Orange Grove Boulevard north. **Open** *noon-3pm Thur-Sun; closed Mon-Wed.* **Admission** *$5; $3-$4 concessions.*

INTERWAR BOOM

During the growth years of the 1920s, Southern California embraced the Mediterranean tradition, building thousands of pocket haciendas, 'Churrigueresque' car showrooms and abstracted Andalusian farmhouses. The city developed an indiscriminate appetite for all things foreign and exotic: Wallace Neff and George Washington Smith set the pace, but all Beaux Arts-trained architects were masters of period style, and every builder could run up a mosque, a medieval castle or an Egyptian tomb to satisfy a devotee of romantic fiction. Hollywood legitimised this exuberant eclecticism, but the impulse came from newcomers who flocked to LA, dreaming of fortune or an easy life in the sun.

The greatest personal fantasy to survive, however, was not a rich man's folly. The **Watts Towers** (1921-54) were built by a poor Italian immigrant, Simon Rodia. Every day he hoisted himself up one of the slender iron frameworks, implanting scraps of broken china and glass in wet cement. The towers – nearly 100 feet (30 metres) tall – are currently covered in scaffolding for restoration; they are scheduled to reopen in early 2001. For more information, *see page 104* **The Watts Towers**. **Spadena House** (Walden Drive, at Carmelita Avenue, Beverly Hills), also known as the Witch's House, is one of the city's favourite fantasy houses. It was built as a movie set in Culver City in 1921 and later moved to its present site.

Mass fantasies found their outlet in exotic movie palaces. Still flourishing is **Mann's Chinese Theater** (6925 Hollywood Boulevard); newly reborn is **El Capitan Theater** opposite (No.6838). Other palaces are now used for the performing arts: art deco fans should catch a show at the **Pantages Theater** (6233 Hollywood Boulevard) or the **Wiltern Theater** (Wilshire Boulevard, at Western Avenue). There is also a cluster of decaying vintage movie palaces on South Broadway. For more information, *see page 215* **Movie palaces**.

Recently restored and expanded by US firm Hardy Holzman Pfeiffer, Bertram Goodhue's **Central Library** in Downtown embodies the civic pride and Beaux Arts scholarship of the 1920s in its Egyptian massing, spirited murals and lofty inscriptions. Likewise, the vast, pyramid-capped 1928 **City Hall** (200 North Spring Street), designed by Austin, Parkinson, Martin, Whittlesey, was intended to impress, to the point of pomposity: until 1957, it was the only exception that had been permitted to the city's 13-storey height limit.

The commercial counterpart was **Bullocks Wilshire** (3050 Wilshire Boulevard, at Vermont Avenue), the grandest of department stores and the first to be designed so that motorists could unload beneath a porte cochère (a drive-through canopy attached to the entrance) and park in the rear. It has recently been transformed into a law school, with its art deco façades and ornament preserved.

For many architecture and design enthusiasts, Los Angeles is best known for the spare, modernist houses made famous by the exotic black-and-white pictures of photographer Julius Shulman. These buildings had their roots in remarkable earlier works by Frank Lloyd Wright and his Austrian-born protégés, Rudolph Schindler and Richard Neutra, who pioneered modern architecture in Southern California from 1920 onwards.

Highlights include Wright's **Hollyhock House** and **Ennis-Brown House** in Los Feliz and the **Schindler House** (now known as the MAK Center) in West Hollywood. Hollyhock House is currently closed for major repairs, as well as re-landscaping of the surrounding Barnsdall Art Park. It is due to reopen in spring 2003; for more info, call the LA Municipal Art

Speaking Frankly

Frank Gehry is one of LA's most famous sons: his 1997 voluptuous, titanium-clad Guggenheim Museum in Bilbao, Spain, firmly established him as one of the world's most extraordinary architects. Gehry's family moved to Los Angeles from Toronto in his youth, and he studied at the University of Southern California before spending several years at corporate architecture firm Victor Gruen & Associates and then set up his own firm, Frank O Gehry & Associates, in his early 30s in 1962. With commercial work for bread and butter, he proceeded to design a string of low-budget studios and residences; an early (1964) notable project is the **Danziger Studio/ Residence** (7001 Melrose Avenue, at Sycamore Avenue, Hollywood), two simple, bold, cubic structures buffered from the busy street by a high surrounding wall.

Gehry drew inspiration from local artists rather than architects, and became increasingly experimental, creating collages of cheap materials and banal building elements. He catapulted himself on to the world stage with the 1978 remodelling of his own house in a polite residential area in Santa Monica (1002 22nd Street, at Washington Avenue), a seemingly chaotic collage of chainlink fencing, plywood and exposed structure.

Although Gehry likes to claim that he is only appreciated outside LA, he has built many buildings in the city. Must-see examples from the 1980s and early 1990s are the **Geffen Contemporary Museum**; **Loyola Law School** in Downtown (1441 W Olympic Boulevard, between Albany and Valencia Streets); the

Edgemar Development (pictured); **Santa Monica Place Shopping Center**, famous for its layered chainlink façade on the parking garage, visible from Second Street to the south; the West Coast headquarters for the **former TBWA Chiat Day** advertising agency (340 Main Street, Venice), with its eye-catching portico in the form of a huge pair of upturned binoculars designed by Claes Oldenburg and Coosje van Bruggen. Also in Venice are several residential projects by Gehry.

With increased stature, up went Gehry's budgets, and in the 1990s his work moved from raw, makeshift construction to complex, sensuous structures clad in rich materials, designed with the aid of sophisticated computer programmes. Buildings from this era include two in Anaheim – the **Team Disney** administration building (800 West Ball Road) with its fabulous undulating yellow façade; the muscular **Disney Ice Arena** (300 West Lincoln Avenue), with its wavy roof – and, of course, the yet-to-be-built **Disney Concert Hall**, an exploding flower of curving forms, which will be the new Downtown home for the LA Philharmonic.

The concert hall, heralded as the pinnacle of Gehry's career, has been held up for cost reasons (and its thunder has arguably been stolen by the Bilbao Guggenheim, which has a similar aesthetic), but, following modifications (wavy walls will be clad in stainless steel, not the intended stone), it is now under construction and set to open in 2003. It will be the first major civic building designed by Gehry for Los Angeles and should further enhance his – and the city's – reputation.

Gallery on 1-213 485 4581. The Schindler House, built as the architect's live-work space, is a dazzling combination of tilt-up concrete walls, redwood partitions, rooftop 'sleeping baskets' and outdoor living rooms. Another major work by Schindler is the concrete-frame **Lovell Beach House** (13th Street, at Beach Walk, Balboa Island, Orange County). Neutra had a 40-year career in Los Angeles: among his finest 'International Modern' residences are the **Lovell Health House** (4616 Dundee Drive, at the southern end of Griffith Park), which starred in *LA Confidential*, and the **Strathmore Apartments**, stacked up a hillside in Westwood (11005 Strathmore Drive, off Gayley Avenue).

'The post-war generation of coffeeshops epitomises 1950s and 1960s futuristic drive-by design.'

Another influential LA architect born out of Frank Lloyd Wright's organic modern tradition was John Lautner, designer of structurally dynamic futuristic buildings, such as the 1960 **Chemosphere** (7776 Torreyson Drive, north of Mount Olympus), most familiar as the exotic setting of choice in James Bond films. Lautner first came to Los Angeles in 1939 to supervise construction of Frank Lloyd Wright's Sturges House and was sickened by the ugliness of what he found in the city. But he realised, as Wright had in the 1920s, that he could realise his vision here, in the soft clay of a burgeoning community, as he never could in the tradition-bound East or Midwest. He settled and built a succession of daring, highly original houses – although he did no more than scrape a living and achieved widespread fame only in the last few years before his death in 1994.

The Los Angeles region fared better than most during the Depression, but the old extravagance was gone and New World 'streamline moderne' replaced European models for many public buildings and a few homes. In Downtown, you can drive by the **Coca-Cola Bottling Plant** (1334 Central Avenue, at 14th Street), which resembles an ocean liner moored amid the warehouses, and take a train from **Union Station** (800 North Alameda Street), last of the great US passenger terminals.

Central Library
630 W Fifth Street, between Flower Street & Grand Avenue, Downtown (1-213 228 7000). Metro Pershing Square or Seventh Street-Metro Center/bus DASH E/I-110 north, exit Sixth Street east. **Open** 10am-5.30pm Mon, Thur-Sat; noon-8pm Tue, Wed; 1-5pm Sun. **Map** p309 B3.

Ennis-Brown House
2655 Glendower Avenue, at Vermont Avenue & Los Feliz Boulevard, Los Feliz (1-323 660 0607). Bus 180, 181/US 101, exit Vermont Avenue north. **Open** *Office* 9am-4pm Mon-Fri. **Tours** *LA County residents only* second Sat in Jan, Mar, May, July, Sept, Nov; *others* by appointment. **Admission** $10. **Map** p308 A1.
This is a private residence and only open for guided tours; book at least two weeks ahead.

MAK Center for Art & Architecture at the Schindler House
835 N Kings Road, between Santa Monica Boulevard & Melrose Avenue, West Hollywood (1-323 651 1510). Bus 4, 105, 304/I-10, exit La Cienega Boulevard north. **Open** 11am-6pm Wed-Sun; closed Mon, Tue. **Admission** $5; free 4-6pm Fri. **Map** p306 B2.

THE GOOGIE LEGACY
When America emerged from the Depression and war, there was a mood of optimism and of faith in technology. Cars were designed to look like jet fighters, and the coffeeshops (like car washes) also strove to look as though they were moving at warp speed. Lloyd Wright (Frank's son) and John Lautner led the charge; in 1949, Lautner designed an angular, wood and glass coffeeshop called Googie's, next door to the legendary Schwab's drugstore on Sunset Strip. Both landmarks have now vanished, replaced by a pastel shopping/movie theatre complex, but the name Googie lives on as shorthand for the post-war generation of coffeeshops that epitomises 1950s and 1960s futuristic drive-by design. Flashing neon signs towered over these single-storey boxes, while the furnishings within were a mix of cosy and gee-whizz: Naugahyde booths and space-age lamps.

Of the survivors, the best may be **Pann's** (*see page 165*) and **Ship's Culver City** (Overland Avenue, at Washington Boulevard). The earliest surviving **McDonald's** (10807 Lakewood Boulevard, at Florence Avenue, Downey), built in 1953, shares the aesthetic.

These designs also drew on the tradition of the building as sign: the oversized doughnuts, windmills and hot-dogs that had lured passing motorists from the 1930s onward. The **Tail-o'-the-Pup** in West Hollywood (329 North San Vicente Boulevard, at Beverly Boulevard), built in 1946, and **Randy's Donuts** in Inglewood (805 West Manchester Boulevard, at La Cienega Boulevard), built in 1954, are surviving examples of this once ubiquitous building type.

POST-WAR GROWTH
The population of Southern California exploded in the 1950s and new suburbs obliterated fields and citrus orchards, extending, with the freeways, over the mountains and into the desert. Business interests spurred the renewal

In Context

of Downtown, razing the decaying Victorian mansions atop Bunker Hill and creating, from the early 1960s onwards, a corridor of office towers. But, as freeways clogged and public transportation lagged, Century City and other commercial hubs grew to serve an increasingly fragmented and suburban metropolis. This period also saw the construction of the landmark **Theme Building** (by Paul Williams, 1961) between Terminals 2 and 6 at LAX, a space-age fantasy that has now slipped into a kitsch-classic middle age.

From 1945 to 1962, the influential magazine *Arts + Architecture* sponsored the Case Study House programme, a visionary project fuelled by post-war optimism, whose mission was to create prototypical low-cost houses using new prefabricated materials and building methods. Although they never achieved the anticipated mass popularity, the Case Study Houses stand as icons of Southern Californian modern design, characterised by the use of glass walls and doors – to make the exterior landscape flow into the interior, and vice versa – and open-plan glass and steel volumes. One of the best was the steel-framed **Eames House**, built in 1949 from off-the-shelf components, and a fusion of poetry and technology by Charles and Ray Eames, the US's most talented husband-and-wife design team.

Just as Frank Lloyd Wright inspired the first generation of modernists in Southern California, so has Toronto-born Frank Gehry (*see page 32* **Speaking Frankly**) served as mentor to several generations of free-spirited architects. There are several must-see buildings by architects influenced by Gehry's idiosyncratic forms and inventive use of materials – often low-cost industrial stuff. One living example of this is a sizzling yellow and blue kit-of-parts building, designed by Hodgetts and Fung; for several years it served as the **'Towell' (Temporary Powell) Library** on the UCLA campus, then was dismantled and now sits in pieces at another college, Cal Poly Pomona, where it is soon to be rebuilt as the architecture school. In Culver City, Eric Owen Moss has remodelled a succession of drab warehouses, creating cutting-edge workspaces, including the **Box** (8520 National Boulevard) and **Samitaur** (3457 South La Cienega Boulevard).

Outstanding examples of contemporary architecture in Downtown include the **Museum of Contemporary Art** (250 South Grand Avenue) – a powerful complex of geometric solids and skylit galleries designed by Japanese architect Arata Isozaki; its sister museum, the **Geffen Contemporary** (152 North Central Avenue), a dramatic remodel of an old police garage by Frank Gehry; and Pei Cobb Freed's soaring extension to the **Convention Center**.

For relaxation, there's **Pershing Square** (at South Olive and Fifth Streets), LA's second-oldest public space. The square was dramatically re-landscaped in 1994 by Laurie Olin, with colourful architectural features added by Ricardo Legorreta.

Neither Gehry nor his acolytes got to build LA's largest civic project of the past decade: the newly opened **Getty Center** (*see chapter* **Museums**).That choice commission went to East Coast architect Richard Meier, who reintroduced cool International Modernism to LA in his hilltop complex. Meier also designed the crisp **Museum of Television & Radio** in Beverly Hills. The original **Getty Museum**, a replica Roman villa in Malibu, is being remodelled by Machado & Silvetti Associates, also from the East Coast, and will reopen in 2002 as a centre for classical antiquities and comparative archaeology.

In Burbank, Robert Stern brings smiles to motorists crawling home on the Ventura Freeway with his cartoon-like **Disney Animation Building** (at Alameda Avenue and Buena Vista Street). To the south, in Orange County, Philip Johnson and John Burgee created the aptly named **Crystal Cathedral** for one of California's leading pop preachers.

Eames House

203 Chautauqua Boulevard, off Pacific Coast Highway, Pacific Palisades (office 1-310 459 9663). Bus 9, 434/I-10, exit PCH north. **Open** by appointment 10am-4.30pm Mon-Fri; closed Sat, Sun. You can see the exterior on a self-guided tour, but phone first to make an appointment.

Crystal Cathedral

12141 Lewis Street, at Chapman Avenue, Garden Grove, Orange County (1-714 971 4000). I-5 south, exit Center Drive to Chapman Avenue west. **Open** 9am-3.30pm Mon-Sat (except during weddings and funerals). *Services* English 9.30am, 11am, 6pm Sun. Spanish 1pm Sun.
On Sundays, the church is only open for services.

THE 1990S

The architecture scene in Los Angeles changed dramatically in the early 1990s, when architects were hit first by the recession, then by the 1992 riots, 1994 earthquake and floods. These cataclysms jolted many architects into a sense of responsibility for the city. With tremendous zeal, architects organised seminars, community workshops and masterplanning sessions, out of which came numerous, well-intentioned plans for LA. In reality, most of these plans gathered dust and the devastated parts of the city were largely rebuilt by developers and politicians in the most expedient way possible.

However, that brief period of reflection did produce some legacies, such as **Inner City**

In Context

Your eyes will pop at **In-N-Out Burger**.

Arts, an arts school for poor kids in Downtown public schools. With a post-riot rush of donations, they were able to move into a new home, an imaginatively converted car repair shop (720 South Kohler Street), designed by Michael Maltzan Architecture. Maltzan, a protégé of Frank Gehry and one of LA's leading young architects, also designed a strong, sculptural arts complex at **Harvard-Westlake School** in North Hollywood (3700 Coldwater Canyon, at Hacienda Drive).

While the 1980s produced a recognisable architectural aesthetic, the 1990s have been less distinctive. The recession produced an aesthetic shift away from the deconstructivist contortions that characterised much of the prominent late-1980s design towards simpler and stylistically varied buildings. On one hand, you can see Googie revisited – for example, in Stephen Ehrlich's **Robertson Library** (1719 South Robertson Boulevard, at Airdrome Street); Kanner Architects' **In-N-Out Burger** in vibrant primary colours on Gayley Avenue in Westwood Village; or head south to the otherwise uninteresting city of Gardena to see the newly opened **Hustler Casino** (1000 Redondo Beach Boulevard, at Vermont Avenue), by Godfredsen-Segal Architects. This is best seen at night, not only for the full effect of the flashing neon-rimmed windows, but also because you might get a peak at *Hustler* publisher Larry Flynt, who sometimes play high-stakes poker there.

A starker minimalism is also evident, as in buildings by David Hertz Work, whose spare **McKinley Residence** (2420 McKinley Avenue, Venice) and **Lehrer Residence** (2238 Stradella Road, Bel Air) are laboratories for environmental sustainability, in the use of solar panels, underfloor heating and a recycled concrete product called 'syndecrete' for surfaces and furnishings. Arguably one of the more interesting examples of recent design in LA was by a Frenchman, and it was mostly an interior:

Philippe Starck's stagey remodel of the **Mondrian Hotel** on Sunset Boulevard. However, now that the stylishly surreal hotels of Starck and Ian Schrager have become a brand, popping up in all major cities, the Mondrian has lost its uniqueness.

Since the economy picked up in the mid-1990s, the biggest source of work for architects has been the entertainment industry. All the studios have embarked on massive expansion plans, and many are developing restaurants, leisure centres and themed entertainment/retail destinations, exemplified by **Universal CityWalk**, an amalgam of LA buildings distilled into an artificial street of exploding noise and colour at Universal City. CityWalk was designed by the Jerde Partnership International, a prominent entertainment architect firm also responsible for the Fremont Street Experience in Las Vegas and Mall of America, the world's largest shopping centre, in Bloomington, Minneapolis. CityWalk II, a slightly less imaginative version of the original, opened in 2000.

An antidote to such excessive architecture is the serene, spacious and elegant **Form Zero**, an architectural bookshop with an interior designed by the store's owner, Andrew Liang, in the Gehry-designed Edgemar Development (2433 Main Street, between Ocean Park Boulevard and Hollister Avenue, Santa Monica). This shop is also a goldmine of information about architecture in Los Angeles.

In recent years, attention has turned once again to the public realm, especially schools, which have suffered from dilapidated buildings and teaching standards that have declined as the school population has grown. The Los Angeles School District has plans for a massive school building programme. Meanwhile, the smaller city of Pomona, to the east of LA, has stunned design enthusiasts with Morphosis Architects' new **Diamond Ranch High School** (100 Diamond Ranch Road), a poetic composition of leaning walls and flying roofs high on a hill above Pomona town centre. It's as breathtaking as Gehry's Guggenheim in Bilbao or anything by Zaha Hadid, but even more remarkable given that it was built on a shoestring budget for a bureaucracy.

The other burgeoning building type in LA are the numerous warehouse conversions, especially on the Westside, for dotcom, film and advertising production companies. Two standout examples – if you can get access to their interiors – are **TBWA Chiat Day** (5353 Grosvenor Boulevard, Playa del Rey), by Clive Wilkinson Architects, and **Ground Zero** (4235 Redwood Avenue, at Maxella Avenue, Marina del Rey), by Shubin + Donaldson.

Ethnic LA

Immigration has turned LA into the multicultural capital of the US, resulting in both interracial fusion and tension.

When the Beach Boys eulogised 'California Girls' in the early 1960s, the image that came to mind was of athletic, tall, blue-eyed blondes who played volleyball and tanned themselves on the beach. Not in that picture were the dark-skinned, brown-eyed beauties that people LA today. In the past 30 years, LA has undergone a huge transformation: from Iowa-on-the-Pacific to the US capital of foreign immigration; from whitebread city to one where Mexicans are fast becoming the majority population and where inter-ethnic relations are the primary social and political concern.

In large part, this change is the result of a 1965 immigration act that transformed patterns of immigration to the US. The Hart-Celler Act abolished the old country-of-origin quotas, which had favoured Europeans, particularly the Irish. Instead, family ties to US citizens or possession of scarce skills became the criteria for entry. Designed to contain immigration, the act, in fact, released a flood of migrants from Latin America, the Caribbean, the Middle East

and (where the reformers least expected) Asia. Well-educated Chinese, Filipinos, Koreans and East Asians (from India) poured in, followed by their less-skilled relatives, making Asians today the third largest group in LA, more numerous than African-Americans. Mexicans, already established in Southern California, jumped from a population of just over one million in 1970 to almost four million in 1990, of whom almost half were immigrants.

Many thousands of people came to the US simply seeking a better life and chose Los Angeles for the traditional reasons – sun, sea and opportunity. But political upheavals overseas in the 1970s and early 1980s also injected a sudden rush of new arrivals. LA became home to exiles from the 1973 Arab-Israeli wars, the Lebanese civil war that began in 1975 and the Iranian revolution of 1978-79; from the collapse of the US-supported regime in South Vietnam and the Communist takeovers in Cambodia and Laos; from the conflicts in El Salvador and Guatamala; and, in the late

1980s, from the fall of the Iron Curtain and the dissolution of the Soviet Union.

The result has been the transformation of the five-county Los Angeles region into a mosaic of communities speaking more than 80 languages. If you drive through LA, you'll see its endless miles of tract housing and strip mall development overlaid with the markings of different cultures: vividly painted walls and murals in heavily Hispanic areas from Pacoima in the north Valley down to Compton in South LA; Chinese and Vietnamese sculptures and signs in Little Saigon in Orange County; and Armenian schools and churches in Glendale.

THE ETHNIC DISTRICTS

Central Americans – 300,000 Salvadorans and 150,000 Guatamalans – are dispersed throughout the city, though concentrated in South Central LA. Many start their US life in the Pico-Union and MacArthur Park area just west of Downtown. Don't be surprised if people tell you to avoid this notoriously dangerous neighbourhood – poverty and gang trouble are common – but, really, it's fine for outsiders and has its share of interesting shops and eateries. For cheap Salvadoran food and plenty of atmosphere, try **El Izalqueno** (1830 West Pico Boulevard, between Union Avenue and Alvarado Street, 1-213 387 2467).

The original **Chinese** heart of LA was old Chinatown, north of Downtown, where a fair number of the 300,000 Chinese-Americans, particularly the older generation, still live. Chinatown is a cute attraction for tourists and the Anglo gallery owners who have recently set up shop there, but it is currently struggling to revive its fortunes, in decline as younger generations and new immigrant Chinese have left for the suburbs.

Chinese people, from Hong Kong, Taiwan and the mainland, have instead moved east, transforming Monterey Park in the eastern San Gabriel Valley into a thriving enclave, thanks to the efforts, in part, of a creative Chinese developer who sold the neighbourhood to his compatriots as the 'Chinese Beverly Hills'. Go there for full immersion in Chinese culture – and, reputedly, the best Chinese food in the US.

Many **Middle Easterners**, now numbering more than 300,000 in LA, have settled in the 'three Bs': Beverly Hills, Brentwood and Bel Air. California's **Vietnamese** also number around 300,000: airlifted from Vietnam by US planes and deposited at Camp Pendleton north of San Diego, they have remained in the region. They have concentrated in Orange County, where the white community tends to be conservative and therefore supported these exiles from a Communist regime. In LA, they have created a

capital in Little Saigon, three square miles of strip malls and industrial buildings centred on Bolsa Avenue in Westminster – a must if you want an authentic flavour of Vietnam, especially its superb French-Vietnamese food, best exemplified at **Song Long** restaurant (9361 Bolsa Avenue, suite 108, between Bushard and Magnolia Streets, 1-714 775 3724).

Koreatown is both home and workplace to many of the city's 200,000 **Koreans**, and is the largest Korean community outside Korea, a fact that became evident in the press attention on the North-South Korean summit in June 2000. Korean-Americans, many of whom have relatives in North Korea, were glued to their TV sets for the duration, their joy and astonishment at the rapprochement palpable in the city. Located north and south of Wilshire Boulevard around Western Avenue, just east of Miracle Mile, Koreatown features such outposts of Korean culture as the fabulous **Beverly Hot Springs** (*see page 194*), a natural mineral water baths that is also a shiatsu massage and treatment centre.

Indians (called East Asians in LA) have dispersed across the basin but there are small concentrations in Artesia, in the South Bay and in the Valley. **Indian Sweets & Spices** is a wonderful chain of Indian groceries, where you can also get fantastic and very cheap platefuls of curry. The most central branch is at 409 Venice Boulevard, at Bagley Avenue, in Culver City (1-310 837 5286).

One nucleus of **African** LA is Fairfax, south of Wilshire Boulevard, where you can find an Ethiopian restaurant row. **Armenians**, 115,000 in total, concentrate in suburban Glendale. Older **Russians**, many of them Jewish (and so with no great reason to love their country of origin), have settled in the social-service-heavy city of West Hollywood. Some 400,000 **Britons** currently live in LA and many of those strange creatures populate the beach – mainly Santa Monica (aka Santa Margate) – and the Hollywood area, making their presence felt in such pubs as **Ye Olde King's Head** and the **Coach & Horses** (*for both, see chapter* **Bars**).

INTERRACIAL TENSIONS

Just because many new immigrants arrived in Los Angeles at the same time did not mean they arrived at the same level. LA is tussling not only with interracial conflicts but race-class conflict, demonstrated most shockingly in he 1992 riots. The rage of blacks following the Rodney King beating was vented not, as expected, on whites, but on Koreans – perceived by blacks as economically better off and exploiters of their neighbourhoods. Some 2,000 Korean businesses were looted, damaged or

Viva Mexico!

For most of the 20th century, Los Angeles's Mexican roots were either 'ignored by Anglo Angelenos or turned into a mythical "Spanish" past,' says sociologist Vilma Ortiz. But the past 25 years of immigration have reconnected LA with its roots and made people of Mexican ancestry the largest ethnic block in the region: 40 per cent of LA County residents, or four million people, are either Mexican-born or trace their origins to Mexico. LA has become the capital of Mexican America, the largest single Mexican concentration outside Mexico City – Mexican politicians even come and campaign among immigrant Mexicans in Los Angeles – and Mexicans are predicted to overtake all other ethnic groups combined by 2020.

MEXICAN INFLUENCES

The number of Mexicans has soared since 1970, but they have lived in Southern California since its inception. When Mexico gained its independence from Spain in 1822, large tracts of land were deeded to local Mexican families, many of whom grew prosperous as ranchers and merchants, until the Mexican-American war in 1848 brought an end to Mexican supremacy. But they left their mark on the region, in the naming of places (Santa Monica, Pasadena, Ventura) and boulevards (La Cienega, La Brea, Figueroa and Sepulveda), and the city itself, formerly the lyrical mouthful El Pueblo de Nuestra Señora la Reina de Los Angeles. Mexican influence is also revealed in adobes and Spanish Mission-style architecture, and in festivals, such as Cinco de Mayo (5 May), celebrating a military victory over French invaders in 1862, and Diez y Seis de Septiembre (16 September), commemorating Mexico's Independence Day.

Under white dominance, Mexicans were reduced to an inferior status, labouring in menial jobs and in the fields of the Central Valley agricultural belt – as a disproportionate number still do. Now, however, a rising number are moving into the middle class, and so great is the Mexican population that an entire economy has arisen around it. Some of the more nationalist Mexicans, and more paranoid anti-immigrants, claim that Mexico, still resentful about losing California in 1848, is conspiring to get it back.

Spanish-speaking radio dominates the airwaves, while publications, sporting events, shops, restaurants, real estate and insurance companies abound, all catering to Mexicans and Central Americans (many of the latter, incidentally, complain of being treated as inferior by Mexicans). Many municipal signs and much official literature are printed in English and Spanish, and the Catholic Church has taken over from Protestantism to become the city's dominant religion, with churches introducing Spanish masses and crying out for Spanish-speaking priests.

LATINO-BLACK TENSION

The emergence of Mexican economic and political power appears threatening to many in the fast-diminishing black and white communities, so much so that the past decade has seen bitter fights over political seats and legislative attempts to slow immigration and stop bilingual education. And, worryingly, tax cuts passed in the past two decades mean that public education and services, now catering increasingly to

destroyed in the three days of trouble; of those, 200 liquor stores were destroyed in South Central LA alone.

Many Middle Easterners were successful entrepreneurs and professionals in their home countries – Iranians, for example, chose to come to LA, says one Iranian journalist, because their children were already there, studying at UCLA and other good California schools. They were able to transfer large sums of money and settle in traditionally affluent white neighbourhoods, and have a reputation for flamboyant wealth. Africans, too, from Ethiopia and Ghana, tend to be well educated and affluent. In a cruel irony,

they seem to move more easily in white professional classes than their distant African-American cousins. Many Africans consider themselves to be very different from African-Americans – they tend not to feel as strongly the racial preoccupations that are the legacy of slavery – and this gives rise to tensions between the two groups.

Indians are often entrepreneurial and very well educated – often better educated than their white US counterparts. They feature prominently in computer and high technology: Bill Gates has upset immigration-control advocates by going to bat for Asian computer

Mexicans, are far inferior to those enjoyed by previous, white generations.

In the poorer communities, the tension between African-Americans and Latinos is mounting, as blacks see their numbers and political power withering. The once predominantly black neighbourhoods, such as Watts and Compton, are now moving towards majority Latino. This is contributing to 'Black Flight' from the inner city to suburban counties, and seething tensions among those left. Some longtime black residents resent the newcomer Mexicans and Central Americans, who they see as bumpkins with their yards full of chickens, washing and cars (a sentiment shared by second- and third-generation Mexican-Americans). There is a feeling that Mexicans took their jobs, and now as black politicians see their seats going to Latinos, are taking their hard-earned, fledgling political power.

This frustration was felt particularly keenly in April 2000 when the city's janitors, many of them immigrant Latinos, went on strike, a strike so effective they won the support of the mayor, the cardinal, various celebs, affluent liberals and, in the end, relatively substantial pay raises. For many African-Americans, who remember when black janitors lost their union jobs to Central Americans who undercut them in the 1980s, this was a bitter pill to swallow.

For people like Joe Hicks, executive director of the Los Angeles City Human Rights Foundation, diffusing Latino-black tension is the city's greatest challenge. But he notes, at a neighbourhood level, people find ways to coexist. They are, for example, uniting to fight for better schools in their neighbourhoods; after 20 years in terrible decline, the Los Angeles School District is attempting to

overhaul the public education system. A darker demonstration of integration is the fact that Latinos now belong to the notorious African-American gangs, the Crips and Bloods, while blacks are being welcomed into the once Latino-only 18th Street gang.

Unfortunately, such camaraderie breaks down in prison; the county jail is one of the most notoriously segregated environments, and, some say, a microcosm of tensions outside. This was highlighted in April 2000 in a vicious attack at a detention centre by Mexican inmates on blacks, whom they outnumbered two to one. The attack was reportedly organised by the notorious old-time Mexican-American gang, active in and outside the prisons, known as the 'Mexican Mafia'.

THE FUTURE

Short of the Mexican birth rate freezing – LA's population is projected to reach 22 million by 2020, due in large part to Mexican population growth – and immigration stopping, the trend will continue, thoroughly transforming Los Angeles from majority white to majority Latino. But, if the trend toward economic self-improvement also continues, most Mexicans will, like all other past immigrants to the US, assimilate into the home-owning, gas-guzzling, Coke-drinking, cheerleading, channel-surfing, God-fearing Americans that many already are.

To really get a sense of Mexican LA, take a walk down Broadway or Olvera Street in Downtown. Or drive into East LA, the heart of the Mexican community. Or head south into South Central on Vermont or Normandie Avenues. Or take Van Nuys Boulevard north into the Valley. Wherever you go, what you'll find is, LA is Mexican LA.

experts, without whom, he says, his company would be short-handed. They have also created a niche market for themselves: motel ownership.

Speaking English on arrival has given Indian immigrants a strong advantage. In West Hollywood, the Russian newcomers' lack of English and seemingly unfriendly manners have given rise to tensions with the gay population that also considers WeHo home. In the city of Glendale, in the San Gabriel Valley, there are sometimes murderous brawling between Armenian and Latinos gangs.

Central Americans have not been made welcome for other reasons. Salvadorans have

arrived fleeing a US-supported right-wing regime, unlike the Indo-Chinese, and are often ill-educated and very poor. Having entered at the bottom of the heap, Central Americans and Mexicans are the backbone of LA's economy, working in disproportionately high numbers in the garment and service industries. Because labour is so cheap and supply so high, an astounding number of middle-class people in Los Angeles have nannies, gardeners, cleaners and sometimes even cooks, giving rise to the charge that LA is a third-world economy. And in addition to helping to grease the wheels of double-income, typically white, Westside family life, many Latin Americans are also sending a portion of their paltry incomes home, to support relatives there. 'Envios' – small businesses that arrange money transfers to Central America and Mexico – can be found throughout Latino neighbourhoods.

ETHNIC ACTION

In the past decade, ethnic LA has become a subject of academic study, material for novels, grist for politicians' mills and scourge of those who hate political correctness. The *Los Angeles Times*, once a bastion of the conservative white establishment, has hired a race relations correspondent, while news programmes bend over backwards to put an 'ethnic' anchor on screen – the preferred type being an indefinable hybrid, clearly not Anglo, but not identifiably another specific race.

The reason for this ethnic appeasement is that over the past ten years or so the tensions have turned into a sense of social and political events. In Monterey Park, inter-ethnic murmurings began in the late 1980s, after the area had gone from being predominantly white then heavily Latino to majority Chinese in the space of 15 years, and triggered a series of ugly racial fights and political battles that have only now settled down.

> **'The five-county Los Angeles region is a mosaic of communities speaking more than 80 languages.'**

The riots in 1992 were the most brutal but arguably most cathartic expression of the stresses. The civil unrest (as the riots are termed in PC parlance) wiped complacency off the face of LA and provoked an unprecedented surge of community and corporate efforts to stimulate economic development and mutual understanding. Promises of greater private and public investment in the inner city have, in reality, translated into limited efforts; Watts, for example, a neighbourhood that has been blighted since earlier riots in 1965, is one of the many South Central areas, now occupied by equal numbers of poor blacks and Latinos, that have missed the late 1990s prosperity train.

One unexpected consequence of the riots was that Korean-Americans found a voice, transforming themselves overnight from a silent to a relatively vocal minority. Angela Oh, one of Los Angeles's most prominent Korean spokeswomen during the riots and their aftermath, became a member of President Clinton's Race Commission. She has often said: 'Korean-Americans were born on 29 April 1992.'

Similarly, Hispanic-Americans were arguably born, or reborn, after the 1994 passage of Proposition 187, a statewide initiative passed convincingly by California voters, which cut off social services and public education to the children of illegal immigrants. It was later deemed unconstitutional by the Supreme Court, and rather than stop the flow of immigrants, as its authors intended, it galvanised the Latino community. Notoriously indifferent to politics, Mexicans and Central Americans rushed to become citizens and activate the voters in their communities, with the result being a sudden, large increase in the number of Latino politicians at local and state level, ousting long-held seats in traditionally white, black and Jewish strongholds.

FUSION CITY

But the counterpart to ethnic tension in Los Angeles is fusion. LA is, after all, the home of the teriyaki hamburger and the kosher burrito. And even though some parts of the city are relatively segregated, many are increasingly mixed. Mike Davis, author of the bestseller *City of Quartz*, once said that the stretch of Vermont Avenue between the I-10 and Hollywood Boulevard has the highest number of different cultures represented on one street in LA, and probably the world. Koreatown shares its neighbourhood with Latinos and blacks, and to the east overlaps with posh, Anglo Hancock Park; the unofficial term for Hancock Park, where 300 Korean families reportedly now live, is 'Han Kook', the native term for Korea.

In the Baldwin Hills area of the predominantly black Crenshaw district (south of the I-10, surrounding Crenshaw Boulevard), you will find the manicured gardens and pagoda-style roofs bequeathed by a former Japanese community (which relocated there after returning from internment camps after World War II), some of whom still live there.

LA is also home to wonderful fusion music groups, such as Ozomatli (a large, multi-ethnic band that mixes Cuban, Brazilian, African, Jamaican, Mexican and jazz influences to perfection), and boasts one of the highest rates of interracial marriage in America. For a taste of inter-ethnic harmony, you need only walk down the Boardwalk in Venice, Third Street Promenade in Santa Monica or CityWalk in Universal City.

Rodney King's poignant plea to the public during the riots – 'Can't we all get along?' – was, and is, heeded by vast numbers in the city. The sense that Los Angeles is a microcosm of the world, a multiracial template for the future, is another reason why this city is such an exciting place to be.

Accommodation

Accommodation 43

Feature boxes

Accommodation

LA is famous for having some of the most glamorous and glitzy hotels in the world, but travellers on a budget are well catered for, too.

What kind of hotel are you after? A city groover, a rural hideaway, a postmodern designer fantasy or a beach belle? whatever you want, Los Angeles has it. And now, even more than ever. In the past couple of years there's been a boom in tourism and the hotels have responded accordingly, madly competing with one another for travellers' attention. Some hotels, such as Loewes in Santa Monica, have undergone multi-million dollar renovations as newcomers Casa Del Mar and Le Merigot have opened their doors by the beach. The Sunset Marquis and the Argyle in West Hollywood have also renovated in the face of competition from the Mondrian and the newer Standard and the Grafton. The latter two belong to a new breed of boutique hotels – others include the Avalon and Maison 140 in Beverly Hills – that are targeting hip travellers with smaller billfolds – *see page 62* **Boutique chic**.

Facilities have improved, too, especially for the business traveller: rooms in all luxury and some standard hotels have at least two phone lines, and often a third one for your computer. You can even get personalised business cards.

PRICES AND SERVICES

Expect to pay $60-$110 in a budget hotel (for a double room, per night), $90-$250 in a mid-range hotel, and from about $250 to any sum you like in a first-class hotel. The cheapest place to stay (bar camping) is in a shared room in a hostel; these start at around $18 per person per night. Budget chain motels can be quite cheap, too (*see page 44* **Chain gang**), especially if there are four of you: double rooms usually have two large double beds, so you can end up paying as little as $25 per person. The rates will be lower the further out you go, and it can be worth the commute, especially since motels are never far from a freeway.

Remember that the quoted rates are 'rack rates' ('official' published rates): the actual cost can be half as much. Ask about corporate, AAA, weekday, promotional and any other kind of discount you can think of. Be aware that, much like an aeroplane, your neighbour is almost certainly not paying the same as you. Room rates usually don't include taxes, which range from 12 to 15 per cent (depending on which city the hotel is in).

Almost all hotels have air-conditioning (we've noted the ones that don't). Except in hostels, rooms will almost always have cable TV, a radio and a telephone (expect to pay a service charge, from 25¢ for a local call, for using it). Many will also have a hairdryer, iron and sometimes a coffeemaker. You can also expect parking facilities: it's usually free at budget and mid-range hotels, but be warned that the overnight charges at the larger and more costly places can increase your bill substantially (charges quoted in the listings below are per night). No-smoking rooms are now more common than smoking ones, so if you want the latter, ask. Most places can accommodate disabled guests.

BOOKING AGENCIES

If you want someone else to search for the options in your price range, contact any of the following services. They'll not only give you a list of hotels, B&Bs and motels, but also make your reservation for you. Some local tourist bureaus (look under the relevant areas in *chapter* **Sightseeing**) have hotel-booking services. The **Los Angeles Convention & Visitors Bureau** (*see page 290*) will not book a room for you, but will send you a copy of its visitor magazine, which contains hotel info.

Bed & Breakfast International
PO Box 282910, San Francisco, CA 94128 (1-800 872 4500/1-408 867 9662/fax 1-408 867 0907/ www.bbintl.com).
Hotel Reservations Network
8140 Walnut Hill Lane, suite 203, Dallas, TX 75231 (1-800 964 6835/1-214 361 7311/fax 1-214 361 7299/www.hoteldiscount.com).
Preferred Hotels & Resorts Worldwide
311 S Wacker Drive, suite 1900, Chicago, IL 60606 (1-800 323 7500/www.preferredhotels.com).

HOTELS ONLINE

Most individual properties now have their own websites, and will take online reservations. There are also hundreds of general websites featuring accommodation in LA.

Try the following: **Los Angeles Hotel Guide** (http://los.angeles.hotelguide.net) and **All-Hotels** (www.allhotels.com). For last-minute discounts, try **Discount Los Angeles Hotels** (www.vacationweb.com/ hotels/la/index.html).

Westside: beach towns

A room in Santa Monica guarantees quick shoreline access, a cooler climate and a beachy California vibe. Venice is grittier and more bohemian, while there are some romantic inns further up the northern shore in Malibu. There are also some good budget options.

First-class

Casa Del Mar

1910 Ocean Way, at Pico Boulevard, Santa Monica, CA 90405 (reservations 1-800 898 6999/front desk 1-310 581 5533/fax 1-310 581 5503/www.hotelcasa delmar.com). Bus Santa Monica 7/I-10, exit Fourth-Fifth Street south. **Rates** $335-$495 single/double; $950-$3,500 suite. **Credit** AmEx, DC, Disc, MC, V. **Map** p304 A3.

In the 1920s, the Casa Del Mar was an exclusive beach club and hotel, frequented by movie stars. In World War II, the US army took it over as an R&R spot for officers. In 1999, and millions of dollars later, it reopened to rave reviews. Set right on the beach with a prime view of the Santa Monica Pier, it brings a taste of the Riviera to LA. Wooden Venetian blinds, gauzy white drapes, bamboo headboards, wicker chairs and Matisse-inspired art adorn the 129 bedrooms and suites. There's also a spa and health club, casual and formal dining and an exquisite pool. **Hotel services** *Bar. Business centre. Concierge. Disabled: adapted rooms. Gym. Laundry. Parking ($18). Pool. Restaurant. Room service (24hr). Spa.* **Room services** *Dataport. Mini-bar. Refrigerator. Turndown. TV: cable/pay movies/VCR.*

Hotel Oceana

849 Ocean Avenue, between Montana & Idaho Avenues, Santa Monica, CA 90403 (reservations 1-800 777 0758/front desk 1-310 393 0486/fax 1-310 458 1182/www.mweb.com/oceana). Bus 22, 333/I-10, exit Fourth-Fifth Street north. **Rates** $325 junior suite; $345-$500 1-bedroom suite; $600-$700 2-bedroom suite. **Credit** AmEx, DC, Disc, MC, V. **Map** p304 A1/2.

Most people choose the bright yellow Oceana because of its proximity to the ocean: it has clear views to Santa Monica beach, and is only two blocks from Third Street Promenade. The 63 one-bedroom suites, many set around the centrepiece pool or with balconies facing the ocean, aim to recall the art deco era of the Côte d'Azur: vivid yellows, pinks and blues, wrought iron and wicker abound. All rooms have Frette linen, down duvets, marble bathrooms and fully equipped kitchens. Breakfast and a free newspaper are delivered daily to the room. There is no on-site restaurant, but room service is provided by the nearby Wolfgang Puck Café. **Hotel services** *Babysitting. Business centre. Concierge. Disabled: adapted rooms. Gym. Laundry. Limousine service. Parking ($18). Pool. Room service (11am-10pm).* **Room services** *CD player. Dataport. Kitchen. Mini-bar. Refrigerator. TV: cable/pay movies.*

Chain gang

There are hundreds of chain hotels, ranging from budget to luxury, in Los Angeles. Try these:

First-class

The Four Seasons 1-800 332 3442/ www.fourseasons.com
Ritz Carlton 1-800 241 3333/ www.ritzcarlton.com
Hilton Hotels 1-800 445 8667/ www.hilton.com
Hyatt 1-800 233 1234/www.hyatt.com
Sheraton Hotels & Inns 1-800 325 3535/ www.sheraton.com

Mid-range

Holiday Inn 1-800 465 4329/ www.basshotels.com/holiday-inn
Howard Johnson 1-800 654 2000/ www.hojo.com
Marriott 1-800 228 9290/ www.marriott.com
Radisson 1-800 333 3333/ www.radisson.com

Budget

Best Western 1-800 528 1234/ www.bestwestern.com
Comfort Inns 1-800 228 5150/ www.comfortinn.com
Days Inn 1-800 325 2525/ www.daysinn.com
Motel 6 1-800 466 8356/ www.motel6.com
Super 8 1-800 800 8000/ www.super8.com
Travelodge 1-800 578 7878/ www.travelodge.com

Le Merigot

1740 Ocean Avenue, at Pico Boulevard, Santa Monica, CA 90401 (reservations 1-800 926 9524/ front desk 1-310 395 9700/fax 1-310 395 9200/ www.LeMerigotHotel.com). Bus Santa Monica 7, 8/ I-10, exit Fourth-Fifth Street south. **Rates** $279-$569 room; $1,200-$1,800 suite. **Credit** AmEx, DC, Disc, MC, V. **Map** p304 A3.

The newest upmarket hotel in Santa Monica is also the most practical and affordable and, arguably, trying the hardest. Slammed between Loews and Shutters, both geographically and aesthetically, the 175-room contemporary European-styled hotel attracts a mix of corporate clients and families. Frette linen, down pillows, terry cloth robes and slippers and Bare Essentials toiletries are standard, as is its signature Butler Express service (one button on the phone for all your needs). The full-service spa – with redwood sauna and eucalyptus steam room – is a big draw, while casual to fine dining is offered in contemporary Cal-French restaurant Cezanne. **Hotel services** *Bar. Business centre. Concierge. Disabled: adapted rooms. Gym. Laundry. Limousine service. Parking ($22). Pool. Restaurant. Room service (6am-1am). Spa.* **Room services** *CD player. Dataport. Mini-bar. Refrigerator. TV: cable/ pay movies.*

Loews Santa Monica Beach Hotel

1700 Ocean Avenue, between Colorado Avenue & Pico Boulevard, Santa Monica, CA 90401 (reservations 1-800 235 6397/front desk 1-310 458 6700/fax 1-310 458 6761/www.loewshotels.com). Bus 33, 333, Santa Monica 1, 7, 8/I-10, exit Fourth-Fifth Street north. **Rates** $240-$445 single/double; $600-$2,750 suite. **Credit** AmEx, DC, Disc, MC, V. **Map** p304 A3.

The 340-room Loews is just what you'd expect from Southern California: light and airy, warm and beachy, casual but elegant, especially after its recent expensive renovation. The four-storey atrium lobby (with newly added palm trees) takes full advantage of its scenic surroundings. The beach is just across the street and the oceanfront park, pier, restaurants and Third Street Promenade are a painless stroll away. Food highlights include a spectacular Sunday brunch, revered French restaurant Lavande and Papillon, a new bar and fireside lounge.

Hotel services *Babysitting. Bar. Beauty salon. Concierge. Disabled: adapted rooms. Fax. Garden. Gym. Laundry. Parking ($15.40-$18). Pool. Restaurants (2). Room service (24hr). Spa.* **Room services** *Dataport. Fax. Mini-bar. Turndown. TV: cable/pay movies.*

Shutters on the Beach

1 Pico Boulevard, at Ocean Avenue, Santa Monica, CA 90405 (reservations 1-800 334 9000/front desk 1-310 458 0030/fax 1-310 458 4589/www.shutters onthebeach.com). Bus 33, 333, 436, Santa Monica 7/ I-10, exit Fourth-Fifth Street south. **Rates** $360-$595 single/double; $895-$3,050 suite. **Credit** AmEx, DC, Disc, MC, V. **Map** p304 A3.

Nothing comes between Shutters' guests and the beach. It opened in 1993 and, except for its sister property Casa Del Mar (*see p44*), is the only hotel in Santa Monica that's actually on the beach. Beyond the lobby – with its two roaring fireplaces (come rain or shine) and original artworks by David Hockney and Roy Lichtenstein – are 198 rooms including 12 suites, custom-furnished in luxury beach decor. Think Ralph Lauren. Many of the bathrooms feature whirlpool tubs with views out to sea. There are two restaurants: the divine and upmarket 1 Pico, and the more modest Pedals Café.

Hotel services *Babysitting. Bar. Bike hire. Concierge. Disabled: adapted rooms. Gym. Laundry. Parking ($17). Pool. Restaurants (2). Room service (24hr). Spa.* **Room services** *CD player. Dataport. Mini-bar. Safe. Turndown. TV: cable/pay movies/VCR.*

Mid-range

Casa Malibu Inn on the Beach

22752 Pacific Coast Highway, between Malibu Pier & Carbon Canyon, Malibu, CA 90265 (reservations 1-800 831 0858/front desk 1-310 456 2219/fax 1-310 456 5418/casamalibu@earthlink.net). Bus 434/ I-10, exit PCH north. **Rates** $119-$199 single/double; $249-$329 suite. **Credit** AmEx, MC, V.

This small, two-storey, 1949 motel, owned by Joan and Richard Page, is the best choice in its price range along the northern shore. Each of its 21 rooms (including two suites) has classy furnishings and a coffeemaker; some have fireplaces, kitchens and/or private decks. Upgraded rooms include Italian tiling and the kind of seriously stunning bathrooms you'd expect from a luxury hotel. The buildings are covered with flowing vines and surround a garden courtyard and a brick patio that looks directly on to the hotel's private beach. Robert de Niro is rumoured to favour the Malibu Suite.

Hotel services *Fax. Garden. Laundry. Limited air-conditioning. Parking (free). Private beach. Room service (10am-9pm).* **Room services** *Dataport. Refrigerator. TV: cable/pay movies.*

Channel Road Inn

219 W Channel Road, between Pacific Coast Highway & Rustic Road, Santa Monica, CA 90422 (1-310 459 1920/fax 1-310 454 9920/www.channel roadinn.com. Bus Santa Monica 9/I-10, exit PCH north. **Rates** $160-$335. **Credit** AmEx, MC, V. **Map** p304 A1.

This historical Colonial Revival house, clad in blue shingle, was moved from its original hilltop site to its current location, one block from the beach and surrounded by four excellent restaurants. It is now run as a romantic country inn by Susan Zolla. Four-poster, sleigh and pencil-post canopy beds adorn the 14 bedrooms, all of which have luxurious private bathrooms; some have wooden balconies. If you're not lucky enough to get first dibs on Room 6 with its own living room and two-person jacuzzi at the foot of the bed, there's a jacuzzi in the garden. Room 3 is also delightful, with a fireplace, and jacuzzi for two.

Hotel services *Business centre. Concierge. Disabled: adapted room. Garden. Limited air-conditioning. Parking (free). Room service (7.30am-10am).* **Room services** *TV: cable/VCR.*

The Georgian

1415 Ocean Avenue, between Broadway & Santa Monica Boulevard, Santa Monica, CA 90401 (reservations 1-800 538 8147/front desk 1-310 395 9945/fax 1-310 451 3374/www.georgianhotel.com). Bus 4, 33, 304, Santa Monica 1, 10/I-10, exit Fourth-Fifth Street north. **Rates** $235-$285 single/double; $350-$500 suite. **Credit** AmEx, DC, Disc, MC, V. **Map** p304 A2.

The best thing about this 84-room hotel is its pale yellow and blue deco façade, complete with veranda and red-boothed basement restaurant (which used to be a speakeasy purportedly frequented by Bugsy

Siegel and Al Capone). Early evening cocktails are served on the veranda, where you can gaze across to the beach. The rooms tend to border on the drab, but have funky charm; the ones with ocean views are best. The bathrooms boast original art deco tiles. The place is also said to be haunted.

Hotel services *Bar. Concierge. Disabled: adapted rooms. Laundry. Parking ($15). Room service (6.30am-10pm).* **Room services** *Dataport. Fax. Mini-bar. Safe. Turndown. TV: cable/pay movies/ Nintendo.*

Inn at Playa Del Rey

435 Culver Boulevard, at Pershing Drive, Playa Del Rey, CA 90293 (1-310 574 1920/fax 1-310 574 9920/ www.innatplayadelrey.com). Bus 220, Commuter Express 438/I-405, exit Culver Boulevard west. **Rates** $160-$225 single/double; $225-$335 suite. **Credit** AmEx, Disc, MC, V.

Under the same ownership as the divine Channel Road Inn (*see p45*), this place is perfect if you have a car or don't need to be right in Venice or Santa Monica. It's a new building designed to look old; in fact, it's the scaled-down inn version of Shutters. Natural sunlight filters through the 21 rooms, each tricked out with tasteful furniture, bright quilts, seaside-inspired doodahs and fresh flowers. The bathrooms – two with two-person whirlpool tubs – are to die for. There's no swimming pool, but there's a beautiful deck for sunbathing and a jacuzzi set among rose bushes. Best of all is the location: it's behind the Ballona Wetlands, home to at least 85 bird species.

Hotel services *Business centre. Disabled: adapted rooms. Garden. Parking (free). Room service (8-10am).* **Room services** *Dataport. Turndown. TV: cable/pay movies/VCR.*

Shangri-La

1301 Ocean Avenue, at Arizona Avenue, Santa Monica, CA 90401 (reservations 1-800 345 7829/ front desk 1-310 394 2791/fax 1-310 451 3351/ www.shangrila-hotel.com). Bus 22, 434, Santa Monica 1, 10/I-10, exit Fourth-Fifth Street north. **Rates** $160 single/double; $205-$310 1-bedroom suite; $330 2-bedroom suite; $450-$540 penthouse. **Credit** AmEx, DC, Disc, MC, V. **Map** p304 A2.

Across from oceanfront Palisades Park, the art deco Shangri-La, built in 1939, prides itself on its spacious rooms and great ocean views. The 54 rooms (including 35 suites and two penthouse suites) are plain and adorned with deco furniture that has seen better days, but most have kitchens, and the bathrooms are clean and roomy. The downsides? There's no pool, room service, restaurant or bar – but you do get breakfast, afternoon tea and free parking.

Hotel services *Fax. Garden. Gym. Laundry. Parking (free).* **Room services** *Dataport. Kitchen. Refrigerator. TV.*

Also recommended

Ritz Carlton Marina Del Rey 4375 Admiralty Way, Marina del Rey, CA 90292 (1-310 823 1700).

Budget

Bayside Hotel

2001 Ocean Avenue, at Bay Street, Santa Monica, CA 90405 (1-310 396 6000/fax 1-396 1000). Bus 33, 333, Santa Monica 7/I-10, exit Fourth-Fifth Street south. **Rates** $84-$119 single/double; $104-$169 single/double with ocean view. **Credit** AmEx, DC, Disc, MC, V. **Map** p304 A3.

A few blocks south of Santa Monica's shopping and dining action and across from the beach, the Bayside is reached through a beautiful oceanfront park. And it's surprisingly well appointed, considering it's an elderly motel. The 44 rooms – some with kitchens, some with ocean views – have been smartened up with furnishings from the legendary Beverly Hills Hotel (*see p49*), better mattresses and cable TV and direct-dial dataport phones. The bathrooms still have their original pale pink, green and blue 1950s tiles. The south-facing rooms are air-conditioned; the rest rely on ceiling fans and sea breezes. The hotel also offers daily morning tours of the area's sights.

Hotel services *Fax. Garden. Limited air-conditioning. Parking (free). Phones.* **Room services** *Dataport. Turndown. TV: cable/pay movies.*

The Cadillac

8 Dudley Avenue, at Speedway Street, Venice, CA 90291 (1-310 399 8876/fax 1-310 399 4536/ www.thecadillachotel.com). Bus 33, 333, 436, Santa Monica 2/I-10, exit Fourth-Fifth Street south. **Rates** $25 hostel bed; $89-$110 single/double; $130 suite. **Credit** AmEx, MC, V. **Map** p304 A4.

Built in 1905, this four-storey hotel was once Charlie Chaplin's summer home. Its front yard is in the heart of Venice Beach, complete with rollerbladers, bikers and sunbathers, and is as vibrant as its beachfront surroundings. It's a popular hangout for young world travellers, who like the location, amenities and deco interior. There are three hostel rooms, each with two bunk beds and a shared bath, and 40 private rooms (on the tackier side of deco, with black lacquer furnishings and industrial carpeting). Common areas include a sun deck and a lounge with pool table.

Hotel services *No air-conditioning. Babysitting. Disabled: adapted rooms. Gym. Laundry. Parking (free). Sauna.* **Room services** *Safe. TV.*

Hotel California

1670 Ocean Avenue, between Pico Boulevard & Colorado Avenue, Santa Monica, CA 90401 (1-310 393 2363/fax 1-310 393 1063/www.hotelca.com). Bus 33, 333, Santa Monica 8/I-10, exit Fourth-Fifth Street north. **Rates** $125-$150 single; $155-$170 2-bedroom suite. **Credit** AmEx, Disc, MC, V. **Map** p304 A3.

Sandwiched between the Loews hotel (*see p45*) and a string of commercial properties, this two-storey inn is a half-block from the beach and entered from a gated cul-de-sac lined with private houses and greenery. The surfboards adorning the front of the property (formerly the Belle Blue Inn) announce its casual vibe. The newly renovated rooms – 21, plus five suites – are on the small side, with bland, minimalist decor and tiny bathrooms. However, many have cute love seats and hardwood floors. It's a smoke-free zone, apart from the courtyard.

Hotel services *No air-conditioning. Courtyard. Disabled: adapted room. Fax. Laundry. Parking ($9).* **Room services** *Dataport. Refrigerator. Turndown. TV: satellite/VCR.*

Hotel Carmel by the Sea

201 Broadway, at Second Street, Santa Monica, CA 90401 (reservations 1-800 445 8695/front desk 1-310 451 2469/fax 1-310 393 4180/www.hotel carmel.com). Bus 4, 33, 434, Santa Monica 7, 8, 10/I-10, exit Fourth-Fifth street north. **Rates** $70-$80 room with shared bath; $109 single; $139 double; $189 suite. **Credit** AmEx, DC, Disc, MC, V. **Map** p304 A2.

Hotel Carmel opened in the 1930s; its walls show their age, but that doesn't stop young visitors from packing the place: its location one block from the beach and around the corner from Third Street Promenade, plus its cheap rates, make it one of the best budget bets in the area. The 102 rooms (16 with shared bathrooms) have wooden furnishings and colourful bedspreads. Bathrooms are basic.

Hotel services *Disabled: adapted rooms. Fax. Laundry. Parking ($7.70).* **Room services** *Dataport.*

Venice Beach House Historic Inn

15 30th Avenue, at Speedway Street, Venice, CA 90291 (1-310 823 1966/fax 1-310 823 1842). Bus 108, Culver City 1, 2, Commuter Express 437/I-10, exit Fourth-Fifth Street south. **Rates** $95-$165. **Credit** AmEx, MC, V. **Map** p304 A5.

This Craftsman-style inn, built in 1911, was the summer home of Abbot Kinney, Venice Beach's founder, and Warren Wilson, who started the *Daily News*. Surrounded by a lush garden, it's a peaceful retreat from the circus of Venice at its back door. Now owned by Vivienne and Phil Boesch, it has nine rooms bedecked with dark wood, beautiful antiques and padded fabric walls. Most have private bathrooms. We recommend the understated Abbot Kinney Room (masculine in feel, with red and green plaid walls), the Pier Suite (a floral pink affair, with a fireplace and peekaboo view of the ocean) or the James Peasgood Room (with a balcony, vaulted ceiling and two-person jacuzzi).

Hotel services *No air-conditioning. Fax. Garden. Parking (free).* **Room services** *TV: cable.*

Also recommended

Best Western Jamaica Inn Bay 4175 Admiralty Way, Marina del Rey, CA 90292 (1-310 823 5333); **Cal Mar Hotel Suites** 220 California Avenue, Santa Monica, CA 90403 (1-310 395 5555); **The Inn at Venice Beach** 327 Washington Boulevard, Venice, CA 90291 (1-310 821 2557).

Westside: inland

Beverly Hills and West Hollywood (in particular Sunset Strip) provide the hotels of myth and legend that have made LA famous. Here you'll find some of the world's most luxurious hotels, from the historic – the Argyle, Beverly Hills Hotel, Chateau Marmont, Hotel Bel-Air, Regent Beverly Wilshire – to more modern contenders – the Mondrian and the new St Regis and W.

Enjoy stunning views from the rooftop pool at the art deco **Argyle**. *See p49.*

Note that the stretch of Santa Monica Boulevard in West Hollywood is in the middle of a massive reconstruction project, which makes driving a nightmare and parking even worse than usual, so avoid it if it you can. Work should be finished by autumn 2001.

First-class

The Argyle

8358 Sunset Boulevard, betweeen Sweetzer Avenue & La Cienega Boulevard, West Hollywood, CA 90069 (reservations 1-800 225 2637/front desk 1-323 654 7100/fax 1-323 654 9287/www.arygle hotel.com). Bus 2, 3, 302/I-10, exit La Cienega Boulevard north. **Rates** $210-$325 single/double; $285-$1,200 suite. **Credit** AmEx, DC, MC, V. **Map** p306 B1.

This 15-storey, 1931 building in the heart of Sunset Strip was formerly the Sunset Tower apartment building (home to Bugsy Siegel, Charlie Chaplin, Marilyn Monroe and Errol Flynn) and later the St James Club. An art deco masterpiece, it has 64 guest rooms, all with spectacular views and period and repro furnishings. The bathrooms, with their deco tiling, are equally stylish; some have steam showers and jacuzzi tubs. There's a functional small gym and sauna, and a fabulously romantic terrace with an azure swimming pool (that appeared in *The Player*) ornamented by fibreglass palm trees. Fenix, the beautiful restaurant and pool-level bar, doubles as a 'Young Hollywood' nightspot.
Hotel services *Babysitting. Bar. Butler (24hr). Concierge (24hr). Disabled: adapted rooms. Fax. Gym. Laundry. Limousine service. Parking ($19.50). Pool. Restaurant. Room service (24hr). Sauna.* **Room services** *CD player. Dataport. Fax. Mini-bar. Refrigerator. Safe. TV: cable.*

Beverly Hills Hotel & Bungalows

9641 Sunset Boulevard, at Crescent Drive, Beverly Hills, CA 90210 (reservations 1-800 283 8885/front desk 1-310 276 2251/fax 1-310 887 2887/www.the beverlyhillshotel.com). Bus 2, 302, 305/I-405, exit Sunset Boulevard east. **Rates** $300-$400 single/double; $600-$3,000 suite; $380-$3,000 bungalow. **Credit** AmEx, DC, MC, V. **Map** p305 B1.

The pink palace opened its doors in 1912, drawing guests such as Charlie Chaplin and Rudolph Valentino. Thanks to its $100-million renovation by new owner, the Sultan of Brunei, it still oozes the sort of grandiose glamour one associates with Old Hollywood. Pink-shirted valets relieve you of your car, where a red carpet (of course) leads you to the ornate front doors. The interior is signature pink spotted with green banana-leaf swirls, and the likes of Arnold Swarzenegger hold court in the famous Polo Lounge restaurant. The rooms are giddy with flouncey drapes, overstuffed chairs, gilded mirrors and bathrooms the size of small sitting rooms. There are 21 bungalows (with their own private entrances): No.5 has its own pool, while No.7 is decorated to Marilyn Monroe's taste. There's also an

Chateau Marmont: hotel of the stars.

Olympic-sized pool with private cabanas, tennis courts with a resident Wimbledon pro and acres of grounds in which to roam.
Hotel services *Babysitting. Bar. Beauty salon. Concierge. Disabled: adapted rooms. Garden. Gym. Jogging trails. Laundry. Limousine service. Parking ($21). Pool. Restaurants (3). Room service (24hr).* **Room services** *CD player. Dataport. Fax. Mini-bar. Turndown. TV: cable/pay movies/VCR.*

Chateau Marmont

8221 Sunset Boulevard, between Sweetzer Avenue & Crescent Heights Boulevard, Hollywood, CA 90046 (reservations 1-800 242 8328/front desk 1-323 656 1010/fax 1-323 655 5311). Bus 2, 3, 302/I-10, exit La Cienega Boulevard north. **Rates** $220 single/double; $290-$450 suite; $675-$975 bungalow; $1,000-$1,950 penthouse. **Credit** AmEx, DC, MC, V. **Map** p306 B1.

Columbia Pictures boss Harry Cohn told young stars William Holden and Glenn Ford: 'If you must get into trouble, do it at the Chateau Marmont.' The seven-storey building above Sunset Strip was modelled after the Loire Valley's Château Amboise, and is known for its discretion as much as for its funky-chic charm. Since 1933, stars such as Greta Garbo, Jean Harlow and Clark Gable have checked in and found it hard to leave. Howard Hughes rented the large penthouse and spied on starlets around the pool. Roman Polanski spent his last two days in the US holed up here. John Belushi fatally ODd in one of the bungalows. A steady stream of partying rock stars took its toll on the place until 1990, when new owner Andre Balazs returned it to its original dignified yet raffish aesthetic. It is set in lush grounds dripping with bougainvillea and eucalyptus. Add the cool and famous clientele, the hotel's lounge and outdoor dining patio, the popular next-door Bar Marmont (*see p168*) and immediate access to Sunset Boulevard into the equation and you've got one of the hippest hotels in town.

Hotel services *Babysitting. Bar. Concierge. Disabled: adapted rooms. Fax. Garden. Gym. Laundry. Limited air-conditioning. Parking ($21). Pool. Restaurant. Room service (24hr).* **Room services** *CD player. Dataport. Mini-bar. Refrigerator. Turndown. Safe. TV: cable/VCR.*

Four Seasons Los Angeles at Beverly Hills

300 S Doheny Drive, at Burton Way, Beverly Hills, CA 90048 (reservations 1-800 332 3824/front desk 1-310 273 2222/fax 1-310 859 9048/www.four seasons.com). Bus 27, 316, 576/I-10, exit Robertson Boulevard north. **Rates** $305-$395 single; $335-$425 double; $490-$4,500 suite. **Credit** AmEx, DC, MC, V. **Map** p306 A3.

The Four Seasons is a hermetically sealed world of soothing luxury; from the moment you walk into the lobby you're enveloped in its sensual embrace. Larry Flynt visits regularly for Sunday brunch at the award-winning Gardens restaurant (where if diners are wearing black they're given a dark napkin rather than the traditional white – a mark of the hotel's rarified service). Dennis Quaid was spotted at the rooftop pool adjacent to the tented outdoor gym, Brenda Blethyn stayed here to promote a recent film and Sean Penn was spied with friends at Windows Bar. Frette linen adorns the legendary beds (which, after countless requests, guests can now purchase). And the hotel has just opened a pristine new spa (*see p194*).

Hotel services *Babysitting. Bar. Concierge. Disabled: adapted rooms. Fax. Garden. Gym. Laundry. Parking (free-$22). Pool. Restaurants (2). Room service (24hr). Spa.* **Room services** *CD player. Dataport. Mini-bar. Refrigerator. Safe. Turndown. TV: cable/pay movies/VCR.*

Hotel Bel-Air

701 Stone Canyon Road, at Bellagio Road, Bel Air, CA 90077 (reservations 1-800 648 4097/front desk 1-310 472 1211/fax 1-310 476 5890). I-405, exit Sunset Boulevard east. **Rates** $325-$435 single/ double; $525-$2,500 suite. **Credit** AmEx, Disc, MC, V.

Built by an oil millionaire and purchased by the Sultan of Brunei's brother, Jeffrey, while on one of his infamous spending sprees, the 1920s, pink, Mission-style Hotel Bel-Air is sophisticated, luxurious and impossibly romantic. Movie stars, dignitaries and world travellers have been retreating to this five-star hideaway long before Marilyn Monroe booked her room by the pool. Warren Beatty and Annette Bening set up home here when their own was ravaged by the 1994 earthquake. The setting is

Hotel Bel-Air: a luxurious, romantic oasis, complete with swans.

heavenly, with a lake where three swans, well, swan around, and a well-designed garden wilderness scattered with courtyards, fountains and arches and dripping with bougainvillea, azaleas and camellias. It's a modest two storeys, so still has the air of a private estate. The 92 rooms are impeccably stylish, and each has a private entrance from the gardens. It's not unusual to see celebs (Nancy Reagan still lunches here and Jack Nicholson's daughter was wed here), but don't attempt commemorative pics – exclusivity means no cameras are allowed.

Hotel services *Babysitting. Bar. Beauty salon. Concierge (24hr). Disabled: adapted rooms. Fax. Garden. Gym. Laundry. Parking ($13.50). Pool. Restaurant. Room service (24hr).* **Room services** *CD player. Dataport. Mini-bar. Safe. TV: cable/pay movies/VCR.*

Le Meridian at Beverly Hills

465 S La Cienega Boulevard, at Clifton Way, Beverly Hills, CA 90048 (reservations 1-800 645 5624/hotel operator 1-310 247 0400/fax 1-310 247 0315). Bus 27, 105, 576/I-10, exit La Cienega Boulevard north. **Rates** $290-$335 single; $315-$360 double; $385-$1,800 suite. **Credit** AmEx, DC, Disc, MC, V. **Map** p306 B3.

Formerly the Asian-inspired Hotel Nikko, Le Meridian may now have a few European accents, but it still offers Eastern minimalism coupled with high-tech chic. The black granite lobby is dominated

by a Japanese-style rock garden with fountains and a towering atrium. Behind the Hana Lounge is the pool area (as seen in the film *Indecent Proposal*) and, upstairs, the 302 rooms range from 'deluxe' to the $1,800-per-night Presidential Suite. Each room has contemporary Japanese-style furnishings, shoji screens, subdued lighting and luxuriously soft, canopied beds. The bathrooms are huge, and some have sunken Japanese tubs. Mobile phones are provided for use anywhere on the property.
Hotel services *Babysitting. Bars (2). Concierge (24hr). Disabled: adapted rooms. Fax. Garden. Gym. Laundry. Parking (free). Pool. Restaurant. Room service (24hr). Spa.* **Room services** *CD player. Dataport. Mini-bar. Refrigerator. Safe. Turndown. TV: cable/satellite/VCR.*

Mondrian Hotel

8440 Sunset Boulevard, at La Cienega Boulevard, West Hollywood, CA 90069 (reservations 1-800 525 8029/front desk 1-323 650 8999/fax 1-323 650 5215/www.mondrianhotels.com). Bus 2, 3, 302/ I-10, exit La Cienega Boulevard west. **Rates** *$285-$340 single/double; $350-$900 suite; $2,100-$2,600 penthouse.* **Credit** *AmEx, DC, Disc, MC, V.* **Map** *p306 A/B1.*
Enter through gargantuan doors into the *Alice in Wonderland*-like world of erstwhile Studio 54 club owner turned hotelier, Ian Schrager. The place oozes with scenesters, celebrities, leggy models, vampy blondes and plain ol' wannabes, posing in the white on white lobby, the über-hip SkyBar (*see p168*) and the newly opened New York import, Asia de Cuba restaurant. Philippe Starck's design may be minimalism at its best (although sometimes horribly uncomfortable), but what the hotel lacks in clutter and colour, it makes up for a thousandfold in pretension and attitude. In the guest rooms, instead of the conventional bible, you'll find a copy of Raymond Chandler's *Farewell My Lovely*.
Hotel services *Babysitting. Bar. Children's play area. Concierge (24hr). Disabled: adapted rooms. Fax. Gym (24hr). Jacuzzi. Laundry. Parking ($20). Pool. Restaurants (2). Room service (24hr). Steam room.* **Room services** *CD player. Dataport. Mini-bar. Safe. Turndown. TV: cable/VCR with video library.*

Peninsula Beverly Hills

9882 S Santa Monica Boulevard, at Wilshire Boulevard, Beverly Hills, CA 90212 (reservations 1-800 462 7899/front desk 1-310 551 2888/fax 1-310 788 2319/www.peninsula.com). Bus 27, 304, 316/I-405, exit Santa Monica Boulevard east. **Rates** *$395-$475 single/double; $725-$3,000 suite.* **Credit** AmEx, DC, Disc, MC, V. **Map** *p305 B2/3.*
Bellhops in the Peninsula's signature snappy white uniforms and gold-crested caps greet the famous, the wealthy and the corporate elite at the hotel's discreet location, eight blocks off Rodeo Drive. The five-star/five-diamond hotel encompasses a whole city block with just under 200 rooms, suites and villas. Highlights include the Belvedere restaurant, the mahogany-lined Club Bar and the

gracious Living Room (*see p163*), where guests sip tea or champagne and look out on to gardens planted with palm trees, vines and magnolias. The tranquil pool with private cabanas is fronted by the patio restaurant, beauty salon and spa, overlooking the city and the hills. There is 24-hour check-in and check-out.
Hotel services *Bar. Beauty salon. Concierge (24hr). Disabled: adapted rooms. Fax. Garden. Laundry. Limousine service & complimentary Rolls-Royce service in Beverly Hills. Gym. Parking ($23). Pool. Restaurants (2). Room service (24hr). Spa.* **Room services** *Dataport. Mini-bar. Refrigerator. Safe. Turndown. TV: cable/VCR.*

Raffles L'Ermitage Beverly Hills

9291 Burton Way, at Elm Drive, Beverly Hills, CA 90210 (reservations 1-800 800 2113/front desk 1-310 278 3344/fax 1-310 278 8247/www.lermitage hotel.com). Bus 27, 316, 576/I-405, exit Wilshire Boulevard east. **Rates** *$418-$448 room; $780-$3,800 suite.* **Credit** AmEx, DC, Disc, MC, V. **Map** *p305 C2.*
The 124-room L'Ermitage, located moments from Beverly Hills' best shops and restaurants, is one of the most popular new hotels with business travellers and those with an extravagant sense of luxury. The standard room (although pricey) is anything but standard in its size, design and accoutrements – such as five phones and a cellphone. The mini-bar is equipped for serious bon vivants, while the lighting and temperature controls remember your preferred settings. A beautiful domed restaurant offers superb French-inspired cuisine, which you can enjoy anywhere you wish – by the rooftop pool with panoramic views, in the VIP cigar lounge or even in the spa. Perks include free local calls and room service, and 24-hour check-in and check-out.
Hotel services *Bar. Beauty salon. Business centre. Concierge. Disabled: adapted rooms. Fax. Garden (rooftop). Gym. Laundry. Limousine service. Parking ($21). Pool. Restaurant. Room service (24hr). Spa.* **Room services** *CD/DVD player. Dataports (4). Fax/printer/copier. Mini-bar. Safe. Turndown. TV: cable/VCR.*

Regent Beverly Wilshire

9500 Wilshire Boulevard, between Rodeo & El Camino Drives, Beverly Hills, CA 90212 (reservations 1-800 421 4354/front desk 1-310 275 5200/fax 1-310 274 2851/www.regenthotels. com). Bus 20, 21, 720/I-405, exit Wilshire Boulevard east. **Rates** *$385-$545 single/double; $570-$7,500 suite.* **Credit** AmEx, DC, Disc, MC, V. **Map** *p305 C2.*
This 395-room, Italian Renaissance-style hotel (as featured in *Pretty Woman*) is one of LA's favourite luxury hotels. Built in 1928, it is renowned for its old-world opulence (vaulted ceilings, columns, Murano glass chandeliers and marble floors) and famous clientele. The rooms (all understated and oversized) are in two wings: the historic Wilshire wing and the more modern Beverly. Warren Beatty, at the height of his playboy career, shacked up here

The fabulous **Argyle** on Sunset Strip, built in 1931. *See p49.*

for 12 years. Visiting heads of state opt for the Presidential Suite ($7,500 a night). There's a cosy bar frequented by cigar-smoking businessmen, tourists and well-heeled women. With its updated spa and fitness centre and Four Seasons management, things couldn't be better.
Hotel services *Ballroom. Bar. Beauty salon. Concierge (24hr). Disabled: adapted rooms. Fax. Gym. Laundry. Limousine service. Parking ($23). Pool. Restaurants (2). Room service (24hr). Spa.* **Room services** *Dataport. Mini-bar. Refrigerator. Safe. Turndown. TV: cable/pay movies.*

The St Regis Los Angeles

2055 Avenue of the Stars, at Constellation Boulevard, Century City, CA 90067 (reservations 1-877 787 3452/front desk 1-310 277 6111/fax 1-310 277 3711/www.stregis.com). Bus 27, 28, 328/ I-405, exit Santa Monica Boulevard east. **Rates** $460-$760 single/double; $850-$1,950 suite; $5,550-$10,000 penthouse. **Credit** AmEx, Disc, DC, MC, V. **Map** p305 B3.

The hotel formerly known as the Westin Century Plaza has undergone a total renovation and is now the most recent luxury addition to the city. Its regal interiors have Spanish overtones and delightful modern twists, with colossal pillars, orange-hued wooden floors, leather chairs, metal chandeliers and a giant fresco of flamenco dancers running the length of the marble-topped lobby bar. Each of the 297 rooms has a small private balcony, while Asian-inspired touches give a new twist to the well turned-out but otherwise orthodox rooms. Close to the attractions of Century City and Beverly Hills, it's a swell place to hole up in, hang out by the new pool and spa or exercise in the glass-covered gym.
Hotel services *Bar. Beauty salon. Concierge (24hr). Disabled: adapted rooms. Garden. Gym. Laundry. Limousine service. Parking ($23). Pool. Restaurant. Room service (24hr). Spa.* **Room services** *CD player. Dataport. Mini-bar. Safe. Turndown. TV: cable/pay movies/VCR.*

Sunset Marquis Hotel & Villas

1200 N Alta Loma Road, at Sunset Boulevard, West Hollywood, CA 90069 (reservations 1-800 858 9758/ front desk 1-310 657 1333/fax 1-310 652 5300). Bus 2, 3, 302/I-10, exit La Cienega Boulevard north. **Rates** $255-$5,000 suite; $350-$1,330 villa. **Credit** AmEx, DC, MC, V. **Map** p306 A1.

In the heart of West Hollywood, but set back on a residential street, the Sunset Marquis was once part of Lionel Barrymore's estate. In the 1980s, it became LA's first all-suite boutique hotel. The 114 rooms have balconies or private patios, many overlooking the pool. Twelve villas clustered around a smaller, more exclusive pool have hosted the likes of Julio Iglesias and Aerosmith's Steven Tyler, and come with their own private butler. It has always been a mecca for the rock 'n' roll, film and media crowd – it's the only hotel to boast its own recording studio in the basement, and a gym personally kitted out by repeat guest Keith Richards. Despite the celebrity clients drinking at the popular Whiskey Bar, the hotel is refreshingly devoid of elitist attitude and makes everyone feel like a VIP in a manner best described as nonchalant charm.
Hotel services *Babysitting. Bar. Concierge. Disabled: adapted rooms. Fax. Laundry. Gym. Parking ($18). Pools (2). Restaurant. Room service (24hr).* **Room services** *CD player. Dataport. Kitchen. Mini-bar. Safe. TV: cable/pay movies/VCR.*

The W

930 Hilgard Avenue, at Le Conte Avenue, Westwood, CA 90024 (reservations US 1-800 421 2317/ UK 0800 897529/front desk 1-310 208 8765/ fax 1-310 824 0355/www.whotels.com). Bus 305, 361, Santa Monica 1, 2, 12/I-405, exit Wilshire Boulevard east. **Rates** $250-£1,099. **Credit** AmEx, Disc, DC, MC, V.

Formerly the Westwood Marquis, the 258-suite W is one of the city's bright new stars. The decor, by former set designer (*Dances with Wolves*) Dayna Lee, seems to be a friendly poke at Philippe Starck's Mondrian (*see p51*), with its oversized scale: giant 1950s-style lamps, monolithic pillars and immense framed mirrors. But whereas Starck stays clear of anything that isn't white on white, Lee has infused the hotel with succulent greens and mauves against a backdrop of white walls, black wooden floors, concrete pillars and wall-to-ceiling frosted glass screens. Bonuses include the lively Mojo restaurant, a full-service spa and two pools: a shell-shaped number and a serious lap pool.
Hotel services *Bars (2). Business centre. Concierge. Disabled: adapted rooms. Garden. Gym. Laundry. Parking ($23). Pools (2). Restaurants (2). Room service (24hr). Spa.* **Room services** *CD players (2). Dataport. Mini-bar. Refrigerator. Safe. Turndown. TV: cable/pay movies/VCR/web TV.*

Wyndham Bel Age Hotel

1020 N San Vicente Boulevard, at Sunset Boulevard, West Hollywood, CA 90069 (reservations 1-800 996 3426/front desk 1-310 854 1111/fax 1-310 854 0926/www.wyndham.com). Bus 2, 3, 105, 305/ I-10, exit La Cienega Boulevard north. **Rates** $199-$275 corporate; $219-$295 suite; $400-$900 grand class suite. **Credit** AmEx, DC, Disc, MC, V. **Map** p306 A1.

Located just below Sunset Strip and around the corner from the Viper Room (*see p242*), this ten-storey, brown stucco structure contains 200 one- and two-bedroom suites. Attractions include the top-class Diaghilev restaurant, the La Brasserie nightclub, which hosts live jazz, and the excellent Alex Roldan hair salon containing Lisa Wilson's beauty salon (*see p198*). A kitschy collection of sculptures and artworks adorns the common areas, while the rooftop pool scattered with palm trees provides city views. The large, comfortable suites have been recently renovated in rather dull grey and burgundy tones. High-tech touches include high-speed wireless Internet access in public areas.
Hotel services *Bars (2). Beauty salon. Concierge. Disabled: adapted rooms. Fax. Gym. Jacuzzi. Laundry. Parking ($19). Pool. Restaurants (2).*

Room service (24hr). **Room services** CD player.
Dataport. Mini-bar. Kitchenette. Refrigerator.
Turndown. TV: cable/ pay movies/satellite/VCR/
web TV.

Also recommended

Century Plaza Hotel & Spa 2025 Avenue of
the Stars, Century City, CA 90067 (1-310 277 2000);
Hotel Sofitel 8555 Beverly Boulevard, West
Hollywood, CA 90048 (1-310 278 5444).

Mid-range

Hilgard House Hotel

927 Hilgard Avenue, at Le Conte Avenue, Westwood,
CA 90024 (reservations 1-800 826 3934/front desk
1-310 208 3945/fax 1-310 208 1972). Bus 305,
361, Santa Monica 1, 2, 12/I-405, exit Wilshire
Boulevard east. **Rates** $119-$139 single/double;
$159-$250 suite. **Credit** AmEx, DC, Disc, MC, V.
Across from the W (*see p53*) is the understated but
elegant 55-room Hilgard House. The lobby looks like
an English library, while the rooms are cosy
European in style, and include three new penthouse
suites. It lacks extras – there's no pool, gym, bar or
restaurant – but with continental breakfast, free
parking and a good location (surrounded by UCLA
and Westwood shopping), it's a darn good deal.
Hotel services *Concierge. Disabled: adapted rooms.*
Fax. Laundry. Parking (free). Room service (7-10am).
Room services *Dataport. Refrigerator. TV: cable.*

Hotel Del Capri

10587 Wilshire Boulevard, at Westholme Avenue,
West LA, CA 90024 (reservations 1-800 444 6835/
front desk 1-310 474 3511/fax 1-310 470 9999).
Bus 20, 22, 720/I-405, exit Wilshire Boulevard east.
Rates $85-$140 single; $95-$140 double; $120-$140
suite. **Credit** AmEx, MC, V. **Map** p305 A3.
This hotel is a floral oasis offering splendid respite
from the surrounding high-rises and Wilshire
Boulevard traffic. It's popular with touring dance
companies and Europeans, who enjoy the community atmosphere, and is adorned with tropical fish
tanks, fountains and other decorative touches rarely
found in such affordable lodgings. The 80 rooms are
divided between a hotel block and a motel-style
building around a lovely courtyard pool (open 24
hours). Perks include continental breakfast and the
close proximity of Westwood Village and UCLA,
both six blocks away.
Hotel services *Concierge. Garden. Laundry.*
Parking (free). Pool (24hr). Room service (7am-3pm).
Room services *Dataport. Turndown. TV: cable.*

Le Montrose Suite Hotel

900 Hammond Street, between Sunset & Santa
Monica Boulevards, West Hollywood, CA 90069
(reservations 1-800 776 0666/front desk 1-310 855
1115/fax 1-310 657 9192/www.lemontrose.com).
Bus 2, 3, 105, 305/I-405, exit Santa Monica
Boulevard east. **Rates** $295 junior suite; $390
executive suite; $475 1-bedroom suite. **Credit** AmEx,
DC, Disc, MC, V. **Map** p306 A2.

Le Montrose offers affordable, comfortable suites
and a central location on a residential street, just
two blocks south of Sunset Boulevard. The 132
suites are spotless, tastefully furnished in contemporary style, and the beds are wonderfully large.
The modest rooftop saltwater pool has a com-
manding view of LA, looking out over the nearby
Beverly Center, and there's a fitness centre, sauna
and tennis court – a rarity for any hotel in LA. Dogs
are not just welcomed, they're treated as VIPs with
in-room pet sitting, pooch massage and grooming.
Its nearby sister property, Le Parc Suite Hotel, is
also an all-suite hotel. Ideal for families and couples.
Hotel services *Babysitting. Bicycles. Concierge*
(24hr). Disabled: adapted rooms. Garden. Gym.
Laundry. Limousine service. Parking ($18). Pool.
Restaurant. Room service (24hr). Spa. **Room**
services *CD player. Dataport. Kitchen. Mini-bar.*
Refrigerator. Safe. Turndown. TV: cable/pay movies/
VCR.
Branch: Le Parc Suite Hotel 733 N West Knoll
Drive, between Hancock Avenue & Westmount
Drive, West Hollywood, CA 90069 (1-310 855 8888).

Luxe Hotel Rodeo Drive

360 N Rodeo Drive, at Brighton Way, Beverly Hills,
CA 90210 (reservations 1-800 468 3541/front desk
1-310 273 0300/fax 1-310 859 8730). Bus 4, 20,

The best Hotels

For a sense of LA lore

Mix with the ghosts of Hollywood past, from
Charlie Chaplin to Marilyn Monroe, at
Chateau Marmont (see page 49), the
impossibly romantic **Hotel Bel-Air** (see
page 50) or the pink palace **Beverly Hills
Hotel** (see page 49).

For beachside chic

If you want a room actually on the beach,
try **Shutters** (see page 45) or new sister
property **Casa Del Mar** (see page 44).
Newcomer **Le Merigot** (see page 44) offers
a sensual spa and top-notch service.

For budget fun

Stars abound at the festive **Best Western
Hollywood Hills Hotel** (see page 57), while
singing cockatoos and a cheerful vibe await
at the **Beverly Terrace** (see page 55). Or
make the most of vibrant Venice at the
Cadillac (see page 47).

For pretension & attitude

The **Mondrian** (see page 51), home to the
ultra-hip SkyBar and Philippe Starck's
whiter than white minimalist decor, is a
narcissist's dream.

Inn at Playa Del Rey:
a tranquil haven. *See p47.*

21, 27/I-405, exit Wilshire Boulevard east. **Rates**
$255-$275 single/double; $325-$375 suite; $925-
$1,400 penthouse. **Credit** AmEx, DC, Disc, MC, V.
Map p305 C2.
The former Summit has reopened as the slick and
very moderne Luxe, right in the heart of Beverly
Hills' prime shopping area. The 88 rooms are decorated in stark white and slate blues and greys, with
oversized gilt mirrors, Roman blinds, wicker chairs,
black-and-white photos and fine striped linen.
There's not much public space apart from the minimalist lobby, second-floor sun deck and gym, and
Café Rodeo (sure to become a hip local spot) – but a
shuttle will take you to its sister property in Bel Air
to swim, play tennis or get pampered in the spa.
Hotel services *Babysitting. Bar. Business centre.
Concierge. Disabled: adapted rooms. Laundry.
Parking ($18). Restaurant. Room service (6am-
10.30pm).* **Room services** *CD player. Dataport.
Mini-bar. Refrigerator. Turndown. TV: satellite.*

Ramada West Hollywood

*8585 Santa Monica Boulevard, between La Cienega
Boulevard & Rugby Drive, West Hollywood, CA
90069 (reservations 1-800 228 2828/front desk
1-310 652 6400/fax 1-310 652 2135/www.ramada-
wh.com). Bus 4, 304/I-10, exit La Cienega Boulevard
north.* **Rates** $165 single/double; $175-$279 suite.
Credit AmEx, DC, Disc, MC, V. **Map** p306 A2.
Slap-bang in the middle of WeHo's 'Boy's Town',
within walking distance of Sunset Strip and the
Beverly Center and next door to a very popular
Starbucks and a fab health food supermarket, the
Ramada is a plain but friendly chain hotel. It has
some nice neo-art deco touches and was completely
redecorated in 1998. The 175 rooms include 25 suites
(each with a refrigerator, mini-bar and microwave),

of which 20 are double-storey. Best of all are the two
monolithic corner suites with spiral staircases and
giant beds. It's popular with a mixed crowd, from
business people to gays and families.
Hotel services *Bar. Concierge. Disabled: adapted
rooms. Gym. Laundry. Parking ($15). Pool.
Restaurant. Room service (5am-11pm Mon-Thur;
5am-2am Fri-Sun).* **Room services** *Mini-bar.
Refrigerator. Safe. Turndown. TV: cable/pay
movies/ VCR.*

Also recommended

Beverly Crescent Hotel 403 N Crescent Drive,
Beverly Hills (1-310 247 0505); **The Beverly Hills
Inn** 125 S Spalding Drive, Beverly Hills, CA 90210
(1-310 278 0303); **Beverly Plaza** 8384 W Third
Street, LA, CA 90048 (1-323 658 6600); **Carlyle Inn**
1119 S Robertson Boulevard, West LA, CA 90035
(1-310 275 4445).

Budget

Beverly Terrace Hotel

*469 N Doheny Drive, at Santa Monica Boulevard &
Melrose Avenue, Beverly Hills, CA 90210 (1-310 274
8141/ fax 1-310 385 1998/www.beverlyterracehotel.
com). Bus 3, 304/I-10, exit Robertson Boulevard
north.* **Rates** $95-$115 single; $115-$165 double.
Credit AmEx, DC, Disc, MC, V. **Map** p306 A2.
This gem of a European-style pension has few
frills, but a cheerful vibe that attracts bohemian
souls for short- or long-term stays. A pair of singing
cockatoos provide a welcome in the lobby. The 39
rooms are pretty basic, but bright, with vivid paintings in gilt frames and painted wooden furniture. All
have en suite bathrooms (some with only showers).

Central Park SummerStage

presented by

Heineken®

CATCH A WORLD OF PERFORMERS AMERICAN MUSIC WORLD MUSIC SPOKEN WORD MODERN DANCE INTERNATIONAL CABARET DJ'S ELECTRONIC MUSIC PERFORMANCE ART OPERA WORLDSHOPS KIDS ROCK N' ROLL AFRICAN MUSIC COUNTRY REGGAE HIP HOP POETRY BRAZILIAN FUNK CALYPSO GOSPEL CELTIC

NEW YORK CITY'S FAVORITE FREE PERFORMING ARTS F E S T I V A L

TRADITIONAL DANCE TRIP-HOP R&B BHANGRA SOUL GYPSY MUSIC BLUEGRASS SALSA SOUL COMPAS MERENGUE SKA SAMBA BLUES LATIN ROCK AFRO-BEAT RAI JAZZ HOUSE MUSIC MBALAX BEAT BOX SOCA ZYDECO QWAALI POPULAR MUSIC CLASSICAL MANGUE BEAT AND MUCH, MUCH MORE CONCERTS DANCE SPOKEN WORD OPERA FAMILY EVENTS MID JUNE - MID AUGUST *www.SummerStage.org*

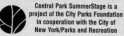

Central Park SummerStage is a project of the City Parks Foundation in cooperation with the City of New York/Parks and Recreation

All shows at Rumsey Playfield,
72nd Street, Mid Park
INFO/VOLUNTEER HOTLINE: 212.360.2777
Pick up a summer issue of *Time Out New York* Magazine
for a complete listing of Central Park SummerStage events.

Some rooms are built around a modest courtyard pool where potted palms and ficus trees provide shade. The excellent continental breakfast includes a fantastic walnut bread. The location, at the junction of Melrose and Doheny, puts it just inside the Beverly Hills frontier – at these rates, that's rare. **Hotel services** *Courtyard. Parking (free). Pool. Restaurant.* **Room services** *Dataport. Refrigerator. TV: cable.*

The Secret Garden B&B

PO Box 46164, LA, CA 90046 (1-323 656 8111/ 3888/fax 1-323 656 9992/www.secretgardenbnb. com). **Rates** from $95 single/double. **Credit** MC, V.
LA's best B&B is so secluded that the management asked us not to print the address. But we can reveal that it's tucked away at the bottom of Laurel Canyon, within walking distance of the most buzzing shopping/eating complex in the area, and is an oasis of tranquillity. Run by the ex-maître d of legendary restaurant Chasen's, the pink, 1923 Spanish-Moorish-style building has five beautiful rooms, all with private bathrooms. As its name suggests, there's a gorgeous fairy tale garden, complete with jacuzzi. While serving his home-cooked breakfasts, host Raymond is happy to regale guests with tales of celebrity goings-on at Chasen's. **Hotel services** *No air-conditioning. Business centre. Garden. Laundry. Parking (free). Piano.* **Room services** *TV: cable.*

Hollywood & Midtown

Hollywood is not the best place for luxury hotels, but it's a good choice for budget travellers looking for funky, characterful options that suit the historical surroundings.

Mid-range

Clarion Hollywood Roosevelt Hotel

7000 Hollywood Boulevard, between N Highland & N La Brea Avenues, Hollywood, CA 90028 (reservations 1-800 252 7466/front desk 1-323 466 7000/fax 1-323 462 8056/www.hotelchoice.com). Metro Hollywood-Highland/bus 1, 180, 181, 212/ US 101, exit Highland Avenue south. **Rates** $143 single; $170-$197 double; $197-$269 suite. **Credit** AmEx, DC, MC, V. **Map** p307 A1.
In the middle of gritty Hollywood Boulevard, opposite Mann's Chinese Theater, stands the surprisingly pleasant if touristy 335-room Hollywood Roosevelt, a 1927 landmark building that was once the hub of Hollywood's party circuit. The first Academy Awards were held here, Marilyn Monroe lived here for eight years and legend has it that Bill 'Bojangles' Robinson taught Shirley Temple how to tap dance up the lobby staircase. Staff say the place is haunted by Montgomery Clift and Marilyn Monroe (her room is still intact, her wardrobe mirror hangs in the lower lobby and some claim they've seen her face in it). The two-storey Spanish Colonial lobby, with its hand-stencilled ceilings and arched doorways, is

Beverly Terrace Hotel: low-key charm. *See p55.*

impressive. The rooms are less glamorous, but are individually decorated. There's a David Hockney painting on the bottom of the pool. **Hotel services** *Babysitting. Bars (2). Disabled: adapted rooms. Fax. Gym. Jacuzzi. Laundry. Parking ($9.50). Pool. Restaurant. Room service (6am-11pm).* **Room services** *Mini-bar. Safe. TV: cable/pay movies.*

Budget

Best Western Hollywood Hills Hotel

6141 Franklin Avenue, between N Gower Street & Vista del Mar, Hollywood, CA 90028 (reservations 1-800 287 1700/front desk 1-323 464 5181/fax 1-323 962 0536). Bus 26, Community Connection 208/US 101, exit Gower Street north. **Rates** $99-$139 single/ double. **Credit** AmEx, DC, Disc, MC, V. **Map** p307 B1.
No budget hotel celebrates Hollywood and festivity like this one. Located near the 101 freeway, this family-run hotel looks grim on the outside, but inside, the lobby is swank and moody, walls throughout are adorned with murals and posters of movie stars and cartoon characters, and every guest room has a glittery star on the door. There are two buildings: the newer one, renovated in 1998, is motel-

like, with a dapper, modern decor and outdoor entrances looking down on the courtyard pool; the older building has larger, less formal rooms. The Hollywood Hills Coffee Shop off the lobby is a fave with hip celebrities.

Hotel services *Disabled: adapted rooms. Fax. Laundry. Parking (free). Pool. Restaurant. Room service (7am-10pm).* **Room services** *Dataport. Kitchenette. Refrigerator. TV: cable.*

Beverly Laurel Motor Hotel

8018 Beverly Boulevard, at N Laurel Avenue, Hollywood, CA 90048 (1-323 651 2441/fax 1-323 651 5225). Bus 14, 217, DASH Fairfax/I-10, exit La Cienega Boulevard north. **Rates** $75 single; $79 double. **Credit** AmEx, DC, MC, V. **Map** p306 B2.

It looks like a 1950s dive from the outside, and is priced accordingly, but the owners' artistic flare has turned the Beverly Laurel into one of the funkier motels around. Its location is good – close to the Beverly Center mall and West Hollywood – and the 52 rooms, although a tad tired, are made original by gold-and-black checked bedspreads, black vinyl chairs, groovy '50s tables and wooden headboards inlaid with arcane photos. In most rooms, one wall is painted cobalt blue. Some rooms have kitchens; all have microwaves and fridges. The adjoining restaurant, Swingers, is a popular breakfast and late-night spot. It's one of the best deals in town – especially for larger groups.

Hotel services *Fax. Parking (free). Pool. Restaurant.* **Room services** *Dataport. Microwave. Refrigerator. TV: cable.*

Bevonshire Lodge Motel

7575 Beverly Boulevard, at Curson Avenue, Hollywood, CA 90036 (1-323 936 6154/fax 1-323 936 6640). Bus 14, DASH Fairfax/I-10, exit La Brea Avenue north. **Rates** $52.50 single; $56.50 double. **Credit** AmEx, MC, V. **Map** p306 C2.

The enormous rubber tree growing from a hole in the Bevonshire's lobby carpet and extending along the two-storey windows is an indication of how long this motel has been around. Though a splash of paint is needed in some areas, every bathroom has been recently remodelled and the carpets are new. The 24 rooms are sizeable and many come with full kitchens; all have cable TV and fridges and circle the unheated courtyard pool. There's no restaurant, but the popular Authentic Café is across the street and health food emporium Erewhon is close by, as are many of Beverly Boulevard's trendy boutiques, coffeehouses and restaurants.

Hotel services *Parking (free). Pool.* **Room services** *Refrigerator. TV: cable.*

Highland Gardens Hotel

7047 Franklin Avenue, at La Brea Avenue, Hollywood Hills, CA 90028 (reservations 1-800 404 5472/front desk 1-323 850 0536/fax 1-323 850 1712). Bus 1, 2, 3, 4, 212, 420/US 101, exit Highland Avenue south. **Rates** $55-$80 single; $60-$80 double; $80-$110 suite. **Credit** AmEx, MC, V. **Map** p307 A1.

Beverly Laurel Motor Hotel: for funky travellers on a budget.

Rooms here may be reminiscent of a *Brady Bunch* set, but they're huge, dirt cheap and only a few blocks from star-paved Hollywood Boulevard. Common areas consist of a simple lobby (with free coffee and pastries) and a heated courtyard pool. The rooms surround the pool and offer the basics in 1970s colours and decor, with enormous bedrooms, kitchens and/or living rooms. Per square foot, no hotel in town can touch this for value. A ghoulish fame claim is that Janis Joplin overdosed here – in Room 105 – on 4 October 1970, when the hotel was called the Landmark.

Hotel services *Disabled: adapted rooms. Fax. Garden. Laundry. Parking (free). Pool.* **Room services** *Dataport. Refrigerator. TV: cable.*

Hollywood Hills Magic Hotel

7025 Franklin Avenue, between La Brea & Orange Avenues, Hollywood, CA 90028 (reservations 1-800 741 4915/front desk 1-323 851 0800/fax 1-323 851 4926/www.magichotel.com). Bus 1, 180, 181, 212, 217, 429/US 101, exit Highland Avenue south. **Rates** $55-$69 single; $69-$85 executive suite; $79-$109 deluxe suite; $105-$139 2-bedroom suite. **Credit** AmEx, Disc, DC, MC, V. **Map** p307 A1.

Across the street from the Highland Gardens (*see p58*) is the motel-like Magic Hotel. The 40 rooms are large and clean, with newish furnishings and carpeting and stiff mattresses. Old magic show posters adorn the walls, in reference to the neighbouring Magic Castle, a private magicians' club. All rooms surround the courtyard, which has a pool and lounge furniture, and each includes a safe, iron, hairdryer, free coffee and cable TV. All (except for the singles) have a kitchenette.

Hotel services *Laundry. Parking (free). Pool. Room service (9am-5pm).* **Room services** *Dataport. Kitchenette. Refrigerator. Safe. TV: cable.*

Downtown

Although Downtown digs generally cater to business travellers, there are some historical gems among the skyscrapers, such as the very regal Regal Biltmore.

Some kind of renaissance also seems to be on its way: successful club owner Marc Smith and money manager Sedd (son of artist Ed) Moses are reopening the El Dorado Hotel, at the corner of Spring and Fourth Streets, in late 2001. The 1913 building will boast its original opulent lobby, as well as 150-plus rooms, a bar, restaurant, brasserie and spa, and be 'arcanely different', they say.

First-class

The New Otani Hotel & Garden

120 S Los Angeles Street, at First Street, LA, CA 90013 (reservations 1-800 273 2294/ front desk 1-213 629 1200/fax 1-213 622 0980/www.newotani. com). Bus 30, 31, 40, 42, DASH A/I-101, exit Los Angeles Street south. **Rates** *$180-$195 single/double; $600 Japanese suite; $500-$1,800 suite.* **Credit** AmEx, DC, Disc, MC, V. **Map** p309 C2.

This Japanese hotel at the gateway of Little Tokyo, steps from the Civic Center and the Performing Arts Center (*see p228* **Dorothy Chandler Pavilion**), has 434 guest rooms, some western, others traditional Japanese tatami rooms with shoji-screen doors, soft futons and deep soaking tubs. Add in shiatsu massage, dinner in A Thousand Cranes restaurant – which overlooks manicured Japanese gardens, replete with ponds and waterfalls – and you might be thousands of miles from LA. There's also the Garden Grill for Tokyo-style teppanyaki dining, Azalea for contemporary California food and three cocktail lounges, one with live entertainment and one with karaoke. Alas, they are short of a swimming pool.

Hotel services *Babysitting. Bars (3). Beauty salon. Business centre. Concierge (24hr). Disabled: adapted rooms. Garden. Gym. Laundry. Limousine service. Parking ($14.85-$19.25). Restaurants (3). Room service (6am-11pm). Spa.* **Room services** *Dataport. Mini-bar. Refrigerator. Safe. TV: cable/ pay movies/VCR.*

Omni Los Angeles Hotel

California Plaza, 251 S Olive Street, at Second Street, LA, CA 90012 (reservations 1-800 442 5251/front desk 1-213 617 3300/fax 1-213 617 3399/www.omnihotels.com). Metro Civic Center-Tom Bradley/bus 14, 76, 78, 378, 379, 401, 402/I-110, exit Fourth Street east. **Rates** *$150-$260 single; $210-$280 double; $350-$1,300 suite.* **Credit** AmEx, DC, Disc, MC, V. **Map** p309 B2.

Formerly called the Inter-Continental, the Omni is a welcome departure from generic business hotels. Located next door to the Museum of Contemporary Art, it blends the traditional with the boldly creative – and the result is impressive. An enormous, light lobby, with grand floral arrangements, a huge, bright yellow sculpture and calming orchestral music, gives way to soothing taupe-and-olive rooms. Each has an en suite bath and shower, chaise longue, comfy love seat and an oversized desk. 'Club level' guests are housed on floors 16 or 17, with access to the hotel's business centre. This is the hotel where OJ Simpson's jury stayed.

Hotel services *Bar. Business centre. Concierge. Disabled: adapted rooms. Gym. Laundry. Limousine service. Parking ($18-$20). Pool. Restaurant. Room service (24hr). Sauna. Steam room.* **Room services** *Dataport. Mini-bar. Refrigerator. Turndown. TV: cable.*

Regal Biltmore

506 S Grand Avenue, at Fifth Street, LA, CA 90071 (reservations 1-800 245 8673/front desk 1-213 624 1011/fax 1-213 612 1545/www.the biltmore.com). Metro Pershing Square/bus 76, 78, 79, 96, 378, 379, 401, 402/I-110, exit Sixth Street east. **Rates** *$145-$235 single/double; $290-$2,000 suite.* **Credit** AmEx, Disc, MC, V. **Map** p309 B3.

Built in 1923, the 11-storey Biltmore is the oldest hotel in Downtown, and still maintains the Italian-Spanish Renaissance elegance that enticed such dignitaries as Winston Churchill, Princess Margaret, Presidents Truman, Kennedy and Ford – and the Beatles. The cathedral-like lobby and common areas have hand-painted frescos (by Italian artist Giovanni Smeraldi, who also contributed to the White House and the Vatican), bas-reliefs, a fountain, beautifully ornate ceilings and stupendous floral arrangements. The rooms are not as impressive as the common parts, but have recently been given a face-lift. Most come with mini-bars and refrigerators. The health club has a Roman-style steam room, pool, jacuzzi and sauna. Sadly, the fabulous Bernard's restaurant has been turned into a steakhouse, but Sai Sai offers excellent Japanese food.

Hotel services *Babysitting. Bars (3). Beauty salon. Concierge. Disabled: adapted rooms. Gym. Laundry. Parking ($17.50). Pool. Restaurants (3). Room service (24hr). Spa.* **Room services** *Dataport. TV: cable/ pay movies.*

Also recommended

Wyndham Checkers Hotel 535 S Grand Avenue, LA, CA 90071 (1-213 624 0000).

Mid-range

Hotel Figueroa

939 S Figueroa Street, at Olympic Boulevard, LA, CA 90015 (reservations 1-800 421 9092/front desk 1-213 627 8971/fax 1-213 689 0305/www.figueroa hotel.com). Bus 81, 434, 439, 460, DASH A, F/-110, exit Ninth Street east. **Rates** $88-$175 single/double. **Credit** AmEx, DC, MC, V. **Map** p309 A4.

An exotic oasis near the Convention Center and the new Staples Center sports arena, the 12-storey, 285-room Figueroa was originally built in the 1920s as a YWCA. It's now Southwestern meets Spanish/Moroccan funky-chic – a whirlwind of hand-painted everything, including elevators, doors and ceilings, with Mexican tables and chairs and huge pots filled with exotic plants. Some rooms are large, some small and each is uniquely decorated. Especially cool are the Clay Pit Indian restaurant and the outdoor Veranda Bar overlooking the pool and garden.
Hotel services *Bar. Disabled: adapted rooms. Garden. Laundry. Parking ($8). Pool. Restaurants (2). Spa.* **Room services** *Dataport. Refrigerator. TV: satellite.*

The Inn at 657

657 W 23rd Street, at Figueroa Street, LA, CA 90007 (reservations 1-800 347 7512/front desk 1-213 741 2200/www.patsysinn675.com). Bus 81, 442, 444, 445, 603/I-110, exit Adams Boulevard west. **Rates** $110-$125. **Credit** MC,V.

One of LA's nicest mid-range B&Bs, located on a safe residential street, and popular with visiting scholars, museum curators and business people. Former teacher and lawyer turned innkeeper Patsy Carter has been running the place for ten years and recently bought the adjacent property. There are five suites (with en suite bathrooms and living rooms) in the original building, and six in the newer one, which has air-conditioning and new bathrooms. All rooms feature a cosmopolitan and elegant array of furniture from different periods. Enjoy the generous breakfast served in the intimate dining room or on the patio, and the unique and friendly atmosphere.
Hotel services *Garden. Laundry. Parking (free).* **Room services** *Dataport. Microwave. Refrigerator. TV: cable/VCR.*

Westin Bonaventure Hotel & Suites

404 S Figueroa Street, at Fourth Street, LA, CA 90071 (reservations 1-800 228 3000/front desk 1-213 624 1000/fax 1-213 612 4800/www.westin. com). Metro Seventh Street-Metro Center/bus 60, 434, 436, 466/I-110 north, exit Third Street east. **Rates** $175-$235 single; $202-$242 double; $308 suite. **Credit** AmEx, DC, Disc, MC, V. **Map** p309 B2.

Five gargantuan, cylindrical, mirrored towers fused together, the Bonaventure is a major contributor to Downtown LA's skyline. From the outside, it's a visual wonder; from the inside, a mini-city. Occupying an entire city block, the hotel has 12 glass elevators that shoot you to your (rather small) room – one of 1,354, each with floor-to-ceiling windows.

Tower suites are twice the size. There's a huge health and tennis centre, a revolving rooftop lounge called Top of Five (*see p170*) and a shopping gallery with more than 40 shops and restaurants. There's also one all-suite tower with a Japanese guest floor (24-hour translation, Japanese newspapers, TV and breakfast), and sky bridges to the World Trade Center. The hotel was renovated in 1998.
Hotel services *Bars (3). Beauty salon. Business centre. Concierge (24hr). Disabled: adapted rooms. Gym. Laundry. Parking ($19). Pool. Restaurants (20). Room service (24hr). Spa.* **Room services** *Dataport. Refrigerator. Safe. Turndown. TV: cable.*

Budget

Stillwell Hotel

838 S Grand Avenue, between Eighth & Ninth Streets, LA, CA 90017 (1-800 553 4774/1-213 627 1151/fax 1-213 622 8940). Metro Seventh Street-Metro Center or Pershing Square/bus 76, 78, 79, 96, 378, 379, 401, 402, DASH C/I-110, exit Ninth Street east. **Rates** $44-$49 single; $54-$59 double. **Credit** AmEx, DC, MC, V. **Map** p309 B3.

Aged and ultra-budget, the 232-room Stillwell isn't much to look at, but it's cheap and located only a few blocks from the LA Convention Center and the California Mart. The staff can be abrupt, but the hotel has both an Indian and a Mexican restaurant and authentic barflies in Hank's Bar (*see p170*). Some rooms have mini-bars and refrigerators.
Hotel services *Bar. Business centre. Disabled: adapted rooms. Laundry. Limousine service. Parking ($4). Restaurants (2).* **Room services** *TV: cable/VCR.*

The Valleys

First-class

Ritz-Carlton Huntington Hotel & Spa

1401 S Oak Knoll Avenue, at Wentworth Avenue, Pasadena, CA 91106 (reservations 1-800 241 3333/front desk 1-626 568 3900/fax 1-626 568 3700). Bus 485/I-110, exit Glenarm Street east. **Rates** $185-$310 single; $200-$1,310 double; $495-$2,000 suite. **Credit** AmEx, DC, Disc, MC, V.

On 23 pristine acres (9.3 hectares), the Ritz's 1907 palace stands amid Japanese gardens and vast grassy expanses – a perfect escape from LA's traffic and crowds. It has 392 rooms, including ten cottages; Jim Carrey rents the Presidential Suite when he's in the neighbourhood. The rooms and cottages are elegant, with plush robes and marble bathrooms. Splash in the Olympic-sized pool, soak in the spa, play on the tennis court, stroll through the gardens, snack on sushi, swing dance on Friday night or indulge in Sunday's champagne brunch – whatever you do, you'll be hard-pressed to find a reason to leave this peaceful (albeit pricey) retreat.
Hotel services *Babysitting. Bar. Beauty salon. Business centre. Concierge (24hr). Disabled: adapted*

rooms. Garden. Gym. Laundry. Limousine service.
Parking ($20). Pool & swimming lessons. Restaurants
(2). Room service (24hr). Spa. **Room services**
Dataport. Mini-bar. Safe. Turndown. TV: cable.

Mid-range

The Sportsmen's Lodge
12825 Ventura Boulevard, at Coldwater Canyon
Avenue, Studio City, CA 91604 (reservations 1-800
821 8511/front desk 1-818 769 4700/fax 1-818 769
4798/www.slhotel.com). Bus 150, 240, 750/I-101,
exit Coldwater Canyon Avenue south. **Rates** $134-
$172 single/double; $187-$290 suite. **Credit** AmEx,
DC, Disc, MC, V.
This relaxed and charming Valley landmark has 191
rooms painted dusty rose, green and blue and decorated in country pine, some with chintzy four-poster
beds. The excessively large pool is the focal point,
and the coffeeshop/diner with its 1950s-style counter
serves good all-American breakfasts. There's also a
pub-style bar, a modest gym and the more elegant
Caribou restaurant set near a man-made lake in
extensive gardens. A lot of TV stars stay here
because it's so convenient for the studios.
Hotel services *Bar. Beauty salon. Disabled:*
adapted rooms. Garden. Gym. Laundry. Parking
(free). Pool. Restaurants (2). Room service (6.30am-
9pm). **Room services** *Dataport. TV: cable.*

Also recommended
Sheraton Universal Hotel 333 Universal
Terrace Parkway, Universal City, CA 91608
(1-818 980 1212).

Orange County & Anaheim

First-class

The Disneyland Hotel
1150 W Magic Way, between Ball Road & Katella
Avenue, Anaheim, CA 92802 (reservations 1-714
520 5005/front desk 1-714 778 6600/fax 1-714
*956 6597/www.disney.com/Disneyland/plan/resort_*
hotels/). Bus 460/I-5, exit Disneyland Drive south.
Rates $180-$275 single/double; $350-$2,000 suite.
Credit AmEx, DC, Disc, MC, V.
Hotel services *Babysitting. Bar. Concierge.*
Disabled: adapted rooms. Garden. Gym. Laundry.
Parking ($10). Pools (3). Restaurants (5). Room
service (5am-1am). **Room services** *Dataport. Safe.*
Turndown. TV: cable.

Disney's Grand Californian Hotel
Reservations 1-877 700 3476/www.disney.com/
Disneyland/plan/resort_hotels/. **Rates** $315-$335
single/double; $590 suite. **Credit** AmEx, DC, Disc,
MC, V.
Hotel services *Babysitting. Business centre.*
Concierge. Disabled: adapted rooms. Garden. Gym.
Laundry. Parking. Pools (3). Restaurants (4). Room
service (24hr). Spas (2). **Room services** *Dataport.*
Safe. TV: cable.

Disney's Paradise Pier Hotel
1717 Disneyland Drive, at Katella Avenue, Anaheim,
CA 92802 (1-714 999 0990/fax 1-714 776 5763/
www.disney.com/Disneyland/plan/resort_hotels/).
Bus 460/I-5, exit Disneyland Drive south. **Rates**
$195-$235 tower; $270-$310 concierge level; $350-
$450 suite. **Credit** AmEx, DC, Disc, MC, V.
Hotel services *Babysitting. Bars. Concierge.*
Disabled: adapted rooms. Garden. Gym (24hr).
Laundry. Parking ($10-$15). Pool. Restaurants (2).
Room service (6am-1am). **Room services** *Dataport.*
Refrigerator. TV: cable.
Both the Disneyland Hotel and Paradise Pier are
adjacent to the Disneyland theme park and surrounded by restaurants, an outdoor pool with a
sandy shore and volleyball court, shops and the
monorail that functions as a shuttle to Disneyland.
The rooms themselves are rather disappointing:
not in quality, but because they're not fantastical
enough. The Disneyland Hotel (990 rooms) features traditional Disney (Mickey, Donald et al)
while the Paradise Pier (502 rooms) honours modern Disney (*The Lion King*). The Paradise Pier, the
fancier of the two, is currently less central, but
when Disney's enormous new extension, California
Adventure, is completed in early 2001, the hotel
will look directly on to the new park. And actually inside the new park will be the Grand
Californian (750 rooms), which marks Disney's
move into the four-star league. It's built in an Arts
& Crafts style and houses the Napa Rose restaurant, helmed by Napa Valley star Andrew Sutton,
a health club and spa and a separate pool for
adults. Big bonus: with the purchase of a basic
Disney passport, guests can enter the park two
hours before the rest of the public.

Ritz-Carlton Laguna Niguel
1 Ritz-Carlton Drive, at Pacific Coast Highway, Dana
Point, CA 92629 (reservations 1-800 241 3333/
front desk 1-949 240 2000/fax 1-949 240 0829/
www.ritzcarlton.com). Bus Orange County Transit
1/I-5, exit Crown Valley Parkway west. **Rates** $375-
$535 single/double; $475-$635 club floor; $495-$3,900
suite. **Credit** AmEx, DC, Disc, MC, V.
This four-star/five-diamond resort perches on a
150ft (46m) bluff in Dana Point, overlooking the
adjoining golf course and the shimmering Pacific
Ocean. A four-storey, Mediterranean-style hotel, it's
about as good as it gets, with 393 rooms, an art
gallery, three renowned restaurants and every type
of resort recreation you could wish for (including
two miles of hotel beachfront). The kids' programme
will keep young folk busy all day while parents
relax, and you can always blast over to Disneyland,
35 miles (56km) away.
Hotel services *Babysitting. Bars. Beauty salon.*
Business centre. Concierge (24hr). Disabled: adapted
rooms. Garden. Golf. Gym. Laundry. Limousine
service. Parking ($20). Pools (2). Restaurants (3).
Room service (24hr). Spa. Sports facilities. **Room**
services *Dataport. Mini-bar. Safe. Turndown.*
TV: cable/pay movies/satellite/VCR.

Accommodation

Boutique chic

These four new boutique hotels – two in Beverly Hills, two on Sunset Strip in West Hollywood – are aiming at a younger, hipper, design-conscious visitor looking for a funky vibe and the charm of a smaller hotel. And they're proving very successful...

Avalon

9400 W Olympic Boulevard, at Robertson Boulevard, Beverly Hills, CA 90212 (reservations 1-800 535 4715/front desk 1-310 277 5221/fax 1-310 277 4928/ www.srs worldhotels.com). Bus 27, 28, 328, Commuter Express 534/I-10, exit Robertson Boulevard north. **Rates** *$199-$249 single/double; $249-$425 suite.* **Credit** *AmEx, Disc, MC, V.* **Map** *p306 A4.*
The recently opened Avalon (pictured below), formerly the Beverly Carlton (where Marilyn Monroe slept) and set in the southern

reaches of Beverly Hills, has already become a magnet for design-conscious hipsters in favour of 1950s eclectic chic. The 88 rooms are in three pale green buildings, the mainstay of which boasts a swirling circular driveway, fabulous boomerang facade and copper reception desk. Furnishings are by the likes of George Nelson, Charles Eames and Isamu Noguchu, to which designer Kelly Wearstler has added her own inventive pieces. The beds are dressed in Frette linens; blue, green and putty colour the walls. The result is a glorious mix of glamour, intimacy, functionality and minimalist attitude.
Hotel services Babysitting. Bar. Concierge (24hr). Disabled: adapted rooms. Pool. Gym. Laundry. Parking ($17). Limousine service. Restaurant. Room service (24hr). **Room services** CD player. Dataport. Mini-bar. Refrigerator. Safe. Turndown. TV: cable/ pay movies/VCR.

The Grafton on Sunset

8462 W Sunset Boulevard, at La Cienega Boulevard, West Hollywood, CA 90069 (reservations 1-800 821 3660/front desk 1-323 654 4600/fax 1-323 654 5918/ www.graftononsunset.com) Bus 2, 3, 302/ I-10, exit La Cienega Boulevard north. **Rates** *$230-$275 single/double; $375-$475 suite.* **Credit** *AmEx, Disc, MC, V.* **Map** *p306 A/B1.*
This newish four-storey hotel competes in price with the nearby Standard (see below). It has 107 rooms, a Mediterranean garden and outdoor heated pool, a gym with sauna and what they promise will become one of LA's hottest lounge, bar and restaurant scenes – though only time will tell. The style is less hip and in your face than at the Standard, leaning toward practicality. Details such as extra down pillows wrapped in gold ribbon, toy frogs for the bathtub and Pro Terra organic bath products provide a contemporary, fun touch.
Hotel services Bar. Concierge (24hr). Disabled: adapted rooms. Garden. Gym. Laundry. Limousine service. Parking ($16). Pool. Restaurant. Room service (6am-1am). **Room services** CD player. Dataport.

Maison 140

140 S Lasky Drive, at Little Santa Monica Boulevard, Beverly Hills, CA 90212 (reservations 1-800 432 5444/front desk 1-310 271 2145/fax 1-310 276 8431). Bus 27, 316/I-405, exit Santa Monica Boulevard

east. **Rates** single/double $140-$215. **Credit**
AmEx, DC, Disc, MC, V. **Map** p305 B3.
The newly opened Maison 140 (formerly
the Beverly House Hotel) is a chic trip into
18th-century Paris with contemporary Asian
twists. It comes from the same design and
management team as the terminally hip
Avalon (see above). Built in the 1930s and
once owned by Lillian Gish, it now has all-
black corridors and 45 rooms that display
ingenious design touches and a surprising
use of vivid oranges and pinks. Enjoy
continental breakfast in the lobby-cum-bar
in the morning and cocktails after dark.
Hotel services Bar. Concierge (24hr).
Disabled: adapted rooms. Laundry. Parking
($15). Restaurant. **Room services** CD player.
Dataport. Mini-bar. Refrigerator. Turndown.
TV: cable.

The Standard

*8300 Sunset Boulevard, at Sweetzer Avenue,
West Hollywood, CA 90069 (1-323 650
9090/ fax 1-323 650 2820). Bus 2, 3,
302/I-10, exit La Cienega Boulevard north.*
Rates $99-$225 single/double; $650 suite.
Credit AmEx, DC, Disc, MC, V. **Map** p306 B1.
In the 1960s, it was the Thunderbird Motel
and, more recently, a run-down retirement
home. Now the Standard is the latest
postmodernist hotel (pictured right) from
Andre Balazs of Chateau Marmont fame
(see page 49) and reminiscent of that funky
New York classic, the Chelsea. It's located in
the centre of Sunset Strip, next to the Argyle
(see page 49), and, with rooms (139 in total)
starting at $99, it's cheap. As the playful
upside-down hotel sign implies, there's little
that's standard here. Electric blue astroturf
around the pool, candy orange tiles in the
bathrooms, a shagadelic carpet in the
lobby... you expect to find Austin Powers
swinging from the suspended bubble chair.
Highlights include a 24-hour diner, a resident
DJ in the lobby and an on-site barber shop
that sells everything from Japanese candy to
sex toys. A hip, 25- to 35-year-old music/
publishing/film biz crowd is keeping the
friendly, exceedingly young staff very busy.
Hotel services Air-conditioning. Bar. Beauty
salon. Concierge. Disabled: adapted rooms.
Laundry. Limousine service. Parking ($18).
Pool. Restaurant. Room service (24hr). Table
tennis. **Room services** CD player. Dataport.
Mini-bar. Refrigerator. TV: cable/VCR.

Mid-range

Candy Cane Inn

*1747 S Harbor Boulevard, at Katella Avenue,
Anaheim, CA 92802 (1-800 345 7057/front desk
1-714 774 5284/ fax 1-714 772 5462). Bus 460/
I-5, exit Harbor Boulevard south.* **Rates** $78-$103
single/double. **Credit** AmEx, DC, Disc, MC, V.

Ask locals where to stay and they'll direct you to the
Candy Cane Inn. Sadly, it's not pink and striped: the
name dates back to the inn's beginnings in the early
days of Disneyland, but it's come a long way since
then, winning Anaheim's own award for most beautiful property in 2000. It's one of the best mid-range
options in the area. The 172 rooms are immaculate
and have recently been renovated in a French floral
motif. There's an abundance of greenery in the
grounds, a pool, jacuzzi and kids' wading area. And
the management really cares about its guests.
Hotel services *Disabled: adapted rooms. Fax.
Garden. Laundry. Parking (free). Pool. Shuttle to
Disneyland (free).* **Room services** *Dataport.
Refrigerator. TV: cable.*

Budget

Penny Sleeper Inn

*1441 S Manchester Avenue, at Harbor Boulevard,
Anaheim, CA 92802 (reservations 1-800 854
6118/front desk 1-714 991 8100/fax 1-714 533
6430/www.pennysleeper.com). Bus 460, Orange
County Transit 43, 46/I-5, exit Harbor Boulevard
south.* **Rates** $36-$46 single/double. **Credit** AmEx,
Disc, MC, V.

You're likely to hear cars passing on the neighbouring freeway, and the beds and furniture look
like they haven't been updated since the 1970s (think
bright orange), but if you're looking for a clean crash
pad with a pool for next to nothing, this 192-room
hotel is the spot.
Hotel services *Disabled: adapted rooms. Fax.
Laundry. Parking (free). Pool. Shuttle to Disneyland
(free).* **Room services** *Dataport. TV: cable.*

Hostels

A useful online guide is **Hostels in Los
Angeles** (www.hostels.com/us.ca.la.html).

Banana Bungalow Hollywood

*2775 W Cahuenga Boulevard, between Mulholland
Drive & Franklin Avenue, Hollywood, CA 90068
(reservations 1-800 446 7835/front desk 1-323 851
1129/fax 1-323 883 1960/www.bananabungalow.
com). Bus 163, Community Connection 208/US 101,
exit Hollywood Bowl/Highland Avenue north.* **Rates**
$18-$20 shared room; $55 single/double. **Credit** MC, V.
This small 'village' just above the Bowl is the perfect
place from which to explore Hollywood. Its location
is a bit removed from the action, but there are daily
shuttles to attractions and nightlife. It has 22 well-
kept bungalows (sleeping four to six, each with its
own bathroom) and 13 private rooms (each with

cable TV, lockers and bathroom). Guests have access
to a pool, kitchen, pool table, video games, a simple
and cheap restaurant and regular dance parties.
Hotel services *No air-conditioning. Airport pick-up
(free-$9). Fax. Gym. Internet access. Kitchen.
Laundry. Parking (free). Pool. Restaurant. Video
room. Vending machines.* **Room services** *Lockers.
No phone.*

Hostelling International Los Angeles

*1436 Second Street, at Santa Monica Boulevard,
Santa Monica, CA 90401 (reservations 1-800 909
4776 ext 105/front desk 1-310 393 9913/fax
1-310 393 1769/www.hiayh.org). Bus 4, 304, Santa
Monica 1, 2, 10/I-10, exit Fourth-Fifth Street north.*
Rates *Members* $21-$23 bed in dorm; $55 single/
double; *non-members* $24-$27 bed in dorm; $58
single/double. **Credit** MC, V. **Map** p304 A2.
If a beach vacation is your thing, book in advance
at this huge Santa Monica hostel located two blocks
from the shore and a few strides from Third Street
Promenade. Rooms are either dorm-style (sleeping
four, six, eight or ten) or private. The latter are small
and basic – just a bed, side table, lamp, mirror and
dresser (no wardrobe) – but spotless. All bathrooms
are shared, so bring flip-flops to wear in the shower.
Hotel services *No air-conditioning. Bike storage.
Disabled: adapted rooms. Fax. Games room. Kitchen.
Laundry. Library. Linen rental (free). Lockers. Pay
phone. Pool table. Restaurant (breakfast only). TV
lounge.* **Room services** *Cooking facility. No phone
or TV.*

Camping

It's worth considering camping: obviously it's
cheap, but it's also pleasant: state campgrounds
tend to be located in beautiful surroundings and
each site has a picnic table and fire ring. Yes, it
involves a drive – but what doesn't in LA?

Leo Carrillo State Park

*35000 Pacific Coast Highway, just north of
Mulholland Highway, Malibu, CA 90265
(reservations 1-800 444 7275/1-818 880 0350/
www.cal-parks.ca.gov). Bus 434/I-10, exit PCH north.*
Rates $8-$17 per site. **Credit** AmEx, MC, V.
Tent camping is allowed in the park, except on the
north side of the beach, which is tarmac and so open
only to camper vans. There are 127 sites, bathrooms,
pay showers, a small shop and access to the beach
and hiking/biking trails.

Malibu Beach RV Park

*25801 Pacific Coast Highway, at Corral Canyon &
Puerco Canyon Road, Malibu, CA 90265
(reservations 1-800 622 6052/1-310 456 6052/
www.malibubeachrv.com). Bus 434/I-10, exit PCH
north.* **Rates** Tents from $17.92; RVs $40.32.
Credit AmEx, Disc, MC, V.
A commercial (and so less lovely) site largely aimed
at recreational vehicle (RV) campers, but with 50 tent
sites and plenty of facilities, including a jacuzzi.

Sightseeing

Introduction

Los Angeles is huge, so you need to know the basics before you start.

It will take a while to get your bearings in Los Angeles. The one sign you will not see when you arrive is one directing you to the city centre – because there isn't one. Greater LA is an amorphous, sprawling agglomeration spread over a huge flood basin, subdivided by freeways and bounded by ocean and mountains: on its western edge by 160 miles (257 kilometres) of Pacific coastline, and then, clockwise, by the Santa Monica, San Gabriel, San Bernadino, San Jacinto and Santa Ana Mountains. Laid over this geography is a dizzying variety of cityscapes and neighbourhoods.

As you drive around what you think is Los Angeles, you may be confused by signs pointing to 'Los Angeles'. This is because the City of Los Angeles is a distinct city within the County of Los Angeles. LA County contains 88 incorporated cities, each with its own downtown (town centres) and jurisdiction, including Malibu, Santa Monica, Beverly Hills, West Hollywood, Culver City, Inglewood, Pasadena and Los Angeles itself. To add to the confusion, some areas, such as East LA, are unincorporated – meaning they are under the jurisdiction of the County, not the City, of LA. West Hollywood used to be unincorporated but formed itself into a city in 1984. On the other hand, Hollywood, which seems to be a distinct place, is not an official city but just one of many neighbourhoods in the amorphous City of LA (which also includes Downtown). In Hollywood, however, as in the San Fernando Valley and San Pedro, there are popular moves afoot to secede from the City of Los Angeles.

There are also broad, unofficial titles distinguishing the different areas and characters, such as the Westside, East LA (mainly Latino), Hollywood and Midtown and South Central (comprising many black and Latino neighbourhoods). Within the Westside is also an area called, confusingly, West LA. This refers to a western portion of LA that encompasses those areas between the cities of Santa Monica, Beverly Hills and Culver City.

LA County is one of the counties in the Los Angeles Five County Area. Together with Riverside, Ventura, Orange and San Bernadino Counties, the Five County Area constitutes a colossal area of 34,000 square miles (88,083 square kilometres) and 14.5 million people.

To make exploring this mega-metropolis a little easier, we have split the LA region into ten areas: **Westside: Beach Towns**; **Westside: Inland**; **Hollywood & Midtown**; **Downtown**; **East of Hollywood**; **East LA**; **South Central**; **the Valleys**; **South Bay & Long Beach** and **Orange County**.

WESTSIDE: BEACH TOWNS

There's more to the Westside beach towns than just sun, sea and sand. **Santa Monica**, **Venice**, **Marina del Rey**, **Pacific Palisades** and **Malibu** are all home to feisty communities who have created neighbourhoods with distinct character and plenty to do. Just remember that the beach cities are not at their best in June, during which they are swathed in morning cloud known as June Gloom. For information on the beaches themselves, *see page 78* **Life's a beach**. This includes areas of West LA.

WESTSIDE: INLAND

Palm-lined streets, movie stars' houses, astronomically pricey shopping; Sunset Strip, UCLA and the Getty Center; if the name 'Los Angeles' puts you in mind of these things, you're thinking about the mostly wealthy, mostly white area that lies east of the beach towns of Venice and Santa Monica, south of the Santa Monica Mountains, north of LAX (the airport) and west of Fairfax Avenue. It contains the rock music and gay heartland of **West Hollywood**, the seriously monied enclaves of **Beverly Hills** and **Bel Air**, the UCLA campus and student **Westwood Village**, wealthy, rustic **Brentwood**, workaday **Culver City** and the Westside's own high-rise business district, **Century City**. In-between districts fall into the West LA category.

Street talk

LA is subdivided by numerous freeways and a loose grid of large arteries (the boulevards and avenues); these non-freeway streets are referred to as 'surface streets'. Boulevards typically (but not exclusively) go east to west – with street numbers starting at one in Downtown and ascending westwards – while avenues usually run north to south. Sometimes the boulevards and avenues are divided into 'North', 'South', 'East' and 'West' and the numbering will restart at a city boundary (North Robertson Boulevard, for example, changes numbers three times as it passes through three cities), so check which stretch of road you want and watch the numbers carefully.

When planning a journey, make sure you find out the nearest cross street – for example, La Cienega and Third. If you're taking the freeway, find out the exit nearest to your destination. Unless you're sure of the district you're heading for, also get the city and the zip code (Highland Avenue, Santa Monica, CA 90405, for example). Remember that the same street name will occur in different cities.

In the central portion of LA County, the geographical basin where you are likely to spend most of the time, the **I-10** freeway traverses Los Angeles from west to east and separates Hollywood and Midtown from South and South Central LA. The **I-405** goes north to south on the west side of the City of Los Angeles, separating the affluent coastal and inland cities from the rest of LA. The **I-110** also goes north to south, on the east side,

separating Downtown and East LA from west and central LA. The **US 101** and the **I-5** head north-west from Downtown into the Valleys.

The freeways have names (often more than one) as well as numbers, so it helps to know both. These are the most useful ones:

I-5 Golden State Freeway/ Santa Ana Freeway
I-10 Santa Monica Freeway/ San Bernadino Freeway
US 101 Hollywood Freeway/ Ventura Freeway
I-110 Harbor Freeway/Pasadena Freeway
Hwy 134 Ventura Freeway
I-210 Foothill Freeway
I-405 San Diego Freeway
I-710 Long Beach Freeway

The coast road, Highway 1, is also known as the Pacific Coast Highway (aka PCH) and becomes Lincoln Boulevard and Sepulveda Boulevard when it moves inland. Similarly, Highway 2 (aka Glendale Freeway) becomes Santa Monica Boulevard when it moves through the Westside.

An essential aid is the annually updated street map, the *Thomas Guide to Los Angeles & Orange Counties*. It costs about $35 and is available from the **Thomas Brothers Maps & Travel Bookstore** (521 W Sixth Street, Downtown, 1-888 277 6277/1-213 627 4018/www.thomas.com). For updates on construction and road closures, call the CalTrans/California Highway Patrol hotline on 1-800 427 7623. For websites providing traffic reports, route planning and handy shortcuts, see page 292.

HOLLYWOOD AND MIDTOWN

If you want LA's contrasts in a nutshell, look no further than the disparate patch known – for want of a better name – as Midtown. It is bounded by **Hollywood** (unique icons at odds with a mostly threadbare reality) to the north, Downtown to the east, Beverly Hills to the west and the I-10 freeway and South Central to the south. This area encompasses both wealthy, residential **Hancock Park**, where you'll be ignoring the suspicious stares of security guards, and the very different MacArthur Park, where the stares will come from the drug dealers, addicts, homeless people and working-class families who populate the district. In between is **Koreatown**, while back west along Wilshire Boulevard is faded **Miracle Mile** – now miraculous only for its profusion of

museums – sandwiched between the monied blocs of Hancock Park and Beverly Hills. The **Fairfax District** also falls into this area.

DOWNTOWN

Stretching south from the eastern end of Sunset Boulevard, Downtown is the site of the original city and home to most of LA's political and financial institutions, many of its major historical landmarks and the Museum of Contemporary Art. As the oldest part of the city, it's an area of contrasts: nowhere else in LA will you find such an intriguing array of comparatively old buildings (many dating from the early 1900s), but nor can any other part of the city match Downtown for soulless 1980s skyscrapers and bank plazas. Compared to the downtowns of Chicago, San Francisco or New

York, LA's is a little pathetic – small, lacking buzz and pretty much lifeless out of office hours – but it does boast some impressive architecture, the Latin enclaves of **Olvera Street** and bustling **Broadway**, **Chinatown** and, less than a mile away, **Little Tokyo**, the heart of LA's Japanese community.

EAST OF HOLLYWOOD

While a tourist's preconception of a visit to Los Angeles might centre on Hollywood and the beaches, it would be an omission not to venture any further east into a part of LA that is both relatively safe and manageable to the casual visitor and has a homey charm that's lacking in the slicker parts of town. Here are the bohemian enclaves of **Silver Lake** and **Los Feliz**, **Echo Park**, home of Dodger Stadium, and **Griffith Park**, a vast hilly open space with the famous Griffith Observatory and open-air sports from golf to horse riding.

EAST LA

One of the most distinctive neighbourhoods of Los Angeles is also the least visited by outsiders: East LA, an unincorporated area of eight square miles (20 square kilometres) east of Downtown and the heartland of LA's Mexican community. 'El Este' has traditionally been the gateway for migrant communities: pre-war East LA and neighbouring Boyle Heights housed a large Jewish population. It has now crystallised into a Mexican hub, and almost 90 per cent of its population is Latino and predominantly Mexican. In fact, East LA is deemed the most homogeneous area in the entire Southern California region.

SOUTH CENTRAL

Everyone's heard of South Central. It's the part of Los Angeles you are told to avoid, the part that is synonymous with gangs, drugs, poverty and violence. But very few people can actually tell you where it is because its fluid boundaries have been linked to the changing migratory patterns of black Angelenos: wherever blacks congregate, that becomes South Central. It's as generic and loose a name as the Westside. Essentially, it includes the areas of the City of Los Angeles that extend south of the I-10 freeway as far as the I-105, bound on the west by the cities of Culver City and **Inglewood** (the latter, because it is predominantly black, is often lumped in with South Central) and, on the east, by the heavily Latino cities of Vernon, Huntington Park and South Gate. And while it does contain many poor and sometimes troubled neighbourhoods, it also, on its outer west edge, can include (depending on who you talk to) the **Crenshaw District**, LA's most affluent black neighbourhood, and the cultural

Don't miss Sights

Hollywood icons
Hollywood Boulevard, the Walk of Fame, the Hollywood sign, Mann's Chinese Theater: touristy but essential. See page 86.

Beaches
Take to the waves at Zuma in northern Malibu or soak up the rays and the neighbourhood vibe at the South Bay beaches. See page 78.

Downtown
Experience culture at Downtown's many museums, join a walking tour or explore the Mexican markets on Olvera Street and Broadway. See page 92.

Griffith Park
Escape the city for a while. View the stars at the Observatory and the animals at the Los Angeles Zoo, or go hiking along the numerous trails. See page 98.

Santa Monica & Venice
Shop on Third Street Promenade and ride the Ferris wheel on the pier (see page 72), then hire a bike and ride along the winding Boardwalk to Venice or just people-watch among the beachfront stalls (see page 75).

Getty Center
For spectacular views over the city, a stunning architectural complex and some impressive artworks. See page 120.

Watts Towers
LA's most eccentric and magical monument – finally reopened after a decade of renovation. See page 104.

centre that is **Leimert Park**. Furthermore, while South Central used to be majority black, in a trend dubbed 'the Browning of LA', much of it has lately been occupied by Central Americans and Mexicans – now surpassing the number of blacks – which has caused tremendous political and social tensions.

THE VALLEYS

These two interior valleys – the **San Fernando Valley** to the north-west of LA and the **San Gabriel Valley** to the north-east – are usually, at best, ridiculed and, at worst, condemned for embodying the horrors of American suburbia: they are hot, often smoggy and covered with unrelenting low-rise sprawl. Cut off from ocean breezes by the mountains, they can be 10-20°F

Sightseeing

(11-17°C) hotter than LA proper in summer – and 10-20°F cooler in winter. Yet they are not without charm. Hidden within are communities and attractions well worth a visit. In particular, they have many small suburban downtowns – business and shopping districts, both old and new, where you can get out of your car and stroll for a few blocks enjoying a small-town atmosphere. Westsiders mock the Valleys, but natives wouldn't live anywhere else.

THE SOUTH BAY AND LONG BEACH

The living is easy in much of the South Bay; but defining exactly what makes up the region is not. Some definitions include everything from condo-crazy Marina del Rey in the north to such hardbitten, inland communities as Compton, Gardena, Lawndale, Hawthorne and Lomita to the south-east. But when LA residents speak of the South Bay, they're usually referring to the coast-hugging cities just south of LAX:

El Segundo, **Manhattan Beach**, **Hermosa Beach** and **Redondo Beach**, plus the landlocked suburb of Torrance just to the east. Drive over the majestic Vincent Thomas Bridge from **San Pedro** and there is **Long Beach**, the old US Navy port that's now a city of nearly 500,000 and a cosmopolitan mix of yuppies, artists, harbour workers, gays and students, as well as a rainbow of races, including the largest Cambodian community outside Cambodia.

ORANGE COUNTY

Bordering LA County to the south-east, Orange County is best known as the home of Disneyland in **Anaheim**. With the additional blessing of a copious coastline, it lures 40 million visitors a year. Angelenos look down on it as a conservative white-collar suburb, with some justification. But if you're making the trip to Disney, it's worth straying off the freeway to have a look around.

Sightseeing

Guided tours

For a personalised tour of LA, contact Anne Block who runs the cheekily dubbed **Take My Mother Please!** tours (1-323 737 2200/ www.takemymotherplease.com). They're expensive – $250 for a half day, $375 for a full day, for up to three people – but fun, and cover all areas of the city. Reservations are required. And to see an often-ignored part of the urban landscape, **Friends of the LA River** offers guided riverside walks on the third Sunday of the month at 4.30pm (1-213 381 3570/www.folar.org).

Angel City Tour

1-310 470 4463. **Tours** Call for a schedule. **Cost** $12.50, plus $3 transit fares.
LA historian Greg Fischer's popular two-hour tour of Downtown shatters two myths about LA: a) that it has no history, and b) you can't do anything without a car. The tour – which is partly on foot, partly by subway, and chock-full of Fischer's arcane facts about Los Angeles – begins at Union Station (where there was once a brothel and vineyard) and proceeds to Olvera Street, Grand Central Market, Angel's Flight, the Central Library and the Bradbury Building.

Los Angeles Conservancy Walking Tours

1-213 623 2489/www.laconservancy.org. **Tours** usually 10am, 11am Sat. **Cost** $8.
The LA Conservancy works to preserve and revitalise LA's urban architectural heritage. Its walking tours, mainly in Downtown and all one to two hours long, include art deco gems, Pershing Square, Seventh Street and specific buildings such as the Biltmore Hotel and Union Station. They're popular, so book ahead.

Nature Adventures for Kids

1-310 998 1151/reservations 1-310 364 3591/www.childrensnatureinst.org. **Tours** Call for a schedule. **Cost** *Requested donation* $5 per individual; $10 per family.
Nature walks in the Santa Monica Mountains and other areas near LA, which aim to introduce families to the outdoors while instilling respect for wilderness areas. Walks are usually held daily and most are pushchair-accessible.

Neon Cruises

1-213 489 9918/www.museneon.org. **Tours** 7.30-10.30pm; call for a schedule. **Cost** $40.
The US's first neon sign was installed in LA in 1923 when auto dealer Earle C Anthony bought two orange and blue signs for his Packard dealerships from the Claude Neon Co of Paris. You can explore this singular art form on the Museum of Neon Art's three-hour tour (at night, of course) in an open-top double-decker bus. The route includes the classic Wilshire and Hollywood Boulevards, Universal CityWalk (where neon displays too big to fit in MONA's Downtown space are on display) and the faux pagodas of Chinatown. Reservations required.

Westside: Beach Towns

Enjoy sand, surf and a laid-back beachside vibe as you explore the streets of liberal Santa Monica, bohemian Venice and exclusive Malibu.

Map p304

Map p304

Santa Monica

With the Santa Monica Mountains to the north, the glistening Pacific Ocean to the west, palm tree-lined cliffs and almost year-round sun tempered by ocean breezes, affluent Santa Monica is indisputably the jewel of LA's Westside. Known locally as 'the people's republic of Santa Monica', it is also the heartland of bourgeois liberalism, noted for its espousal of environmental causes, rent control and tolerance of the homeless. The hipper denizens of Hollywood and Silver Lake see Santa Monica as totally uncool – because it's short on nightclubs and long on Starbucks coffeehouses. Well, Santa Monica may not be cool, but it is comfortable and casual: shorts, healthy bodies and rollerblades are the uniform. Get yours on and take to the beach (town).

The Santa Monica area was inhabited for centuries by the Gabrieleno Native Americans, then by Spanish settlers who named the city and many of its major streets. It was acquired by Anglo pioneers in the late 19th century and snowballed from a small holiday resort into today's city of about 87,000. Brits abound in Santa Monica (also known to some as Santa Margate) as do Iranians (since the fall of the Shah), many other immigrant groups, retirees (octogenarians on wheels are the biggest danger on the city's streets), health fanatics, beach bums and entertainment industry titans. One famous local, Arnold Schwarzenegger, also owns a chunk of commercial property in the town and a mediocre restaurant, **Schatzi on Main** (3110 Main Street, 1-310 399 4800).

As well as the tourist-oriented beaches, pier and shops, Santa Monica also boasts some of the best restaurants in the LA basin, a burgeoning creative business centre and a thriving art, coffeehouse and literary scene. It has some great modern architecture: much of Frank Gehry's work is here, including his own house, as well as some art deco landmarks, such as the **Shangri-La** hotel (*see page 47*) and good 1950s 'modern' architecture.

Santa Monica has three main shopping and entertainment areas: Montana Avenue, Third Street Promenade and Main Street.

Third Street Promenade. *See p73.*

Montana Avenue

Montana Avenue runs parallel to Wilshire Boulevard (the city's main east–west artery) towards the northern, affluent end of Santa Monica bordering on the Santa Monica Canyons. Montana Avenue metamorphosed in the 1970s from a bland commercial strip into the Rodeo Drive of the coast, and is very popular with wealthy liberals in north Santa Monica and Brentwood. Locals get a workout with a spiritual dimension at **Yoga Works** (*see page 256*), which is very similar in character to the yoga studio depicted in Madonna's yoga

Sightseeing

movie *The Next Best Thing*; they buy their wheatgrass juice and wholesome groceries at **Wild Oats Market** opposite (No.1425, 1-310 576 4707), drink microbrews at **Father's Office** (No.1018, 1-310 393 2337), LA's first smoke-free bar, and eat delicious non-dairy Indian food at **Pradeep's** (No.1405, 1-310 393 1467). North of Montana Avenue, at Fourth Street and Adelaide Drive, are the infamous **Fourth Street Steps**: 189 concrete steps that serve as a cliffside stairmaster and, reputedly, a pick-up place for fit singles.

Running parallel to Montana Avenue a few blocks north is **San Vicente Boulevard**, a wide street lined with grass verges that is very popular with joggers. The east end of San Vicente, around Bundy Drive, also features some eating haunts popular with the Brentwood set (Mezzaluna restaurant, made notorious because Nicole Brown Simpson ate her last meal there, finally closed down in 1997). Trendy haunts on San Vicente include **Pizzicotto**, a cosy Italian (No.11758, 1-310 442 7188) and **Zenzoo Tea**, a tea emporium (No.13050, 1-310 576 0585), which is very popular with the yoga and pilates set who work out on a higher floor of the same building.

Third Street Promenade

South of Montana Avenue, below Wilshire Boulevard at Third Street, is the wildly popular Third Street Promenade. Anchored by three cineplexes, the Frank Gehry-designed Santa Monica Place shopping mall at the southern end (approach from Main Street to the south for a surprising façade) and adjacent parking structures, these four blocks of pedestrianised streets are, by day and night, a hugely popular shopping, eating and entertainment zone.

Third Street Promenade is constantly active with street performers, farmers markets on Wednesday and Saturday mornings, seasonal festivals and numerous shops and hangouts. These include two popular bookshops – the ubiquitous **Barnes & Noble** branch and café and the independent **Midnight Special** bookshop (*see page 225*), both of which offer regular readings – hip clothing chain **Urban Outfitters**; **Ultrahouse**, a popular housewares store run by two pretty German boys, selling blow-up furniture and Pop Bauhaus houseware; and **Gotham Hall** pool club (*see page 249*).

Main Street

Even further south is Main Street, an upmarket commercial strip two blocks west of the Santa Monica Boardwalk. A popular breakfast-time haunt for early-morning joggers, Main Street offers an eclectic mix of fashion and knick-knack shops, as well as numerous coffeehouses and eateries. Highlights include the **Novel Café**, an extremely laid-back bookshop/coffee bar, Wolfgang Puck's **Chinois on Main** (*see page 129*) and the Frank Gehry-designed **Edgemar Complex** (No.2437), a sculptural mall that houses the MOCA store (a great place for presents), **Form Zero**, an elegant bookstore, the high-class **Röckenwagner** restaurant (*see page 130*) and a branch of coffee chain **Peet's**, considered by its regulars to offer the best coffee. Main Street runs through **Ocean Park**, a hilly, bohemian neighbourhood at the south end of Santa Monica, whose intense light and tranquillity were celebrated on canvas by late resident Richard Diebenkorn in a celebrated series of paintings. It hosts a very popular farmers market on Sunday mornings (*see page 192*).

If you head west from Third Street Promenade or from Ocean Park, you'll get to Santa Monica beach and its three miles of newly renovated boardwalk. Popular stop-off points include the **Santa Monica Pier** (at Colorado Avenue) and **Shutters** hotel at the boardwalk and Pico Boulevard (*see page 45*); the terrace bar is a great place to watch sunset.

Farmers market in Ocean Park.

Worth visiting inland is the new **Bergamot Station**, a complex of art galleries created at a former Red Trolley terminus (accessible from Michigan Avenue, off Cloverfield Boulevard), and **Santa Monica Airport**. Built before much of the rest of Santa Monica, the airport is the hip hangout for plane enthusiasts. Top gun Tom Cruise keeps his Pitts Special biplane here; mere mortals (with a licence) can rent a plane for only $60 an hour or take a simulated flight at the **Museum of Flying** (*see page 210*). Large parties are held at the airport, architects and designers have offices in hangars and there are two good restaurants: **DC-3** (*see page 208*) and **Typhoon** (*see page 130*), both serving very good food in full view of the planes.

For one of the most beautiful and sweeping views of the coast, have a drink or meal at Toppers, the Mexican restaurant on the top floor of the **Radisson Huntley Hotel** (1111 Second Street, between Wilshire Boulevard and California Avenue, 1-310 394 5454). On a clear day, you can see all the way to Catalina Island and the endless roll of the San Bernardino Mountains. Take the outside glass elevator to the top. Since the city has ruled against the erection of buildings over eight storeys, the Huntley (which featured memorably in John Boorman's movie *Point Blank*) is in no danger of losing its exquisite view. The bar closes at 1.30am daily.

Santa Monica Visitor Center

1400 Ocean Avenue, at Santa Monica Boulevard, Santa Monica, CA 90401 (1-310 393 7593/ www.santamonica.com). **Open** 10am-4pm daily. **Map** p304 A2.

Venice

Santa Monica is very pleasant but it can, in some areas, seem a bit precious, something that could never be said of its southerly neighbour, Venice. Despite gentrification during the 1980s, Venice remains the bohemian quarter of LA, populated by ageing hippies, artists, students and young professionals in creative industries who can't yet afford a place in Santa Monica. It is also home to transients and a poor black – and increasingly Latino – community beset by drug dealing and periodic gang fights that make the Oakwood area (circumscribed by Lincoln and Venice Boulevards and Sunset and Electric Avenues) a bit dodgy after dark, though it is far safer than it was in the early 1990s.

Formerly a beach resort, the section of Venice west of Lincoln Boulevard has rows of sometimes dishevelled clapboard beachhouses on 'walk-streets' (pedestrian-only alleyways leading to the beach) and, in the more affluent southern end, one of LA's best-kept secrets, a

completely idyllic enclave of eclectic architecture, waterways, bridges, and churpy ducks, known as the Venice Canals.

Venice owes its existence to entrepreneur Abbot Kinney, who founded the once independent city in 1900 (Venice is now under the jurisdiction of Los Angeles), envisaging it as the hub of a cultural renaissance in America. He oversaw the construction of canals, a lagoon and buildings in the Venetian style, even importing two dozen genuine gondoliers to complete the effect (one of whom apparently got so homesick that he tried to sail back to Italy; he made it as far as San Pedro). Although Kinney failed to achieve the cultural rebirth – visitors were far more interested in amusing themselves – he did succeed in creating a successful resort known in its heyday as the 'Playland of the Pacific'.

Venice's main commercial street, **Abbot Kinney Boulevard**, is named in his honour and well worth visiting for its collection of art galleries, bric-a-brac and design shops and good eateries – including **Hal's Bar & Grill** (*see page 133*), the eternally hip hangout for local meedja folk (the atmosphere compensates for the overpriced food). Also try **Joe's** (*see page 134*) for excellent food in simple surroundings, **Axe** (*see page 133*) and the **Abbot's Habit** (*see page 161*) for coffee and snacks.

In the 1980s, Venice became a hotbed of architectural activity. You can see several buildings by acclaimed contemporary local architects, such as Frank Gehry's Norton and Spiller houses; the Bergren, Sedlak and 2-4-6-8 houses by Morphosis; Dennis Hopper's residence by Brian Murphy; and Frank Gehry's Chiat/Day Building. You can't miss the latter as its entrance is marked by an enormous pair of Claes Oldenburg-designed binoculars. The binoculars are one of the better examples of public art that can be found in Venice. A more controversial art piece is Jonathan Borofsky's unmissable *Dancing Clown*, perched on the corner of Main Street and Rose Avenue. For a tour of the public artworks, many of which are near Ocean Front Walk (aka Venice Boardwalk), contact SPARC on 1-310 822 9560.

Many renowned Southern Californian artists have maintained studios in Venice for years, among them Laddie John Dill, Guy Dill, Billy Al Bengston, Ed Moses and Chuck Arnoldi. If you are here in May, you might catch the yearly **Venice Artwalk**, a charitable event in aid of the Venice Family Free Clinic, in which you can tour more than 60 artists' studios.

Venice is known as a mecca for kooky California culture and fitness fanaticism. Stroll along the **Venice Boardwalk** to see the best of both worlds: street performers, con artists, assorted weirdos, pumped-up guys working out

Beachfront stall on **Venice Boardwalk.**

at **Muscle Beach** and rows of beachfront stalls selling everything from henna tattoos to Tarot readings to tacky T-shirts. Two of LA's most famous gyms are here: **Gold's** (*see page 256*) and the Schwarzenegger-owned **World Gym** (812 Main Street, 1-310 827 8019). Their buff clientele can be seen strutting their stuff in many Venice locales; you can't miss them chowing down on protein-packed brunches at the **Firehouse Restaurant** (1-310 396 6810), a vivid, red-painted, former fire station at Rose Avenue and Main Street.

Other notable Venice spots include **St Marks** restaurant/club at the beach end of Windward Avenue; go there for salsa lessons on Sundays. This is one block south of Market Street, where you can take in the prominent **LA Louver** art gallery and trendy restaurant **72 Market Street** (*see page 133*). The other key strip is Rose Avenue, an east–west commercial street at the north end of Venice. There are a few interesting second-hand shops, but the main attraction is the **Rose Café** (No.220, 1-310 399 0711), adorned with large painted roses; it's a self-serve and sit-down restaurant with an attractive garden and crafts store.

For more information on what Venice has to offer, visit website www.venice.net.

Marina del Rey

An unsung aspect of Los Angeles life is its sailing. Many Angelenos keep boats, others live in them, at the **Marina del Rey Harbor**, a resort and residential complex just south of Venice in an area bounded by Washington Boulevard, Admiralty Way, Fiji Way and Via Marina. Conceived a century ago and finally completed in 1965, the Marina consists of a picturesque artificial harbour with eight basins named to evoke the South Seas (Tahiti Way,

Bora Bora Way and so on). They are filled with 6,000 bobbing yachts, motor boats and flashy cruisers, and surrounded by low- and high-rise apartment buildings and generic hotels, as well as many touristy restaurants.

Perceived as a haven for swinging singles, the Marina is actually home to many retirees and young families for whom the complex is a reasonably priced and charming – if somewhat sterile – place to live. It is livened up, however, by a motley crew of impecunious boat-dwellers. Simply to experience a pure 1970s period piece, the Marina is definitely worth seeing.

It's no place for culture vultures, however; except for a small public library, all the Marina's attractions are recreational. You can picnic, jog and cycle (the Marina is a link in the 21-mile coastal bike path) in the **Burton W Chace Park** and **Admiralty Park** at the northern end; fish from a dock at the west end of the Burton W Chace or rent a boat to go ocean-fishing at **Fisherman's Village**, 13755 Fiji Way, at Lincoln Boulevard (Green Boathouse). You can also rent boats or join excursions at a number of charter companies located in the Marina; there are whale-watching trips in winter. If you want to park your own boat, contact the visitor information centre.

There are plenty of touristy shops, most of them concentrated in **Fisherman's Wharf**, a cheesy replica of a New England fishing town. The many eateries are to be recommended for their waterside charm rather than for their food, which does not rank among Los Angeles's best. The **Cheesecake Factory** and the ultimate beach supershack, the **Warehouse Restaurant** (go on a full stomach), all on Admiralty Way, are among the better ones.

At the south end of Marina del Rey (just north of LAX) is **Playa del Rey**, a largely residential beach neighbourhood and an artificial lagoon. **Tanner's Coffee Company** (200 Culver Boulevard, 1-310 574 2739) is one of the more lively local cafés in an area whose attractions are mainly beach-oriented. Playa del Rey is also a magnet for nature lovers and birdwatchers, who come to observe the great grey herons, white egrets and other creatures that converge on the **Ballona Wetlands**, a natural sanctuary just east of Playa del Rey, in Playa Vista.

Pacific Palisades

Between Santa Monica and Malibu lies Pacific Palisades, a small, wealthy, residential community that has managed to keep a lower profile than its neighbours. The perfect, clipped, shiny green lawns and large bungalows of Pacific Palisades are straight out of *Leave It to Beaver* – but contained within its Santa Monica Mountains location are some wonderful places to visit.

The original Getty Museum, J Paul Getty's Roman fantasy, is just visible from Pacific Coast Highway but is closed to the public until it reopens as a museum for antiquities in 2002. For rugged nature, there's **Rustic Canyon Park** (1-310 454 5734), **Temescal Canyon Park** (1-310 459 5931) and **Will Rogers Historic State Park** (*see below*). The latter is the former home of the late 'cowboy philosopher', trick roper, journalist and media personality Will Rogers. For a more manicured, but unbelievably lovely retreat, try the **Self-Realization Fellowship Lake Shrine** (*see below*).

Will Rogers State Beach was once used as a location for *Baywatch*, which, sadly, is a victim of what's known here as Runaway Production – the filming of *Baywatch*, like that of many other TV series and movies, has moved out of state where costs are lower. By the way, the real male lifeguards are a lot hunkier than David Hasselhof, whose famously spindly legs are carefully kept out of the TV frame.

Self-Realization Fellowship Lake Shrine

17190 Sunset Boulevard, just off Pacific Coast Highway (1-310 454 4114/www.yogananda-srf.org/temples/lakeshrine/). Bus 2, 302, 576, Commuter Express 430/I-10, exit PCH north. **Open** 9am-4.30pm Tue-Sat; 12.30-4.30pm Sun; closed Mon. **Admission** free.

Opened in 1950, this Buddhist retreat is an oasis of peace and beauty, run by the Self-Realization Fellowship Church. There's a spring-fed lake, trees, flowers, paths, birds and turtles. You can stroll the grounds, ponder in private garden nooks or meditate in the Windmill Chapel. There's another SRF temple at 4860 Sunset Boulevard in Hollywood (1-323 661 8006).

Will Rogers Historic State Park

1501 Will Rogers State Park Road, at Sunset Boulevard (1-310 454 8212). Bus 2, 302, 576 Commuter Express 430/I-405, exit Sunset Boulevard west. **Open** 8am-sunset daily. **Admission** $3 per car.

Will Rogers was a busy man. Humorist, writer, performer, cowboy and rope-trickster, he was also the first honorary mayor of Beverly Hills. Since Rogers was the only man in Hollywood who 'never met a man he didn't like', it seems fitting that upon his death, his ranch house and land became a park welcoming one and all. The 31-room house is maintained as it was when the 1930s box-office star lived there, the living room full of Western-style furniture, Indian rugs and lariats. The grounds give access to some good hikes – one path takes you to the aptly named Inspiration Point, from where you get a breathtaking view of mountains and sea – and also host polo matches on Saturdays and Sundays.

Malibu

Malibu is not a place so much as a long stretch of the Pacific Coast Highway (PCH) – 27 miles (43 kilometres) of it – which winds through some of Southern California's most magnificent coastal terrain. Parts of it are lined, on the ocean side, by beach houses of varying sizes and styles, with largely mediocre commercial buildings on the inland side, nestling against the Santa Monica Mountains.

The location is so desirable that residents are willing to live with the threat of seasonal (often destructive) fires and floods, and they form a cohesive community dedicated to preventing new development from marring their bucolic lifestyle. Incorporated as a city in 1990, Malibu is extremely wealthy (average income $150,000), due to its numerous entertainment industry residents, many of whom inhabit a private beachside street known as the **Malibu Colony**. It also contains several trailer parks whose spectacular hillside sites make them the most enviable low-rent accommodation in the country.

Malibu has neither major industry nor major culture. Its treats for visitors lie mainly in the beaches, restaurants, cafés and canyons: within yards of the entrance to one of the many canyon trails, you can be completely out of view of the city. Malibu eating experiences include top-notch California cuisine at Wolfgang Puck's **Granita** (*see page 135*), coffee and ornamental cakes at **Xanadu French Bakery** (3900 Cross Creek Road, 1-310 317 4818) or, if you prefer a grittier atmosphere, you can join bikers and surfers for burgers and all-day breakfast at the notorious **Malibu Inn & Restaurant** (22969 PCH, 1-310 456 6106).

Malibu has one significant landmark, the **Adamson House** (23200 PCH, 1-310 456 8432): a stunning 1929 Spanish-style building that sits, together with the Malibu Lagoon Museum, in Malibu Lagoon State Park. The house is adorned with decorative tiles manufactured at the once celebrated, now closed Malibu Tile Works. It's open only for guided tours ($2), from 11am to 3pm Wednesday to Saturday.

To learn about conservation techniques for trees and flowers, and visit some historic homes, take one of the Wednesday afternoon garden tours at **Ramirez Canyon Park**, an estate previously owned by Barbra Streisand and now belonging to the Santa Monica Mountains Conservancy (www.ceres.ca.gov). Book in advance on 1-310 589 2850 ext 144.

Malibu Chamber of Commerce

23805 Stuart Ranch Road, suite 100, at Civic Center Way, Malibu, CA 90265 (1-310 456 9025/www.malibu.org). **Open** 10am-4pm Mon-Fri; closed Sat, Sun.

Life's a beach

Ever since Vasco Núñez de Balboa first laid eyes on the Pacific Ocean in 1513, the world has gazed upon the Southern California coastline with wonder. With its gorgeous interface of sea and sky against a chiselled, lush mountain backdrop, the 30-mile (48km) stretch of beaches along LA County's coastline – from Malibu south through Santa Monica and Venice to the South Bay – is incomparable.

Summer temperatures hover near 100°F (38°C) and the notorious smog is at its worst in late summer and early autumn. The sun's rays are strong, so use proper sunblock. Despite LA's surf city reputation, the Pacific Ocean is chillingly cold nine months of the year. In July and August, however, the water temperature can reach 70°F (21°C). As for pollution, generally, the further you are from Santa Monica Bay (where waste is pumped into the ocean), the cleaner the water – though the water there has improved under the auspices of Heal the Bay (1-310 453 0395), an environmental outfit devoted to monitoring pollution levels and keeping local waters clean. The worst time to swim in the ocean is immediately after a rainstorm because flood channels empty into the sea. Fortunately, it rarely rains in LA and the ocean water generally is clean and refreshing.

Beaches officially open at sunrise and close at sunset. Many have space and rental gear for rollerblading, roller-hockey, bicycling, surfing and volleyball, as well as refreshment stands, showers and toilets. On LA County beaches, lifeguards are on duty daily, year-round. Alcohol, pets and nudity are prohibited. Bonfires are permitted (in designated cement fire rings) only at Dockweiler State Beach (in Vista del Mar) and Cabrillo Beach (in San Pedro).

Parking can be difficult, and sometimes expensive, but it's better to pay for a legit space than have your vehicle towed while you're off having fun. Limited free parking is available along Pacific Coast Highway. For more info on the beach of your choice, call the Department of Beaches & Harbors on 1-310 305 9503.

The following are the pick of LA's beaches, from north to south:

El Matador State Beach

Small, beautiful and dominated by rocky outcrops, El Matador looks like a European beach. It's six miles (9.5km) north of Malibu,

just past Zuma Beach, then a walk down a steep gravelly path. Wear shoes and don't bring too much heavy gear or picnic paraphernalia. There are no lifeguards or other facilities, so you should be able to find some privacy; spread your towel in the cupped hands of the rocks. Arriving early or staying late should reward you with a memorable dawn or sunset. Nearby El Pescador and La Peidra beaches are also worth visiting.

Zuma Beach

Zuma, in northernmost Malibu, is about as good as it gets. The four-mile (6.5km) sprawl of immaculate sand is ideal for surfing, swimming, volleyball, sunbathing and long walks. The water is clean and the sand soft beneath your feet. Zuma can get crowded, and getting there along traffic-congested PCH can be a challenge. Some parking spots along PCH are a short walk to the sand, but unless you arrive early, it's better to fork out $5 to park and then you're set for the day. There are

Santa Monica Be

Venice B

lifeguards, restrooms and showers. You can buy food from stands, but packing a picnic basket is a better idea. Zuma is ideal for families or large gatherings.

Malibu

Unfortunately, the nicest beaches in Malibu are the private property of the rich and famous (most, by law, must have public access, but finding the routes down to them can be very difficult). The public beaches, spotted with commercial restaurants, are nothing out of the ordinary, making tourists wonder where the real Malibu could be. Nonetheless, swimming, sunning and playing here is popular, especially among those who enjoy watching the do-or-die surfers riding the waves at Surfrider Beach. There are also tidepools, a marine preserve and volleyball and picnic areas. Drive out towards Point Dume to see the opulent houses of the rich and famous – some built precariously on the edge of rocky bluffs.

...and **Pier**.

Manhattan Beach.

Santa Monica

Accessible and near the heart of LA, this big, famous beach is usually crowded and has a fun, festive, summer-holiday feel to it. Santa Monica Pier is the big attraction. Recently renovated, it is about three city blocks in length and offers typical and endearingly low-tech distractions: pier fishing, video arcades, free twilight dance concerts in summer, fortune tellers, shops, fairground games, snack foods, rides and an 11-storey Ferris wheel – from the top of which, on a clear day or night, you can see forever.

Venice

Venice Beach has the feel of a country all its own, with the least homogeneous set of residents and visitors you could imagine. People-watching is the raison d'être here, and you'll soon tick off every last category in your *I Spy* book, Californian wackos included. Pedestrian-only Ocean Front Walk offers shops, restaurants, food stands and one of the most varied selection of cheap sunglasses on earth. Seawards from the Walk, jump into the flow of the winding Venice Boardwalk, where you can rollerblade or cycle, watch or play volleyball or basketball, check out the Incredible Hulk-sized men and women who work out endlessly at Muscle Beach, the almost legendary (but now rather outmoded) outdoor gym. Venice Pier, to the south, is amusing, but second fiddle to Ocean Front Walk. Street parking is usually jammed solid, but there are several beachside parking lots – try the end of Rose Avenue or Windward Avenue, off Pacific Avenue ($5-$7).

The South Bay

Manhattan, Huntington and Hermosa Beaches are the best of the South Bay beaches (though less cosmopolitan in their mix of people). Right out of a postcard of Southern California, they offer clean water, sand that stretches out of sight, small piers and all kinds of activities: volleyball, sailing and oceanfront paths for walking, running, cycling and rollerblading. The charm of these beaches is the local flavour; visitors can swim, picnic and bask in the sun alongside residents and local fishermen. The surf isn't bad either. Huntington Beach picks up swells from a variety of directions, which makes for good waves, and the water is often less crowded than at Malibu's Surfrider Beach. For those who prefer dry land, Manhattan Beach hosts an annual Volleyball Open.

Westside: Inland

This is the LA of legend: from the hotels and rock clubs of West Hollywood to the designer shops and film stars' mansions of Beverly Hills.

Maps p305 & p306

West Hollywood

West Hollywood, which became an independent city in 1984, is actually three bustling communities in one. Most famously, perhaps, the tiny city (1.9 square miles/4.9 square kilometres) is the epicentre of gay and lesbian life in Los Angeles, with **Santa Monica Boulevard** as its main strip. But it is also home to the (straight scene) nightclubs of the fabled **Sunset Strip**. Both these communities are thriving impressively, thanks to the active nightlife that draws fun-seekers of every persuasion to Santa Monica and Sunset, where a string of restaurants, coffee bars and nightclubs are hopping nearly every night of the week. The third community comprises immigrant Russians who live and run businesses in the east end of the city, around Fairfax; relations with their Western-hedonist neighbours are not especially harmonious. There is also a sizeable – and influential – elderly population in the area.

Sunset Strip, the stretch of Sunset Boulevard (one of the longest streets in LA) that runs approximately from Doheny Drive to Laurel Canyon, was originally developed in 1924. By the 1930s, it was Hollywood's playground, home to clubs like the Trocadero, Mocambo, the Players and Ciro's, where performers such as Lena Horne and Edith Piaf belted out their sets. In the 1940s and '50s, mobsters Mickey Cohen and Bugsy Siegel called it home, and in 1963 the **Whisky A Go-Go** (still breaking new acts; *see page 237*) became the first discotheque on the West Coast.

With Whisky's success, clubs such as Gazzarri's, the Zodiac, the Galaxy, Filthy McNasty's (named after a WC Fields movie) and the Trip opened. The Byrds, Love, the Doors and countless other bands played on the Strip, starting a musical revolution, which ended in a riot in 1966, when young clubgoers protested in the streets against the proposed redevelopment of such key venues as Pandora's Box. In the 1970s, the moguls moved in: David Geffen, Phil Spector and disco giant Casablanca Records. The Strip is still home to DreamWorks Records, Island Records and other major record

The legendary **Whisky** on Sunset Strip.

companies. Although the famous Marlboro man billboard has been replaced by a liquor ad, the area's glitzy, Las Vegas quality is still readily apparent to anyone who traverses the Strip by night.

The **Comedy Store** (*see page 243*) helped to break stars like Robin Williams, David Letterman and Whoopi Goldberg, and still hosts comedic legends, while music clubs, such as the **House of Blues**, the **Roxy** (for both, *see chapter **Music***) and Johnny Depp's **Viper Room** (*see page 242*), continue to present the latest sounds. The legend of the Strip is also kept alive by restaurants such as **Le Dôme** , and hotels such as **Chateau Marmont** (where Greta Garbo lived and John Belushi died) and the **Mondrian** (for both, *see chapter **Accommodation***), still brim-full with celebs. Newcomer **Hustler Hollywood** (*see page 195*) brings a touch of class and sophistication to the sex shop, while old-timer **Book Soup** (*see page 178*) is well loved for its huge selection of literature and magazines, and late opening hours. For more Strip lore, *see page 237* **Sunset Strip**.

West Hollywood is one of the few districts that is easily walkable. In fact, while the Santa Monica Boulevard Reconstruction Project grinds on, walking is probably your best bet. A massive facelift that includes new pavements and the planting of more than a thousand new trees, the construction work has turned the stretch of Santa Monica Boulevard from Holloway Drive in the west to La Brea Avenue in the east into a veritable two-lane nightmare. The finishing touches will supposedly be in place by the end of summer 2001, but until then, you're better off traversing the area on foot. Bear in mind you have to drive there before you can walk, though, and note that parking is horrid in West Hollywood – so always check all parking signs.

Head a few blocks south of Sunset Boulevard to find exclusive restaurants such as **Morton's** on Melrose Avenue, the **Ivy** on North Robertson Boulevard (famed for its celebrity clientele and Hollywood deals), **Le Colonial** on Beverly Boulevard, a string of excellent French restaurants along La Cienega Boulevard, and **Tail-o'-the-Pup** on North San Vicente Boulevard, a landmark 1946 hot dog stand built in the shape of a huge hot dog. For all, *see chapter* **Restaurants**.

Urth Caffè (8565 Melrose Avenue, 1-310 659 0628) is a popular spot, while next door, the **Bodhi Tree** (*see page 178*) is a well-known Buddhist bookshop and lecture room. The **Sunset Marquis Hotel & Villas** (*see page 53*) on Alta Loma Road at Sunset Boulevard is still a music celeb hangout, while over on Robertson Boulevard, **LunaPark** (*see page 234*) is a popular restaurant and eclectic nightclub. Tucked away at the northern end of Kings Road, the **Schindler House** and its garden is an oasis of minimalist architecture (it's also known as the MAK Center; *see page 33*), and the **Lloyd Wright Home & Studio** on Doheny Drive, designed by Frank Lloyd Wright's eldest son, is a masterpiece of quirky architecture.

The West Hollywood skyline is dominated by the **Pacific Design Center** (8687 Melrose Avenue). A gigantic blue and green glass building, it was designed by Cesar Pelli in 1975 to house outlets for the interior design trade. Fondly known as the 'Blue Whale', it is somewhat underused for its size except when it hosts the bustling West Week design convention each March. South of the PDC on Beverly Boulevard and La Cienega Boulevard is the monstrous **Beverly Center** mall (*see page 174*), a huge 'brown whale' much bigger than the PDC, which houses the usual chainstore outlets and is where the Paul Mazursky film *Scenes from a Mall* was shot. Complete your consumer tour at **Koontz** (8914 Santa Monica Boulevard, 1-310 652 0123), which has the best selection of fixtures and fittings in LA and very helpful staff.

West Hollywood Convention & Visitors Bureau

Pacific Design Center, 8687 Melrose Avenue, at San Vicente Boulevard, suite M25, West Hollywood, CA 90096 (1-800 368 6020/1-310 289 2525/www.visit westhollywood.com). **Open** 8.30am-5.30pm Mon-Fri; closed Sat, Sun. **Map** p306 A2.

Beverly Hills

Swimming pools, movie stars, Rolls-Royces: when it comes to Beverly Hills, all the clichés are true. Expensively manicured and policed to the point of sterility, it comes across as a theme park for the rich, where shopping, eating and looking good in your car are the major activities. It's brimming with lavish mansions and celebrities – Douglas Fairbanks and Mary Pickford were the first to move here, to their mansion Pickfair, in 1920 – and is now populated by rich immigrants from Iran and Israel, with the second most-spoken language being Farsi. The area is replete with lushly planted streets, lilac-flowering jacaranda trees that bloom in April and May and every architectural style imaginable.

Beverly Hills extends either side of Santa Monica and Sunset Boulevards, south-west of West Hollywood. The best way to experience its opulent living is to drive around the residential streets that run north to south from Sunset to Santa Monica Boulevards, between Linden and Doheny Drives. Or check out the hillside houses in and around Benedict and Coldwater Canyons, north of Sunset. Just don't drive too slowly or the vigilant BH cops will be on your tail. Celeb-watchers should note that the public toilets in Will Rogers Memorial Park, at the intersection of Beverly Drive and Sunset Boulevard, is

Even the palm trees are manicured in Beverly Hills.

Beverly Hills' grandiose **Civic Center**.

Avenue and Walden Drive). Built in 1921, with peaked, shingled roofs, tilted windows and a fabulous witch-and-broomstick spirit, it was originally a film company's administration building and was often used as a movie set. It is now a private residence, so be careful not to incite the wrath of the resident witch, warlock or other homeowner.

The recently refurbished **Beverly Hills Hotel** (*see page 49*) on Sunset Boulevard, aka 'the Pink Palace', was one of the first buildings to be constructed in the city and remains a popular celebrity hangout. Its bar, the **Polo Lounge** (*see page 143*), is still the place for power lunching and movie dealing. The **Peninsula Beverly Hills** (*see page 51*) on Little Santa Monica Boulevard is also a good place for celebrity-spotting, while next door stands the IM Pei-designed **CAA** (Creative Artists Agency) building, all minimalist white marble and cantilevered glass.

The stretch of Beverly Drive south of Wilshire Boulevard to Pico Boulevard is a wonderful example of the kind of 1950s architecture that LA is renowned for. **Nate & Al** (*see page 142*) on Beverly Drive is one of the best New York-style delis in the city, while upmarket diner **Kate Mantilini** (*see page 142*) on Wilshire Boulevard, named after a 1940s boxing promoter, is a feast of high-art architecture by noted firm Morphosis.

Away from the shopping frenzy, **Greystone Mansion** (905 Loma Vista Drive, 1-310 550 4796), set in 18 landscaped acres (7.3 hectares), is an oasis of peace and quiet that's suitable for romantic afternoon strolls. Built in 1927 by oil millionaire Edward L Doheny (who was murdered by his secretary within three weeks of moving into the place), the 55-room Tudor-style home has been used in such films as *The Witches of Eastwick*, *The Bodyguard* and *Indecent Proposal*. The gardens are open 10am to 6pm daily; the house is closed to the public.

Beverly Hills Visitors Bureau

239 S Beverly Drive, between Charleville Boulevard & Gregory Way, Beverly Hills, CA 90212 (1-800 345 2210/1-310 248 1015/www.bhvb.org). **Open** 9am-5pm Mon-Fri; closed Sat, Sun. **Map** p305 C3.

UCLA & Westwood Village

The University of California at Los Angeles (UCLA) is a sprawling 400-acre (162-hectare) campus, originally built on a bean field in the city of Westwood in 1929. Diverse architectural styles blend in beautifully landscaped grounds, highlighting the enormous wealth and influence of the school. The university is noted for its library (among the largest in the world), school of business administration, centre for health

where singer George Michael was arrested in the spring of 1998.

The Spanish baroque-style **Civic Center**, which straddles Santa Monica Boulevard and Rexford Drive, is a unique reflection of the city's wealth, so carefully coiffed it looks like a film set. In direct contrast to such pomposity is the Union 76 gas station (on the corner of Little Santa Monica Boulevard and Rexford Drive), with its magnificent 1950s cantilevered concrete canopy.

The real reason most people visit Beverly Hills is the 'Golden Triangle' – the shopping area bounded by Wilshire Boulevard, Canon Drive and Little Santa Monica Boulevard – that includes **Rodeo Drive**, **Dayton Way** and **Brighton Way**. It contains some of the most expensive shopping outlets in the world, among them Gucci, Armani, Ralph Lauren, Prada, Chanel and Cartier. **Two Rodeo Drive**, a $200-million ersatz European cobbled walkway that boasts an even greater selection of exclusive shops, is always busy with both window-shopping tourists and serious spenders. For more info on LA's shopping delights, *see chapter* **Shops & Services**.

If you're in the area, also take a look at the fairy tale folly of **Spadena House**, also known as the Witch's House (at Carmelita

Sightseeing

Greystone Mansion's gardens. See p83.

sciences and sports facilities. Schoenberg Hall – named after the composer, who taught here in the 1940s – and Royce Hall are popular concert and performance venues.

Due to the sheer size of the campus, students are always buzzing around the area. Nearby Westwood Village – just south of UCLA and one of the few walkable neighbourhoods in Los Angeles – is a good place for inexpensive food and, south of Wilshire Boulevard, for bookshops and Italian and Persian restaurants.

Westwood Memorial Cemetery (1218 Glendon Avenue, 1-310 474 1579), on the edge of the Village, is famous for its celebrity graves, including those of Marilyn Monroe and Natalie Wood, but the **Mormon Temple** (best seen from Santa Monica Boulevard) is by far the most powerful presence in the area. The 257-foot (84-metre) tower, crowned with a gold-leaf statue of the angel Moroni, is the largest temple of the Church of Jesus Christ of Latter-day Saints outside Salt Lake City, Utah. The temple itself is only open to church members (there is a visitor centre for infidels; 10777 Santa Monica Boulevard, 1-310 474 1549), but the beautifully green, manicured lawn and clean, white stone building, which is lit up at night, are always an awe-inspiring sight.

Rhino Records (*see page 180*) and **Border's Books & Music** (*see page 178* **Bookshops**) are both fine and famed outlets for music on Westwood Boulevard, south of Wilshire Boulevard: Rhino's for its knowledgeable, friendly staff and eclectic selection of CDs and vinyl; Border's for the sheer volume of its merchandise.

Westside Pavilion on Pico Boulevard is the epitome of the many 1980s shopping malls in Los Angeles: pastel colours juxtaposed with a glass-vaulted atrium and the obligatory selection of high-fashion shops that are in every other mall. However, it also houses the excellent Samuel Goldwyn four-screen cinema, which often has exclusive runs of independent films.

Also notable for its adventurous, independent movie screenings is the **Nuart** (*see page 214*), one of Los Angeles's last surviving movie repertory houses.

Across the road from Westside Pavilion is the **Apple Pan** (*see page 145*), home of the homely hamburger and waiters who have worked there 40 years or more. **John O'Groats** (10516 Pico Boulevard, 1-310 204 0692) is a Scottish-style eatery that serves great fish and chips, and porridge (honest), while those seeking authentic East Coast-style Italian grub will hit the proverbial jackpot at **Matteo's Hoboken** (2323 Westwood Boulevard, 1-310 474 1109).

Bel Air

Bel Air is a posh, sleepy, hillside community between Brentwood and Beverly Hills: developed by Alphonzo E Bell in the early 1920s, it rapidly became a preferred location for celebrities who valued privacy and a good view. There's not much for the outsider to see along the winding roads, as the best houses are hidden behind huge, imposing walls. Celebs who still inhabit the area include Joni Mitchell, Tom Jones, Barry Manilow, Elizabeth Taylor and Lionel Ritchie.

Colourful sounds, too, at **Rhino Records**.

There's not much to do in Bel Air either, except take a jaunt to the **Hotel Bel-Air** on Stone Canyon Road (*see page 50*). This ultra-expensive inn reflects the tranquil, dripping-with-money neighbourhood, with its beautifully manicured gardens, a lake with a bridge and swans, fireplaces in the rooms and a cosy bar. It has an expensive but delicious Sunday brunch and is also rumoured to entertain Prince Charles for a drink or two when he's in town. Grace Kelly lived in the hotel during her Hollywood years.

Century City

This tiny neighbourhood, between Beverly Hills and West LA, was once a movie backlot and the site of Tom Mix Westerns. It was bought by Alcoa from 20th Century Fox in 1961 and today is still dominated by Fox Studios and an over-abundance of high-rise office buildings: 8.6 million square feet (800,000 square metres) of office space on only 176 acres (71.3 hectares). Amid these nondescript buildings, however, are two designed by Minoru Yamasaki (who also designed New York's World Trade Center towers): the triangular Century Plaza towers and the **Century Plaza Hotel** (2025 Avenue of the Stars), a huge, high-rise ellipse enlivened at night by orange lighting and a blue-lit fountain that sits in front of the hotel.

Century City Shopping Center is a vast upmarket mall with a bustling food court. It is also home to the AMC Century 14, claimed to be the second-largest cinema in the States. **Houston's** is a good place to grab a Martini and a french dip sandwich after a film. But give yourself time to park; the underground parking at Century City is one of LA's largest, and most confusing.

Brentwood

Novelist Raymond Chandler wrote *High Window* and *Lady in the Lake* while living at 12216 Shetland Place, and Marilyn Monroe died a lonely death just down the road at 12305 Fifth Helena Drive. This exclusive residential neighbourhood west of Beverly Hills was farms and fields until 1915, when a real estate agent named Bundy developed them into streets. Landscape architects and engineers were commissioned to create 'flora, arbor and artistic park attractions'. Everything that suggested a formal city street was avoided, which means Brentwood is like a small town and the main street, San Vicente Boulevard, has a line of coral trees (the official tree of Los Angeles) running down its centre.

The hills north of San Vicente are very rustic, very expensive and, needless to say, home to yet more celebrities. One in particular, OJ Simpson, has done much to put the neighbourhood on the map. The condo of murdered Nicole Brown Simpson on Bundy Drive became a regular tourist attraction, but has now been re-landscaped to deter ghoulish sightseers; OJ's own house, on Rockingham Avenue, was bulldozed in the summer of 1998.

On San Vicente Boulevard, the **Cheesecake Factory** (No.11647, 1-310 826 7111) has a busy bar scene, while the **New York Bagel Company** (No.11640, 1-310 820 1050), designed by Frank Gehry, is the place to have breakfast. **Dutton's** (No.11975, 1-310 476 6263) is one of the best bookshops in LA, sprawling its collection of books both new and used over four requisitioned condo units.

Nowadays, most people visit Brentwood to see the hugely popular **Getty Center** (*see page 120* **Getty Center**) designed by architect Richard Meier. Set on a fantastic hillside site, this complex houses everything but the Greek and Roman collections, which remain at the original J Paul Getty Museum in Malibu (scheduled to reopen in 2002).

Culver City

An incorporated city with its own police force, Culver City, at the south-eastern crux of the I-10 and I-405 intersection, is renowned for being safe, if boring. At one time it was the home of three major motion picture studios – Metro Goldwyn Mayer, Hal Roach Studios and Selznick International Studios – and produced half the films made in the US. MGM, which claimed to have 'more stars than there are in heaven', gave up its last piece of turf to the producers of *Dallas* and *Falcon Crest*. Sony Film Studios dominates the area and there is a host of art and photography warehouse conversions by some of LA's most progressive architects, such as Eric Owen Moss and the late Frank Israel. The old Helms Bakery building on Helms Avenue now houses a collection of furniture shops, both contemporary and antique, as well as an acclaimed jazz venue, the **Jazz Bakery** (*see page 237*).

Further west on Venice Boulevard is **Versailles** (*see page 147*), a cheap and cheerful Cuban restaurant worth visiting; there's another branch nearby on La Cienega Boulevard. Also worth a trip is **Johnnie's Pastrami** (4017 South Sepulveda Boulevard, 1-323 734 6003), a local landmark whose deliciously greasy sandwiches are upstaged only by the cartoonish flair of the building's Googie-style 1950s architecture.

Sightseeing

Hollywood & Midtown

Hollywood may be run-down and touristy, but it's still thrilling. And some of LA's best museums are congregated in Midtown.

Maps p306 & p307

Hollywood

Los Angeles is a city of contrasts, and one of the most depressing is that between the glittering Hollywood of legend and the grim Hollywood of reality. Certainly, the floodlit paradise of filmic immortality that the name conjures up was mostly the creation of over-imaginative press officers, but the area's genuine traces of glamour are all but gone today. In any case, you are about as likely to spot a bona-fide movie star strolling along Hollywood Boulevard as you are to see Zeus cavorting on Mount Olympus. The area has no official status, either: it's merely part of the City of Los Angeles, while, confusingly, West Hollywood next door is an independent city.

The 1990s were a particularly difficult time for the stretch of **Hollywood Boulevard** that runs between La Brea Avenue and Western Avenue. Severely damaged by riots, earthquakes and subway construction, the Boulevard also became home to countless squatters and teenage runaways. However, the old lady is about to receive a billion-dollar facelift, courtesy of the newly inaugurated Hollywood Entertainment District. The makeover includes plans for the Hollywood & Highland Development Project, which will renovate the wonderfully opulent **Mann's Chinese Theater** (*see page 213*) and add a four-storey entertainment complex next door, featuring restaurants, shops, cinemas, a hotel and a 3,300-seat auditorium that will become the new home of the annual Academy Awards ceremony. The project should reach completion in 2002, as should the new Hollywood History Museum, which will be located in the renovated Max Factor Building at the corner of Hollywood Boulevard and Highland Avenue. At least, the construction has meant that Hollywood Boulevard is now well served by the Metro, with three stops on the Red Line.

Also going under the knife is the famous **Cinerama Dome** (*see page 215* **Movie palaces**). Though preservationists were able to thwart plans to demolish its eye-catching geodesic exterior, they were sadly unable to prevent Pacific Theaters, the venue's owner,

from carving up the spacious interior into a 15-screen multiplex. Plans for the new Cinerama Dome Theater Center, which is scheduled to open in 2001, also call for the addition of offices, restaurants, shops and a 3,000-capacity car park. Adjacent to the property will be the new Hollywood Marketplace, a three-acre 'urban entertainment and retail village' supposedly inspired by the Hollywood architecture of the 1940s.

Whether all this activity will actually give Hollywood a new lease of life remains to be seen; until then, expect massive traffic delays, especially around the intersection of Highland Avenue and Hollywood Boulevard.

In the meantime, despite the seediness, Hollywood Boulevard does retain a sense of magic, particularly the stretch between Sycamore Avenue and Argyle Avenue. For a sense of the area's history, try the self-guided walking tour along Hollywood Boulevard and

The star-studded **Walk of Fame**. See p87.

The Hollywood sign

This perennially fascinating sign, symbol, logo, sculpture and icon in one stands north of Hollywood on Mount Lee. Built in 1923, the gargantuan sign was originally an advertisement for a real-estate development called 'Hollywoodland'. In 1949, the city  tore down the last four of the 50-foot (15-metre) high letters and kept the rest as a landmark.

It has now become such a potent symbol of stardom that it's a surprise to hear that it's been the jumping-off point for only one suicide – a young starlet, Lillian Millicent Entwistle, known as Peg, who threw herself off the 'H' one breezy September night in 1932 after RKO studios declined to pick up her option when they saw her first film.

Today, the sign is repainted five times a year and defended by a million-dollar security system. But even this cannot keep out the trespassers who want to get their messages out to the world. For brief moments, the sign and its 5,000 lights have become 'Ollywood' (after Iran-Contra messenger Colonel Oliver North), 'Hollyweed' (in appreciation of the powers of marijuana) and a support message to the US troops fighting in the Gulf War, when a massive yellow ribbon was tied around the letters.

A good place from which to see the sign is the corner of Sunset Boulevard and Bronson Avenue; another is Paramount Studios, at Melrose Avenue and Gower Street. For more sign lore, visit www.hollywoodsign.org.

surrounding streets, where 46 signs mark sites of historical, architectural or other significance. For details, visit www.hollywoodbid.org/hist/historic_sites.html.

You can still commune with the ghosts of old Hollywood at **El Capitan Theater** (No.6838), the newly renovated **Egyptian Theater** (*see page 214* **American Cinematheque**), as well as Mann's Chinese Theater, or share a drink and a meal with them at Tinseltown standbys **Musso & Frank** (*see page 170*) or **Miceli's** (1646 Las Palmas Avenue, 1-323 466 3438). For the chance of seeing some real ghosts, there's no better place than the celeb-filled **Hollywood Forever Cemetery** (*see page 89*), which abuts **Paramount Studios** – the only film studio still located in Hollywood – and is open for tours (*see page 217*).

Of course, you can always take a stroll down the **Walk of Fame** (on Hollywood Boulevard between La Brea and Argyle Avenues), with its star-shaped pavement plaques bearing the names of 2,000-plus entertainment greats – and anyone else with $7,500 and a decent publicity agent. A first glimpse of the huge **Hollywood sign** (*see box above*) is always a thrill, and the outdoor **Hollywood Bowl** (*see page 229*) won't disappoint either, especially if you take a picnic to a summer evening concert. Further bucolic pleasures can be had at the **Hollywood Reservoir & Dog Park** and **Sunset Ranch**,

which offers horse riding in the Hollywood Hills – for both, *see page 89*.

Yamashiro (*see page 150*), on Sycamore Avenue at Franklin Avenue, serves Japanese cuisine in an ancient pagoda with phenomenal views. Imported from Japan, the pagoda – originally a brothel, according to legend – is more than 600 years old, making it the oldest building in Los Angeles. Any music fan worth his or her salt will experience a sense of wonder on seeing the **Capitol Records** building (on Vine Street, just north of the intersection with Hollywood Boulevard) – it's shaped like a stack of records and topped with a stylus, allegedly the idea of songwriter Johnny Mercer and singer Nat 'King' Cole.

Back on Hollywood Boulevard, the art deco interior of the **Pantages Theater** (*see page 231*) is so disorientatingly beautiful that it verges on the psychedelic. Anyone with a fetish for underwear or a taste for the camp should pay a visit to the Celebrity Lingerie Hall of Fame – an exhibition of underwear worn by stars both living and dead – at **Frederick's of Hollywood** (*see page 188*). Underwear shop **Playmates of Hollywood** (No.6438, 1-323 464 7636) occasionally holds transvestite lingerie shows that are not to be believed.

If you feel the need to unleash the tourist within, pay a visit to the **Hollywood Wax Museum** (No.6767, 1-323 462 5991). Rather ragged around the edges, the museum is still

Sightseeing

amusing, even if the sets do seem to have been locked in a time capsule for a decade. Its redeeming feature is the Chamber of Horrors, which, despite its campness, can be a bit spooky – as is the waxen re-creation of the Last Supper, covered with pennies thrown by visitors. Combo discount admission is available for the Wax Museum and the **Guinness World of Records Museum** across the street (No.6764, 1-323 463 6433). But make sure you leave off psychedelic drugs beforehand – both contain exhibits that, if viewed in a fragile state of mind, could warp you for life.

More intentional oddness can be found at **Ripley's Believe it or Not!** (No.6780, 1-323 466 6335), a tourist trap of bizarre 'facts' that stretches the definition of the term museum. For cheesy film and TV memorabilia, including sets from *Star Trek* and *Cheers*, there's the **Hollywood Entertainment Museum** (*see page 123*). If you do want to visit the Entertainment Museum, consider investing in a **Hollywood CityPass**, which gets you into that and seven LA other sights – the El Egyptian Theater, Universal Studios, Autry Museum of Western Heritage, Petersen Automotive Museum, Museum of Television & Radio, Museum of Tolerance, Reagan Presidential Library & Museum – for a cost of $49.75 ($38 3-11s). The pass is valid for nine days and available from any of the attractions or the Hollywood Tourist Bureau.

Those looking for a more reverent view of Hollywood history should check out the mini-museum of cinematic memorabilia on the mezzanine of the **Clarion Hollywood Roosevelt Hotel** at No.7000 (*see page 57*), while memorabilia collectors and film fans should plan to drop some cash at **Hollywood Book & Poster** (No.6349, 1-323 465 8764), a shop jammed to the rafters with obscure videos, rare lobby cards (promotional signs that used to be displayed in cinema foyers) and stills from just about every movie ever made.

Sunset Boulevard east of Fairfax Avenue is pretty sleazy as well (Hugh Grant was nicked in this part of town), but it somehow seems a lot more vital than its counterpart to the north. Maybe it's the constant, furtive comings and goings from the hourly rate motels or the equally busy string of guitar shops. Anyone interested in the latter should pay a visit to the **Guitar Center** (No.7425, 1-323 874 1060): the selection of axes is dizzying in the extreme, and it's entertainment enough just to listen to the 'Hey, dude!' patois of the long-haired, beflannelled shop assistants and customers. **Crossroads of the World** (No.6671), a charming little outdoor shopping plaza built in 1936, predates Los Angeles's strip mall

Famous undies at **Frederick's**. See p87.

explosion by 50 years: too bad its successors couldn't follow the example of its eye-catching mixture of English, French, Moorish and Spanish architecture.

The buildings that comprise **A&M Studios** (1416 North La Brea Avenue) have resonated not only to the sounds of the Rolling Stones and the Carpenters (among the thousands of other acts that have recorded here over the past few decades), but with cinematic history as well: the core of the complex was built in 1918 by Charlie Chaplin, who used it as his movie studio. Jazz musician Herb Alpert purchased the place for A&M Records in 1966, but concrete prints of Chaplin's feet are (allegedly) still visible outside Studio 3. Unfortunately, the record company closed its doors in early 1999, and the property's future is rather up in the air at the moment.

Hollywood Chamber of Commerce

7018 Hollywood Boulevard, CA 90028 (1-323 469 8311/www.hollywoodchamber.net). **Open** 9am-5pm Mon-Fri; closed Sat, Sun. **Map** p307 A1.

Hollywood Tourist Bureau

The Janes House, 6541 Hollywood Boulevard, at Hudson Avenue, CA 90028 (1-213 236 2331/ www.lacvb.com). **Open** 9am-5pm Mon-Sat; closed Sun. **Map** p307 A1.

Located in the historic Janes House, this is the Hollywood branch of the main tourist office.

Hollywood Forever Cemetery

6000 Santa Monica Boulevard, between Gower Street & N Van Ness Avenue (1-323 469 1181/ www.forevernetwork.com). Bus 156, 304/US 101, exit Santa Monica Boulevard west. **Open** *Summer 8.30am-7pm daily. Winter 8.30am-6.30pm daily.* **Admission** *free.* **Map** p307 B2.

Formerly called the Hollywood Memorial Cemetery, Hollywood Forever is unquestionably the best place to look for the Ghost of Hollywood Past. The new owners have come under criticism for promoting the place as a tourist attraction, but certainly any place that houses the remains of such luminaries as Tyrone Power, Cecil B De Mille, Douglas Fairbanks Snr, Adolph Menjou, Nelson Eddy, Jayne Mansfield, studio mogul Harry Cohn (who wanted to be buried facing his beloved Columbia Studios), Peter Lorre, Peter Finch and silent star Renee Adoree is worth a look. Located just north of Paramount Studios, Hollywood Forever is also the final resting place of Rudolph Valentino; legend has it that a mysterious 'Woman in Black' still stalks the place, mourning the demise of Hollywood's original Latin lover. The grounds are incredibly peaceful, the decades-old monuments unique in design and, overall, it's still much less of a downer than walking along Hollywood Boulevard. As the headstone of Mel Blanc – the voice of Porky Pig, Elmer Fudd et al – reads: 'That's all, folks!'

Hollywood Reservoir & Dog Park

Lake Hollywood Drive, Hollywood Hills. Bus 156, 163, 426/US 101, exit Barham Boulevard north.

Set in the Hollywood Hills, above the Hollywood Bowl and below the Hollywood sign and Madonna's former enormous estate, the Hollywood Reservoir attracts runners, walkers and the occasional cyclist. It's at its best when the gates open at 6.30am: the aroma of dew-moist pines envelops you as you run or walk on the three-mile (5km) pebbly dirt road around the reservoir. From one side of the water, you get a fantastic view of the Hollywood sign. Tucked behind the reservoir up Beachwood Canyon is the Hollywood Dog Park. It's not uncommon to catch a glimpse of jogging celebs who think they're incognito under their baseball caps.

Mann's Chinese Theater

6925 Hollywood Boulevard, between La Brea & Highland Avenues (1-323 464 8111/www.mann theatres.com). Metro Hollywood-Highland/bus 156, 163, 180, 181, 426/US 101, exit Hollywood Boulevard west. **Tickets** *$9; $6 concessions.* **Credit** MC, V. **Map** p307 A1.

Mann's is where you'll find the famous courtyard where movie greats have made imprints of their hands and feet. Master showman Sid Grauman, in true Hollywood style, commissioned architects Meyer and Holler to create a Chinese temple as a new stage on which to perform his prologues. Legend insists that Norma Talmadge accidentally stepped into the wet cement outside the new building and, in spirited response, Sid fetched Mary Pickford and

Douglas Fairbanks to repeat the 'mistake' with their feet and hands. And so it began. Mann's was the spot where the first gala premières took place – with limousines, fur-wrapped starlets, the works. The courtyard is sometimes choked with camera-snapping tourists measuring their own hands and feet against the likes of John Wayne, Jimmy Stewart and Judy Garland, but the cinema itself is well preserved, clean and still a great place to catch a movie. *See also p215* **Movie palaces**.

Sunset Ranch

3400 N Beachwood Drive, off Franklin Avenue (1-323 469 5450/www.sunsetranchhollywood.com). US 101, exit Beachwood Drive north. **Open** *9am-5pm daily.* **Horses** *$20 per hour.* **Credit** MC, V.

Sunset Ranch offers riding lessons, moonlight rides and hourly rentals in the Hollywood Hills. Don't miss the evening Margarita ride, which takes you up and over the hills and into the Valley, where you stop at a Mexican restaurant – and at least one person always falls off on the way home.

Fairfax District

Although LA's first major Jewish community settled in the East LA neighbourhood of Boyle Heights, the stretch of Fairfax Avenue between Beverly Boulevard and Melrose Avenue has been Los Angeles's main Jewish drag since the 1940s. If you're shopping for a new menorah or

Pay tribute at **Hollywood Forever Cemetery**.

the latest in Israeli pop music, this is the place to go: and the neighbourhood's heavy Hasidic population makes it the safest place in LA to jog on a Friday evening.

Kosher grocers, butcher's shops, restaurants and bakeries line the street; all are excellent, and almost all are closed on Saturdays. Open 24 hours a day, however, is the legendary **Canter's** (*see page 150*), a World War II-era kosher restaurant, deli and bakery. The food is delicious and authentic (homesick New Yorkers eat here regularly), and portions are generous. Another good lunch spot is **Eat-a-Pita** (No.465), a pleasant outdoor stand that serves some of the best Middle Eastern fast food in town. Just south of the Beverly-Fairfax intersection lies **CBS Television City**, home to many a game show and sitcom. Next door is the retail experience of the **Farmers Market**; for the more authentic farmers markets that are held all over Los Angeles, selling locally grown and often organic produce, *see page 192*.

Farmers Market

6333 W Third Street, at Fairfax Avenue (1-213 549 2140/www.farmersmarketla.com). Bus 16, 217/I-10, exit Fairfax Avenue north. **Open** 9am-7pm Mon-Sat; 10am-6pm Sun. **Map** p306 B2.

Originally a co-op where people could buy produce from local farmers, today the Farmers Market has more than 165 stalls selling foods both homely and exotic, as well as shops offering knick-knacks, clothes and tourist tat. It's best on Thursday and Saturday evenings, when bands play; karaoke on Friday nights is also popular. Plans to turn the neighbouring car park into a mall bode ill for the low-key atmosphere.

Miracle Mile & Midtown

So named because of its tremendous commercial growth during the 1920s, Miracle Mile's appellation now seems somewhat ironic, given the rate at which businesses on the strip – which stretches along Wilshire Boulevard from Fairfax to La Brea Avenues – have been shutting their doors.

Opened in 1940, the gigantic May Co department store (6067 Wilshire Boulevard) was one of the commercial mainstays of the district, but a shift in consumer habits (huge shopping malls such as the Beverly Center now reign supreme) and the psychological residue of the 1992 riots (as far as most suburbanites were concerned, anywhere south of Ventura Boulevard was South Central) forced it to close in 1993. Recently renovated by the **Los Angeles County Museum of Art** (*see page 117*), the building reopened its doors in 1998 as LACMA West. In desperate need of a similar reprieve is the neighbouring

diner, Johnie's (No.6101), a rare and rather run-down example of 1950s Googie architecture, which closed for good in early 2000.

This stretch of Wilshire is also known as Museum Row, and for good reason. The **Los Angeles County Museum of Art,** the **Petersen Automotive Museum,** the **Carole & Barry Kaye Museum of Miniatures** and the **George C Page Museum of Tar Pit Discoveries** (for all, *see chapter* **Museums**) are all within easy walking distance of each other. The last has the added attraction of the La Brea Tar Pits, a huge, bubbling swamp of primordial ooze. Recently re-landscaped, the Tar Pits are a wonderful place to while away an afternoon. The renovated **El Rey Theatre** (No.5519), built in 1936 in the Streamline Moderne style, is now a popular rock concert and nightclub venue (*see page 232*).

The area just south of the Miracle Mile is primarily residential, inhabited by an ethnically mixed, middle- and lower-middle-class community. Some of the finest soul food north of South Central can be found here, at **Maurice's Snack 'n' Chat** (*see page 152*) and **Roscoe's House of Chicken 'n' Waffles** (5006 West Pico Boulevard, 1-323 934 4405), while **Uncle Darrow's** (5301 Venice Boulevard, 1-323 938 0518) dishes up the best no-frills Cajun cooking in town.

A few miles and many generic strip malls to the east, the **Wiltern Center** (at Wilshire Boulevard and Western Avenue) is thriving nicely. A breathtaking, green art deco pile built in 1931, it lingered in a state of advanced decrepitude during much of the 1970s and 1980s before being rescued from the wrecking ball and turned into a performing arts and commercial centre. Pop acts regularly strut their stuff inside the stunning **Wiltern Theater** (*see page 232*) on the corner of the Center, which also regularly hosts such popular black theatrical productions as *Beauty Shop* and *Mama I'm Sorry*. The neighbouring **Atlas Supper Club** (*see page 150*) is a must for Californian cuisine and cabaret in a deliciously camp interior. For a more authentically Mid-Wilshire experience, stop for some 'food and grog' at the **HMS Bounty** (*see page 169*), a convivial gathering place for neighbourhood characters.

Across the street from the Bounty, the **Ambassador Hotel** (No.3400) – known to most as the site of Robert F Kennedy's assassination on the eve of the 1968 California primary elections – is certainly due for a revival, but plans to reopen the building have recently been delayed; there is talk, in fact, that it might be razed to make way for a school. But new life has come to the glorious **Bullocks**

Grand but a bit grim: **MacArthur Park**.

Wilshire (No.3050); one of the first department stores to open (in 1929) outside Downtown, it closed its doors in the wake of sagging revenues and the 1992 riots. Now it has been given a new life as a law school.

Revitalisation is still light years away, however, for **Lafayette Park** and its larger neighbour, **MacArthur Park** (on Wilshire Boulevard, between Alvarado and Park View Streets). The latter, with its recently restored lake and 500-foot (150-metre) high water spout, is an especially grand example of urban landscaping – that is, if you can ignore the crackheads, drug dealers and Central American gang members who populate it. It's a shame; even in its present state, it's still not difficult to see how the park could have inspired Jimmy Webb's epic ballad. But these days, the only thing left out in the rain is the park's resident encampment of homeless individuals.

Two notable remnants of the area's better days are the imposing **Park Plaza Hotel** (607 South Park View Street, 1-213 384 5281) and **Langer's Delicatessen** (704 South Alvarado Street, 1-213 483 8050). The latter, considered by many to have the best pastrami sandwich in town, has a kerbside takeaway service for customers too scared to park their cars on the surrounding mean streets. On Sixth Street, hamburger fans should seek out nearby **Cassell's**, where the home-made patties may well be the best you've ever tasted.

Hancock Park

A gorgeous residential neighbourhood dating back to 1910, Hancock Park is home to some of the most jaw-droppingly opulent mansions found outside Beverly Hills and Bel Air. Bounded by Wilshire Boulevard and Van Ness, Highland and Melrose Avenues, Hancock Park is best toured by car – the local security services are apt to be suspicious of anyone on foot. Historically an Anglo enclave, it excluded blacks and Jews (who moved west) until 1948,

when Nat 'King' Cole was the first African-American to live there. (Don't confuse the area with Hancock Park, an actual park further west on Wilshire Boulevard.)

For a 'Main Street USA' experience in the middle of Los Angeles, stop for refreshment on the nearby stretch of Larchmont Boulevard, between Beverly Boulevard and First Street, known as **Larchmont Village**. This charming couple of blocks has a variety of restaurants, antique shops and other small businesses, many of them housed in buildings built in the 1920s. Even more of a must-see is **Youngwood Court**, a private residence located a few blocks to the west, at the south-east corner of Third Street and Muirfield Road. Though the ranch-style home is nothing special in itself, the owner's decision to decorate his lawn with 30 or so replicas of Michaelangelo's *David* makes for a jaw-dropping visual experience. In fact, the whole stretch of Third Street between Rimpau Boulevard and Van Ness Avenue is a must-drive during the Christmas holidays, when local homeowners try to outdo each other with eye-popping displays of yuletide decorations.

Koreatown

Torched during the 1992 riots, Koreatown – the Midtown neighbourhood roughly comprising the area south of Wilshire Boulevard and along Pico Boulevard between Western and Vermont Avenues – has made a remarkable comeback. Tensions between the Korean and African-American communities (and the area's Central American population) haven't exactly abated, but, for the shopowners, at least, things seem to be back to business as usual. Korean banks, men's clubs, shopfront grocers and golf driving ranges abound, especially along Pico and Olympic Boulevards, and several Korean car dealerships are currently thriving. The area is also becoming popular with artsy white folks who've found the sky-rocketing rents in Silver Lake and Los Feliz to be too prohibitive.

There are also plenty of Korean eateries, of course. Although Korean cooking, with its heavier, meat-based dishes, hasn't quite caught on with non-Koreans, adventurous eaters should take the opportunity to have a spot of lunch in the area. The pricey **Woo Lae Oak** on Western Avenue (*see page 153*) gets regular raves, while holes-in-the-wall such as **Ham Hung** (809 South Ardmore Avenue, 1-213 381 1520) offer delicious but cheaper regional cooking. For a carnivorous – and non-Korean – experience, try **Taylor's Steakhouse** (3361 West Eighth Street, 1-213 382 8449), a chop house with enormous buttoned-and-tufted booths and almost equally enormous steaks.

Sightseeing

Downtown

The city's civic and business centre also contains some of its best arts institutions and most vibrant ethnic districts.

Map p309

It's hard to imagine now, but Downtown LA was once quite literally the heart of the city: a place where lavish film premières were held, where movie stars socialised in swanky restaurants and where a large portion of Angelenos actually went to work every day. Today, there are plenty of LA residents who have never been to Downtown at all, except perhaps to board a train at Union Station or catch the latest hot musical at the Mark Taper Forum. It's a pity, really; though its best days may well be behind it, Downtown still offers plenty of enjoyment.

After decades of post-war decline, the area attracted a lot of investment in the 1980s, much of it from the Far East. Now it's packed during the week with commuting office workers, while the main drag, Broadway, is a buzzing Latino shopping zone, particularly at weekends. Many Angelenos hoped that the arrival in summer 2000 of the Democratic Convention would inspire the city to implement a rebeautification project like the one that recently revitalised downtown Chicago, but no such plan emerged. Likewise, the $375-million Staples Center sports arena (*see page 253*) was supposed to rejuvenate the southern end of Downtown, but shop owners – who bore the brunt of the rioting that followed the LA Lakers' 2000 championship victory – haven't exactly thrived in its garish shadow. On the other hand, the Democratic Convention seemed to pass without any great incident, and the city's sports fans (at least the ones who can afford to get in) seem to love the new arena. Perhaps it's only a matter of time before the surrounding blocks begin to blossom again.

Downtown is one of the few areas of LA where it's better to walk than drive. Everything can be seen in a day and DASH buses (*see page 279*) serve the area at frequent intervals. Although it's not the best place in Los Angeles for star-spotting, you may well see film crews at work: it's a popular location for movies and television shows. Most notably, perhaps, Ridley Scott immortalised Downtown's skyline and its landmark Bradbury Building in *Blade Runner*, a seminal LA movie.

No one really knows how many people live in Downtown and it's certainly not a conventional residential area. It also attracts a considerable number of homeless people. Avoid walking round the area at night and, if you're arriving or departing from the Greyhound bus terminal on Seventh Street, be careful in its immediate vicinity. However, Downtown is currently undergoing a revival as a few savvy property developers have recognised there is gold in them thar defunct commercial buildings, which are rapidly being turned into apartment buildings for would-be urban dwellers. One of these developers has also purchased the once doomed St Vibiana's Cathedral, which is being turned into a theatre, school and housing complex and, together with the pending Walt Disney Concert Hall and new Catholic Cathedral, actually promises to make Downtown more of a magnet than its naysayers would believe.

Chinatown

Located at the northern end of Downtown and starting where Broadway meets Sunset Boulevard, Chinatown has suffered in recent years from an exodus of residents to the San Gabriel Valley, now the best area for Chinese food. Nevertheless, this small but busy neighbourhood is home to an estimated 30,000 people and remains the spiritual centre of LA's Chinese community. It is also undergoing a revival of sorts, with the arrival of a cluster of art galleries, which have moved from the Westside and opened up in Chinatown Plaza, making for an interesting juxtaposition of dusty old Chinese-owned bric-a-brac stores cheek by jowl with trendily spartan white galleries.

North Broadway and **North Spring Street** are the main thoroughfares – the site of banks, businesses and traditional markets – while the streets running off them are also worth a look: the small row of shops between Bamboo Lane and Bernard Street is an especially good place for souvenir shopping. Come February or March, giant dragons snake down Broadway during celebrations for **Chinese New Year** (*see page 207*).

There are plenty of restaurants in the area. **Ocean Seafood** (Chunsan Plaza, 747 North Broadway, 1-213 687 3088) and **Yang Chow** (819 North Broadway, 1-213 625 0811) are both good bets, though the former can get very busy

Olvera Street: Mexican gifts and culture.

at weekends. Apart from eating, there's little to do here at night unless there are openings at the galleries, when Chinatown Plaza becomes a magnet for art world hipsters.

Olvera Street

Just across Sunset Boulevard from Chinatown is **El Pueblo de Los Angeles Historical Monument**, a newly restored 44-acre (18-hectare) historic park and museum on the site of the original settlement of Los Angeles. In fact, the very first settlement was about half a mile from here, but no trace of it remains: LA's official birthday is 4 September 1781, the day that the first Spanish settlers began farming and building ranches. There's a visitor centre (1-213 628 1274) within the museum (open 10am to 3pm Monday to Saturday, closed Sunday) and the museum courtyard is occupied by taco stands and a gift shop. Next door is the oldest Catholic church in LA: **Our Lady, Queen of the Angels**, known as La Placita (*see page 16* **Let's get spiritual**). Established in 1784, it's still very much in use and has some impressive ceiling murals.

Cross Main Street and you reach the Plaza. With a bandstand in the middle, it's a popular place for performances by dancers and musicians and the trees offer some shade from the sun. In one corner is the **Mexican Cultural Institute**. The Plaza is the site of

two annual festivals, the **Blessing of the Animals at Easter** and **Las Posadas** just before Christmas. The yearly **Cinco de Mayo** celebrations include a parade down Olvera Street and then a fiesta commemorating the Mexican victory at the Battle of Puebla in 1862. For details of all, *see chapter* **By Season**.

Running off the eastern side of the Plaza is **Olvera Street**, a narrow thoroughfare full of stalls selling postcards and Mexican handicrafts. Renovated in 1930 as a Mexican marketplace, it's now just a tourist trap – albeit a vibrant and generally enjoyable one. The **El Pueblo Gallery**, which shows local art, is worth checking out. Olvera Street also contains **Avila Adobe**, the oldest house in Los Angeles. Built in 1818, this small ranch-style house has been restored, furnished with period pieces and now operates as a museum.

There are also numerous Mexican restaurants along Olvera, all pretty average. If you're not in the mood for Mexican or Chinese, try **Philippe's The Original Sandwich Shop** (1001 North Alameda Street), an ancient eaterie two blocks north of Olvera Street, which has been serving up delicious 'French Dip' sandwiches and 10¢ coffee for the best part of the past century. It's open 24 hours a day, and always crowded (*see also page 154*).

Visible from the Plaza is **Union Station** (800 North Alameda Street), one of the most accomplished structures in the city. Opened in 1939 on the site of the original Chinatown, which was later moved to its present location, it was the last of the great American train stations to be built, and unified the three railroads that then served LA. With its distinctive, Spanish Mission-style exterior, marble floors, high ceilings and gorgeous decorative tiles, it's an evocative place at which to arrive or depart from LA (but don't confuse the station with the imposing piece of Spanish colonial architecture that stands next to it: that's the post office).

Union Station is also home to the easternmost stop on LA's new subway line, which has branches that extend to Wilshire Boulevard and Western Avenue to the West, and Universal CityWalk to the north. Unlike the subway systems in New York or Chicago, the Red Line is spotlessly clean and almost entirely free of graffiti. We'll see how long that lasts.

Little Tokyo

Head south down Alameda Street for a few blocks, past Temple Street to Central Avenue, and you reach the **Geffen Contemporary Wing** of MOCA (*see page 118*), housed in an old warehouse converted by Frank Gehry. It's a more flexible space than MOCA's other

Sightseeing

site (at California Plaza, 250 South Grand Avenue) and concentrates mainly on post-World War II art. The always provocative exhibitions change frequently.

Just down Central Avenue, on the corner of First Street, is the **Japanese American National Museum** (*see page 117*). It's an appropriate place to start a tour of Little Tokyo, which begins at First Street and spreads west and north. The museum, which has a new 85,000-square foot (7,900-square metre) pavilion, is dedicated to recording and relating the extensive history of the Japanese-American community – Little Tokyo has been in existence for over a century – and mixes exhibits with films and, occasionally, performance art.

Cross First Street from the museum and you enter the **Japanese Village Plaza** (335 East Second Street), a two-storey mini-mall with restaurants, shops and karaoke bars. Pop into **Rascal's** or **Frying Fish** for good ramen or sushi, respectively. Restaurants here generally stay open later than most of LA's eating places: you can turn up after midnight and still get served.

At the end of the plaza is the Fire Tower with its distinctive tiled roof. Nearby is the **Japanese American Cultural & Community Center** (244 South San Pedro Street, 1-213 628 2725), which has an art gallery and Japanese garden. Kabuki, dance and music performances are held in the **Japan America Theater** on the same site. Also in the area is the **Higashi Honganji Buddhist Temple** (505 East Third Street, at Central Avenue), which blends neatly into its very Western surroundings.

If you continue west past the Higashi Temple, you'll enter the **Artists'/Loft District**. The name is something of a misnomer: there are more homeless people here than artists. During the 1980s, when both Downtown and the LA art scene were booming, artists began converting the derelict warehouses that are scattered throughout this area into studios and apartments. Developers quickly started doing the same thing in the hope of reproducing New York's SoHo on the West Coast, but the expected rush of tenants never materialised. But now they are trying again, only this time they are aiming at a higher-income class of tenants.

The beautiful and historic **St Vibiana's Cathedral** (which was profoundly damaged by the Northridge Quake) is about to be transformed into Cathedral Place, plopping a 75-room boutique hotel and restaurant, 150 apartments and a performing arts centre and school down on the corner of Second and Main Streets. Construction is due to begin in 2001.

Civic Center

A few blocks north of Little Tokyo along First Street is the area where many of LA's administrative and political institutions are based. The first you'll encounter is the **Times-Mirror Building** (202 West First Street), home to the *Los Angeles Times*. The building is a slightly tatty example of 1930s architecture and the newspaper is the subject of derision for East Coasters (with good reason), but it's an important LA institution, founded in the late 1800s by the Chandler family, one of the elite WASP families that used to run Los Angeles and played a major part in the development of Downtown.

Conveniently for *Times* reporters, **City Hall** is just across the road on Spring Street. Surrounded by uninspired modern office blocks, its graceful art deco lines have appeared in many movies and television shows (it was destroyed most memorably in *War of the Worlds*), and until 1957 it was the tallest building in LA. Unfortunately, the building has yet to completely recover from the millions of dollars in damage caused by the Northridge Quake of 1994, and is still surrounded by tarpaulins and scaffolding.

Union Station: for trains and a fine building.

Nearby, in the Los Angeles Mall, an utterly soulless shopping area, is the **Children's Museum of Los Angeles** (*see page 210*). Partly designed by the ubiquitous Frank Gehry, it's an ambitious and fun museum with plenty of interactive exhibits and installations. Around the corner, on Aliso and Los Angeles Streets, is the **Metropolitan Detention Center**, LA's newest high-tech prison. Designed to blend in with the office blocks around it, the building looks nothing like a conventional jail; local legend has it that a group of Japanese tourists once tried to check into it, thinking it was a hotel. Also of note is the **Los Angeles County Courthouse**: located on Temple Street between Spring Street and Broadway, this imposing structure was the scene of the OJ Simpson trial in 1995.

Slated to open in 2001 is the city's new Catholic cathedral – **Our Lady of the Angels** – located on Temple Street between Grand Avenue and Hill Street. Designed by Spanish architect Rafael Moneo, the $163-million project is intended to serve as a 'spiritual home to all Angelenos,' and will feature Spanish Mission-style colonnades and a huge plaza.

Broadway

If you want a taste of what a real Mexican shopping street looks like, as opposed to the tourist tack of Olvera Street, then **Broadway** is the place to explore. Running the whole length of Downtown, it's one of the most fascinating streets in the area: a place where old Los Angeles, in the shape of the once grandiose and now mostly decrepit buildings that line it, meets the new, increasingly Hispanic city.

Back in the 1920s and '30s it was the most fashionable shopping and entertainment zone in the city. But the post-war decline of Downtown hit Broadway hard and many of the buildings are boarded up or in a state of disrepair. Despite this, there's a vitality to the street, particularly at the weekends, that you don't find anywhere else in LA. The stores sell mainly electronic goods, cut-price clothes (this is a good place to buy jeans) and jewellery (LA's jewellery district starts below Fifth Street and Broadway) – but don't come here for the shopping so much as for the atmosphere.

Start at Second Street and Broadway and wander south. At the corner of Third Street and Broadway, you'll find the **Bradbury Building** (*see page 31*), one of the unquestionable highlights of the city's architecture. Across the street, there's the Million Dollar Theater, first opened by impresario Sid Grauman in 1918 and now an

Little Tokyo's **Japanese Plaza**. *See p94.*

evangelical church. Next door is **Grand Central Market** (*see page 190*), an enclosed market in the Mexican tradition. It's one of the busiest places in Downtown, with a host of fresh fruit stalls, butchers and fishmongers. If you want lunch and a beer, there are also plenty of taco stands, Chinese fast-food counters and pizza joints.

Alternatively, further down Broadway, just past Sixth Street, you can eat at **Clifton's Brookdale Cafeteria** (No.648, 1-213 627 1673). Built in the 1930s, the restaurant boasts a sumptuous array of inexpensive food items, but is also notable for its bizarre interior, which is half hunting lodge, half redwood forest.

Just across the street is the **Los Angeles Theater**, which was built in 90 days for the première of Charlie Chaplin's *City Lights* in 1930. It's now boarded up, but the extravagant façade is still visible. Other resplendent movie theatres include the **Palace** (630 South Broadway), which may be reopening soon as a live music venue, and the huge **Orpheum** (No.842), built in 1926 in a wacky blend of colonial Spanish and French Gothic styles. It's the only one of the old Broadway movie palaces that's still a working cinema, although others open in June for the Last Remaining Seats film festival (*see page 215* **Movie palaces**). Across the street from the Orpheum is the old **Eastern Columbia Building**, a gorgeous, 13-storey, turquoise art deco pile built in 1929 by Claude Beelman.

For a break from the hustle of Broadway, turn west at Fifth Street and head for **Pershing Square**. Named after the commander of the US Army in World War I, the square hosts free jazz, blues and salsa concerts during the summer and is a good place to catch your breath. Dominating the western corner of the square is the **Regal Biltmore** (*see page 59*), built in 1923 and one of the grandest hotels in Los Angeles. Past guests have included Winston Churchill and various American presidents.

For a self-guided tour of Downtown, try **Angels Walk**. Modelled on Boston's Freedom Trail (no one said LA was the home of originality), illustrated bronze tableaux tell the stories of 15 landmarks of urban art and architecture – including the Bradbury Building, Grand Avenue, Bunker Hill steps, Pershing Square and Central Library – that span more than a century of the city's history. Pick up a leaflet from the **LA Convention & Visitors Bureau** (*see page 290*).

Financial District

A block west of Pershing Square and you enter the land of the skyscraper. The major banks have their huge, gleaming offices here, dwarfing everything around them. This neighbourhood used to be known as Bunker Hill: a century or so ago it was where LA's rich built their houses, but most of the mansions are now long gone. The only remnant of that era is **Angels Flight**, the world's shortest railway (*see below*).

A minute west of Bunker Hill and you reach the **Central Library** on Fifth Street (*see page 284*). Completed in 1926 and recently refurbished after a fire, it's an excellent library and a striking Beaux Arts building with a dramatic, tiled pyramid tower. Virtually opposite is the **Westin Bonaventure Hotel** (*see page 60*), the most distinctive skyscraper in Downtown. With its interior pools and bubble-shaped elevators, it offers a refreshing change from the uniformity of most of the district's tall buildings.

If you feel the need to watch a film while in the area, head for **Laemmle's Grande** (349 South Figueroa Street, 1-213 617 0268), a modern four-screen cinema that's rarely crowded. Also near here is the **Los Angeles Convention & Visitors Bureau**, the main info centre for the city (*see page 290*). Backtrack from the library down Fifth Street to Grand Avenue and then head north up the sharp little hill: the Wells Fargo Center is on your left. Apart from being the headquarters of the Wells Fargo bank, it also houses the **Wells Fargo History Museum** (333 South Grand Avenue, 1-213 253 7166), which tells the story of the bank founded in the heyday of the California Gold Rush. There's a 100-year-old stagecoach and gold nuggets on display. Just up from the Wells Fargo Center on the other side of the road is the other **Museum of Contemporary Art** site (*see page 118*). Part of the billion-dollar California Plaza development, the museum is unmissable – there's a huge Swiss Army knife, designed by Claes Oldenburg, in front of it.

Carry on walking up Grand Avenue and on the left, at First Street, you'll come to the vast **Performing Arts Center**. Gathered together in one complex are the **Dorothy Chandler Pavilion** (*see page 228*), where the Oscars have taken place and the LA Philharmonic currently lives, the **Mark Taper Forum** and the **Ahmanson Theater** (for both, *see page 257*), regarded as two of LA's better theatres. Guided tours are available for the Center, which will be significantly upgraded over the next few years. The biggest addition to the complex will be the much-ballyhooed **Walt Disney Concert Hall**, which is slated to open in time for the 2002-2003 concert season. Designed by Frank Gehry, the 2,290-seat venue will be adjoined by public gardens, restaurants, an art gallery and, of course, a gift shop.

Angels Flight

Hill Street, between Third & Fourth Streets (1-213 626 1901/www.westworld.com/~elson/larail/angels flight.html). Metro Pershing Square/bus 1, 2, 3, 4, 10, 11, 48, 304/I-110, exit Fourth Street east. **Open** 6.30am-10pm daily; closed 6.30-8am 1st & 3rd Tue of the mth. **Tickets** 25¢. **Map** p309 B2.
Opened in 1901, this funicular was designed to connect Bunker Hill with the business district that was then located around Hill and Spring Streets; it saved the residents from having to walk the steep slope back to their houses. The railway reopened in 1996, with its two original wooden passenger cars, Sinai and Olivet, and connects to the fountain-filled Watercourt at California Plaza. A ride costs 25¢ (one way) and takes a mere two minutes (up and down), but it's considerably more charming than any Disneyland or Universal Studios attraction.

Angels Flight: the world's shortest railway.

East of Hollywood

Head east for funky and increasingly gentrified Los Feliz and Silver Lake, and the bucolic delights of Griffith Park.

Map p308

Los Feliz

Los Feliz is a truly cohesive neighbourhood, a casual coffee-klatch community where on-the-go hipsters and yuppies mix with a significant Armenian population and pensioners. In the Los Feliz Hills, above Los Feliz Boulevard and just below Griffith Park, there are posh, secluded homes, including the fabulous **Lovell House** (4616 Dundee Drive), designed by Richard Neutra in 1929 and featured in *LA Confidential*. The proximity of the neighbourhood to Griffith Park means you can combine a ramble in the park and a visit to the observatory with shopping, eating and entertainment.

The area was home to a number of film studios during the silent era: DW Griffith built his gigantic set for *Intolerance* at the north-east corner of Sunset Boulevard and Hillhurst Avenue, now the site of the **Vista**, a fine single-screen cinema offering the most leg room of any in Los Angeles. On the culinary side, two good bets in this part of town are **Jitlada** (5233 W Sunset Boulevard, 1-323 667 9809) and **Zankou Chicken** (5065 W Sunset Boulevard, 1-323 665 7845). Jitlada offers excellent Thai cuisine at extremely reasonable prices, while Zankou Chicken serves up cheap and very tasty Middle Eastern food. Visitors with a taste for the seedier side of life can pay a visit to the **Sunset Theater** at the corner of Sunset Boulevard and Western Avenue, one of the town's few remaining triple-X grind houses ('free admission for ladies').

At the opposite end of the cultural spectrum is the lush oasis known as **Barnsdall Art Park** on Hollywood Boulevard (between Edgemont Street and Vermont Avenue), currently closed for re-landscaping. This peaceful, verdant park is home to the lovely **Hollyhock House** (built between 1917 and 1920, it was Frank Lloyd Wright's first Los Angeles commission), an art gallery and a number of arts and crafts centres, all of which are overseen by the City of Los Angeles Department of Cultural Affairs. Hollyhock House is also closed for repairs; like the Art Park, it is scheduled to reopen in spring 2003.

Though the once delightful view of the city is now largely blocked by a nearby hospital complex, Barnsdall Art Park remains an enjoyable escape from the madness of LA.

The spine of Los Feliz, **Vermont Avenue** – between Franklin Avenue and Hollywood Boulevard – is a couple of blocks south of the park and very much alive and kicking. Both Vermont Avenue, and the nearest major street to the east, **Hillhurst Avenue**, are hopping with a multicultural cocktail of clothing shops, bookshops and bars. The resurgent hipness of the neighbourhood has resulted in a number of fly-by-night outfits, but certain mainstays are worth visiting. They include eateries such as the **House of Pies** (1869 North Vermont Avenue, 1-323 666 9961), good for breakfast, and – a touch on the greasy side – the tiny stand **Yuca's** (2056 Hillhurst Avenue), where you can get a delicious $2.70 Yucatan pork burrito, or the 'No Name' Japanese fast-food restaurant right next door to the **Los Feliz Three Cinemas** (1822 North Vermont Avenue, 1-323 664 2169). For shopping, try novelty shops such as **Uncle Jer's** (4459 Sunset Boulevard, 1-323 662 6710) and **Wacko** (4633 Hollywood Boulevard, 1-323 663 0122), where you can find all kinds of funky things, including Farrah Fawcett posters, festive Chilean Christmas lights and beaded curtains.

Mixing with these established names are more recent and more upmarket additions, a reflection of the changing demographics of the neighbourhood. On North Vermont Avenue, the recently arrived **vermont** restaurant (*see page 155*) serves contemporary American food, while at **Mexico City** you'll find decent Cal-Mex fare and Margaritas and occasionally the odd recognisable face. **X-Large** (*see page 183*) sells hip, generally quite spendy Gen-X clothes, and **Squaresville** (No.1800, 1-323 669 8464) has a good selection of second-hand clothes for men and women.

Bookworms should stop at **Skylight Books** (No.1818, 1-323 660 1175) for its wide selection and frequent literary readings. For vinyl record hounds, **Fat Beats** (*see page 180*) has a comprehensive selection of hip hop and rare groove. You'll find more new and used records and CDs – progressive house, trance, hard house, down tempo, rock, goth and industrial –

Sightseeing

at **Vinyl Fetish** (No.1750, 1-323 660 4500) with accessories at its adjacent sister shop **Sinister Store** (1-323 666 5100).

The area is also home to some of LA's more interesting drinking holes. You can bar-hop on foot from the smoke-filled sports bar **Ye Rustic Inn** (1831 Hillhurst Avenue, 1-323 662 5757) to the hipper **Good Luck Bar** (*see page 171*), with its Chinese opium den-style interior, and into the darkness at **Akbar** (4356 Sunset Boulevard, 1-323 665 6810). True swingers squeeze into **Tiki-Ti**, tiny home of Polynesian kitsch (*see page 171*).

For live music and dancing, head back to Vermont Avenue, for the fabulously upholstered, white leather **Dresden Room** (*see page 171*), as seen in *Swingers*, a classy joint featuring the lounge musical stylings of Marty and Elayne in the evening. A young swing-dancing crowd is centred on the **Derby** on Hillhurst Avenue (*see page 241*), with its large parquet dancefloor and circular bar, and the newly arrived **Los Feliz Jazz Club** (2138 Hillhurst Avenue, 1-323 666 8666), right opposite the Derby.

Silver Lake

Heading eastward – and a little further down the economic totem pole – Los Feliz gives way to the ethnically, culturally and sexually diverse Silver Lake, populated by an equally vital mix of artists and labourers (and home to folk rapper Beck), with a small pocket of wealthier individuals ensconced in homes overlooking the Silver Lake Reservoir, many of whom hobnob while their trophy pooches trot at the dog park adjacent to the reservoir. Some of LA's finest architects, including RM Schindler, Richard Neutra and John Lautner, built houses in this area in the 1920s and 1930s.

This bohemian segment of LA continues to experience an upswing in popularity – and prices. However, although an article in *Vanity Fair* dubbing Silver Lake 'the coolest neighbourhood in Los Angeles' is indicative of its recent gentrification, cheesy chainstores have yet to truly invade and independently owned shops and restaurants give it an undeniable flair. Most of the shops are found along the sun-baked stretch of Sunset Boulevard between Sanborn Avenue and Silver Lake Boulevard, but extend with lesser frequency west to Hillhurst Avenue. You can browse the punk selection at **Destroy All Music (**No.3818, 1-323 663 9300), and search for vintage clothes at **Rag Mopp Vintage** (No.3966, 1-323 666 0550). Local pirate radio station KBLT (104.7 FM) is temporarily off the air but may be back soon.

Griffith Park

Mining tycoon Griffith J Griffith donated 4,000 acres (1,600 hectares) to the city in 1896. Today, this land is the largest city-run park in the US (five times the size of New York's Central Park) and, despite recent fires and the flooding from El Niño that followed, is a paradise for hikers, picnickers, cyclists, families and tennis, golf, soccer and horse enthusiasts. The park's myriad attractions include the **Griffith Observatory** (pictured right), **Los Angeles Zoo**, the **Travel Town Museum**, Western memorabilia at the **Autry Museum** (see page 122), open-air concerts at the 1930 **Greek Theater** see page 231), Andy Gibb's burial slot at Forest Lawn Memorial Park and a 1926 merry-go-round (as seen in *Face/Off*). There are 53 miles (85 kilometres) of hiking trails – the 1,625 feet (495 metre) peak of Mount Hollywood is only a half-hour hike from the Observatory – and the Sierra Club (1-213 387 4287) organises regular guided hikes and moonlight rambles. The park is open sunrise to sunset daily; for more information, call 1-213 665 5188. For details of the four golf courses, 24 tennis courts and the Los Angeles Equestrian Center, *see chapter* **Sport & Fitness**.

Griffith, 'it would revolutionise the world.'
The formidable deco-modern building has
starred in many films, from the acclaimed
(*Rebel Without a Cause, Terminator 2* and
Wim Wenders's *The End of Violence*) to the
disdained (*Flesh Gordon*). It houses a triple-
beam solar telescope and a 12in (30.5cm)
Zeiss refracting telescope. When there are
eclipses or comets to be seen, local
astronomy clubs set up 'scopes on the lawn
and talk shop to anyone who will listen.
Don't miss the traditional Planetarium show,
and leave time for the Hall of Science and
a gander at the Foucault pendulum, the
cosmic ray cloud chamber, the seismograph
and the giant Tesla coil.

Los Angeles Zoo

*5333 Zoo Drive (1-323 666 4650/www.lazoo.
org). Bus 96/I-5, exit Zoo Drive west.* **Open**
10am-5pm daily; last entry 4pm. **Admission**
$8.25; $3.25-$5.25 concessions; free
under-2s. **Credit** AmEx, Disc, MC, V.
One of the park's biggest draws for families,
the LA Zoo continues to make improvements,
such as the new $6.5-million Red Ape
Rainforest, where orang-utans live in an
imitation Indonesian rainforest, complete
with tropical vegetation. Visitors can walk
through the rainforest and observe the apes
through glass. And when your visit to the
more than 1,200 reptiles, birds, mammals
and amphibians threatens to become too
much, cool down in the eucalyptus forest
environment inside the Ahmanson Koala
House. If you've got kids in tow, take them
to Adventure Island, specially designed for
small children, where they can meet and
touch animals with the Animal Encounters
programme.

Griffith Observatory

*2800 E Observatory Road (1-323 664 1181/
recorded information 1-323 664 1191/
Laserium 1-818 901 9405/www.griffithobs.
org). Bus Community Connection 203/
I-5, exit Los Feliz Boulevard west.* **Open**
Summer 12.30-10pm daily. *Winter* 2-10pm
Tue-Fri; 12.30-10pm Sat, Sun; closed Mon.
Admission *Telescope* free (cloudless nights
only). *Planetarium shows* $4; $2-$3
concessions. *Laserium shows* $9; $8
concessions; under-5s not admitted.
Credit AmEx, Disc, MC, V (Laserium only).
The outside deck of the Observatory, at the
southern edge of the park, provides the best
overview of the sprawl of LA; even when the
curdled haze of smog inhibits visibility, the
view stretches over Chavez Ravine into
East LA, down Western Avenue towards
Inglewood and across Sunset Boulevard
towards Santa Monica. On clear nights when
the city sparkles below, the beauty of LA's
psychogeography is mind-blowing.

The Observatory's bronze domes have
been part of the Hollywood Hills landscape
since 1934. 'If every person could look
through that telescope,' declared Griffith J

Travel Town Museum

*5200 Zoo Drive (1-323 662
5874/www.cityofla.org/RAP/grifmet/tt/
index.htm). Bus Commuter Express 549/
Hwy 134, exit Forest Lawn Drive.* **Open**
10am-4pm Mon-Fri; 10am-5pm Sat, Sun.
Admission free.
A fine outdoor museum, set up in the 1950s,
with restored railroad cars from the Union
Pacific, Atchison and Santa Fe lines, an early
20th-century milk delivery truck, more than a
dozen steam and diesel locomotives and a
nifty miniature train that gives visitors a ride
around the museum grounds.

The venerable **Dodger Stadium** in Echo Park: home of the LA Dodgers.

Casual dining venues include **Netty's** (1700 Silver Lake Boulevard, 1-323 662 8655), famed for its cornbread and blackened snapper, and the superb Mexican eaterie **Alegria** (3510 Sunset Boulevard, 1-323 913 1422). For a great breakfast and some 'service with a fuck you' (their phrase!), try **Millie's** (3524 Sunset Boulevard, 1-323 664 0404). **Café Tropical** (2900 Sunset Boulevard, 1-323 661 8391) is a more upmarket coffeehouse serving potent café con leche and guava empanadas. If you'd like to peruse your newspaper in peace, try the **Coffee Table** (*see page 164*) or pick up a take-out coffee and breakfast at **Say Cheese** or **Trader Joe's** (2800 and 2730 Hyperion Avenue) and head for the hills of Griffith Park.

At the annual **Sunset Junction Street Faire** in late August (*see page 206*), a mile of Sunset Boulevard is blocked off to traffic for three days, allowing celebrants to stroll the bazaar of craft stalls, ethnic food stands, live entertainment stages and beer trucks without incident.

Echo Park

Echo Park is the final funky link between Hollywood and the predominantly Latino East LA, although most LA residents only venture into the area to visit **Dodger Stadium** (*see page 252*), home of the Los Angeles Dodgers

baseball team. Defined as the area to the north of the Hollywood Freeway (US 101) and east of Alvarado Street, Echo Park was a 19th-century farming area that used Echo Park Lake for irrigation, and the area's winding hills retain a rustic feel. **Elysian Park** offers some fine views of Downtown and, like its bigger neighbour, Griffith Park, has trails and picnic and barbecue spots. **El Carmelo Bakery** (1800 West Sunset Boulevard, 1-213 484 9255) is a gem, an obscure Cuban restaurant with delicious soups, sandwiches and coffee. For a relaxing drink out of the heat or for fairly priced French fare, try **Taix** (1911 West Sunset Boulevard, 1-213 484 1265), a Hollywood institution since 1927.

Although surrounded by some particularly dicey blocks, the 1300 block of **Carroll Avenue** is worth visiting for its painstakingly restored Victorian mansions, colourful remnants of the area's brief 1880s incarnation as a popular suburb for the monied classes. **Echo Park** itself (just below the junction of Sunset and Glendale Boulevards), laid out in the 1890s by architect Joseph Henry Taylor to resemble an English garden, serves during the summer as a focal point for various festivals presented by the neighbourhood's Cuban, Filipino, Vietnamese and Samoan communities. At the lake you can take a paddle-boat ride through the blossoming lotuses.

East LA

Despite years of neglect and widespread poverty, El Este remains the spiritual centre of Latino Los Angeles.

It may not have a statue to mark it, but East LA is Los Angeles's own Ellis Island. Many non-Anglo immigrant groups arrived here first, starting with Jews in the early 20th century, followed by Asians, blacks, Italians and, of course, Mexicans, who have dominated the area since the 1960s. Now largely a staging post for immigrants who move to less dense suburbs when they can afford it, East LA (or El Este) remains very poor, with a reported average annual income per capita of $5,000 and 30 per cent of its households living below the poverty line. It is the site of some of the most noxious industries in LA, and suffers from virulent gang problems. And in the past its political clout was so negligible (these days Latinos have much more power) that it was torn asunder in the late 1960s by freeway construction: the intersection of the I-5, the I-10 and Highway 60 is a feat of engineering remarkable to behold, but it destroyed a neighbourhood and severed East LA from Downtown and the western part of the city.

However, East LA is also a lively and characterful area, distinguished from typically Anglo neighbourhoods by its vibrant street life and strong sense of Latino identity. Just as gays all over LA consider West Hollywood their capital, and Koreans see Koreatown as theirs, so East LA is ground zero for Latinos in the region. Not only do people hang out on the street, they almost live in their front yards – creating lavish fenced-in gardens with patio tables and chairs – a kind of outdoor living room. East LA is also literally very colourful, with bright murals decorating many of the buildings; some of LA's best murals, dating from the Chicano movement in the 1960s, are here – and on Broadway in Downtown, which many consider East LA's Main Street.

East LA encompasses the hilly district of Boyle Heights (part of the City of Los Angeles) and extends, unofficially, east from the Los Angeles River to just beyond Atlantic Boulevard, and from Olympic Boulevard north to the I-10. Officially, it starts even further east, at Indiana Avenue, but the true spiritual starting point is **Olvera Street**, to the west, at the corner of Cesar E Chavez Avenue and Alameda Street in Downtown. Pretty much all that remains from the days of Spanish, then Mexican rule, Olvera Street is now a touristy

stretch of mariachi singers and stalls selling Mexican trinkets (*see page 93*).

Much of the action in East LA takes place on **First Street**, **Whittier Boulevard** and **Cesar E Chavez Avenue**. The latter (formerly Brooklyn and renamed a few years ago after the United Farm Workers Union president) is actually a continuation of Sunset Boulevard and runs from north of Downtown through Boyle Heights into East LA. At the intersection of Cesar E Chavez and Soto Street, in Boyle Heights, you can see several murals by local artists on such subjects as the social, economic and political life of the Mexican people and East LA neighbourhood scenes. For tours of these and other Eastside murals, contact **SPARC** (Social & Public Art Resource Center) on 1-310 822 9560. At the same intersection is the **Paseo of Peace**, a landscaped memorial walkway honouring local veterans of the Vietnam war.

Chavez Avenue is home to immigrant Latino street vendors, selling bargain silver items, bootleg tapes and mangoes and papayas, and strolling musicians, who will play a romantic bolero or two on their well-worn guitars for a reasonable fee as you dine at **La Parilla** (*see page 156*). For fresh Mexican pastries, try **La Mascota Bakery** (2715 Whittier Boulevard, 1-323 263 5513).

Just east of Downtown, at First Street and Boyle Avenue, is the famous **Mariachi Plaza**, one of the largest congregations of freelance mariachi musicians outside Mexico City's Garibaldi Square. Sporting traditional black ranchero outfits, they assemble at the Olympic Donut Shop (1803 E First Street) and wait for passing drivers to hire them to play at social and family events. Also on First Street is the relatively expensive **La Serenata di Garibaldi** (*see page 156*), which specialises in Mexican haute cuisine, and, further east, **El Mercado** (No.3425), a multi-level marketplace reminiscent of those found in Mexican cities. Upstairs are restaurants with duelling mariachi bands, each seeking to lure clientele from the others, while downstairs teems with stalls selling all manner of goods.

On Chavez Avenue you'll also find one of East LA's best-known arts institutions, **Self-Help Graphics** (No.3802, 1-323 264 1259),

Traditional musician at **Mariachi Plaza**.

Chavez Avenue at Echandia Street), another legacy of the Jewish community. Another open space worth visiting is the **Evergreen Cemetery**, with its grand Beaux Arts gates and handsome Ivy Chapel, at First and Lorena Streets. Dating from 1877, it's one of the oldest cemeteries in LA.

South of Highway 60, in the southern end of East LA, is **Whittier Boulevard**, known as 'the Boulevard', the street some consider the unofficial 'capital' of East LA. This stretch of Whittier Boulevard, heading east towards Atlantic Boulevard, offers a wealth of clothes shops, restaurants, department stores, botanicas selling healing herbs and incense, bakeries, nightclubs, bars and other commercial establishments. On 29 August 1970, the Boulevard was the scene of a 'police riot' when a Chicano anti-war demonstration in a nearby park was attacked by police. Noted Chicano journalist Ruben Salazar was killed in the Silver Dollar Café on Whittier Boulevard by a police tear-gas pellet to the head. Salazar's death was thought by many to be retribution for his criticism of the sheriff's department's abusive behaviour towards people of colour. The park was renamed **Salazar Park** in his honour and is a symbol of the 1970s Chicano Movement.

Whittier Boulevard also used to be the main drag for fabulous displays of lowrider hot rod cars – until police put a stop to them. But East LA continues to be the LA capital of hot rod design and, if you're lucky, you'll see a spectacular example cruising the street. Look out for customised lowrider motorbikes, too: turning bikes into bejewelled fantasies fit only for display, not functional use, is as much a craze in Latino culture as customising cars. (If you want to find out more about goings-on in the hot rod world, pick up a copy of *Hot Rod Magazine* from newsstands.)

East LA life also spills over into its north-eastern neighbour, the city of **Monterey Park**. Try **Luminarias** (3500 Ramona Boulevard, 1-323 268 4363) for dinner and a night of salsa, merengue and more contemporary music. From their hilltop perch, both offer a splendid view of the San Gabriel Mountains to the north.

For other typically Mexican entertainments in East LA, the banda or norteño aficionado could try bar-restaurant **La Zona Rosa** (1010 East Cesar E Chavez Avenue, 1-323 223 5683). And for a feast of burritos and tacos, do as the Romans do and head east to **King Taco** (4504 East Third Street, 1-323 264 4067). Open 24 hours, it began as a solitary taco truck and is now a chain of restaurants (there's another branch on Chavez Avenue and Soto Street) and a cultural icon – as well as an early-morning stop for many an Eastsider on their way home after a hectic night of partying.

with its distinctive façade of multicoloured pottery encased in plaster walls. The gallery shows work by established and up-and-coming Latino artists and also runs community art workshops: it has launched the careers of several successful Latino artists. The annual **Dia de Los Muertos** (Day of the Dead) celebration at the gallery in autumn has become an East LA tradition, presenting the cream of the Latino counter-culture crowd of poets, performance artists and agit-prop theatre groups; it's a 'must be seen at' event for Latino and other local hipsters (*see page 207*).

For breakfast or lunch, head west on Chavez Avenue to Evergreen Avenue, to the always crowded **El Tepeyac Café** (812 N Evergreen Avenue, 1-323 268 1960) to try a 'Hollenbeck Special', an oversized burrito that could choke a horse. Or amble south to **Ciro's** (705 North Evergreen Avenue, 1-323 267 8637) for more traditional Mexican food.

East LA also boasts three very pleasant parks, the largest being **Lincoln Park**, at 3540 North Mission Road, north of the I-10. It contains statues of Mexican revolutionary heroes and the Plaza de la Raza, a popular arts centre in a converted boathouse by the lake, which offers arts classes to children after school and hosts evenings of music, dance and theatre. There is also **Hollenbeck Park** (at Fourth and Cummings Streets) built on the English model, and the heart-shaped **Prospect Park** (off

South Central

Welcome to the cultural heart of black LA and the home of one of the city's most enduring monuments.

South Central owes its black identity to the era of restrictive covenants – legal restrictions on who could reside in a property or neighbourhood – that were instituted in the early part of the 20th century and finally repealed in 1948. These heinous laws, which also put restrictions on Jews, Chinese and Mexicans and helped to shape LA into the relatively segregated place it still is, confined African-Americans to a tight area around Central Avenue. Though congested, Central Avenue enjoyed a cultural boom in the jazz age.

Following the lifting of restrictive covenants, blacks gradually moved west, making the Crenshaw District its cultural and commercial centre. In the past two decades, they have vacated South Central in growing numbers to head to the suburbs. Their homes have been taken over by Latino families, who've made their mark in the form of brightly painted *mercados* (shops), cheap Mexican restaurants and the numerous hole-in-the-wall evangelical churches that are wooing Latinos away from the Catholic Church.

While South Central is not necessarily dangerous – it's highly unlikely you'll get caught in the crossfire between the rival gangs that riddle the area – it is bleak. Many of the homes and gardens in the area are as pretty and sizeable as the single-family bungalows found throughout the Los Angeles region, but missing are shops, restaurants, public landscaping and parks. Unrelieved by hills or sea, South Central seems to consist of relentless flatlands of concrete and asphalt. But it has a rich history and some of its neighbourhoods are worth checking out.

Central Avenue

At the turn of the 20th century, the black community lived in what is now Little Tokyo in Downtown. Following World War I, Los Angeles's black population increased sharply as stories of the successes of local blacks circulated around the country. Thus began the steady migration of blacks west and south along the Central Avenue corridor, to which they were then restricted. Central Avenue's significance in the history of black Los Angeles cannot be underestimated. It was the West

Coast equivalent of Ellis Island to migrating blacks between the 1920s and the 1950s and home to some of the first financial enterprises, theatres, churches and social institutions established exclusively to serve blacks.

Built in 1928 by a wealthy professional couple, the **Dunbar Hotel** (4225 South Central Avenue) was the first hotel built by and for blacks. Along with several nightclubs in the area, including the now extinct Club Alabam, it brought to Central Avenue a worldwide reputation for its jazz scene, which is re-created every August with the free **Central Avenue Jazz Festival** (*see page 206*). To get a vivid picture of pre- and post-war Central Avenue, read Walter Mosley's Easy Rawlins detective mysteries. Modern-day Central Avenue is far less alluring – many of its buildings are vacant and in disrepair – but the Dunbar, now operated by the Dunbar Economic Development Corporation as low-income residential units, continues to be a centre of jazz culture.

Watts

After the jazz era, blacks continued their migration south along Central Avenue towards Watts, known primarily for the **Watts Towers** (*see page 104*) – designed, in fact, by an Italian but adopted as a symbol of black pride – and the rioting in 1965 and 1992. The towers are currently under restoration but are scheduled to reopen in spring 2001. The adjacent community art centre hosts exhibitions of Third World and African-American art, workshops and a couple of festivals a year, including the **Day of the Drum/Simon Rodia Watts Towers Jazz Festival** in September (*see page 206*).

Though many parts of the area are still neglected, Watts is cautiously re-emerging as a centre for black community pride, embodied by the **Watts Labor Community Action Committee** (10950 South Central Avenue, 1-323 563 5600), about a mile from the towers. A victim of both the 1965 and 1992 riots, it has now been completely rebuilt. A one-stop social and cultural centre that features live theatre, blues and jazz, the WLCAC also showcases work by local inner-city artists and houses *Countdown to Eternity*, an exhibit on the 1960s Civil Rights movement and the final days of

The Watts Towers

The Watts Towers have been called a monument to humanity, and a testament to a single man's will. They were constructed over three decades (1921-1954) by Simon Rodia, an Italian-born tilesetter who employed nothing more than the tools of his trade in their fabrication. Using salvaged steel rods and cast-off pipe structures, bed frames and cement, Rodia incorporated glass, mirrors, rocks, ceramic tiles, pottery and marble shards into his folk-art masterpieces. He scaled the 92ft (28m) towers on a window-washer's belt and bucket, and decorated them with over 25,000 seashells.

A patchwork of found materials, Rodia's confabulation is also a reliquary of early and mid 20th-century consumer objects. The glass is predominantly green and comes from bottles of 7-Up or Milk of Magnesia. Many of the tiles probably came from Malibu Potteries, where Rodia was employed in the late 1920s. Pieces of costume jewellery have also found their way into the coarse, gaudy 'skin' of the complex. Surrounding the ensemble of four towers is a more stolid but no less colourful wall whose topside undulates in rhythm with the arcs climbing the towers' sides.

The towers' construction under the hands of an individual working without any assistance (save the casual aid of passers-by and local children), are part of their legend. But so is their sheer beauty. Like skeletal echoes of Antoni Gaudi's voluptuous Barcelona church steeples, the towers reach for the sky in an elaborate network of spindly, curved tendrils, connected with equally playful, decorous webs.

They occupy an odd triangular lot (with a neighbouring arts centre) in the middle of low-income Watts. When Rodia moved there

the neighbourhood was ethnically mixed; by time he left, it was predominantly black and Latino, and had come to be regarded as the heart of LA's African-American community. That association was driven home in 1965 when Watts erupted in riots. By then, the towers had become a source of local pride and they went untouched in the uprising. (Coincidentally, Rodia had died only weeks before.)

Durable as the towers may be, their surfaces, composed of mosaic-like inlay in cement, gradually deteriorated over the years. The inlaid material that provides the riot of colour and texture for which the towers are famed came loose in places. But the lengthy repair job, which kept the structures enmeshed for over a decade, is complete, as is the shoring-up necessitated by damage wrought by the 1994 quake. Weekend self-guided public tours recommence in May 2001.

The Watts Towers may not be the town's most exciting ride, flashiest tourist attraction or star-studded watering hole. They sit in the middle of nowhere (a very safe nowhere, certainly during the day), viewable from no freeway (although the Blue Line tram has a stop a block

away). But they are as fantastical a spectacle as anything Los Angeles has to offer. They're pure magic.

Watts Towers & Arts Center

1727 & 1765 E 107th Street, between Alameda Street & Central Avenue, Watts (arts centre 1-213 847 4646). Metro 103rd Street/bus 56, 251/I-10, exit Century Boulevard north. **Open** *Arts centre 10am-4pm Tue-Sat; noon-4pm Sun; closed Mon. Towers call to check.* **Admission** *free.*

Martin Luther King, plus interactive installations on the history of the movement. The centre's public art piece, *The Mother of Humanity*, is the largest bronze sculpture of a black woman in the world, and the building's main façade is the setting for *Mudtown Flats*, a mural depicting historic sites on Central Avenue. The centre also runs historical and cultural bus tours of Watts, taking in about 18 sights including the Watts Towers; price is $12.50 per person and it's run on a by appointment basis (book on 1-323 563 5639). You can also park your car at the centre, and take a shuttle bus to the Towers.

The Crenshaw District

The Crenshaw District is the area surrounding Crenshaw Boulevard south of the I-10 as far as Florence Avenue. It was the site of the 1932 Olympic Village (now Village Green Apartments on Rodeo Road, near La Brea Avenue) and of the first airport in Los Angeles. Though it's now one of the few predominantly black communities in LA County, the influence of earlier Japanese residents who moved there and established themselves as landscape gardeners after returning from World War II internment camps is still visible, notably in residential landscaping.

The Hills – Baldwin Hills, Windsor Hills, View Park and Ladera Heights – which lie west of Crenshaw Boulevard around Slauson Avenue, are home to some of LA's most prominent upper middle-class and professional blacks. At the base of these well-manicured hills is an area known as the Jungle. The name originally derived from its lush tropical plantings, but the Jungle is better known these days as a haven for drug dealing and other illicit activities, so exercise caution.

In the 1940s, the first shopping plaza in the US was built at the intersection of 'King' and Crenshaw Boulevards (the former is properly called Martin Luther King Jr Boulevard). Now transformed into the **Baldwin Hills Crenshaw Plaza**, it is the perfect place to park and see what's going on in this community. While there, visit the **Magic Johnson Theaters** (*see page 216*). Owned by basketball great Irvin 'Magic' Johnson, these cinemas have the friendliest staff in LA and show first-run films. And going to movies there is an experience: the audience doesn't simply watch the picture, it joins in with the action, loudly rooting for, shouting advice to and yelling at the actors.

For memorable soul food, leave your car in the plaza parking lot and walk half a block east on King to **M&M's Soul Food** (9506 Avalon

Boulevard, 1-323 777 9250), required eating for locals, and get in line. Another good place to eat is **Golden Bird Fried Chicken** (1-323 735 5686) inside the floundering Santa Barbara Plaza, a dilapidated mall that is about to be turned into a large CityWalk-style entertainment retail centre by Magic Johnson's company, Magic Johnson Enterprises.

Don't, incidentally, expect the same stellar service as at the Magic Theaters: some of these restaurants are well known for their rude, temperamental staff and less-than-attractive decor. And leave your diet behind: the food may be salty and loaded with fat and calories, but it's worth every artery-clogging bite. Also worth visiting is the **Museum of African American Art** (on the third floor of the Robinsons-May store in the plaza – 1-323 294 7071).

For a rousing black religious experience, visit the **West Angeles Church of God** on Crenshaw Boulevard (*see page 16* **Let's get spiritual**). Presided over by bishop Charles Blake, it is one of the most popular black Pentecostal churches, with 16,000 members – including celebrities such as Denzel Washington and Magic Johnson. With the help of fat donations from these two ($5 million from Johnson, $2.5 million from Washington), Blake is now building a new cathedral. The West Angeles Church is more than just a church, it is a major economic generator in the area. Not

The ever-popular **West Angeles Church of God.**

Sightseeing

only does it have a school, an arts centre and a bookstore, but it also invests in housing and economic development. Together, the church and Magic Johnson's company are kick-starting the revitalisation of the Crenshaw District.

On the far west side of Crenshaw, sprawling between La Cienega Boulevard and La Brea Avenue, north of Stocker Street, is an unsung public amenity, the **Kenneth Hahn State Recreation Area**. Named after a former and much-beloved councillor, this park is a delight. It's huge, with a pond that you can fish in, ducks, swans, a Japanese bridge over a gurgling waterfall, undulating hills, volleyball and basketball courts and fab views (from an unusual vantage point) of Los Angeles.

Once a year for the last two weekends in August and concluding on Labor Day, the Crenshaw District lights up with the **African Marketplace**, a celebration of diverse African cultures with a feast of foods, crafts and non-stop entertainment (for details, *see page 206*).

Leimert Park

Leimert (pronounced 'Luh-murt') Park, anchored by the park itself and 43rd Street, is LA's most talked-about black neighbourhood. In recent years, it has become what Central Avenue was in its heyday. The neighbourhood is experiencing a cultural revolution, with art galleries, jazz clubs, speciality shops, poetry readings and restaurants replacing the pawn shops and beauty salons that once lined the streets.

On most weekends you will find street fairs in the Leimert Park village and there is usually live music every weekday. Don't miss the annual **Leimert Park Jazz Festival** if you're visiting in September (*see page 206*).

For terrific live entertainment, **Fifth Street Dick's Coffee Company** (*see page 236*) is famous for its jazz and the chess games that take place on tables outside; **Babe & Ricky's Inn** (*see page 234*), relocated from Central Avenue, for the blues; and the **World Stage** (*see page 237*) for a mix of live jazz every night of the week except Wednesday, when it hosts a cutting-edge poetry workshop. Along Degnan Boulevard, the neighbourhood's main drag, there are also several Afrocentric art galleries and the charming **Lucy Florence Coffeehouse** (No.4305, 1-323 293 2395).

Off Degnan Boulevard, at 4307 Leimert Boulevard, you'll find the famous **Phillip's Barbecue** (1-323 292 7613): prepare to queue for a take-out order of some of the best ribs in town. Alternatively, **Earle's Wieners** (4326 Crenshaw Boulevard, 1-323 299 2867) has an assortment of hot dogs, links (sausages) and vegetarian finger foods, or try **Coley's Kitchen** (No.4335, 1-323 290 4010) for Caribbean fare.

Inglewood

Although outside the Los Angeles city limits, Inglewood is often considered part of South Central. It's best known for being the home of the Great Western Forum, where the Los Angeles Lakers basketball team and Los Angeles Kings hockey teams played before they changed locations to the new state-of-the-art Staples Center in Downtown. Just south of the Forum is the **Hollywood Park Race Track & Casino** (*see page 253*), which features horse racing and an impressive array of live music each weekend for a reasonable price.

Jazz and poetry at **World Stage**.

The Valleys

Amid the TV studios and suburban sprawl are some of LA's most popular attractions and prettiest towns.

San Fernando Valley

The San Fernando Valley is perhaps most famous for its girls. The gum-popping, air-headed Valley Girl – immortalised by Frank and Moon Unit Zappa's song 'Valley Girl' and the movie of the same name – is a quintessential 1980s phenomenon. Then there are the porn stars. While the *Brady Bunch* was being filmed in a perfect, split-level 1970s ranchhouse, in other San Fernando backyards, girls in curls and guys in tight polyester trousers were doing a lot more than playing ball. Paul Thomas Anderson, the Valley's latest self-appointed scribe, famously exposed suburbia's sordid past (and present) in *Boogie Nights*, his look at the 1970s porn industry. As archetypal suburb, the Valley has also been the target of hilarious barbs from Sandra Tsing Loh – author of *Depth Takes a Holiday* – who both celebrates its increasingly multi-ethnic culture and trashes it for suburban monotony.

The earlier history of the San Fernando Valley, fictionalised in the movie *Chinatown*, is a colourful tale of betrayal and greed. At the start of the 20th century, LA's land barons hoodwinked voters into approving bonds for an aqueduct and then diverted the water away from the city to the San Fernando Valley so they could cash in on the increased land values.

Today, Valley and city are once again arguing over distribution of those contentious water rights. The Valley is still part of the City of Los Angeles, but secessionists have recently led a move to break away and create a separate city. A vote is planned for 2002. If the Valley does become independent, it would be the sixth largest city in America, with a population of approximately 1.5 million. The contracted Los Angeles, with a population of about 2.5 million, would be only the third largest, behind Chicago. Its demography would change dramatically: fewer whites, more Latinos and Asians. *See also page 13* **Independence day**.

The massive 1994 Northridge earthquake had its epicentre in the Valley; federal relief money inspired a great deal of construction, so there are plenty of shiny new shopping centres and renovated houses. The Valley is also home to California State University, Northridge, and is a business centre, linked to Los Angeles by three freeways – US 101 (Hollywood Freeway), the I-405 (San Diego Freeway) and I-5 (Golden State Freeway) – and numerous winding canyon roads. The long-awaited Metrolink commuter rail system also serves the Valley; call 1-800 371 5465 for information.

As in other parts of LA, new life is being injected into once-decaying urban areas of the Valley, and it is developing pleasant walking districts, especially along Ventura Boulevard near Van Nuys Boulevard in **Sherman Oaks** and further east on Ventura Boulevard in **Studio City**. **Glendale** and **Burbank**, which are separate cities, also feature pedestrian-friendly downtown areas that have been revived in recent years. Glendale is also home to the **Forest Lawn Memorial Park** (1712 South Glendale Avenue, 1-800 204 3131), the final resting place of a stack of celebrities including Walt Disney, Errol Flynn, Spencer Tracy, Humphrey Bogart, Nat 'King' Cole, Clark Gable and Carole Lombard. Unfortunately, the place is huge and staff will not disclose grave locations, so those in the mood for morbid sightseeing are on their own.

Unexpected modernist gems dot the Valley, including two Googie-style buildings: the **First Lutheran Church of Northridge** (18355 Roscoe Boulevard, Northridge, 1-818 885 6861), sometimes called the 'First Church of Elroy Jetson', and **Bob's Big Boy** diner in Burbank (4211 Riverside Drive, 1-818 843 9334), where muscle-car aficionados gather on Friday nights to show off their El Camino motors in true LA fashion. There are also homes by Richard Neutra and Frank Lloyd Wright; call the LA Conservancy on 1-213 623 2489 for more information.

The Valley is also the gateway to the **Santa Monica Mountains**, one of the country's most beautiful and environmentally fragile urban mountain ranges. Separating the Valley from the city basin and the ocean, the Santa Monicas are covered with hiking and biking trails, and contain many ranches that once belonged to movie stars and studios. The **Paramount Ranch** (2813 Cornell Road, off Kanan Road, Agoura), has stood in for Tombstone and Dodge City, and was used for the now-defunct TV series *Dr Quinn, Medicine Woman*. For more information on the area, contact the Santa

Make a splash at
Universal Studios

Monica Mountains National Recreation Area, 401 West Hillcrest Drive, Thousand Oaks, CA 91360 (1-805 370 2300).

Six Flags Magic Mountain Parkway (*see below*), a theme park and thrill-seeker's paradise, is in Santa Clarita at the north end of the Valley. For a glimpse of history along the way, make the easy detour to one of the earliest Californian missions, **Mission San Fernando Rey de Espa** in Mission Hills, founded in 1797 and rebuilt after the 1971 Sylmar earthquake.

Many of the sound stages where TV shows and movies are actually filmed can be found in the Valley – especially in Burbank and at Universal City, both located off US 101 at the Valley's east end. Dapper studio execs and the occasional TV personality from Warner Brothers, NBC and Walt Disney Studios eat in the restaurants around Burbank's 'Media District', along Riverside Drive. The Disney complex is hard to miss: the Animation Building, designed by post-modernist architect Robert Stern, has a two-storey wizard's hat like the one worn by Mickey in the Sorcerer's Apprentice sequence in *Fantasia* and the word 'animation' spelt out in 14-foot (4.3-metre) high capital letters. Studio tours are available at **Warner Brothers**, and most TV shows offer free tickets to their tapings (for details on both, *see chapter* **Film**).

From Burbank, it's just a short drive on Barham Boulevard into Cahuenga Pass, home of the **Universal Studios & CityWalk** complex (*see below*). The Universal Studios tour, a jolly tram trip across the back lot, still exists, but is now surrounded by a theme park to rival Disneyland.

Burbank and Universal are also close to the northern edge of **Griffith Park**, home to Los Angeles Zoo, the Griffith Park Observatory and sundry other attractions (*see page 98*).

San Fernando Valley Conference & Visitors Bureau

15205 Burbank Boulevard, 2nd floor, Van Nuys, CA 91411 (1-818 782 7282/www.valleyofthestars.org). **Open** 8.30am-4.30pm Mon-Fri; closed Sat, Sun. You can't visit the office, but they will send out information – and the website is very impressive.

Six Flags California

Magic Mountain Parkway, off the I-5, Valencia (1-818 367 5965/www.sixflags.com). I-5, exit Magic Mountain Parkway. **Open** *Magic Mountain Summer* from 10am daily. *Winter* from 10am Fri-Sun; closed Mon-Thur. Call for closing times. *Hurricane Harbor Summer* from 10am daily; call for closing times. *Winter* closed. **Admission** *Magic Mountain* $40.99; $20.50 concessions (incl children under 48in/122cm); free under-2s. *Hurricane Harbor* $19.99; $12.99 concessions (incl children under 48in/122cm); free under-2s. *Combined ticket* $50.99. **Credit** AmEx, Disc, MC, V.

Six Flags California comprises Six Flags Magic Mountain and its newer watery cousin, Six Flags Hurricane Harbor. There are rollercoasters and water rides for every level of screamer. Perhaps the most famous is the Colossus, the largest wooden-framed rollercoaster ever built. Those whose idea of fun is to feel their internal organs shifting around should not miss the Viper, the world's tallest loop-the-loop rollercoaster. The Suspended Ninja sends passengers whizzing over the treetops, and the technological wizardry of Superman, the Escape catapults you straight up a 41-storey tower at 100mph (160kmph) – in seven seconds – then you freefall down at the same speed. Two new rides, the Riddler's Revenge and Goliath, also rack up the scare points with rollercoaster lovers. Set scenically on the hip of the San Fernando Mountains, this is fun with a screamingly huge capital 'F'.

Universal Studios & CityWalk

100 Universal City Plaza, Universal City (1-818 508 9600/www.universalstudios.com). Metro Universal City/bus 420/US 101, exit Universal Center Drive.

Open *Summer* 8am-10pm daily; last tram tour 5.15pm. *Winter* 9am-6pm or 7pm daily; last tram tour 4.15pm. **Admission** $41; $31-$36 concessions; under-3s free. **Credit** AmEx, DC, Disc, MC, V.
Angelenos usually send their visitors off to Universal for at least one day of good, cheesy Hollywood fun. Make time for the low-key but enjoyable tram ride, which takes you through the back lot of the working studio, where you will see the likes of King Kong moving rather arthritically, the shark from *Jaws* leaping out of the water and snapping its mechanical mouth at you, the parting of the Red Sea, the 'Big One' earthquake simulation (nothing like the real thing) and the *Psycho* house. The real highlights of the ride, however, are the glimpses of studio life: casts and crews rushing about, fake New York streets and Western towns, dilapidated old props stashed here and there. You can also come face to face with dinosaurs on the 'Jurassic Park' water ride (wear waterproof clothing), take a trip on the flight simulator in 'Back to the Future' and recoil at the 3D effects in 'Terminator 2: 3D'.

Allow a full day and start early to make the most of the complex, which also houses Universal Amphitheater – one of LA's larger concert venues – an 18-screen cinema and CityWalk, an LA-themed shopping and eating 'street', which has recently expanded to include more upmarket shops and restaurants, a bowling alley and virtual Nascar racing. CityWalk has been ridiculed for its fake, collaged architecture – but then, what could be more appropriate for Tinseltown?

San Gabriel Valley

Like the San Fernando Valley, the San Gabriel Valley, east and north-east of downtown Los Angeles, hides a collection of charming small towns. Though crowded with suburban development and often choking with traffic and smog, the Valley is set picturesquely against the striking San Gabriel Mountains to the north. It is now perhaps LA's most diverse area, with Asian and Latino communities scattered throughout. Unlike the San Fernando Valley, the San Gabriel Valley is not part of the City of Los Angeles, but is divided into many small suburban communities. You can reach it from LA via a series of east–west freeways, including the I-210 (Foothill Freeway), I-10 (San Bernardino Freeway) and US 60 (Pomona Freeway), as well as the north–south I-110 (Pasadena Freeway).

If this Valley has an image in America's popular imagination, it's as the 'white trash heaven' of the 1950s and '60s, described vividly by crime writer James Ellroy in his book *My Dark Places* – a search for the killer of his mother, who was murdered in the San Gabriel Valley town of El Monte. This town still has its dark side: a few years ago, it hit the headlines

after Thai sweatshop workers were discovered living in virtual slavery. But the San Gabriel Valley towns that pre-date the 1950s are charming and pleasant: Pasadena, San Marino and La Verne contain some of LA's most beautiful neighbourhoods.

Pasadena, first settled by wealthy retired farmers from the Midwest, remains one of the most attractive towns in the area and one of the few parts of Southern California where having 'old money' still means something. **Old Town Pasadena** (centred on Colorado Boulevard and bounded by Arroyo Parkway, De Lacey Avenue and Holly and Green Streets) is a 1920s retail district turned shopping and entertainment centre. Its revival has been astonishing: as late as the mid 1980s, it was a run-down collection of boarded-up commercial buildings. Today, packs of teenagers mingle with local families and older couples, thronging the pavements after midnight. Demand for retail space has become so great that even alleys have been opened up, redesigned and decorated with public art. Although there are more chain restaurants and well-known brands than offbeat boutiques, Colorado Boulevard is nonetheless a pleasant place to have dinner and a stroll.

Pasadena has a clutch of museums, including the **Norton Simon Museum**, the **Pacific Asia Museum** (for both, *see chapter* **Museums**) and **Kidspace** for children (*see page 210*). It is also home to the **California Institute of Technology** (CalTech, 1-626 395 6327) and the **Jet Propulsion Laboratory** (1-818 354 9314), one of the nerve centres of the US space programme. Tours can be arranged at both, but must be booked in advance.

Other sights include the **Gamble House**, designed by Charles and Henry Greene in 1908. The leading example of Southern California's indigenous 'Craftsman' bungalow, influenced – in typical Californian fashion – by both Japanese and Swiss architecture, it is open to the public; for details, *see page 31*. The Greenes also built many other houses in adjacent streets, notably Arroyo Terrace and Grand Avenue.

The **Rose Bowl** stadium in Brookside Park is the home of college football and the LA Galaxy, LA's soccer team, and each New Year's Day the **Rose Parade** (*see page 207*) travels through Pasadena with lavishly decorated floats. If you're a flower lover and in town in the last couple of weeks in December, you can volunteer to help with last-minute decorating.

North-west of Pasadena is the picturesque hillside community of **La Cañada Flintridge**, home of the beautiful and peaceful **Descanso Gardens** (*see page 110*). And just south of the town is the expensive suburb of **San Marino**, developed by land and railroad baron Henry

The 1908 **Gamble House**. *See p109.*

Huntington at the start of the 20th century. His former estate (*see below*) now houses a world-class collection of books and manuscripts and has some beautiful gardens. Near to San Marino, Pasadena's Lake Street district and the Fair Oaks area of South Pasadena are pleasant walking and shopping areas.

To the east of Pasadena is the lovely town of **Arcadia**, home of **Santa Anita Park**, one of LA's best-known race tracks (*see page 254*). Though dwarfed by a surrounding sea of suburbia, many older foothill communities along the Foothill Freeway, including **Sierra Madre** and **Monrovia**, have charming early 20th-century downtown areas. Both are north of the I-210; Sierra Madre is reached by the Santa Anita exit, Monrovia by the Mountain exit. They lie in the shadow of the San Gabriel Mountains, one of the most geologically unstable mountain ranges in the world.

Further south in the Valley is one of the largest Chinese settlements in the US, larger even than San Francisco's famed Chinatown. The bustling suburbs of **Monterey Park**, **Alhambra** and **San Gabriel** have largely Chinese or Chinese-American populations – many of them immigrants from Taiwan and Hong Kong – though there is also a significant Latino minority. The commercial strips of Atlantic Boulevard and Garfield Avenue contain Chinese restaurants of every sort, as well as Chinese groceries, bakeries and herb shops. For a crash course in Chinese food, visit the Universal Shopping Plaza, a garishly pink behemoth of a mall on Del Mar Avenue and Valley Boulevard.

The San Gabriel Valley is also home to several universities, including **California State University** (off the I-10 in East LA), **California State Polytechnic University** Pomona – a beautifully landscaped campus f the Kellogg Drive exit of the I-10 – and the **Claremont Colleges**, a collection of six distinguished colleges near East Foothill Boulevard in Claremont. The town of

Claremont and the campus offer shady streets and an academic vibe reminiscent of East Coast Ivy League schools. Claremont's 'Village' (east of Indian Hill Boulevard, between First and Fourth Streets) is another delightful downtown area, featuring buildings from the 1920s, many restaurants and a train station – you can get there from Downtown LA via Metrolink.

The eastern San Gabriel Valley is the site of the **LA County Fair**, an annual two-week event held in autumn at the Fairplex in Pomona (*see page 207*). LA County remains an important agricultural centre, so you'll get to see the same giant vegetables and prize-winning pigs as you would in the Midwest.

Descanso Gardens

1418 Descanso Drive, La Cañada Flintridge (1-818 952 4400/www.descanso.com). Hwy 2, exit Verdugo Boulevard. **Open** 9am-5pm daily. **Admission** $5; $1-$3 concessions; free under-5s. **No credit cards.**
Descanso Gardens is a delightful tribute to the horticultural magic of SoCal. It includes more than 600 varieties of camellia (best between mid February and early May), and five acres of roses. There are also lilac, orchid, fern and California native plant areas, as well as an Oriental tea house donated by the Japanese-American community.

The Huntington Library, Art Collections & Botanical Gardens

1151 Oxford Road, off Huntington Drive, San Marino (recorded information 1-626 405 2141/ www.huntington.org). Bus 79/I-110, exit Arroyo Parkway north. **Open** June-Aug 10.30am-4.30pm Tue-Sun; Sept-May noon-4.30pm Tue-Fri; 10.30am-4.30pm Sat, Sun. Closed Mon. **Admission** $8.50; $6-$8 concessions; free under-12s. Free 1st Thur of month. **Credit** MC, V.
Founded in 1919 by Henry E Huntington, his institution reflects the passions of this savvy businessman: books, art and gardens. The library holds six million items: the star attractions are a Gutenberg Bible, several early Shakespeares and the earliest known edition of Chaucer's *Canterbury Tales*, with an impressive supporting cast of rare books and manuscripts on British and American history and literature. The museum has one of the most comprehensive collections of British and French art from the 18th and 19th centuries, while the vast gardens contain more than 14,000 different plant varieties, including fantastic cacti in the 12-acre (5ha) Desert Garden. It's an enchanting place to spend an afternoon, topped off with cakes and sandwiches served in the Rose Garden Tea Rooms ($13.80; reservations essential). There's a second entrance to the estate at the corner of Orlando Road and Allen Avenue.

Pasadena Convention & Visitors Bureau

171 S Los Robles Avenue, Pasadena, CA 91101 (1-626 795 9311/www.pasadenavisitor.org). **Open** 8am-5pm Mon-Fri; 10am-4pm Sat; closed Sun.

Heading South

Here you can explore some of Southern California's most beautiful beaches, and the man-made delights of Disneyland.

The South Bay & Long Beach

The South Bay

El Segundo, Manhattan Beach, Hermosa Beach & Redondo Beach

Getting to the South Bay is half the fun. The road Vista del Mar, which runs right along the beach, starts about a mile (1.5 kilometres) south of Marina del Rey, off Culver Avenue at Dockweiler State Beach, and it's the most picturesque gateway to the area. Zip past LAX airport and you're in the district of **El Segundo**. The best non-aquatic attraction here is an old-fashioned cinema: the **Old Town Music Hall** (140 Richmond Street), open weekends only, features pre-1960s classics, a pipe organ and singalongs.

But for a true flavour of the South Bay, continue south on Vista del Mar (which becomes Highland Avenue) until you reach Manhattan Beach Boulevard and then make a right towards the ocean. On sunny weekends, the **Manhattan Beach** strand and pier are mobbed with skaters, cyclists and sun-worshippers. Cleaner than Venice, the strands in Manhattan and neighbouring Hermosa Beach offer some of the same people-watching pleasures (though with a less ethnically diverse crowd). Good casual dining is available nearby at the **Kettle** (at the corner of Highland Avenue and Manhattan Beach Boulevard, 1-310 545 8511), easily one of the best 24-hour restaurants in the LA area, and a French/Italian/Japanese mix at **Michi** (1-310 376 0613). The surfside flavour continues southward into **Hermosa** and **Redondo Beaches**. Visitors might even catch a pro beach volleyball championship, surf festival or rollerblading exhibition.

Those who prefer shade to sun can check out the **Lighthouse Café** (30 Pier Avenue, off the coastal Hermosa Avenue, 1-310 372 6911), a watering hole since the 1950s where beach volleyball players and scenesters hang and listen to live music; the **Comedy & Magic Club** (*see page 243*) where the likes of Jay Leno

are said to try out new material; **Java Man Coffee** (157 Pier Avenue, 1-310 379 7209), a trendy place to sip a latte; **Spot** (110 Second Street, 1-310 376 2355), a well-known vegetarian restaurant that, rumour has it, is a favourite of Paul McCartney; and **Ragin' Cajun**, an authentic Louisiana-style café (422 Pier Avenue, 1-310 376 7878).

Continuing south, Redondo Beach's **King Harbor** (at the end of Portofino Way), with shops, restaurants, fish markets and marina, is one of the area's most developed piers. Purists might find it a bit naff, but Redondo is the most family-oriented of these beaches. In the nearby inland city of Torrance, there's a phenomenal neighbourhood restaurant, **Gina Lee's Bistro** (211 Palos Verdes Boulevard, 1-310 375 4462) and the excellent **Coffee Cartel** café (1820 South Catalina Avenue, 1-310 316 6554).

Palos Verdes & San Pedro

One of the best ocean drives in SoCal is the loop around scenic Palos Verdes Peninsula. Take the Pacific Coast Highway (Highway 1, aka PCH) south to Palos Verdes Boulevard (at Redondo State Beach, a mile or so south of the eponymous city), go south again to Palos Verdes Drive West and then Palos Verdes Drive South. On the way, stop at the lovely glass and stone **Wayfarer's Chapel** (5755 Palos Verdes Drive South), the most visited building by architect Lloyd Wright (Frank's son), and the **South Coast Botanic Gardens** (26300 Crenshaw Boulevard, 1-310 544 6815), 87 acres (35 hectares) of botanical beauty.

Ironically, ritzy Palos Verdes shares the peninsula with one of LA's most colourful working-class communities, **San Pedro**. The traditional home of fishermen, dockworkers, Navy staff and Mediterranean immigrants, San Pedro – also home of the massive Port of Los Angeles – often used to seem more Boston than Burbank. Gentrification and cuts in defence spending have changed much of that, but a walk along quaint Sixth Street and a Greek meal at **Papadakis Taverna** (301 West Sixth Street, 1-310 548 1186), a Croatian one at **Ante's** (729 South Palos Verdes Street, 1-310 832 5375), or a classic film at the

Warner Grand Theatre (478 West Sixth Street, 1-310 548-7672), a restored 1931 movie palace, can make the years vanish.

There's a spectacular view of the ocean from nearby **Angels Gate Park** (3601 South Gaffey Street), home to the giant Korean Friendship Bell, a bicentennial gift to the US from South Korea. Below this bluff, **Point Fermin Park**, with its 1874 wooden lighthouse, is a great picnic spot. For families, the **Cabrillo Marine Aquarium** (3720 Stephen White Drive, 1-310 548 7562), housed in a Frank Gehry-designed building, and the **Los Angeles Maritime Museum** (Berth 84, at the end of Sixth Street, 1-310 548 7618) are both fun to explore.

The pier at **Manhattan Beach**. *See p111.*

Long Beach

Long Beach is easy to reach by public transport: it takes about an hour from Downtown LA on the Metro Blue Line. The city has been given short shrift by its more well-heeled neighbours to the north and south; the Long Beach of popular imagination is one of dockworkers, swing shifts and drunken sailors on leave. But since the factories closed and Navy work dwindled in the 1980s, it has changed almost out of recognition. The city's latest attempt to shake off its gritty past is the **Long Beach Aquarium of the Pacific** (*see page 113*), opened to fanfare in the summer of 1998; with 10,000 creatures representing 550 Pacific Ocean species, it ranks as one of the US's largest and most spectacular aquariums.

The Aquarium is the first fruit of redevelopment for the area known as Queensway Bay; some restaurants and a park have already opened nearby, a larger retail complex will be built soon. (Note: the circular building with whales painted on its exterior is not the aquarium but the Long Beach Arena, where the local minor league ice hockey team, the feisty Ice Dogs, play. The building was given its aquatic theme in 1992 by famed Southern California muralist Wyland.) But there's more to the LBC – as local rappers call Long Beach – than a fish tank. An anchor's toss from the Aquarium is the **Queen Mary** (*see page 113*), one of the largest passenger ships ever built, now a hotel and restaurants.

Downtown Long Beach has sprouted some cool restaurants in recent years, such as the beautifully designed **La Traviata** (at the corner of Cedar Avenue and Third Street, 1-562 432 8022), the nouveau-Brazilian **Cha Cha Cha** (762 Pacific Avenue, 1-562 436 3900) and a string of haunts along or near once-blighted Pine Avenue. Try bar and grill **M** (No. 213A, 1-562 435 2525), cigar lounge and dance club **Cohiba** (entrance through Mum's restaurant at

144 Pine Avenue, 1-562 491 5220) and rock club **Blue Café** (210 The Promenade North, 1-562 983 7111). Every April, the streets of downtown come alive with the sound of revving engines, when the **Long Beach Grand Prix** takes over for three days (*see page 204*).

Lesser-known things to do: catch a performance by the extremely avant-garde **Long Beach Opera** (Carpenter Performing Arts Center, 6200 Atherton Street, 1-562 439 2580), arguably the most eccentric opera company in the US; visit the small but ambitious **Long Beach Museum of Art** (2300 East Ocean Boulevard, 1-562 439 2119), which shows mainly contemporary Californian artists and is located in a recently renovated seaside house built in 1912; or try the **Museum of Latin American Art** (628 Alamitos Avenue, 1-562 437 1689).

Also worth exploring are eclectic Broadway, between Alamitos and Ximeno Avenues, with such remarkable restaurants as the 1920s bordello-themed **House of Madam Jo Jo's** (2941 East Broadway, 1-562 439 3672); Fourth Street (near Cherry Avenue), a funky strip of thrift stores; Belmont Shore (Second Street, from Park to Bayshore Avenues) where Cal State students shop and bar-hop. Check out the excellent second-hand record shop **Fingerprints** (4612 Second Street, 1-562 433 4996), and what is unofficially known as Little Phnom Penh, Anaheim Street, between Atlantic and Cherry Avenues, a struggling area and home to many Cambodian shops and eateries.

Naples (off Second Street, between Bay Shore and Marina Avenues) is an expensive neighbourhood laid out around picturesque canals; it's similar to Venice up the coast, but with none of the latter's decay. Gondola rides are offered by **Gondola Getaway** (5437 East Ocean Boulevard, 1-562 433 9595, reservations required). In recent years, Long Beach has earned a rep for its rap scene. Snoop Doggy Dogg, Warren G and Dr Dre are some of the local hitmakers. Unfortunately, many of these performers have left the city and there is no hip hop club as such.

Avoid the beaches here: pollution is a problem in this industrial town, especially since the breakwaters were built years ago to hold back the (cleansing) waves. Long Beach and San Pedro are both jumping off points for nearby **Catalina Island**.

Long Beach Aquarium of the Pacific

100 Aquarium Way, at Shoreline Drive (1-562 590 3100/www.aquariumofpacific.org). Metro First Street or Transit Mall/Long Beach Transit bus C/I-710, exit Shoreline Drive east. **Open** 9am-6pm daily. **Admission** $14.95; $7.95-$11.95 concessions. **Credit** AmEx, MC, V.

The $117-million aquarium with its wave-shaped profile has been turning 'em away since opening in June 1998 – and it's easy to see why. Start in the Great Hall of the Pacific, where a life-size replica of a blue whale with calf hangs from the ceiling, and then move through the Pacific Ocean's three regions: Southern California/Baja, the Tropical Pacific and the Northern Pacific. A three-storey-high predator tank, coral reef and kelp forest are among the simulated environments, and there's a seal and sea lion habitat, giant Japanese spider crabs and plenty of interactive exhibits to keep the kids amused.

Kids will love **Long Beach Aquarium**.

Queen Mary

1126 Queens Highway (1-562 435 3511/hotel booking 1-800 437 2934/www.queenmary.com). Metro Transit Mall/I-405, then I-710 south. **Open** Summer 9am-6pm Mon-Fri; 9am-9pm Sat, Sun. Winter 9am-6pm daily. **Admission** $17; concessions $10-$13. **Credit** AmEx, DC, Disc, MC, V.

Having retired from active duty in 1967, the *Queen Mary* is now a popular tourist attraction. Though only mildly diverting unless you have a thing for cruise ships, the majestic liner offers fun like the Ghost Tour, Engine Room Tour and terrifying haunted house at Hallowe'en. Also, the bar up front is a great place for a Martini.

Long Beach Convention & Visitors Bureau

1 World Trade Center, Long Beach, CA 90831 (1-562 436 3645/www.golongbeach.org). **Open** 8am-5pm Mon-Fri; closed Sat, Sun.

Orange County

The South Coast

Seal Beach and **Sunset Beach**, near the LA County border, begin the 50-mile (80-kilometre) expanse of beach bliss that is coastal Orange County. The Pacific Coast Highway (PCH, or Highway 1) runs the length of it. While Seal Beach and Sunset Beach are unpretentious fun, the real action starts just to the south in **Huntington Beach**, aka 'Surf City'. Hang out at the pier (Main Street, off PCH) or on the sand and you'll see how the city got its nickname. From dawn to dark, surfers are out searching for the perfect wave; the best appear in the many pro championships held every summer. Main Street has been refurbished in recent years, and includes numerous surfboard shops and bars, and at least one perfect greasy spoon – the **Sugar Shack** (213 Main Street, 1-714 536 0355) – where you can hang with local surfers.

Newport Beach, further south, is something else altogether. From the multi-million-dollar homes overlooking Newport Harbor to the outdoor **Fashion Island** mall and the **Orange County Art Museum** (850 San Clemente Drive, at Santa Barbara Drive, 1-949 759 1122), which specialises in California art, Newport Beach is where the American leisure class can live out its life in sun-soaked splendour. **Balboa Island** (Jamboree Road Bridge, near PCH) and Balboa Peninsula (Balboa Boulevard and PCH) are both prime walking areas, and a ferry ushers visitors between the two. The island is full of small shops, restaurants and homes; just off the ferry on the peninsula is a carnival with a Ferris wheel and old-style arcade.

Laguna Beach began as an artists' colony and is the home of the admired **Laguna Beach Museum of Art** (307 Cliff Drive, at PCH, 1-949 494 6531), which has a collection of Californian art. The city hosts an annual Festival of the Arts in August and September, which includes a surreal live-action 'Pageant of the Masters' in which models pose as famous paintings. It's more intriguing than it sounds. **Main Beach**, with its pick-up basketball and volleyball games, is a must for people-watching. The scuba-diving is also good here.

Further down the coast, **San Juan Capistrano** is famous for the swallows that return to **Mission San Juan Capistrano** (Camino Capistrano and Ortega Highway) each spring. But the 1776-built mission is worth visiting on its own account. One of the area's best rock clubs, the **Coach House** (33157 Camino Capistrano, 1-949 496 8930), is nearby. At the county's end, **San Clemente** has all the sun and waves but few of the crowds of its neighbours. Richard Nixon's western White House, a Spanish-inspired mansion called Casa Pacifica, can be seen from San Clemente State Beach.

Central Orange County

Costa Mesa (which isn't on the coast) likes to bill itself as another city of the arts. It's the home of the **Orange County Performing Arts Center** (*see page 260*) and the much-admired **South Coast Repertory Theatre Company** (655 Town Center Drive, 1-714 957 5500). But it's really a city of commerce, thanks to an array of malls, including **South Coast Plaza**, one of the largest in the world (just off the I-405 at Bristol Avenue); **Triangle Square** (at the end of the I-55), a massive altar to consumerism that includes a Nike Town and Virgin Megastore; and the **Lab** (2930 Bristol Street), the 'anti-mall' for the young and the pierced. Current tenants include Urban Outfitters, Tower Records Alternative, Spanish Fly for dance and rave wear, and Stateside Garment Traders for vintage clothing. Eat at **Habana** (1-714 556 0176), a postmodern Cuban restaurant and one of OC's best eateries.

Antiseptic **Irvine**, an early masterplanned 'city of the future' (so futuristic when built that part of the *Planet of the Apes* series was shot there), is home to the University of California, Irvine, and the large **Irvine Spectrum** outdoor mall (at the intersection of the I-5 and I-405 freeways, known as El Toro) with its 3-D IMAX cinema. The Spectrum also houses the popular singalong bar **Sing Sing** (1-949 453 8999), where you can watch Southern Californians get very drunk and sing very badly.

To the north, **Santa Ana** is a distinctively Latino city. Strolling along busy Fourth Street, between French and Ross Streets, with its colourful storefronts and hum of Spanish, is like walking through a small city in Mexico. Santa Ana is also home to the **Bowers Museum** (2002 North Main Street, at 20th Street, 1-714 567 3600), which has a strong collection of Latin and African arts and crafts, and a budding artists' district between Broadway, Bush, First and Third Streets. Near the Costa Mesa border is the **Galaxy** (3503 South Harbor Boulevard, 1-714 957 0600), a small concert venue and dance club. Rock artists such as Beck have been known to play intimate rehearsal shows there.

Another lively neighbourhood is **Little Saigon** in Westminster, the largest Vietnamese community outside Vietnam. It's too big to walk, but well worth a visit for the Vietnamese and other South-east Asian foods served at restaurants such as **Seafood Paradise** (8602 Westminster Boulevard, 1-714 893 6066).

Anaheim & inland

This area of Orange County is filled with some of the best-known icons of middle Americana, of which **Disneyland** (*see page 115*) is king. The area around Disneyland, for years known for its cheap motels and strip mall seediness, has been revitalised (unfortunately, losing its wacky 1950s Googie architecture in the process). A new Disney theme park, **California Adventure**, just adjacent to Disneyland, is scheduled to open in February 2001.

Anaheim Stadium, where the California Angels baseball team plays, has been redesigned, given a bit of personality and rechristened **Edison International Field**. The glitzy new **Arrowhead Pond** is a huge arena presenting everything from the Mighty Ducks hockey team to Barbra Streisand concerts. **Linda's Doll Hut** (107 South Adams Street, at Manchester Boulevard, 1-714 533 1286) is the cramped rock club where such OC bands as the Offspring got started. Expect a lot of punk and ska.

For a more traditional slice of American pie, hop over to Beach Boulevard near La Palma Avenue in **Buena Park**. Here you'll find **Knott's Berry Farm**, a smaller, more homely version of Disneyland (*see page 115*), **Movieland Wax Museum** (7711 Beach Boulevard, 1-714 522 1154) and **Medieval Times** (7662 Beach Boulevard, 1-714 523 1100), the knights-and-knaves eatery where the food is beside the point.

Two other shrines to the American way of life deserve a visit. The **Crystal Cathedral**, an all-glass house of worship (*see page 34*) is a

Angels Gate Park in San Pedro. *See p112.*

marvel of sheer excess, while the **Nixon Library & Birthplace** in Yorba Linda (*see chapter* **Museums**) is a combination of library and pro-Nixon propaganda machine (note how the display glosses over his resignation). At the other end of the scale, some alternative, college-style life can be found around the Cal State campus in **Fullerton**, including the **Off-Campus Bar** (2736 East Nutwood Avenue, 1-714 879 8094), where rock bands play from Wednesday to Saturday nights.

If you're a shopaholic, visit the new **Block** shopping mall in **Orange** (20 City Boulevard W, 1-800 284 3256/1-714 769 4000). With more than 100 shops, restaurants and attractions, it's as much an outdoor playground as a mall, and includes **Vans Skate Park** (*see page 251*), the world's largest indoor skateboard arena, where you can watch OC skate punks do their tricks.

Disneyland

1313 Harbor Boulevard, between Katella Avenue & Ball Road, Anaheim (1-714 781 4000/recorded information 1-714 781 4565/www.disneyland.com). Bus 460, Orange County Transit 205, 430/I-5, exit Disneyland Drive. **Open** *Summer* 8am-midnight daily. *Winter* 10am-8pm Mon-Thur; 10am-midnight Fri, Sat; 9am-9pm Sun. Hours can vary, so call in advance. **Admission** $41; $31-$39 concessions. **Credit** AmEx, DC, Disc, MC, V.

Called 'the Happiest Place on Earth', Disneyland is all it's cracked up to be – if you like that kind of thing. If you don't, you may need sectioning after your visit. In this immaculate world (deliveries and rubbish removal are all done underground), new rides come on line with movie-studio productivity rates. But some of the old favourites still draw enormous crowds: Space Mountain, which takes you, in utter darkness, on a fast, scream-inducing ride through time, space and black holes; the Matterhorn, where you take a bobsled rollercoaster ride around a Swiss Alp; the Haunted Mansion, where Disney ghosts trill and smile; and the Pirates of the Caribbean, where pirates sing as you float by. A

word of advice: if you hate having a song stick in your head, skip It's a Small World, which is outdated and no more than an incitement to strangle the composer of that inane tune. Disneyland is fun, but get there early to beat the crowds, be prepared to queue and pace yourself – it's very big.

Disney's new California Adventure, slated to open early in 2001, has rides, live shows, shopping and eating in three 'lands' – all with distinctly Californian themes. The Golden State is based on Californian people, places and ideas; the Hollywood Pictures Backlot centres on a make-believe studio backlot; and Paradise Pier is a nostalgic look at California beach culture.

Knott's Berry Farm

8039 Beach Boulevard, at La Palma Avenue, Buena Park (recorded information 1-714 220 5200/www.knotts.com). Bus 460, Orange County Transit 38/I-5, exit Beach Boulevard south. **Open** *Summer* 9am-midnight daily; hours can vary; call ahead. *Winter* hours vary; call ahead. **Admission** $40; $30 concessions; $16.95 all ages after 4pm. **Credit** AmEx, DC, Disc, MC, V.

Knott's Berry Farm started as a farm selling home-made preserves of one Mrs Cordelia Knott. Although Ma Knott and her family are long gone, her jams are still on sale, as are tasty fried chicken dinners at the restaurant outside the gates. Inside the park, which portrays an idealised, kinder America, there are water rides, the 20-storey Sky Jump parachute ride and Montezooma's Revenge, a seemingly tame rollercoaster that still gives you a stomach-flying-out-of-your-mouth sensation. Many of the buildings in the park have been transplanted from old mining towns, which heightens the feeling of nostalgia that hovers in the air. Children will like the Ghost Town, with its smiling cancan girls and gun-slinging cowboys.

Anaheim/Orange County Visitor & Convention Bureau

800 W Katella Avenue, Anaheim, CA 92801 (1-714 765 8888/www.anaheimoc.org). **Open** 8am-5.30pm Mon-Fri; closed Sat, Sun.

Museums

LA's museums may not be as impressive as New York's or Washington's, but it has some world-class holdings and some eccentric one-offs, too.

Los Angeles's museums have a hard fight for attention in the world's entertainment capital, but they're in good health and taking their responsibilities more seriously than ever. The worst of the last decade's budgetary crises seem to have passed, though individual museums may yet face constriction or even extinction. Alongside sober, professionally curated institutions, LA also has a rich seam of lone devotees displaying eccentric amassments for the public's edification.

Though museums and art galleries (*see* chapter **Galleries**) tend to cluster in particular locations, these are beginning to overlap: you can find important galleries, for instance, in the museum-intensive Miracle Mile along Wilshire Boulevard, while there is now a museum at the heart of the region's premier gallery enclave, Bergamot Station in Santa Monica. Individual venues are scattered far and wide, so be prepared to venture out to Pasadena or Malibu, or to look for parking in Beverly Hills or Chinatown. Your reward will be some of the best expressions of culture that Southern California – and the entire US – has to offer.

Many museums are closed on Mondays.

Don't miss Museums

Autry Museum
The Autry features Hollywood's Wild West along with the true Wild West of legend, but makes clear the distinction between the two. See page 122.

California Science Center
Filled with neat stuff. Don't miss Gertie, the 50ft transparent woman (actually, it's very hard to miss her). See page 119.

The Huntington Library, Art Collections & Botanical Gardens
Everybody's sentimental favourite for the lovely gardens and the teahouse in their midst. See page 117.

Los Angeles County Museum of Art
The region's great all-around art museum, with a good gift/bookshop, very good restaurant and cafeteria and superb film and music programme. See page 117.

Museum of Contemporary Art
Probably the American West's best showcase for contemporary art, displayed in two architectural landmark buildings. See page 118.

Norton Simon Museum of Art
Newly renovated, with an impressive array of European old masters – and it's in charming Pasadena. See page 118.

Art & culture

Barnsdall Art Park
4800 Hollywood Boulevard, between Edgemont Street & Vermont Avenue, Los Feliz (1-323 660 4254/ Hollyhock House 1-323 913 4157/Junior Arts Center 1-213 485 4474/LA Municipal Art Gallery 1-213 485 4581). Metro Sunset-Vermont/bus 204, 354, Community Connection 203/US 101, exit Sunset Boulevard east. **Map** p308 A2.
The city's official 'art park', perched on a green hill where tawdry Hollywood meets bohemian Silver Lake, boasts a complex of small institutions, each housed in a structure designed by Frank Lloyd Wright and/or his son, the unjustly overshadowed Lloyd Wright. Hollyhock House, one of the senior Wright's signal middle-period residential structures, features architectural exhibits, while the Municipal Art Gallery and Junior Arts Center sponsor one-person and themed group shows of Southern Californian artists. The entire complex was closed in 2000 for extensive renovation and re-landscaping. The project is scheduled for completion in 2003, but individual pavilions may open earlier, so it's best to call for more information.

California African-American Museum
600 State Drive, at Figueroa Street, Exposition Park, Downtown (1-213 744 7432/www.caam.ca.gov). Bus 81, 102, 550, DASH F/I-110, exit Exposition Boulevard west. **Open** 10am-5pm Tue-Sun; closed Mon. **Admission** free; donation requested.
A research library and museum focusing on the cultural and historical achievements of African-Americans, with permanent exhibits of sculpture, landscape painting and African tribal art. Past shows have included a survey of African puppetry,

LACMA: it's got something for everyone.

black art and black music in 1960s LA, the history of black children's book illustration and retrospectives of famed photographer-musician Gordon Parks and local artists Betye Saar and John Outterbridge.

The Huntington Library, Art Collections & Botanical Gardens

1151 Oxford Road, off Huntington Drive, San Marino (recorded information 1-626 405 2141/ www.huntington.org). Bus 79, 379/I-110, exit Arroyo Parkway north. **Open** *June-Aug* 10.30am-4.30pm Tue-Sun; *Sept-May* noon-4.30pm Tue-Fri; 10.30am-4.30pm Sat, Sun. Closed Mon. **Admission** $8.50; $6-$8 concessions; free under-12s. Free 1st Thur of the month. **Credit** MC, V.

Located in the Pasadena suburb of San Marino, the bequest of entrepreneur Henry E Huntington has some very, very rare old books and manuscripts, a large collection of 18th- and 19th-century French and British art – Gainsborough's *Blue Boy* is here, as is a new collection of William Morris designs – and a temporary exhibition schedule revitalised by the conversion of a former stable into handsome new galleries. All this sits amid sumptuous botanical gardens, along with a teahouse.

Japanese American National Museum

369 E First Street, between Alameda Street & Central Avenue, Downtown (1-800 461 5266/1-213 625 0414/www.janm.org). Bus 30, 31, 40, 42,

DASH A/US 101, exit Alameda Street south. **Open** 10am-5pm Tue, Wed, Fri-Sun; 10am-8pm Thur; closed Mon. **Admission** $6; $3-$5 concessions; free under-5s. Free 5-8pm Thur & the 3rd Thur of the mth. **Credit** AmEx, MC, V. **Map** p309 C2.

Two years ago, the JANM, located in the heart of Little Tokyo, expanded into new quarters, which quadrupled its exhibition space. The museum has an impressive record of documentary and art exhibitions, including a survey of Asian-influenced American art from the 1950s and 1960s, several collaborations with other ethnically based institutions, and wrenching yet nostalgia-laden displays of images and artefacts from the internment camps into which Japanese-Americans were herded in World War II. The JANM – not to be confused with the nearby Japanese American Cultural Center – is the largest of a growing number of museums devoted to the arts and culture of particular sections of LA's polyglot population.

Los Angeles County Museum of Art

5905 Wilshire Boulevard, between La Brea & Fairfax Avenues, Miracle Mile (1-323 857 6000/ www.lacma. org). Bus 20, 21, 720/I-10, exit Fairfax Avenue north. **Open** noon-8pm Mon, Tue, Thur; noon-9pm Fri; 11am-8pm Sat, Sun; closed Wed. **Admission** $7; $1-$5 concessions. Free 2nd Tue of the mth. **No credit cards. Map** p306 C3.

The multipurpose Getty Center may be vaster, but LACMA's five pavilions ringing a central courtyard, augmented by a whole huge annexe a block away (at the old May Co building on the corner of Fairfax), constitute LA's largest purely museological complex. In some ways, it's more like the Getty than the Getty. It's got a bit of everything, but in certain areas stands with the world's greatest museums. Notable collections include modern and contemporary masterpieces, incorporating a small but impressive sculpture garden (heavy on the Rodins), textiles, photos and pre-Columbian, Indian, South-east Asian and Japanese art (a whole building is devoted to the latter). Recent shows have included surveys of Van Gogh, Charles and Ray Eames, a provocative survey of the face in photography, the Harlem Renaissance, and 'Made in California', a hugely ambitious overview of the state's art and culture, high and low, in the 20th century. There are also lectures, films and classical and jazz concerts.

Los Angeles Craft & Folk Art Museum

5814 Wilshire Boulevard, between Curson & Stanley Avenues, Miracle Mile (1-323 937 4230). Bus 20, 21, 720/I-10, exit Fairfax Avenue north. **Open** 11am-5pm Wed-Sun; closed Mon, Tue. **Admission** $3.50; $2.50 concessions; free under-12s. **Credit** AmEx, MC, V. **Map** p306 C3.

Although its beloved old café, the Egg & the I, is gone, the Craft & Folk Art Museum has been saved from oblivion by the city's Cultural Affairs Department, which took it over from private ownership in 1998 when it went bankrupt. Now, LA's

Arts & Entertainment

only public showcase devoted entirely to functional and informal art has actually broadened its programming. Charming and informative shows of Slovenian craft, Venetian Carnivale masks and musical instruments 'of trance and ecstasy', among others, have appeared at the resurrected museum. It is also bringing back its popular schedule of events and festivals.

Museum of Contemporary Art & Geffen Contemporary

MOCA: 250 S Grand Avenue, at Third Street, Downtown (1-213 621 2766). Metro Pershing Square/bus 37, 76, 78, 96, DASH B/I-110, exit Fourth Street east. Map p309 B2. Geffen: N Central Avenue, at First Street, Downtown (1-213 621 2766/www.moca-la.org). Bus 30, 31, 40, 42, DASH A/US 101, exit Alameda Street south. Map p309 C2. Both Open 11am-5pm Tue, Wed, Fri-Sun; 11am-8pm Thur; closed Mon. Admission $6; $4 concessions; free under-12s. Free 5-8pm Thur. Credit AmEx, MC, V.

The city's – and perhaps the American West's – premier showcase for art made after the middle of the 20th century, MOCA started life in a vast bus barn on the edge of Little Tokyo. Long known as the 'Temporary Contemporary', this building is now the Geffen Contemporary (with an interior designed by Frank Gehry). When MOCA's main building (the work of Japan's Arata Isozaki) was completed a block from the Civic Center, the museum was able both to mount ambitious survey exhibitions and to showcase items from an excellent and rapidly expanding permanent collection. Thus, upwards of half a dozen shows can be viewed at any time in the two MOCAs. Such recent displays as 'At the End of the Century: 100 Years of Architecture', 'Out of Actions', an exhaustive history of post-war performance art, and retrospectives of individual artists travel to all corners of the world. The MOCA bookshop, including its offshoot at the Geffen, is one of the best places in LA to find publications about new art. A free shuttle bus runs between the two sites.

Museum of Television & Radio

465 N Beverly Drive, at Little Santa Monica Boulevard, Beverly Hills (1-310 786 1000/ www.mtr. org). Bus 3, 14, 27, 316/I-10, exit Robertson Boulevard north. Open noon-5pm Wed, Fri-Sun; noon-9pm Thur; closed Mon, Tue. Admission free; suggested donation $6; $3-$4 concessions. No credit cards. Map p305 C2.

The MT&R's permanent collection consists of nearly 100,000 TV and radio programmes, duplicating the holdings of the museum's New York counterpart and easily accessible via a computer catalogue. Does that make it a 'museum without walls', in André Malraux's phrase? (Perhaps it should be renamed 'Malraux's Place'.) Not entirely: the MT&R also has a lively, changing programme of artefact exhibitions, such as the wedding dresses from soap operas, costumes and make-up from *Star Trek*, and a history of *TV Guide* through its covers.

Museum of Tolerance at the Simon Wiesenthal Center for Holocaust Studies

9786 W Pico Boulevard, at Roxbury Drive, West LA (1-310 553 8403/Simon Weisenthal Center 1-310 553 9036/www.wiesenthal.com/mot). Bus Santa Monica 5, 7, 12/I-10, exit Overland Boulevard north. Open 11.30am-6.30pm Mon-Thur; Nov-Mar 11.30am-3pm Apr-Oct 11.30am-5pm Fri; 11am-7.30pm Sun; closed Sat. Admission $8.50; $3.50-$6.50 concessions. Credit AmEx, MC, V. Map p305 C3.

One section of the permanent exhibit area confronts contemporary racism in the US, with exhibits about the 1992 LA riots, the Civil Rights movement, hate groups and racial stereotypes; the other, more extensive area guides visitors through the Holocaust, with dioramas, photos and stories. At the start of this section, you get a 'passport' with a child's photo on it: their fate is revealed to you at the end of the tour. Upstairs, in the Multimedia Learning Center, you can explore the subject further by computer. Book in advance. Note that last entry is usually two hours before closing time.

Norton Simon Museum of Art

411 W Colorado Boulevard, at Orange Grove Boulevard, Pasadena (1-626 449 6840/www.norton simon.org). Bus 180, 181/I-110, exit Orange Grove Boulevard north. Open noon-6pm Mon, Wed, Thur, Sat, Sun; noon-9pm Fri; closed Tue. Admission $6; $3 concessions. No credit cards.

The Norton Simon recently underwent extensive interior renovation (design courtesy of the ubiquitous Frank Gehry), and beefed up its temporary programming and events schedule. This is helping it to emphasise the different aspects of its collection more evenly, hanging choice items and programming special exhibitions with a wider perspective. It is still best known for its impressive collection of old masters, notably superb examples of 17th-century Dutch and 19th-century French painting, as well as some excellent modern works (including the Galka Scheyer collection of modern German painting), and extensive collections of European prints and Far Eastern art and artefacts.

Pacific Asia Museum

46 N Los Robles Avenue, at Colorado Boulevard, Pasadena (1-626 449 2742). Bus 180, 181, 188/ I-110, exit Colorado Boulevard east. Open 10am-5pm Wed, Fri-Sun; 10am-8pm Thur; closed Mon, Tue. Admission $4; $2 concessions. No credit cards.

Art and artefacts from Asia and the Pacific Rim are displayed in the historic Grace Nicholson Building, a re-creation of a northern Chinese palace, with charming Chinese Garden Court to match. Exhibitions include contemporary as well as traditional Asian arts. The museum's most popular events, however, are its family-oriented festival days, each featuring the culture and cuisine of a different Asian nation or people.

The **Norton Simon** in Pasadena. *See p118*.

Santa Monica Museum of Art

Bergamot Station, 2525 Michigan Avenue, building G1, at Cloverfield Boulevard, Santa Monica (1-310 586 6488). Bus Santa Monica 7/I-10, exit Cloverfield Boulevard north. **Open** 11am-6pm Tue-Sat; noon-5pm Sun; closed Mon. **Admission** free; suggested donation $3. **Credit** AmEx, MC, V. **Map** 2 C3.

Greater LA's best contemporary *kunsthalle* occupies a corner of Bergamot Station, the region's most art-intensive neighbourhood, where it attracts sizeable crowds with its lively programme of work by local and international artists and its Friday Night Salon, a series of discussions and performances. Since moving into the Bergamot 'art mall' in 1997, museum shows have included collages and drawings by the late Fluxus-Happenings artist Al Hansen and his grandson, pop singer Beck; installations by Californian artists such as Michael McMillen, Carl Cheng, and Jennifer Steinkamp; and a survey of the elaborate auto-erotic photographs of French post-Surrealist Pierre Molinier.

Skirball Cultural Center & Museum

2701 N Sepulveda Boulevard, at I-405, West LA (1-310 440 4500/www.skirball.org). Bus 561, Culver City 6, Commuter Express 430/I-405, exit Skirball Center/Mulholland Drive. **Open** noon-5pm Tue-Sat; 11am-5pm Sun; closed Mon. **Admission** $8; $6 concessions; free under-12s. **Credit** MC, V.

Concerned primarily with American Judaism, this offshoot of Hebrew Union College houses a reconstruction of a Middle Eastern archeological dig, a room-sized exhibit devoted to religious decorative arts and a collection of art that chronicles Jewish migration to America. Its temporary exhibitions display both art and historical documentation, and often bridge over to cover LA's other ethnic groups. The Skirball also features lectures, readings and musical and theatrical performances. Hebrew Union College should not be confused with the University of Judaism, across the I-405, which has a much smaller exhibition space, the Platt Gallery, which shows work by mainly Jewish local artists.

Southwest Museum

234 Museum Drive, at Avenue 43, Mt Washington (1-323 221 2164/www.southwestmuseum.org). Bus 81, 83/I-110, exit Avenue 43 north. **Open** 10am-5pm Tue-Sun; closed Mon. **Admission** $6; $3-$4 concessions; free under-6s. **No credit cards**.

Located atop a hill in the Mount Washington area, in an impressive building that reconstructs the hacienda style of the area's Spanish settlers, the Southwest displays selections from its huge collection of Native American art and artefacts, as well as old-fashioned dioramas. The unusual entrance tunnel (originally installed in 1920 after the first director had a heart attack and died while climbing the hill) has recently been reopened and a new lift installed. At the time of writing, the museum is still mounting exhibitions at its (much more convenient) annexe in the art deco May Co building, which it shares with LACMA.

UCLA Armand Hammer Museum of Art & Cultural Center

10899 Wilshire Boulevard, at Westwood Boulevard, Westwood (1-310 443 7000/www.arts.ucla.edu/ hammer). Bus 20, 22, 720, Santa Monica 1, 2, 8, 12/I-405, exit Wilshire Boulevard east. **Open** 11am-7pm Tue, Wed, Fri, Sat; 11am-9pm Thur; 11am-5pm Sun; closed Mon. **Admission** $4.50; $3 concessions; free under-17s. Free Thur. **Credit** AmEx, MC, V.

Industrialist Armand Hammer founded this museum in his Occidental Petroleum building primarily to house his personal collection of art. After his death in 1990 and several years of lacklustre programming, the 'Oxy' board ceded the museum to nearby UCLA, which moved its art collections and substantial exhibition schedule there. The latter favours modern and contemporary Western work, and there is a further bias towards Californian culture: shows have included a scholarly look at pre-war Californian modernism; the controversial 'Sunshine & Noir' show that surveyed contemporary LA art from a European standpoint; and a huge exhibition documenting the architecture and planning of Disney's amusement parks. Renovation and expansion will make the exhibition programme even more adventurous, introduce a ground-level café and make the superb bookshop more accessible.

UCLA Fowler Museum of Cultural History

UCLA campus, between the Dance Building & Royce Hall, Westwood (1-310 825 4361/www.fmch.ucla. edu). Bus 2, 302, 305, 561, Santa Monica 2, 8/I-405, exit Sunset Boulevard east. **Open** noon-5pm Wed, Fri-Sun; noon-8pm Thur; closed Mon, Tue. **Admission** $5; $3 concessions; free under-17s. Free Thur.

Tucked away on the UCLA campus, the Fowler presents exciting, in-depth exhibitions on diverse ethnographic themes: shows have included Haitian voodoo flags, African headrests, recycled 'junk' art and craft in Africa and in Southern California's own car-body shops, and northern Mexican *corrido* ballads and their singers. The shows are invariably well researched and handsomely installed.

Science

California Science Center

700 State Drive, between Figueroa & Menlo Streets, Exposition Park, Downtown (1-213 744 7400/IMAX 1-213 744 2014/www.casciencectr.org). Bus 102,

Arts & Entertainment

The Getty Center

Los Angeles's very own acropolis occupies the top of a hill in the Santa Monica Mountains, in the wealthy Westside neighbourhood of Brentwood, overlooking the 405 freeway, on land once destined to be the site of a co-operative housing development.

The complex was conceived as a home for the hitherto disparate entities of the J Paul Getty Trust and was the brainchild of former CEO and president of the trust, Harold Williams. On taking over in 1981, he invested and – substantially increased – the late oil baron's $700 million bequest to the J Paul Getty Museum. He then expanded the trust's mission, created new institutes, announced a commitment to reaching out to the local community and hired a new museum director, John Walsh. Before his retirement in 2000, Walsh oversaw the expansion of the museum's holdings from a laughable hotchpotch of gaudy rococo furniture and a few insignificant paintings to a competitive store of post-Renaissance European paintings, drawings and sculpture, decorative arts, antiquities and an outstanding photography collection.

The new campus was built partly to get rid of millions of spare dollars: to keep its tax-exempt status, the Getty has to spend 4.25 per cent of its endowment in three out of every four years (the endowment currently stands at $4.3 billion – work that out). In 1984, the trust hired East Coast-based Richard Meier, then America's most celebrated architect. As the building slowly went up, stories about its excesses were legion – the escalation of cost from $733 million to $1 billion (due to an expanded programme and earthquake retrofitting costs, explained the Getty); the 16,000 tons of split travertine blocks quarried in italy; the first-of-its-kind, computer-operated tram installed to ferry people up the hill. Then there were the feuds between the architect and various antagonists: the locals, who objected to Meier's original plans for a white metal building; Walsh, who rejected Meier's minimalist interiors and instead hired interior designer Thierry Despont to create lavish backdrops; and artist Robert Irwin, selected over Meier's head to landscape the Central Garden.

When the Getty Center finally opened, it surprised many doubting Thomases by turning out to be a stunner. Getting there to see it, however, is tiresome, to say the least. By car, it means a drive, invariably at a slow crawl, up the congested I-405, then a queue for the parking lot, then another queue for the tram. But once you are on the little train, winding up the ravine and into the clouds, leaving freeway and city behind, it becomes a truly marvellous – albeit slightly Disneyish – experience (some refer to the Getty Center as 'Gettyland').

On arrival at the top of the hill you find yourself in a large plaza with a stupendous panoramic view of Los Angeles, from the hills and ocean in the west right around to Downtown in the east. (The view is probably the biggest hit with the casual visitor.) The complex is a little baffling because there are several buildings, some open to the public, others not, and signs are few and confusing.

To the west of the plaza is a decent self-service café, a restaurant and the circular Research Institute, which houses a private scholarly centre and changing public exhibits. North are the other institutes (some off-limits to the public) and the Harold M Williams Auditorium, where scholarly lectures and symposia alternate with less academic fare. To the south, up a grand Spanish Steps-style

stairway, is the museum lobby, an airy, luminous rotunda that gives on to a fountain-filled open courtyard surrounded by the Getty Museum's six pavilions, housing the permanent collection and temporary exhibitions. Continue past the pavilions to cascading terraces and at the end you'll find a charmingly quirky garden of cacti and succulents – and an even more breathtaking view.

In its entirety, the collection of pristine buildings, all clad in varying amounts of travertine and white metal panelling, can feel a little like a very expensive office park, and Irwin's Central Garden pseudo-maze is lush in blooming seasons but can seem overly fussy. There is much to offset these shortcomings, however: the elegant modernism of some of the spaces; the glorious light (inside and out); the spaciousness; the fountains and pools; the pretty landscaping; the many outside terraces, balconies, nooks and crannies for panoramic viewing; and the Center's overall sense of civic grandeur, a quality rare in Los Angeles.

When it opened the museum proved so phenomenally successful – with almost double the expected attendance – that it had to back-pedal from its initial statement that the Getty was open to all who could get there, whether by car, bus, bicycle, taxi, or on foot. Now that the novelty has worn off, the institute has been able to loosen its reservation requirements some, allowing for free, non-reserved parking – usually on

Saturday and Sunday and after 4pm on Thursday and Friday (call for exact information and save yourself $5 and a headache). The shortage of toilets remains, however.

The Getty Center was a Johnny-come-lately to collecting European art; its acquisitions budget may be the envy of museums the world over, but until, say, the Vatican has a fire sale, the Getty's collections will never amount to that of the great old art museums. Certain of its holdings, however – such as post-Renaissance decorative arts, for instance, or the ever-expanding photography holdings – are magnificent in their capacity and breadth.

The original Getty Villa, perched on another bluff directly over the ocean in Malibu, is closed until 2002 for extensive renovation (the fate of a planned amphitheatre is less certain, as the Getty grapples legally with recalcitrant, and very well-heeled neighbours). It will house the Getty's great collections of antiquities, which until then are being sampled in a cycle of exhibitions at the new museum.

The Getty Center

1200 Getty Center Drive, at the I-405, Brentwood (information & reservations 1-310 440 7300/hearing-impaired 1-310 440 7305/www.getty.edu). Bus 561, Santa Monica 14/I-405, exit Getty Center Drive. **Open** 10am-7pm Tue, Wed; 10am-9pm Thur, Fri; 10am-6pm Sat, Sun; closed Mon. **Admission** free.

Arts & Entertainment

204, 354, 550, DASH F/I-110, exit Martin Luther King Boulevard. **Open** 10am-5pm daily. **Admission** *Museum* free; *IMAX* $6.50; $3.50-$4.50 concessions. **Credit** (IMAX) MC, V.

The Science Center, incorporating the California Museum of Science and Industry and the Aerospace Museum, consists of four themed wings: World of Life, Creative World, World of the Pacific and Worlds Beyond. World of Life unravels biological mysteries: its main feature is Gertie, a 50ft (15m) long transparent human female body. Creative World focuses on human adaptability and our relationship with technology. World of the Pacific examines the varied forms nature and culture take on either side, and in the middle, of the ocean at LA's edge, while Worlds Beyond heads out into deep space. The Center also houses the improved seven-storey 3-D IMAX cinema.

George C Page Museum of La Brea Discoveries

5801 Wilshire Boulevard, between La Brea & Fairfax Avenues, Miracle Mile (1-323 934 7243/ 1-323 857 6311/www.tarpits.org). Bus 20, 21, 720/ I-10, exit La Brea Avenue north. **Open** 10am-5pm daily. **Admission** $6; $2-$3.50 concessions; free under-5s. Free 1st Tue of the mth. **Credit** AmEx, Disc, V. **Map** p306 C3.

Inside the half-underground Page Museum, check out old bones found in the surrounding La Brea Tar Pits, along with reconstructed, life-size skeletons of mammoths, wolves, sloths and eagles and an animatronic sabre-toothed tiger. Walk around the park

and look for stray puddles of oozing black tar, still seeping from the ground. In the summer, you can see palaeontologists at work in the ongoing excavation of Pit 91 and smell the tang of tar in the air. A giant re-creation of a mastodon sinking into a pit as his 'wife' and 'child' look on is heart-rending.

Los Angeles County Museum of Natural History

900 Exposition Boulevard, between Hoover & Menlo Streets, Exposition Park, Downtown (1-213 763 3466/ recorded information 1-213 744 3466/ www.nhm.org). Bus 40, 42, 102, 550, DASH F/ I-110, exit Exposition Boulevard west. **Open** 10am-5pm daily. **Admission** $8; $2-$5.50 concessions; free under-5s. **No credit cards**.

The huge Spanish-Renaissance building – one of the few old-fashioned museums left in LA – opened in 1913. It's the third-largest natural history museum in the US, its 35 halls and galleries packed with stuffed birds, mammals, gems, a Tyrannosaurus Rex skull and Native American pottery, textiles and baskets. One highlight, a perennial favourite with pre-teens, is the Insect Zoo, full of stick insects, Madagascan hissing cockroaches, scorpions, tarantulas and lots of ants.

Only in LA

Autry Museum of Western Heritage

4700 Western Heritage Way, opposite LA Zoo, Griffith Park (1-323 667 2000/www.autry-museum. org). Bus 96/I-5, exit Zoo Drive west. **Open** 10am-

Mastodons still walk the earth at the **George C Page Museum**.

Beverly Hills entrepreneur Barry Kaye (author of *Die Rich & Tax Free*) and his wife Carole began collecting miniatures – miniature everything – a decade ago, acquiring items at such a rate that they had soon established their own museum. Classic and kitsch stand cheek by jowl here: you'll find both a miniature 'Alexander's Siege Tent at Halicarnassus' and a Lilliputian version of the OJ Simpson trial. But the emphasis is on historic curios, such as those found in the Great Palaces of Europe exhibit.

Frederick's of Hollywood Celebrity Lingerie Hall of Fame

6608 Hollywood Boulevard, at Hudson Avenue, Hollywood (1-323 466 8506). Metro Hollywood-Vine/ bus 212, 217/US 101, exit Highland Avenue south. **Open** 10am-9pm Mon-Fri; 10am-7pm Sat; 11am-6pm Sun. **Admission** free. **Map** p307 A1.

This 'museum' is housed in a few rooms in the back of the well-known lingerie emporium. On display, next to an oil painting of founder Frederick Mellinger, are brassières with names like the 'Peek-a-boo' and the 'Depth Charge'. Madonna's black-and-gold sequinned bustier is on show, along with the bra Marilyn Monroe wore in *Let's Make Love*, and, inexplicably, a bra that was thrown on stage during a Kiss concert. Still as trashy as ever, the rest of the store is almost a museum itself. Amazing shoes, too.

Hollywood Entertainment Museum

7021 Hollywood Boulevard, at N Sycamore Avenue, Hollywood (1-323 465 7900/www.hollywood entertainment.com). Metro Hollywood-Highland/ bus 163, 180, 212, 217/I-10, exit Highland Avenue south. **Open** 11am-6pm Mon, Tue, Thur-Sun; closed Wed. **Admission** $7.50; $4-$4.50 concessions; free under-5s. **Credit** AmEx, DC, MC, V. **Map** p307 A1.

This huge state-of-the-museological-art facility is dedicated to the history of Hollywood, its people and its productions. It features original sets, Tinseltown memorabilia – including stars' wigs and cosmetics from the Max Factor Museum of Beauty, which the Entertainment Museum incorporates – an educational wing, a recording studio, a library and archives, as well as temporary exhibitions.

International Surfing Museum

411 Olive Avenue, between Main & Fifth Streets, Huntington Beach, Orange County (1-949 960 3483/ www.surfingmuseum.org). Bus Orange County Transit 25, 29/I-405, exit Beach Boulevard south. **Open** *Summer* noon-5pm daily. *Winter* noon-5pm Wed-Sun; closed Mon, Tue. **Admission** $2; $1 concessions; free under-6s. **Credit** AmEx, MC, V.

This small museum in Orange County honours Duke Kahanamoku, the father of surfing, and celebrates surf music, the women of surfing and the heroes of surf life-saving. It's staffed with friendly volunteers full of stories; ask to hear about Dick 'King of the Surf Guitar' Dale's guitar, which was stolen from the museum's original building and now hangs in the rear gallery. If you want a taste of contemporary beach culture, however, head for the beach, which is within walking distance.

Frederick's of Hollywood: bras of the stars.

5pm Tue, Wed, Fri-Sun; 10am-8pm Thur; closed Mon. **Admission** $7.50; $3-$5 concessions. **Credit** AmEx, MC, V.

At the Autry Museum, the real history of the West is presented side by side with images and props from its various silver-screen interpretations – such as a life-size bronze sculpture of Gene Autry (aka the 'Singing Cowboy') and his horse, Champion. Kids will enjoy the re-creations of Wild West saloons and the 1873 fire engine. Unlike Hollywood (or the Hollywood president, Ronald Reagan), the museum distinguishes between the real and the artificial — and does both justice. Its serious exhibitions have included a survey of women artists in the pre-war West, revealing their significance in frontier regions. And to celebrate California's 150th anniversary, it hosted a sober, un-jingoistic documentary show about the Mexican-American War.

Carole & Barry Kaye Museum of Miniatures

5900 Wilshire Boulevard, between Ogden Drive & Spaulding Avenue, Miracle Mile (1-323 937 6464/ www.museumofminiatures.com). Bus 20, 21, 720/ I-10, exit Fairfax Avenue north. **Open** 10am-5pm Tue-Sat; 11am-5pm Sun; closed Mon. **Admission** $7.50; $3-$6.50 concessions. **Credit** MC, V. **Map** p306 C3.

Arts & Entertainment

Museum of Jurassic Technology

9341 Venice Boulevard, at Bagley Avenue, Culver City (1-310 836 6131). Bus 33, 333, 436/I-10, exit Robertson Boulevard south. **Open** 2-8pm Thur; noon-6pm Fri-Sun; closed Mon-Wed. **Admission** free; suggested donation $4. **No credit cards.**

From its name, you would expect this museum to go under the heading 'Science'. But this is science fiction, taken to an especially subtle and sublime level. The brainchild and handiwork of artist Richard Wilson, the MJT presents itself as a museum of curiosities, scientific wonders (a bat that can fly through walls without harming itself or the wall) and artistic miracles (the 'microminiature' painting of Hagop Sandaldjian, who painted on needles, sculpted human hair and specks of dust the likenesses of famous people, including the Pope and several Disney characters). Fact (Sandaldjian did, indeed, craft such microscopic objects) is mixed with fantasy through the elaborate treatment accorded each display, right down to extensive wall labels and dramatically lit vitrines.

Museum of Neon Art

Grand Hope Park, 501 W Olympic Boulevard, between Hope Street & Grand Avenue, Downtown (1-213 489 9918). Metro Pico or Seventh Street-Metro Center/bus 27, 28, 83, 84, 328/I-110, exit Ninth Street east. **Open** 11am-5pm Wed-Sat; noon-5pm Sun; closed Mon, Tue. **Admission** $5; $3.50 concessions. **Credit** AmEx, MC, V. **Map** p309 B4.

MONA is a celebration of the many uses of neon, including signage and fine art. Permanent exhibits include works by kinetic-art pioneers Lili Lakich (founder of the museum) and Candace Gawne, and a well-wrought neon interpretation of the Mona Lisa. You'll also find work by other neon artists from around the country and the world, and a lively and topical temporary exhibition programme.

Nethercutt Collection

15200 Bledsoe Street, at San Fernando Road, Sylmar (1-818 367 2251). Bus 94/I-5, exit Roxford Street east. **Open** *Booking office* 9-11.30am, 1-3pm Tue-Sat; closed Mon, Sun. *Tours* (2hrs) 10am, 1.30pm Tue-Sat. **Admission** free; booking essential. No under-12s.

Housed in an innocuous building in an even more innocuous industrial suburb north of LA, Dorothy and JB Nethercutt, heirs to a cosmetics fortune, have assembled a huge collection of functional objects, all of which somehow fit their very personal concept of beauty. Their principles also dictate that everything must be in working order: the Rolls-Royces are all driven to a picnic once a year and the gargantuan Mighty Wurlitzer Pipe Organ is played at scheduled recitals. Visitors are also treated to a huge collection of Steuben Glass hood ornaments, nickelodeons, French furniture, clocks and watches, and a painted ceiling depicting the members of the immediate Nethercutt family as cherubs. Shorts and jeans are prohibited out of respect for the stuff.

Petersen Automotive Museum

6060 Wilshire Boulevard, at Fairfax Avenue, Miracle Mile (1-323 964 6315/1-323 930 2277/www.nhm. org/petersen/index1.htm). Bus 20, 21, 720/I-10, exit Fairfax Avenue north. **Open** 10am-6pm Tue-Sun; closed Mon. **Admission** $7; $3-$5 concessions. **Credit** AmEx, MC, V. **Map** p306 B3.

A monster pick-up truck embedded in the wall marks the entrance to LA's version of the car museum. Inside, life-size dioramas of garages, supermarkets and restaurants re-create the early days of the drive-in lifestyle, complete with a full range of classic cars parked at the front. Upstairs, changing exhibitions showcase various aspects of car culture, from film stars' cars to fancy racing machines to motorcycles. Among the typical shows: 'It's a Duesy!', with more than 20 examples of the glamorous Duesenberg Model J (owned by, among others, Elvis Presley and Tyrone Power).

Presidential libraries

The LA area is home to two presidential libraries/museums. The museums are open to the general public, while the libraries are open for research. The tone of the two is very different: Reagan's banks on sentimentality, while Nixon's focuses more on the intellectual rigour required of a president. Both libraries are some way out of LA, in opposite directions.

Richard Nixon Library & Birthplace

18001 Yorba Linda Boulevard, at Imperial Highway, Yorba Linda, Orange County (1-714 993 5075/ www.nixonfoundation.org). Bus Orange County Transit 22/Hwy 90, exit Yorba Linda Boulevard west. **Open** 10am-5pm Mon-Sat; 11am-5pm Sun. **Admission** $5.95; $2-$3.95 concessions. **Credit** AmEx, Disc, MC, V.

Located in the out-of-the-way suburb where Nixon was born, the library provides an overview of his presidency as well as a tour of the modest house, built from a kit by his father, in which Tricky Dicky was born. The gifts section includes a gun from Elvis Presley and a rock in the shape of Nixon's profile from Barry Goldwater, as well as the usual assortment of buckles and paintings. Richard and Pat Nixon are buried in the gardens.

Ronald Reagan Library & Museum

40 Presidential Drive, at Madera Road, Simi Valley, Ventura (1-805 522 8444). Metrolink Simi Valley/ US 101, exit Hwy 23 north. **Open** 10am-5pm daily. **Admission** $5; $3 concessions; free under-15s. **No credit cards.**

This place is great for fans of the Gipper, but liberal types will probably see red. The museum has a CD-Rom display containing Reagan's most endearing quips, photos of him as a young lad with a football and a re-creation of the Oval Office, plus awesome gifts received over the years, such as a beaded gown given to Nancy by Imelda Marcos and a White House-shaped Kleenex box made from white yarn.

Eat, Drink, Shop

Feature boxes

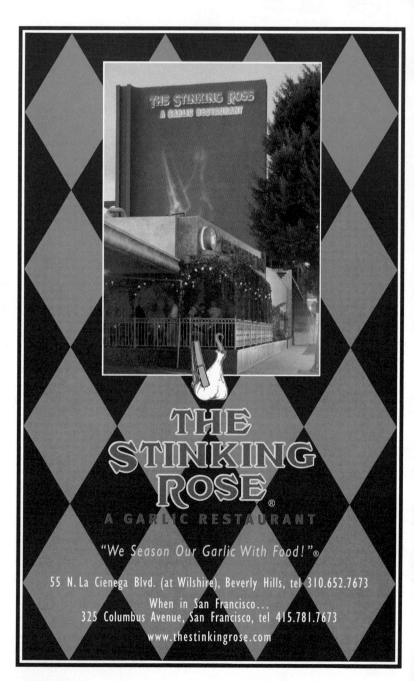

THE STINKING ROSE®

A GARLIC RESTAURANT

"We Season Our Garlic With Food!"®

55 N. La Cienega Blvd. (at Wilshire), Beverly Hills, tel 310.652.7673

When in San Francisco...
325 Columbus Avenue, San Francisco, tel 415.781.7673

www.thestinkingrose.com

Restaurants

Los Angeles is one of the world's great dining destinations: from celebrity chefs to ethnic cafés, there's something for all tastes.

At one time, choosing a restaurant in Los Angeles was mainly a matter of fashion. But, while there are still plenty of restaurants catering to the see-and-be-seen ethos, there's a new emphasis on the integrity of the food. Tasting menus have become *de rigueur*, and there has been a revival of the almost forgotten neighbourhood restaurant, with places such as **Los Feliz, vermont** and **Pastis** experiencing new-found popularity. The city's celebrity chefs are still much in evidence, of course, with the likes of Wolfgang Puck (**Spago, Chinois on Main, Granita**), Piero Selvaggio (**Posto, Valentino**), Nobuyuki Matsuhisa (**Nobu, Matsuhisa, Ubon**) and Hans Röckenwagner (**Rock, Röckenwagner**) still pulling in diners in their droves.

The city has always had lots of Italian restaurants, but the spaghetti-with-meatballs kind are now being superseded by places producing more authentic northern and contemporary Italian cuisine, such as **Orso**, . Decent French bistros, on the other hand, used to be thin on the ground, but now there's a slew, including **Les Deux Café**, **Mimosa**, **Le Petit Bistro** and the **Little Door**. And Japanese restaurants, having started the sushi craze, are now feeling courageous enough to introduce other Japanese specialities. It's no longer a surprise to find things such as natto (fermented soya beans) or, heaven forbid, sashimi, at places such as **Hirozen**, **Ita Cho** or **Yabu**. Nuevo Latino is another new trend, with places such as **Mojo** at the trendy W hotel and the delightful **Boca del Conga Room** doing good business.

Los Angeles really comes into its own with its amazing range of truly ethnic food. With everything from Korean barbecue through superb Oaxacan specialities to Thai treasures, this is a city where those with a sense of adventure, whatever their budget, can explore the culinary outer limits.

INSIDE INFORMATION

Although LA has a reputation for closing early, Angelenos are rediscovering their sense of *joie de vivre* and restaurants are staying open later and later. It's always best to book, to valet park

Enjoy sweeping views and fine seafood at the **Lobster** by Santa Monica Pier. *See p129*.

Eat, Drink, Shop

Landmarks

Apple Pan
This tiny sandwich bar in West LA (pictured) has been in business since 1947. See page 145.

Chez Jay
After 50 years, this funky beachside roadhouse in Santa Monica is as popular as ever. See page 129.

Dan Tana's
An old-fashioned Italian restaurant in West Hollywood, packed with film industry types. See page 137.

The Los Angeles Palm
Expect to wait for a table at this venerable steakhouse in West Hollywood. See page 139.

Musso & Frank Grill
The decor and menu have hardly changed in 70 years at this vintage grill on Hollywood Boulevard. See page 149.

The Polo Lounge
The power breakfast was invented at this legendary lounge inside the Beverly Hills Hotel. See page 143.

and show your appreciation with a minimum 15 per cent tip; 20 per cent is not considered exorbitant. Also, check out the bold letter on the front of the restaurant where you're intending to eat. The LA County Health Services Department grades restaurants on their health-code compliance. A 'C' rating or lower is questionable. You can also enjoy smoke-free eating, thanks to the city's anti-smoking law. And remember this is California: casual dress is usually fine, although shorts and jeans are not allowed at some more refined establishments.

Westside: Beach towns

Santa Monica

1 Pico
Shutters on the Beach, 1 Pico Boulevard, at Ocean Avenue (1-310 587 1717). Bus 33, 333, Santa Monica 7/I-10, exit Fourth-Fifth Street south. **Open** 11.30am-2.30pm, 6-10.30pm Mon-Sat; 11am-2.30pm, 6-10.30pm Sun. **Main courses** brunch & lunch $14-$20; dinner $14-$30. **Credit** AmEx, DC, Disc, MC, V. **Map** p304 A3.
Think ocean, sunsets and Ralph Lauren, and you've got 1 Pico. Dip your toes in the sand before settling into a well-prepared meal, served with grace. We recommend brunch. *See also p45.*

The Beach House
100 W Channel Road, at Pacific Coast Highway (1-310 454 8299). Bus 434, Santa Monica 9/I-10, exit PCH north. **Open** from 6pm Tue-Sun; closed Mon. **Main courses** $19-$32. **Credit** AmEx, MC, V. **Map** p304 A1.
Simple American food in an elegant candlelit setting. Try baby back ribs, with french fries and beans, buckets of clams and oversized marinated shrimps.

Border Grill
1445 Fourth Street, between Broadway & Santa Monica Boulevard (1-310 451 1655). Bus 4, 304, Santa Monica 1, 2, 10/I-10, exit Fourth-Fifth Street north. **Open** 5-10pm Mon-Thur; 5-11pm Fri; 4.30-11pm Sat; 4.30-10pm Sun. **Main courses** lunch $9-$16; dinner $16-$25. **Credit** AmEx, DC, Disc, MC, V. **Map** p304 A2.
With its orange walls, vivid paintings, pulsating music, sharp Margaritas, crowded bar and dining area and spicy New Mexican cuisine, this place is hot. Celebrity chefs/owners Mary Sue Milliken and Susan Feniger (who host a TV food show called *Too Hot Tamales*) have been instrumental in putting healthy gourmet cuisine on the map. Recommended: green corn tamales with salsa fresca, and Pescado Vera-cruzano: Chilean sea bass, pan-seared in a white wine broth with olives, onions, tomatoes and jalapeños.

Cezanne Le Merigot
Le Merigot, 1740 Ocean Avenue, at Pico Boulevard (1-310 395 9700). Bus 33, Santa Monica 8/I-10, exit Fourth-Fifth Street south. **Open** 6am-2.30pm,

6-10pm Mon-Fri; 7am-2pm, 6-11pm Sat; times vary Sun. **Main courses** breakfast $12-$22, lunch & dinner $16-$23. **Credit** AmEx, MC, V. **Map** p304 A3.
Cezanne is trying to put the oomph and panache back into hotel dining. The new chef had yet to revamp the French menu as this guide went to press, but all the food we sampled was inventive and polished. A welcome addition to an area where so-so beach dining proliferates. The dining room is all over-the-top opulence. *See also p44.*

Chez Jay
1657 Ocean Avenue, between Pico Boulevard & Colorado Avenue (1-310 395 1741). Bus 33, 333, Santa Monica 7, 8/I-10, exit Fourth-Fifth Street north. **Open** noon-2pm, 6-10.30pm Mon-Fri; 9am-10.30pm Sat; 9am-11pm Sun. **Main courses** $15-$24. **Credit** AmEx, MC, V. **Map** p304 A3.
Ten tables, a dozen bar stools, a massive schooner wheel, real portholes and sawdust on the floor: this is the beachfront roadhouse that owner Jay Fiondella opened in 1959. It's low-key and funky, and the clientele includes a few celebrities in search of anonymity (Sean Penn, Warren Beatty and Henry Kissinger). The simple fare (steak au poivre or fish in old-fashioned, heavy sauces) isn't bad either.

Chinois on Main
2709 Main Street, at Hill Street (1-310 392 9025). Bus 33, 333, Santa Monica 8/I-10, exit Fourth Street south. **Open** 6-10.30pm Mon, Tue, Sat; 11.30am-2pm, 6-10.30pm Wed-Fri; 5.30-10pm Sun. **Main courses** $22-$36. **Credit** AmEx, DC, Disc, MC, V. **Map** p304 A4.
Some people believe this Wolfgang Puck eaterie is his finest. The cuisine goes by the name of Pacific New Wave, which means a mélange of different ethnicities (Asian, French, Californian) rolled into one, sometimes creating confusion, sometimes delighting, all with the backdrop of wife Barbara Lazaroff's kitsch design and the deliriously friendly staff. New chef Louis Diaz still cooks up some of the city's best barbecued baby pork ribs in a honey-chilli sauce and Shanghai lobster in spicy curry. *See also p143* Spago and *p135* Granita.

Gallego's
1424 Broadway, at 15th Street (1-310 395 0162). Bus Santa Monica 2/I-10, exit Lincoln Boulevard north. **Open** 7.30am-6pm Mon-Fri; 7.30am-4pm Sat; closed Sun. **Main courses** $2-$6. **Credit** AmEx, Disc, MC, V. **Map** p304 A2.
Economically priced fresh Mexican food. All the expected classics, such as tacos and burritos, with home-made tortillas. Take out or eat in.

Giorgio Baldi
114 W Channel Road, at Pacific Coast Highway (1-310 573 1660). Bus 434, Santa Monica 9/I-10, exit PCH north. **Open** 6-10pm daily. **Main courses** $15-$35. **Credit** AmEx, MC, V. **Map** p304 A1.
One of the few classic Italian restaurants by the beach. A slew of tables are tightly clustered in one room and enclosed patio where attentive waiters

cater to your every whim (if they can hear you above the din). It's pricey but worth it for the langoustine, home-made pasta dishes and star-spotting.

The Hump
Santa Monica Airport, 3221 Donald Douglas Loop South, off Stewart Avenue (1-310 313 0977). Bus Santa Monica 14/I-10, exit Bundy Drive south. **Open** noon-2pm, 6.30-10pm Mon-Thur; noon-2pm, 6-10pm Fri; 6-10pm Sat; closed Sun. **Main courses** $6-$10. **Credit** AmEx, DC, MC, V. **Map** p304 C4.
One of the city's coolest – albeit pricey – Japanese restaurants, divinely situated overlooking the runway within Santa Monica's small airport.

The Ivy at the Shore
1541 Ocean Avenue, at Colorado Avenue (1-310 393 3113). Bus 33, 333, Santa Monica 8/I-10, exit Fourth-Fifth Street north. **Open** 11.30am-10.30pm Mon-Fri; 11am-11.30 pm Sat, Sun. **Main courses** $25-$35. **Credit** AmEx, DC, MC, V. **Map** p304 A2.
This venerable institution is a mite pretentious, despite its beach-shack decor. Nevertheless, the American food (Caesar salads, crab cakes, pasta dishes) is unquestionably good, and it's fertile celebrity-spotting ground.

JiRaffe
502 Santa Monica Boulevard, at Fifth Street (1-310 917 6671). Bus 4, 304, Santa Monica 1, 10/I-10, exit Fourth-Fifth Street north. **Open** noon-2pm, 6-10pm Tue-Fri; 5.30-11pm Sat; 5.30-9pm Sun; closed Mon. **Main courses** lunch $11-$13; dinner $18-$24. **Credit** AmEx, DC, MC, V. **Map** p304 A 2/3.
Raphael Lunetta (sans partner; *see below* Melisse) continues the tradition of breathtaking French fare with flare: different pasta specials every day, duck breast from Sonoma with pineapple chutney and creamy polenta, roasted halibut with morel mushrooms, asparagus and tomato concasse in a black truffle mushroom sauce. One of Santa Monica's best restaurants.

The Lobster
1602 Ocean Avenue, at Colorado Avenue (1-310 458 9294). Bus 434, Santa Monica 2, 8/I-10, exit Fourth-Fifth Street south. **Open** 11.30am-10pm daily. **Main courses** $17-$24. **Credit** AmEx, DC, Disc, MC, V. **Map** p304 A2/3.
Housed in a sweeping glass structure that teeters at the foot of the Santa Monica pier, this new venture is a gentrified affair, offering attentive service and an upmarket wine list to accompany fish or meat choices. Crab Martini or romaine and endive salad with fried oysters are sublime to whet your appetite for hefty steamed Maine lobster.

Melisse
1104 Wilshire Boulevard, at 11th Street (1-310 395 0881). Bus 20, 720, Santa Monica 2/I-10, exit Lincoln Boulevard north. **Open** 6-10pm Mon, Tue, Sat; noon-1.30 pm, 6-10pm Wed-Fri; 6-9pm Sun. **Main courses** lunch $17-$21; dinner $25-$40. **Credit** AmEx, DC, Disc, MC, V. **Map** p304 B2.

When most partners split, it's a sad affair. Not so with Josiah Citrin, who left long-time surfing buddy and cooking partner Raphael Lunetta and restaurant JiRaffe (*see p129*). With his own restaurant, Melisse, a few blocks away, devotees get to double their pleasure. His classic-with-a-twist Provençal fare is presented with panache: the cucumber soup is served like a cappucino, complete with foam, in a espresso cup, while a poached egg whooshed up with lemon-infused crème fraîche is put back into its shell and then into a silver eggcup. Or there's roasted Maine lobster in a swirl of Thai green curry. All in all, it puts one in mind of a painting produced by the colliding talents of Georgia O'Keefe and Salvador Dali.

Michael's

1147 Third Street, between California Avenue & Wilshire Boulevard (1-310 451 0843). Bus 20, 720, Santa Monica 4/I-10, exit Fourth-Fifth Street north. **Open** 11.30am-2.30pm, 6-10.30pm Tue-Fri; 6-10.30pm Sat; closed Mon, Sun. **Main courses** lunch $16-$22; dinner $25-$34. **Credit** AmEx, MC, V. **Map** p304 A2.
Andrew Pastore is now at the helm of one of LA's oldest and most venerated restaurants – and also one of the prettiest. Sit in the garden beside trickling fountains and consume some of the best nouvelle food where it was first conceived. The service is witty and charming. It's pretty expensive, though.

Rae's

2901 Pico Boulevard, at 29th Street (1-310 828 7937). Bus Santa Monica 7/I-10, exit Pico Boulevard south. **Open** 5.30am-10pm daily. **Main courses** $4-$6. **No credit cards. Map** p304 C3.
A slick, turquoise, classic 1950s diner, so popular there are often queues around the block. Great for breakfast – try the '2 plus 2': two eggs, two strips of bacon or sausages and two pancakes.

Röckenwagner

2435 Main Street, at Ocean Park Boulevard (1-310 399 6504). Bus 33, 333, Santa Monica 8/I-10, exit Fourth-Fifth Street south. **Open** 11.30am-2.30pm, 6-10pm Tue-Fri; 9am-2pm, 5.30-10pm Sat, Sun; closed Mon. **Main courses** brunch $9-$17; dinner $23-$32. **Credit** AmEx, DC, MC, V. **Map** p304 A3.
Located in architect Frank Gehry's sculptural Edgemar Complex, this is the high-end restaurant that made German chef Hans Röckenwagner's name. It epitomises California cuisine in its marriage of eclectic and artistic food and decor; crab soufflé with sliced mango and lobster-butter sauce is his most popular dish. Also check out his new funkier restaurant Rock (*see p134*).

Rosalynn Thai Restaurant

2308 Lincoln Boulevard, at Pearl Street (1-310 397 2647). Bus Santa Monica 3/I-10, exit Lincoln Boulevard south. **Open** 11am-10pm daily. **Main courses** $6-$12. **Credit** MC, V. **Map** p304 B3.
Thai restaurants are two-a-penny in the Southland, but it's hard to find an exceptional one. This place is distinctive, with its 76-item menu, some unusual

dishes and attentive service. Recommendations: krathongtong, spicy scallops, duck salad, pad see yew, shrimp curry, and ginger ice-cream.

Royal Star Seafood Restaurant

3001 Wilshire Boulevard, at Stanford Avenue (1-310 828 8812). Bus 20, 720, Santa Monica 2/ I-10, exit Bundy Drive north. **Open** 11am-3pm, 5.30-10pm daily. **Main courses** from $4. **Credit** MC, V. **Map** p304 C2.
Outstanding Hong Kong-style Chinese food in opulent surroundings. Try the giant shrimp and the duck served with dumpling-like pancakes.

Sushi Roku

1401 Ocean Avenue, at Santa Monica Boulevard (1-310 458 4771). Bus 22/I-10, exit Fourth-Fifth Street north. **Open** 11.30am-2.30pm, 5.30-11.30pm Mon-Fri; noon-11.30pm Sat; 5.30-10pm Sun. **Main courses** lunch $13-$19; dinner $13-$30.**Credit** AmEx, DC, MC, V. **Map** p304 A2.
No prosaic California roll in a minimalist white-walled setting here. Designed in bizarre Zen-meets-Frank-Lloyd-Wright style, Sush Roku is an eclectic, sensual and complete dining experience. And its owners have had no problems drawing an upmarket hipster crowd. Try crispy tuna sashimi spring rolls with a chilli oil and beurre blanc sauce or seared yellow tail with balsamic dressing.

Typhoon

Santa Monica Airport, 3221 Donald Douglas Loop South, off Stewart Avenue (1-310 390 6565). Bus Santa Monica 14/I-10, exit Bundy Drive south. **Open** noon-3pm, 5.30-10.30pm Mon-Fri; 5.30-10.30pm Sat; 11.30am-3pm, 5.30-10.30pm Sun. **Main courses** lunch $8-$12; dinner $16-$28. **Credit** AmEx, DC, Disc, MC, V. **Map** p304 C4.
This Pan-Asian restaurant sits right on the runway of Santa Monica Airport, providing fabulous views of planes landing and taking off, as well as the mountains and city. You can sample excellent food from more than seven countries and scan for celebrities: Robert De Niro, Goldie Hawn and Val Kilmer love this place.

Valentino

3115 Pico Boulevard, at Centinela Avenue (1-310 829 4313). Bus Santa Monica 7/I-10, exit Centinela Avenue south. **Open** 5-11pm Mon-Thur, Sat, Sun; 11.30am-2.30pm, 5-11pm Fri. **Main courses** $22-$30. **Credit** AmEx, DC, Disc, MC, V. **Map** p304 C3.
Piero Selvaggio has awards coming out of his ears for this, his flagship restaurant; according to *Wine Spectator* magazine, it is one of the top Italian restaurants in the country. His wine cellar is also said by some to be the finest in the US. Ask Piero to put together a 'tasting plate' for you, and if you've got the money, splurge. *See also p157* Posto.

Also recommended

Capo (Italian) 1810 Ocean Avenue (1-310 394 5550); **Fritto Misto** (Italian) 601 Colorado Avenue (1-310 458 2829); **Remi** (Italian) 1451 Third Street Promenade (1-310 393 6545).

The adorably pretty **Ivy**: popular with celebs at lunchtime. *See p138.*

Venice

5 Dudley

5 Dudley Avenue, at Rose Avenue (1-310 399 6678).
Bus 33, 333, 436/I-10, exit Lincoln Boulevard south.
Open 6-10pm Tue-Sat; closed Mon, Sun. **Main**
courses $17-$32. **Credit** AmEx, MC, V.
Map p304 A4.
One of the city's hottest reservations. In part, this is
because the beachside restaurant is so small, but
also because the food – French-California eclectic –
is just great. There is no menu. The food (such as
Caesar salad designed to be eaten with the hands, or
rabbit en croute or venison) is joyfully recited and
often served by one of the four young chefs (all
friends or extended family). The place has a casual
vibe accented by a trip hop/acid jazz drum beat.

72 Market Street

72 Market Street, between Pacific Avenue &
Speedway (1-310 392 8720). Bus 33, 333, 436,
Santa Monica 2/I-10, exit Lincoln Boulevard south.
Open 11.30am-2.30pm, 6-10pm Mon-Thur; 11.30am-
2.30pm, 6-11pm Fri, Sat; 5.30-10.30pm Sun.
Main courses $13-$20. **Credit** AmEx, MC, V.
Map p304 A5.
The local artist community makes up the backbone
of the clientele at this upmarket restaurant, housed
in a minimalist space. Chef Robert Roaquin gives a
French, Asian and even Latin twist to the cooking.
But the staple American comfort foods instituted by
Leonard Schwartz (*see p142* Maple Drive) – such as
kick-ass chilli, meatloaf and the best mashed pota-
toes west of Ireland – linger proudly on the menu.
The oyster bar and grand piano remain, and you
may catch sight of the founding owners – actor
Dudley Moore and filmmaker Tony Bill.

Angels

636 Venice Boulevard, at Abbot Kinney Boulevard
(1-310 827 5878). Buses 33, 333, 436/I-405, exit
Venice Boulevard south. **Open** noon-2.30pm, 6-10pm
Mon-Wed; 10am-2pm, 6-10pm Thur-Sun. **Main**
courses brunch & lunch $9-$12; dinner $15-$25.
Credit AmEx, DC, Disc, MC, V. **Map** p304 A5.
British restaurateur Martin has taken over this airy
indoor/outdoor space and created a joyful, quasi-
Moroccan vibe, with orange and brown cushions
scattered over bench seating. The food, prepared by
Jason (the eldest OJ Simpson son), is clean, creative
world cuisine with Californian flair: turkey meatloaf, noodles with littleneck clams, paella and
Moroccan spiced lamb. On Sundays, there's an all-
you-can-eat barbecue.

Axe

1009 Abbot Kinney Boulevard, at Main Street
(1-310 664 9787). Bus 33, 333, 436, Santa Monica
1, 2/I-10, exit Lincoln Boulevard south. **Open**
11.30am-3pm, 6.30-10.30pm Tue-Fri; 9am-3pm,
6.30-10.30pm Sat; 9am-3pm Sun; closed Mon. **Main**
courses lunch $4-$14; dinner $10-$26. **Credit**
AmEx, DC, Disc, MC, V. **Map** p304 A4.
Fabulous minimalist setting – think Japan meets

Sweden – with wood benches, wicker chairs and
long wooden tables; and a short but esoteric menu
of beers and wines by the glass along with healthy,
organic and simple cuisine featuring salads, sandwiches, buckwheat soba noodles and hearty bowls
of chicken over rice. At night, things get more complex, with dishes such as black mussels drenched
in a broth of green curried coconut.

The Canal Club

2025 Pacific Avenue, at Venice Boulevard (1-310
306 6266). Bus Culver City 1/I-10, exit Lincoln
Boulevard south. **Open** 6-10pm Mon-Thur, Sun;
6-11pm Fri, Sat. **Main courses** $12-$30. **Credit**
AmEx, DC, MC, V. **Map** p304 A5.
A stylish new restaurant housed in an early Frank
Gehry landmark building, with an enormous sushi
and oyster bar. While away the evening with exotic
cocktails and everything from sushi to beef tacos
to swordfish to porterhouse. Make sure you're not
seated at the back.

The Fig Tree

429 Ocean Front Walk, at Rose Avenue (1-310 392
4937). Bus 33, 333, 436/I-10, exit Lincoln Boulevard
south. **Open** 9am-9pm daily. **Main courses** $7-$15.
Credit AmEx, DC, MC, V. **Map** p304 A4.
Get front seats for the spectacle that is Venice
Boardwalk and eat healthily and heartily at the
locals' favourite oceanside brunch hangout. All the
vegetables are organic; cakes and desserts are
sweetened only with honey or fruit juice. Highly
recommended (if you go on an empty stomach) are
the oat or cornmeal pancakes stuffed with blue-
berries or banana and served with apple butter and
pure maple syrup.

Hal's Bar & Grill

1349 Abbot Kinney Boulevard, at California Avenue
(1-310 396 3105). Bus Santa Monica 2/I-10, exit
Lincoln Boulevard south. **Open** 11.30am-3pm, 6pm-
midnight Mon-Fri; 6pm-midnight Sat, Sun. **Main**
courses lunch $8-$14; dinner $14-$22. **Credit**
AmEx, DC, Disc, MC, V. **Map** p304 A5.
A mainstay for the local Venetian bourgeoisie, real
and wannabe artists and artistes. The place is a bit
like an aircraft hangar, with the same horrible
acoustics, but the bar is long, the booths enticing and
the Californian food upmarket (though overpriced).
Supposedly an excellent pick-up spot.

James' Beach

60 N Venice Boulevard, at Pacific Avenue (1-310
823 5396). Bus 333, 436/I-10, exit Lincoln
Boulevard south. **Open** 6-10.30pm Mon, Tue;
11.30am-3pm, 6-10.30pm Wed-Fri; 10am-3pm,
6-10.30pm Sat, Sun. **Main courses** lunch $9-$30;
brunch $9-$15; dinner $12-$30. **Credit** AmEx, DC,
MC, V. **Map** p304 A5.
Formerly located on Market Street, James Evans's
restaurant serves American favourites such as
chicken pot pie, with a new spin. There's a bar inside
and another on the covered patio, adding to the fun,
neighbourhood vibe.

Eat, Drink, Shop

Joe's

*1023 Abbot Kinney Boulevard, between Broadway &
Westminster Avenues (1-310 399 5811). Bus 33,
333, 436, Santa Monica 2/I-10, exit Lincoln
Boulevard south.* **Open** 11.30am-2.30pm, 6-11pm
Tue-Fri; 11am-3pm, 6-11pm Sat, Sun; closed Mon.
Main courses lunch $11-$14; dinner $18-$24.
Credit AmEx, MC, V. **Map** p304 A4.

Joe's unassuming shopfront – which stands out
wildly in this restaurant-heavy, artsy section of
town – has expanded next door. The place still has
that hard-to-find low-key feel, though, and the
French-Californian food will bring tears of joy to
your eyes. Try warm onion tart with gravadlax
and crème fraîche, followed by roast pork tender-
loin, potatoes, wild mushrooms and roasted garlic
juice. There's also a small bar, a small patio and a
fixed-price menu.

Venus of Venice

*1234 Venice Boulevard, between Grand View Avenue
& Inglewood Boulevard, Mar Vista (1-310 391
7674). Bus 33, 333, 436/I-10, exit Bundy Drive
south.* **Open** 11am-3pm, 5-8pm Tue-Fri; 11am-8pm
Sat, Sun; closed Mon. **Main courses** lunch $5-$10;
dinner $7-$12. **No credit cards.**

Although it's moved from Venice to Mar Vista, this
restaurant is still one of a kind, reminiscent of a
Southern truckstop, wherein eccentric owner Venus
is a law unto herself. She whispers like Blanche
Dubois, usually dresses in long pink dresses and
serves up an array of home-made, vegetarian health
food at a leisurely pace.

Also recommended

Abbot's Pizza (pizza) 1407 Abbot Kinney
Boulevard (1-310 396 7334).

Marina del Rey

Alejo's Trattoria

*4002 Lincoln Boulevard, at Washington Boulevard
(1-310 822 0095). Bus Culver City 1, 2, Santa
Monica 3/Hwy 90, exit Lincoln Boulevard north.*
Open 11am-10pm Mon-Fri; 4-10.30pm Sat, Sun.
Main courses $6-$10. **Credit** AmEx, Disc, MC, V.

This Italian- and Argentinian-owned joint is a fabulous, cheap and fun place to eat spaghetti with
clams or any other authentic Italian trattoria-style
food you care to name. It doesn't have a licence, so
pop to the shop next door and buy some wine to
accompany your meal.

Aunt Kizzy's Back Porch

*Villa Marina Marketplace, 4325 Glencoe Avenue,
between Mindanao Way & Maxella Avenue (1-310
578 1005). Bus 108, 220/Hwy 90, exit Mindanao
Way north.* **Open** 11am-10pm Mon-Thur; 11am-
11pm Fri, Sat; 4-10pm Sun. **Set menus** lunch $6.95;
dinner $11.95, $12.95. **Credit** AmEx.

Signed photos of black celebs line the walls of this
cheerful, popular soul-food haunt tucked away in a
mini-mall. If you're not cholesterol-conscious, it's a
great place to sample comfort food, Southern style.

Benny's BBQ

*4077 Lincoln Boulevard, between Maxella Avenue &
Washington Boulevard (1-310 821 6939). Bus Santa
Monica 3/Hwy 90, exit Lincoln Boulevard north.*
Open 11am-10pm Mon-Fri; noon-10pm Sat; 3-10pm
Sun. **Main courses** $4-$9. **Credit** AmEx, MC, V.

This is a Marina del Rey institution, providing the
neighbourhood with smoky ribs and fab hot links
(sausages) from an oakwood barbecue.

Café del Rey

*4451 Admiralty Way, between Bali & Palawan Ways
(1-310 823 6395). Bus 108, Santa Monica 3/Hwy
90, exit Mindanao Way west.* **Open** 11.30am-2.30pm,
5.30-10pm Mon-Thur; 11.30am-2.30pm, 5.30-10.30pm
Fri, Sat; 10.30am-2.30pm, 5-10pm Sun. **Main
courses** lunch $8-$16; dinner $24-$39. **Credit**
AmEx, DC, Disc, MC, V.

A beautiful setting overlooking the marina, coupled
with an excellent fusion of French and Pacific Rim
cuisine by executive chef Katsuo Nagasawa, makes
Café del Rey an excellent choice for Sunday brunch,
a watery dinner or simply when you're peckish after
dropping off someone at LAX. Prices are reasonable.

Killer Shrimp

*523 Washington Street, at Ocean Avenue (1-310
578 2293). Bus 108, Culver City 1/Hwy 90, exit
Lincoln Boulevard north.* **Open** 11.30am-10pm
Mon-Thur, Sun; 11.30am-11pm Fri, Sat. **Set menus**
$13.95, $15.95. **Credit** MC, V.

For some of the best shrimp west of the Bayou, head
to this chain chow house. Eat shrimps, peeled or
unpeeled, with Bayou butter or pepper sauce, served
with bread, rice or spaghetti, on paper plates.

Rock

*13455 Maxella Avenue, at Lincoln Boulevard (1-310
822 8979). Bus 108, Commuter Express 437/Hwy
90, exit Lincoln Boulevard north.* **Open** 11.30am-
2pm, 5-10pm Mon-Fri; 5-10pm Sat; closed Sun.
Main courses lunch $9-$14; dinner $11-$18. **Credit**
AmEx, DC, MC, V.

A funkier and more affordable spin-off of Hans
Röckenwagner's restaurant in Santa Monica (*see
page 130* Röckenwagner). A mishmash of a menu
with mains including a series of 'ciabattas' – home-
made bread with fillings such as red pepper and aioli
or fontina, asparagus or mushrooms drizzled with
white truffle oil. Or there's more traditional filet
mignon with truffle fries or crispy skinned striped
bass with a curry sauce, tomato fondue and rice.

Malibu

Geoffrey's

*27400 Pacific Coast Highway, at Latigo Canyon
Road (1-310 457 1519). Bus 434/I-10, exit PCH
north.* **Open** noon-10pm Mon-Thur; noon-11pm Fri;
11am-11pm Sat; 10.30am-10pm Sun. **Main courses**
lunch $16-$22; dinner $18-$30. **Credit** AmEx, MC, V.

Dining on Geoffrey's cliffside deck, you could swear
you're on the French Riviera. But the hearty, eclectic
Californian menu, the California-heavy wine list and

Eat, Drink, Shop

A carnivore's delight: **Nick & Stef's** steakhouse. *See p154.*

the Ray Ban-clad waiters soon set you straight. The good food, exceptional view (featured in films *The Player* and *Guilty by Suspicion*) and the harmonious service make the drive worthwhile. A good choice for Sunday brunch.

Gladstone's 4 Fish
17300 Pacific Coast Highway, at Sunset Boulevard (1-310 454 3474). Bus 434/I-10, exit PCH north. **Open** 7am-11pm Mon-Thur, Sun; 7am-midnight Fri, Sat. **Main courses** lunch $10-$17; dinner $10-$40. **Credit** AmEx, DC, Disc, MC, V.
The busiest Greyhound refuelling stop on the PCH: seagulls and tourists alike flock here for fresh seafood right on the beach. If you don't like having your name called over a megaphone and being treated like one of the hungry 3,000 (which is the average number of customers served per day), this isn't the place for you.

Granita
23725 W Malibu Road, at Webb Way (1-310 456 0488). Bus 434/I-10, exit PCH north. **Open** 6-10pm Mon, Tue; 11.30am-2pm, 6-10pm Wed-Fri; 11am-2pm, 5.30-11pm Sat, Sun. **Main courses** $26-$34. **Credit** MC, V.
Wolfgang Puck's restaurant in Malibu Colony Plaza. The food is California-Provençal with Asian influences; the interior is beach chic, styled, as always, by Puck's wife and partner Barbara Lazaroff. The open kitchen allows you to see new chef Jennifer Naylor prepare such dishes as crispy tempura softshell crab with radicchio-kaiware salad, pickled

ginger and black bean vinaigrette. The fashionable bar has become a place to spy celebs from the Colony. *See also p143* Spago and *p129* Chinois on Main.

Neptune's Net
42505 Pacific Coast Highway, just north of Leo S Carrillo State Beach (1-310 457 3095). Bus 434/I-10, exit PCH north. **Open** 10.30am-8pm daily. **Main courses** $2-$100. **Credit** AmEx, MC, V.
A funky seafood joint that's been around for 30 or so years, where you'll find plenty of locals diving into steamed, grilled or fried plates of shellfish. Eat inside or outside with everyone from bikers and their chicks to surfing pals.

Nobu
Malibu Country Mart, 3853 Cross Creek Road, at Pacific Coast Highway (1-310 317 9140). Bus 434/I-10, exit PCH north. **Open** 5.45-10pm Mon-Thur, Sun; 5.45-11pm Fri, Sat. **Main courses** $8-$30. **Credit** AmEx, DC, MC, V.
This is renowned chef Nobuyuki Matsuhisa's Malibu joint. Expect the usual array of non-traditional surprises – with the chef's well-judged use of garlic, fresh chilli and sauces – at this elegant Japanese-with-a-hint-of-Peruvian spot. *See also p142* Matsuhisa and *p141* Ubon.

Taverna Tony
23410 Civic Center Way, at Cross Creek Road (1-310 317 9667). Bus 434/I-10, exit Pacific Coast Highway north. **Open** 11.30am-11.30pm daily. **Main courses** $8-$25. **Credit** AmEx, Disc, MC, V.

Nic's: great bar and music. *See p142.*

A Greek taverna loved by locals for its good food, hospitable service and general party atmosphere, not to mention the breathtaking views of the Santa Monica Mountains from the outside patio.

Tra di Noi

3835 Cross Creek Road, at Pacific Coast Highway (1-310 456 0169). Bus 434/I-10, exit PCH north. **Open** 11.30am-3pm, 5.30-10.30pm daily. **Main courses** $12-$19. **Credit** AmEx, MC, V.
Popular – if pricey – local haunt with a delightful patio, serving solid, upscale Italian favourites.

Westside: Inland

West Hollywood & Melrose

Asia de Cuba

Mondrian Hotel, 8440 Sunset Boulevard, at La Cienega Boulevard (1-323 848 6000). Bus 2, 3, 302/I-10, exit La Cienega Boulevard north. **Open** 11.30am-3.30pm, 6-11pm, 11.30pm-2am daily. **Main courses** $55-$65 for two people. **Credit** AmEx, DC, MC, V. **Map** p306 A/B1.
Alice in Wonderland-like giant doors lead the way into Ian Schrager's ultimate hip creation. You'll find yourself in the minimalist, all-white interior (where the table legs have painted socks) or outside between gargantuan flower pots, overlooking the pool or the city, or gazing longingly at the SkyBar (*see p168*) – it may be the closest you'll get to it. Try the fried calamari salad and Hunan wok-fried fish with crab dressing and the lamb palmetto. The prices are sky-high, the Latino-inspired food a bit hit and miss. But oh, what a setting!

Boxer

7615 Beverly Boulevard, between Curson & Stanley Avenues (1-323 932 6178). Bus 14, 316/ I-10, exit Fairfax Avenue north. **Open** 11.30am-2.30pm, 6.30-11.30pm Tue-Fri; 10am-2.30pm, 6.30-11.30pm Sat; 10am-2pm, 6.30-11.30pm Sun; closed Mon. **Main courses** $16-$22. **Credit** AmEx, DC, Disc, MC, V. **Map** p306 C2.
Owner Steven Arroyo wanted to give a certain 'punchiness' to his one-room restaurant – hence the name. It's difficult to choose from the inventive Cal-eclectic menu, but we recommend the New York steak with roasted Peruvian potatoes and grilled asparagus, and the butter-roasted lobster tail with carrot ricotta ravioli and black mussels. The place attracts a stylish but unpretentious crowd.

Cadillac Café

359 N La Cienega Boulevard, between Beverly Boulevard & Oakwood Avenue (1-310 657 6591). Bus 14, 105, 576/I-10, exit La Cienega Boulevard north. **Open** 11am-11pm Mon-Thur; 11am-midnight Fri; 10am-midnight Sat, Sun. **Main courses** $9-$18. **Credit** AmEx, MC, V. **Map** p306 A/B2.
A funky, friendly café serving up some very competent American comfort food with an ironic twist in a kitschy Jetsons-style setting. We cannot recommend the French toast enough, nor the coconut banana pancakes for brunch and the blackened meatloaf with a side order of 'curly Q' fries.

Café Med

8615 Sunset Boulevard, at Sunset Plaza (1-310 652 0445). Bus 2, 3, 302/I-10, exit La Cienega Boulevard north. **Open** 11am-11.30pm Mon-Thur; 11.30am-midnight Fri-Sun. **Main courses** $11-$14. **Credit** AmEx, Disc, MC, V. **Map** p306 A1.
This could be the least pretentious and most fun of the Sunset Plaza pavement restaurants – if it weren't for the Eurotrash clientele. Try piadina bread with stracchino cheese and rocket, then the pasta al mare with a beautifully dressed tricolore salad.

Chaya Brasserie

8741 Alden Drive, at Robertson Boulevard (1-310 859 8833). Bus 220, DASH Fairfax/I-10, exit La Cienega Boulevard north. **Open** 11.30am-2.30pm, 6pm-midnight Mon-Fri; 6pm-midnight Sat; 6-10pm Sun. **Main courses** lunch $9-$20; dinner $14-$28. **Credit** AmEx, DC, MC, V. **Map** p306 A3.
This posh but friendly restaurant serves excellent Mediterranean-French dishes with Pacific Rim influences, in a pretty colonial-style setting, with large trees stretching to the high ceiling. It's been a mainstay of the area for some time, attracting surgeons from nearby Cedars Sinai hospital, film execs from New Line Cinema, and art and antiques dealers from Robertson Boulevard and Beverly Hills.

Chianti Cucina

7383 Melrose Avenue, at Martel Avenue (1-323 653 8333). Bus 10, 11/I-10, exit Fairfax Avenue north. **Open** *Chianti* 5.30-10.30pm Mon-Thur, Sun; 5.30-11pm Fri, Sat. *Cucina* 11.30am-11.30pm Mon-Thur; 11.30am-midnight Fri, Sat; 4-11pm Sun. **Main**

Eat, Drink, Shop

courses *Chianti* $18-$35; *Cucina* $17-$23. **Credit** AmEx, DC, MC, V. **Map** p306 C2.
Two restaurants that share the same kitchen. On the left is Chianti: opened in 1938, it's dark, formal, expensive and romantic, with a bar. On the right is Cucina: contemporary and airy. The food in both places is outstanding modern northern Italian.

China One
8290 Santa Monica Boulevard, at Sweetzer Avenue (1-323 656 2215). Bus 4, 304/I-10, exit Fairfax Avenue north. **Open** 11.30am-10.30pm Mon-Thur, Sun; noon-midnight Fri, Sat. **Main courses** $8-$15. **Credit** AmEx, DC, Disc, MC, V. **Map** p306 B1.
Cheap, festive, one-room Chinese restaurant, with a small patio, owned in part by Wesley Snipes. Don't leave without sampling the crackerjack shrimp and spicy cashew pork and shrimp with lobster sauce.

Dan Tana's
9071 Santa Monica Boulevard, at Doheny Drive (1-310 275 9444). Bus 4, 304/I-10, exit Robertson Boulevard north. **Open** 5pm-1am daily. **Main courses** $16-$40. **Credit** AmEx, DC, Disc, MC, V. **Map** 4 A2.
This friendly, vivacious late-night restaurant and bar has been hanging in there since 1964 and is still bursting at the seams with film and TV stars, sports personalities and the rank and file of the movie industry. It offers consistently good, if simple, old-fashioned Italian food served with panache and humour by a loyal staff.

Dominick's
8715 Beverly Boulevard, between Robertson & San Vicente Boulevards (1-310 652 7272). Bus 14, 220, DASH West Hollywood/I-10, exit La Cienega Boulevard north. **Open** 7pm-12.30am Mon-Thur, Sun; 7pm-2am Fri, Sat. **Main courses** $12-$28. **Credit** AmEx, MC, V. **Map** p306 A2.
John Sidell, former husband of Rosanna Arquette and founder of such hip joints as the Good Luck Bar (*see p171*) and Jones (*see p138*) is also responsible for Dominick's. It's his spin on the renowned hang-out (a favourite of Frank Sinatra and his Rat Pack), reopened one door down from the original. It has a nautical-meets-cabana motif with a patio, an intimate bar and racing green-coloured booths. It appeals to musicians, artists, writers and the odd actor, who appreciate a late-night watering hole. Pared-down American classic menu.

El Coyote
7312 Beverly Boulevard, between Poinsettia Place & Fuller Avenue (1-323 939 2255). Bus 14/I-10, exit La Brea Avenue north. **Open** 11am-10pm Mon-Thur, Sun; 11am-11pm Fri, Sat. **Main courses** $7-$10. **Credit** MC, V. **Map** p306 C2.
People generally don't come here for the food but to soak up the carefree atmosphere and the Margaritas in the indoor red booths or on the outdoor enclosed front patio. After 65 years in business, it's an institution, maybe because of its anti-snob vibe. If you're not a courageous eater, try the chicken and rice.

Fenix at the Argyle
8358 Sunset Boulevard, betweeen Sweetzer Avenue & La Cienega Boulevard (1-323 654 7100). Bus 2, 3, 302/I-10, exit La Cienega Boulevard north. **Open** 7am-2.30pm, 6-10.30pm Mon-Sat; 10am-3pm Sun. **Main courses** lunch $14-$20; dinner $23-$34. **Credit** AmEx, DC, MC, V. **Map** p306 B1.
This authentic art deco hotel is a delightful, upmarket spot for brunch, lunch or dinner – with Sunday brunch a favourite. Sit on the patio overlooking the pool for an extraordinary view of the city. The food is upscale Californian.

Gaucho Grill
7980 Sunset Boulevard, at Crescent Heights Boulevard (1-323 656 4152). Bus 2, 3, 105, 302/I-10, exit Fairfax Avenue north. **Open** 11am-11pm Mon-Thur, Sun; 11am-midnight Sat. **Credit** AmEx, DC, MC, V. **Map** p306 B1.
Part of a fun, well-priced Argentinian restaurant chain. This branch is perfectly located for a bite before or after watching a movie or browsing around the Virgin Megastore at the adjacent Sunset 5 mall. Excellent beef ribs and boneless, skinless, spicy chicken dishes served with rice or 'curly Q' fries.

The best Upmarket

Citrus
Head to Hollywood for imaginative Californian-French food in a classy 'inside outside' setting. See page 148.

La Cachette
Chef Jean-François Meteigner presides over this award-winning French restaurant in Century City. See page 148.

L'Orangerie
In business for 20 years, this aristocratic spot in West Hollywood is the place for classic French cuisine. See page 139.

Melisse
Classic Provençal fare – with an inventive twist – at Josiah Citrin's new venture in Santa Monica. See page 129.

Patina
Hollywood stars flock to Joachim Splichal's esoteric Californian restaurant on Melrose Avenue. See page 149.

Valentino
Piero Selvaggio's flagship Italian restaurant in Santa Monica. One of the best in the US – and a fantastic wine cellar, too. See page 130.

Eat, Drink, Shop

Dine in the gorgeous garden at the hidden **Les Deux Café**. *See p149.*

Branch: 1251 Third Street Promenade, between Arizona Avenue & Wilshire Boulevard, Santa Monica (1-310 394 4966).

Hirozen

8385 Beverly Boulevard, between Orlando Avenue & La Cienega Boulevard (1-323 653 0470). Bus 14, 105/I-10, exit La Cienega Boulevard north. **Open** 6-10pm daily. **Main courses** $20-$25. **Credit** AmEx, DC, Disc, MC, V. **Map** p306 B2.

Hidden in a corner of a nondescript mini-mall, this is one of the finest and most unpretentious Japanese restaurants in town. Apart from traditional sushi offerings, iconoclast chef Hiro conjures up some truly ethereal dishes. Any conoisseur of Japanese food knows about this joint, so come early or be prepared to wait.

Indochine

8225 Beverly Boulevard, between Harper & La Jolla Avenues (1-323 655 4777). Bus 14/I-10, exit Fairfax Avenue north. **Open** 6-11pm daily. **Main courses** $15-$20. **Credit** AmEx, DC, Disc, MC, V. **Map** p306 B2.

This Vietnamese restaurant housed in the old Monkey Bar has become as much an institution in LA as has its cousin in Manhattan, attracting a bustling crowd of artistes, beautiful people and star-gazers, who enjoy the sultry tropical decor and the light fare. Try the oxtail broth with sliced fillet of beef, rice noodles and bean sprouts or the spicy sliced chicken breast with lemongrass, Asian basil and sweet-potato crisps.

Ita Cho

7311 Beverly Boulevard, between Fuller Avenue & Poinsettia Place (1-323 938 9009). Bus 14/I-10, exit La Brea Avenue north. **Open** noon-3pm, 6-11pm Mon-Thur; noon-3pm, 6pm-midnight Fri; 6pm-midnight Sat; closed Sun. **Main courses** $12-$25. **Credit** MC, V. **Map** p306 C2.

Now moved from its funkier location in a strip mall on an iffy side of town, Japanese Ita Cho serves some sublime sashimi and vegetable dishes, but no sushi.

Itana Bahia

8711 Santa Monica Boulevard, between Hancock Avenue & Huntley Drive (1-310 657 6306). Bus 4, 304, DASH West Hollywood/I-10, exit La Cienega Boulevard north. **Open** noon-11pm Tue-Fri; noon-10pm Sat, Sun; closed Mon. **Main courses** $8-$20. **Credit** AmEx, MC, V. **Map** p306 A2.

A tiny and increasingly popular Brazilian restaurant decorated with indigenous musical instruments, serving some of the more exotic and challenging foods of the Bahia region.

The Ivy

113 N Robertson Boulevard, between Third Street & Beverly Boulevard (1-310 274 8303). Bus 220, DASH Fairfax/I-10, exit Robertson Boulevard north. **Open** 11.30am-4.30pm, 5-11pm daily. **Main courses** lunch $16-$33; dinner $18-$35. **Credit** AmEx, MC, V. **Map** p306 A1/2.

Service sometimes borders on rude or inattentive, but that doesn't seem to affect the status of this landmark Californian restaurant in a converted house complete with adorably pretty patio. It's great for star-spotting, especially at lunchtime; it also serves excellent salads, crab cakes and fresh fish dishes. The white-chocolate lemon and walnut cake covered in flowers and fruit is otherworldly.

Jones

7205 Santa Monica Boulevard, between Poinsettia Place & Formosa Avenue (1-323 850 1726/7). Bus 4, 304, DASH West Hollywood/I-10, exit La Brea Avenue north. **Open** noon-4.30pm, 7.30pm-1.30am Mon-Fri; 7.30pm-1.30am Sat, Sun. **Main courses** lunch $7-$25; dinner $10-$25. **Credit** AmEx, Disc, MC, V. **Map** p306 C1.

Sean MacPhearson has the trend thing down. His 1930s-retro restaurant/bar has a nightclub atmosphere and attracts the hippest younger set plus a spattering of celebs. There's even a stern doorman who checks your reservation before letting you in. Try the Caesar salad with a pizza and ignore the sometimes supercilious attitude of the other diners. Reservations or connections a must.

Joss

9255 Sunset Boulevard, at Doheny Drive (1-310 276 1886). Bus 2, 3, 302/I-10, exit La Cienega Boulevard north. **Open** noon-3pm, 6-10.30pm Mon-Thur; noon-3pm, 6-11pm Fri; 6-11pm Sat; 6-10.30pm Sun. **Main courses** lunch $10-$15; dinner $15-$20. **Credit** AmEx, DC, MC, V. **Map** p306 A1.

At last, a restaurant where you can eat dim sum for both lunch and dinner. It's an upmarket celeb hangout with a minimalist design, where the food is innovative and the atmosphere cool. An eclectic mix of Cantonese, Mandarin and Szechuan dishes, but lobster is a speciality.

Jozu

8360 Melrose Avenue, between Flores Street & Kings Road (1-323 655 5600). Bus 10, 11/I-10, exit La Cienega Boulevard north. **Open** 6-10pm Mon-Thur, Sun; 5.30-10.30pm Fri, Sat. **Main courses** $17-$25. **Credit** AmEx, DC, Disc, MC, V. **Map** p306 B2.

One of LA's A-list restaurants, offering tranquillity, exquisite Pacific New Wave dishes and lots of sake.

Le Colonial

8783 Beverly Boulevard, at Robertson Boulevard (1-310 289 0660). Bus 14, 220, DASH West Hollywood/I-10, exit Robertson Boulevard north. **Open** 11.30am-2pm, 5.30-11pm Mon-Wed, Sun; 11.30am-2pm, 5.30pm-midnight Thur-Sat. **Main courses** lunch $12-$20; dinner $18-$30. **Credit** AmEx, DC, MC, V. **Map** p306 A2.

Athough the designers have outdone themselves evoking a French-Vietnamese colonial joint – with a hip and inviting lounge bar – some say it's quicker to order a pizza on your mobile phone; it will arrive long before the waitress does. However, if you can get a table outside, Le Colonial is really very romantic and the banh cuon (Vietnamese ravioli stuffed with shrimp, chicken and mushroom) will take a long time to forget.

Le Dôme

8720 Sunset Boulevard, between Horn Avenue & Sunset Plaza Drive (1-310 659 6919). Bus 2, 3, 302, DASH West Hollywood/I-10, exit La Cienega Boulevard north. **Open** noon-11.30pm Mon-Fri; 6pm-midnight Sat; closed Sun. **Main courses** $18-$45. **Credit** AmEx, DC, Disc, MC, V. **Map** p306 A1.

An LA institution where all the major players of the film industry chow down for lunch and sometimes dinner. Where they seat you, dahling, is everything – personally, we prefer the new front patio. There are some creative and hedonistic dishes on the New French menu, with quite a few options for those ever-shrinking 'salad girls'.

Lola's

945 N Fairfax Avenue, at Romaine Street (1-213 736 5652). Bus 217/I-10, exit Fairfax Avenue north. **Open** 5.30pm-2am daily. **Main courses** $10-$15. **Credit** AmEx, MC, V. **Map** p306 B2.

As much a place to hang out as a restaurant, Lola's has an exceptional Martini list (we recommend the dark-and-white-chocolate variety) and an international menu that allows you to snack (crispy calamari, crab cakes and chicken satay) at the bar, in the living room or while playing a game of pool. Or dine more sedately on less-than-stellar entrées at high prices in the dining room or on the patio.

L'Orangerie

903 N La Cienega Boulevard, between Melrose Avenue & Santa Monica Boulevard (1-310 652 9770). Bus 10, 11, 105/I-10, exit La Cienega Boulevard north. **Open** 6-11pm Tue-Sun; closed Mon. **Main courses** $36-$50. **Credit** AmEx, DC, Disc, MC, V. **Map** p306 A/B2.

Classic French cuisine in an aristocratic setting, now celebrating its 20th year. Owners Gérard Ferry and his wife Virgine have imported 26-year-old Ludovic Lefèbvre, who worked at two three-star restaurants in Paris, and the food remains as inspired as ever. The restaurant is dripping with towering flower arrangements and the more private garden room has a ceiling that pulls back to reveal the stars. Plenty of stars seated at the tables, too.

The Los Angeles Palm

9001 Santa Monica Boulevard, at Robertson Boulevard (1-310 550 8811). Bus 4, 220, 304, DASH West Hollywood/I-10, exit Robertson Boulevard north. **Open** noon-10.30pm Mon-Fri; 5-10.30pm Sat; 5-9.30pm Sun. **Main courses** lunch $16-$30; dinner $20-$60. **Credit** AmEx, MC, V. **Map** p306 A2.

A spin-off of the Palm in NYC, which opened in the 1920s, the LA version has survived intact for more than 20 years and is still doing a rip-roaring trade, so expect to wait for your table. The chop-house fare – steak and lobster – all comes in man-sized portions, only fitting for the predominantly macho crowd that comes to celebrate freshly inked deals.

Mandalay

611 N La Brea Avenue, between Melrose Avenue & Beverly Boulevard (1-323 933 0717). Bus 212/I-10, exit La Brea Avenue north. **Open** 6pm-midnight daily. **Main courses** $10-$18. **Credit** AmEx, DC, Disc, MC, V. **Map** p306 C2.

Red leatherette booths, Asian tapestries and an abundance of dark wood furnish the main dining room at this hip, sophisticated restaurant. The menu is California Asian, and there's also a sushi bar.

Morton's

8764 Melrose Avenue, at Robertson Boulevard (1-310 276 5205). Bus 10, 11, 220, DASH West Hollywood/I-10, exit Robertson Boulevard north. **Open** noon-3pm, 6-11.30pm Mon-Fri; 6-11.30pm Sat; closed Sun. **Main courses** $16-$30. **Credit** AmEx, DC, MC, V. **Map** p306 A2.

Hard Rock Café founder Peter Morton owns this upmarket restaurant, a bastion of the power luncheon and dinner crowd. Reminiscent of a cosy aircraft hangar, if such a thing could exist, it offers a tranquil setting at tables masked by tall palms or at the bar presided over by Jack Martin (voted LA's best bartender by *Los Angeles* magazine). The American menu with a Californian twist isn't overly ambitious, but it's very serviceable.

Orso

8706 W Third Street, at Hamel Road (1-310 274 7144). Bus 16, DASH Fairfax/I-10, exit La Cienega Boulevard north. **Open** 11.45am-11pm daily. **Main courses** $12-$27. **Credit** MC, V. **Map** p306 A3.

Sitting on the back patio, you could feel as if you were taking a vacation from Los Angeles – if it weren't for all those celebrities. Regular Faye Dunaway is known to the waiting staff as Fadin' Away. Timid Jennifer Jason Leigh chooses a corner table, close to the foliage. The house wine is excellent, the pizzas are thinner than the girls that dine on them and the liver and onions is tremendous. And the pasta, particularly the taglierini served with clams, is superb.

Pastis

8114 Beverly Boulevard, between Fairfax Avenue & La Cienega Boulevard (1-323 655 8822). Bus 14, 316/I-10, exit La Cienega Boulevard north. **Open** noon-2.30pm, 6-10pm Mon-Thur; noon-2.30pm, 6-11pm Fri; 6-11pm Sat; 5.30-9pm Sun. **Main courses** lunch $9-$12; dinner $15-$18. **Credit** AmEx, DC, Disc, MC, V. **Map** p306 B2.

A fabulously authentic French restaurant that is perfect for romantic evenings or business lunches, with excellent, unpretentious service, a few pavement tables and real French waiters.

The Pig

612 N La Brea Avenue, between Melrose Avenue & Beverly Boulevard (1-323 935 1116). Bus 212/I-10, exit La Brea Avenue north. **Open** 11am-11pm Tue-Thur; 11am-1am Fri, Sat; 11am-9pm Sun; closed Mon. **Main courses** $6-$16. **Credit** AmEx, DC, MC, V. **Map** p306 C2.

The Pig attracts a late-night crowd, especially chefs coming off duty – and what better validation can a restaurant have? BBQ is the order of the day (and night) here: hickory-smoked baby back ribs, Cajun crusted Mississippi catfish and Memphis-style ribs.

Pink's Hot Dogs

709 N La Brea Avenue, at Melrose Avenue (1-323 931 4223). Bus 10, 11, 212/I-10, exit La Brea Avenue north. **Open** 9.30am-2am Mon-Thur, Sun; 9.30am-3am Fri, Sat. **Main courses** $2-$3. **No credit cards. Map** p306 C2.

This little hot dog stand has been pulling in the punters consistently since Paul Pink started his business with a pushcart in 1939. His chilli dogs went on to become the most popular in LA. It's one of the city's few late-night eateries – and the burgers and dogs are OK, too.

The Porch at the House of Blues

8430 Sunset Boulevard, at Olive Drive (1-323 848 5100). Bus 2, 3, 429/I-10, exit La Cienega Boulevard north. **Open** 11.30am-11pm Mon-Thur; 11.30am-midnight Fri, Sat; 9.30am-11pm Sun (brunch sittings 9.30am, noon, 2.30pm Sun). **Main courses** $10-$15. **Credit** AmEx, DC, Disc, MC, V. **Map** p304 B1.

The newly revamped upstairs restaurant inside this well-known blues club on Sunset Strip is now a separate and complete dining experience, serving hearty but refined Southern tucker and a wild Gospel Brunch on Sundays. Choose from Louisiana crawfish cakes, shrimp étouffée and smoked baby back ribs with Jack Daniels BBQ sauce.

Real Food Daily

414 N La Cienega Boulevard, between Melrose Avenue & Beverly Boulevard (1-310 289 9910). Bus 105, DASH Fairfax/I-10 exit La Cienega Boulevard north. **Open** 11.30am-11pm daily. **Main courses** $5-$12. **Credit** AmEx, MC, V. **Map** p306 B2.

Real Food is one of the few organic vegetarian restaurants in town. Freshly juiced fruits and vegetables, brown rice, tofu, aduki beans, salads and low-fat desserts are served in a strangely moderne setting. Stay away from the new-fangled specials and you'll be OK.

The Seabar at the Mondrian

Mondrian Hotel, 8440 Sunset Boulevard, at La Cienega Boulevard (1-323 848 6055). Bus 2, 3, 302/I-10, exit La Cienega Boulevard north. **Open** 6-11.30pm Tue-Thur; 6pm-1am Fri, Sat; closed Sun, Mon. **Main courses** $6-$18. **Credit** AmEx, DC, Disc, MC, V. **Map** p306 A/B1.

One long white marble table, dramatically lit from underneath, seats 32 guests. If you don't mind staring into the eyes of strangers opposite, it can be a culinary delight. High-grade flavoured sakes served at room temperature in wooden boxes accompany new-fangled dishes such as langoustine tempura rolls or 'fire & ice' (spicy fish served on ice). You can also order from the menu at the hotel's Asia de Cuba restaurant (*see p136*). To avoid the astronomical valet parking fees, park across the street at Pink Dot for $6 for the whole night.

Tail-o'-the-Pup

329 N San Vicente Boulevard, at Beverly Boulevard (1-310 652 4517). Bus 14, 550, DASH West Hollywood/I-10, exit La Cienega Boulevard north. **Open** 6am-5pm Mon-Sat; closed Sun. **Main courses** $2-$5. **No credit cards. Map** p306 A2.

You don't visit Tail, as it's familiarly called, for a gourmet experience. You visit it for a taste of the carefree, pre-cholesterol-conscious LA of the 1950s. It's a classic: a hot dog stand shaped like a giant hot dog, one of the few remaining examples of the buildings-as-signs that used to proliferate here. The Mexican Olé chilli dog and the Baseball Special are recommended.

Talesai

9043 Sunset Boulevard, at Doheny Drive (1-310 275 9724). Bus 2, 3, 302/I-10, exit La Cienega Boulevard north. **Open** 11.30am-2.30pm, 6-10.30pm Mon-Fri; 6-10.30pm Sat; closed Sun. **Main courses** $9-$20. **Credit** AmEx, MC, V. **Map** p306 A1.

The city is jammed with bargain Thai restaurants, but this is the upgraded gourmet version and it's well worth the trip into its cool and dark interiors. Order the Hidden Treasures (Thai versions of dim sum served in little clay covered pots), the pineapple fried rice and Phuket chicken.

Ubon

Beverly Center, 8500 Beverly Boulevard, at La Cienega Boulevard (1-310 854 1115). Bus 14, 105, 316/I-10, exit La Cienega Boulevard north. **Open** noon-10pm daily. **Main courses** $10-$15. **Credit** AmEx, MC, V. **Map** p306 A/B2.

Nobuyuki Matsuhisa's bistro – albeit Japanese-eclectic style – is conveniently located within the Beverly Center mall. It's decked out in minimalist modernist style in mustard and white, with an over-sized photo of the chef peering down over diners. While noodles, soba and udon with a variety of toppings are the specialities of the house, there are daily lunch and dinner specials that are nothing if not eclectic, plus a few sushi dishes. *See also p135* Nobu and *p142* Matsuhisa.

Yabu

521 N La Cienega Boulevard, between Melrose & Rosewood Avenues (1-310 854 0400). Bus 10, 11, 105/I-10, exit La Cienega Boulevard north. **Open** 11.30am-2.30pm, 6-10.30pm Mon-Thur; 11.30am-2.30pm, 6-11pm Fri-Sun. **Main courses** $6-$10. **Credit** AmEx, DC, Disc, MC, V. **Map** p306 A/B2.

Adorable, upmarket version of the original noodle shop in West LA. The small shopfront has been redesigned with a vaulted wooden ceiling and small Japanese-style patio. Noodles are the mainstay, but a sushi bar offers some unusual cooked and raw fish dishes and feather-light tempura.
Branch: 11820 W Pico Boulevard, at Bundy Drive, West LA (1-310 473 9757).

Yujean Kang's

8826 Melrose Avenue, at Robertson Boulevard (1-310 288 0806). Bus 105, DASH West Hollywood/I-10, exit Robertson Boulevard north. **Open** noon-2.30pm, 6-10.30pm daily. **Main courses** lunch $8-$15; dinner $10-$20. **Credit** AmEx, DC, Disc, MC, V. **Map** p306 A2.

The second startlingly good Chinese restaurant with a modern California twist from chef Yujean Kang, making Melrose and Robertson one of the hottest restaurant corners in West Hollywood. It's a cavernous contemporary space, offset with antiques. Recommended: the crispy Szechuan beef and spicy Beijing noodles.

Also recommended

Authentic Café (Southwestern) 7605 Beverly Boulevard (1-323 939 4626); **Caffè Luna** (Italian) 7463 Melrose Avenue (1-323 655 8647); **Chin Chin** (Californian-Chinese) 8618 Sunset Boulevard (1-310 652 1818); **Duke's** (diner) 8909 Sunset Boulevard (1-310 652 3100); **Hugo's** (American-Italian) 8401 Santa Monica Boulevard (1-323 654 3993); **Marix Tex Mex Café** (Mexican) 1108 N Flores Street (1-323 656 8800); **Mishima** (Japanese) 8474 W Third Street (1-323 782 0181); **Newsroom Café** (healthy) 120 N Robertson Boulevard (1-310 652 4444); **North** (American) 8029 Sunset Boulevard (1-323 654 1313); **Pane e Vino** (Italian) 8265 Beverly Boulevard (1-323 651 4600).

Beverly Hills

Café Roma

350 N Canon Drive, between Wilshire & Santa Monica Boulevard (1-310 274 7834). Bus 3, 14, 316, 576/I-405, exit Santa Monica Boulevard east. **Open** noon-2am daily. **Main courses** lunch $10-$14; dinner $16-$23. **Credit** AmEx, DC, Disc, MC, V. **Map** p305 C2.

Old Beverly Hills folk and a good many Italian-Americans frequent this Italian café run by two brothers – it's a virtual institution. Lasagne, a robust glass of Sangiovese, dessert and espresso in the courtyard, surrounded by boutiques on all sides, makes for a perfect afternoon repast.

Ed Debevic's

134 N La Cienega Boulevard, at Wilshire Boulevard (1-310 659 1952). Bus 21, 105, 576, 720/I-10, exit La Cienega Boulevard north. **Open** 11.30am-3pm Mon-Thur; 11.30am-midnight Fri, Sat; 11.30am-10pm Sun. **Main courses** $7-$12. **Credit** AmEx, DC, Disc, MC, V. **Map** p306 B3.

Extremely loud, 1950s diner-cum-tourist-trap, plastered with fun memorabilia. Worth visiting just for the ridiculous waiting staff and their entertaining schtick or if you have kids in tow.

The Fountain Coffee Shop

Beverly Hills Hotel, 9641 Sunset Boulevard, at Crescent Drive (1-310 276 2251). Bus 2, 302, 305/I-405, exit Sunset Boulevard east. **Open** 7am-7pm daily. **Main courses** $15-$25. **Credit** AmEx, MC, V. **Map** p305 B1.

This cute pink-and-pistachio soda bar is just as much the stuff of legend as the hotel's Polo Lounge (*see p143*). Sit on one of the 20 bar stools at the counter (built in 1949) and order omelettes, pancakes or waffles for breakfast or salads, sandwiches or burgers for lunch or dinner. Wash it all down with a soda, float or home-made ice-cream.

Kakemoto

456 N Bedford Drive, between Santa Monica & Wilshire Boulevards (1-310 989 9467). Bus 3, 4, 21, 304, 316, 720/I-405, exit Santa Monica Boulevard east. **Open** noon-3pm, 5.30-10.30pm Mon-Thur; noon-3pm, 5.30-11pm Fri; 5.30-11pm Sat; closed Sun. **Main courses** lunch $15-$20; dinner $20-$25. **Credit** AmEx, DC, MC, V. **Map** p305 B2.

A small new Japanese restaurant and sushi bar with modern twists. It serves some of the freshest sushi you'll find and brave creations by chef Nono, who claims to be one of the few traditionally trained Japanese chefs in town. We recommend the tuna and salmon sashimi, shrimp and mango spring roll and his original version of tiramisu for dessert.

Kate Mantilini

9101 Wilshire Boulevard, at Doheny Drive (1-310 278 3699). Bus 21, 720/I-10, exit Robertson Boulevard north. **Open** 7.30am-1am Mon-Thur; 7.30am-2am Fri; noon-midnight Sat; 10am-4pm Sun. **Main courses** lunch $8-$20; dinner $10-$30. **Credit** AmEx, MC, V. **Map** p306 A3.

This cavernous restaurant has some rather strange 1980s artworks suspended from the high ceiling. The large American menu is nothing to write home about, but it's open late (by LA standards), there are some inviting wooden booths and, if you order carefully, you can have an enjoyable if overpriced meal, served by white-aproned, friendly staff. Brunch is served on Saturday and Sunday.

Mako

225 S Beverly Drive, at Charleville Boulevard (1-310 288 8338). Bus 21, 720/I-405, exit Santa Monica Boulevard east. **Open** 6-10pm Mon, Tue, Sat; 11.30am-2pm, 6-10pm Wed-Fri; closed Sun. **Main courses** lunch $13-$22; dinner $20-$30. **Credit** AmEx, DC, MC, V. **Map** p305 C3.

Anchored by a beautifully lit open kitchen, chef Makoto's restaurant has counter seating and is adorned with some of his wife Lisa's whimsical artwork. Although the contemporary Asian food references Makoto's work at Chinois on Main (*see p129*) and Spago (*see p143*), it's more subtle, humorous and edited fare. Try the crispy oysters, served in their shell with psychedelic green (pesto) and red (beetroot) dipping sauces.

Maple Drive

345 N Maple Drive, at Burton Way (1-310 274 9800). Bus 27, 315, 576/I-405, Santa Monica Boulevard east. **Open** 11.30am-2.45pm, 6-10pm Mon-Thur; 11.30am-2.45pm, 6-11pm Fri, Sat; closed Sun. **Main courses** lunch $18-$20; dinner $18-$25. **Credit** AmEx, DC, Disc, MC, V. **Map** p305 C2.

Maple Drive has been a lunchtime fave for years with the entertainment crowd and a dinner-time choice for Beverly Hills residents. Sit in a booth and listen to the jazz combo, chill out on the patio or loll at the long maplewood bar, where cigars can be puffed and, at happy hour, hors d'oeuvres are free. Wherever you sit, you cannot fail to be impressed by Leonard Schwartz's fine new American food.

Matsuhisa

129 N La Cienega Boulevard, between Wilshire Boulevard & Clifton Way (1-310 659 9639). Bus 105, 576/I-10, exit Wilshire Boulevard north. **Open** 11.45am-2.15pm, 5.45-10.15pm Mon-Fri; 5.45-10.15pm Sat, Sun. **Main courses** $6-$28. **Credit** AmEx, DC, MC, V. **Map** p306 B3.

Chef Nobuyuki Matsuhisa's fusion of Japanese and Peruvian cuisines attracts expense-account eaters and celebrities. Although traditional sushi is available, his additions of garlic, fresh chilli and special sauces are a shrewd delight. Try the squid 'pasta' with garlic sauce, or sea scallops filled with black truffles and topped with caviar. *See also p135* Nobu and *p141* Ubon.

Mr Chow's

344 N Camden Drive, between Wilshire Boulevard & Brighton Way (1-310 278 9911). Bus 4, 14, 304/ I-405, exit Wilshire Boulevard east. **Open** noon-2.30pm, 6-11.30pm Mon-Fri; 6-11.30pm Sat, Sun. **Main courses** $18-$30. **Credit** AmEx, DC, MC, V. **Map** p305 C2.

Breathe a sigh of relief as you enter the comforting cocoon that is Mr Chow's, which started in London, and has a sister restaurant in Manhattan. The night we were there, Steve Martin was chewing on some tender duck alongside artist Cindy Sherman. Be prepared to pay top dollar.

Mulberry Street Pizzeria

347 N Canon Drive, between Brighton & Dayton Ways (1-310 247 8100). Bus 3, 14, 576/I-405, exit Santa Monica Boulevard east. **Open** 11am-midnight Mon-Sat; 11am-11pm Sun. **Main courses** $7-$20. **Credit** MC, V. **Map** p305 C2.

A no-frills pizza joint that looks like it might have been lifted from a Scorsese movie. The idea is not so far-fetched: the owner is *Raging Bull* co-star Cathy Moriarty. The walls are covered in autographed photos of her celebrity friends and clientele and you may even find Ms Moriarty herself, with sleeves rolled high, serving some fine pizza or old-fashioned Sicilian favourites such as spaghetti and meatballs.

Nate & Al

414 N Beverly Drive, between Brighton Way & Little Santa Monica Boulevard (1-310 274 0101). Bus 4, 27, 304/I-405, exit Santa Monica Boulevard east. **Open** 7.30am-8.45pm Mon-Fri, Sun; 7.30am-9.30pm Sat. **Main courses** $6.75-$13. **Credit** AmEx, MC, V. **Map** p305 C2.

Despite its tawdry exterior, this 50-year-old establishment is a big industry hangout, serving excellent, traditional Jewish deli fare. The blintzes and velvety cornbeef hash are particularly good.

Nic's

453 N Canon Drive, between Brighton Way & Santa Monica Boulevard (1-310 550 5707). Bus 3, 14, 576/I-405, exit Santa Monica Boulevard east. **Open** 5-11pm Mon-Sat (cocktail hour 5-6pm); closed Sun. **Main courses** $15-$20. **Credit** AmEx, Disc, MC, V. **Map** p305 C2.

Nic's restaurant and Martini bar sits on the edge of Beverly Hills in more ways than one. Although the setting for Larry Nicola's inspired menu is upscale lounge, the vibe is closer to bohemian cool, and it attracts the full gamut from punk to politician. The food is a little off-kilter, too: Nicola calls it American with ethnic flair. Don't miss the famous sautéed

The stars are watching you at **Fred 62**, open 24 hours. *See p155.*

oysters on spinach with walnuts and garlic. With a fine selection of Martinis and almost nightly live blues or jazz, it's the kind of place you'll want to linger in and entertain your friends.

The Polo Lounge
Beverly Hills Hotel, 9641 Sunset Boulevard, at Crescent Drive (1-310 276 2251). Bus 2, 302, 305/ I-405, exit Sunset Boulevard east. **Open** 7am-1.30am daily. **Main courses** breakfast $6-$16; lunch $18-$34; dinner $23-$35. **Credit** AmEx, DC, MC, V. **Map** p305 B1.

A not-to-be-missed piece of Old Hollywood, where the power breakfast was invented and having a phone brought to your table was made a famous Hollywood tactic. The hotel was recently over-hauled, but the lounge has been left intact and million-dollar deals are still sealed over eggs benedict, while romantic interludes are shared on the charming patio over a fine steak or myriad fish preparations. They also serve the best hamburger in town.

Raffles L'Ermitage Beverly Hills
9291 Burton Way, at Elm Drive (1-310 385 5307). Bus 27, 316, 576/I-405, exit Wilshire Boulevard east. **Open** 6.30-11am, 11.30am-2.30pm, 6-11pm daily. **Main courses** breakfast $9-$12; lunch $12-$15; dinner set menus $55, $75. **Credit** AmEx, Disc, MC, V. **Map** p305 C2.

This upmarket Beverly Hills hotel houses a terribly elegant and intimate restaurant, with a magnificent domed ceiling and huge glass windows overlooking a modern fountain sculpture that roars like a fire. At the time of writing, David Myers had just signed on as the new executive chef. We recommend the tasting menu, so you won't miss out on anything. Service par excellence.

Reata
421 N Rodeo Drive, between Little Santa Monica Boulevard & Brighton Way (1-310 550 8700). Bus 4, 14, 304/I-405, eixt Santa Monica Boulevard east. **Open** 11.30am-10.30pm daily. **Main courses** lunch $8-$10; dinner $12-$29. **Credit** AmEx, MC, V. **Map** p305 C2.

A bit of cowboy Texas in the middle of Rodeo Drive. Chef Grady Spears, ex-cowhand and cattle broker, serves up down-home cowboy food with a delicate Southwestern touch in a facsimile of a cattle baron's ranch house, complete with large bar. The house speciality is predictably meaty: a mean-looking rib eye steak. There's also the likes of penne with south Texas quail, smoked tomatoes and brown sage broth, or enchilladas filled with smoked shrimp.

Spago of Beverly Hills
176 N Canon Drive, between Clifton Way & Wilshire Boulevard (1-310 385 0880). Bus 3, 14, 576/I-405, exit Wilshire Boulevard east. **Open** 11.30am-2pm, 6-11pm daily. **Main courses** $21-$33. **Credit** AmEx, DC, Disc, MC, V. **Map** p305 C2.

Wolfgang Puck opened the original Spago off Sunset Boulevard umpteen years ago. One of the US's first celebrity chefs, he and his partner/designer/wife

Barbara Lazaroff opened Spago of Beverly Hills in 1998. It's a huge, stunning extravaganza with Italian glass chandeliers, a romantic garden, an impressive art collection including a Hockney and a Picasso, a long bar and an expanse of glass that exposes the chefs at work. They create most of Puck's classic dishes: designer pizzas and light California cuisine with Far Eastern influences, with the addition of Puck's spin on sturdier Austrian dishes. *See also p129* Chinois on Main and *p135* Granita.
Branch: Spago 1114 Horn Avenue, at Sunset Boulevard (1-310 652 4025).

Trattoria Amici
469 N Doheny Drive, between Melrose & Rangely Avenues (1-310 858 0271). Bus 4, 304/I-10, exit Robertson Boulevard north. **Open** noon-2.30pm, 5.30-10.30pm Mon-Fri; 5.30-10.30pm Sat, Sun. **Main courses** $10-$17. **Credit** AmEx, MC, V. **Map** p306 A2.
Sit on the leafy patio with twinkly Christmas lights and dream of Europe. Amici serves good Italian standards plus seafood specials and excellent thin-crusted pizza napolitano, which attracts well-heeled locals and wistful Europeans.

X'ian
362 N Canon Drive, between Brighton & Dayton Ways, Beverly Hills (1-310 275 3345). Bus 3, 14, 576/I-405, exit Wilshire Boulevard east. **Open** 11am-10pm Mon-Wed, Sat; 11.30am-10pm Thur, Fri; closed Sun. **Main courses** $15-$18. **Credit** DC, Disc, MC, V. **Map** p305 C2.
X'ian is an upmarket Chinese health spot in downtown Beverly Hills, with a contemporary minimalist interior and a few pavement tables. Hearts dot the extensive menu, signifying healthy, low-fat, low-sodium ingredients.

Also recommended
Barney Greengrass (American) Barneys New York, 9570 Wilshire Boulevard, at Camden Drive, Beverly Hills (1-310 276 4400); **Bombay Palace** (Indian) 8690 Wilshire Boulevard (1-310 659 9944); **Il Buco** (pizza) 107 N Robertson Boulevard (1-310 657 1345); **Il Pastaio** (Italian) 400 N Canon Drive (1-310 205 5444); **McCormick & Schmick's** (seafood) Two Rodeo, 206 N Rodeo Drive (1-310 859 0434); **Porta Via** (Italian) 424 N Canon Drive (1-310 274 6534).

Westwood & UCLA

Eurochow
1099 Westwood Boulevard, at Wilshire Boulevard (1-310 209 0066). Bus Santa Monica 8/I-405, exit Wilshire Boulevard east. **Open** 11.30am-midnight Mon-Wed, Sun; 11.30am-1am Thur-Sat. **Main courses** $16-$20. **Credit** AmEx, Disc, MC, V. **Map** p305 A4.
This restaurant screams for attention, with its white and silver padded chairs, glass staircases up to the theatrical balcony seating and cathedral-like ceilings. It was once a bank and the old vault is now

a wine cellar. It's a definite scenester hangout, serving Chinese-meets-Italian fare – pizza, pasta, seafood and even sandwiches – and some hearty entrées.

Maui Beach Café
1019 Westwood Boulevard, between Kinross & Weyburn Avenues (1-310 209 0494). Bus Culver City 6, Santa Monica 3, 8/I-405, exit Wilshire Boulevard east. **Open** 11.30am-10pm Mon-Thur; 11.30am-11pm Fri-Sat; 4-10pm Sun. **Main courses** lunch $8-$14; dinner $15-$24. **Credit** AmEx, DC, MC, V.
The menu is as much fun as the decor, and both are designed to make you think Pacific. Try tea-smoked pot-stickers with a lilikoi sweet and sour sauce as an appetiser, followed by macadamia nut-dusted swordfish with fresh banana salsa and mashed potatoes, polished off with jasmine rice pudding with fresh papaya. Paradise on a plate.

Mojo at the W
930 Hilgard Avenue, at Le Conte Avenue (1-310 208 8765). Bus 305, 361, Santa Monica 1, 2, 12/I-405, exit Wilshire Boulevard east. **Open** 11am-2.30pm, 5.30-11pm daily. **Main courses** lunch $7-$14; dinner $21-$30. **Credit** AmEx, Disc, MC, V.
Mojo is as much about imbibing the spirited atmosphere of the W hotel, with all its pristine modernist twists, as the vibrant nuevo Latino food. You could try clams roasted in beer, with toasted garlic, lime, coriander and chillies, followed by hot paprika prawns served on smoky gazpacho with sweet mango and green almond rice. Desserts are a little over the top, but fun: tequila ice-cream float, for example, arrives complete with a bottle of pineapple soda pop on the side.

Shaharazad
1422 Westwood Boulevard, at Ohio Avenue (1-310 470 3242). Bus Santa Monica 1, 8/I-405, exit Wilshire Boulevard east. **Open** 11.30am-midnight Mon-Thur; 11.30am-4am Fri, Sat; closed Sun. **Main courses** $9-$14. **Credit** AmEx, DC, MC, V.
Good Persian food at great prices – and it's open late.
Branch: 138 Beverly Drive, between Wilshire & Charleville Boulevards (1-310 859 8585).

Also recommended
Asuka (Japanese) 1266 Westwood Boulevard (1-310 474 7412); **Delphi** (Greek) 1383 Westwood Boulevard (1-310 478 2900); **The Gardens on Glendon** (Californian) 1139 Glendon Avenue (1-310 824 1818); **Koutoubia** (Moroccan) 2116 Westwood Boulevard, West LA (1-310 475 0729); **Thai House** (Thai) 1049 Gayley Avenue (1-310 208 2676).

Bel Air, Brentwood & West LA

Apple Pan
10801 W Pico Boulevard, at Glendon Avenue, West LA (1-310 475 3585). Bus Culver City 3, Santa Monica 7, 8, 12, 13/I-10, exit Overland Avenue north. **Open** 11am-midnight Tue-Thur, Sun; 11am-1am Fri, Sat; closed Mon. **Main courses** $4-$6. **No credit cards. Map** p305 A4.

Eat, Drink, Shop

The Baker family bought a vacant lot in 1947 and literally built the Apple Pan from the ground up. It was an instant hit, and at lunchtime people still line up for one of the 26 coveted stools at the 1950s horse-shoe counter, to eat from the simple selection of seven sandwiches. They're all served on paper plates and washed down with Coke, Dr Pepper or root beer served in paper cups. For dessert, choose from their myriad home-baked cream pies.

Bombay Café

12021 W Pico Boulevard, at Bundy Drive, West LA (1-310 473 3388). Bus Santa Monica 10, 14/I-10, exit Bundy Drive north. **Open** 11am-10pm Tue-Thur; 11am-11pm Fri; 4-11pm Sat; 4-10pm Sun; closed Mon. **Main courses** lunch $7-$10; dinner $10-$15. **Credit** MC, V.

At its new, more accommodating location, the queues that used to plague this popular restaurant are thankfully gone. If you do have to wait for a table, there's a large bar. Try the masala dosas or the Frankies (egg-dipped tortillas, filled with chicken, lamb or cauliflower), with by Indian beer or chai (tea). Finish with rice pudding or home-made mango kulfi.

Chan Dara

11940 W Pico Boulevard, at Bundy Drive, West LA (1-310 479 4461). Bus Santa Monica 10, 14/I-10, exit Bundy Drive north. **Open** 11am-11pm Mon-Fri; 5-11pm Sat, Sun. **Main courses** $7-$15. **Credit** AmEx, DC, Disc, MC, V.

The best of this very popular chain of rock 'n' roll Thai restaurants. The food is reliably good: try the spicy garlic chicken and the Thai bouillabaisse with brown rice. Some joke that people come less for the good food and more for the pretty, provocatively dressed waitresses.

Delmonico's Seafood Grille

9320 W Pico Boulevard, between Beverly & Doheny Drives, West LA (1-310 550 7737). Bus Santa Monica 5, 7, 12/I-10, exit Robertson Boulevard north. **Open** 11.30am-10pm Mon-Fri; 5-10pm Sat; 4-10pm Sun. **Main courses** lunch $15-$20; dinner $20-$40. **Credit** AmEx, MC, V.
Map p305 C3.

While its sign, 'If it swims, we've got it', may not be entirely truthful, Delmonico's is dependable for a few fishy things. The Maine lobster is reliable and

The best Ethnic

Chinese
For the best dim sum outside Hong Kong, visit **Empress Harbor** in Monterey Park. See page 159.

Indian
Head to West LA for masala dosas and chai at the **Bombay Café**. See page 146.

Japanese
Try traditional sushi and chef Hiro's (pictured) creative concoctions at **Hirozen** in West Hollywood. See page 138.

Korean
Custom-make your own meal at traditional Korean barbecue joint **Woo Lae Oak**. See page 153.

Mexican
Join Mexican families and mariachi musicians at **La Serenata di Garibaldi** in LA's Latino heartland. See page 156.

Nuevo Latino
Inventive food and great Latin music at **La Boca del Conga Room** on Miracle Mile. See page 152.

Thai
Discover Hidden Treasures at gourmet eaterie **Talesai** in West Hollywood. See page 141.

South American
Try hole-in-the-wall **Mario's** in Hollywood for budget Peruvian dishes (see page 149) or pretty **Itana Bahia** in West Hollywood for Brazilian regional fare (see page 138).

Vietnamese
It's better than OK at **Pho Okay** near Koreatown. See page 153.

there are some good variations on grilled and sautéed fish, but too often the dishes are drowning in rich, old-fashioned sauces. The setting, with plush booths and tables adorned with the finest linen, oozes old-world charm.
Branch: 16358 Ventura Boulevard, at Havenhurst Avenue, Encino (1-818 986 0777).

Hotel Bel-Air

701 Stone Canyon Road, at Bellagio Road, Bel Air (1-310 472 1211). I-405, exit Sunset Boulevard east. **Open** 7.30am-2pm, 6.30-10pm Mon-Sat; 7am-2pm, 6.30-10pm Sun. **Main courses** breakfast $11-$21; brunch $32.50; lunch $15-$25; dinner $25-$30. **Credit** AmEx, DC, Disc, MC, V.
Driving up Stone Canyon Road to the 1920s Mission-style Hotel Bel-Air – one of LA's most luxurious hotels – is a romantic experience in itself. Crossing the wooden bridge by the swan garden is an added bonus, but taking a leisurely brunch, lunch or dinner on the bougainvillea-draped terrace makes for an earthbound version of heaven. They serve great hamburgers and very good pasta, fish, meat and salads. *See also p50.*

Hymie's Fish Market

9228 W Pico Boulevard, between Beverly & Doheny Drives, West LA (1-310 550 0377). Bus Santa Monica 5, 7, 12/I-10, exit Robertson Boulevard north. **Open** 11.30am-2pm, 4-9pm Mon-Fri; 4-9pm Sat, Sun. **Main courses** lunch $10-$17; dinner $15-$39. **Credit** AmEx, DC, Disc, MC, V. **Map** p305 C4.
Hymie's is a fish market by day and a pricey fish restaurant by night. The fish is very fresh, the preparation simple and the service painstaking. It's a bare-bones sort of place.

Milky Way

9108 W Pico Boulevard, at Doheny Drive, West LA (1-310 859 0004). Bus Santa Monica 5, 7, 12/ I-10, exit Robertson Boulevard north. **Open** 11.30am-2.30pm, 5.30-8.30pm Mon-Thur, Sun; 11.30am-2pm Fri. **Main courses** lunch $7-$12; dinner $10-$15. **Credit** AmEx, MC, V. **Map** p305 C3.
A restaurant owned by Steven Spielberg's mother, offering strictly kosher food and a warm atmosphere. Traditional choices such as cheese blintzes and potato pancakes are always popular, but the menu also branches out into the likes of pistachio-nut pasta and Cajun blackened snapper. 'Reservations are sometimes a good idea here,' says a modest Mrs Spielberg Sr.

Monte Alban

11927 Santa Monica Boulevard, at Bundy Drive, West LA (1-310 444 7736). Bus 4, 304, Santa Monica 10, 14/I-10, exit Bundy Drive north. **Open** 8.30am-midnight daily. **Main courses** $5-$10. **Credit** AmEx, DC, Disc, MC, V.
This amicable and pristine hole-in-the-wall is famous for its Oaxacan specialities, particularly its complex mole sauces.

Red Moon Café

Westdale Plaza, 11267 National Boulevard, at Sawtelle Boulevard, West LA (1-310 477 3177). Bus Commuter Express 437, 574/I-405, exit National Boulevard west. **Open** 11am-3.30pm, 5-9pm Mon-Thur; 11am-3.30pm, 5-10pm Fri; noon-3.30pm, 5-10pm Sat; closed Sun. **Main courses** $10-$18. **Credit** AmEx, DC, Disc, MC, V.
Located in a hard-to-find cul-de-sac (under the 405 freeway), with parking around the corner off Sawtelle Boulevard, Red Moon Café offers a delightful selection of Chinese and Vietnamese dishes. Mouth-watering favourites include grilled mussels, Red Moon duck, Luc Lac steak with a hint of coconut and bean sauce, and Dungeness crab served with garlic and shrimp.

Versailles

1415 S La Cienega Boulevard, at Pico Boulevard, West LA (1-310 289 0392). Bus Santa Monica 5, 7, 12, 105/I-10, exit La Cienega Boulevard south. **Open** 11am-7pm daily. **Main courses** $8. **Credit** AmEx, MC, V. **Map** p306 B4.
Well-known, funky, no-frills Cuban joint where the food is good, the prices great (even the LAPD can afford it) and the service to the point. Try the garlic chicken served with sweet raw onion and fried plantains on white rice and black beans.
Branch: 10319 Venice Boulevard, at Motor Avenue, Culver City (1-310 558 3168).

Vincenti

11930 San Vicente Boulevard, between Bundy Drive & Montana Avenue, Brentwood (1-310 207 0127). Bus 22, Santa Monica 3/I-405, exit Wilshire Boulevard west. **Open** 6-10.30pm Tue-Sat; 6-9.30pm Sun, closed Mon. **Main courses** $17-$30. **Credit** AmEx, MC, V.
Flawless and exciting contemporary Italian cuisine in a sleek but warm setting –wood floors and teal-and-aubergine walls. Specialities are gnocchi in a robust tomato-squab sauce, and meat and whole fish dishes from the wood-burning rotisserie. It's frequented by the local haute bourgeoisie.

VIP Harbor Seafood Restaurant

11701 Wilshire Boulevard, suite 16, at Barrington Avenue, West LA (1-310 979 3377). Bus 20, 22, Santa Monica 2/I-405, exit Sunset Boulevard west. **Open** 11am-3pm, 5-10pm Mon-Fri; 10am-10pm Sat, Sun. **Main courses** $7-$15. **Credit** AmEx, MC, V.
This popular Cantonese-style seafood restaurant on Wilshire Boulevard has live tanks of lobster, crab, abalone and shrimp. Excellent dim sum is served every day until 3pm.

Also recommended

Asahi Ramen (Japanese) 2027 Sawtelle Boulevard, West LA (1-310 479 2231); **Pizzicotto** (Italian) 11758 San Vicente Boulevard, Brentwood (1-310 442 7188); **Sushi Sasabune** (Japanese) 11300 Nebraska Avenue, West LA (1-310 268 8380); **U-Zen** (Japanese) 11951 Santa Monica Boulevard, West LA (1-310 477 1390).

Eat, Drink, Shop

Century City

Houston's
Century City Shopping Center, 10250 Santa Monica Boulevard, between Century Park W & Avenue of the Stars (1-310 557 1285). Bus 27, 28, 316, 328/I-405, exit Santa Monica Boulevard east. **Open** 11.30am-10.30pm Mon-Thur, Sun; 11.30am-11.30pm Fri, Sat. **Main courses** $10-$18. **Credit** AmEx, MC, V. **Map** p305 B3.
Houston's is a frenetic place, so relax, if you can, at the bar and wait for your pager to go off, signalling that your table is ready. The food is consistently good, fast-food-type fare; try the very thin pizzas, hickory burgers or the barbecue ribs. The decor is upmarket and womb-like, with plenty of dark wooden panels and booths.

La Cachette
10506 Little Santa Monica Boulevard, between Beverly Glen & Overland Avenue (1-310 470 4992). Bus 4, 304/I-405, exit Santa Monica Boulevard east. **Open** 11.30am-2pm, 5.30-9pm Mon-Fri; 5-10pm Sat, Sun. **Main courses** $16-$26. **Credit** AmEx, DC, MC, V. **Map** p305 A3/4.
Jean-François Meteigner is arguably the top French chef in town, and this is his upscale romantic joint. Apprenticed in Michelin-starred restaurants in Paris, in LA he worked as the executive chef at L'Orangerie (*see p139*) before opening Cicada, then this award-winning place. The cuisine is French, but with a restrained use of butter and cream. Signature dishes include Muscovy duck with sherried brandy sauce, and rock shrimp ravioli with lobster sauce.

Culver City

Bamboo
10835 Venice Boulevard, between Overland Avenue & Sepulveda Boulevard (1-310 287 0668). Bus 33, 333, 436/I-10, exit Overland Avenue south. **Open** 11am-10.30pm daily. **Main courses** $10-$15. **Credit** AmEx, DC, Disc, MC, V.
A casual neighbourhood spot for 'tropical' food: crab cakes, jerk chicken and Bahia shrimp in coconut milk, all at reasonable prices.

Café Brasil
10831 Venice Boulevard, at Westwood Boulevard (1-310 837 8957). Bus 33, 333, 436/I-10, exit Overland Avenue south. **Open** 11.30am-11pm daily. **Main courses** $10-$13. **Credit** MC, V.
A funky shack that prides itself on its low-priced authentic Brazilian food – fish and meat marinated and then grilled, served with rice and beans and Brazilian salsa.

JR's Bar-B-Que
3055 S La Cienega Boulevard, at Woodrow Wilson Drive (1-310 837 6838). Bus 105, 576/I-10, exit Fairfax Avenue south. **Open** 11am-9pm Mon-Thur; 11am-10pm Fri, Sat; closed Sun. **Main courses** $5-$8. **No credit cards.**

Arguably one of the best places in town for barbecue food to eat in at the horseshoe-shaped counter or take away. There are baby ribs, rib tips, beef brisket (as spicy as you want it), sweet potato pie, crumble of the day and long glasses of lemonade – not to mention a very hospitable atmosphere.

Also recommended
Tito's Tacos (Mexican) 11222 Washington Place (1-310 391 5780).

Hollywood & Midtown

Hollywood

Ammo
1155 N Highland Avenue, at Santa Monica Boulevard (1-323 871 2666). Bus 4, 156, 304, 426/I-5, exit Highland Avenue south. **Open** 8am-3pm, 6-10pm Mon-Thur; 8am-3pm, 6-11pm Fri; 9am-3pm, 6-11pm Sat; 9am-3pm Sun. **Main courses** lunch $7-$9; dinner $18-$20. **Credit** AmEx, DC, Disc, MC, V. **Map** p307 A2.
Sandwiched between photo labs, film equipment rental houses and industrial manufacturing companies, Ammo is a groovy, low-key *boîte* where you're as likely to hear Ella as the Chemical Brothers emanating from the sound system. Film stylists and editors chow down on simple but well-prepared comfort food, otherwise known as 'fuel for thought': turkey burgers, breakfast burritos, field green salad strewn with parmesan. Enjoy!

Citrus
6703 Melrose Avenue, at Citrus Avenue (1-323 857 0034). Bus 10, 11/I-10, exit La Brea Avenue north. **Open** noon-2.30pm, 6.30-10.30pm Mon-Fri; 6-11pm Sat; closed Sun. **Main courses** lunch $13-$17; dinner $17-$31. **Credit** AmEx, DC, MC, V. **Map** p307 A3.
One of LA's most imaginative menus (Californian-French) in a carelessly classy 'outside inside' setting. Sit under white umbrellas and watch masterful chefs create in their glass kitchen. Try the smoked salmon terrine, the snails in white wine and mushroom sauce, the sea bass dipped in a sauce of black chanterelles, the wafer-thin onion rings and the chocolate hazelnut bars.

Hollywood Canteen
1006 Seward Street, at Santa Monica Boulevard (1-323 465 0961). Bus 4, 304, DASH West Hollywood/I-10, exit Santa Monica Boulevard west. **Open** 11.30am-10pm Mon-Fri; 5-10pm Sat; closed Sun. **Main courses** $13-$19. **Credit** AmEx, DC, MC, V. **Map** p307 A2.
Bang in the middle of Nowheresville, surrounded by film post-production houses, is this cool, retro-styled grill. A simple sushi bar greets you at the front, while a more sophisticated collection of booths furnishes the centre room. There's also a small garden, with a silver Airstream trailer for decoration. The menu offers good Caesar salads, pastas, chowders, steaks and fish.

Eat, Drink, Shop

Hollywood Hills Coffee Shop

Best Western Hollywood Hills Hotel, 6145 Franklin Avenue, between Gower & Vine Streets (1-323 467 7678). Bus 26, Community Connection 208/US 101, exit Gower Street north. **Open** 7am-10pm daily. **Main courses** $7-$13. **Credit** AmEx, Disc, MC, V. **Map** p307 B1.

A banner outside alerts motorists to the 'Last cappuccino before the 101 freeway'. This non-greasy-spoon diner is favoured by celebs like Sandra Bullock, Quentin Tarantino and Tim Roth as a great place to meet or simply to read the morning paper with a terrific breakfast of blueberry pancakes or huevos rancheros.

Les Deux Café

1638 Las Palmas Avenue, between Hollywood Boulevard & Selma Avenue (1-323 465 0509). Metro Hollywood-Highland/bus 163, 180, 181, 217/US 101, exit Highland Avenue south. **Open** 6.30pm-2am daily. **Main courses** $18-$32. **Credit** AmEx, MC, V. **Map** p307 A1.

Despite an almost secret location (you have to go through the back of Grant's parking lot), Michele Lamy's café has attracted a madly fashionable crowd. It's pricey, reservations are often not honoured, and when they are, the service can be erratic. But the French food can be good and the ambience is a sort of Euro-chic only found in LA, with an eclectic interior and a stunning garden.

Mario's Peruvian Seafood

5786 Melrose Avenue, at Vine Street (1-323 466 4181). Bus 10, 11, 201, 310, 426/I-10, exit La Brea Avenue north. **Open** 11.30am-8.30pm Mon-Thur, Sun; 11.30am-10pm Fri, Sat. **Main courses** $7-$11. **Credit** MC, V. **Map** p307 B3.

You'll probably have to queue at this economical Peruvian hole-in-the-wall joint that serves siete mares (seven seas seafood soup), lomo saltado (strips of beef sautéed with onions and tomatoes, served with french fries) and a hot guacamole sauce to eat with bread.

Musso & Frank Grill

6667 Hollywood Boulevard, at Cherokee Avenue (1-323 467 7788). Metro Hollywood-Highland/ bus 163, 180, 181, 212, DASH Hollywood/ US 101, exit Highland Avenue south. **Open** 11am-11pm Tue-Sat; closed Mon, Sun. **Main courses** $18-$40. **Credit** AmEx, DC, MC, V. **Map** p307 A1.

In 1919, Musso & Frank's opened its double doors on what was then just a muddy strip of Hollywood Boulevard. Everything about the area has changed, but this old-style grill is immortal, with its original, high-backed, red leatherette booths, dark stained wood and faded hunting-scene wallpaper. If you're not deterred by the undertaker-like demeanour of the waiting staff, nor by a menu that hasn't changed in 70 years (lamb kidneys, short ribs and sauerbraten), and you don't mind ruining your palate with a Sidecar or a Highball, this is a landmark must. Hollywood dining at its most vintage.

Off Vine

6263 Leland Way, at Seward Street (1-323 962 1900). Bus 2, 3, 302/US 101, exit Sunset Boulevard west. **Open** 11.30am-2.30pm, 5-11pm Mon-Fri; 5-11.30pm Sat; 10am-2.30pm, 4-11.30pm Sun. **Main courses** $7-$16. **Credit** AmEx, MC, V. **Map** p307 A2.

California-chic casual restaurant where the food is a mite ambitious, but the Arts and Crafts cottage hideaway setting is just too cute to pass up. It's worth coming for the dessert soufflés alone. It's also a lovely spot for Sunday brunch.

Patina

5955 Melrose Avenue, at N Cahuenga Boulevard (1-213 467 1108). Bus 10, 11/US 101, exit Melrose Avenue west. **Open** 6-10pm Mon-Fri, Sun; 5.30-10pm Sat. **Main courses** $24-$27. **Credit** AmEx, DC, Disc, MC, V. **Map** p307 B3.

Joaquim Splichal's flagship restaurant opened in 1989 and was completely revamped in 2000 – a sort of 'new urban' interior and exterior reigns, along with high-tech video cameras that monitor the progress of customers' meals, particularly useful for the popular tasting menus. Its location, handily near many of the movie studios, and Splichal's esoteric creations mean Patina has long been a favourite with Hollywood players: Madonna loves the foie gras, Warren Beatty the lobster. We're rather partial to the grouse flown in daily from Scotland.

Pinot Hollywood

1448 N Gower Street, at Sunset Boulevard (1-323 461 8800). Bus 2, 3, 302/US 101, exit Gower Street south. **Open** 11.30am-10.30pm Mon-Thur; 5.30-11pm Fri, Sat; closed Sun. **Main courses** lunch $16; dinner $22. **Credit** AmEx, DC, Disc, MC, V. **Map** p307 B2.

Also owned by Joachim Splichal (see *p149* Patina and *p153* Café Pinot, *p157* Pinot Bistro), this is a sparky, upmarket French bistro with a great bar and patio dining. It's the only posh restaurant in the heart of Hollywood, and worth a visit even if you're not already on this side of town.

Roscoe's House of Chicken 'n' Waffles

1514 N Gower Street, between Selma Avenue & Sunset Boulevard (1-213 466 7453). Bus 2, 3, 302/ US 101, exit Gower Street south. **Open** 8am-midnight Mon-Thur, Sun; 8am-4am Fri, Sat. **Main courses** $4-$10. **Credit** AmEx, Disc, DC, MC, V. **Map** p307 B1/2.

One of a chain of funky Southern joints that are beloved for their late opening, low prices and tasty down-home dishes.

Tidal Wave

6122 Sunset Boulevard, at Gower Street (1-323 466 9917). Bus 2, 3, 302/US 101, exit Sunset Boulevard west. **Open** 11am-10pm Mon-Sat; closed Sun. **Main courses** $6-$16. **Credit** AmEx, DC, Disc, MC, V. **Map** p307 B2.

Juan Mercado presides over this funky restaurant. The interior is nothing to write home about (brown synthetic fabric, booths, vinyl tablecloths), but there's excellent seafood – crab cakes with a fine butter sauce, hearty jambalaya and more delicate fish specials – alongside quesadillas, a mean cheeseburger and simple, poached salmon salads. And, oh, such sweet prices.

Yamashiro

1999 N Sycamore Avenue, at Franklin Avenue (1-213 466 5125). Bus 180, 181/US 101, exit Highland Avenue south. **Open** 5.30-10pm Mon-Thur; 5.30-11pm Fri, Sat; closed Sun. **Main courses** $15-$39. **Credit** AmEx, DC, Disc, MC, V. **Map** p307 A1.

You don't visit Yamashiro for the so-so Japanese food. You visit it for the chance to consume cocktails and so-so Japanese food in a truly magnificent setting: a hilltop palace (imported from Kyoto, complete with ornamental gardens) with a spectacular, panoramic view of LA. No shorts allowed.

Also recommended

360 (supper club) 6290 Sunset Boulevard (1-323 461 8600); **Las Palmas** (International) 1714 N Las Palmas Avenue (1-323 464 0171). **Lucy's Café El Adobe** (Mexican) 5536 Melrose Avenue (1-323 462 9421); **Prizzi's Piazza** (pizza) 5923 Franklin Avenue (1-323 467 0168).

Fairfax & Midtown

Canter's

419 N Fairfax Avenue, at Oakwood Avenue (1-323 651 2030). Bus 217, 218, DASH Fairfax/I-10, exit Fairfax Avenue north. **Open** 24 hours daily. **Main courses** $8-$13. **Credit** MC, V. **Map** p306 B2.

Visiting 50-year-old Jewish deli Canter's is a unique experience. The service can be charmless and the food tasteless, but, hell, it's open 24 hours. Staff make their own pickles and sell some excellent chocolate-chip rugala and bagels covered with melted cheddar and poppy seeds. After midnight, the place fills up with young folk in search of sustenance after a night of clubbing. The next-door Kibbutz Room and the bar have live music.

Linq

8338 W Third Street, between Sweetzer & Orlando Avenues (1-323 655 4555). Bus 218, 316, DASH Fairfax/I-10, exit La Cienega Boulevard north. **Open** 11.30am-3pm, 6pm-1.30am daily. **Main courses** lunch $6-$16; dinner $18-$28. **Credit** AmEx, DC, Disc, MC, V. **Map** p306 B3.

One of the new 'it' places in town, Linq is marked by a strange silver sculpture of a naked man outside and a slick interior. The food is surprisingly good; we suggest the lobster ravioli, sea bass and New York pepper steak.

The Little Door

8164 W Third Street, at La Jolla Avenue (1-323 951 1210). Bus 218, 316, DASH Fairfax/I-10, exit Fairfax Avenue north. **Open** 6.30pm-midnight daily. **Main courses** $18-$30. **Credit** AmEx, MC, V. **Map** p306 B3.

One of the prettiest restaurants in the neighbourhood and so hip that it doesn't even need a sign out front. Alas, the place is so overrun with Eurotrash clad in attitude, leather pants and rakish hairstyles, smoking madly, that it's hard to get a table inside or outside on the idyllic patio. Avoid such frustrations: go for a drink and a gander at the scene.

Mimosa

8009 Beverly Boulevard, at Edinburgh Avenue (1-323 655 8895). Bus 14, 316/I-10, exit Fairfax Avenue north. **Open** 11.30am-3pm, 5.30pm-midnight Mon-Fri; 5.30pm-midnight Sat; closed Sun. **Main courses** $14-$20. **Credit** AmEx, DC, MC, V. **Map** p306 B2.

Beautifully decked out in bewitching Mediterranean hues, Mimosa offers excellent French bistro fare – mussels marinière, fried steak and andouillette sausages in French bread – for your enjoyment inside or outside on the pavement patio.

Nyala Ethiopian Restaurant

1076 S Fairfax Avenue, between Olympic Boulevard & Whitworth Drive (1-323 936 5918). Bus 217/ I-10, exit Fairfax Avenue north. **Open** 11.30am-11.30pm daily. **Main courses** lunch $5-$7; dinner $8-$10. **Credit** AmEx, DC, Disc, MC, V. **Map** p306 B4.

Enjoy spicy food scooped up with bread, eaten with your mitts only, served by Ethiopian waitresses, often to the accompaniment of live music. An unusual and fun experience.

Tahiti

7910 W Third Street, at Fairfax Avenue, (1-323 651 1213). Bus 217, DASH Fairfax/I-10, exit Fairfax Avenue north. **Open** 11.30am-2.30pm, 6-10pm Mon-Thur; 6-11pm Fri, Sat; 5-9pm Sun. **Main courses** lunch $10-$15; dinner $13-$29. **Credit** MC, V. **Map** 4 B3.

Leopard- and alligator-print booths, peacock-feather lamps, thatched umbrellas, oversized Ali Baba urns and a small lava rock and bamboo garden exemplify the theatricality of this restaurant, the work of film designer Damon Medlen. The food is just as striking and whimsical, inspired by the islands, cooked by Tony Di Lembo, formerly a personal chef to Barbra Streisand. Dishes include Yucatan-style Chilean sea bass, baked in banana leaves, with achote spices, orange sticks and chillis; chicken in red curry coconut sauce; plus an unbeatable beer menu.

Also recommended

Du-Par's (diner) Farmers Market, 6333 W Third Street (1-323 933 8446); **Vim** (Thai) 831 S Vermont Avenue (1-213 386 2338).

Miracle Mile, Mid Wilshire & Westlake

Atlas Supper Club

3760 Wilshire Boulevard, at Western Avenue (1-323 380 8400). Metro Wilshire-Western/bus 20, 21, 207, 357, 720/I-10, exit Western Avenue north. **Open**

Make tracks for **Traxx** – located on the concourse of Union Station. *See p154.*

Restaurant 11am-3pm Mon; 11am-10pm Tue-Fri; 6-10pm Sat, Sun. *Bar* 11am-2am Mon-Fri; 6pm-2am Sat, Sun. **Main courses** $10-$15. **Credit** AmEx, DC, MC, V. **Map** p307 C4.

Atlas is the legacy of flamboyant restaurateur Mario Tomayo, who died of AIDS in his early 30s after establishing three highly successful restaurants in run-down neighbourhoods. Atlas followed the smaller Cha Cha Cha (still going – *see p154*) and Café Mambo (now closed) and instantly attracted a mixed Midtown business and gay crowd with its gold-painted room the size of a tennis court, super-camp decor and charming waiters. Its eclectic menu is fine enough, but with live blues, jazz and Latin music most nights, dining here is more than just eating out.

Campanile

624 S La Brea Avenue, between Sixth Street & Wilshire Boulevard (1-323 938 1447). Bus 20, 21, 212, 720/I-10, exit La Brea Avenue north. **Open** 11.30am-2.30pm Mon-Thur; 11.30am-2.30pm, 5.30-11pm Fri; 9.30am-1.45pm, 5.30-11pm Sat; 9.30am-1.45pm Sun. **Main courses** brunch $6-$15; lunch $14-$18; dinner $22-$35. **Credit** AmEx, DC, Disc, MC, V. **Map** p307 A4.

Chef/owner Mark Peele provides an original spin on Mediterranean food at one of the city's prettiest restaurants. The likes of risotto and barley cake with roasted autumn vegetables, or duck breast stuffed with Swiss chard and dried cherries in a port sauce are complemented by now-famous bread and pastries

that are sold all over town, made by Peele's wife, Nancy Silverton. We recommend Sunday brunch, and Monday for the well-priced set menus.

Cassell's

3266 W Sixth Street, at Berendo Street (1-213 480 8668). Bus 18, 20, 21, 720/I-10, exit Vermont Avenue north. **Open** 10.30am-4pm Mon-Sat; closed Sun. **Main courses** $5-$7. **No credit cards.** **Map** p308 A5.

Perhaps hamburgers are to Americans what pizzas are to Italians: the discourse can be endless as to where to commandeer the best in town. Many are faithful to this lunch-only joint, which serves up a mean and greasy burger with home-made mayonnaise and great potato salad.

El Cholo

11121 S Western Avenue, between Pico & Olympic Boulevards (1-323 734 2773). Bus 207, 357/I-10, exit Western Avenue north. **Open** 11am-10pm Mon-Thur; 11am-11pm Fri, Sat; 11am-9pm Sun. **Main courses** $9-$11. **Credit** AmEx, MC, V. **Map** p307 C5.

This LA landmark opened in 1927. The service is old-style ceremonious by ladies in flowing floral dresses. The Mexican food is traditional CalMex – basically Mexican but favouring dishes that have done well in California. What to order: tortilla soup and blue corn enchilada.

Branch: 1025 Wilshire Boulevard, between Tenth & 11th Streets, Santa Monica (1-310 899 1106).

The best Brunch

Café del Rey
Enjoy French/Pacific New Wave cuisine while overlooking the yachts at Marina del Rey. See page 134.

Campanile
Inventive Mediterranean food at one of the city's prettiest restaurants, on Miracle Mile. See page 151.

Geoffrey's
Soak up the Malibu view from this Californian restaurant's cliffside deck. See page 134.

Hotel Bel-Air
Exquisite gardens, a lake with swans and a terrace dripping in bougainvillea at one of LA's most romantic hotels. See page 147.

Off Vine
Escape the noise of Hollywood Boulevard at this Arts and Crafts cottage restaurant. See page 149.

Farfalla
143 N La Brea Avenue, between First Street & Beverly Boulevard (1-323 938 2504). Bus 212/I-10, exit La Brea Avenue north. **Open** 11.30am-2.30pm, 6-11pm Mon-Thur; 11.30am-2.30pm, 6pm-midnight Fri; 6pm-midnight Sat; 5.30-10pm Sun. **Main courses** $18-$20. **Credit** AmEx, DC, Disc, MC, V. **Map** p307 C3.

A very popular Italian restaurant that attracts a hip thirtysomething crowd. Sample the pizzas and pastas, many of which are home-made: especially good is the fusilli dell' aristocratico: truffle oil, roasted artichokes, shitake mushrooms and crumbled ricotta. There's live music upstairs some nights.

La Boca del Conga Room
5364 Wilshire Boulevard, between Cloverdale Avenue & Detroit Street (1-323 938 1696). Bus 20, 21, 22, 212/I-10, exit La Brea Avenue north. **Open** 6-10.30pm Wed-Sat; closed Mon, Tue, Sun. **Main courses** $15-$24. **Credit** AmEx, MC, V. **Map** p306 C3.

Decked out in 1950s tropical style – orange and white walls, white leatherette booths bathed with spots of orange light and some unusual artwork – this club hosts some of the best Latin dance music in the world: José Feliciano, Tito Nieves and Celia Cruz have all played here. And the restaurant serves up some very palatable festive nuevo Latino food – lobster empanadas on grilled octopus, white bean salad with a passionfruit truffle vinaigrette, and grilled rib-eye on mashed tamale. *See also p235.*

La Fonda
2501 Wilshire Boulevard, at Coronado Street (1-213 380 5055). Bus 20, 21, 26/I-10, exit Vermont Avenue north. **Open** seatings 6.30pm, 9.30pm, 11pm Mon-Sat, closed Sun. **Main courses** $10-$18. **Credit** AmEx, DC, MC, V. **Map** p308 B5.

People have come to La Fonda for 30 years, mainly to hear the famous mariachi musicians, Los Camperos, but also to eat Mexican food.

Maurice's Snack 'n' Chat
5549 W Pico Boulevard, at Sierra Bonita Avenue (1-323 931 3877). Bus 30, 31, Santa Monica 5, 7, 12, 13/I-10, exit Fairfax Avenue north. **Open** 7am-midnight Mon-Thur; 7am-2am Fri, Sat; closed Sun. **Main courses** $10-$16. **Credit** AmEx, MC, V. **Map** p306 C4.

Visit Maurice at her funky soul-food restaurant. She makes the best home-fried chicken in town, as well as great liver and onions and smothered pork chops with brown sauce, cooked with a low-fat content – that's what she says, anyway!

Sonora Café
180 N La Brea Avenue, between First & Second Streets (1-323 857 1800). Bus 212, DASH Fairfax/ I-10, exit La Brea Avenue north. **Open** 11.30am-9.30pm Mon-Thur; 11am-11pm Fri; 5-11pm Sat; 5-10pm Sun. **Main courses** $18-$27. **Credit** AmEx, DC, Disc, MC, V. **Map** p306 C3.

A huge – and hugely successful – Southwestern restaurant, immaculately done up in an elegant style, with lush carpets, roaring fireplaces, heavy wooden furniture – and some great grub.

Hancock Park

Girasole
225½ N Larchmont Boulevard, between Beverly Boulevard & W First Street (1-323 464 6978). Bus 14, 316/I-10, exit La Brea Avenue north. **Open** 11.30am-3pm Tue; 11.30am-3pm, 5.30-10pm Wed-Sat; closed Mon, Sun. **Main courses** $23-$25. **Credit** AmEx, Disc, MC, V. **Map** p307 B3.

An authentic Italian trattoria run by a northern Italian couple. Ermanno takes care of things out front, while Sonia cooks up a storm in the back. The rigatoni with sausage, olives and a slightly spicy tomato sauce is especially good.

Prado
244 N Larchmont Boulevard, at Beverly Boulevard (1-323 467 3871). Bus 14, 316/I-10, exit La Brea Avenue west. **Open** 11.30am-3pm, 5-10pm Mon-Thur; 1.30-3pm, 4.30-10pm Fri, Sat; 5.30-10pm Sun. **Main courses** $9-$18. **Credit** AmEx, DC, Disc, MC, V. **Map** p307 B3.

Prado is split into two, with twin themes of night and day depicted on the walls and ceilings. We suggest the Prado sampler: moist corn tamales served with sour cream, caviar and tomatillo sauce, shrimp in black pepper sauce, crab cakes with tartare sauce and a portion of Pacifico-style chilli relleno. The tarte tatin (a brief European excursion) is sublime.

Koreatown

Dong Il Jang
3455 W Eighth Street, at Hobart Boulevard (1-213 383 5757). Metro Wilshire-Western/bus 66/I-10, exit Western Avenue north. **Open** 11am-10pm daily. **Main courses** $8-$10. **Credit** AmEx, MC, V. **Map** p307 C4.

An upmarket affair in the heart of Koreatown. Dine at the sushi bar, in a booth, or, more privately, sitting on cushions on the floor. For Korean barbecue, we recommend the galbi-marinated beef short ribs, which you cook at your table yourself. These arrive with myriad side dishes: pickled vegetables, sweet potatoes, glass noodles and rice. Shika, made from rice and sugar, is a good way to cleanse your palate at the end of the meal.

Guelaguetza
3337½ W Eighth Street, at Irolo Street (1-213 427 0601). Bus 66/I-10, exit Vermont Street north. **Open** noon-10.30pm daily. **Main courses** $10-$15. **Credit** MC, V. **Map** p307 C4.

A spotless and informal restaurant painted in happy colours and dedicated to the food of Oaxaca – the Mexican region famed for its seven moles (sauces). Here you can try at least four: mole negro, made with four types of chilli, sesame seeds, tomatoes, garlic, onions, bananas, raisins and secret spices, usually served over chicken; red mole coloradito, which includes chocolate, sugar and peanuts; or the green and yellow moles.
Branch: 11127 Palms Boulevard, at Sepulveda Boulevard, West LA (1-310 837 1153).

Noshi Sushi
4430 Beverly Boulevard, at N Hobart Place (1-323 469 3458). Bus 14, 207, 357/I-10, exit Western Avenue north. **Open** 11.30am-9pm Tue-Sun; closed Mon. **Main courses** $9-$13. **No credit cards.** **Map** p307 C3.

This is the perfect complement to an expensive day at the Beverly Hot Springs spa across the street (*see p194*). It's almost a fast-food sushi bar: basic, cheap and popular with the masses. Try halibut sushi in special sauce or spicy tuna handrolls.

Pho Okay
4220 Beverly Boulevard, at Normandie Avenue (1-213 487 5002). Bus 14, 206, 316/I-10, exit Normandie Avenue north. **Open** 10am-10pm Tue-Sun; closed Mon. **Main courses** $5-$8. **Credit** MC, V. **Map** p308 A4.

When we visited, the 'P' had lost its neon glimmer, but this spotless family-run Vietnamese place, located in a mini-mall in a Korean-Latino neighbourhood, is still a gem. Pho, spring rolls and shrimp cakes are all fabulous, and you can eat like a prince for $10.

Soot Bull Jeep
3136 W Eighth Street, between Berendo & Catalina Streets (1-213 387 3865). Metro Wilshire-Western/bus 66/I-10, exit Vermont Avenue north.

Open 11am-11pm daily. **Main courses** $11-$15. **Credit** AmEx, MC, V. **Map** p308 A5.

This is one of the best Korean barbecue joints in Los Angeles. Even before you're seated, a waitress scatters a trowel full of glowing coals into a pit set in the middle of your table.

Woo Lae Oak
623 S Western Avenue, between Wilshire Boulevard & Sixth Street, Koreatown (1-213 384 2244). Metro Wilshire-Western/bus 20, 21, 720/I-10, exit Western Avenue north. **Open** 11.30am-10.30pm daily. **Main courses** lunch $8; dinner $9-$18. **Credit** AmEx, DC, MC, V. **Map** p307 C4.

Another traditional Korean barbecue restaurant, where you can cook a custom-made meal on your own hwaro (table-top grill). The sister restaurant in Beverly Hills serves near-psychedelic dishes culled from a mixture of French and Korean cuisines – we suggest ke sal mari (crab and spinach crêpes), chap chae (fried glass noodles and assorted vegetables) and pajun (seafood and spring onion pancakes).
Branch: 170 N La Cienega Boulevard, at Wilshire Boulevard, Beverly Hills (1-310 452 4187).

Downtown LA

Café Pinot
700 W Fifth Street, between Flower Street & Grand Avenue (1-213 239 6500). Bus 16, 104, DASH B, C, F/I-110, exit Sixth Street east. **Open** 11.30am-2.30pm, 5.30-9pm Mon; 11.30am-2.30pm, 5.30-9.30pm Tue-Thur; 11.30am-2.30pm, 5.30-10pm Fri; 5-10pm Sat; 5-9pm Sun. **Main courses** lunch $15-$18; dinner $16-$26. **Credit** AmEx, DC, Disc, MC, V. **Map** p309 B3.

Surreally located in the shadow of the Central Library, this restaurant is made almost entirely of glass: even if you're not seated on the pretty patio outside, you feel just as liberated. It's part of the Pinot family, so expectations are high, but they're more than fulfilled by chef Bernhard Renk's Californian-French menu.

Ciudad
445 S Figueroa Street, at Ninth Street (1-213 486-5171). Bus 66, 362, 434, 436, 439, 460, DASH A, F/I-110, exit Ninth Street west. **Open** 11.30am-9pm Mon; 11.30am-10pm Tue-Thur; 11.30am-11pm Fri; 4.30-11pm Sat; 4.30-10pm Sun. **Main courses** lunch $7-$20; dinner $15-$24. **Credit** AmEx, Disc, MC, V. **Map** p309 A3.

Ciudad is a tribute to Latin world cuisine, which celebrity chefs Susan Feniger and Mary Sue Milliken (*see p128* Border Grill) have researched in markets and private homes throughout South America. The predominantly soft yellow paintwork adorned with Miro-esque graphic swirls, paper-like cube lanterns, stubby wooden chairs and tables with giant, sculptured edible crackers, provide a distinctly 1950s feel. The waiting staff are dressed in embroidered, '50s-style Mexican shirts and striped trousers – this is a place with a sense of fun.

Eat, Drink, Shop

Empress Pavillion

Bamboo Plaza, suite 201, 988 N Hill Street, at
Bernard Street (1-213 617 9898). Bus 81, 90, 91,
94, 401, 402, 410, 418/I-110, exit Hill Street east.
Open 9am-3pm, 3.30-9.45pm daily. **Main courses**
$11-18. **Credit** DC, MC, V.

Come with a crowd to this outstanding – and vast –
Cantonese-style restaurant, so you can flag down
more of the dim sum waitresses. The main menu is
good, too.

Mon Kee's

679 N Spring Street, at Ord Street (1-213 628
6717). Metro Union Station/bus 81, 90, 91, DASH
B/I-110, exit Hill Street east. **Open** 11am-10pm
Mon-Thur, Sun; 11am-10.30pm Sat. **Main courses**
$18-$20. **Credit** AmEx, DC, MC, V.
Map p309 C1.

Arguably the best Chinese seafood in the area. Pick
out your own live Maine lobster or crab and have it
cooked in garlic sauce, or get down and dirty with
crispy shrimp served with a secret-recipe sauce.

Nick & Stef's

330 S Hope Street, between Third & Fourth Streets
(1-213 680 0330). Bus Metrolink Shuttle Bunker
Hill/US 101, exit Hill Street south. **Open** 11.30am-
2.30pm, 5.30-9.30pm Mon-Thur; 11.30am-2.30pm,
5.30-10.30pm Fri, Sat; 5-9pm Sun. **Main courses**
$19-$32. **Credit** AmEx, DC, MC, V. **Map** p309 B2.

The new joint from Joachim Splichal (*see also p149*
Patina, *p153* Café Pinot, *p157* Pinot Bistro and *p149*
Pinot Hollywood), this is a steakhouse extraordinaire.

The Pacific Dining Car

1310 W Sixth Street, at Witmer Street (1-213 483
6000). Bus 18, 316/I-110, exit Third Street west.
Open 24hrs daily. **Main courses** breakfast $8-$15;
lunch $20-$25; dinner $41-$46. **Credit** AmEx, DC,
MC, V. **Map** p309 A3.

When this 24-hour, all-American steak house opened
in 1921, LA barely extended west of Downtown. It
was immediately adopted as a hangout by local
politicians, businessmen, lawyers and sportsmen
(from nearby Dodger Stadium). The front room
resembles a Pacific Rail dining car, service is attentive and the menu is fastidiously realised: corn-fed
beef from the Midwest, which the chefs age themselves and cook over mesquite charcoal, a good
selection of fish and shellfish and inventive breakfast dishes such as eggs sardu (with spinach) and
roast beef hash.

Philippe's Original Sandwich Shop

1001 N Alameda Street, at Ord Street (1-213 628
3781). Metro Union Station/bus 76, DASH B, Santa
Monica 10/US 101, exit Alameda Street north.
Open 6am-10pm daily. **Main courses** $5-$7.
No credit cards. Map p309 C1.

Philippe Mathieu invented the French Dip Sandwich
in 1908: freshly carved roast beef, lamb, pork or
turkey served on a soft bun dipped in the meat's
juices. Choose from a fine selection of wines by the
glass to accompany said creation.

vermont: pretty as a picture. *See p155.*

Traxx

Union Station, 800 N Alameda Street, between Cesar
E Chavez Avenue & US 101 (1-213 625 1999).
Metro Union Station/bus 40, 42, 436, 444, 445,
446, 447, DASH B/US 101, exit Alameda Street
north. **Open** 11.30am-2pm, 5.30-9pm Mon-Fri; 5.30-
9.30pm Sat; closed Sun. **Main courses** $10-$28.
Credit AmEx, MC, V. **Map** p309 C1.

This restaurant on the concourse of Union Station,
wittily incorporates some of the station's art deco
details. And the Californian-French food is excellent, with such creations as endive with gorgonzola
and walnuts, lamb sandwiches and pumpkin risotto
with shrimp.

Also recommended

R-23 (Japanese) 923 E Third Street (1-213 687 7178);
Yagura Ichiban (Japanese) Japanese Village Plaza
Mall, 335 E Second Street (1-213 623 4141).

East of Hollywood

Café Stella

3932 Sunset Boulevard, at Hyperion Avenue (1-323
666 0265). Bus 2, 3, 4, 175, 176/US 101, exit Silver
Lake Boulevard north. **Open** 6-11pm Tue-Sat; closed
Mon, Sun. **Main courses** $18-$20. **Credit** AmEx,
MC, V. **Map** p308 B2.

An amazing casual *boite* of a French bistro with
additional pavement patio, where the menu is anything but fussy nouvelle. Poulet à l'estragon, excellent steak au poivre with pommes lyonnaise or
transcluscent pomme frites, and ratatouille. Small
and popular – so we strongly advise that you book.

Cha Cha Cha

656 N Virgil Avenue, at Melrose Avenue (1-323 664
7723). Bus 10, 11, 26/I-10, exit Vermont Avenue
north. **Open** 8am-10.30pm daily. **Main courses**

Eat, Drink, Shop

lunch $7-$10; dinner $8-$17. **Credit** AmEx, DC, Disc, MC, V. **Map** p308 A3.
One of Mario Tomayo's restaurants: a festive, funky place whose Latin American menu draws all the best people to the worst neighbourhood. We thoroughly recommend the jerked dishes. *See also p150 Atlas Supper Club.*

Electric Lotus
4656 Franklin Avenue, at Vermont Avenue (1-323 953 0040). Bus 2, 3, 204, 217, 354/US 101, exit Vermont Avenue north. **Open** 10.30am-midnight Mon-Thur; 10.30am-1am Fri, Sat; closed Sun. **Main courses** $8-$12. **Credit** AmEx, MC, V. **Map** p308 A2.
A hip, late-night Indian restaurant with a chic and contemporary interior and brightly coloured plastic chairs, plus traditional live entertainment or electronica-inspired DJs almost every night.

Fred 62
1850 N Vermont Avenue, at Russell Avenue (1-213 667 0062). Bus 204, 354/US 101, exit Vermont Avenue north. **Open** 24hrs daily. **Main courses** $8-$12. **Credit** AmEx, DC, Disc, MC, V. **Map** p308 A2.
At the latest whimsical venture of Fred Eric (of Vida fame, *see p155*), on the increasingly hipper-than-thou Vermont Avenue, you can satisfy your hunger pangs at any time of day or night. The menu is stylised fast food, with a health-conscious and vegetarian edge. It's done out like a 1950s diner with some 1960s style overlap, and the jukebox is stacked with 1970s funk to add to the mix.

Los Feliz
2138 Hillhurst Avenue, at Los Feliz Boulevard (1-323 666 8666). Bus 180, 181/I-5, exit Los Feliz Boulevard west. **Open** 11.30am-3pm, 5.30-11pm Tue-Thur; 5.30-11pm Fri, Sat; 11.30am-11pm Sun; closed Mon. **Main courses** brunch $23; dinner $17-$26. **Credit** AmEx, DC, MC, V. **Map** p308 A1.
Los Feliz is one of the most exciting additions to this burgeoning hip neighbourhood. Chef Collin Crannell's inventive and subtle creations are a perfect beginning to an evening that is best ended next door at the Jazz Spot. Aubergine timbale with herbed goat's cheese, or lobster salad on fava beans are popular starters, followed, perhaps, by duck breast on stone-ground grits with pears, or vegetarian cassoulet with root veg, mushrooms and navy white beans.

Mexico City
2121 Hillhurst Avenue, at Los Feliz Boulevard (1-323 661 7222). Bus 180, 181/I-5, exit Los Feliz Boulevard west. **Open** 5-10pm Mon, Tue; noon-3pm, 5-10pm Wed-Fri; noon-11pm Sat, Sun. **Main courses** $9-$15. **Credit** AmEx, MC, V. **Map** p308 A1.
The ambience is 1950s Mexican. The food is brave – myriad enchiladas with eclectic sauces and Yucatan specialities including carne and shrimp. The scene: young hipsters.

Millie's
3524 W Sunset Boulevard, between Maltman Avenue & Griffith Park Boulevard (1-323 664 0404). Bus 2, 3, 4, 302, 304/US 101, exit Silver Lake Boulevard north. **Open** 8am-10pm Mon-Thur, Sun; 8am-midnight Fri, Sat. **Main courses** $5-$7. **No credit cards. Map** p308 B3.
This quaint little all-American diner – complete with a counter-top jukebox that plays everything from Tony Bennett to Nick Cave – has gone through a lot of owners since it opened in 1926. Local eccentrics swarm here for home-made food at good prices. Or is it because you can bring your own booze? Try the Eleanor R (for Roosevelt): two eggs over easy, cheddar, salsa and sour cream on rosemary potatoes.

vermont
1714 Vermont Avenue, at Hollywood Boulevard (1-323 661 6163). Bus 180, 181, 204, 217, 354/US 101, exit Vermont Avenue north. **Open** 11.30am-3pm, 5.30-10.30pm Tue-Thur; 11.30am-3pm, 5.30-11.30pm Fri, Sat; 5.30-10pm Sun; closed Mon. **Main courses** $13-$19. **Credit** AmEx, DC, Disc, MC, V. **Map** p308 A2.
Everything about vermont is warm, from hospitable owners Michael and Miguel to the back-to-basics decor and the well-turned-out contemporary American-meets-French comfort food. Michael's salad – a couple of perfectly poached eggs perched atop bacon and frisée with a warmed vinaigrette – is hard to beat. Lamb shank on lentils is excellent, as is the delicate fish bouillabaisse. They've just taken over the former bakery next door, where they plan to open a bar serving finger food.

Also recommended
El Chavo (Mexican) 4441 W Sunset Boulevard (1-213 664 0871); **Café Figaro** (French) 1802 N Vermont Avenue (1-323 662 1587); **Jay's Jay Burger** (hamburgers) 4481 Santa Monica Boulevard (1-323 666 5204); **Katsu** (Japanese) 1972 Hillhurst Avenue (1-323 665 1891).

Vida
1930 Hillhurst Avenue, between Franklin & Clarissa Avenues (1-323 660 4446). Bus 26, 180, 181/US 101, exit Vermont Avenue north. **Open** 6-10pm Mon-Fri; 6-11pm Sat, Sun. **Main courses** $15-$25. **Credit** AmEx, DC, MC, V. **Map** p308 A2.
One of the wave of Californian restaurants that serve inventive, offbeat, usually vertically constructed and whimsically named food. There is an array of different corners at which you can dine, and a busy bar. The crowd is chic.

East LA

Boca del Rio
3706 E Whittier Boulevard, at Indiana Street (1-323 268 9339). Bus 18, 65, 720/Hwy 60, exit Whittier Boulevard east. **Open** 9am-9pm daily. **Main courses** $8-$11. **Credit** AmEx, Disc, MC, V.
This family restaurant specialises in food from Veracruz in the southern part of Mexico. Try

grilled lobster, steamed and stuffed crab served with rice and flavoured with enough garlic to ward off the most persistent vampires, or red snapper marinated with garlic and dried chillis. The atmosphere is convivial.

La Parilla

2126 Caesar E Chavez Avenue, between Cummings & St Louis Streets (1-323 262 3434). Bus 68, 70, 71, 78, 378, 379/I-10, exit Cesar E Chavez Avenue east. **Open** 8am-11pm daily. **Main courses** $8-$10. **Credit** AmEx, MC, V.

Slap-bang in the middle of run-down Boyle Heights, this hospitable Mexican restaurant is the real thing. Its speciality is grilled meats, especially sweet and spicy spare ribs, as well as seafood, mole sauce, cactus and sangria. Beware of the parillada for two: it's way too large.

La Serenata di Garibaldi

1842 E First Street, between State Street & Boyle Avenue (1-323 265 2887). Bus 30, 31/I-10, exit Boyle Avenue north. **Open** 11am-3.30pm, 5-10pm daily. **Main courses** lunch $9-$15; dinner $11-$21. **Credit** DC, MC, V.

This small, simple place in Boyle Heights serves fresh fish in exquisite sauces. Call in advance, get directions, park in the back and you'll dine at red-and-white checked tables with Mexican families, mariachi musicians and Downtown artists. La Serenata Gourmet is the less formal and less expensive Westside version – try the fish tacos and empanadas stuffed with pink shrimp – while the newest branch is in Santa Monica.

Branches: 1416 Fourth Street, between Broadway & Santa Monica Boulevard, Santa Monica (1-310 656 7017); **La Serenata Gourmet** 10924 W Pico Boulevard, at Westwood Boulevard, West LA (1-310 441 9667).

Semitas Poblanas

3010 E First Street, at Evergreen Avenue (1-323 881 0428). Bus 30, 31, 253/I-10, exit Cesar E Chavez Avenue east. **Open** 10am-10pm daily. **Main courses** $4-$7. **No credit cards.**

Need a fast snack in East LA? Then head here for puebla-style beef sandwiches.

Also recommended

Tacos Clarita (Mexican) 3049 E Fourth Street (1 323 262 3620).

South Central

Coley's Place

300 E Florence Avenue, at La Brea Avenue, Inglewood (1-310 672 7474). Bus 107/I-10, exit La Brea Avenue south. **Open** 8am-9pm Mon; 8am-10pm Tue-Thur; 8am-11pm Fri, Sat; closed Sun. (Breakfast 8-11am, by reservation only). **Main courses** $9-$12. **Credit** AmEx, MC, V.

A very hospitable Jamaican restaurant where you will be greeted by an out-of-this-world shrimp St James: tender shrimp surrounded by okra nestling

in a coconut cream sauce with conch fritters. Or there's chicken Lockerton, a breast of chicken stuffed with bananas and then deep-fried. Don't even think about asking for the bill before you've indulged in an order of peach cobbler.

Harold & Belle's

2920 W Jefferson Boulevard, between Arlington Avenue & Crenshaw Boulevard, Jefferson Park (1-323 735 9023). Bus 38/I-10, exit Crenshaw Boulevard south. **Open** 11.30am-10pm Mon-Thur, Sun; 11.30am-11pm Fri, Sat. **Main courses** lunch $9-$18; dinner $16-$32. **Credit** AmEx, Disc, MC, V.

If you have a hankering for upmarket Southern food, you're in luck (though the area is not the safest for visitors). Once inside, you're cosseted in elegance and, of course, good ol' Southern hospitality. Try breaded fish with crayfish sauce, soft-shell crabs or Louisiana oysters.

M&M's Soul Food Café

9506 S Avalon Boulevard, at 95th Street, Watts (1-323 777 9250). Bus 51/I-110, exit Century Boulevard east. **Open** 8am-8pm Tue-Sat; 8am-6pm Sun; closed Mon. **Main courses** $8-$11. **Credit** (Mon-Fri only) MC, V.

All the branches of this soul-food chain claim to be the original – this one has been around for 30 years. With only five burgundy leatherette booths, seven stools at the counter and four tables in the middle, it's a small, basic place. People who try the newer, more user-friendly branches generally end up back here because, quite simply, its short ribs (served barbecued or smothered), oxtail, pork chops and chitlins (chitterlings) are the best.

The Valleys

San Fernando Valley

Art's Deli

112224 Ventura Boulevard, between Laurel Canyon Boulevard & Whitsett Avenue, Studio City (1-818 762 1221). Bus 150, 240, 750, DASH Van Nuys/US 101, exit Laurel Canyon Boulevard south. **Open** 6.30am-9.30pm Mon-Thur; 6.30am-10.30pm Fri, Sat; 6.30am-9pm Sun. **Main courses** $10-$14. **Credit** AmEx, MC, V.

Many people think this is one of LA's best delis. Seating is mainly in booths, with large photos of their famous sandwiches on the walls – try the corned beef and pastrami.

Chili My Soul

4928 Balboa Boulevard, at Ventura Boulevard, Encino (1-818 981 7685). Bus 150, 240, 750/US 101, exit Balboa Boulevard south. **Open** 11am-9pm daily. **Main courses** $5-$7. **Credit** AmEx, MC, V.

Randy Hoffman prepares 28 different kinds of chilli, their spiciness indicated by numbers from one to ten. We recommend the habanero/mango, chicken and Irish whiskey. They all come with a choice of three amazing toppings.

Joe Joe's

*13355 Ventura Boulevard, between Coldwater
Canyon Boulevard & Woodman Avenue, Sherman
Oaks (1-818 990 8280). Bus 150, 240, 750/
US 101, exit Coldwater Canyon Boulevard south.
Open 11.30am-2.30pm, 6-10pm Mon-Thur;
6-11pm Fri; 11am-2pm, 6-11pm Sat; 11am-2pm
Sun.* **Main courses** $13-$18. **Credit** AmEx,
MC, V.

This casual, one-room place in Sherman Oaks is
adorned with illustrations from children's books.
Although chef Leon Cruz's heart-warming food is
frequently presented in the hip, vertical pile-up
style, it is also grounded in earthiness, with the
likes of lamb sirloin crusted with porcini mushrooms sitting alongside a plate of shrimp towering
over saffron risotto, crowned with shredded and
sautéed carrots and green beans. The four-course
set menu is tough to beat at $28.

Le Petit Bistro

*13360 Ventura Boulevard, at Fulton Avenue,
Sherman Oaks (1-818 501 7999). Bus 150, 240,
750/US 101, exit Coldwater Canyon Boulevard
south.* **Open** 11.30am-2.30pm, 5.30-11pm Fri;
5.30-11.30pm Sat; 5-11.30pm Sun. **Main courses**
lunch $9-$13; dinner $11-$19. **Credit** AmEx, Disc,
MC, V.

A French bistro with very good roast chicken and
pommes frites among other serviceable fare. It's
always bustling with hungry locals.

Pinot Bistro

*12969 Ventura Boulevard, between Coldwater
Canyon Avenue & Valley Vista Boulevard, Studio
City (1-818 990 0500). Bus 150, 240, 750/US 101,
exit Coldwater Canyon Boulevard south.* **Open**
11.30am-2.30pm, 6-10pm Mon-Thur; 11.30am-2.30pm,

6-10.30pm Fri; 5.30-10.30pm Sat; 5.30-9.30pm Sun.
Main courses lunch $15-$18; dinner $16-$21.
Credit AmEx, MC, V.

This is part of Joachim Splichal's Pinot empire,
where executive chef Jose Flores conjures up
French bistro-style food. The smart (if a mite staid
and masculine) decor of wood panelling, ochre
walls and chequered floor, the attentive service and
the eclectic menu make it one of the most prized
spots in the area. See also *p149* Patina and *p154*
Nik & Stef's.

Poquito Mas

*3701 Cahuenga Boulevard, between Lankershim
Boulevard & Barham Boulevard, Studio City (1-818
760 8226). Bus 156, 426/US 101, exit Cahuenga
Boulevard south.* **Open** 10am-midnight Mon-Thur,
Sun; 10am-1am Fri, Sat. **Main courses** $4-$7.
Credit AmEx, MC, V.

The strongest link in this chain of fast-food Mexican
joints, serving some of the freshest fish this side of
Baja. You can eat on the small patio or take out. Try
the shrimp tacos San Felipe or the ahi tuna tacos –
and the beans, of course.

Posto

*14928 Ventura Boulevard, at Kester Avenue,
Sherman Oaks (1-818 784 4400). Bus 150, 240,
561, 750/US 101, exit Sepulveda Boulevard south.*
Open 11.30am-2.30pm, 5-10.30pm Mon-Fri;
5-10.30pm Sat; closed Sun. **Main courses** $13-$25.
Credit AmEx, DC, MC, V.

The child of Piero Selvaggio's Valentino restaurant
(*see p130*) on the Westside, Posto achieves the
impossible: serious class without pretension. Chef
Steve Sampson's dishes include duck breast marinated in balsamic vinegar and served with fruit
mostarda, stuffed veal rolled with prosciutto and

Saladang Song: amazing architecture and inventive Thai food. *See p160.*

fontina cheese and a blackberry brown-butter tart
served with vanilla ice-cream. Posto also boasts one
of the finest wine collections in California. Go on,
spoil yourself.

Saddle Peak Lodge
419 Cold Canyon Road, off Piuma Road,
Calabasas (1-818 222 3888). I-10, exit Pacific
Coast Highway north. **Open** 6-9pm Wed-Sat;
11.30am-2pm, 6-9pm Sun; closed Mon, Tue.
Main courses $20-$40; Sunday brunch $22.50.
Credit AmEx, MC, V.
Saddle Peak Lodge is a fabulous escape from the
crowded streets of the city: it's only a 30-minute
drive from Santa Monica to a rustic hunting lodge
setting, complete with fireplaces, waterfalls and
Malibu views. Game is the speciality here in safari
park proportions: antelope, kangaroo, buffalo, venison, pheasant and even ostrich are usually on the
menu. Saddle Peak is impossibly romantic – if you
don't mind being stared at by stuffed deer heads at
almost every turn, that is.

Sushi Nozawa
11288 Ventura Boulevard, between Tujunga &
Vineland Avenues, Studio City (1-818 508 7017).
Bus 96, 150, 240, 750/US 101, exit Vineland
Avenue south. **Open** noon-2pm, 5.30-10pm Mon-Fri;
5.30-10pm Sat; closed Sun. **Main courses** $4-$6
per piece. **Credit** MC, V.
The Valley's best-kept secret, hidden in a ordinary-
looking strip mall. Queue with others in the know
who adore this café-style restaurant serving just one
thing: sushi. Above the somewhat taciturn chef is a
large sign that brusquely announces 'No California
Roll' and 'Tonight's Special: Trust Me'. Trust us: you
will become a devotee.

Also recommended
Anajak Thai 14704 Ventura Boulevard,
Sherman Oaks (1-818 501 4201); **The California
Canteen** (Mediterranean) 3311 Cahuenga Boulevard
W, Universal City (1-213 876 1702); **Sushi on Tap**
(Japanese) 11056 Ventura Boulevard, Studio City
(1-818 985 2254).

Restaurants by cuisine

American

Ammo see p148; **The Beach House** p128;
Benny's BBQ p134; **Cadillac Café** p136;
Chez Jay p129; **Chili My Soul** p156;
Dominick's p137; **Hollywood Canteen** p148;
Houston's p148; **Jones** p138; **JR's Bar-B-Que**
p148; **Kate Mantilini** p142; **Lola's** p139;
The Los Angeles Palm p139; **Maple Drive**
p142; **Maui Beach Café** p145; **Morton's**
p139; **Musso & Frank Grill** p149; **Nick &
Stef's** p154; **The Pacific Dining Car** p154;
The Pig p140; **Reata** p143.

Californian

5 Dudley p133; **72 Market Street** p133;
Angels p133; **Boxer** p136; **Café Pinot** p153;
Campanile p151; **Chaya Brasserie** p136;
Chez Melange p160; **Citrus** p148; **Fenix at
the Argyle** p137; **Fred 62** p155; **French 75**
p160; **Geoffrey's** p134; **Granita** p135; **Hal's
Bar & Grill** p133; **Hotel Bel-Air** p147; **The Ivy**
p138; **The Ivy at the Shore** p129; **James'
Beach** p133; **Joe Joe's** p157; **Joe's** p134;
Le Dôme p139; **Linq** p150; **Los Feliz** p155;
Michael's p130 (french cal); **Michi** p160;
Nic's p142; **Off Vine** p149; **Patina** p149;
Pinot Bistro p157; **Pinot Hollywood** p149;
The Polo Lounge p143; **Rock** p134;
Röckenwagner p130; **Saddle Peak Lodge**
p158; **Spago of Beverly Hills** p143; **Traxx**
p154; **vermont** p155; **Vida** p155.

Caribbean & soul food

Aunt Kizzy's Back Porch p134; **Bamboo**
p148; **Coley's Place** p156; **Harold & Belle's**
p156; **M&M Soul Food** p156; **Maurice's
Snack 'n' Chat** p152; **Porch** p140; **Roscoe's
Chicken 'n' Waffles** p149; **Versailles** p147

Chinese

China One p137; **Empress Harbor** p159;
Empress Pavillion p154; **Joss** p139; **Lake
Spring Shanghai** p159; **Mon Kee's** p154; **Mr
Chow's** p142; **Royal Star** p130; **VIP Harbor**
p147; **X'ian** p145; **Yujean Kang's** p141.

Delis, diners & fast food

Apple Pan p145; **Art's Deli** (deli) p156;
Canter's p150; **Cassell's** p156; **Ed
Debevic's** p141; **The Fountain Coffee Shop**
p141; **Hollywood Hills Coffee Shop** p149;
Milky Way (kosher) p147; **Millie's** p155;
Nate & Al p142; **Philippe's Original
Sandwich Shop** p154; **Pink's Hot Dogs**
p140; **Rae's** p130; **Tail-o'-the-Pup** p140.

Fish & seafood

Delmonico's p146; **Gladstone's 4 Fish** p135;
Hymie's Fish Market p147; **Killer Shrimp**
p134; **The Lobster** p129; **Neptune's Net**
p135; **Tidal Wave** p149.

San Gabriel Valley & Pasadena

All India Café

39 S Fair Oaks Avenue, between Green Street & Colorado Boulevard, Pasadena (1-626 440 0309). Bus 188, 256, 483/I-110, exit Colorado Boulevard west. **Open** 11.30am-10pm Mon-Thur, Sun; 11am-11pm Fri, Sat. **Main courses** $9-$11. **Credit** AmEx, DC, Disc, MC, V.

There's little on the West Coast in the way of decent Indian food, but this excellent, eclectic restaurant in Pasadena offers distinguished curries and innumerable interesting vegetable dishes.

Babita

1823 S San Gabriel Boulevard, at E Norwood Place, San Gabriel (1-626 288 7265). Bus 76, 264, 487, 489/I-10, exit San Gabriel Boulevard north. **Open** 11.30am-2.30pm, 5.30-9.30pm Tue-Thur; 11.30am-2.30pm, 5.30-10pm Fri; 5.30-10pm Sat; closed Sun, Mon. **Main courses** $10-$16. **Credit** AmEx, Disc, MC, V.

Modern spin on honest Mexican favourites prepared with the panache of soophisticated French cooking, courtesy of chef Roberto Berrelleza.

Empress Harbor

111 N Atlantic Boulevard, at E Garvey Avenue, Monterey Park (1-626 300 8833). Bus 70, 260/I-10, exit Atlantic Boulevard south. **Open** 10am-8pm daily (dim sum 11am-2.30pm Mon-Fri). **Main courses** $15-$20. **Credit** AmEx, Disc, MC, V.

Possibly the best dim sum (served lunchtime only) you'll eat outside Hong Kong. Also good are the shark's fin soup and the lobster.

Lake Spring Shanghai Restaurant

219 E Garvey Avenue, at Russell Avenue, Monterey Park (1-626 280 3571). Bus 70, 262/I-10, exit Garfield Avenue south. **Open** 11am-3pm, 5-10pm daily. **Main courses** lunch $5-$6; dinner $10. **Credit** MC, V.

This is an awe-inspiring Shanghai café, a place to experiment with hairy crabs, pork pump (pork encased in fat) and jade shrimp.

French

Café Stella p154; Cezanne Le Merigot p128; JiRaffe p129; JW's p160; La Cachette p148; Le Petit Bistro p157; Les Deux Café p149; The Little Door p150; L'Orangerie p139; Melisse p129; Mimosa p150; Pastis p140.

Indian

All India Café p159; Bombay Café p146; Electric Lotus p155.

International

1 Pico p128; Café del Rey p134; The Canal Club p133; Chinois on Main p129; Eurochow p145; Raffles L'Ermitage Beverly Hills p143.

Italian & pizza

Alejo's Trattoria p134; Café Med p136; Café Roma p141; Chianti Cucina p136; Dan Tana's p137; Farfalla p152; Giorgio Baldi p129; Girasole p152; Mulberry Street Pizzeria p142; Orso p140; Posto p157; Tra di Noi p136; Trattoria Amici p145; Trattoria Tre Venezie p160; Valentino p130; Vincenti p147.

Japanese

Hirozen p138; The Hump p129; Ita Cho p138; Kakemoto p141; Matsuhisa p142; Nobu p135; Noshi Sushi p153; Sushi Nozawa p158; Sushi Roku p130; Ubon p141; Yabu p141; Yamashiro p150.

Korean, Thai & Vietnamese

Chan Dara p146; Le Colonial p139; Dong Il Jang, Jeep, Pho Okay all p153 Red Moon p147; Rosalynn p130; Saladang Song p160; Soot Bull Woo Lae Oak p153; Talesai p141.

Mexican

Babita p159; Boca del Rio p155; El Cholo p151; El Coyote p137; Gallego's p129; Guelaguetza p153; La Fonda p152; La Parilla p156; La Serenata di Garibaldi p156; Mexico City p155; Monte Alban p147; Poquito Mas p157; Semitas Poblanas p156.

Nuevo Latino/Southwestern

Asia de Cuba p136; Atlas Supper Club p150; Border Grill p128; Cha Cha Cha p154; Ciudad p153; La Boca del Conga Room p152; Mojo at the W p145; Prado p152; Sonora Café p152; Xiomara p160.

Pan-Asian

Indochine p138; Jozu p139; Mako p142; Mandalay p139; Tahiti p150; Typhoon p130.

South American

Café Brasil p148; Gaucho Grill p137; Itana Bahia p138; Mario's Peruvian Seafood p149.

Healthfood/vegetarian

Axe p133; Fig Tree p133; Real Food p140; Venus p134.

Eat, Drink, Shop

Saladang Song

383 S Fair Oaks Avenue between California & Del Mar Boulevards, Pasadena (1-626 793 5200). Bus 177, 485/I-110, exit Del Mar Boulevard west. **Open** 6.30am-10pm daily. **Main courses** lunch $8-$10; dinner $6-$16. **Credit** AmEx, DC, MC, V.

The splendid architectural setting (it looks more Moorish than Thai) with indoor and outdoor seating, and honest Thai food served by beautiful Thai girls in elaborate silk dresses, will transport you. There are deep-fried spicy fishcakes, rice noodles in a transluscent pink dripping in coconut milk, and pork spare ribs – things you would find at the best Thai cafés and outdoor carts.

Trattoria Tre Venezie

119 W Green Street, at Fair Oaks Avenue, Pasadena (1-626 795 4455). Bus 256, 483/I-110, exit Colorado Boulevard west. **Open** 11.30am-2.30pm, 5.30-10.30pm Tue-Thur; 5.30-10.30pm Fri-Sun; closed Mon.* **Main courses** lunch $8-$20; dinner $13-$24. **Credit** AmEx, Disc, MC, V.

Chef Gianfranco Minuz's Austro-Hungarian and Venetian-influenced cuisine is causing a stir at this elegant, light-filled trattoria. Dishes include ravioli filled with ricotta, parmigiano reggiano and beet-roots, finished with more beetroot, julienne-style.

Xiomara

69 N Raymond Avenue, at Colorado Boulevard, Pasadena (1-626 796 2520). Bus 181, 188, 256, 401/I-110, exit Colorado Boulevard west. **Open** 11.30am-11pm Mon-Fri; 5-11pm Sat, Sun. **Main courses** lunch $8-$13; dinner $18-$26. **Credit** AmEx, Disc, MC, V.

Eating at this nuevo Latino restaurant is a mystical, one-of-a-kind experience. It's owned by Cuban-born Xiomara Ardolina, with Steven Herrman master-minding in the kitchen.

Also recommended

Arirang (Korean) 114 W Union Street, Pasadena (1-626 577 8885); **Market City Caffè** (Italian) 33 S Fair Oaks Avenue, Pasadena (1-626 568 0203); **The Raymond** (Californian) 1250 S Fair Oaks Avenue, Pasadena (1-626 441 3136); **Sushi Polo** (Japanese) 927 E Colorado Boulevard, Pasadena (1-626 356 0099).

The South Bay

Chez Melange

Palos Verdes Inn, 1716 Pacific Coast Highway, between Prospect Avenue & Palos Verdes Boulevard, Redondo Beach (1-310 540 1222). Bus 225, 232/I-405, exit Artesia Boulevard west. **Open** 7am-10pm Mon-Thur; 7.30am-11pm Fri, Sat; 7-10pm Sun. **Main courses** breakfast $8-$11; lunch $9-$13; dinner $17-$21. **Credit** AmEx, Disc, MC, V.

In 1982, in the middle of the recession, Englishman Michael Franks and New Yorker Robert Bell walked into a bank with no collateral and came out with a $200,000 loan to build Chez Melange. They now have five hugely successful restaurants in the South

Bay. The food at their flagship operation is nouvelle eclectic, but doesn't take itself too seriously – how could it, when it's housed in a late-1950s diner? There are also vodka, champagne and caviar bars.

Michi

903 Manhattan Avenue, at Ninth Street, Manhattan Beach (1-310 376 0613). Bus 126, 439, Commuter Express 438/I-405, exit Hawthorne Boulevard north. **Open** 6-10.30pm Mon; 11.30am-2.30pm, 6-10.30pm Tue-Fri; 6-11pm Sat; closed Sun. **Main courses** $12-$23. **Credit** AmEx, DC, MC, V.

Michi Takahashi is one of the Southland's hippest chefs, thanks to his cross-cultural culinary treat – inspired by French, Italian and Japanese cuisines. We like the oysters on roast potatoes as a starter, followed by seafood paella for two as an entrée, and absolutely anything for dessert.

Also recommended

The Crab Pot (seafood) 215 Marina Drive, Long Beach (1-562 430 0272); **L'Opéra** (Italian) 101 Pine Avenue, Long Beach (1-562 491 0066); **Reed's** (New American-French) 2640 N Sepulveda Boulevard, Manhattan Beach (1-310 546 3299); **Splash!** (Californian) 350 N Harbor Drive, at Beryl Street, Redondo Beach (1-310 798 5348).

Orange County & Anaheim

French 75

1464 Pacific Coast Highway, between Calliope & Mountain Streets, Laguna Beach (1-949 494 8444). Bus Orange County Transit 1/Hwy 133, exit PCH south. **Open** 5-11pm Mon-Sat; 11am-3pm, 5-11pm Sun. **Main courses** brunch $9-$16; dinner $16-$30; set menu $35. **Credit** AmEx, MC, V.

This is still the hottest thing to hit Laguna Beach in years: a little Parisian bistro and champagne bar, with oversized tables, overstuffed chairs, a surfeit of velvet and a patio, from which, if you crank your head enough, you can see the ocean. Dishes run the gamut from heavenly to earthbound: 'langoustine and crayfish cappuccino' and 'rustic French soul food'. There's live jazz in the evenings from Wednesday until Saturday.

JW's

Anaheim Marriott, 700 W Convention Way, at Harbor Boulevard, Anaheim (1-714 750 8000). Bus 460/I-5, exit Harbor Boulevard south. **Open** 5-10pm daily. **Main courses** $20-$25. **Credit** AmEx, DC, Disc, MC, V.

You have to see it to believe it. A French château, or at least a good facsimile thereof, slap-bang in the middle of the Marriott Hotel. Seafood and steaks with typically fussy hotel service. At least it's a safe haven from Disneyland.

Also recommended

Café Zoolu (Californian) 860 Glenneyre Street, Laguna Beach (1-714 494 6825); **The White House** (Italian) 887 S Anaheim Boulevard, Anaheim (1-714 772 1381).

Coffeehouses

In this hard-working, clean-living, car-driving city, coffee – in all its myriad forms –
rules as Angelenos' favourite beverage.

It's hard – outside the city's numerous fast-food
joints – to find a bad cup of coffee in Los
Angeles. In the city of the automobile, caffeine
is favoured over alcohol as the social drink of
choice and coffeehouses outnumber bars.
Whether you like to spend hours or just minutes
on your java intake, whether you're looking for
rocket fuel or just a rockin' good time, you will
find whatever your little caffeinated heart
desires in the City of Angels.

The sheer number of coffeehouses as well as
the sheer variety of coffee drinks is bewildering
to any first-timer. From vintage mom-and-pop
institutions where a good strong cup of joe is
poured straight up, to more hip and health-
conscious minimalist cafés where you can order
a non-fat decaff organic mocha with extract of
ginseng blended in, Angelenos bask in the
diversity that is inherent in every part of the
sprawling metropolis.

The past few years has seen a trend for siting
cafés within bookshops and record shops.
Chains such as **Borders Books & Music**
(*see below*) and independent shops such as
Opus Café (*see page 165*) allow you to browse
through magazines and books or flip through
CDs while sipping on your favourite latte.
There is also an increasing number of places
that specialise in teas from around the world –
Hugo's (*see page 163*) in West Hollywood is
a good example.

Cybercafés are still popular, and useful for
visitors wanting to get online: try **CyberJava**
in Hollywood (7080 Hollywood Boulevard, at La
Brea Avenue, 1-323 466 5600/www.cyberjava.
com). Another attraction is the outdoor patio:
smoking is prohibited in bars in California, so
many smokers have now chosen their local
coffeehouse with its outdoor seating over their
local pub for the evening's entertainment.

COFFEE CHAINS

There are a number of chain coffeehouses that
have literally hundreds of locations in the Los
Angeles area. While their product and design
standards are high, and reassuringly consistent,
their corporate sameness can seem bland
compared with the independents. We've
reviewed one branch of each of the Big Three:
Starbucks, the **Coffee Bean & Tea Leaf**
and **Peet's Coffee & Tea**.

Westside: beach towns

Abbot's Habit
*1401 Abbot Kinney Boulevard, at California Avenue,
Venice (1-310 399 1171). Bus Santa Monica 2,
Venice 33/I-10, exit Lincoln Boulevard south.* **Open**
6am-11pm daily. **No credit cards. Map** p304 A5.
By its very nature, Venice attracts a weirdly capti-
vating crowd, and the Abbot's Habit is no exception to this. Affluent canal home owners mix with
starving artists here. There's always plenty of local
art on the walls, but this is something of a hit-and-
miss experience: you may be sitting next to something that could shade your day in beautiful hues
or make you want to heave up your muffin. A
colourful experience all around.

Anastasia's Asylum
*1028 Wilshire Boulevard, between Tenth & 11th
Streets, Santa Monica (1-310 394 7113). Bus 20,
21, 22/I-10, exit Lincoln Boulevard north.* **Open**
6.30am-1am Mon-Thur; 6.30am-2am Fri; 8am-2am
Sat, Sun. **Credit** DC, Disc, MC, V. **Map** p304 B2.
This arty (and some say haunted) coffeehouse has
comfy armchairs, live music at night and great,
ever-changing artwork on the walls. There is some
mystery about the relationship between the owner
and the Russian Princess Anastasia, so secrets
abound in this little café.

Borders Books & Music
*1415 Third Street Promenade, between Broadway &
Santa Monica Boulevard, Santa Monica (1-310 393
9290/www.borderstores.com). Bus 4, 304, Santa
Monica 1, 2, 3, 7/I-10, exit Fourth Street north.*
Open 9am-11pm Mon-Thur, Sun; 9am-midnight Fri,
Sat. **Credit** AmEx, MC, V. **Map** p304 A2.
Once you've perused the extensive selection of books
on the multiple floors of this well-known bookshop
chain, take a break at the in-house café. It's a great
place to sit and read all those magazines you don't
want to pay for and/or lug around, and the coffee
and pastries are excellent.
Branches: throughout the city.

Interactive Café
*215 Broadway, at Second Street, Santa Monica
(1-310 395 5009). Bus 4, 33, 434, Santa Monica 7,
8, 10/I-10, exit Fourth Street north.* **Open** 6.30am-
1am Mon-Thur, Sun; 6.30am-2am Fri, Sat. **Credit**
MC, V. **Map** p304 A2.
Interactive sells newspapers and magazines, so you
can grab one as you sink into its velvet sofas. Then
take a deep breath and smell the incredible – and

incredibly large – flower arrangements and raise your eyes to the ceiling to take stock of the huge mixed-media installation. Great fruit shakes and sandwiches, with the added attraction that it's just around the corner from the shopping mecca that is Third Street Promenade.

Joni's Coffee Roaster Café
552 Washington Boulevard, at Via Marina Way, Marina del Rey (1-310 305 7147). Bus 108, Culver City 1/I-405, exit Venice Boulevard west. **Open** 5am-4pm Mon-Fri; 6am-4pm Sat, Sun. **Credit** AmEx, Disc, MC, V.
Opening early in the morning, Joni's has at its heart an antique iron coffee roasting machine. The extensive menu makes it a very popular place for breakfast, and it attracts a creative crowd of actors, producers and photographers for its brews of Kona, French and Jamaica Blue roasts.

Legal Grind
2640 Lincoln Boulevard, at Ocean Park Boulevard, Santa Monica (1-310 452 8160/www.legal-grind. com). Bus Santa Monica 3, 7/I-10, exit Lincoln Boulevard. **Open** 6.30am-6.30pm Mon-Thur; 6.30am-2pm Fri-Sun. **No credit cards**. **Map** p304 B3/4.
Coffee and counselling are the order of the day at this law centre, where the caffeinated meet a multitude of lawyers giving out advice ($10-$20) on various subjects. Lawyers are there every weekday towards the latter half of the afternoon and on Saturday mornings. The website lists the topics for each day, and don't forget to leave a donation to keep the centre running. California State Bar-certified.

Peet's Coffee & Tea
2439 Main Street, between Ocean Park Boulevard & Hollister Avenue, Santa Monica (1-310 399 8117/ www.peets.com). Bus 33, 333/I-10, exit Lincoln Boulevard. **Open** 6.30am-7pm daily. **Credit** Disc, MC, V. **Map** p304 A3.
Many coffee aficionados will claim that the best hit is to be found at Peet's, which started in San Francisco and was once a David against the Goliath of Starbucks, but is now pretty ubiquitous, too. And the best Peet's is arguably this one in Ocean Park. The hub of a small and stylish shopping mall designed by Frank Gehry – which contains the groovy MOCA Store and Rockenwagner restaurant – it is jam-packed in the mornings and is a favourite with local designers and architects.
Branches: throughout the city.

Starbucks
334 Third Street Promenade, at Wilshire Boulevard, Santa Monica (1-310 260 9947/www.starbucks.com). Bus 4, 304, Santa Monica 1, 2, 3, 7/I-10, exit Fourth Street north. **Open** 7am-11pm Mon-Thur; 7am-1am Fri, Sat; 8am-11pm Sun. **Credit** AmEx, MC, V. **Map** p304 A2.
Probably one of the most happening Starbucks on the Westside, this one is located on the pedestrianised Third Street Promenade, one of the busiest shopping streets near the ocean. Bring a book, but

remember to occasionally glance up: its locale is great for people-watching.
Branches: throughout the city; call 1-800 235 2883 to find your nearest.

Van Gogh's Ear
796 Main Street, between Rose Avenue & Abbot Kinney Boulevard, Venice (1-310 396 1987). Bus 33, 436, Santa Monica 1, 2/I-10, exit Fourth Street south. **Open** 24hrs daily. **No credit cards**. **Map** p304 A4.
This colourful, 24-hour café attracts an eclectic bunch of people because of its location. From the bodybuilders in the morning to the Venice hippies in the afternoon, there is certainly plenty of gossip and people-watching. Although the menu is slightly tongue-in-cheek (all the dishes are named after ne'er-do-well celebs – check out the Woody Allen or the John Belushi), the food is superb.

Also recommended
Panini Coffee & Café 4325 Glencoe Avenue, Marina del Rey (1-310 823 4446); **Tudor House** 1403 Second Street, Santa Monica (1-310 451 4107); **UnUrban Coffee House** 3301 Pico Boulevard, Santa Monica (1-310 315 0056); **World Café** 2820 Main Street, Santa Monica (1-310 394 7113).

Westside: inland

The Abbey
692 N Robertson Boulevard, at Santa Monica Boulevard, West Hollywood (1-310 289 8410). Bus 4, 10, 22, West Hollywood A, B, N/I-10, exit La Cienega Boulevard north. **Open** 7am-2am Mon-Thur; 7am-3am Fri; 8am-3am Sat; 8am-2am Sun. **Credit** AmEx, MC, V. **Map** p306 A2.
Right in the heart of West Hollywood, the Abbey is a beautiful space and set just far enough from the street to be quiet (at least during the day). It attracts a fairly mixed crowd in the day, and is much more gay – and much busier – in the evening (it's close to the big gay clubs, such as Rage and Micky's). The desserts are excellent. *See also p222.*

Buzz Coffee
8000 Sunset Boulevard, at Crescent Heights Boulevard, West Hollywood (1-323 656 7460). Bus 26, 163, 212, 217/I-10, exit Fairfax Avenue north. **Open** 7am-12.30am Mon-Thur, Sun; 7am-1.30am Fri, Sat. **Credit** AmEx, MC, V. **Map** p306 B1.
Housed in a fashionable outdoor mall, together with the celeb-filled Crunch gym, the upscale Burke-Williams spa, the indie cinema Sunset 5 and Virgin Megastore, this is as buzzy as its name suggests.
Branches: 8200 Santa Monica Boulevard, at Havenhurst Avenue, West Hollywood (1-323 650 7742); 7623 Beverly Boulevard, at Stanley Avenue, West Hollywood (1-323 634 7393).

Caffe Latte
6254 Wilshire Boulevard, at Crescent Heights Boulevard, Beverly Hills (1-323 936 5213). Bus 20, 21, 22/I-10, exit La Cienega Boulevard north. **Open**

Eat, Drink, Shop

Elixir: tonics, teas and tranquillity.

7am-9pm Mon-Fri; 8am-3.30pm Sat, Sun. **Credit** AmEx, MC, V. **Map** p306 B3.
Located in a mini-mall, so it's easy to miss, Caffe Latte is one of the best-kept secrets in Beverly Hills. It's kinda homey, has great food (try the muffins and French toast) and the coffee is roasted on the premises. A discovery that's as kind to your wallet as it is to your stomach.

Chado Tea Room
8422½ W Third Street, between Croft Avenue & La Cienega Boulevard, West Hollywood (1-323 655 2056). Bus 16, DASH Fairfax/I-10, exit La Cienega Boulevard north. **Open** 11.30am-6pm Mon-Sat; 11.30am-4.30pm Sun. **Credit** AmEx, DC, Disc, MC, V. **Map** p306 B3.
Probably the only place in LA where you can get Afternoon Tea without attitude. All the big hotels will serve it – at a price and with a hint of snobbishness – but at Chado, you'll not only get delicious

scones and whipped cream, but friendly staff. Just east of the Beverly Center mall, it's a great place to relax after a shopping session.

Coffee Bean & Tea Leaf
8591 Sunset Boulevard, at Sunset Plaza Drive, West Hollywood (1-310 659 1890/www.coffeebean.com). Bus 2, 3, 105, DASH West Hollywood/I-10, exit La Cienega Boulevard north. **Open** 6.30am-midnight Mon-Fri; 7am-midnight Sat, Sun. **Credit** MC, V. **Map** p306 A1.
In Los Angeles, location is everything and coffeehouses are no exception to this rule. This branch of the popular Coffee Bean chain is located directly opposite the designer shopping heaven that is Sunset Plaza. A-list celebs frequent it every day. **Branches**: throughout the city.

Elixir
8612 W Melrose Avenue, between Huntley & Westbourne Drives, West Hollywood (1-310 657 9300) Bus 10, 11, 105, DASH Fairfax, West Hollywood/I-10, exit La Cienega Boulevard north. **Open** 9am-9pm Mon-Sat; 9am-7pm Sun. **Credit** AmEx, MC, V. **Map** p306 A2.
Bringing the orient to West Hollywood, Elixir offers tonics and teas plus a zen garden, incense and the sounds of a babbling brook. There's even a doctor of Chinese medicine on staff. Elixir promises, among other things, to increase your sex drive, cure a hangover and even make the world a more peaceful place.

Hugo's
8401 Santa Monica Boulevard, at Kings Road, West Hollywood (1-323 654 3993). Bus 4, 304/I-10, exit La Cienega Boulevard north. **Open** 7.30am-3.30pm Mon-Fri; 7.30am-4pm Sat, Sun. **Credit** AmEx, DC, Disc, MC, V. **Map** p306 B1.
A number of tea specialists have opened in LA in recent years, including Hugo's, which occupies the back room of this venerable WeHo Italian-American eatery. It looks very low key but actually draws the power breakfast/lunch crowd. Choose from more than 120 varieties of tea – black, green, red and white – including rare teas from China and yogi teas.

Kings Road Café
8361 Beverly Boulevard, at Kings Road, West Hollywood (1-323 655 9044). Bus 14/I-10, exit La Cienega Boulevard north. **Open** 7.30am-11pm daily. **Credit** MC, V. **Map** p306 B2.
Kings Road Café has kept its appeal for more than a decade. Some say it's the European feel or the take-out pastry counter next door, but the fact that their coffee is strong enough to drive a 18-wheeler may be the crucial factor. If you're feeling at all sluggish, this rocket fuel masquerading as coffee is guaranteed to keep you going all day.

The Living Room
Peninsula Hotel, 9882 Little Santa Monica Boulevard, at Wilshire Boulevard, Beverly Hills (1-310 551 2888). Bus 4, 304/I-405, exit Wilshire Boulevard east. **Open** 8am-midnight Mon-Thur, Sun;

8am-1am Fri, Sat; reservations required. **Credit** AmEx, DC, Disc, MC, V. **Map** p305 B2/3.

You need to book ahead to be able to enjoy English High Tea here, inside the Peninsula, one of LA's most prestigious hotels. If you can get a table, you'll love the huge range of teas, salmon sandwiches and heavenly tea cakes. In keeping with all things in Beverly Hills, it ain't cheap.

Also recommended

Il Fornaio 301 N Beverly Drive, Beverly Hills (1-310 550 8330); **Paddington's Tea Room** 355 S Robertson Boulevard, Beverly Hills (1-310 652 0624); **Petterson's Frisch Rost** 10019 Venice Boulevard, Culver City (1-310 839 3359); **Revival Café** 7149 Beverly Boulevard, West Hollywood (1-323 930 1210); **Sweet Lady Jane** 8360 Melrose Avenue, West Hollywood (1-213 653 7145); **Zen Zoo Tea** 13050 San Vincente Boulevard, Brentwood (1-310 576 0585).

Hollywood & Midtown

Bourgeois Pig

5931 Franklin Avenue, at Tamarind Avenue, Hollywood (1-323 962 6366). Bus 26, Community Connection 208/US 101, exit Gower Street north. **Open** 9am-1.30am daily. **No credit cards.** **Map** p307 B1.

A coffeeshop for the late-night caffeine crawler, the Pig is replete with black lights and chandeliers. And although legally you aren't supposed to smoke in here, that doesn't seem to stop the hip crowd. Sandwiched between a couple of popular bars and a good newsstand, it's definitely one not to miss.

Insomnia

7286 Beverly Boulevard, at N Poinsettia Place, Fairfax District (1-323 931 4943). Bus 14/I-10, exit Fairfax Avenue north. **Open** 9am-4am daily. **No credit cards.** **Map** p306 C2.

Insomnia is a late-night café generally frequented by actors and writers. With some of the comfiest couches in Los Angeles, plus high ceilings and changing artwork, it's the place to go if you need to study – so bring your script.

Stir Crazy

6917 Melrose Avenue, between Highland & La Brea Avenues, Hollywood (1-323 934 4656). Bus 10, 11/ I-10, exit La Brea Avenue. **Open** 9am-midnight daily. **No credit cards.** **Map** p307 A3.

The big attraction here is the $1.50 bottomless cup of coffee, but the couches, relaxed atmosphere, art on the walls, good pastries, magazines and chess boards also make this a fun place to hang out.

Also recommended

Hollywood Hills Coffee Shop & Café Best Western Hollywood Hills Hotel, 6145 Franklin Avenue, Hollywood (1-323 467 7678).

East of Hollywood

The Coffee Table

2930 Rowena Avenue, at Hyperion Avenue, Silver Lake (1-323 644 8111). Bus 175/I-5, exit Los Feliz Boulevard south. **Open** 7am-11pm Mon-Thur, Sun; 7am-midnight Fri, Sat. **Credit** AmEx, MC, V. **Map** p308 B1.

Pann's: pure nostalgia. *See p165.*

It already had the vibe of a neighbourhood hangout, but the new outdoor patio seating means the Coffee Table is even nicer now. The tabletops are decorated with mosaic tiles and the outside wooded area is hard to beat. The breakfast burritos are unsurpassed and the desserts scrumptious.

La Belle Epoque
2128 Hillhurst Avenue, at Avocado Street, Los Feliz (1-323 669 7640). Bus 154, 156/I-5, exit Riverside Drive south. **Open** *7.30am-10pm Tue-Sat; 8am-8.30pm Sun; closed Mon.* **Credit** *AmEx, MC, V.* **Map** p308 A1.
In the past couple of years, Los Feliz has become home to a lot of cool young actors, and this is one of the coffeeshops that has benefited from the area's star appeal. It's a quaint place with an obvious French feel. Sit by the bakery counter and try out the amazing desserts. They also provide full and inexpensive dinners to consume before you go off to some fabulous Hollywood party.

Also recommended
Angeles Bohemia 3200 Sunset Boulevard, Silver Lake (1-323 667 1083); **Tsunami** 4019 Sunset Boulevard, Silver Lake (1-323 661 7771).

South Central

Pann's
6710 La Tijera Boulevard, at La Cienega Boulevard, Inglewood (1-323 776 3770). Bus 625/I-10, exit La Cienega Boulevard south. **Open** *10am-10.30pm daily.* **Credit** *AmEx, MC, V.*
One of the oldest coffeeshops in the city, Pann's harks back to the golden era of the 1950s when LA seemed to be the coffeeshop capital of the world. It's built in the art deco style and the waitresses still wear those pointy hats. If it's nostalgia you're looking for with your cup of joe, this is the place.

The Valleys

Aaah! Capella
5907 Lankershim Boulevard, between Burbank & Oxnard Boulevards, North Hollywood (1-818 509 6738). Bus 154, 156/Hwy 170, exit Burbank Boulevard east. **Open** *6pm-6am daily.* **Credit** *AmEx, Disc, MC, V.*
This place belongs to actor Carl David (Lieutenant Russell in various *Star Trek* movies), and so attracts plenty of actors, including Dennis Hopper. You can catch a poetry reading one night and watch a drag queen revue the next. It's funky and fun, with seating ranging from comfy sofas to lawn chairs. There is also a small games room.

Lulu's Beehive
13203 Ventura Boulevard, between Coldwater Canyon & Fulton Avenue, Studio City (1-818 986 2233). Bus 424, 522/US 101, exit Coldwater Canyon south. **Open** *8am-1am Mon-Fri; 8am-2am Sat; 11am-2am Sun.* **No credit cards.**

Java joints
The best

Anastasia's Asylum
LA's best (probably only) haunted coffeehouse, with great artwork and comfy chairs. See page 161.

Bourgeois Pig
The coffeehouse of choice for late-night caffeine addicts. See page 164.

Coffee Bean & Tea Leaf
Enjoy the best celeb-spotting in town at this Sunset Plaza spot. Be fabulous! See page 163.

Interactive Café
For the best – and biggest – flower arrangements in town. See page 161.

Opus Café
If you want to combine music with your mocha, this is the only café with built-in cup holders on the CD racks. See page 165.

Pann's
Hark back to a golden era of coffeeshops at this slice of 1950s nostalgia. See page 165.

Situated on the now trendy Ventura Boulevard in Studio City, Lulu's is a homely joint. The staff are very friendly, and there is a variety of entertainment from staged readings to stand-up comedy.

Opus Café
36 E Colorado Boulevard, between Fair Oaks & Raymond Avenues, Pasadena (1-626 685 2800). Bus 180, 181, 188, 256, Foothill Transit 237/I-210, exit Colorado Boulevard west. **Open** *11am-11pm Mon-Thur, Sun; 11am-midnight Fri, Sat.* **Credit** *AmEx, Disc, MC, V.*
Combining a music shop with a coffeehouse, Opus Café in Old Town Pasadena has listening stations amid its industrial decor, and allows you to sip on your latte as you peruse the shelves – there are even built-in cup holders in the CD racks. Plus Internet access and live gigs.

Also recommended
Boom Boom Room 11651 Riverside Drive, North Hollywood (1-818 753 9966); **Hot House Café** 12123 Riverside Drive, North Hollywood (1-818 506 7058); **Kulak's Woodshed** 5230½ Laurel Canyon Boulevard, North Hollywood (1-818 766 9913); **Nudie's Custom Java** 11651 Riverside Drive, Valley Village (1-818 753 9966); **Rose Tree Cottage** 828 E California Boulevard, Pasadena (1-626 793 3337).

Eat, Drink, Shop

Bars

LA isn't much of a drinking town, but you can still find some swanky bars and atmospheric dives in which to drown your sorrows.

Woe betide the weary travellers who find themselves thirsty in Los Angeles. For unlike New York, Chicago, San Francisco, Boston, New Orleans or Seattle – or any other American metropolis that's worth a damn – LA is painfully short of worthwhile watering holes. In other cities, you're never more than a few blocks away from a cold beer and a comfy bar stool; in LA, it's more like a 20-minute car ride.

Unsurprisingly, bars tend to play a much smaller role in the social life of your average resident than they do elsewhere. While most Angelenos would rather drive to their favourite bar than brave LA's rotten public transport system (especially after sundown), stringent drink-driving laws generally discourage the consumption of more than two cocktails at a sitting, and the sheer distance between most nightspots makes pub crawling an expensive prospect if you're travelling by cab. The early-to-bed, early-to-rise ethos of the entertainment industry means that many bars empty out well before closing time, and '12-step' meetings (Alcoholics Anonymous and the like) have notoriously supplanted bars as popular pick-up spots. The lack of a drinking culture also means that what Brits, say, might consider a normal level of drinking would be seen as over-indulgence in Los Angeles.

Angelenos themselves are hardly discerning imbibers, a fact that seems inextricably linked to the city's utter lack of talented bartenders. You can always order a beer, of course, but don't expect an inspiring variety: with the microbrew boom of the early 1990s supplanted by today's Martini revivalism, most bars tend to stick to such insipid American standbys as Rolling Rock and Miller Genuine Draft. Bass, Newcastle Brown, Harp, Guinness and Foster's are the most commonly found foreign beers.

Despite all these caveats, it must be said that LA's bar scene has been far more vibrant in the past half-decade than it's been for years, thanks in part to the recent 'lounge revival' (which, unfortunately, came too late to save some classic Polynesian-themed 'tiki' bars) and to the appearance of several local watering holes in films such as *Ed Wood* and *LA Confidential*. Note that smoking has been banned inside bars since the mid 1990s – you can smoke on outdoor patios or immediately outside the front door.

The government enforces the law erratically at best, and many bar owners would prefer to pay the $500 fine (smokers themselves are not fined), rather than suffer the greater financial hit that would go with losing their smoking customers. Smart, high-profile bars tend to enforce the ban more stringently than dark and dingy dives, but asking the bartender for an ashtray is the simplest way to ascertain whether or not you'll be allowed light up.

Helpful hint: it's proper etiquette to tip the bartender. The simple act of tipping one or two dollars per round will win you a friend for life – or, at least, attentive service throughout the evening. In return, you can expect that most bartenders will be happy to call a cab for you.

Some bars have live music: if so, you may have to pay a cover charge of up to $5. For bars serving a specifically gay or lesbian clientele, *see chapter* **Gay & Lesbian**.

BOOZE & THE LAW

All bars are subject to California's alcohol laws: you have to be 21 or over to buy and consume the stuff (take photo ID even if you look much older), and alcohol can be sold only between the hours of 6am and 2am. Almost every bar calls last orders at around 1.45am; technically, staff are obliged to confiscate unconsumed alcohol after 2am.

Westside: beach towns

The Arsenal

12012 W Pico Boulevard, at Bundy Drive, West LA (1-310 479 9782). Bus 30, 31, 209/I-10, exit Bundy Drive north. **Open** 10am-2am daily. **Credit** AmEx, DC, Disc, MC, V.

Boasting an alarming array of decorative weapons on its walls, this tiny restaurant-bar more than lives up to its name. The service is friendly, however, and the drinks are inexpensive. The framed *Playboy* centrefolds in the men's room are a nice touch, too.

Encounter

209 World Way, between Terminals 2 & 6, LAX (1-310 215 5151). Bus 11, 42, 120, 225, 232, Culver City 6, 11/I-405, exit La Tijera Boulevard west. **Open** 11am-midnight Mon-Thur, Sun; 11am-2am Fri, Sat. **Credit** AmEx, DC, MC, V.

The service is variable, the drinks expensive and the food is mediocre at best, but the *Star Trek-meets-Austin Powers* vibe of this nostalgically futuristic restaurant-bar (hanging aloft in LAX's fabulous 1960s Theme Building) makes it more than worth the trip. Lava lamps adorn the kidney-shaped bar, 'space-age bachelor pad' music plays in the elevators and you can watch the endless parade of flight departures and arrivals while sipping your beverage. Altogether an essential LA experience.

Liquid Kitty
11780 W Pico Boulevard, between Barrington Avenue & Bundy Drive, West LA (1-310 473 3707). Bus 30, 31, 209/I-10, exit Bundy Drive north. **Open** 6pm-2am Mon-Fri; 8pm-2am Sat, Sun. **No credit cards**
This small, dimly lit establishment brings a touch of lounge-revival elegance to an otherwise drab stretch of Pico Boulevard. Obscure drink requests are handled with aplomb, and live bands and DJs often stoke the atmosphere with appropriately retro sounds.

Red Carpet Lounge
Bay Shore Bowl, 234 Pico Boulevard, between Main & Third Streets, Santa Monica (1-310 399 7731). Bus 20, 33, 434, Santa Monica 1, 7, 8/I-10, exit Lincoln Boulevard south. **Open** 9am-midnight Mon-Thur, Sun; 9am-1am Fri, Sat. **Credit** AmEx, MC, V. **Map** p304 A3.
Identical twins Jean and Pat preside over this Googie-style bowling alley's bar, mixing incredible $2.75 Martinis. The lure of this place – where the Coen brothers threw *The Big Lebowski*'s wrap party – is its seedy, supine, unintentional re-creation of a Southern brothel. *See also p246* **Bay Shore Lanes**.

Ye Olde King's Head
116 Santa Monica Boulevard, between Ocean Avenue & Second Street, Santa Monica (1-310 451 1402). Bus 4, 20, 22, 33, Santa Monica 1, 7, 8, 10/ I-10, exit Fourth-Fifth Street north. **Open** 11am-1.30am Mon-Thur; 10am-1.30am Fri-Sun. **Credit** AmEx, DC, MC, V. **Map** p304 A2.
Santa Monica's large British contingent pretty much keeps this pub in business. Darts, fish and chips, and stout in abundance make a suitable home away from home; it's also the best place in the area to watch televised European soccer matches, which is why you'll usually find various British rock stars hanging out here when they're in town.

Also recommended
The Brig 1515 Abbot Kinney Boulevard, Venice (1-310 399 7537); **Circle Bar** 2926 Main Street, Santa Monica (1-310 392 4898); **My Father's Office** 1018 Montana Avenue, Santa Monica (1-310 451 9330); **Voda** 1449 Second Street, Santa Monica (1-310 394 9774).

Westside: inland

Argyle Hotel Bar
8358 Sunset Boulevard, between Sweetzer Avenue & La Cienega Boulevard, West Hollywood (1-323 654 7100). Bus 2, 3, 429, West Hollywood A, B/ I-10, exit La Cienega Boulevard north. **Open** 11am-1.30am daily. **Credit** AmEx, DC, Disc, MC, V. **Map** p306 B1.
Located in the breathtaking art deco structure that is the Argyle Hotel, this bar – which appeared in Robert Altman's *The Player* – has one of the finest selections of whisky in town. Dress to impress.

Blasts from the past
Top five

The Dresden Room
You'd almost expect to see Sammy Davis Jr propping himself up at the piano bar, but lounge duo Marty & Elayne (pictured) make a fine subsitiute. See page 171.

Formosa Café
Take a seat in an overstuffed red leather booth, order a drink and pretend you're a

private detective or a matinée idol. Elvis drank here, and so should you. See page 169.

Hank's Bar
This hotel bar is a warm and intimate throwback to the days when reporters wore fedoras, cops patrolled Downtown on foot and the Dodgers still played in Brooklyn. See page 170.

Musso & Frank Grill
After two heavenly Martinis at this old-fashioned landmark on Hollywood Boulevard, you'll forget you even wanted dinner in the first place. See page 170.

Trader Vic's
Return to the 1950s at this old-school 'tiki' bar inside the Beverly Hilton. Another Tiki Puka-Puka, please, and don't spare the rum! See page 168.

Bar Marmont

8171 Sunset Boulevard, between Sweetzer Avenue & Crescent Heights Boulevard, West Hollywood (1-323 650 0575). Bus 2, 3, 429/US 101, exit Highland Avenue south. **Open** 6pm-1.30am daily. **Credit** AmEx, MC, V. **Map** p306 B1.

This bar's luxurious, opium den-like interior hides within a deceptively ugly, shanty-like structure down the street from the Chateau Marmont hotel on Sunset Boulevard. Bar Marmont has become the place for Hollywood's élite to lap up prohibitively priced but nicely confected libations. It's sensible to call in advance for table reservations, otherwise you run the risk of standing around in the waiting area for hours on end.

C

8442 Wilshire Boulevard, at Hamilton Drive, Beverly Hills (1-323 782 8157). Bus 20, 21, 22, 320/I-10, exit La Cienega Boulevard north. **Open** 5.30pm-2am Mon-Fri; 6.30pm-2am Sat, Sun. **Credit** AmEx, DC, Disc, MC, V. **Map** p306 B3.

Prepare to dress smartly and pay through the nose for a classy, deco-era LA experience. The architecture and design of this small bar and restaurant in Beverly Hills dates back to 1929, and looks it: sumptuous, red-stained African wood panelling, real leather booths, bronze-toned drapes, plus smoked windows to keep the real world at bay. The globe-trotting assortment of vodkas, vintage champagnes, single malt whiskies, ports, cognacs and tequilas sure helps, too.

Coronet Pub

370 N La Cienega Boulevard, between Beverly Boulevard & Oakwood Avenue, West Hollywood (1-310 659 4583). Bus 14,104/I-10, exit La Cienega Boulevard north. **Open** 6pm-2am Mon-Sat; closed Sun. **No credit cards. Map** p306 B2.

Located right next door to the Coronet Theater, this tiny, straight outta Chicago dive is extremely popular with pre- and post-show crowds. The awkwardly designed booths may be a little uncomfortable for some, and the decor itself is nothing to write home about, but you won't find a more unpretentious (or more budget-friendly) bar in all of West Hollywood.

North

8029 W Sunset Boulevard, between Laurel Canyon Boulevard & Laurel Avenue, Hollywood (1-323 654 1313). Bus 26, 163, 212/I-10, exit La Cienega Boulevard north. **Open** 6pm-2am daily. **Credit** AmEx, DC, Disc, MC, V. **Map** p306 B1.

This hard-to-find throwback to the Rat Pack era has a pretty decent dinner menu, but the expertly mixed cocktails are the real reason to visit. Sinking back into one of the comfy leather booths while sipping a Mojito (a rum-intensive version of a Mint Julep) or a Last Harrah (Scotch and ginger ale), it's easy to imagine that you're in a speakeasy that's several hundred miles (and decades) removed from the Sunset Strip.

SkyBar

Mondrian Hotel, 8440 Sunset Boulevard, at La Cienega Boulevard, West Hollywood (1-213 848 6025). Bus 2, 3, 429/I-10, exit La Cienega Boulevard north. **Open** 11am-2am daily. **Credit** AmEx, DC, MC, V. **Map** p306 A/B1.

This grotesquely trendy poolside watering hole in the Mondrian Hotel is a great place for spotting celebs, provided you can actually get in – to gain entry, you must first make reservations by phone (even if you're staying at the hotel, you're allowed only two guests). The unceasing parade of beautiful Hollywood types (including the servers) is the main visual interest: the fixed decor is rather plain, and the view from the windows is far from impressive – don't be fooled by the high-flying name, as the bar is actually situated on one of the Mondrian's lower floors, but it does look on to the hotel's terrace and swimming pool, with fantastic views.

Trader Vic's

Beverly Hilton Hotel, 9876 Wilshire Boulevard, at Santa Monica Boulevard, Beverly Hills (1-310 274 7777). Bus 4, 20, 21, 22, 27/I-405, exit Wilshire Boulevard east. **Open** 5pm-1am daily. **Credit** AmEx, DC, Disc, MC, V. **Map** p305 B2.

The **Formosa**: classic Hollywood. *See p169.*

Renowned for its absurdly overpriced Polynesian menu and its expensive-but-worth-it tropical drinks, Trader Vic's is an old-school 'tiki' bar. Wizened bartenders of South Sea descent create alchemical wonders with various liquors and fruit juices – ordering the ridiculously potent Tiki Puka-Puka will earn you their undying respect and admiration – while Hawaiian entertainer Don Ho's 1960s classic *Tiny Bubbles* seems to play at five-minute intervals. Extremely crowded with the young and beautiful at weekends, the place usually has a barstool or two free during the week. Be warned: drinking more than two of Trader Vic's tropical concoctions can lead to total inebriation and/or severe insulin shock.

Also recommended

Avalon Hotel Lounge 9400 Olympic Boulevard, Beverly Hills (1-310 277 5221); **Barney's Beanery** 8447 Santa Monica Boulevard, West Hollywood (1-213 654 2287); **Cava** 8384 W Third Street, West Hollywood (1-213 658 8898); **Max's** 442 N Fairfax Avenue, Fairfax District (1-323 651 4421).

Hollywood & Midtown

Boardner's

1652 N Cherokee Avenue, at Hollywood Boulevard, Hollywood (1-323 462 9621). Bus 1, 180, 181, 210, 212/US 101, exit Highland Avenue south. **Open** 11am-2am daily. **No credit cards.** **Map** p307 A1.
Cheap beer and even cheaper entertainment – that is, if you find slumming starlets and drunken former members of 1980s heavy metal acts entertaining – make a trip to this seedy Hollywood mainstay worthwhile. It also appeared in the Johnny Depp film *Ed Wood*. Multiple bars and an airy back patio add to its frayed-at-the-edges appeal. Smoking is definitely not discouraged here.

Cat & Fiddle Pub

6530 Sunset Boulevard, between Highland Avenue & N Cahuenga Boulevard, Hollywood (1-323 468 3800). Bus 2, 3, DASH Hollywood/US 101, exit Sunset Boulevard west. **Open** 11.30am-2am daily. **Credit** AmEx, MC, V. **Map** p307 A2.
This popular spot for expatriate Brits and visiting rock musicians, run by former Creation/Ashton Gardner & Dyke bassist Kim Gardner, offers fish and chips as well as several draught English brews. The front patio is an exceedingly pleasant place to enjoy a pint, though the interior may be a trifle brightly lit for some nightcrawlers.

Coach & Horses

7617 Sunset Boulevard, at Stanley & Curson Avenues, Hollywood (1-323 876 6900). Bus 2, 3, 429/US 101, exit Highland Avenue south. **Open** 11.30am-2am Mon-Thur; noon-2am Sat; 5pm-2am Sun; closed Fri. **No credit cards.** **Map** p306 C1.
A dartboard, a variety of lagers and a crew of unbelievably ill-tempered barmaids attract many of LA's British subjects to this tiny pub on Sunset

Boulevard's 'Guitar Row'. The presence of an Indian restaurant next door is a further attraction for homesick Brits.

El Carmen

8138 W Third Street, between Kilkea Drive & La Jolla Avenue, Fairfax District (1-213 852 1556). Bus 16, DASH Fairfax/I-10, exit Fairfax Avenue north. **Open** 5pm-2am Mon-Fri; 7pm-2am Sat, Sun. **Credit** AmEx, MC, V. **Map** p306 B3.
Arguably the best tequila bar in LA, this haven of Mexican kitsch is always packed for good reason: it stocks more than 60 brands of mescal and tequila, from Patrón to Chicicapa. Bring a designated driver.

Formosa Café

7156 Santa Monica Boulevard, at Formosa Avenue, Hollywood (1-323 850 9050). Bus 4, 212, West Hollywood A, B/I-10, exit La Brea Avenue north. **Open** 11.30am-2am daily. **Credit** AmEx, MC, V. **Map** p306 C1.
One of the few real remnants of Old Hollywood. The darkened interior of this charming oriental box (which allegedly boasts the world's largest collection of Elvis decanters) is covered with autographed photos of movie stars who have imbibed here in the past six decades. The Formosa has experienced a recent surge in popularity, thanks to a memorable appearance in *LA Confidential*, but the addition of upstairs and outdoor bar areas (the latter handily sidestepping the smoking ban) helps to keep it from getting unbearably crowded. Steer clear of the food, which is unutterably awful.

Frolic Room

6245 Hollywood Boulevard, at Vine Street, Hollywood (1-323 462 5890). Bus 1, 180, 181, 217, 429/US 101, exit Hollywood Boulevard west. **Open** 10am-2am daily. **No credit cards.** **Map** p307 B1.
Stepping over the squatter overflow from the lobby of the neighbouring Pantages Theater will work up a thirst in even the hardiest of individuals, so refresh yourself with a visit to this tiny, hard-boiled relic from the 1940s, which featured in several scenes in *LA Confidential*. Shrinking violets should probably take their business elsewhere, as the joint's high-decibel level of conversation means that you usually have to shout to get the barkeeper's attention.

HMS Bounty

3357 Wilshire Boulevard, at S Catalina Street, Mid Wilshire (1-213 385 7275). Metro Wilshire Western/bus 20, 21, 22/I-10, exit Western Avenue north. **Open** 11am-10pm Mon, Sun; 11am-2am Tue-Sat. **Credit** AmEx, Disc, MC, V.
'Food and Grog' reads the sign outside this tatty Mid Wilshire treasure, a nautical-themed dive where office workers, hipsters, drag queens, junkies and down-at-heel senior citizens eat and drink together, exhibiting the sort of easygoing camaraderie that's usually absent from LA's hotter establishments. The food's not bad (the oversized burgers are always a good bet), but cheap drinks and excellent people-watching are the Bounty's real attractions.

Lava Lounge

*1533 N La Brea Avenue, at Sunset Boulevard,
Hollywood (1-323 876 6612). Bus 2, 3, 212,
302, 429/I-10, exit La Brea Avenue north.*
Open 9pm-2am daily. **Credit** Disc, MC, V.
Map p306 C1.
Located in a fairly grim strip mall, Lava Lounge
updates the Polynesian pleasure palaces of the Rat
Pack era with an attractive mirrors-and-bamboo
look, while the triangle-backed leather barstools are
the last word in bachelor-pad luxury. Along with the
usual beers and hard liquor, the bartenders mix a
mean selection of tropical drinks. The Lava Lounge
sometimes has DJs and live bands, often of the surf
or lounge music variety.

Molly Malone's Irish Pub

*575 S Fairfax Avenue, at Sixth Street, Miracle Mile
(1-323 935 1577/music hotline 1-323 935 2707).
Bus 20, 21, 22, 217/I-10, exit Fairfax Avenue north.*
Open 10.30am-2am daily. **Credit** AmEx, MC, V.
Map p306 B3.
Irish to the nth degree, Molly's stout-brown walls
are adorned with paintings of Brendan Behan,
James Joyce and Ms Malone herself. A friendly
place to enjoy a pint of Guinness – though it can
become uncomfortably crowded on weekend
nights – the pub attracts an odd mix of musicians,
twentysomething actors and actresses and incredibly aged Irishmen. It also books a rootsy combination of country, folk and Irish-influenced
performers, so there's usually a cover charge
after 8pm.

Musso & Frank Grill

*6667 Hollywood Boulevard, at Cherokee Avenue,
Hollywood (1-323 467 7788). Bus 163, 180, 181,
212, DASH Hollywood/US 101, exit Highland
Avenue south.* **Open** 11am-11pm Tue-Sat;
closed Mon, Sun. **Credit** AmEx, DC, MC, V.
Map p307 A1.
A worthwhile stop on any self-guided tour of Old
Hollywood, Musso's was a favourite hangout of
novelist and poet Charles Bukowski, who supped
here in his more moneyed later years. Dinner at
this post-World War I relic – it opened in 1919 –
can cost you an arm and a leg, but plenty of
Angelenos come just to sit at the bar, sip Martinis
(easily the best in town) and soak up the wood-
panelled atmosphere.

The Room

*1626 N Cahuenga Boulevard, between Selma Avenue
& Hollywood Boulevard, Hollywood (1-323 462
7196). Bus 1, 180, 210, 212/US 101, exit Sunset
Boulevard west.* **Open** 8pm-2am daily. **Credit** MC,
V. **Map** p307 B1.
This dark dive's hard-to-find location (the entrance
is down an alley at the back of the building) makes
it the ultimate in 'if you don't know, don't go' hipness, though the atmosphere inside is friendly and
very laid-back. The extremely spacious booths and
seemingly endless bar ensure there's almost always
a place to sit and sip, even at weekends.

The Snake Pit

*7529 Melrose Avenue, at Sierra Bonita Avenue,
Hollywood (1-323 653 2011). Bus 10, 11/I-10, exit
La Cienega Boulevard north.* **Open** 11am-10pm Mon,
Sun; 11am-2am Tue-Sat. **Credit** MC, V. **Map** p306 C2.
Don't be put off by the fearsome name; if anything,
this cosy corner bar is one of the most unassuming
and down-to-earth watering holes west of La Brea.
If the Melrose Avenue shopping experience has left
you craving liquid refreshment (or at least some
peace and quiet), slip inside the Snake Pit and knock
back a couple of cool ones, and maybe catch some
football, baseball or basketball on the bar TV.

Three of Clubs

*1123 Vine Street, at Santa Monica Boulevard,
Hollywood (1-323 462 6441). Bus 4, 210, 420, 426/
US 101, exit Vine Street south.* **Open** 8.30pm-2am
daily. **Credit** AmEx, MC, V. **Map** p307 B2.
Cloaked in anonymity on the edge of one of
Hollywood's more dilapidated strip malls – look for
the Bargain Clown Mart sign overhead, or you'll miss
it completely – the Three of Clubs is a cavernous
wonder, complete with flocked velvet wallpaper and
a ceiling decorated to look like a sparkling night sky.
Although it looks (on the inside, at least) like the sort
of place that Don Vito Corleone would hold court in,
you're more likely to find beautiful twentysome-
things packed into the dark booths, exchanging
phone numbers to the music of yesterday's easy-
listening icons. The bar also features occasional live
performances by local acts.

Also recommended

Burgundy Room 16212 N Cahuenga Boulevard,
Hollywood (1-323 465 7530); **Daddy's Lounge**
1610 N Vine Street, Hollywood (1-323 466 7777);
The Power House 836 N Highland Avenue,
Hollywood (1-323 460 6630).

Downtown

Hank's Bar

*Stillwell Hotel, 840 S Grand Avenue, between Eighth
& Ninth Streets, Downtown (1-213 623 7718).
Metro Seventh Street-Metro Center or Pershing
Square/bus 40, 78, 79, 96, DASH C, E/I-110, exit
Ninth Street east.* **Open** 10am-2am daily. **Credit**
AmEx, MC, V. **Map** p309 B3/4.
If you're strolling around Downtown or on your way
to a game at Staples Center, be sure to stop in at this
piece of Los Angeles history, a popular meeting
place for policemen, reporters and politicians since
before World War II. Just about the only thing that's
changed since then is the price of the drinks.

Top of Five

*Westin Bonaventure Hotel, 404 S Figueroa Street, at
Fourth Street, Downtown (1-213 624 1000). Metro
Seventh Street-Metro Center/bus 53, 60, 471/US 101
north, exit Third Street south.* **Open** 5.30-10pm
daily. **Credit** MC, V. **Map** p309 A/B2.
If the thought of watching sunset from a slowly
revolving bar at the top of a Downtown hotel

Visit **Tiki-Ti** for Polynesian paraphernalia and wicked cocktails.

appeals to you, give this place a visit. The overpriced drinks and early 1990s decor are nothing special, but the view is – on a clear day, you get a panoramic eyeful of the city – and the ride in the glass elevator isn't bad, either.

Also recommended

Little Pedro's 901 E First Street, Downtown (1-213 687 3766); **The Gallery Bar** Regal Biltmore Hotel, 506 S Grand Avenue, Downtown (1-213 624-1011); **Otani Hotel Bar** 120 S Los Angeles Street, Downtown (front desk 1-213 629 1200).

East of Hollywood

The Dresden Room

1760 N Vermont Avenue, between Franklin Avenue & Hollywood Boulevard, Los Feliz (1-213 665 4294/ www.thedresden.com). Bus 26, 180, 181, Community Connection 203/US 101, exit Vermont Avenue north. **Open** 11am-2am Mon-Sat; 3-10pm Sun. **Credit** AmEx, MC, V. **Map** p308 A2.
This Los Feliz landmark has experienced something of a renaissance in the past few years, thanks to its appearance in the movie *Swingers*. An eye-popping white leather and corkboard interior – and regular appearances by lounge duo Marty & Elayne – are the main attractions, but experienced bartenders also make it a real pleasure for discerning drinkers. The overpriced food is best avoided, however.

Good Luck Bar

1514 N Hillhurst Avenue, at Hollywood & Sunset Boulevards, Los Feliz (1-323 666 3524). Bus 1, 2, 3, 26, 302/US 101, exit Hollywood Boulevard east. **Open** 7pm-2am Mon-Fri; 8pm-2am Sat, Sun. **Credit** MC, V. **Map** p308 A2.
This popular spot is packed to the rafters most nights of the week, which can make it hard to appreciate (or even see) its gloriously gaudy oriental

decor. Many intriguing Chinese liqueurs and brandies are listed on the drinks menu, although the predominantly college-age crowd seems to prefer shots and beers (Tsingtao, of course). You can get a pretty solid Martini here, too.

Smog Cutter

864 N Virgil Avenue, between Normal & Burns Avenues, Silver Lake (1-323 667 9832). Bus 26/US 101, exit Melrose Avenue east. **Open** noon-2am daily. **No credit cards. Map** p308 A3.
If karaoke's your passion, don't miss the Smog Cutter. Tough-talking Asian barmaids encourage you to have another, while folks from all walks of life get up to take their turn at the microphone.

Tiki-Ti

4427 W Sunset Boulevard, between Hillhurst & Fountain Avenues, Silver Lake (1-213 669 9381). Bus 1, 2, 3, 26, 175/US 101, exit Vermont Avenue north. **Open** 6pm-2am Wed-Sat; closed Mon, Tue, Sun. **No credit cards. Map** p308 A/B2.
A tiny Polynesian gem in the shadow of Silver Lake's KCET television studios, the Tiki-Ti dares to ask the inebriated question: how much South Seas-related junk can you pack into an outhouse-sized shack while still leaving room for a few customers? Ray, the bar's lovable and inscrutable founder, sadly passed away in late 1999, but his legacy lives on in the form of such potent tropical libations as Blood and Sand, the Stealth and Ray's Mistake.

Also recommended

Akbar 4356 Sunset Boulevard, Silver Lake (1-323 665 6810); **Big Foot Lodge** 3172 Los Feliz Boulevard, Atwater Village (1-323 662 9227); **Lowenbrau Keller** 3211 Beverly Boulevard, Silver Lake (1-213 382 5723); **Red Lion Tavern** 2366 Glendale Boulevard, Silver Lake (1-213 662 5337); **Ye Rustic Inn** 1831 Hillhurst Avenue, Los Feliz (1-323 662 5757).

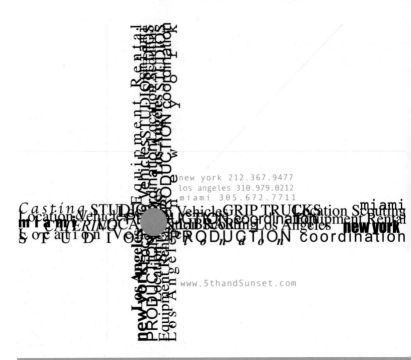

new york 212.367.9477
los angeles 310.979.0212
miami 305.672.7711

www.5thandSunset.com

Shops & Services

Calling all fashion victims and shopaholics: you want it? LA's got it.

The shopping districts

Beverly Hills, particularly the Rodeo Collection and Two Rodeo on **Rodeo Drive**, is for those with money to burn and less-than-radical taste. Hidden among the Chanels and Pradas, however, are the odd, one-off boutique and hip California designer. It's also home to some of the best department stores, such as Neiman Marcus and Barneys New York. **Brentwood** has a range of upmarket restaurants, bookshops, clothing boutiques and the petite Brentwood Gardens mall near **San Vincente Boulevard**. San Vincente, particularly the five blocks between Bundy Drive and Darlington Avenue, is also a nice high-end stroll of trattorias, stationery shops and hip clothing stores.

Sunset Plaza on Sunset Strip in **West Hollywood**, is another posh neighbourhood, scattered with high-end shops and pavement cafés, and great for a spot of people-watching. **Robertson Boulevard** between Alden Drive and Third Street is teeming with antique and design shops and is getting more fashionable by the nano-second, with a flurry of hip, upmarket boutiques and shoe shops moving in. **Third Street** itself (anchored by the Beverly Center mall) is an unconventional shopping stretch chock-full of rare bookshops, art pottery and cool vintage clothing, with the best stuff located between La Cienega Boulevard and Sweetzer Avenue.

Just north of Third Street, **Melrose Avenue** is akin to the King's Road in London, once hip and avant-garde and now a somewhat tired-looking row of shops, cafés and restaurants that change hands quicker than a dealer at a poker table. It also suffers from a lack of decent parking. However, it's still popular with the young and a great place to spot young girls baring their pierced belly buttons.

North La Brea Avenue is Rodeo Drive's younger, hipper, cheaper sibling, the place for retro fashion and clubwear; **South La Brea**, particularly the 100 to 600 blocks, is a more weathered, with antique and vintage clothing shops and outdoor cafés. **Larchmont Village** is an oddity in LA – a four-block stretch of boutiques, shops and restaurants plonked slap-bang in the middle of expensive, residential Hancock Park – and not to be missed.

In **Hollywood**, **Hollywood Boulevard** – not unlike the **Venice Boardwalk** in Venice – is fun and seedy, packed with one-off vendors selling T-shirts, trashy lingerie, cloned designer goods, sunglasses, bargain leather and naff gifts. If both are two obnoxiously touristy, **Franklin Avenue**, just above Hollywood Boulevard, has a quieter, loosely aggregated collection of used bookshops, funky coffeehouses and pavement cafés.

East of Hollywood, edgy clothing and furniture shops and cafés have sprung up in the past couple of years on **Silver Lake Boulevard** and **Rowena Avenue**. For a funky, unconventional vibe, **North Vermont Avenue** and **Hillhurst Avenue** in **Los Feliz** offer a booming alternative-retail experience of the sacred, the profane and the often disturbing.

Westwood near Beverly Hills offers the kind of shopping you would find in a mall, but without the structure. It also has a very limited choice of shops. Its popularity has been usurped by **Third Street Promenade** in **Santa Monica**, which – rather like **Old Town Pasadena** in the San Gabriel Valley, especially Colorado Boulevard – is a retro-fitted downtown area that emulates the mall experience.

Main Street in the **Ocean Park** area of Santa Monica is a revamped early 1900s seaside resort, made into a delightful shopping area with antique shops, fashion outlets, art galleries and speciality shops. The nearby nine-block strip of **Abbot Kinney Boulevard** in **Venice** is like a bohemain beachfront fair, where fine art galleries, home furnishings, antiques and fine food mix with upstart media companies and artist's lofts. On **Montana Avenue**, in the northern part of Santa Monica, you are spoilt for choice with furniture shops, antique and gift shops, restaurants, cafés, galleries, clothing shops and gourmet food shops. It combines high quality with eclectic range and has a pleasant, albeit affluent, neighbourhood vibe.

Further up the coast, **Swarthmore Avenue** in **Pacific Palisades** is a bustling, if rather bland, enclave where the wealthy families of the area shop – you may just run into Tom Hanks and his family here. North from there is **Cross Creek Road** in **Malibu**, which eschews valet parking and designer stores for a slightly rustic, casual beach town vibe – save for the *très* Malibu pricing.

Malls of fame

Shopping malls sprang up in the 1950s and '60s to service suburbanites newly lured away from downtown areas. In LA, the ultimate suburban sprawl, malls have all but taken over, and a visit to one often takes the place of other activities, since it can combine shopping, dining, exercise, movie-going and driving in one experience. The same shops and franchises appear again and again – Ann Taylor, Z Gallerie, the Gap, Banana Republic, the Limited, Express, Hold Everything, Crabtree & Evelyn, Victoria's Secret, Joan & David – usually anchored by a generic department store, adding to the general homogeneity. Malls also usually house fast-food venues, cafés, cinemas and often a large supermarket, as well as the occasional restaurant and one-off shop.

That last holdout of Valley Girl culture, the **Sherman Oaks Galleria** (at Ventura and Sepulveda Boulevards), which shut down in 1998, is reopening in spring 2001. It will shed its concrete-box look, morphing into an open-air complex with pedestrian promenades, anchored by a 16-screen cinema and a Tower Records store that will be the nation's largest. Other new malls include the massive **Block at Orange**, in Orange County (see page 115).

Below are the best and most centrally located of LA's malls.

Beverly Center (pictured)

8500 Beverly Boulevard, at La Cienega Boulevard, West Hollywood (1-310 854 0070). Bus 14, 105, 316/I-10, exit La Cienega Boulevard north. **Open** 10am-9pm Mon-Fri; 10am-6pm Sat; 11am-6pm Sun. **Map** p306 A2/3.
All you could possibly want in a mall, including two department stores (Macy's and Bloomingdale's), a MAC Cosmetics, a Diesel (one of only two branches in LA), stalwarts like Banana Republic, some good shoe shops and high-end, one-off boutiques and a multi-screen cinema. Opposite is the Beverly Connection, a small and slightly shabby mall, with a Bookstar, Sport Chalet and Starbucks.

Brentwood Gardens

11677 San Vicente Boulevard, at 26th Street, Brentwood (1-310 820 7646). Bus 22, Santa Monica 4, 8/I-405, exit Wilshire Boulevard west. **Open** Individual shops vary.
A mini-mall housing some excellent designer-filled boutiques.

Century City Shopping Center

10250 Santa Monica Boulevard, between Century Park W & Avenue of the Stars, Century City (1-310 277 3898/www.century cityshopping center.com). Bus 27, 28, 316, Santa Monica 5, Commuter Express 534/ I-405, exit Santa Monica Boulevard east. **Open** 10am-9pm Mon-Fri; 10am-6pm Sat; 11am-6pm Sun. **Map** p305 B3.
An outdoor set-up, comprehensive for both shopping, eating and movie-watching.

Glendale Galleria

Central Avenue & Broadway, Glendale (1-818 240 9481). Bus 177, 180, 181, 201, 410/ I-5, exit Colorado Street east. **Open** 10am-9pm Mon-Fri; 10am-8pm Sat; 11am-7pm Sun.
The largest shopping mall in the Valley, with around 260 stores. It has a Neiman Marcus, so we approve.

Sherman Oaks Fashion Square

14006 Riverside Drive, between Woodman & Hazeltine Avenues, Sherman Oaks (1-818 783 0550).Bus 6, 158/US 101, exit Woodman Avenue north. **Open** 10am-9pm Mon-Fri; 10am-7pm Sat; 11am-6pm Sun.
You'll find Macy's, Bloomingdale's and the usual suspects, including fabulous kitchen accessories at Williams Sonoma.

Westside Pavilion

10800 W Pico Boulevard, at Westwood Boulevard, West LA (1-310 474 6255/www. westsidepavilion.com). Bus Culver City 3, Santa Monica 7, 8, 12, 13, Commuter Express 431/I-10, exit Overland Boulevard north. **Open** 10am-9pm Mon-Fri; 10am-8pm Sat; 11am-6pm Sun. **Map** p305 A4/5.
This Westside shopping complex has some good kids' toys and clothes shops, the only Nordstrom department store in the centre of LA, a fine art-house cinema – and difficult parking.

Downtown LA is home to the fashion and garment districts (extending roughly from Broadway and Sixth to San Pedro and 16th Streets), jewellery trade centres, flower and furniture markets and the California Mart, the country's largest wholesale apparel centre. **Seventh Street** has the city's largest collection of shoe shops and its original department stores. **Little Tokyo**, bustling **Broadway**, **Chinatown**, and Mexican **Olvera Street** offer a good few hours of fun. Broadway is one of LA's main Latino streets and is full of discount clothing and knick-knack shops, bodegas (which sell religious kitsch and folkloric remedies for everything from indigestion to unrequited love), jewellers' shops and also features the vibrant Grand Central Market, which is a must.

Leimert Park in the **Crenshaw District** is a 12-block shopping and eating experience that mixes with the cultural celebration of black LA at the turn of the 21st century.

Moving into the **San Fernando Valley**, there's **Ventura Boulevard** ('Beverly Hills without the attitude'), especially the stretch of high-end shops between Laurel and Coldwater Canyons. If it's low-end you want, the 2400 to 2900 blocks of **Magnolia Boulevard** in **North Hollywood** offer many vintage clothing shops and cool prop rental houses. The recently expanded **Universal CityWalk** in Universal City has the feel of a futuristic shopping centre with a mélange of shops and cafés. The sheer magnitude of the place and the wacky designs of the buildings make it worth a visit.

HOURS AND TAXES

Shop and shopping mall opening hours are usually 10am to 7pm or 8pm, depending upon the neighbourhood. Return policies in the chainstores are nearly always in the buyer's favour; but watch out for smaller boutiques, which will go to the other end of the world to avoid giving you your money back. Parking is usually not too difficult, but if you're visiting the more expensive shops, use their valet parking: it's a small indulgence (compared to what you'll be laying out for the merchandise) and far better than a traffic ticket.

LA County adds an 8.25 per cent sales tax to the marked price of all merchandise and services; Orange County taxes at 7.75 per cent.

Department stores

You'll also find branches of **Sears** (Hollywood branch: 1-323 769 2600/www.sears.com) and **Robinsons-May** (Beverly Hills branch: 1-310 275 5464/www.robinsonsmay.com) throughout the city; call one branch to find your nearest.

Barneys New York

9570 Wilshire Boulevard, at Camden Drive, Beverly Hills (1-310 276 4400). Bus 20, 21, 720/I-10, exit Robertson Boulevard north. **Open** 10am-7pm Mon-Wed; 10am-8pm Thur-Sat; noon-6pm Sun. **Credit** AmEx, MC, V. **Map** p305 C2.
A good facsimile of the now legendary New York store, with four floors of cosmetics, jewellery, shoes, the best in designer clothes for both sexes, lingerie and home accessories. Above sits more elegance: Barney Greengrass, a classy rooftop restaurant and bar, with one of the best views into Beverly Hills.

Bloomingdale's

Century City Shopping Center, 10250 Santa Monica Boulevard, between Century Park W & Avenue of the Stars (1-310 772 2100/www.bloomingdales.com). Bus 27, 28, 316, Santa Monica 5, Commuter Express 534/I-405, exit Santa Monica Boulevard east. **Open** 10am-9pm Mon-Fri; 10am-8pm Sat; 11am-6pm Sun. **Credit** AmEx, Disc, MC, V. **Map** p305 B3.
Known as Bloomies by its fans, this upmarket chain store is located in only a few large US cities. It specialises in designer clothing, shoes, jewellery and accessories, along with its own-brand clothing. **Branches**: Beverly Center, 8500 Beverly Boulevard, at La Cienega Boulevard, West Hollywood (1-310 360 2700); Fashion Square, 14060 Riverside Drive, between Woodman & Hazeltine Avenues, Sherman Oaks (1-818 325 2200).

Macy's

Beverly Center, 8500 Beverly Boulevard, at La Cienega Boulevard, West Hollywood (1-310 854 6655/www.macys.com). Bus 14, 105, 316/I-10, exit La Cienega Boulevard north. **Open** 10am-9.30pm Mon-Sat; 11am-7pm Sun. **Credit** AmEx, MC, V. **Map** p306 A2/3.
Once just a New York store, Macy's has spent the past decade expanding across the nation. Its moderate to expensive offerings include costly garments from mostly US designers, plus more affordable clothing lines, accessories and cosmetics. **Branches**: throughout the city.

Neiman Marcus

9700 Wilshire Boulevard, at Roxbury Drive, Beverly Hills (1-310 550 5900/www.neimanmarcus.com). Bus 20, 21, 720/I-10, exit Robertson Boulevard north. **Open** 10am-6pm Mon-Fri; 10am-7pm Sat; noon-6pm Sun. **Credit** AmEx. **Map** p305 B3.
Neiman Marcus may be nicknamed 'Needless Markups', but nothing is really overpriced here. It's simply a store selling top-of-the-line goods that, naturally, cost a lot of money. It has one of the best women's shoe departments in town and a good cosmetics department.

Nordstrom

Westside Pavilion, 10800 W Pico Boulevard, at Westwood Boulevard, Century City (1-310 470 6155/ www.nordstrom.com). Bus Culver City 3, Santa Monica 7, 8, 12, 13, Commuter Express 431/I-10, exit Overland Boulevard north. **Open** 10am-9pm

Eat, Drink, Shop

Check out LA's fashion scene (clockwise from top left): **Costume National** (*see p183*); **Liza Bruce** (*see p184*); **Decades** (*see p186*); and **Earl Jean** (*see p184*).

Mon-Thur; 10am-9.30pm Fri; 10am-8pm Sat; 11am-6pm Sun. **Credit** AmEx, Disc, MC, V. **Map** p305 A4/5.
On the department store scale of things, where Macy's is the least expensive and Neiman Marcus the costliest, Nordstrom falls neatly in the middle in terms of both price and selection.
Branches: 200 W Broadway, at Central Avenue, Glendale (1-818 502 9922).

Saks Fifth Avenue

9600 & 9634 Wilshire Boulevard, at Bedford Drive, Beverly Hills (1-310 275 4211/www.saksfifth avenue.com). Bus 3, 20, 21, 720/I-405, exit Wilshire Boulevard east. **Open** 10am-6pm Mon-Wed, Fri, Sat; 10am-8.30pm Thur; noon-5pm Sat. **Credit** AmEx, MC, V. **Map** p305 B/C2.
Saks has been a part of Beverly Hills since 1938 and offers everything you could possibly want in expensive glamour. The men's department, the Fifth Avenue Club for Men, is claimed to offer the most comprehensive personal shopping service in the US.
Branches: 35 N De Lacey Street, at Fair Oaks Avenue, Pasadena (1-626 396 7100); South Coast Plaza, I-405 & Bristol Street, Costa Mesa, Orange County (1-714 540 3233).

Factory stores

If you're willing to drive further afield, factory outlet stores offer factory seconds, discontinued lines and some very good deals on major brand names such as Sony, Nike and Guess. Some items are not returnable.

Citadel Factory Stores

5675 E Telegraph Road, at Citadel Drive, City of Commerce (1-323 888 1220/www.citadelfactory stores.com). Bus 462/I-5, exit Washington Boulevard north. **Open** 10am-8pm Mon-Sat; 10am-6pm Sun. **Credit** varies.

The Cooper Building

860 S Los Angeles Street, at Ninth Street, Downtown (1-213 627 3754). Bus 27, 28, 40, 42, 83, 84, 85/I-110, exit Ninth Street east. **Open** 8.30am-5.30pm Mon-Sat; 11am-5pm Sun. **Credit** varies. **Map** p309 B4.

Desert Hills Factory Outlets

48400 Seminole Road, at the I-10, Cabazon (1-909 849 6641). I-10, exit Seminole Road north. **Open** 10am-8pm Mon-Fri, Sun; 9am-8pm Sat. **Credit** varies.
A two-hour drive east of LA, this is probably California's most sought-after factory outlet, with Gucci and Barney's New York stores. The Prada outlet goes under the name of Space.

Antiques

Most of LA's antique shops are concentrated in West Hollywood, along Robertson and Beverly Boulevards and La Brea Avenue. It's also worth looking around near the Pacific Design Center on Melrose Avenue and La Cienega Boulevard.

Antique Guild

3225 Helms Avenue, at Venice Boulevard, Culver City (1-310 838 3131/www.theantiqueguild.com). Bus 33, 333, 436/I-10, exit National Boulevard south. **Credit** AmEx, MC, V.
An antiques collective located in the Old Helms Bakery Building in the heart of charming, revived Culver City.

Blackman/Cruz

800 N La Cienega Boulevard, at Waring Avenue, West Hollywood (1-310 657 9228/www.blackman cruz.com). Bus 105/I-10, exit La Cienega Boulevard north. **Open** 10am-6pm Tue-Sat; noon-6pm Sun; closed Mon. **Credit** AmEx, Disc, MC, V. **Map** p306 A/B2.
Searching for an old operating-room light fixture? Or an animal-cage coffee table? Adam Blackman and David Cruz offer a delectable, cutting-edge mix of bibelots, lighting and period furniture. A haunt for celebs and local and national decorators – even Banana Republic's product developers come here.

Wells

2209 Sunset Boulevard, at Mohawk Street, Echo Park (1-213 413 0558). Bus 2, 3, 4, 302, 304/ US 101, exit N Alvarado Boulevard north. **Open** 11am-6pm Mon-Sat; closed Sun. **Credit** AmEx, MC, V. **Map** p308 C4.
Probably the largest collection of Southern Californian antique tiles and pottery, dating from 1900 to the 1940s.

Antiques malls

Pasadena Antique Center (1-626 449 7706), open 10am to 6pm daily, is also worth a visit.

Cranberry House

12318 Ventura Boulevard, between Whitsett & Laurel Grove Avenues, Studio City (1-818 506 8945). Bus 150, 218, 240, 750/US 101, exit Laurel Canyon south. **Open** 11am-6pm daily.
Some 15,000sq ft (1,395sq m) of antique clothing, furniture and accessories on two floors of a 1930s building. The ambience and service are welcoming.

Santa Monica Antique Market

1607 Lincoln Boulevard, between Colorado Avenue & Olympic Boulevard, Santa Monica (1-310 314 4899). Bus Santa Monica 2, 3, 9/I-10, exit Lincoln Boulevard north. **Open** 10am-6pm Mon-Sat; noon-5pm Sun. **Map** p304 B3.
This 20,000sq ft (1,860sq m) mall has more than 200 different dealers.

Flea markets & swap meets

Along **Santee Alley**, between Maple and Santee Streets in the LA Fashion District in Downtown LA, vendors hawk clothing, accessories and fabrics for shockingly low prices in a colourful bazaar setting, from 10am

Eat, Drink, Shop

to 5pm daily. Just remember there is a price to be paid: LA has become an international manufacturing centre for fake designer accessories; you don't know which item was made by sweatshop labour in Downtown and its surrounding suburban industrial parks.

Also in Downtown is the **Alameda Swap Meet** – similar to a car boot sale (501 South Alameda Street, 1-213 233 2764). It's open from 8am to 7pm every day except Tuesdays. At Alvarado Street, between Sixth and Eighth Streets (near MacArthur Park), four swap meets happen simultaneously on Sunday afternoons, the best of which is the **Westlake Swap Meet** (710 South Alvarado Street, 1-213 483 9300) at the former Westlake Theater.

The best flea market in the area is held at the **Rose Bowl** in Pasadena on the second Sunday of the month; details on 1-323 560 7469 or www.rgcshows.com/rosebowl.asp.

Long Beach Outdoor Antique & Collectible Market

Long Beach Veterans Memorial Stadium, Clark Avenue & Conant Street, Long Beach (1-562 655 5703). Bus Long Beach Transit 93, 112/I-405, exit Lakewood Boulevard north. **Open** 5.30am-3pm 3rd Sun of the mth. **Admission** $4.50-$10.
The largest antiques and collectibles market in the West, with more than 800 dealers.

Melrose Trading Post

Fairfax High School parking lot, 7850 Melrose Avenue, at Fairfax Avenue, Hollywood (1-323 651 5200). Bus 10, 11, 217, DASH Fairfax/I-10, exit Fairfax Avenue north. **Open** 9am-5pm Sun. **Admission** free. **Map** p306 B2.

Art supplies

The **Art Store** in West Hollywood (7301 West Beverly Boulevard, 1-323 933 9284/www.art store.com) is also a good source for everything from frames and portfolios to art books.

Aaron Brothers Art Mart

1645 Lincoln Boulevard, between Colorado Avenue & Olympic Boulevard, Santa Monica (1-310 450 6333/www.aaronbrothers.com). Bus Santa Monica 9/ I-10, exit Lincoln Boulevard north. **Open** 9am-9pm Mon-Sat; 10am-6pm Sun. **Credit** AmEx, Disc, MC, V. **Map** p304 B3.
This the Westside's biggest art supply shop, with a huge range of stuff and good prices.
Branches: throughout the city.

Bookshops

There are three main bookshop chains, with branches all over town, many with in-shop cafés. Phone one branch to find your nearest: **Barnes & Noble** (Westwood branch, 1-310

475 4144/www.bn.com), **Borders Books & Music** (Santa Monica branch, 1-310 393 9290/www.borderstores.com) and **Bookstar** (Beverly Connection branch, 1-310 289 1734). Below are the best of the independent, specialist and second-hand bookshops.

Bodhi Tree

8585 Melrose Avenue, at Westbourne Drive, West Hollywood (1-310 659 1733/www.bodhitree.com). Bus 10, 11, 105, DASH Fairfax, West Hollywood A, B/I-10, exit La Cienega Boulevard north. **Open** 10am-11pm daily. **Credit** MC, V. **Map** p306 A2.
Once frequented only by underground mystics and some pretty odd people, the Bodhi Tree is now recognised as the best metaphysical bookshop in LA. It also hosts 'alternative' workshops, poetry readings and seminars. The annexe at 606 Westbourne Drive sells second-hand books.

Book Soup

8818 Sunset Boulevard, at Horn Avenue & Holloway Drive, West Hollywood (1-310 659 3110/www.book soup.com). Bus 2, 3, 105, 302/I-10, exit La Cienega Boulevard north. **Open** 9am-midnight daily. **Credit** AmEx, DC, Disc, MC, V. **Map** p306 A1.
If you only have time to visit one bookshop in Los Angeles, make it Book Soup. It has a huge, diverse collection, as well as readings and signings. There's also an extensive newsstand with domestic and international publications.

Children's Book World

10580¾ W Pico Boulevard, between Prosser & Manning Avenues, Rancho Park (1-310 559 2665). Bus Culver City 3, Santa Monica 7, 13, Commuter Express 431/I-10, exit Overland Avenue north. **Open** 10am-5.30pm Mon-Fri; 10am-5pm Sat; closed Sun. **Credit** MC, V. **Map** p305 B4.
A huge children's bookshop, with devoted and knowledgeable staff. There are storytelling sessions three Saturdays a month.

Elliot M Katt

8568 Melrose Avenue, at Westmount Drive, West Hollywood (1-310 652 5178). Bus 10, 11, DASH Fairfax, West Hollywood A, B/I-10, exit La Cienega Boulevard north. **Open** 11am-5.45pm Mon-Sat; closed Sun. **Credit** AmEx, MC, V. **Map** p306 A2.
A huge array of books on any and every aspect of the performing arts in the US.

Eso-Won

3655 S La Brea Avenue, between Coliseum & Rodeo Avenues, Crenshaw (1-323 294 0324). Bus 212/ I-10, exit La Brea Avenue south. **Open** 10am-7pm Mon-Sat; noon-5pm Sun. **Credit** AmEx, Disc, MC, V.
One of the biggest black-interest bookshops in the country, with more than 15,000 titles on subjects as diverse as Black Power, the Harlem Renaissance, slavery, Egyptology and male-female relationships, as well as African-American fiction.

Eat, Drink, Shop

Hot off the press at **Book Soup**. *See p178.*

valuable oddities such as a transcription of the conversation between NASA and the first men on the moon ($950 – only 50 in existence).

Mysterious Bookshop

8763 Beverly Boulevard, between Robertson & San Vicente Boulevards, West Hollywood (1-310 659 2959). Bus 14, 220/I-10, exit La Cienega Boulevard north. **Open** 10am-6pm Mon-Sat; noon-5pm Sun. **Credit** AmEx, Disc, MC, V. **Map** p306 A2.
The city's oldest and largest mystery bookshop, selling new, second-hand and rare mystery, spy, detective and crime books, plus thrillers.

Samuel French Theater & Film Bookshop

7623 Sunset Boulevard, at Stanley Avenue, West Hollywood (1-323 876 0570/www.samuelfrench. com). Bus 2, 3, 302/I-10, exit Fairfax Avenue north. **Open** 10am-6pm Mon-Fri; 10am-5pm Sat. **Credit** AmEx, Disc, MC, V. **Map** p306 C1.
Just about every film script in print, plus myriad theatre scripts and many books about drama and film.
Branch: 11963 Ventura Boulevard, at Laurel Canyon Boulevard, Studio City (1-818 762 0535).

Talking Book World

7164 Beverly Boulevard, at La Brea Avenue, Hollywood (1-323 932 8111/www.talkingbookworld. com). Bus 14, 316/I-10, exit La Brea Avenue north. **Open** 9am-9pm Mon-Fri; 9am-6pm Sat; 11am-5pm Sun.* **Credit** AmEx, Disc, MC, V. **Map** p307 A3.
This is where Angelenos come to stock up on audio book versions of their favourite tomes – there are more than 5,000 titles to select from. Why? To while away the hours spent in traffic in a positive, creative manner, of course!

Vroman's

695 E Colorado Boulevard, between N El Molino & N Oak Knoll Avenues, Pasadena (1-626 449 5320). Bus 180, 181, 188, 485/I-110, exit Colorado Boulevard east. **Open** 9am-9pm Mon-Thur, Sat; 9am-10pm Fri; 10am-7pm Sun. **Credit** AmEx, Disc, MC, V.
The largest independent bookshop in Southern California. It's 102 years old and still going strong.

Hollywood Book City

6627 Hollywood Boulevard, between Cherokee & Whitley Avenues, Hollywood (1-323 466 2525/ www.hollywoodbookcity.com). Metro Hollywood-Highland or Hollywood-Vine/bus 163, 180, 181, 212/US 101, exit Cahuenga Boulevard south. **Open** 10am-10pm Mon-Fri; 9am-9pm Sat; 10am-8pm Sun. **Credit** AmEx, DC, Disc, MC, V. **Map** p307 A1.
A gargantuan, well-organised space filled with used books on myriad subjects.
Branch: **Sam's Book City of Burbank** 308 N San Fernando Boulevard, between E Palm Avenue & Magnolia Boulevard, Burbank (1-818 848 4417).

Koma

Room 1033, 548 S Spring Street, at Sixth Street, Downtown (1-213 239 0030/www.komabookstore. com). Metro Pershing Square/bus 33, 55, 83, 92/ I-110, exit Sixth Street east. **Open** noon-7pm daily. **Credit** MC, V. **Map** p309 B3.
Could this be the strangest bookshop in the world? It certainly has enough tomes on cults, fetishes, obsessions, serial killers, Nazis, anarchy, Satanism, self-mutilation and general craziness to qualify.

Michael R Thompson Books

8312 W Third Street, at Sweetzer Avenue, West Hollywood (1-323 658 1901). Bus 16, 316/I-10, exit La Cienega Boulevard north. **Open** 10am-6pm Mon-Sat; closed Sun. **Credit** AmEx, MC, V. **Map** p306 B3.
Used, dusty books in an academic bookshop setting, with a bent towards Western philosophy, plus

CDs, tapes & records

Los Angeles has the overwhelming selection of recorded music that you'd expect to find in a big city and, as a music industry hub, is also fantastic for used vinyl. A whole 'beat junkie' culture has grown around finding rare records for next to nothing, and even the casual buyer can make great finds.

You'll find **Tower Records** on Sunset Strip (8801 Sunset Boulevard, at Horn Avenue, 1-310 657 7300/www.towerrecords.com). It doesn't always carry the range you would expect, forcing customers to flee to the nearby, much nicer and better stocked **Virgin Megastore** (8000 Sunset Boulevard, at Crescent Heights

Eat, Drink, Shop

Boulevard, 1-213 650 8666/www.virginrecords. com). We've listed the best of the independent shops below.

If you want to make music rather than just listen to it, visit the **Guitar Center** in Hollywood (7425 Sunset Boulevard, 1-323 874 1060), which stocks most kinds of musical instruments as well as vintage guitars. Or try the lower-key **West LA Music** (11345 Santa Monica Boulevard, 1-310 477 1945). In East LA, **Candelas Guitars** (2427 Cesar Chavez Avenue, 1-323 261 2011), a family-run operation for more than 50 years, makes handcrafted Mexican instruments that are favoured by everyone from Andres Segovia to members of Los Lobos and Ozomatli.

Benway Records

1600 Pacific Avenue, at Windward Avenue, Venice (1-310 396 8898). Bus 33, 333, 436/I-405, exit Venice Boulevard south. **Open** 11am-8pm daily. **Credit** AmEx, MC, V. **Map** p304 A5.

Ron and Kelly Jackson, along with their psychedelic used CD and vinyl shack, are the ultimate Venice Beach fixtures. Drop by to peruse the old and second-hand jazz CDs, trash videos, and the wall full of cassettes, T-shirts, stickers and posters or to jaw with part-time staffer Ronnie, drummer for local punk legends, the Muffs.

Fat Beats

1722 N Vermont Avenue, between Hollywood Boulevard & Franklin Avenue, Silver Lake (1-323 663 3717). Bus 180, 181, 206/US 101, exit Vermont Avenue north. **Open** noon-9pm Mon-Thur; noon-10pm Fri, Sat; noon-6pm Sun. Closed last Sun of the month. **Credit** MC, V. **Map** p308 A2.

A comprehensive hip hop shop with 200-plus wall-mounted racks selling the newest of the new, complemented nicely by a rare groove wall.

Global Grooves

2400 Main Street, at Hollister Avenue, Santa Monica (1-310 450 1484). Bus 33, 333, Santa Monica 2, 8/I-10, exit Fourth-Fifth Street south. **Open** 11am-7pm daily. **No credit cards.** **Map** p304 A3.

The owners are partners in Giant (*see p240*), currently the hottest, and best, of LA's weekly dance clubs, so this might be the place to tap into LA's electronic scene. It also has nice British staff who won't sneer at your vinyl selections.

Head Line Records

7708 Melrose Avenue, between Genesee & Spaulding Avenues, Melrose District (1-323 655 2125/www. headlinerecords.com). Bus 10, 11/I-10, exit Fairfax Avenue north. **Open** noon-8pm daily. **Credit** MC, V. **Map** p306 C2.

Not the first punk rock store in LA, but by far the most dangerous. Mild-mannered French owner Jean Luc Gaudry's shop used to be in Westwood but had to move to Melrose because the in-store punk performances got so out of control.

House of Records

3328 Pico Boulevard, between 33rd Street & Centinela Avenue, Santa Monica (1-310 450 1222/ www.houseofrecords.com). Bus Santa Monica 7/I-10, exit Centinela Avenue south. **Open** 11am-7pm daily. **Credit** AmEx, Disc, MC, V. **Map** p304 C3.

Opened in 1952, this place claims to be the oldest record shop in LA. It carries thousands of out-of-print records, used records and CDs, and videos.

Music Man Murray

5055 Exposition Boulevard, at S La Brea Avenue, Crenshaw (1-323 734 9146). Bus 38, 212/I-10, exit La Brea Avenue. **Open** usually noon-5pm Tue-Sat; closed Mon, Sun. **Credit** AmEx, Disc, MC, V.

Yes, it's one guy and he's one of the oldest record dealers in Los Angeles. His incredibly cluttered shop contains more than 200,000 rare and discontinued records (78s, 45s and 33s) of everything from classical, jazz, West African, mariachi, operas, marching bands and salsa to Broadway tunes. Prices range from $3-$2,000.

Music Zone

4004 Vermont Avenue, at Martin Luther King Jr Boulevard, South Central (1-323 233 8333). Bus 40, 42, 204, 354/I-110, exit Martin Luther King Jr Boulevard west. **Open** 10am-7pm Mon-Sat; 2-5pm Sun. **Credit** MC, V.

This new addition to LA's hip hop map features the best of hard-to-find, underground or independent hip hop, reggae and Latin in album, CD and vinyl form. The Zone also makes custom CDs and hosts live DJ performances on Saturday afternoons.

The Record Recycler

4659 Hollywood Boulevard, at Vermont Avenue, Los Feliz (1-323 666 7361). Bus 180, 181, 206/US 101, exit Vermont Avenue north. **Open** 11am-8pm Mon-Sat; noon-6pm Sun. **Credit** AmEx, Disc, MC, V. **Map** p308 A1.

This Los Feliz shop is a place for vinyl buffs, with a huge selection of clean, well-filed, used vinyl, with decks to listen before you buy.

Rhino Records

1720 Westwood Boulevard, between Massachusetts Avenue & Santa Monica Boulevard, Westwood (1-310 474 8685). Bus 4, 304, Santa Monica 8, 12/ I-405, exit Santa Monica Boulevard east. **Open** 10am-11pm Mon-Thur, Sun; 10am-midnight Fri, Sat. **Credit** AmEx, Disc, MC, V. **Map** p305 A4.

For serious collectors and ol' fashioned lovers of fine rock, jazz, blues, folk and reggae. You'll find new and second-hand records and all other formats, indie and imports, plus regular live performances in the shop. A new shop opens at 2028 Westwood in early 2001.

Rockaway Records

2395 Glendale Boulevard, at Silver Lake Boulevard, Silver Lake (1-323 664 3232/www.rockaway.com). Bus 92, 603/I-5, exit Glendale Boulevard south. **Open** 10am-9.30pm daily. **Credit** AmEx, MC, V. **Map** p308 C2.

Used CDs, rare vinyl, new alternative and LA-based bands, 1960s memorabilia and videos. The ultimate place to check out Silver Lake indie bands.

Vinyl Fetish

1750 N Vermont Avenue, at Kingswell Avenue, Los Feliz (1-323 660 4500). Bus 180, 181, 206/US 101, exit Vermont Avenue north. **Open** noon-8pm daily. **Credit** AmEx, MC, V. **Map** p308 A2.

One of the best places for vinyl imports of punk, goth, industrial grindcore and other strange shit.

Wentzel's Music Town

13117 Lakewood Boulevard, at Gardendale Street, Downey (1-562 634 2928). Bus 265, 266, 631/I-105, exit Lakewood Boulevard south. **Open** 9am-6pm Mon, Wed-Sat; 11am-5pm Sun; closed Tue. **Credit** AmEx, Disc, MC, V.

Downey is famous for two things: the oldest McDonald's in the US and this delightful place, open for over 40 years, where the Chantays recorded their seminal surf instrumental 'Pipeline' in the back room. (Owners Tom and Maxine Wentzel still receive royalties.) The decor is a bit shabby, but you'll find bins full of country, rock, doo-wop, easy listening, big band and even disco.

Electronics & computers

There are branches of electronics superstore **Circuit City** throughout LA (Midtown branch: 1-310 280 0700/www.circuitcity.com.

CompUSA

11441 Jefferson Boulevard, between Slauson Boulevard & I-405, Culver City (1-310 390 9993/ www.compusa.com). Bus 108, 110, 561, Culver City 2, 4, 6/I-405, exit Jefferson Boulevard east. **Open** 9am-9pm Mon-Fri; 10am-7pm Sat; 11am-7pm Sun. **Credit** AmEx, MC, V.

Computer supplies and systems. At last, a shop that celebrates the Macintosh (whaddya think this book was built on?). **Branches:** throughout the city.

Fry's

3600 Sepulveda Boulevard, at Rosecrans Avenue, Manhattan Beach (1-310 364 3797/www.frys.com). Bus 125, 232/I-405, exit Rosecrans Avenue west. **Open** 8am-9pm Mon-Fri; 9am-8pm Sat; 9am-7pm Sun. **Credit** Disc, MC, V.

A dizzying array of computers, software and gadgetry, plus an excellent choice of games.

Fashion: general

You'll find virtually every international designer label under the sun in Los Angeles, as the city becomes the new status address on every top designer's shopping bag. With that said, LA also boasts a growing stable of home-grown fashion designers, mixing Hollywood glitz, hippie chic and sportswear – *see page 185* **Local talent**.

Reliable chainstores the **Gap** (Santa Monica branch: 1-310 453 4551/www.gap.com) and **Banana Republic** (Beverly Hills branch: 1-310 858 7900/www.bananarepublic.com) are plentiful. **J Crew**, offering the ultimate in preppie-style casual togs for both sexes, has branches in the Century City Shopping Center (1-310 286 9562), on Third Street Promenade and in Pasadena. Self-consciously cool Italian label **Diesel** pops up in Santa Monica (1-310 899 3055) and the Beverly Center, while **Urban Outfitters** appears in Santa Monica (1-310 394 1404), on Melrose and Pasadena. Call any branch to find the one nearest to you.

Aero & Co

4651 Kingswell Avenue, at N Vermont Avenue, Los Feliz (1-323 665 4651/www.aeroandco.com). Bus 180, 181/US 101, exit Vermont Avenue north. **Open** 11am-7pm Mon-Wed, Fri; 11am-9pm Thur; noon-8pm Sat; noon-7pm Sun. **Credit** AmEx, MC, V. **Map** p308 A2.

A showcase for one of LA's leading designers, Cynthia Vincent, and her fashion chums. Aside from Cynthia's St Vincent line, Victorian-inspired works by emerging LA designer Magda Berliner are flying out the door. Plus men's fashions, including Grey Ant, and T-shirts by Brit duo Antoni & Alison.

Calypso

8635 Sunset Boulevard, at La Cienega Boulevard, West Hollywood (1-310 652 4454). Bus 2, 3, 302/ I-10, exit La Cienega Boulevard north. **Open** 11am-7pm Mon-Sat; noon-6pm Sun. **Credit** AmEx, MC, V. **Map** p306 A/B1.

In Los Angeles you get to wear the sunny stuff year-round, so expand your wardrobe (or suitcase) with tropical sarongs, sandals and straw bags.

Club Monaco

Beverly Center, 8500 Beverly Boulevard, at La Cienega Boulevard, West Hollywood (1-310 657 1818). Bus 14, 105, 316/I-10, exit La Cienega Boulevard north. **Open** 10am-9pm Mon-Fri; 10am-8pm Sat; 11am-6pm Sun. **Credit** AmEx, MC, V. **Map** p306 A2/3.

This popular chain offers hip basics inspired by key looks from the runways. Hot items don't hang around, so as soon as you arrive in town, head straight for your nearest branch.

Branches: 401 N Beverly Drive, at Brighton Way, Beverly Hills (1-310 858 0204); 8569 Sunset Boulevard, between La Cienega Boulevard & Holloway Drive, West Hollywood (1-310 659 3821).

CP Shades

2937 Main Street, at Marine & Pier Avenues, Santa Monica (1-310 392 0949). Bus 22, Santa Monica 1/I-10, exit Lincoln Boulevard south. **Open** 11am-7pm Mon-Fri; 11am-6pm Sat; noon-5pm Sun. **Credit** AmEx, MC, V. **Map** p304 A4.

Comfortable sportswear for men and women, all in muted and solid colours. **Branches:** throughout the city.

Curve

154 N Robertson Boulevard, between Clifton Way &
Wilshire Boulevard, Beverly Hills (1-310 360 8008).
Bus 21, 220/I-405, exit Wilshire Boulevard east.
Open 11am-7pm daily. **Credit** AmEx, MC, V.
Map p306 A3.
Delia Seaman and Nevena Borissova have combined
their fashion styles – Delia's is classic and conserv-
ative and Nevena's is street-funky – at Curve, a
women's clothing and accessory shop.

Dari

12184 Ventura Boulevard, at Laurel Canyon
Boulevard, Studio City (1-818 762 3274). Bus 150,
218, 230, 240, 750/US 101, exit Laurel Canyon
Boulevard. **Open** 11am-7pm Mon-Sat; noon-5pm Sun.
Credit AmEx, MC, V.
Only in LA will you find a psychic giving readings
in a clothes shop. This Bali-esque oasis within the
frumpy San Fernando Valley, owned by Melanie
Shatner (daughter of William), also serves up elixirs
and tea while you browse the racks of clothes by
Anna Sui, Bella Freud and local talent Anna Huling.

Emma Gold

8115 Melrose Avenue, at Crescent Heights
Boulevard, Melrose District (1-323 651 3662). Bus
10, 11, DASH Fairfax/I-10, exit La Cienega
Boulevard north. **Open** 11am-7pm Mon-Sat; noon-
5pm Sun. **Credit** AmEx, MC, V. **Map** p306 B2.
Don't let the wide selection of clothes, shoes and
accessories overpower you. One rack at a time, you'll
discover clothing by leading European designers,
including Clements Ribeiro, Ann Demeulemeester
and Matthew Williamson, plus feng shui candles
and aromatherapy items. Plus footwear by the likes
of Prada, Fendi and Marc Jacobs.

Fred Segal/Ron Herman Melrose

8100 Melrose Avenue, at Crescent Heights
Boulevard, Melrose District (1-323 651 4129). Bus
10, 11, DASH Fairfax/I-10, exit La Cienega
Boulevard north. **Open** 10am-7pm Mon-Sat; noon-
6pm Sun. **Credit** AmEx, MC, V. **Map** p306 B2.
Fred Segal is a mecca for those with style, taste and
money. A cornucopia of shops under one roof, with
everything from hip casual wear to expensive
designer gear for men, women and small children,
plus gifts, furniture and beauty goods. It's a great
platform for local designers, including Josephine
Loka and William B. At Lee & Life Size, you'll find
adorable clothes for trend-setting babies and children aged up to 14.
Branch: 500 Broadway, at Fifth Street, Santa
Monica (1-310 393 4477).

Govinda

3764 Watseka Avenue, at Venice Boulevard, West
LA (1-310 204 3263). Bus 33, 333, 436/I-405, exit
Venice Boulevard north. **Open** 11am-8.30pm Mon-
Sat; noon-8.30pm Sun. **Credit** AmEx, MC, V.
This Aladdin's cave of a shop will get your heart
pumping. Govinda is a popular Hari Krishna out-
post among fashion stylists, boasting the city's

largest range of pashmina shawls, embroidered
handbags, Indian blouses, skirts, trousers and beaded slippers – all at bargain basement prices. One of
LA's best kept secrets.

Kate Spade

105 N Robertson Boulevard, at Alden Drive, Beverly
Hills (1-310 271 9778). Bus 220, DASH Fairfax/
I-405, exit Wilshire Boulevard east. **Open** 11am-7pm
Mon-Sat; noon-5pm Sun. **Credit** AmEx, Disc, MC, V.
Map p306 A3.
Wacky bags and a small line of classic clothes by
the famous New York handbag/purse designer.

Madison

106 N Robertson Boulevard, between W Third Street
& Alden Drive, Beverly Hills (1-310 275 1930). Bus
220, DASH Fairfax/I-10, exit Robertson Boulevard
north. **Open** 11am-7pm Mon-Sat; noon-5pm Sun.
Credit AmEx, MC, V. **Map** p306 A3.
A good mix of hiply classic clothes for sophisticated
women. As well as Madison's own label, you'll find
clothing by Alberto Biani, Blumarine, Tocca and
Ann Demeulemeester and shoes and handbags by
Miu Miu and Dolce & Gabbana.

Ma Meg

11925 Montana Avenue, off I-405, Brentwood
(1-310 826 4142). Bus Santa Monica 3/I-405, exit
Montana Avenue **Open** 10am-6pm Mon-Fri; 11am-
5pm Sat; closed Sun. **Credit** AmEx, MC, V.
When top fashion mag editors harp on about a shop,
you know something's cooking. Ma Meg sells work
by Europe's best designers, including Helmut Lang,
Balenciaga and Comme des Garçons. It's ruinously
expensive, but that goes with the territory.

Maxfields

8825 Melrose Avenue, at Robertson Boulevard, West
Hollywood (1-310 274 8800). Bus 10, 11, 220/I-10,
exit Robertson Boulevard north. **Open** 11am-7pm
Mon-Sat; closed Sun. **Credit** AmEx, DC, Disc, MC, V.
Map p306 A2.
The Sistine Chapel of designer gear and accessories
for cutting-edge men and women: Gigli, Gucci,
Prada, Comme des Garçons, Yohji Yamamoto, Jil
Sander, Gaultier, Galliano, Dries Van Noten, as well
as local designers such as Rick Owens. Enjoy the
personal service and drink the shop's own-label
designer water while you mix and match. Visit sister
shop Maxfield Bleu for year-round discounts on
Gucci, Jil Sander, Prada and Dolce & Gabbana.
Branch: **Maxfield Bleu** 151 N Robertson
Boulevard, at Beverly Boulevard, West Hollywood
(1-310 275 7007).

Naked

181 N Martel Avenue, at Beverly Boulevard, Fairfax
District (1-323 964 0222). Bus 14, 316/I-10, exit
La Brea Avenue north. **Open** 11am-6pm Mon-Sat;
closed Sun. **Credit** AmEx, MC, V. **Map** p306 C2.
Behind Naked's etched glass windows, hipsters will
find solace with avant-garde men's and women's
European fashions, including Hussein Chalayan,
Mandarina Duck and Seraph.

Eat, Drink, Shop

Noodle Stories

8223 W Third Street, at Sweetzer Avenue, Fairfax District (1-323 651 1782). Bus 218, 316/I-10, exit La Cienega Boulevard north. **Open** 10am-6pm Mon-Sat; noon-5pm Sun. **Credit** AmEx, MC, V. **Map** p306 B3.

Stock up on easy-to-wear styles by European labels for both sexes, including Martin Margiela, Mandarina Duck and New York. Covet the finely spun 100% cotton underwear by Ripcosa and John Smedley, and other top brands.

Steinberg & Sons

4712 Franklin Avenue, at N Vermont Avenue, Los Feliz (1-323 660 0294). Bus 26, 180, 181, DASH Hollywood/US 101, exit Hollywood Boulevard east. **Open** noon-7pm Tue-Sun; closed Mon. **Credit** AmEx, Disc, MC, V. **Map** p308 A2.

Tatiana Von Furstenburg, daughter of Diane, runs this tiny store in an unassuming neighbourhood in Los Feliz. It's filled with her mum's famous silk jersey dresses, as well as cutesy T-shirts, tank tops and itsy-bitsy crocheted underwear by Petit Oiseau and stylised streetwear by other local designers.

Tracy Ross

8595 Sunset Boulevard, between Alta Loma Road & La Cienega Boulevard, West Hollywood (1-310 854 1996). Bus 2, 3, 302/I-10, exit La Cienega Boulevard north. **Open** 10am-7pm Mon-Sat; noon-5pm Sun. **Credit** AmEx, MC, V. **Map** p306 A1.

T-shirts, mini dresses, pyjamas and perfumes for the cool girl-woman about town.

Union

110 N La Brea Avenue, between First & Second Streets, Fairfax District (1-323 549 6950). Bus 212/I-10, exit La Brea Avenue north. **Open** 11am-7pm Mon-Sat; noon-6pm Sun. **Credit** AmEx, MC, V. **Map** p306 C3.

Casual clothes and active wear by young designers.

X-Large & X-Girl

1756 N Vermont Avenue, between Hollywood Boulevard & Franklin Avenue, Los Feliz (1-323 666 3483). Bus 180, 181, 204/ US 101, exit Vermont Avenue north. **Open** noon-7pm Mon-Sat; noon-6pm Sun. **Credit** AmEx, MC, V. **Map** p308 A2.

Three lines of actionwear for grown-up boys and girls – Grand Royal, X Large and Mini – plus work by other hip designers, including the Milk Fed line.

Designer

The area in Beverly Hills bounded by Crescent Drive, Wilshire Boulevard and Little Santa Monica Boulevard is known as the 'Golden Triangle'; it contains the swanky shopping meccas of Rodeo Drive and Brighton Way, where you'll find boutiques for most of fashion's top names. In Two Rodeo, a European-style outdoor shopping complex at the corner of Rodeo Drive and Wilshire Boulevard, is Christian Dior (1-310 859 4700).

On Rodeo Drive itself, top designers include Dolce & Gabbana (No.312, 1-310 888 8701); Hermès (No.343, 1-310 278 6440); Chanel (No.400, 1-310 278 5500); Giorgio Armani (No.436, 1-310 271 5555); Prada (No. 343, 1-310 385 5959); Fendi (No. 355, 1-310 276 8888) and Gucci (No.443, 1-310 278 3451). Brighton Way is home to Emporio Armani (No.9533, 1-310 271 7790).

Agnès B

100 N Robertson Boulevard, at Alden Drive, Beverly Hills (1-310 271 9643). Bus 220, DASH Fairfax/I-10, exit Robertson Boulevard north. **Open** 11am-7pm Mon-Sat; noon-6pm Sun. **Credit** AmEx, MC, V. **Map** p306 A3.

Modern-day classics for men and women, plus a line for teenagers, entitled Lolita.

Andrew Dibben

1618 Silver Lake Boulevard, at Effie Street, Silver Lake (1-323 662 9189). Bus 201/I-5, exit Glendale Boulevard south. **Open** noon-6pm Wed-Sun; closed Mon, Tue. **Credit** AmEx, MC, V. **Map** p308 C3.

Andrew Dibben spent stints with Helmut Lang, Liza Bruce and Mark Eisen before setting up shop to sell his own take on modern menswear. Find techno-fibre casualwear teamed with Dibben's hand-selected vintage Levi's, and a backdrop of changing avant-garde art installations. Be nice to the resident Weimaraner. Well worth the trek out to Silver Lake.

Ann Taylor

357 N Camden Drive, between Wilshire Boulevard & Brighton Way, Beverly Hills (1-310 858 7840). Bus 21, 720/I-405, exit Wilshire Boulevard east. **Open** 10am-7pm Mon-Fri; 10am-6pm Sat; noon-5pm Sun. **Credit** AmEx, MC, V. **Map** p305 C2.

Well-priced, sensible day and evening womenswear.

Betsey Johnson

8050 Melrose Avenue, at Laurel Avenue, Melrose District (1-323 852 1534). Bus 10, 11/I-10, exit La Brea Avenue north. **Open** 11am-7pm Mon-Sat; noon-6pm Sun. **Credit** AmEx, MC, V. **Map** p306 B2.

Hip, sexy, affordable fashion for women with little girls' hearts. Everything from polyester minis to Lurex trousers.

Branches: throughout the city.

Costume National

8001 Melrose Avenue, between Crescent Heights Boulevard & Fairfax Avenue, Melrose District (1-323 655 8160). Bus 10, 11, DASH Fairfax/I-10, exit Fairfax Avenue north. **Open** 11am-7pm Mon-Sat; noon-5pm Sun. **Credit** AmEx, MC, V. **Map** p306 B2.

Designed by groovy Santa Monica architect Marmol and Radziner, this is a striking modern space divided by glass, steel and lacquered panels, and housing the popular Italian designer label for men and women. The footwear and accessories are highly covetable.

Daryl K

8125 Melrose Avenue, at Crescent Heights Boulevard, Melrose District (1-323 651 2251). Bus 10, 11, DASH Fairfax/I-10, exit La Cienega Boulevard north. **Open** 10am-6pm Mon-Sat; noon-5pm Sun. **Credit** AmEx, MC, V. **Map** p306 B2.

This New York-based, urban-chic designer has found a key spot on Melrose Avenue, in a white box opposite Fred Segal, to sell her sought-after jeans and separates. Every fashionista should own a pair of these designer denims.

Earl Jean

141½ N Larchmont Boulevard, between First Street & Beverly Boulevard, Hancock Park (1-323 463 1556). Bus 14, 316/I-10, exit La Brea Avenue north. **Open** 11am-6pm Mon-Fri; noon-5pm Sat, Sun. **Credit** AmEx, MC, V.

Designer Suzanne Costas Freiwald is sending women into a frenzy with her 'perfect fit' jeans. Her line also includes leather pieces, denim blazers, snap-front shirt-dresses in vintage denim, low-rise cord jeans and cord jean jackets. The shop is equally stylish, using dark wood, leather and marble, and subtle Western motifs.

Ghost

125 N Robertson Boulevard, at Wilshire Boulevard, Beverly Hills (1-310 246 0567). Bus 21, 220, 720/I-10, exit Robertson Boulevard north. **Open** 11am-7pm Mon-Sat; closed Sun. **Credit** AmEx, MC, V. **Map** p306 A3.

British designer Tanya Sarne's traditional romantic look, reinforced by embroidery and flowing shapes, has recently been augmented by sharper pieces in silk jersey and lightweight wool.

Henry Duarte

8747 Sunset Boulevard, at Sherbourne Drive, West Hollywood (1-310 652 5830). Bus 2, 3, 302/I-10, exit La Cienega Boulevard north. **Open** noon-7pm Mon-Sat; closed Sun. **Credit** AmEx, Disc, MC, V. **Map** p306 A1.

LA designer Henry Duarte's leather creations appeal to a rock 'n' roll crowd. His 1960s-inspired pieces for men and women draw the likes of Nicholas Cage, Roseanne Arquette and Mickey Rourke to this corner of Sunset Strip. You can buy off the shelf or made-to-measure. The gallery-like shop hosts regular art installations.

Laura Urbinati

8667 Sunset Boulevard, at Sunset Plaza Drive, West Hollywood (1-310 652 3183). Bus 2, 3, 302/I-10, exit La Cienega Boulevard north. **Open** 10am-7pm Mon-Fri; 10am-6pm Sat; noon-5pm Sun. **Credit** AmEx, MC, V. **Map** p306 A1.

Two floors of Urbinati wear, including her famous bathing suits in earth-toned cottons, and knitwear, along with a few other classy, wearable designers-with-edge, such as Helmut Lang, Costume National and Martin Margiela. The latest addition is an entire floor devoted to local designer Christina Kim's popular label Dosa.

Liza Bruce

7977 Melrose Avenue, between Fairfax Avenue & Crescent Heights Boulevard, Melrose District (1-323 655 5012). Bus 10, 11, DASH Fairfax/I-10, exit Fairfax Avenue north. **Open** 11am-6pm Mon-Sat; closed Sun. **Credit** AmEx, MC, V. **Map** p306 B2.

Women collect them. Men admire them. Fashion editors can't get enough of them. Liza Bruce's show-stopping swimwear and lingerie engage bold graphic cuts using her signature lycra. The pop-artsy shop (designed by her husband, Nicholas Alivis Vega) also offers made-to-measure designs.

Malia Mills

7972 Melrose Avenue, between Fairfax Avenue & Crescent Heights Boulevard, Melrose District (1-323 655 4709). Bus 10, 11, DASH Fairfax/I-10, exit Fairfax Avenue north. **Open** noon-7pm Mon-Sat; closed Sun. **Credit** AmEx, MC, V. **Map** p306 B2.

You'll find a designer bikini or one-piece swimsuit to suit every body type, plus lingerie by Cosa Bella, Andrea Stewart handbags and Three Dot T-shirts.

Richard Tyler

7290 Beverly Boulevard, between Poinsettia Place & Alta Vista Boulevard, Melrose District (1-323 931 6769). Bus 14, 316/I-10, exit La Brea Avenue north. **Open** 10am-6pm Mon-Fri; 11am-6pm Sat; closed Sun. **Credit** AmEx, MC, V. **Map** p306 C2.

Although Tyler doesn't actively discourage off-the-street business (if you ring the bell, they should let you in), staff do spend most of their time with by-appointment clients known to include Julia Roberts, Brad Pitt and Seal, who come for ballgowns and fine tailored suits. It's all very Melrose.

Fashion: specialist

Children

Gap Kids is everywhere (general information 1-800 427 7895). Many of the shops listed elsewhere also sell children's clothes; see individual entries.

98% Angel

Malibu Country Mart, unit 5A, 3835 Cross Creek Road, off Pacific Coast Highway, Malibu (1-310 456 0069). Bus 434/I-10, exit PCH north. **Open** 10am-6pm Mon-Sat; 11am-5pm Sun. **Credit** AmEx, MC, V.

A hip shop for all your little darlings' wardrobe needs, overlooking a sandbox in a cute shopping plaza in the heart of Malibu. Brands carried include Mini Man, Metropolitan Prairie and Cacharel.

Flap Happy

2330 Michigan Avenue, at Cloverfield Avenue, Santa Monica (1-310 453 3527). Bus Santa Monica 9/I-10, exit Cloverfield Avenue north. **Open** 10am-5pm Mon-Sat; closed Sun. **Credit** Disc, MC, V. **Map** p304 C3.

Colourful, patterned cotton clothes (up to age five) from this Venice-based clothing manufacturer.

Local talent

LA always suffered a bit of an image problem in the style department until Hollywood and fashion became official bedfellows. Today, Hollywood and fashion equals high billings. There's more money than ever in the entertainment arena, and with it has emerged a new breed of local fashion designers. Here are some names to look out for.

Richard Tyler has a penchant for minimalist gowns and is a favourite among Hollywood stars. **Rick Owens**'s avant-garde creations are best summed up as Courtney Love meets gothic chic, with his fabulous leather jackets and deconstructed ensembles in diaphanous fabrics. **Michelle Mason**'s work also fits the avant-garde bill, especially when it comes to her high-concept footwear. New girl on the block **Magda Berliner** is already finding a celebrity following with her Victorian-inspired gothic chic in contrasting fabrics and complex cuts. Along the rock 'n' roll vein is **Henry Duarte** and his tailor-made gothic-cum-cowboy leather outfits. Continuing this theme are

Kelly and John Chirpas's **Josephine Loka** line, which is infused with hippie chic.

While the influence of Hollywood style resonates throughout the fashion world, equally significant is LA's sportswear clothing. The city's year-round sunshine has spawned an entire look, inspiring designers across the world with its relaxed dress code. Discover **Earl Jean**'s 'perfect fit' jeans (pictured above) or William Beranek of the **William B** label, who focuses on modern cuts and slim-fitted silhouettes. Brit import **Andrew Dibben** marries technofibres with his well-tailored classic menswear items with a twist (his Silver Lake shop is pictured below), while **Christina Kim** keeps women swooning for her unique ethnic chic creations and has created a loyal following for her **Dosa** line, which puts sustainable business practices at the forefront of her brand.

Vintage couture is also making headlines in the fashion world, and LA's Cameron Silver is leading this trend with his store **Decades**, stocking the best in Rudi Gernreich, Ossie Clarke and Hermès.

Stockists

Richard Tyler: see page 184. Rick Owens: **Maxfields**, see page 182. Michelle Mason: **Diavolina**, see page 189. Magda Berliner: **Aero & Co**, see page 181. **Henry Duarte**: see page 184. Josephine Loka: **Fred Segal**, see page 182. **Earl Jean**: see page 184. William B: **Fred Segal**, see page 182. **Andrew Dibben**: see page 183. Dosa: **Laura Urbinati**, see page 184. **Decades**: see page 186.

Eat, Drink, Shop

FlapJack's

2462 Overland Avenue, at Pico Boulevard, West LA (1-310 204 1896). Bus Santa Monica 7, Commuter Express 431/I-10, exit Overland Avenue north. **Open** 10am-6pm Mon-Sat; closed Sun. **Credit** AmEx, MC, V. **Map** p305 A4.

Pay a visit to this West LA shop for a huge selection of second-hand clothes (up to age ten).

Pom D'Api

9411 Brighton Way, between Beverly & Canon Drives, Beverly Hills (1-310 278 7663). Bus 3, 14, 576/I-10, exit Robertson Boulevard north. **Open** 10am-6pm Mon-Sat; noon-5pm Sun. **Credit** AmEx, MC, V. **Map** p305 C2.

Tony Brand opened this cool kids' shoe shop, the only one of its kind in the US (the chain started in France), where he stocks a smorgasbord of chic French footwear, from 'Smellies' (scented plastic beach sandals) to clogs in crazy colours.

Discount

Loehmans

333 La Cienega Boulevard, between Third Street & Wilshire Boulevard, Mid Wilshire (1-310 659 0674). Bus 105, 316/I-10, exit La Cienega Boulevard north. **Open** 10am-9pm Mon-Sat; 11am-7pm Sun. **Credit** Disc, MC, V. **Map** p306 B3.

Discount women's and men's clothes and shoes. Be sure to check out the Back Room, devoted to more upmarket designer names, including Perry Ellis and Bill Blass.

Ross Dress for Less

1751 Westwood Boulevard, at Santa Monica Boulevard, Westwood (1-310 477 1707). Bus 4, 304, Santa Monica 1, 8, 12/I-405, exit Wilshire Boulevard east. **Open** 9.30am-9pm Mon-Sat; 9.30am-7pm Sun. **Credit** AmEx, MC, V. **Map** p305 A4.

Men's and women's clothing and accessories.

Saks SFO

652 N La Brea Avenue, between Clinton Street & Melrose Avenue, Melrose District (1-323 939 3993). Bus 10, 11, 212/I-10, exit La Brea Avenue north. **Open** 11am-8pm Mon-Fri; 11am-7pm Sat, Sun. **Credit** MC, V. **Map** p306 C2.

Many a bargain for men, women and children. **Branch**: 9608 Venice Boulevard, at Robertson Boulevard, Culver City (1-310 559 5448).

Dress hire

One Night Affair

2370 Westwood Boulevard, between Tennessee Avenue & Pico Boulevard, West LA (1-310 652 4334/474 7808). Bus Culver City 3, Santa Monica 7, 8, 12, 13/I-10, exit Santa Monica Boulevard east. **Open** 11am-7pm Tue-Sat, by appointment only; closed Mon, Sun. **Credit** AmEx, Disc, MC, V. **Map** p305 A4.

Everything from cocktail dresses to wedding gowns, by designers from Gianni Versace to Bill Blass.

Tuxedo Center

7360 Sunset Boulevard, at N Martel Avenue, West Hollywood (1-323 874 4200). Bus 2, 3, 302/I-10, exit La Brea Avenue north. **Open** 9am-7pm Mon, Fri; 9am-6pm Tue-Thur; 9am-5pm Sat; 11am-3pm Sun. **Credit** AmEx, MC, V. **Map** p306 C1.

Traditional formal wear for men.

Dry cleaners

Brown's

1223 Montana Avenue, between 12th & 13th Streets, Santa Monica (1-310 451 8531). Bus Santa Monica 3/I-10, exit Lincoln Boulevard north. **Open** 7am-6pm Mon-Fri; 8am-2pm Sat; closed Sun. **Credit** MC, V. **Map** p304 B1.

It may be the most expensive dry cleaner in the western world, but it's been around (and family-owned) since 1939. And staff still box your shirts up the old-fashioned way.

Imperial Cleaners

502 S Western Avenue, at Fifth Street, Hancock Park (1-213 487 5470). Bus 207, 357/I-10, exit Western Avenue north. **Open** 6am-9pm Mon-Fri; 6am-7pm Sat; closed Sun. **Credit** MC, V. **Map** p307 C4.

Quite possibly the hippest cleaners in LA: there are TVs embedded in the walls, free doughnuts, popcorn and coffee all day, and a security guard who will help you with the clothes to the car.

Vintage & second-hand

American Rag

150 N La Brea Avenue, between First & Second Streets, Park La Brea (1-323 935 3154). Bus 212/I-10, exit La Brea Avenue north. **Open** 10am-9pm Mon-Sat; noon-7pm Sun. **Credit** AmEx, DC, MC, V. **Map** p306 C3.

One of the largest collections of vintage clothing in LA, housed in a relaxed, warehouse-sized setting. The shop also has new clothes, housewares, shoes and a café.

Decades

8214½ Melrose Avenue, between La Cienega Boulevard & Crescent Heights Boulevard, Melrose District (1-323 655 0223). Bus 10, 11, DASH Fairfax/I-10, exit La Cienega Boulevard north. **Open** 11.30am-6pm Mon-Sat; closed Sun. **Credit** AmEx, MC, V. **Map** p306 B2.

Owner Cameron Silver has created the nation's premier vintage couture store on Melrose Avenue by specialising in men's and women's clothes from the 1960s and '70s. It's virtually a religious experience, with original Ossie Clark, Hermès and Courreges outfits and other rare fashions and designer accoutrements on display. Next door, at sister store **Decades Two**, resale and nearly new clothing and accessories from Prada, Gucci, John Galliano, Chloe, Chanel and Jil Sander et al are sold for around a quarter or one-third of their original retail price.

Decades: vintage couture temple. *See p186.*

Lily

9044 Burton Way, between Doheny & Wetherly Drives, Beverly Hills (1-310 724 5757). Bus 27, 316, 576/I-405, exit Wilshire Boulevard east. **Open** 10am-6pm Mon-Fri; 11am-4pm Sat; closed Sun. **Credit** AmEx, MC, V. **Map** p306 3A.

Not a thrift shop, but a place to discover treasures from the past. An excellent range of clothes from the 1920s to the 1960s, in splendid condition.

The Paper Bag Princess

8700 Santa Monica Boulevard, at La Cienega Boulevard, West Hollywood (1-310 358 1985). Bus 4, 304, 105/I-10, exit La Cienega Boulevard north. **Open** noon-7pm Mon-Sat; noon-5pm Sun. **Credit** MC, V. **Map** p306 A2.

Everything from little black cocktail vintage designer dresses to shoes.

Resurrection Vintage Clothing

8006 Melrose Avenue, at Olive Drive, Melrose District (1-323 651 5516). Bus 10, 11/I-10, exit La Cienega Boulevard north. **Open** 11am-7pm Mon-Sat; noon-5pm Sun. **Credit** AmEx, MC, V. **Map** p306 B2.

Don't be intimidated by the big windows overlooking Melrose Avenue. This is a popular venue for vintage clothing from the 1960s and '70s for both sexes, with a broad spectrum of designer evening wear by Pucci, Giorgio S'Ant Angelo and Courreges. It's worth a visit just to scope out the vintage Gucci handbags.

Wasteland

7428 Melrose Avenue, at N Edinburgh Avenue, Melrose District (1-323 653 3028). Bus 10, 11/I-10, exit La Brea Avenue north. **Open** 11.30am-8.30pm Mon-Sat; noon-8.30pm Sun. **Credit** AmEx, MC, V. **Map** p306 C2.

Look out for Pucci dresses, and anything from the 1960s and '70s.

Fashion: accessories

Jewellery

Harry Winston

371 N Rodeo Drive, at Brighton Way, Beverly Hills (1-310 271 8554). Bus 20, 21, 720/I-405, exit Wilshire Boulevard north. **Open** 10am-5.30pm Mon-Fri; 10am-5pm Sat; closed Sun. **Credit** AmEx, DC, MC, V. **Map** p305 C2.

This is where the Oscar nominees get their shinies for the big night. Winston's has been in business for more than 100 years, supplying the finest diamonds, rubies, sapphires and emeralds in traditional settings. Prices run from $800 to several million.

Slane & Slane

120 N Robertson Boulevard, at Beverly Boulevard, West Hollywood (1-310 854 3804). Bus 14, 220/I-10, exit Robertson Boulevard north. **Open** 11am-6pm Mon-Fri; 10.30am-5pm Sat; closed Sun. **Credit** AmEx, MC, V. **Map** p306 A2.

Sisters Heath and Landon Slane fuse mythological and architectural influences from ancient Greece and Rome as the foundation for their designs. They work in gold, silver, gemstones and pearls.

Tiffany & Co

210 N Rodeo Drive, between Dayton Way & Wilshire Boulevard, Beverly Hills (1-310 273 8880). Bus 20, 21, 720/I-405, exit La Cienega Boulevard north. **Open** 10am-6pm Mon-Fri; noon-6pm Sat, Sun. **Credit** AmEx, DC, MC, V. **Map** p305 C2.

The West Coast branch of the Fifth Avenue breakfast joint, er, classic jeweller.

Lingerie

Lingerie chain store **Victoria's Secret** (Beverly Center shop: 1-310 657 2958) has branches everywhere.

Agent Provocateur

7961 Melrose Avenue, between Sweetzer Avenue & Crescent Heights Boulevard, Melrose District (1-323 653 0229) Bus 10, 11/I-10, exit Fairfax Avenue north. **Open** 11am-7pm Mon-Sat; closed Sun. **Credit** AmEx, MC, V. **Map** p306 B2.

The first outpost of raunchy Brit lingerie shop to hit American shores opened in autumn 2000. It has all the boudoir essentials, including flirty underwear, swimwear and slippers, keeping customers like Julia Roberts, Nicole Kidman and Courtney Love coming back for more.

Eat, Drink, Shop

Frederick's of Hollywood

*6608 Hollywood Boulevard, at Highland Avenue,
Hollywood (1-800 323 9525/1-323 466 8506). Bus
180, 181, 212, 217/US 101, exit Hollywood
Boulevard west.* **Open** 10am-9pm Mon-Fri; 10am-
7pm Sat; 11am-6pm Sun. **Credit** AmEx, Disc, MC, V.
Map p307 A1.

This legendary Hollywood shop has survived earthquakes, riots and even subsidence (caused recently
by the building of the Metro subway). Don't forget
to visit the Celebrity Lingerie Hall of Fame in the
back (*see chapter* **Museums**).

Trashy Lingerie

*402 La Cienega Boulevard, at Oakwood Avenue,
West Hollywood (1-310 652 4543). Bus 105/I-10,
exit La Cienega Boulevard north.* **Open** 10am-7pm
Mon-Sat; closed Sun. **Credit** AmEx, Disc, MC, V.
Map p306 A/B2.

Drew Barrymore and Elizabeth Berkley are among
the celebs who frequent this bright pink shop full of
leather, lace, made-to-measure corsets and G-strings.
You have to become a member to shop; it's only a
formality, though.

Optical & sunglasses

LA Eyeworks

*7407 Melrose Avenue, at N Martel Avenue, Melrose
District (1-323 653 8255). Bus 10, 11/I-10, exit
La Brea Avenue north.* **Open** 10am-7pm Mon-Fri;
10am-6pm Sat; noon-5pm Sun. **Credit** AmEx, MC, V.
Map p306 C2.

If you don't wear glasses, you'll wish you did when
you've seen LA Eyeworks' frames. A clean white
interior is home to a wide range of simply designed
sunglasses and spectacles, including Paul Smith and
Cutler & Gross.

Oliver Peoples

*8642 Sunset Boulevard, at Sunset Plaza, West
Hollywood (1-310 657 2553). Bus 2, 3, 302/I-10, exit
La Cienega Boulevard north.* **Open** 10am-7pm Mon-
Fri; 10am-6pm Sat; closed Sun. **Credit** AmEx, MC,
V. **Map** p306 C2.

White walls, a maple floor and clean lines make
sense for a modern optical store. Some of LA's sex-
iest glasses are found here by Oliver Peoples, Paul
Smith and Beau Soleil.

See Optical

*8000 Sunset Boulevard, at Crescent Heights
Boulevard, West Hollywood (1-323 848 8686).
Bus 2, 3, 218, 302/I-10, exit La Cienega Boulevard
north.* **Open** 10am-8pm Mon-Thur; 10am-9pm Fri,
Sat; noon-5pm Sun. **Credit** AmEx, MC, V.
Map p306 B1.

People no longer have one pair of sunglasses for
every occasion. The fashion-conscious Angeleno of
today needs See Optical. Located in the fashionable
8000 Sunset Mall, this shop offers 600 personality-
defining frames, from serious tortoise horn-rimmed
frames to sexy rhinestone-studded cat-eye frames,
all for less than $199 each.

Get into some **Trashy Lingerie**.

Shoes, luggage & repairs

Shoe chain store **Payless Shoes** (Hollywood
branch 1-323 469 5926) offers all the high street
fashions at discount prices. There are branches
throughout the city.

Artistic Shoe Repair

*9562 Dayton Way, at Rodeo Drive, Beverly Hills
(1-310 271 1956). Bus 20, 21, 720/I-10, exit
Robertson Boulevard north.* **Open** 8.30am-5.30pm
Mon-Fri; 8.30am-3pm Sat; closed Sun. **No credit
cards. Map** p305 C2.

John Yegeyan and Mike Shadoian have been mend-
ing shoes for the Beverly Hills set for over 15 years.

Beverly Hills Luggage

*404 N Beverly Drive, at Brighton Way, Beverly Hills
(1-310 273 5885). Bus 3, 14, 576/I-10, exit
Robertson Boulevard north.* **Open** 9.30am-6pm Mon-
Fri; 9.30am-5.30pm Sat; closed Sun. **Credit** AmEx,
MC, V. **Map** p305 C2.

This shop is more than 100 years old, sells all major
brands of luggage and will repair anything.

Charles David

*Beverly Center, 8500 Beverly Boulevard, at La
Cienega Boulevard, West Hollywood (1-310 659
7110). Bus 14, 105, 316/I-10, exit La Cienega
Boulevard north.* **Open** 10am-9pm Mon-Fri; 10am-
8pm Sat; 10am-6pm Sun. **Credit** AmEx, MC.
Map p306 A2/3.

Shoes and more shoes. An excellent selection of up-to-the-moment designs in a good array of colours and materials. And handbags, too.

Cole Haan

Two Rodeo, 260 N Rodeo Drive, between Dayton Way & Wilshire Boulevard, Beverly Hills (1-310 859 7622). Bus 20, 21, 720/I-10, exit Wilshire Boulevard east. **Open** 10am-7pm Mon-Sat; noon-5pm Sun. **Credit** AmEx, DC, Disc, MC, V. **Map** p305 C2.

Solidly traditional US designs to complete your uptown preppie look. Cole Haan's signature loafers and moccasins have become quite a status symbol, and are particularly popular, for some reason, in Australia and Germany.

Delvaux

8647 Sunset Boulevard, at Sunset Plaza Drive, West Hollywood (1-310 289 8588). Bus 2, 3, 302/I-10, exit La Cienega Boulevard north. **Open** 10am-6pm Mon-Sat; closed Sun. **Credit** AmEx, DC, Disc, MC, V. **Map** p306 A1.

Exclusive, exclusive, exclusive. Founded in 1829, Delvaux was once the licensed supplier of quality luggage to the Belgian court. It now makes scarves, handbags, briefcases and gloves; this is its only US shop and there is a feeding frenzy for its limited stock of haute-couture designs.

Diavolina

7383 Beverly Boulevard, at Martel Avenue, West Hollywood (1-323 936 3000). Bus 14, 316/I-10, exit La Brea Avenue north. **Open** 11am-7pm Mon-Sat; noon-6pm Sun. **Credit** AmEx, MC, V. **Map** p306 C2.

Set foot inside this shoe haven, and you'll never want to leave. Diavolina's white padded walls, belle époque fixtures and rococo-style chandeliers evoke a French boudoir, the perfect setting for a broad range of designer stilettos, wedges and platforms, from Patrick Cox, Costume National and Michelle Mason.

Branch: **Diavolina 2** 334 S La Brea Avenue, between Third & Sixth Streets, West Hollywood (1-323 936 5444).

Freelance

113 N Robertson Boulevard, between Alden Drive & Third Street, Beverly Hills (1-310 247 8727). Bus 16, 220, DASH Fairfax/I-10, exit Roberston Boulevard north. **Open** 11am-7pm Mon-Sat; noon-5pm Sun. **Credit** AmEx, DC, Disc, MC, V. **Map** p306 A3.

Eclectically chic footwear with a grand sense of fun, care of French designing brothers Yvon and Guy Rautureau, lands with a resounding, happy thud in West Hollywood.

Jimmy Choo

469 N Canon Drive, between Wilshire Boulevard & Little Santa Monica Boulevard, Beverly Hills (1-310 860 9045). Bus 3, 14, 576/I-10, exit Robertson Boulevard north. **Open** 10am-6pm Mon-Sat; closed Sun. **Credit** AmEx, MC, V. **Map** p305 C2.

Move over Manolo, Jimmy Choo is the new shoe guy on the block. This chic British export serves up impossibly sexy stilettos.

Kenneth Cole

8752 Sunset Boulevard, between N San Vicente & La Cienega Boulevards, West Hollywood (1-310 289 5085). Bus 2, 3, 302/I-10, exit La Cienega Boulevard north. **Open** 10am-7pm Mon-Thur, Sat; 10am-8pm Fri; noon-5pm Sun. **Credit** AmEx, MC, V. **Map** p306 A1.

This New York-based shoe company offers designer shoes, briefcases and outerwear at affordable prices. Outside the shop are footprints in the concrete, including those of Richard Gere, Liz Taylor and Matthew Modine, and on their respective birthdays, 10% of the shop's proceeds that day go to the star's choice of AIDS charity.

Branches: Third Street Promenade, at Broadway, Santa Monica (1-310 458 6633); Century City Shopping Center, 10250 Santa Monica Boulevard, Century City (1-310 282 8535).

Peter Fox Shoes

712 Montana Avenue, between Lincoln Boulevard & Seventh Street, Santa Monica (1-310 393 9669). Bus Santa Monica 3/I-10, exit Lincoln Boulevard north. **Open** 10am-6pm Mon-Sat; noon-5pm Sun. **Credit** AmEx, MC, V. **Map** p304 A/B1.

Handmade shoes inspired by ladies' footwear dating from the Victorian era up until the 1940s, with a 1970s edge. They're not unlike Patrick Cox shoes. Too cute for words.

Vans

400 Broadway, at Fourth Street, Santa Monica (1-310 394 1413). Bus 4, 20, 21, 22, 320, 561, Santa Monica 2, 8/I-10, exit Fourth Street north. **Open** 10am-8pm daily. **Credit** AmEx, Disc, MC, V. **Map** p304 A2.

Visit this Santa Monica store for a multitude of designs from the leading trainer/casual shoe brand.

Branches: throughout the city.

Film memorabilia & props

The annual **Animation Art & Hollywood Collectibles Auction** (8775 Sunset Boulevard, at Horn Avenue, West Hollywood; 1-800 223 5328) takes place in late August.

Chic-a-Boom

6817 Melrose Avenue, between Orange Drive & Mansfield Avenue, Melrose District (1-323 931 7441/www.chic-a-boom.com). Bus 10, 11/I-10, exit La Brea Avenue north. **Open** 11am-6pm Mon-Sat; closed Sun. **Credit** AmEx, Disc, MC, V. **Map** p306 C2.

Toys, magazines, ads, movie posters and bumper stickers from the 1930s to the 1970s.

Cinema Collectors

1507 Wilcox Avenue, at Sunset Boulevard, Hollywood (1-323 461 6516/www.cinemacollectors.com). Bus 163, 180, 181, 212, 217/US 101, exit Cahuenga Boulevard south. **Open** 10am-6pm Mon-Sat; noon-5pm Sun. **Credit** AmEx, MC, V. **Map** p307 A2.

Posters and photographs.

Eat, Drink, Shop

Global snacking

Los Angeles's multicultural make-up means there is a vast array of shops specialising in foodstuffs from around the world. Here are a few of the best.

Bangkok Supermarket

4757 Melrose Avenue, between Normandie & Western Avenues, Hollywood (1-323 662 9705). Metro Hollywood-Western/bus 10, 11, 207/US 101, exit Melrose Avenue west. **Open** 9am-9pm daily. **Credit** AmEx, MC, V. **Map** p307 C3.

One of LA's landmark Thai markets and an excellent source of all ingredients for your Thai meal. Be prepared: not all products are labelled in English.

C&K Importing Co

2771 W Pico Boulevard, at Normandie Avenue, Midtown (1-323 737 2970). Bus 30, 31, 206/I-10, exit Normandie Boulevard north. **Open** 9am-7pm Tue-Sat; 9am-4pm Sun; closed Mon. **Credit** AmEx, MC, V. **Map** p307 C5.

One of the oldest Greek delis in the city, selling everything from feta and spanakópitta to baklava. Through an archway is Papa Cristo's Taverna, which offers delicious and inexpensive lunch and dinner. Park in the rear and enter via the back door.

El Camaguey Market

10925 W Venice Boulevard, at Veteran Avenue, Culver City (1-310 839 4037). Bus

33, 333, 436/I-405, exit Venice Boulevard east. **Open** 8am-8pm Mon-Sat; 8am-6pm Sun. **Credit** AmEx, Disc, MC, V.

Although this market originated as a Cuban haunt – as evidenced by the hand-rolled cigars perched by the till – it also purveys foodstuffs from South and Central America.

Grand Central Market

317 S Broadway, between Third & Fourth Streets, Downtown (1-213 624 2378). Metro Pershing Square/bus 2, 3, 4, 45, 46, 48, 302, 304, Commuter Express 413, 423, DASH DD/I-110, exit Third Street east. **Open** 9am-6pm Mon-Sat; 10am-6pm Sun. **No credit cards**. **Map** p309 B2.

This fabulous market is worth a visit just for the overwhelming fun of it all. With Korean vendors who speak fluent Spanish, along with Latin-style seafood cocktails at Maria's Fresh Seafood and forditas at Ana-Maria's, you can't go wrong.

India Sweets & Spices

9409 Venice Boulevard, at Bagley Avenue, Culver City (1-310 837 5286). Bus 33, 333, 436/I-10, exit Robertson Boulevard south. **Open** 9.30am-9.30pm daily. **Credit** AmEx, Disc, MC, V.

One of a chain of shops, which are all individually owned and vary drastically. This friendly Culver City branch sells some fantastic food and desserts, which you can take away or eat on the premises.

Elliot Salter's

7760 Santa Monica Boulevard, at Genesee Avenue, West Hollywood (1-323 656 9840). Bus 4, 304/I-10, exit Fairfax Avenue north. **Open** 9.30am-5.30pm Mon-Fri; 10am-4pm Sat; closed Sun. **Credit** AmEx, MC, V. **Map** p306 C1.

Less a pawnshop (OK, it is a pawnshop) than a celebrity hand-me-down museum. Its reputation for fair prices and don't-ask, don't-tell policy has established this as *the* place many celebs visit – though you won't know who provided what stuff.

Tri-Ess Sciences

1020 W Chestnut Street, at N Victory Boulevard, Burbank (1-818 848-7838). Bus 154, 164/I-5, exit Burbank Boulevard west. **Open** 8.30am-5pm Mon-Fri; 8am-noon Sat; closed Sun. **Credit** AmEx, MC, V.

Unassuming owner Ira Kaplan has been supplying the Hollywood SFX industry (as well as the odd enterprising freelance magician) for almost 50 years; he helped to design the bridge demolition that closes James Cameron's *True Lies*. You'll find

gallons of theatrical blood, snap-together transparent cows, flame-proofing materials, liquid latex, skeleton models, shelves of bottled animal organs, plus three kinds of 'Super-Goop'. Just ignore the explosions coming from the 'off-limits, highly restricted areas'.

Food & drink

Bakeries

Beverlywood Bakery

9128 Pico Boulevard, at Oakhurst Drive, Beverly Hills (1-310 278 0122). Bus 3, Santa Monica 5, 7/ I-10, exit Robertson Boulevard north. **Open** 6am-6.30pm Mon-Fri; 6am-6pm Sat; 6am-5pm Sun. **No credit cards**. **Map** p305 C3.

This old-fashioned Jewish bakery is an institution in the neighbourhood: it still gives free biscuits to children and sells some of the best challah, rye bread and rugelach to their parents.

Some claim this is the best tamale shop in town. Watch the ladies make both sweet or savoury versions to take away.

Koreatown Plaza Market

928 S Western Avenue, at Ninth Street, Koreatown (1-213 385 1100). Metro Wilshire-Western/bus 207, 357/I-10, exit Western Avenue north. **Open** 10am-9pm daily. **Credit** MC, V. **Map** p307 C5.

The Harrod's of Korean supermarkets, with a fab selection of fresh and prepared foods.

Safe & Save

2030 Sawtelle Boulevard, at Olympic Boulevard, West LA (1-310 479 3810). Bus Santa Monica 5, 9/ I-405, exit Santa Monica Boulevard west. **Open** 10am-7pm daily. **Credit** MC, V.

This small market has all the fixings for sushi and sukiyaki, with good advice from the friendly staff.

Sorrento's Italian Market

5518 Sepulveda Boulevard, at Jefferson Boulevard, Culver City (1-310 391 7654). Bus Culver City 6/I-405, exit Jefferson Boulevard east. **Open** 7am-7pm Mon-Sat; 7am-4pm Sun. **Credit** AmEx, MC, V.

Fine Italian oils and balsamic vinegars, home-made bread, eggs, salami and fantastic spicy sausages are a few of the goodies on sale at this cluttered Italian market, where nothing is too much trouble.

Juanito's Tamales

4214 E Floral Drive, at Eastern Avenue, East LA (1-323 268 2365). Bus 30/I-710, exit Floral Drive west. **Open** 9am-6pm Mon-Fri; 7am-6pm Sat; 7am-3pm Sun. **No credit cards**.

Mani's Bakery

519 S Fairfax Avenue, between Fifth & Sixth Streets, Miracle Mile (1-323 938 8800). Bus 217/ I-10, exit Fairfax Avenue north. **Open** 6.30am-11pm Mon-Thur; 6.30am-midnight Fri; 7.30am-midnight Sat; 7.30am-11pm Sun. **Credit** AmEx, Disc, MC, V. **Map** p306 B3.

A hip, back-to-basics bakery selling a good selection of muffins, cookies, cakes and tarts. They use only fruit juice to sweeten and organic flour. You can sip coffee and cake on the premises.
Branch: 2507 Main Street, at Ocean Park Boulevard, Santa Monica (1-310 396 7700).

La Brea Bakery

624 S La Brea Avenue, between Wilshire Boulevard & Sixth Street, Mid Wilshire (1-323 939 6813). Bus 20, 21, 212/I-10, exit La Brea Avenue north. **Open** 7.30am-6pm Mon-Fri; 8am-4pm Sun. **No credit cards**. **Map** p306 B3.

LA's most high-profile bakery, supplying many of the better markets and restaurants with owner Nancy

Silverton's outstanding sour-dough baguettes and some more arcane bready delights: chocolate cherry, rye currant and focaccia, and outstanding pastries. Go early in the morning.

Sweet Lady Jane

8360 Melrose Avenue, at Kings Road, West Hollywood (1-323 653 7145). Bus 10, 11/I-10, exit La Cienega Boulevard north. **Open** 8.30am-11.30pm Mon-Sat; closed Sun. **Credit** AmEx, DC, Disc, MC, V. **Map** p306 B2.

A WeHo institution, loved for its cheesecake, lemon meringue tarts and signature three-berry cake.

Beer & wine

Du Vin

540 N San Vicente Boulevard, at Melrose Avenue, West Hollywood (1-310 855 1161). Bus 10, 11, 550, West Hollywood A, B/I-10, exit Robertson Boulevard north. **Open** 10am-7pm Mon-Sat; closed Sun. **Credit** AmEx, MC, V. **Map** p306 A2.

Eat, Drink, Shop

Enter via a cobblestoned courtyard that looks more European than West Hollywood. Du Vin resembles someone's personal, albeit large, wine cellar, and it's filled with sophisticated Italian, French and Californian wines. There are also grappas, eaux de vie and caviar.

Wally's
2107 Westwood Boulevard, between Mississippi Avenue & Olympic Boulevard, West LA (1-310 475 0606). Bus Santa Monica 5, 8, 12/I-405, exit Santa Monica Boulevard east. **Open** 9am-8pm Mon-Sat; 10am-6pm Sun. **Credit** AmEx, MC, V. **Map** p305 A4.

One of the best wine and beer shops in town, with a great selection of grappas, cognacs and single malts, and a full-service gourmet deli. It also offers gift baskets and delivery.

Farmers markets

In a city that often seems fuelled by junk food alone, it's a pleasure to discover that there are weekly markets where you can buy fresh, seasonal produce, some of it organic, directly from small local farmers. In fact, farmers markets have grown to become the hottest new shopping phenomenon in LA. Many have stalls peddling flowers, fresh juices, coffee, hot food and handmade knick-knacks. Some offer live music, donkey rides, pottery classes for children and massage services.

Below we've listed the best markets, but you should be able to find a farmers market somewhere in the city on any given day of the week. For more information, call the Southland Farmers Market Association (1-213 244 9190).

Santa Monica
Information 1-310 458 8712.
Arizona Avenue, at Second Street. **Open** 9am-2pm Wed. **Map** p304 A2.
Pico Boulevard, at Cloverfield Boulevard. **Open** 8am-1pm Sat. **Map** p304 C3.
Arizona Avenue, at Third Street. **Open** 8.30am-1pm Sat (organic market).* **Map** p304 A2.
Heritage Museum, Ocean Park Boulevard & Main Street. **Open** 9.30am-1pm Sun. **Map** p304 A3.

There are four weekly markets in Santa Monica. The main ones are held on Wednesday and Saturday mornings; a smaller, but delightful, one is held in the parking lot of the Heritage Museum on Sundays. There's also an organic market on Arizona Avenue on Saturdays.

Hollywood
Ivar & Selma Avenues, between Hollywood Boulevard & Sunset Boulevard (1-323 463 3171). **Open** 8.30am-1pm Sun. **Map** p307 A/B1

West Hollywood
Plummer Park, Santa Monica Boulevard, at Fuller Avenue (1-323 848 6502). **Open** 9am-2pm Mon. **Map** p306 C1.

Retro emporium **Chic-a-Boom.** *See p189.*

Gourmet

Bristol Farms
7880 Sunset Boulevard, at Fairfax Avenue, West Hollywood (1-323 874 6301). Bus 2, 3, 302/I-10, exit Fairfax Avenue north. **Open** 9am-10pm daily. **Credit** AmEx, DC, MC, V. **Map** p306 B1.

This rather pricey place has excellent meat, fish and fresh produce departments, an interesting deli and bakery and a fine selection of wine and beer. It's also a source of hard-to-find British chocolate.

Gelsons Market
Century City Shopping Center, 10250 Santa Monica Boulevard, between Century Park W & Avenue of the Stars, Century City (1-310 277 4288). Bus 4, 27, 28, 304, 316, Santa Monica 5, Commuter Express 534/I-405, exit Santa Monica Boulevard east. **Open** 8am-10pm daily. **Credit** AmEx, Disc, MC, V. **Map** p305 B3.

A first-rate gourmet market.
Branches: throughout the city.

Trader Joe's
7304 Santa Monica Boulevard, at Poinsettia Place, West Hollywood (1-323 851 9772). Bus 4, 304/I-10, exit La Brea Avenue north. **Open** 9am-9pm daily. **Credit** Disc, MC, V. **Map** p306 C1.

Angelenos swear by this store, which sells dry goods, organic produce and fantastic pre-packed meals with a health bent at bargain prices.
Branches: phone 1-800 746 7857 and punch in your zip code to find your nearest branch.

Organic & wholefoods

Co-Opportunity
1525 Broadway, at 16th Street, Santa Monica (1-310 451 8902). Bus 4, 304, Santa Monica 1, 2, 10/I-10, exit Cloverfield Avenue/26th Street north. **Open** 8am-10pm daily. **Credit** AmEx, Disc, MC, V. **Map** p304 B2.

A wide range of macrobiotic and organic foods and complementary medicines. The shop is a collective, owned and run by subscribing members, who get a 5% discount. You don't have to join to shop, though.

Erewhon Natural Foods

7660 Beverly Boulevard, at Stanley Avenue, Fairfax District (1-323 937 0777). Bus 14, 316, DASH Park La Brea/I-10, exit Fairfax Avenue north. **Open** 8am-10pm Mon-Sat; 9am-9pm Sun. **Credit** AmEx, Disc, MC, V. **Map** p306 C2.

The best organic supermarket in town, selling organic produce, food supplements, eco-friendly cosmetics and bath products. They create juices on the spot at the excellent cold and hot food counter.

Wholefoods

239 N Crescent Drive, between Clifton & Dayton Ways, Beverly Hills (1-310 274 3360). Bus 20, 21, 720/I-10, exit Wilshire Boulevard east. **Open** 8am-9pm daily. **Credit** AmEx, Disc, MC, V. **Map** p305 C2.

Arguably the best in natural gourmet food shopping. Great fish, meat, cheese and deli counters, and excellent fresh pastas.

Speciality foods

Also try **Barney Greengrass** at department store Barneys New York (*see page 175*).

Al Gelato

806 S Robertson Boulevard, between Olympic & Wilshire Boulevards, Beverly Hills (1-310 659 8069). Bus 220/I-10, exit Robertson Boulevard north. **Open** 10am-midnight daily. **No credit cards.** **Map** p306 A3.

Forget Häagen-Daz, this is ice-cream heaven: a wicked selection of intense and exotic flavours.

Aristoff Caviar & Fine Foods

321 N Robertson Boulevard, at Rosewood Avenue, West Hollywood (1-310 271 0576). Bus 14, 220/ I-10, exit Robertson Boulevard north. **Open** 8am-6pm Mon-Fri; 10.30am-4pm Sat; closed Sun. **Credit** AmEx, DC, Disc, MC, V. **Map** p306 A2.

Purveyors of fine caviar: beluga, sevruga and American paddle fish. Savvy Jack Nicholson plumps for the latter – it's half the price of the famous sturgeon varieties.

Cheese Store of Beverly Hills

419 N Beverly Drive, at Santa Monica Boulevard, Beverly Hills (1-310 278 2855). Bus 4, 14, 27, 304/ I-405, exit Santa Monica Boulevard east. **Open** 10am-6pm Mon-Sat; closed Sun. **Credit** AmEx, MC, V. **Map** p305 C2.

You'll find every cheese known to science, olives, baguettes, foie gras, pâté, sausages, wine, balsamic vinegars and olive oils, housed in an old-world setting and served by serious men and women in long denim pinnies. A fabulous shop.

Delmarus Lox

9340 W Pico Boulevard, at Rexford Drive, Beverly Hills (1-310 273 3004). Bus Santa Monica 5, 7, 13/ I-10, exit Robertson Boulevard north. **Open** noon-6pm Mon-Fri; 9am-6pm Sat; 8am-3pm Sun. **Credit** AmEx, Disc, MC, V. **Map** p305 C3.

Lox (smoked salmon) in weird flavours – lemon-dill, rosemary-mint and jalapeño-cilantro (coriander).

Divine Pasta Company

615 N La Brea Avenue, between Clinton Street & Melrose Avenue, Melrose District (1-323 939 1148). Bus 10, 11/I-10, exit La Brea Avenue north. **Open** 11am-8pm daily. **Credit** AmEx, MC, V. **Map** p306 C2.

An extraordinary array of fresh pasta, home-made sauces, and all the things that go with them. Take it home or eat at the pasta bar. **Branch**: 1303 Montana Avenue, at 13th Street, Santa Monica (1-310 394 7930).

Godiva Chocolatier

Beverly Center, 8500 Beverly Boulevard, at La Cienega Boulevard, West Hollywood (1-323 651 0697). Bus 14, 105, 316/I-10, exit La Cienega Boulevard north. **Open** 10am-9pm Mon-Fri; 10am-8.30pm Sat; 11am-6.30pm Sun. **Credit** AmEx, MC, V. **Map** p306 A2/3.

The place for excellent chocolates, beautifully presented in ritzy gold packaging, at high prices.

Heavenly fish and shellfish at **Santa Monica Seafood**. *See p195.*

Spas & masseurs

As you might expect, Tinseltown is not short of places to pamper body and soul. Relax, lie back and let someone else do all the work. Rates start at about $40.

For spas and retreats further out of Los Angeles, *see chapter* **Trips Out of Town**.

Aida Thibiant's European Day Spa

449 N Canon Drive, at Little Santa Monica Boulevard, Beverly Hills (1-310 278 7565). Bus 3, 4, 14, 27/I-405, exit Santa Monica Boulevard east. **Open** 8am-7pm Mon-Wed, Fri, Sat; 8am-8pm Thur; closed Sun. **Credit** AmEx, Disc, MC, V. **Map** p305 C2.

An upmarket, totally aesthetic experience. Purified air and a waterfall are some of the bonuses to go with the usual range of face and body treatments.

Beverly Hot Springs

308 N Oxford Avenue, between Oakwood Avenue & Beverly Boulevard, Mid Wilshire (1-323 734 7000). Bus 14, 207, 357/I-10, exit Western Avenue north. **Open** 9am-9pm daily. **Credit** AmEx, Disc, MC, V. **Map** p307 C3.

Escape the hurly-burly at BHS, the city's only natural spring. Spend the day jumping from hot to cold baths, relaxing in a funky artificial grotto, steam rooms, massage rooms and facial rooms, or get the full body treatment: lie naked and be scrubbed, hosed down and anointed with milk, sesame oil and cucumber.

Burke Williams

8000 Sunset Boulevard, at Crescent Heights Boulevard, West Hollywood (1-323 822 9007). Bus 2, 3, 429/US 101, exit Sunset Boulevard west. **Open** 9am-10pm daily. **Credit** AmEx, MC, V. **Map** p306 B1.

Treatments to uplift your body and spirit, from a manicure or scalp treatment to a more exotic herbal wrap. Create your own simple rejuvenation package: warm up in the jacuzzi, cool down in the plunge pool, then detoxify in the sauna and steam rooms.
Branch: 1460 Fourth Street, at Broadway, Santa Monica (1-310 587 3366).

Four Seasons Spa

Four Seasons Beverly Hills, 300 S Doheny Drive, at Burton Way, Beverly Hills (1-310 786 2229/www.fourseasons.com). Bus 27, 316, 576/I-10, exit Robertson Boulevard north. **Open** 7am-10pm daily. **Credit** AmEx, Disc, MC, V. **Map** p305 C2.

This newly opened spa is just what you would expect from the luxury hotel. Positioned just off the outdoor pool, it offers a rich menu of California-flavoured skin and body treatments, including anti-jetlag massages and custom facials by renowned aesthetician Steven Miller. The signature oils and spa products – designed around the four seasons of the year – will linger in your sensual memory banks for many moons. It's open to non-guests from Monday to Wednesday.

Hahm's Rejuvenation Center

8474 W Third Street, suite 204, at La Cienega Boulevard, West Hollywood (1-323 966 4141). Bus 16, DASH Fairfax/I-10, exit La Cienega Boulevard north. **Open** 9am-9pm daily. **Credit** AmEx, DC, Disc, MC, V. **Map** p306 A3.

Experience the most uplifting 55 minutes in Los Angeles with the blind Korean master of shiatsu massage, Suk Hahm. Follow your massage with a sizzling steam bath and bracing body scrub.

Ole Henrikson

8601 Sunset Boulevard, between La Cienega Boulevard & Sweetzer Avenue, West Hollywood (1-310 854 7700). Bus 2, 3, 302/I-10, exit La Cienega Boulevard north. **Open** 8am-5pm Mon; 8am-7pm Tue-Sat; 9.30am-4.30pm Sun. **Credit** AmEx, MC, V. **Map** p306 B1.

Ole (pronounced 'ooh laa') Henrikson – pictured enjoying his own spa – has been making faces glow and bodies gleam for more than 15 years, inside his zen-style salon-retreat. Sip green tea as you luxuriate in a Japanese tub, then try a salt-glow head-to-toe scrub and and clay body mask.

Santa Monica Seafood

1205 Colorado Boulevard, at 12th Street, Santa Monica (1-310 393 5244). Bus 4, 304, Santa Monica 1, 2/I-10, exit Lincoln Boulevard north. **Open** 9am-7pm Mon-Fri; 9am-6pm Sat; closed Sun. **Credit** AmEx, MC, V. **Map** p304 B2.

The Cigliano family has run this wholesale and retail enterprise since 1969, supplying restaurants throughout SoCal. The shop is beautiful: aquamarine tiles, sunken ceiling lights and glistening silver fixtures set off a heavenly array of fish and shellfish. They also have a great selection of prepared foods, from smoked trout cakes to breaded frogs' legs.

Gifts

Museum and art gallery shops are often a good source for gifts. Two definitely worth visiting are at the **Getty Center** and **Museum of Contemporary Art** (*see chapter* **Museums**).

Espiritu de Vida

5913 Franklin Avenue, at Bronson Avenue, Hollywood (1-323 463 0281/www.espiritudevida. com). Bus 26, Community Connection 203/US 101, exit Gower Street north. **Open** noon-midnight daily. **Credit** AmEx, Disc, MC, V. **Map** p307 B1.

Bric-a-brac madness. The shop's name is Spanish, but its wares have a distinctive Asian sensibility: Japanese tea sets, feng-shui guides and chocolate-scented, Buddha-shaped soap bars. Plus creative toys and books for children, and henna tattoos.

Farmacía Million Dollar

301 S Broadway, at Third Street, Downtown (1-213 687 3688). Bus 2, 3, 4, 30, 31, 40, 42/I-110, exit Fourth Street east. **Open** 9am-6.30pm daily. **No credit cards**. **Map** p309 B2.

All the local santeros (witch doctors) go to this botanica for herbs, candles and love potions – not to mention aerosol sprays that are supposed to help you win your lawsuit, bath oil to quell gossip, and medallions to protect your children.

Hustler Hollywood

8920 Sunset Boulevard, at Hammond Street, West Hollywood (1-310 860 9009/www.hustler.com). Bus 2, 3, 302/I-10, exit La Cienega Boulevard north. **Open** 10am-2am daily. **Credit** AmEx, Disc, MC, V. **Map** p306 A1.

Step inside the perverted, patriotic mind of porn impresario and publisher Larry Flynt. 'Relax, it's just sex' is the motto. Check out the chiffon panties, pink fur cowboy hats, dildos, blow-up dolls and gay, straight and fetish porn in a light, airy, friendly setting. There's a pretty nice coffeeshop, too.

Panpipes Magickal Marketplace

1641 N Cahuenga Boulevard, between Selma Avenue & Hollywood Boulevard, Hollywood (1-323 462 7078/www.panpipes.com). Metro Hollywood-Vine/bus 180, 181, 212, 217/US 101, exit Cahuenga Boulevard south. **Open** 11am-7pm daily. **Credit** AmEx, MC, V. **Map** p307 B1.

LA's oldest full-service occult shop, selling everything from voodoo dolls and mojo bags (for casting spells) to crystal balls. The place to visit if you want to improve your love life or your bank account.

The Pleasure Chest

7733 Santa Monica Boulevard, between Genesee & Stanley Avenues, West Hollywood (1-323 650 1022/ www.pleasurechest.com). Bus 4, 304/I-10, exit Fairfax Avenue north. **Open** 10am-midnight Mon-Thur, Sun; 10am-12.45am Fri, Sat. **Credit** AmEx, DC, MC, V. **Map** p306 C1.

The best in naughty, erotic and X-rated toys, and said to be Madonna's favourite shop. Worth a visit if only to view the limos parked in the lot and the oddly dressed folk inside.
Branches: throughout the city.

Sable Images

4343 Crenshaw Boulevard, at 43rd Street, Leimert Park (1-323 296 8665). Bus 40, 210, 310/I-10, exit Crenshaw Boulevard south. **Open** 3-6pm Mon-Fri; 11am-6pm Sat, Sun. **Credit** AmEx, MC, V.

Long-time collector Gail Deculus-Johnson opened this unusual gift shop with a historical twist: minstrel figurines, tubes of 'Darkie Toothpaste', old restaurant signs that read 'Colored Served in the Rear'. If this sounds bit unpleasant – and it is, some patrons burst out crying – remember that Damon Wayans, Rick James and Spike Lee shop here with great satisfaction.

Skeletons in the Closet

LA County Department of the Coroner, 2nd floor, 1140 N Mission Road, at Marengo Street, Downtown LA (1-323 343 0760). Bus 70, 71, 620/ I-10, exit Marengo Street. **Open** 8am-4.30pm Mon-Fri; closed Sat, Sun. **No credit cards**.

Gallows humour meets capitalism. The nation's one-of-a-kind coroner's department gift shop has some items 'to die or kill for', including beach towels, doormats and T-shirts emblazoned with corpse outlines, toe-tag key chains and 'Sherlock Bones' tote bags.

Soolip Paperie & Press/ Soolip Bungalow

8646 Melrose Avenue, at Norwich Drive, West Hollywood (1-310 360 0545). Bus 10, 11/I-405, exit Santa Monica Boulevard east. **Open** 11am-7pm Mon-Sat; noon-5pm Sun. **Credit** AmEx, MC, V. **Map** p306 A2.

The Paperie & Press sells scented ink, exotic ribbons, notepaper made of bamboo, a huge array of cards and exquisite wrapping paper and also offers a calligraphy service. The Bungalow is through the adjacent garden courtyard and has sleek pyjamas and bed linen, satin pillows, sensuous candles and beauteous bath products.

Yamagushi's

2057 Sawtelle Boulevard, at Olympic Boulevard, West LA (1-310 479 9531). Bus Santa Monica 5, 9/ I-405, exit Santa Monica Boulevard west. **Open** 9.30am-7pm Mon-Fri; 9.30am-6pm Sat; closed Sun. **Credit** MC, V.

A Japanese-style gift store in West LA, where colourful koi kites set off other Asian accessories, cookware and clothing.

Y-Que Trading Post

1770 N Vermont Avenue, at Hollywood Boulevard, Hollywood (1-323 664 0021/www.y-que.com). Bus 180, 181, 204/US 101, exit Vermont Avenue north. **Open** 11am-7pm daily. **Credit** AmEx, MC, V. **Map** p308 A2.

A tiny space packed with funky, kitschy stuff, from T-shirts and hats to a Virgin of Guadalupe holy water holder and Charlie's Angels lunch boxes.

Health & beauty

The **Apothia**, part of the Fred Segal empire (*see page 182*), is a beauty paradise for spoilt princesses, carrying a rainbow of skin, body and haircare products, including Kiehls, Jean Laporte, Thymes and Molton Brown.

Belle De Jour Apothecary & Salon

329 S Robertson Boulevard, between Wilshire & Olympic Boulevards, Beverly Hills (1-310 659 7486). Bus 220/I-10, exit Robertson Boulevard north. **Open** 10am-7pm Mon-Sat; by appointment Sun. **Credit** AmEx, MC, V. **Map** p306 A3/4.

It's a small shop but every square inch is jammed with fabulous beauty and home products, such as Votivo candles, Archipelago bath salts, MOP hair products, white truffle shampoo by Philip B and skin products by Osea and Nuxe.

Homebody

8500 Melrose Avenue, at La Cienega Boulevard, West Hollywood (1-310 222 3971). Bus 10, 11/I-10, exit La Cienega Boulevard north. **Open** 10am-6pm Mon-Sat; closed Sun. **Credit** AmEx, MC, V. **Map** p306 A/B2.

Sandra Bullock and Seal are devotees of Homebody, where custom blends of oils are infused into perfume, shower gel or body lotion. There's also a fine assortment of soaps and candles.

Larchmont Beauty Centre

208 N Larchmont Boulevard, at Beverly Boulevard, Hancock Park (1-323 461 0162). Bus 14, 316/I-10, exit La Brea Avenue north. **Open** *Jan-Oct* 8.30am-7pm Mon-Sat; *Nov, Dec* 11am-5pm Mon-Sat. Closed Sun. **Credit** AmEx, Disc, MC, V. **Map** p307 B3.

This Larchmont Village shop has everything you need for prettifying yourself, including high-end hair and skincare products by Decleor, Thymes, Neal's Yard and JF Lazartigue, plus aromatherapy products from Aroma Vera, Tisserand and Essential Elements.

MAC Cosmetics

133 N Robertson Boulevard, at Beverly Boulevard, West Hollywood (1-310 854 0860). Bus 14, 220, DASH Fairfax/I-10, exit Robertson Boulevard north. **Open** 10.30am-7pm Mon-Sat; noon-5pm Sun. **Credit** AmEx, Disc, MC, V. **Map** p306 A2.

This Canadian-based outfit sells politically sound cosmetics (they have not been tested on animals) in an artist's palette of colours and formulas.
Branches: throughout the city.

Complementary & alternative medicine

Elixir

8612 Melrose Avenue, between La Cienega & N San Vicente Boulevards, West Hollywood (1-310 657 9300). Bus 10, 11/I-10, exit La Cienega Boulevard north. **Open** 9am-9pm Mon-Sat; 11am-7pm Sun. **Credit** Am Ex, MC, V. **Map** p306 A2.

Elixir is an oasis of exotic teas, Chinese tonics and potions, with a tranquil zen garden. You might also get an impromptu tarot card reading.

Healing Waters

136 N Orlando Avenue, at Beverly Boulevard, West Hollywood (1-323 651 4656). Bus 14/I-10, exit La Brea Avenue north. **Open** 1-5pm Mon-Sat or by appointment; closed Sun. **No credit cards**. **Map** p306 B2.

At this cute West Hollywood shop, you can get a Bach Flower or Aura-Soma colour consultation by appointment from Jennifer. Both aim to rejuvenate mind and spirit. She also does herbal body wraps for detoxification and weight loss, and has a cornucopia of other goodies – candles, incense, essential oils and holistic skin and body remedies.

Ron Teagarden's Herbal Emporium

9001 Beverly Boulevard, at Wetherly Drive, West Hollywood (1-310 205 0104). Bus 14, 316/I-10, exit Robertson Boulevard north. **Open** 11am-7pm Mon-Sat; 11am-5pm Sun. **Credit** AmEx, MC, V. **Map** p306 A2.

When you're suffering from *une crise de nerfs*, leave your therapist and run to Ron Teagarden's for Shen Chinese herbs. If your libido is lacking, forget Viagra, purchase extract of deer antler.

Sun Moon Acupuncture Health Clinic

300 N Beverly Drive, suite 105, at Dayton Way, Beverly Hills (1-310 286 1598). Bus 3, 20, 21/I-10, exit Robertson Boulevard north. **Open** 10am-8pm Mon-Sat; closed Sun. **No credit cards**. **Map** p305 C2.

If you want to lose a few pounds, give up smoking, rid yourself of asthma, depression or any physical pain, Balgit Khalsa and his wife Martha will acupuncture your troubles away. Balgit does house calls, and also teaches yoga and meditation and creates his own herbal tinctures. Martha mixes her own essential oils and offers otherworldly massages.

Hairdressers

Art Luna Salon

8930 Keith Avenue, at Robertson Boulevard, West Hollywood (1-310 247 1383). Bus 4, 304, 305/I-10, exit Robertson Boulevard north. **Open** 8.30am-7pm Tue-Fri; 9am-5pm Sat; closed Mon, Sun. **Credit** MC, V. **Map** p306 A2.

Enter a quaint garden, dripping with exotic blooms, and go through a white wooden door to a 1940s cottage. This is Art Luna's workplace and, unlike most hair salons, it's a tranquil refuge. Expect to pay $85-$200 for a cut.

Clark Nova

81182 W Third Street, at Crescent Heights Boulevard, Fairfax District (1-323 655 1100). Bus 218, 316/I-10, exit La Cienega Boulevard north. **Open** 10am-6pm Tue, Wed; 10am-7pm Thur, Fri; 9am-4pm Sat; closed Mon, Sun. **Credit** MC, V. **Map** p306 B3.

There's no Clark or Nova at this smooth barber shop-cum-salon for men and women (although readers of William Burroughs' *Naked Lunch* will get the reference). While owners Mick and Eusebio are both unassuming, lighthearted and very talented cutters, their two resident bulldogs, Fred and Mr Monty, look perennially unamused. Cuts cost from $60 to $75.

Estilo

7402 Beverly Boulevard, at Martel Avenue, Fairfax District (1-323 936 6775). Bus 14, 316/I-10, exit La Brea Avenue north. **Open** 9am-6.30pm Tue-Sat; closed Mon, Sun. **No credit cards**. **Map** p306 C2.

One of LA's fashion-forming salons, with a casual and bohemian vibe. Chris McMillan invented the Jennifer Aniston cut here and also prunes Patricia Arquette's mop, while Philip Carreon tends to the likes of Jodie Foster, Heather Graham and Winona Ryder.

Point De Vue

152 N Wetherly Drive, at Beverly Boulevard, West Hollywood (1-310 273 1231). Bus 14, 316/I-10, exit Robertson Boulevard north. **Open** 9am-6pm Tue-Sat; closed Mon, Sun. **Credit** AmEx, MC, V. **Map** p306 A2.

At this newly opened hair salon tricked out in pale blue and white mosaic tiles, complete with a fountain pool and cappuccino bar, the vibe is as casual as the setting is pretty. Haircuts cost from $75.

Make-up artists

Anastasia

438 N Bedford Drive, at Little Santa Monica Boulevard, Beverly Hills (1-310 273 3155). Bus 4, 14, 304/I-10, exit Robertson Boulevard north. **Open** 9am-6pm Tue-Sat; closed Mon, Sun. **Credit** AmEx, MC, V. **Map** p305 B2.

The latest queen of eyebrow reshaping and makeovers. Expect to pay $40 for Anastasia or $25 for any one of her fabulous colleagues to do your brows. Makeovers cost $75.

The Cloutier Agency

1026 Montana Avenue, between Tenth & 11th Streets, Santa Monica (1-310 394 8813). Bus Santa Monica 3/I-10, exit Lincoln Boulevard north. **Open** 9am-6pm Mon-Thur; 9am-5.30pm Fri; closed Sat, Sun. **No credit cards**. **Map** p304 B1.

Arcona's Studio: a treat for skin. *See p198.*

Some of Chantal Cloutier's top make-up artists, usually booked out for several thousand dollars per day on commercials and fashion shoots, are now available to paint your face. They will come to your home or hotel. Go glamour, girl!

Valerie Cosmetics Boutique & Studio

460 N Canon Drive, at Little Santa Monica Boulevard, Beverly Hills (1-310 274 7348). Bus 3, 4, 14, 576/I-10, exit Robertson Boulevard north. **Open** 10am-6pm Mon-Sat; closed Sun. **Credit** AmEx, MC, V. **Map** p305 C2.

Ex-make-up artist extrordinaire Valerie launched her own line of cosmetics and opened this shop. Try the Secret Weapon foundation or Fairy Dust, a face and body powder with the airiest of finishes.

Manicures & pedicures

Beauty Bar

1638 N Cahuenga Boulevard, between Hollywood Boulevard & Selma Avenue, Hollywood (1-323 464 7676). Metro Hollywood-Vine/bus 2, 3, 212, 217/US 101, exit Hollywood Boulevard west. **Open** 8pm-midnight Mon-Wed, Sat, Sun; 6pm-midnight Thur, Fri. **Credit** AmEx, MC, V. **Map** p307 B1.

Can't decide between a Martini and a manicure? Well, at the Beauty Bar, you can have both. Like its New York and San Francisco counterparts, the LA location offers cocktails with names like Blue Rinse, served by beauty school dropouts. Then grab a seat at one of the vintage manicure tables or hairdryers.

Eat, Drink, Shop

Rejuvenate your mind, body and spirit the holistic way at **Healing Waters**. *See p196.*

Kendall at Lather Hair Shop

727 N Fairfax Avenue, at Melrose Avenue, Melrose District (1-323 658 8585). Bus 10, 11, 217, 218/I-10, exit Melrose Avenue north. **Open** 10am-7pm Mon-Sat; closed Sun. **Credit** AmEx, MC, V. **Map** p306 B2.
One of the best manicurists in the city.

The Paint Shop

319½ S Robertson Boulevard, between Olympic & Wilshire Boulevards, Beverly Hills (1-310 652 5563). Bus 220/I-10, exit Robertson Boulevard north. **Open** 10am-7pm Tue-Wed; 10am-8pm Thur, Fri; 11am-6pm Sat; 11am-4pm Sun; closed Mon. **Credit** AmEx, MC, V. **Map** p306 A3/4.
The Paint Shop resembles a Balinese temple in design. Staff are dedicated to providing healing beauty by targeting the 'nadis' (tiny rivers of electric current) in the feet.

Skin & body care

Arcona's Studio

12030 Riverside Drive, at Laurel Canyon Boulevard, North Hollywood (1-818 506 5192). Bus 96, 230/ US 101, exit Riverside Drive west. **Open** 9am-4.30pm Tue-Sat; closed Mon, Sun. **Credit** AmEx, MC, V.
Holistic skin and body care in a luxurious, retreat-like setting. German-born Arcona's signature contouring treatment is also known as the non-surgical face-lift, reversing skin damage and rejuvenating and toning.

Esthetica Skin Care

9312 La Cienega Boulevard, between Santa Monica Boulevard & Waring Avenue, West Hollywood (1-310 659 5152). Bus 105/I-10, exit La Cienega Boulevard north. **Open** By appointment only. **Credit** AmEx, MC, V. **Map** p306 A/B2.
In a secluded, quaint cottage screened from the hustle and bustle of La Cienega, ex-model Brandy provides a sanctuary where she pampers you with revolutionary facials, body treatments, waxing and tinting. For both men and women.

Lisa Wilson Skin Care

Alex Roldan Hair Salon, Wyndham Bel Age Hotel, 1020 N San Vicente Boulevard, at Sunset Boulevard, West Hollywood (1-310 657 5791). Bus 2, 3, 105, 305/I-10, exit La Cienega Boulevard north. **Open** 9am-5pm Mon; 9am-6pm Tue-Sat; closed Sun. **Credit** AmEx, MC, V. **Map** p306 A1.
Expat Brit Lisa works solo and provides some of the best skincare and body therapies in town. She employs traditional treatment techniques, which she combines with modern ingredients (including the Dermalogica line).

Sona Chaandi Beauty Center

18307 Pioneer Boulevard, at 183rd Street, Artesia (1-562 924 7274). Bus 362/Hwy 91, exit Pioneer Boulevard south. **Open** 10.30am-8pm Tue-Sun; closed Mon. **Credit** AmEx, MC, V.
If you happen to be shopping in Artesia for Indian saris, stop at this immaculate salon, which offers great deals on mehndi (henna body painting), threading (a form of hair removal) and other Indian beauty and hair treatments.

Tattooing

Body Electric

72742 Melrose Avenue, at Poinsettia Place, Melrose District (1-323 954 0408). Bus 10, 11/ I-10, exit La Brea Avenue north. **Open** noon-8pm Wed-Sun; closed Mon, Tue. **Credit** AmEx, MC, V. **Map** p306 C2.
One of LA's safest and oldest tattoo parlours, situated above Angeli's restaurant. Prices start at $45.

Photography

If you're in a hurry, try **Fromex** (Santa Monica branch: 1-310 395 5177) or **One Hour Motophoto** (Midtown branch: 1-310 275 4685) for one-hour film processing.

Bel-Air Camera & Video

10925 Kinross Avenue, at Gayley Avenue, Westwood (1-310 208 5150/1-800 200 4999/www.belair camera.com). Bus Santa Monica 3, Culver City 6/ I-405, exit Wilshire Boulevard east. **Open** 9am-7pm Mon-Fri; 9.30am-6pm Sat; noon-5pm Sun. **Credit** AmEx, MC, Disc.

Look for the giant camera lens overlooking this comprehensive discount camera and video superstore.

Freestyle Camera Co

5124 Sunset Boulevard, between Normandie Avenue & Winona Boulevard, Hollywood (1-800 292 6137/ 1-323 660 3460/www.freestylecamera.com). Bus 2, 3, 302/US 101, exit Sunset Boulevard east. **Open** 9am-6pm Mon-Fri; 9am-5pm Sat; 10am-5pm Sun. **Credit** AmEx, Disc, MC, V. **Map** p307 C1/2.

These guys don't just sell cameras. They are on a mission to educate everyone who comes through their doors about the wonders of shutterbugging. Check out their info- compulsive website.

Samy's Camera

200 N La Brea Avenue, between Second & Third Streets, Mid Wilshire (1-213 938 2420). Bus 16, 212, 316, DASH Fairfax/I-10, exit La Brea Avenue north. **Open** 9am-7pm Mon-Fri; 9.30am-6pm Sat; closed Sun. **Credit** AmEx, Disc, MC, V. **Map** p306 C3.

Some 20,000sq ft (1,860sq m) of photographic heaven (including digital and video rentals and sales) for both amateurs and professionals. The shop also does processing and repairs.

Environmentally friendly **Patagonia**.

Sport & adventure

The ultimate sports chainstore, **Sports Chalet**, has branches throughout the city, including one at the Beverly Connection mall in West Hollywood (1-310 657 3210).

Adventure 16

11161 W Pico Boulevard, between Sepulveda Boulevard & I-405, West LA (1-310 473 4574/ www.adventure16.com). Bus Santa Monica 7, Culver City 6/I-10, exit Overland Boulevard north. **Open** 10am-9pm Mon-Fri; 10am-6pm Sat; 11am-6pm Sun. **Credit** AmEx, MC, V. **Map** p305 A5.

The city's best outward-bound shop. Helpful staff cater for your every camping need, and there's a great selection of travel books.

The Nike Store

9560 Wilshire Boulevard, at Rodeo Drive, Beverly Hills (1-310 275 9998). Bus 20, 21, 720/I-10, exit Robertson Boulevard north. **Open** 10am-7pm Mon-Wed, Fri, Sat; 10am-8pm Thur; noon-6pm Sun. **Credit** AmEx, DC, Disc, MC, V. **Map** p305 C2.

A vast array of Nike shoes and clothing.

Patagonia

2936 Main Street, at Marine Street, Santa Monica (1-310 314 1776/www.patagonia.com). Bus Santa Monica 1/I-10, exit Fourth Street south. **Open** 10am-7pm Mon-Sat; 10am-5pm Sun. **Credit** AmEx, Disc, MC, V. **Map** p304 A4.

This shop sells only – guess what? – environmentally friendly Patagonia outdoor clothing.

ZJ Boarding House

2619 Main Street, at Ocean Park Boulevard, Santa Monica (1-310 392 5646/www.zjboardinghouse. com). Bus 33, 333/I-10, exit Lincoln Boulevard south. **Open** 10am-8pm Mon-Sat; 10am-6pm Sun. **Credit** AmEx, Disc, MC, V. **Map** p304 A3.

You can buy or rent top-of-the-line skateboards, snowboards and boots, surfboards and wetsuits from this popular shop one from the beach.

Toys

The Glendale Galleria houses the famous New York toyshop **FAO Schwarz** (1-818 547 5900), and there's a large branch of **Toys-R-Us** at 402 Santa Monica Boulevard, Santa Monica (1-310 451 1205). The Beverly Center has the educational but fun shop **Learningsmith** (1-310 854 7722).

Allied Model Trains

4411 S Sepulveda Boulevard, at Braddock Drive, Culver City (1-310 313 9353). Bus Culver City 5, 6/ I-405, exit Culver Boulevard east. **Open** 10am-6pm Mon-Thur, Sat; 10am-7pm Fri; closed Sun. **Credit** Disc, MC, V.

Housed in a replica of Union Station, you'll find trains, trains, and train accessories. Makes include Thomas the Tank Engine and Brio for kids, and LGB, Fleishmann and Lionel for adult enthusiasts.

Shopping by area

Westside: Beach towns

Santa Monica & Venice

Aaron Brothers Art Mart (Art supplies, see p178); **Benway Records** (CDs, tapes & records, p180); **Brown's** (Dry cleaners, p186); **The Cloutier Agency** (Make-up artists, p197); **Co-Opportunity** (Organic & wholefood, p192); **CP Shades** (Fashion, p181); **Farmers market** (Farmers markets, p192); **Flap Happy** (Children's fashion, p184); **Global Grooves** (CDs, tapes & records, p180); **House of Records** (CDs, tapes & records, p180); **Patagonia** (Sport & adventure, p199); **Peter Fox Shoes** (Shoes & luggage, p189); **Santa Monica Antique Market** (Antiques malls, p177); **Santa Monica Seafood** (Speciality foods, p195); **Vans** (Shoes & luggage, p189); **ZJ Boarding House** (Sport & adventure, p199).

Westside: Inland

Adventure 16 (Sport & adventure, see p199); **Allied Model Trains** (Toys, p199); **Antique Guild** (Antiques, p177); **Brentwood Gardens** (Malls, p174); **Children's Book World** (Bookshops, p178); **CompUSA** (Computers, p181); **El Camaguey Market** (Global snacking, p190); **FlapJack's** (Children's fashion, p186); **Govinda** (Fashion, p182); **India Sweets & Spices** (Global snacking, p190); **Lakeshore Learning Materials** (Toys, p202); **Ma Meg** (Fashion, p182); **One Night Affair** (Dress hire, p186); **Rhino Records** (CDs, tapes & records p180); **Ross Dress for Less** (Discount fashion, p186); **Sorrento's Italian Market** (Global snacking, p191); **Star Toys** (Toys, p202); **Wally's** (Beer & wine, p192); **Westside Pavilion** (Malls, p174); **Yamagushi's** (Gifts, p195).

Beverly Hills

Agnès B (Designer fashion, see p183); **Aida Thibiant's European Day Spa** (Spas & masseurs, p194); **Al Gelato** (Speciality foods, p193); **Anastasia** (Make-up artists, p197); **Ann Taylor** (Designer fashion, p183); **Artistic Shoe Repair** (Shoes & luggage, p188); **Barneys New York** (Department stores, p175); **Belle De Jour** (Health & Beauty, p196); **Beverly Hills Luggage** (Shoes & luggage, p188); **Beverlywood Bakery** (Bakeries, p190); **Cheese Store of Beverly Hills** (Specialist foods, p193); **Cole Haan** (Shoes & luggage, p189); **Curve** (Fashion, p182); **Delmarus Lox** (Specialist foods, p193); **Four Seasons Spa** (Spas & masseurs, p194); **Freelance** (Shoes & luggage, p189); **Ghost** (Designer fashion, p184); **Harry Winston** (Jewellery, p187); **Jimmy Choo** (Shoes & luggage, p189); **Kate Spade** (Fashion, p182); **Lily** (Vintage fashion, p187); **Madison** (Fashion, p182); **Neiman Marcus** (Department stores, p175); **The Nike Store** (Sport & adventure, p199); **The Paint Shop** (Manicures, p198); **Pom D'Api** (Children's fashion, p186); **Saks Fifth Avenue** (Department stores, p177); **Sun Moon Acupuncture Clinic** (Complementary medicine, p196); **Tiffany & Co** (Jewellery, p187); **Valerie** (Make-up artists, p197); **Wholefoods** (Organic & wholefood, p193).

Century City

Bloomingdale's (Department stores, see p175); **Century City Shopping Center** (Malls, p174); **Gelsons Market** (Gourmet, p192); **Nordstrom** (Department stores, p175).

West Hollywood & Melrose District

Agent Provocateur (Lingerie, see p187); **Aristoff Caviar** (Specialist foods, p193); **Art Luna** (Hairdressers, p196); **Betsey Johnson** (Designer fashion, p183); **Beverly Center** (Malls, p174); **Blackman/Cruz** (Antiques, p177); **Bodhi Tree** (Bookshops, p178); **Book Soup** (Bookshops, p178); **Body Electric** (Tattoing, p198); **Bristol Farms** (Gourmet, p192); **Burke Williams** (Spas & masseurs, p194); **Calypso** (Fashion, p181); **Charles David** (Shoes & luggage, p188); **Chic-a-Boom** (Film memorablilia, p189); **Club Monaco** (Fashion, p181); **Costume National** (Designer fashion, p183); **Daryl K** (Designer fashion, p184); **Diavolina** (Shoes & luggage, p189); **Decades** (Vintage fashion, p186); **Delvaux** (Shoes & luggage, p189); **Divine Pasta Company** (Specialist foods, p193); **Du Vin** (Beer & wine, p191); **Elixir** (Complementary medicine, p196); **Elliot M Katt** (Bookshops, p178); **Elliot Salter's** (Film memorablilia, p190); **Emma Gold** (Fashion, p182); **Esthetica** (Skincare, p198); **Farmers market** (Farmers markets, p192); **Fred Segal/Ron Herman Melrose** (Fashion, p182); **Godiva**

Chocolatier (Specialist foods, p193); **Hahm's Rejuvenation Center** (Spas & masseurs, p194); **Healing Waters** (Complementary medicine, p196); **Head Line Records** (CDs, tapes & records, p180); **Henry Duarte** (Designer fashion, p184); **Homebody** (Health & beauty, p196); **Hustler Hollywood** (Gifts, p195); **Kendall at Lather Hair Shop** (Manicures, p198); **Kenneth Cole** (Shoes & luggage, p189); **LA Eyeworks** (Optical, p188); **Laura Urbinati** (Designer fashion, p184); **Lisa Wilson** (Skincare, p198); **Liza Bruce** (Designer fashion, p184); **MAC** (Health & beauty, p196); **Macy's** (Department stores, p175); **Malia Mills** (Designer fashion, p184); **Maxfields** (Fashion, p182); **Michael R Thompson** (Bookshops, p179); **Mysterious Bookshop** (Bookshops, p179); **Ole Henriksen** (Spas & masseurs, p194); **Oliver Peoples** (Optical, p188); **The Paper Bag Princess** (Vintage fashion, p187); **The Pleasure Chest** (Gifts, p195); **Point De Vue** (Hairdressers, p197); **Resurrection Vintage Clothing** (Vintage fashion, p187); **Richard Tyler** (Designer fashion, p184); **Ron Teagarden's Herbal Emporium** (Complementary medicine, p196); **Saks SFO** (Discount fashion, p186); **Samuel French Theater & Film Bookshop** (Bookshops, p179); **See Optical** (Optical, p188); **Slane & Slane** (Jewellery, p187); **Soolip** (Gifts, p195); **Sweet Lady Jane** (Bakeries, p191); **Tracy Ross** (Fashion, p183); **Trader Joe's** (Gourmet, p192); **Trashy Lingerie** (Lingerie, p188); **Tuxedo Center** (Dress hire, p186); **Wasteland** (Vintage fashion, p187); **Wound & Wound Toy** (Toys, p202).

Hollywood & Midtown

American Rag (Vintage fashion, see p186); **Bangkok Supermarket** (Global snacking, p190); **Beauty Bar** (Manicures, p197); **Beverly Hot Springs** (Spas & masseurs, p194); **C&K Importing Co** (Global snacking, p190); **Cinema Collectors** (Film memorabilia, p189); **Clark Nova** (Hairdressers, p197); **Earl Jean** (Designer fashion, p184); **Erewhon Natural Foods** (Organic & wholefood, p193); **Espiritu de Vida** (Gifts, p195); **Estilo** (Hairdressers, p197); **Farmers market** (Farmers markets, p192); **Frederick's of Hollywood** (Lingerie, p188); **Freestyle Camera Co** (Photography, p199); **Hollywood Book City** (Bookshops, p179); **Hollywood Toys & Costumes** (Toys, p202); **Imperial Cleaners** (Dry cleaners, p186); **Koreatown**

Plaza Market (Global snacking, p191); **La Brea Bakery** (Bakeries, p191); **Larchmont Beauty Centre** (Health & beauty, p196); **Loehmans** (Discount fashion, p186); **Mani's Bakery** (Bakeries, p191); **Melrose Trading Post** (Flea markets & swap meets, p178); **Naked** (Fashion, p182); **Noodle Stories** (Fashion, 183);**Panpipes Magickal Marketplace** (Gifts, p195); **Safe & Save** (Global snacking, p191); **Samy's Camera** (Photography, p199); **Talking Book World** (Bookshops, p179); **Union** (Fashion, p183); **Y-Que Trading Post** (Gifts, p196).

Downtown LA & East LA

Farmacía Million Dollar (Gifts, see p195); **Grand Central Market** (Global snacking, p190); **Juanito's Tamales** (Global snacking, p191); **Koma** (Bookshops, p179); **Skeletons in the Closet** (Gifts, p195).

East of Hollywood

Aero & Co (Fashion, see p181); **Andrew Dibben** (Designer fashion, p183); **Fat Beats** (CDs, tapes & records, p180); **The Record Recycler** (CDs tapes & records, p180); **Rockaway Records** (CDs, tapes & records, p180); **Steinberg & Sons** (Fashion, p183); **Vinyl Fetish** (CDs etc, p181); **Wells** (Antiques, p177); **X-Large** (Fashion, p183).

South Central

Eso-Won (Bookshops, see p178); **Music Man Murray** (CDs, tapes & records, p180); **Music Zone** (CDs, tapes & records, p180); **Sable Images** (Gifts, p195).

The Valleys

Arcona's (Skincare, see p198); **Cranberry House** (Antiques malls, p177); **Dari** (Fashion, p182); **Glendale Galleria** (Malls, p174); **Sherman Oaks Fashion Square** (Malls, p174); **Tri-Ess Sciences** (Film memorabilia, p190); **Vroman's** (Bookshops, p179).

The South Bay

Fry's (Electronics & computers, see p181); **Long Beach Outdoor Antique & Collectible Market** (Flea markets & swap meets, p178); **Zany Brainy** (Toys, p202).

Eat, Drink, Shop

Hollywood Toys & Costumes

6600 Hollywood Boulevard, at Whitley Avenue, Hollywood (1-323 464 4444/www.hollywoodtoys. com). Bus 180, 181, 212, 217/US 101, exit Hollywood Boulevard west. **Open** 9.30am-7pm Mon-Fri; 10am-7pm Sat; 10.30am-7pm Sun. **Credit** AmEx, Disc, MC, V. **Map** p307 A1.

Costumes, wigs, masks, make-up and Halloween accessories – all at low prices.

Kids' Universe

15327 Sunset Boulevard, between Swarthmore Drive & Via de la Paz, Pacific Palisades (1-310 454 6867). Bus 2, 303, 576, Santa Monica 9/I-10, exit Pacific Coast Highway north. **Open** 10.30am-7pm Mon-Fri; 10am-6pm Sat; 10am-4.30pm Sun. **Credit** AmEx, Disc, MC, V.

Eschewing violent games, mind-numbing cartoon merchandising and toy guns, KU is more about unique toys that educate kids while they play: chemistry sets, art projects, dressing-up kits, magic tricks, bubble blowers and CD-Roms.

Lakeshore Learning Materials

8888 Venice Boulevard, at National Boulevard, Culver City (1-310 559 9630/www.lakeshore learning.com). Bus 33, 220, 333, 436, Santa Monica 12/I-10, exit National Avenue south. **Open** 9am-6.30pm Mon-Sat; 11am-5pm Sun. **Credit** AmEx, Disc, MC, V.

A warehouse full of stimulating, politically correct, educational toys. We recommend the Frog Hatchery Kit, the Giant Ant Farm and the jigsaw puzzles.

Star Toys

130 Barrington Place, at Sunset Boulevard, Brentwood (1-310 472 2422). Bus Santa Monica 14/I-405, exit Sunset Boulevard west. **Open** 9.30am-6pm Mon-Sat; 10am-5pm Sun. **Credit** AmEx, MC, V.

This store has 2,200sq ft (205sq m) of toys, from boxed games to collectable dolls. 'If Toys-R-Us carries it, I try not to,' says the owner.

Wound & Wound Toy Company

7374 Melrose Avenue, at N Martel Avenue, Melrose District (1-323 653 6703). Bus 10, 212, 217/ US 101, exit Melrose Avenue west. **Open** 11am-8pm Mon-Thur; 11am-11pm Fri, Sat; noon-7pm Sun. **Credit** MC, V. **Map** p306 C2.

If you can wind it up, they've got it, including lots of retro Soviet-style robots and animals.
Branch: CityWalk, Universal City (1-818 509 8129).

Zany Brainy

3842 Sepulveda Boulevard, at Hawthorne Boulevard, Torrance (1-310 791 6200). Bus 444, Torrance Transit 8/I-405, exit Hawthorne Boulevard south. **Open** 9am-8pm Mon-Sat; 11am-6pm Sun. **Credit** AmEx, Disc, MC, V.

Part of a national chain of multimedia educational superstores, Zany Brainy proclaims it has 'a zillion neat things for kids'. Indeed, there is a huge selection of toys, games, puzzles, audio and video tapes, books, software, dolls and electronic toys.
Branches: throughout the city.

Travel

For general travel services, try **Global Travel Management** in Northridge (1-818 701 7272); after 20 years in business, there's not much they haven't done. Other local firms include **Cheap Seats** (1-800 451 7200/1-323 873 2838/www. cheapseats.com), **All Continents Travel** (1-310 337 1641), and **Cheap Tickets** (1-800 377 1000/1-310 645 5054/1-323 233 6977/www. cheaptickets.com).

The Travel Medical Center

131 N Robertson Boulevard, at Wilshire Boulevard, Beverly Hills (1-310 360 1331). Bus 20, 21, 22, 320, 322/I-10, exit Robertson Boulevard north. **Open** 9am-5pm Mon-Fri; 11am-3pm Sat; closed Sun. **Credit** AmEx, DC, Disc, MC, V. **Map** p306 A3.

Vaccinations, customised first-aid kits for your chosen destination, mosquito nets, travel-sized hairdryers and much more.

Video sales & rentals

To find your nearest branch of the ubiquitous **Blockbuster** chain, call 1-800 800 6767.

Laser Blazer

10587 Pico Boulevard, at Glendon Avenue, West LA (1-310 475 4788/www.laserblazer.com). Bus Culver City 3, Santa Monica 7/I-10, exit Overland Boulevard north. **Open** 11am-9pm Mon-Sat, Sun. **Credit** AmEx, Disc, MC, V. **Map** p305 A4.

The largest laser disc shop in LA carries more than 10,000 disc titles, as well as 5,000-plus DVDs.

Rocket Video

726 N La Brea Avenue, between Melrose & Waring Avenues, Hollywood (1-323 965 1100/www.rocket video.com). Bus 10, 11, 212/I-10, exit La Brea Avenue north. **Open** 11am-10pm Mon-Thur, Sun; 11am-11pm Fri, Sat. **Credit** AmEx, MC, V. **Map** p306 C2.

The cinephile's video shop: Rocket is likely to have that obscure masterpiece when no one else does.

Video West

805 W Larrabee Street, at Santa Monica Boulevard, West Hollywood (1-310 659 5762). Bus 4, 304, 305/I-405, exit Santa Monica Boulevard east. **Open** 10am-midnight daily. **Credit** AmEx, MC, V. **Map** p306 A2.

Large, eclectic collection that includes many foreign, classic and cult titles, documentaries, art-house, gay and lesbian-themed films. A friendly place.

Vidiots

302 Pico Boulevard, at Third Street, Santa Monica (1-310 392 8508). Bus Santa Monica 1, 2, 3, 7, 8/ I-10, exit Lincoln Boulevard north. **Open** 10am-11pm Mon-Thur, Sun; 10am-midnight Fri, Sat. **Credit** AmEx, MC, V. **Map** p304 A3.

Foreign and hard-to-find films as well as regular commercial fare.

Arts & Entertainment

By Season

From Mexican music to Chinese celebrations, you can revel in LA's multicultural diversity throughout the year.

Los Angeles is somewhat tiresomely known as a 'place with no seasons' – not that its natives necessarily take much notice (or are moaning about the average 330 days of sunshine). Most Angelenos clock the seasons by celebrating traditions imported from their place of origin, which results in the diverse displays of cultural pride that the city is celebrated for. The *Los Angeles Festival Guide*, a free booklet available from the **LA Convention & Visitors Bureau** (*see page 290*), lists more than 150 different festivals throughout the year.

For details of the numerous film festivals held in Los Angeles, *see page 216*. For information on the best time to visit, *see page 291*, and for more on local weather patterns, *chapter* **Geography & Climate**.

Spring

LA Marathon
Citywide; check newspapers for route (information 1-310 444 5544/www.lamarathon.com). **Date** 1st Sun in Mar.
With 20,000 runners taking part, the 15-year-old LA Marathon is an all-city traffic-clogging festival, so if you're located within the course, join in the fun. Eleven 'entertainment centres' and more than 100 live bands and performers line the route.

The Academy Awards
Information www.oscar.com/www.oscar.org. **Date** mid/late Mar.
You'll have to camp out all night and hang out all day for even the vaguest chance of spotting any celebs – best to watch the whole shebang on TV, like the rest of the world. If you have friends in town, you're certain to be invited to join an unofficial Oscars bash – everybody has them. Traditionally, the Oscars have alternated between the Dorothy Chandler Pavilion and the Moroccan-motif Shrine Auditorium; the 2001 event will be at the latter, but in 2002 the awards will probably move back to Hollywood, for the first time in decades, to a new purpose-built home at the Hollywood & Highland development. For more on the Oscars and other awards ceremonies, *see p26*.

Santa Clarita Cowboy Poetry & Music Festival
Melody Ranch, just north of Hwy 14, Santa Clarita (information 1-661 286 4021/www.melodyranch studio.com). **Date** late Mar/early Apr.

Relive the Old West with a weekend of trail rides, poetry, storytelling, Western swing dance, chuck wagon food and music by top cowboy artists, held at Gene Autry's former ranch, as seen in the movies *High Noon* and *Gunsmoke*. This is the only time the ranch is open to the public.

Blessing of the Animals
El Pueblo de Los Angeles Historical Monument, Olvera Street, Downtown (information 1-213 625 5045). **Date** Easter weekend.
A bedecked cow leads a procession of farm animals and local pets to be sprinkled with holy water by the Cardinal of Los Angeles in a Roman Catholic tradition dating from the fourth century.

Long Beach Grand Prix
Downtown Long Beach (information 1-800 752 9524/1-562 436 9953/www.longbeachgp.com). **Date** mid Apr.
Thousands come to watch this annual motor race around downtown Long Beach. It's a serious affair, with world-class racing drivers taking part as well as Hollywood stars in a separate celebrity challenge (Paul Newman is a regular).

Fiesta Broadway/Cinco de Mayo
Broadway, Hill & Spring Streets, Downtown (information 1-310 914 0015). **Date** last Sun in Apr.
Billed as 'the nation's largest Cinco de Mayo celebration' – which commemorates the Battle of Puebla in 1862, when the Mexicans defeated the French – but a bit commercial. Ignore the corporate sponsors and zero in on a feast of Latino music.

Ramona Pageant
Ramona Bowl, 27400 Ramona Bowl Road, Hemet, Riverside County (information 1-800 645 4465/ 1-909 658 3111/www.ramonapageant.com). **Date** late Apr-early May.
With a cast of 350, this hokey/wonderful spectacular is based on an early California interracial love story. Set in a stunning mountain amphitheatre, the show features mariachis, dancing, Native American rituals and hordes of charging horsemen. A then-unknown Raquel Welch once took part.

Topanga Banjo Fiddle Contest, Dance & Folk Arts Festival
Paramount Ranch, 2813 Cornell Road, off Mullholland Highway, Agoura (information 1-818 382 4819). **Date** mid May.
A five-day bluegrass blowout, with old-time, railroad and hobo music, cowboy poetry and traditional dances. Bring your instrument and a blanket.

Arts & Entertainment

West Hollywood turns into one big party for **Gay & Lesbian Pride**.

Summer

Summer is the season for outdoor concerts. The most famous are at the **Hollywood Bowl**, the summer home of the LA Philharmonic (for details, *see page 229*).

Playboy Jazz Festival

Hollywood Bowl, 2301 N Highland Avenue, at Odin Street, Hollywood (information 1-310 449 4070).
Date June.
The place to be if you love jazz. All strains of this singular art form – Latin, fusion, bebop, avant-garde, big band, blues and Dixieland – are represented in two days (more than 17 hours) at this event sponsored by *Playboy* magazine.

The Fetish Ball

Information 1-323 644 1811/www.fetishball.com.
Date mid June.
Nightclub luminary James Stone presents this ode to 'debauchery and sensory stimulation'. Supposedly North America's largest erotic-themed event, the devilish fantasy weekend – with fashion, photography, DJs and, er, 'performance art' – takes place at various venues around town.

Gay & Lesbian Pride Celebration

Festival: West Hollywood Park, 647 N San Vicente Boulevard, at Robertson Boulevard, West Hollywood; Parade: travels west along Santa Monica Boulevard, from Crescent Heights Boulevard, to the park (information 1-323 969 8302/www.lapride.com).
Tickets Festival $10. **Date** mid/late June.
A weekend celebration, with a two-day festival, free

concerts and a colourful parade on Sunday morning. Politics and pride, flamboyance and freedom. And lots of fun.

Woodland Hills Concerts in the Park

Warner Ranch Park, 5800 Topanga Canyon Boulevard, between Califa & Marylee Streets, Woodland Hills (information 1-818 704 1587).
Date Sun, June-Aug.
Warner Park is the setting for this viable alternative to the crowded Hollywood Bowl. The 13-week programme (Sundays only) features classical recitals, big bands, Latin combos, reggae bands and much more – all on the grass, under the moon and next to a picnic basket.

Independence Day

Date 4 July.
Americana, LA-style. Picnic, barbecue, go to the beach, take in a parade and watch some fireworks. Check the papers for details of the 50 or so fireworks displays, from the Rose Bowl to Dodger Stadium, Marina del Rey to Magic Mountain, as well as oddities such as the Mr & Ms Muscle Beach Venice Physique Contest.

Lotus Festival

Echo Park Lake, 1020 Glendale Boulevard, at Bellevue Boulevard, Echo Park (information 1-213 485 1310). **Date** 2nd weekend in July.
With the largest lotus bed in the States, this festival celebrates Asia and the Pacific Islands with dance, music, martial arts, exotic plants and, best of all, dragon boat races.

Blessing of the Cars

Verdugo Park, 1621 Canda Boulevard, at Verdugo Road, Glendale (information 1-323 663 1265). **Date** late July.

In Car City, the most important summer pilgrimage is this annual mecca of carbon monoxide. A priest is on hand to bless the cars – but only if they're pre-1968. Plus live punkabilly bands with more tattoos than most of the attending petrolheads.

Festival of the Chariots

Venice Beach Pavilion, Windward Avenue & Ocean Front Walk, Venice (information 1-310 836 2676). **Date** 1st Sun in Aug.

The best thing this side of Benares. See Krishna transported from Santa Monica Pier to Venice on three huge and ornate chariots. Booths promote Indian culture and there's also rock 'n' roll and food.

Nisei Week Japanese Festival

Little Tokyo, Downtown (information 1-213 687 7193/www.niseiweek.org). **Date** late July/early Aug.

This eight-day event (*nisei* refers to the first generation of Japanese born in America) includes martial arts, the tea ceremony, Taiko drumming, Japanese arts, a parade and lots more.

Central Avenue Jazz Festival

Around the Dunbar Hotel, 4225 S Central Avenue, between 42nd & 43rd Streets, South Central (information 1-213 485 2437). **Date** late July/early Aug.

The ghosts of Dizzy Gillespie, Charlie Parker, Miles Davis et al still haunt this West Coast jazz mecca. Extending from Downtown to Watts, Central Avenue was the gold vein of black Los Angeles from the 1920s to the '50s, and this two-day festival recaptures the excitement of those times with jam sessions by local musicians.

US Open of Surfing & 'Surf City' Beach Exposition

Huntington Beach Pier, Main Street, at Pacific Coast Highway, Huntington Beach, Orange County (information 1-888 672 6737). **Date** 1st week in Aug.

Part of the ASP World Championships tour, this six-day event draws internationally top-rated surfers among the 400 competitors. Enthusiasts cheer them on at summer's biggest beach party.

Southern California Indian Center Pow Wow

Orange County Fairgrounds, 88 Fair Drive, between Fairview & Arlington Roads, Costa Mesa, Orange County (information 1-714 663 1102/www.indian center.org). **Date** early Aug.

The biggest Native American event of the year features a weekend of drumming and dancing, food and exhibits from American Indians across the US.

Watts Summer Festival

109th Street Recreation Center, 10950 S Central Avenue, at 109th Street, Watts (information 1-323 789 7304/www.wattsfestival.org). **Date** early Aug.

The oldest African-American culture festival in California – often referred to as the 'Grandfather of the African Festivals' – began in 1966 and continues its cavalcade of the best of the revivified New Watts, including art exhibits, a carnival, live music, a film festival, sports and a grand parade.

Sunset Junction Street Faire

3600-4600 blocks of Sunset Boulevard, between Edgecliff & Fountain Avenues, Silver Lake. (information 1-323 661 7771/www.sunsetjunction. org). **Tickets** $3. **Date** late Aug.

One of the few legitimate street fairs in a city where pedestrians are generally regarded with suspicion, Sunset Junction's popular weekend event means everyone from Latino gang members to outrageously camp transvestites can strut their stuff in a festive and friendly environment. Plus carnival rides, three stages, a disco, food and craft stalls.

LA African Marketplace & Cultural Faire

Rancho Cienega Park, 5001 Rodeo Road, at Martin Luther King Jr Boulevard, Baldwin Hills (information 1-323 734 1164). **Date** last three weekends in Aug.

A dusty African village environment where more than 350 merchants show their wares and six stages provide non-stop entertainment. Enjoy African, Afro-Caribbean, roots and contemporary African-American music, dance and food.

Autumn

Leimert Park Jazz Festival

Leimert Park Village, 43rd Place & Crenshaw Boulevard, Crenshaw (information 1-213 960 1625). **Date** late Sept.

Top jazz artists converge on the creative centre of LA's African-American community.

Day of the Drum Festival/Simon Rodia Watts Towers Jazz Festival

1727 E 107th Street, between Willowbrook Avenue & 103rd Street, Watts (information 1-213 847 4646). **Date** late Sept.

These back-to-back events feature international drumming, jazz, gospel and R&B bands. It's a great excuse to visit one of Los Angeles's quirkiest and most beautiful landmarks.

LA County Fair

Pomona County Fairplex, 1101 W McKinley Avenue, at N White Avenue, Pomona (information 1-909 623 3111/ www.fairplex.com). **Date** mid Sept-early Oct. **Admission** free Mon-Fri; $5-$10 Sat, Sun.

This fair in Pomona, west from Los Angeles, is a two-week kitsch-fest of livestock beauty contests, sewing and garden exhibits, row after row of blue-ribbon winning fruits and vegetables, shows and amusements in a 1930s time-warp setting. And it's been going almost 80 years.

Hallowe'en in West Hollywood
Santa Monica Boulevard, between La Cienega & Robertson Boulevards, West Hollywood (information 1-323 848 6547). **Date** 31 Oct.
In a city full of parties, this one is probably LA's most popular spot for costume viewing. Expect food, music and entertainment – the lip-sync competition is a must. Dress up, but be prepared to hike in; the parking is a nightmare.

Dia de Los Muertos (Day of the Dead)
Self-Help Graphics, 3802 Cesar E Chavez Avenue, at Gage Avenue, East LA (information 1-213 625 5045). **Date** 2 Nov; art exhibition until end of Nov.
This hip organisation of Latino artists brings together art, altars and musical and theatrical groups to celebrate the Mexican tradition of honouring the dead. Skeletons galore.

Mariachi Festival
Mariachi Plaza, First, Boyle & Pleasant Streets, Boyle Heights (information 1-213 485 2437). **Date** mid Nov.
A fun and funky opportunity to experience a range of mariachi styles – right beside the doughnut shop that serves these musicians as an employment agency. Great Mexican food.

Doodah Parade
Old Town Pasadena; parade starts at Raymond Avenue & Holly Street, travels west on Colorado Boulevard, ends at Union Street (information 1-626 449 3649). **Date** Sun before Thanksgiving.
A spoof version of the Rose Parade with just-plain-folks goofing on whatever is topical. Perennial favourites include the Precision Marching Briefcase Drill Team and the Lounge Lizards, a group of Sinatra-crooning reptiles.

Winter

Hollywood Christmas Parade
Hollywood: parade starts at Mann's Chinese Theater, travels east on Hollywood Boulevard, south on Van Ness Avenue, east on Sunset Boulevard (information 1-323 469 2337/www.hollywood christmas.com). **Date** Sun after Thanksgiving.
Join one million fans for an evening of festooned floats, hundreds of B-list celebrities, bands and equestrian units. The streets get very crowded and parking is practically impossible, so take the subway and arrive early.

The Glory of Christmas
Crystal Cathedral, 12141 Lewis Street, at Chapman Avenue, Garden Grove, Orange County (information 1-714 971 4000/reservations 1-714 544 5679). **Date** late Nov-Dec.
Hollywood values make this spectacular 'living nativity' a must. Set in the famous glass-and-steel church (see p34), home of the ministry that originated drive-in churches, it has a cast of hundreds, a breathtaking starlit sky and live camels.

Downtown Tree Lighting Ceremony
Citicorp Plaza, 777 S Figueroa Street, at Seventh Street, Downtown (information 1-213 236 3900). **Date** 1st week of Dec.
LA's answer to New York's Rockefeller Plaza Christmas tree is the lighting of Citicorp's 70ft (21m) white fir, the focus of a host of free events such as carol singing, orchestral concerts, refreshments and photos with Santa and his elves.

Las Posadas
Olvera Street, at Cesar E Chavez Avenue, Downtown (information 1-213 622 3694/625 5045). **Date** 16-24 Dec.
This nine-day re-enactment of Joseph and Mary's search for shelter includes a candlelit procession and finishes with traditional Mexican Christmas music and a piñata party for children.

Tournament of Roses Rose Parade
Pasadena: parade starts at S Orange Grove Boulevard & Ellis Street, travels east on Colorado Boulevard, north on Sierra Madre Boulevard, ends at Paloma Street (information 1-626 795 4100/www.tournamentofroses.com). **Date** 1 Jan.
What is supposedly the world's largest parade started as a marketing ploy to show off California's great climate. And it still works a treat.

Tet Festival
Atlantis Park, at Westminster Avenue & Bushard Street, Westminster, Orange County (information 1-714 531 6296). **Date** Feb.
Little Saigon in the Orange County city of Westminster is the heart of the Vietnamese community in Southern California (and also the largest Vietnamese community outside Vietnam). This three-day festival celebrating the Lunar New Year features music, food, dragon dancers and karaoke.

Riverside County Fair & National Date Festival
Riverside County Fairgrounds, at US 111, Indio, Riverside County (information 1-800 811 3247). **Date** Feb.
This ten-day event presents a uniquely Middle Eastern take on the traditional American county fair. In addition to agricultural exhibits, expect to find daily camel and ostrich races, date milkshakes and weirdly costumed desert denizens.

Chinese New Year
Chinatown: parade travels along N Broadway, between Cesar E Chavez Avenue & Bernard Street (information 1-213 617 0396/www.lachinese chamber.org). **Date** Feb/Mar.
Watch Chinatown come alive with this two-day street fair, including a carnival, races and, best of all, the spectacular Golden Dragon parade.

▶ For dates of **national public holidays**, see page 291.

Children

Yep, it's a very big city, but the beaches, parks, museums and year-round sunshine make it easy to keep the kiddies amused.

At first sight, Los Angeles is not a child-friendly city. Miles of urban sprawl, dominated by freeways that demand a car to get around with any ease, a poor public transport system, not to mention the perceived danger of gun-toting gangs: this is hardly a recipe for an idyllic childhood experience. On the other hand, the city actually has an abundance of attractions for children. There are child-oriented museums, theatres and theme parks, sandy beaches, numerous parks and, of course, the fantastic weather, which turns LA into a sun-drenched playground year round.

For children's book, clothes and toy shops, *see chapter* **Shops & Services**.

Babysitters

Babysitters Agency of Santa Monica

1105 Garfield Avenue, Marina del Rey, CA 90291 (1-310 306 5437/fax 1-310 827 0556). **Open** *Office* 9am-5pm Mon-Sat; closed Sun. **No credit cards.**
Babysitters aged at least 21 will take the kids out for a bike ride, a swim or other activities. They need 24 hours' notice and charge $10 per hour ($12 at hotels) plus transport costs, with a four-hour minimum. The agency services most of the Westside.

Babysitters Guild

6399 Wilshire Boulevard, Suite 812, Los Angeles, CA 90048 (1-323 658 8792/fax 1-323 852 1422). **Open** *Office* 8am-3pm Mon-Fri; closed Sat, Sun. **No credit cards.**
LA's largest and oldest babysitting service, the Babysitters Guild was recently named the city's best babysitting agency by *Los Angeles* magazine. Sitters are aged at least 21, speak English, know how to drive and some have CPR (cardiopulmonary resuscitation) training. They serve hotels all over the city for $8-$11 per hour (four-hour minimum) plus petrol and parking costs.

Eating out

Although LA's smarter restaurants are not very child-friendly, there are plenty of fast-food joints, coffeehouses and great ethnic cafés to be found throughout the city, which welcome youngsters. The following are particularly good places to take children.

Angeli Caffe

7274 Melrose Avenue, between Alta Vista Boulevard & Poinsettia Place, Melrose District (1-323 936 9086). Bus 10, 11, DASH Fairfax/I-10, exit La Brea Avenue north. **Open** noon-10pm Mon-Thur; noon-11pm Fri, Sat; 5-10pm Sun. **Credit** AmEx, DC, Disc, MC, V. **Map** p306 C2.
Ask any parent in LA and they will tell you that Angeli Caffe is the most child-friendly restaurant around, and one they enjoy, too. It offers fresh, simple, rustic food from all over Italy, at moderate prices, in a comfortable, modern setting. Staff are very friendly, there are crayons at every table and each child gets some pizza dough, which they can cook in the oven and then eat or take home.

DC-3

2800 Donald Douglas Loop N, at 28th Street, Santa Monica (1-310 399 2323/http://gtesupersite.com/dc3). Bus Santa Monica 8/I-10, exit Bundy Drive south. **Lunch served** 11.30am-2.30pm Mon-Fri. **Dinner served** 6-9.30pm Tue-Sat. Closed Sun. **Credit** AmEx, MC, V. **Map** p304 C4.
The city's most fashionable restaurant back in the late 1980s, DC-3 offers a service from Tuesday to Friday (6-9.30pm) whereby children are fed and entertained by babysitters while their parents eat. Main courses cost $17-$26; kids' meals average $5.95. Children must be out of nappies and walking.

The Newsroom

120 N Robertson Boulevard, between Alden Drive & Beverly Boulevard, Beverly Hills (1-310 652 4444). Bus 20, 21, 105, 220, 320/I-10, exit Robertson Boulevard north. **Open** 8am-10pm Mon-Thur; 8am-11pm Fri; 9am-11pm Sat; 9am-10pm Sun. **Credit** AmEx, DC, Disc, MC, V. **Map** p306 A2.
You won't have to worry about your kids making too much noise in this big, boisterous restaurant. Located opposite kids' bookstore and art gallery Storyopolis (*see p209*), the Newsroom has healthy and organic food, and tables outside. Overhead TV screens play news reports or music videos.

Entertainment

For listings of theme parks such as Universal Studios and Disneyland, and other family attractions, *see chapter* **Sightseeing**. For more entertainment suggestions, check the 'Calendar' section of the Sunday *LA Times*, the *LA Weekly*, *New Times* and the monthly *LA Parent*, which can be found in any location that caters for children.

Activities

Color Me Mine
1109 Montana Avenue, between 11th & 12th Streets, Santa Monica (1-310 393 0069/www.color memine.com). Bus 3, Santa Monica 3/I-10, exit Lincoln Boulevard north. **Open** 10am-9pm Mon-Thur, Sun; 10am-11pm Fri, Sat; closed Sun. **Credit** AmEx, Disc, MC, V. **Map** p304 B1.
For a few hours of creative fun, visit any of the Color Me Mine locations across Los Angeles. Choose from a wide selection of ceramic plates, bowls, teapots or animals, which you then paint and have fired. There's an hourly charge ($6 adults, $4 children) and the items themselves cost $2-$50. Check the website to find the branch nearest to you.
Branches: throughout the city.

Storyopolis
116 N Robertson Boulevard, plaza A, at Alden Drive, Beverly Hills (1-310 358 2500/1-800 958 2537/ www.storyopolis.com). Bus 20, 21, 105, 220, 320/ I-10, exit Robertson Boulevard north. **Open** 10am-6pm Mon-Sat; 11am-4pm Sun. **Credit** AmEx, Disc, MC, V. **Map** p306 A3.
An airy space that is part kids' bookstore and part gallery (exhibiting original artwork from children's books), Storyopolis hosts numerous family events, including regular book signings with children's book authors and illustrators, themed Saturday craft and story hours, musical events and weekly story-times for babies and toddlers. The atmosphere is relaxed and there are always children roaming about. Afterwards, step across the plaza to the Newsroom (*see p208*) for lunch.

Libraries

Most public libraries have regular storytelling and workshops. To learn about other events and performances, ask for the Childrens' Activities pamphlet, available free of charge at most branches.

Central Library
630 W Fifth Street, between Flower Street & Grand Avenue, Downtown (1-213 228 7000/children's tour reservation line 1-213 228 7055/children's library 1-213 228 7250/www.lapl.org). Metro Seventh Street-Metro Center/bus 16, 18, 78, 79, 96, DASH E, Foothill Transit 492/I-110 north, exit Sixth Street east. **Open** 10am-5.30pm Mon, Thur-Sat; noon-8pm Tue, Wed; 1-5pm Sun. **Map** p309 B3.
The children's section inside LA's main public library is well equipped and very active, and on any given day you will find storytelling, dancing, music, crafts and more throughout the library and its grounds. The Ronald McDonald multimedia centre features eight interactive workstations; to locate books, children can use Kid Cat, a computer catalogue system that uses icons so there's no need to spell. The KLOS Story Theater has music and dance, storytelling and puppet shows (2pm Sat).

Music & theatre

If you're stuck in the car, tune to **KDIS** (710 AM), Disney's 24-hour radio station, offering music, character voices and call-in contests. On weekdays during July and August, **Open House at Hollywood Bowl** (*see page 229*) lays on performances and workshops for children aged three to 12. From October to May, **Open House at the Music Center** schedules a concert and workshop series for children aged from three upwards at the Dorothy Chandler Pavilion (*see page 228*).

Bob Baker Marionette Theater
1345 W First Street, at Glendale Boulevard, Echo Park (1-213 250 9995). Bus 14/I-110, exit Third Street west. **Open** Box office 9am-5pm Tue-Fri; closed Mon, Sat, Sun. *Shows* 10.30am Tue-Fri; 2.30pm Sat, Sun; closed Mon. **Tickets** $10; $8 concessions; free under-2s. **Credit** AmEx, MC, V. **Map** p308 C5.
Original puppet productions. Booking essential.

Santa Monica Playhouse
1211 Fourth Street, between Arizona Avenue & Wilshire Boulevard, Santa Monica (1-310 394 9779/ www.santamonicaplayhouse.com). Bus 20, 320, Santa Monica 2, 3, 8, 9/I-10, exit Fourth Street north. **Open** Box office 11.30am-5.30pm Mon-Fri. *Shows* 12.30pm, 3pm Sat, Sun. **Tickets** $8. **Credit** MC, V. **Map** p304 A2.
Five or six family musicals are staged each year at this Santa Monica theatre by the Playhouses Actors Repertory Theatre Company.

Pasadena Symphony Musical Circus
Pasadena Civic Auditorium, 300 E Green Street, at Euclid Avenue, Pasadena (box office 1-626 449 7360/Pasadena Symphony 1-626 793 7172/ www.pasadenasymphony.com). Bus 180, 181, 188, 256, Foothill Transit 187/I-110, exit Green Street east. **Open** Box office 10am-5pm Mon-Sat; closed Sun. **Tickets** free.
Musicians and teachers help children aged under ten discover the joy of music-making through a hands-on session with various instruments, and a mini performance. Held on the morning of each concert.

Museums

In the **California Science Center**, children can experience a simulated earthquake, watch chicks hatch, design a bicycle and see the body's inner workings in Tess, a recumbent 50-foot (15-metre) human model. The **Natural History Museum** has an interactive gallery and a giant ant farm. At the Discovery Center at the **Skirball Cultural Center**, young archaeologists can play at being Indiana Jones, and woolly mammoths still roam the earth at the **George C Page Museum of La Brea**

Discoveries. Also recommended is the **Petersen Automotive Museum**. For all, *see chapter* **Museums**. Below are museums aimed especially at kids.

Angels Attic Museum

516 Colorado Avenue, between Fifth & Sixth Streets, Santa Monica (1-310 394 8331). Santa Monica 2, 3, 9/I-10, exit Fifth Street north. **Open** 12.30-4.30pm Thur-Sun; closed Mon-Wed. **Admission** $6.50; $3.50-$4 concessions. **Credit** MC, V. **Map** p304 A2/3.

Doll lovers of all ages can covet more than 60 antique doll's houses along with dolls from around the world at this museum housed in a charming Victorian house in Santa Monica.

Children's Museum of Los Angeles

310 N Main Street, at Temple Street, Downtown (1-213 687 8801/recorded information 1-213 687 8800/www.lacm.org). Metro Civic Center-Tom Bradley/bus 434, 436, 439, 442, DASH D/US 101, exit Los Angeles Street south. **Open** 11.30am-5pm Mon-Fri; closed Sat, Sun. **Admission** $5; free under-2s. **No credit cards. Map** p309 C2.

At this Downtown museum, children can record a song in a professional recording studio, make a television show in the Videozone (US-format videos only), learn about recycling, make an animated cartoon and much more. The theatre hosts shows and workshops by storytellers, musicians, dancers, actors, artists, animal handlers and puppeteers. Aimed at kids aged two to ten.

Kidspace Children's Museum

390 S El Molino Avenue, between California & Del Mar Boulevards, Pasadena (1-626 449 9143). Bus 267/I-110 to Arroyo Parkway, exit California Boulevard east. **Open** *June-Aug* 1-5pm Mon-Thur, Sun; 10am-5pm Fri, Sat; *Sept-May* 1-5pm Mon, Wed-Fri, Sun; 1.30-5pm Tue; 10am-5pm Sat. **Admission** $5; $2.50-$3.50 concessions. **Credit** MC, V.

At this museum in Pasadena, curious kids can visit a simulated beach, shop in a mini-supermarket, make masks, observe animal and insect habitats and ecosystems, play with computers and a fire engine, be a TV news anchor and study California's night skies. There are also plenty of games and building blocks to play with. Toddler Territory is especially designed for wee ones, with padded walls and floors.

Museum of Flying

2772 Donald Douglas Loop N, at 28th Street, Santa Monica (1-310 392 8822/www.mof.org). Bus Santa Monica 8/I-10, exit Bundy Drive south. **Open** 10am-5pm Wed-Sun; closed Mon, Tue. **Admission** $7; $3-$5 concessions. **Credit** AmEx, MC, V. **Map** p304 C4.

There are more than 40 aircraft in and around this Santa Monica museum. Aspiring young aviators can clamber into cockpits, attend workshops, watch videos and learn about designing and flying aircraft in the Airventure area.

Outdoors & nature

The rolling hills of **Griffith Park** (*see page 98*) make a great one-stop outdoor experience for children. It contains picnic areas, miles of hiking and horse riding trails, the Travel Town Museum, a merry-go-round built in 1926, the famous Griffith Observatory and the must-see **Los Angeles Zoo** (*see below*). In fact, all the parks are good for kids: also try **Will Rogers Historic State Park** in Pacific Palisades (*see page 77*) and **Kenneth Hahn State Recreation Area**. For an in-depth look at LA's beaches, *see page 78* **Life's a beach**. The **Long Beach Aquarium of the Pacific** is also a must for children; *see page 113*.

Cabrillo Marine Aquarium

3720 Stephen White Drive, at Pacific Avenue, San Pedro (1-310 548 7562/www.cabrilloaq.org). Bus 446/I-110, exit Harbor Boulevard west. **Open** noon-5pm Tue-Fri; 10am-5pm Sat, Sun; closed Mon. **Admission** (suggested donation) $2; $1 concessions.

This 60-year-old aquarium is dedicated to California marine life. It's home to a jellyfish farm, a hands-on tidal pool exhibit and 30 ocean-life tanks. Special seasonal events include two-hour whale-watching trips, guided walks to the tidal pools at Point Fermin Marine Life Refuge and grunion runs (which are held during the migrating season of this small, pencil-sized fish – an opportunity to catch and eat grunion, but not recommended if you get seasick).

Los Angeles Zoo

5333 Zoo Drive, inside Griffith Park (1-323 666 4650/www.lazoo.org). Bus 96/I-5, exit Zoo Drive west. **Open** 10am-5pm daily. **Admission** $8.25; $3.25-$5.25 concessions; free under-2s. **Credit** AmEx, MC, V.

Housing more than 1,600 animals in lushly landscaped settings, the zoo's highlights include a reptile house, a koala house, gorilla and tiger exhibits and animal shows. The Safari Shuttle tram takes the pain out of the zoo's steep slopes. Phone for details of special workshops – where children accompany zookeepers as they give the animals breakfast – and sleepovers, where children can have a night-time stroll with the keepers.

TreePeople

12601 Mulholland Drive, at Coldwater Canyon Drive, Beverly Hills (1-818 753 4620/www.treepeople. org). Bus 245/US 101, exit Coldwater Canyon Boulevard south. **Open** *Park* sunrise-sunset daily; *nursery* 10am-noon Wed; 2-4pm Sat. **Admission** free.

Spend a delightful day with TreePeople. This non-profit group plants and cares for trees both native and exotic, while also working to enlighten the people of LA about protecting the environment. At the centre in the 45-acre (18ha) Coldwater Canyon Park, visitors can enjoy guided walks and educational displays. Children can garden, learn about conservation and explore the recycling area.

Film

As the capital of the world's film and TV industries, LA has everything to keep the cineaste happy, from extravagant movie palaces to film festivals galore.

HOLLYWOOD: THE BEGINNINGS

The old filmmakers liked to say that it was the perfect shooting weather that brought them to Hollywood as early as 1908, but the reality was more prosaic: Los Angeles was a long way from New York and the tough patent laws that controlled filmmaking there. The sunshine was an added advantage, though, and by the beginning of World War I, Hollywood was jammed with film companies operating out of old barns and warehouses.

Star actors soon became a big part of the fledgling movie business, notable among them Charlie Chaplin and Mary Pickford. As early as 1915, studio executives were complaining about the high price of stars' salaries. Carl Laemmle, who started Universal, even took out an ad to claim he was the first producer to 'buck the star system – the ruinous practice that has been responsible for high-priced but low-grade features'. Pickford, however, was a shrewd judge of her own worth and in 1919, along with Chaplin, Douglas Fairbanks and DW Griffith – America's first great film director – she founded United Artists to distribute their own work, becoming, in the process, one of the richest women in America.

Hollywood's first golden age began in the 1920s. Legendary bosses such as Sam Goldwyn, Louis B Mayer and Carl Laemmle were running highly productive studios such as MGM, RKO, Fox, Paramount, Universal and Columbia. Paramount alone was putting out four features a week. At the same time, Hollywood was rocked by a series of scandals, most notable the accusation that popular comedian Roscoe 'Fatty' Arbuckle was involved in the death of a starlet. Frightened of government censorship, the producers put in place a self-regulatory organisation, the Motion Picture Producers and Distributors of America, also known as the Hayes Office after its chief, Will Hayes.

The arrival of sound with *The Jazz Singer* in 1927 further consolidated the studios' power: the new technology meant immediate pay cuts for the silent stars, who had to prove they could make the transition to talkies. Not all of them did, but by now American talent was being bolstered increasingly by new arrivals from Europe. The Brits had been here since the beginning, but the rise of Hitler prompted much

of the German film industry, the artistic powerhouse of world cinema in the 1920s, to up and move to Hollywood. LA was now the world capital of filmmaking, its lure so powerful that even Sergei Eisenstein, the great Soviet director, stopped by in 1932 for a brief visit.

THE PRODUCTION LINE

The Great Depression reached Hollywood four year after the 1929 stock market crash – but it hit hard. President Franklin Roosevelt came to the rescue with the National Industrial Recovery Act, which permitted certain monopolistic practices. It allowed the studios to control every aspect of movie-making, locking the talent into long-term contracts that granted them extravagant salaries while ensuring they had no control over what they did. The studios were factories: actors and directors were assigned to projects whether they liked them or not, writers clocked in every day at the writers' building and an army of technicians kept the cameras rolling. This new atmosphere displeased many actors and filmmakers, but it meant there was no shortage of jobs, and some films were enormously accomplished.

The moguls also worked on Hollywood's somewhat dissolute public image. Nearly all were immigrants from Eastern Europe, but they were determined to make the film industry as American as baseball. Scandals were kept quiet, donations were made to political parties and the outbreak of World War II allowed Hollywood to show that it could wave the flag better than anyone.

After the war, the dark side of this studied patriotism emerged: studios hastily complied with a congressional inquiry into Communism in the motion picture industry. From 1947 until the early 1960s, hundreds of writers, actors and directors were blacklisted from working in Hollywood because of Senator Joe McCarthy's mission to root out Communist sympathisers in all walks of public life.

The 1940s also saw the first cracks in the studio system; by the end of the 1950s, competition from TV had more than halved the movie audience, and stars' desire to control their own destinies appeared to signal its demise. But after some lean times in the late

1960s and early '70s when the studios sold off a lot of their property (20th Century Fox, for example, now occupies a mere quarter of its former massive backlot), they have bounced back. They no longer have the stars on a string and are owned by the Japanese, the banks and, in the case of Fox, by Rupert Murdoch, but the studios are still here. Indeed, the 1990s saw the establishment of a brand new one – the powerhouse of Dreamworks SKG, set up by Steven Spielberg, Jeffrey Katzenberg and David Geffen. After a shaky start, this newest kid on the Hollywood block has been enjoying a stream of big successes. And all the studios have regained much of their financial clout through their ever-expanding non-movie interests: merchandising, running theme parks and owning sports teams.

Hollywood the place and Hollywood the industry have, of course, been quite distinct for decades. However, the massive new Hollywood and Highland development on Hollywood Boulevard, currently under construction next door to Mann's Chinese Theater, is an important attempt to marry the two once again, and in the process revive what has become a profoundly depressing area. The symbolic importance of this new development, which will house a permanent home for the Oscar ceremony, amid a mall and reconstructions of the set of DW Griffith's *Intolerance*, is immense.

TINSELTOWN TODAY

Although Los Angeles is the centre for all the entertainment industries, film still dominates, and for the thousands of young hopefuls who continue to flock here every year, movie stardom remains the highest aspiration. It is, of course, possible to get away from 'the industry' (as it's known in shorthand), but with the hundreds of thousands working or trying to work in it, this is quite a task. And although it may be a city for dreamers and the self-invented, LA is also a harsh place, ruthlessly exposing one's position in the hierarchy of success and, consequently, not a place in which to be 'resting' for too long. It's no coincidence that the city has such a massive 'self-help' and 'self-realisation' industry; the struggling thousands, crazed with lack of recognition, need all the validation they can get.

It's both a strength and a weakness of the Hollywood movie industry that it constantly and ruthlessly discards the old in favour of the new. Among those working in the industry today, this translates into a level of ignorance about Hollywood's history that will perplex the outside visitor; despite outward shows to the contrary, there is virtually no room for sentimentality.

For the film fanatic, it would require a substantial stay to start to get a sense of quite how Hollywood works. Although this is a town just as wedded to a single industry as Detroit once was to the automobile, business is done largely behind closed doors by seemingly invisible people, and to the new visitor it might appear that nothing is happening.

However, the sheer all-pervasiveness of movies means that in terms of actual cinema-going and film-related activities, there are a huge number of choices. There are film courses aplenty at just about every college in and around LA, a couple of film festivals a month, workshops everywhere and, if you're here for a longish time, you're almost certain to come across a location shoot.

INFORMATION AND FILM RATINGS

The best sources are the *LA Times* Calendar section, the *LA Weekly* and *New Times*, which all list festivals and special screenings as well as standard movie reviews and info. There are thousands of cinema screens in LA; we have listed a selection of the most interesting below. For bog-standard local multi-screens, check the newspapers.

Producers pay the Motion Picture Association of America to protect the innocent by rating their movies. NC-17 has replaced the X rating, which embarrassed the MPAA because of its association with porn. The ratings are: G (unrestricted); PG (parental guidance suggested); PG-13 (under-13s must be accompanied by an adult); R (under-17s must be accompanied by an adult); and NC-17 (no one under 17).

Cinemas

Los Angeles isn't a good place to catch the latest European releases: only the big hits tend to make it over. However, you'll find that a lot of European cinema is shown in tributes, retrospectives and special seasons, and not just in art-house cinemas. When it comes to first-run Hollywood fare – what most people choose to see – it's worth remembering that you can catch new releases in Los Angeles months if not years before they make it overseas.

Remember that cinemas are always called movie theatres in LA.

First-run & mainstream

The multiplex, usually attached to a mall, is king, of course. Below are some of the most popular and/or accessible to the visitor. You can get show information and purchase tickets on 1-323 777 3456.

AMC Century 14

10250 Santa Monica Boulevard, between Century Park W & Avenue of the Stars, Century City (1-310 553 8900/www.amctheatres.com). Bus 22, 27, 28, 316, Santa Monica 5, Commuter Express 534/ I-405, exit Santa Monica Boulevard east. **Tickets** $9; $5-$6 before 6pm, concessions. **Credit** AmEx, Disc, MC, V. **Map** p305 B3.

Cineplex Odeon Beverly Center

Beverly Center, 8500 Beverly Boulevard, at La Cienega Boulevard, West Hollywood (1-310 652 7760/www.cineplexodeon.com). Bus 14, 104/I-10, exit La Cienega Boulevard north. **Tickets** $8.50; $5.50 before 6pm; $5 concessions. **Credit** AmEx, MC, V. **Map** p306 A2/3.

Cineplex Odeon Universal City Mutiplex

100 Universal City Plaza, Universal City (1-818 508 0711/www.cineplexodeon.com). Metro Universal City/ bus 420/US 101, exit Universal Center Drive. **Tickets** $8.50; $5.50 before 6pm; $5 concessions. **Credit** AmEx, MC, V.

General Cinema Beverly Connection

100 N La Cienega Boulevard, between Beverly & Third Streets, West Hollywood (1-310 659 5911/ www.generalcinema.com). Bus 14, 104/I-10,

Mann's Chinese: LA's most famous cinema.

exit La Cienega Boulevard north. **Tickets** $9; $6 before 6pm, concessions. **Credit** MC, V. **Map** p306 B3.

General Cinema Hollywood Galaxy

7021 Hollywood Boulevard, at La Brea Avenue, Hollywood (1-323 957 9246/www.generalcinema. com). Bus 180, 181, 212/US 101, exit Hollywood Boulevard west. **Tickets** $9; $6 before 6pm, concessions. **Credit** AmEx, MC, V. **Map** p307 A1.

Among the other first-run cinemas, showing either Hollywood studio films or smaller independent movies, there are a number that are particularly worth a visit, including the following:

Bruin Westwood

948 Broxton Avenue, at Weyburn Avenue, Westwood (1-310 208 8998/www.manntheatres. com). Bus 20, 21, 22/I-405, exit Wilshire Boulevard east. **Tickets** $9; $6 before 6pm; $6-$6.50 concessions. **Credit** AmEx, Disc, MC, V.
Positioned bang opposite the white spired Mann's Westwood (*see below*), this is another handsome white building, which manages also to be intimate. 'Sneak previews' of new films are often held here.

Cecchi Gori Fine Arts

8556 Wilshire Boulevard, between Le Doux Road & Stanley Drive, Beverly Hills (1-310 652 1330/ www.landmarktheatres.com). Bus 20, 21, 22/I-10, exit La Cienega Boulevard north. **Tickets** $8.50; $5.50 concessions. **No credit cards. Map** p306 A3.
A beautiful little jewel box of a cinema that was completely restored recently, this is the perfect place to see the newest art-house features.

Mann's Chinese Theater

6925 Hollywood Boulevard, between La Brea & Highland Avenues, Hollywood (1-323 464 8111/ www.manntheatres.com). Metro Hollywood-Highland/ bus 156, 163, 180, 181, 426/US 101, exit Hollywood Boulevard west. **Tickets** $9; $6 concessions. **Credit** MC, V. **Map** p307 A1.
Probably the most famous cinema in Los Angeles. Best known for the handprints of the stars that decorate its forecourt, the Chinese Theater is also a full-time cinema and hosts many premieres. *See also page 215* **Movie palaces**.

Mann's Westwood

1050 Gayley Avenue, between Kinross & Weyburn Avenues, Westwood (1-310 208 7664/www.mann theatres.com). Bus 21, 22, 23/I-10, exit Wilshire Boulevard east. **Tickets** $9; $6 before 6pm; $6-$6.50 concessions. **Credit** AmEx, Disc, MC, V.
A beautifully elegant, stuccoed white building crowned by a huge steeple, this is one of the most popular venues for major premieres, which happen at least once a week. Showing mainstream block-buster Hollywood fare, it's in Westwood Village, slightly off the typical tourist's beaten track, but if you want to take in Hollywood's latest, and can't face the hordes at an ugly multiplex, this is the place.

Arts & Entertainment

Regent Showcase

*614 N La Brea Avenue, between Clinton Street &
Melrose Avenue, Hollywood (1-323 934 2944/
www.regententertainment.com). Bus 10, 11, 212/
I-10, exit La Brea Avenue north.* **Tickets** $8.50;
$4.40 before 4pm Mon-Fri; $5.50 concessions.
Credit MC, V. **Map** p307 A3.
A good old-fashioned movie theatre with a large
screen, showing a mix of mainstream and more offbeat new releases.

Sunset 5

*8000 Sunset Boulevard, at Crescent Heights
Boulevard, West Hollywood (1-323 848 3500/
www.laemmle.com). Bus 2, 3, 217, 302, 429/I-10,
exit Fairfax Avenue north.* **Tickets** $8.50; $5.50-
$6.50 concessions. **No credit cards. Map** p306 B1.
There are eight Laemmle cinemas scattered across
LA and the Valleys, of which this is perhaps the best
known. It shows the newest independents and
'smaller' studio films; it would be the best place to
catch the new Woody Allen, for example. It also has
mini-seasons and tributes, and the location is
excellent, if you can deal with the busiest parking
lot this side of the San Andreas fault. Other
Laemmle cinemas worth visiting are the Monica 4-
Plex (1332 Second Street, Santa Monica, 1-310 394
9741); Royal (11523 Santa Monica Boulevard, West
LA, 1-310 477 5581); and Music Hall (9036 Wilshire
Boulevard, Beverly Hills, 1-310 274 6869).

Mann's Westwood. *See p213.*

Repertory

New Beverly Cinema

*7165 Beverly Boulevard, at N Detroit Street, Fairfax
District (1-213 938 4038/www.michaelwilliams.com/
beverlycinema). Bus 14, 212/I-10, exit La Brea
Avenue north.* **Tickets** $6; $3-$5 concessions.
No credit cards. Map p306 C2.
The New Beverly is nothing special in terms of comfort, but extraordinary in terms of programming. As
well as independent and foreign films, it revives
older films. The bill changes every couple of days.

Nuart

*11272 Santa Monica Boulevard, at Sawtelle
Boulevard, West LA (1-310 478 6379/www.
landmarktheatres.com). Bus 4, 304, Santa Monica 1,
5/I-405, exit Santa Monica Boulevard west.* **Tickets**
$8.50; $5.50 concessions. **No credit cards.**
Owned by the Landmark chain, the Nuart is the best
rep house on the Westside. It often gets exclusive
engagements of independent and foreign movies. It
also runs classics, including a midnight screening
of *The Rocky Horror Picture Show* on Saturdays, as
well as other midnight screenings.

Rialto

*1023 Fair Oaks Avenue, at Oxly Avenue, South
Pasadena (1-626 799 9567/www.landmarktheatres.
com). Bus 176, 483/I-110, exit Fair Oaks Avenue
south.* **Tickets** $7.75; $5.50 concessions. **No credit
cards.**
Another Landmark Theater where you can catch
The Rocky Horror Picture Show as well as the latest
art-house releases. Some people love the balcony,
though the mediocre sound is worse up there. It's a
useful standby if you're ever in Pasadena, and a
charming looker to boot. Film fans will recognise
this as the cinema where Tim Robbins's character
in *The Player* comes to see *Bicycle Thieves.*

Classic, archive & experimental

Both **Museum of Contemporary Art** sites
screen experimental and classic films and
videos as part of exhibitions, while the **LA
County Museum of Art** runs regular film
seasons and tributes and, on Tuesday afternoons,
shows classic movies for the bargain price of $1.
For both, *see chapter* **Museums**. The
American Film Institute (1-323 856 7600/
www.afionline.com) is dedicated to preserving
old films and sometimes organises screenings
for the general public at venues around the city.

American Cinematheque

*Egyptian Theater, 6712 Hollywood Boulevard,
between Highland & La Palmas Avenues, Hollywood
(1-323 466 3456/www.americancinematheque.com).
Metro Hollywood-Highland/bus 1, 163, 180, 181,
212, 217/US 101, exit Highland Avenue south.*
Tickets $7; $5 concessions. **Credit** AmEx, MC, V.
Map p307 A1.

Movie palaces

For a generation used to watching movies in the bland rabbit warren that is the modern multiplex, Los Angeles offers some spectacular examples of theatres from a more elegant past, when the surroundings were all part of the magic offered by the silver-screen experience.

One of the city's best-kept secrets is Broadway in Downtown; yes, LA had its own Great White Way, which was the thriving centre of the city before it gradually but inexorably moved westward. On South Broadway, an area designated as a Historic Theater District in 1979, stand three of the most beautiful theatres you will see anywhere in the world. The excellent **Los Angeles Conservancy** (1-213 623 2489/ www.laconservancy.org) conducts a fascinating walking tour of the district on Saturday mornings, which takes in the best of these monumental buildings.

The oldest of these, built in 1911, is the **Palace** (630 South Broadway, at West Sixth Street), loosely styled on a Florentine palazzo, with an interior that features exquisite panels by Spanish artist Domingo Mora. As the current initiative to revive Downtown gathers pace, the Palace, which has been closed for some time, could well get a new lease of life soon as an all-purpose performance theatre.

The 2,000-seat **Orpheum** (842 South Broadway, at Eighth Street, 1-213 239 0937), completed in 1926, houses the last of the great theatre organs. With its enormous chandeliers and marble pilasters, it has an atmosphere reminiscent of the Paris Opera. But by far the most impressive is the **Los Angeles Theater** (615 South Broadway, at West Sixth Street), the most lavish and, opening in 1931, the last of the great movie palaces. A French baroque extravaganza, the lobby (pictured) has to be seen to be believed. In a very progressive gesture, the builders incorporated 'crying rooms', to which mothers with crying babies could retire to watch the film relayed to a second, smaller screen.

The best way to experience these theatres is, of course, to see a film in them; thanks to the LA Conservancy's **Last Remaining Seats** festival in June (see page 216), this is now possible – and it's an opportunity that no self-respecting movie-lover should miss.

Travelling west into the heart of Hollywood, you will find **Mann's Chinese Theater** (see page 213), as much a symbol of Hollywood

as St Paul's Cathedral is of London. This strange pagoda-style cinema, with its elaborate but slightly spooky interior, is well known for its famous forecourt, featuring the foot and handprints of stars from the past 80 years. But be warned: it's always besieged by coachloads of tourists.

Almost opposite Mann's is the **El Capitan** (6838 Hollywood Boulevard, 1-323 467 7674), which was dilapidated for years until Disney stepped in and gave it a superb makeover. The best place to see the latest Disney releases, it has a great organ and a spotlight on the roof that lights up the sky at night (and is a great orientation point for where you are in the city).

Further east on Hollywood Boulevard is the recently restored **Egyptian Theater** (see page 214 **American Cinematheque**) with its forecourt full of palm trees. And a few blocks south on Sunset is the **Cinerama Dome** (No.6360, at Ivar Avenue). Currently closed but scheduled to reopen in 2001 as part of a big new retail development, the Dome doesn't exactly qualify as a movie palace, but, built in the 1960s, with its space-age look and massive screen, it vividly conjures up another era of movie-going.

Specialising in tributes and retrospectives, the Cinematheque has a growing reputation for innovative programming. Its permanent home is in the heart of Hollywood, at the beautifully restored historic Egyptian Theater, a visit to which is worth the price of a ticket alone (see p215 **Movie palaces**). Many screenings are followed by a Q&A session with those connected to the film.

IMAX
California Science Center, 700 State Drive, between Figueroa & Menlo Streets, Exposition Park (1-213 744 2014/www.casciencectr.org). Bus 81, 102, 200, 442, 445, 446/I-110, exit Exposition Boulevard west. **Tickets** $6.50; $3.50-$4.75 concessions. **Credit** MC, V.

The seven-storey-high and 70ft (21m) wide screen at the IMAX cinema is perfectly suited to capturing vast landscapes and showing off the natural world – and documentaries on these subjects are what the theatre mostly screens. It's located at the California Science Center, which also has a 3-D theatre, where the prices are a dollar more.

Silent Movie
611 N Fairfax Avenue, at Melrose Avenue, Fairfax District (1-323 655 2520/www.silentmovietheater. com). Bus 10, 212, 217/I-10, exit Fairfax Avenue north. **Closed** Mon-Wed. **Tickets** $10; $8 concessions. **No credit cards. Map** p306 B2.

Reopened at the end of 1999, this is probably the only cinema in the world devoted solely to silent movies. It's certainly worth visiting if you want to see a silent in an authentic environment, with, of course, an organist playing the accompaniment live.

UCLA Film & Television Archive
UCLA campus, 405 Hilgard Avenue, Westwood (recorded information 1-310 206 3456/www.cinema. ucla.edu). Bus 2, 21, 429, 576, Culver City 6, Santa Monica 1, 2, 3/I-10, exit Sunset Boulevard east. **Tickets** $10; $7 concessions. **No credit cards.**

UCLA's massive archives are a treasure trove of little-seen silents and classics from the 1930s heyday of Hollywood, as well as newsreels and documentaries. But screenings aren't just limited to archive material: there's usually something for everyone in any week.

African-American cinema

Magic Johnson Theaters
4020 Marlton Avenue, at Martin Luther King Jr Boulevard, Crenshaw (1-323 290 5900). Bus 105, DASH Crenshaw-Midtown/I-10, exit Crenshaw Boulevard south. **Tickets** $8; $5-$5.25 concessions. **Credit** AmEx, MC, V.

Owned by the now-retired star of the Los Angeles Lakers, this is the one venue in the city that shows African-American films after they've left most mall multiplexes, as well as those that don't make it to general release. It also hosts the annual Pan African Film Festival (see below).

Film festivals

Festival seems the wrong word to use in Los Angeles, where such special programmes go on non-stop. Here are some highlights.

Cinecon Annual Classic Film Festival
Information 1-800 411 0455/www.cinecon.org.
This five-day show, usually held over Labor Day weekend, screens almost-never-seen early films.

Last Remaining Seats
Information 1-213 623 2489/www.laconservancy. org/ remaining.
On Wednesdays in June you can see old films – both silents and talkies – with live musical accompaniment in the grand old movie palaces on Broadway reopened especially for the event. *See also p215* **Movie palaces**.

Los Angeles Asian Pacific Film & Video Festival
Information 1-213 680 3004/1-310 206 3456/ www.vconline.org/filmfest.
Takes a look at what's coming out of the other side of the Pacific Rim each May.

Los Angeles Independent Film Festival
Information 1-323 937 9155/www.laiff.com.
Started in 1995 and held each April, this event showcases the work of young American filmmakers.

Los Angeles International Film Festival
Information 1-323 856 7707/www.afionline.org/ afifest.
The American Film Institute's festival (hence its 'AFI Fest' nickname). Held over about two weeks in October, it always attracts big crowds for both American and foreign films.

Los Angeles International Latino Film Festival
Information 1-323 960 2419/www.latinofilm.org.
First held in 1997 and now an annual July event, this festival focuses on movies from Mexico and Central and South America.

Outfest: The Los Angeles Gay & Lesbian Film Festival
Information 1-323 951 1247/www.outfest.org.
One of the most comprehensive festivals of its kind in the world, Outfest runs for ten days every July. Events tend to sell out quickly.

Pan African Film Festival
Information 1-213 896 8221/www.paff.org.
In addition to African-American films, this festival spotlights movies from Africa and from African communities on other continents. It has a permanent home at the Magic Johnson Theaters (see above) and takes place in January or February.

Arts & Entertainment

Preview screenings

There are endless industry and press screenings in LA, but getting in isn't easy unless you have connections. However, it's more than possible that at certain locations around the city you will be accosted by studio movie recruiters offering free tickets to a preview – popular sites include outside Laemmle's Monica 4-Plex (*see page 214* **Sunset 5**) and the Cineplex Odeon Beverly Center (*see page 213*).

Such previews are often used for audience testing and if you're approached, you will almost certainly be asked what you do for a living; if there's a whiff of 'industry' about you (and that includes journalists of any kind), the invitation will be withdrawn, so a few white lies won't go amiss. It's something of a standing joke that previews are more often than not full of fake social workers.

Official 'sneak previews' of movies opening the following week are open to everybody and are advertised in advance in the *LA Times* and the *LA Weekly*; many of them are held at the Bruin in Westwood (*see page 213*).

Studio tours

The Universal Studios tour (*see page 108*) is justly famous for its spectacular rides, but if you want a tour that shows how a studio

Location shoots

About 150 crews take to the streets of LA each day for everything from TV to fashion to film shoots. Although this is the best chance of seeing a movie being made, bear in mind that it can be like watching paint dry. If there's a big star involved, forget any ideas about maybe approaching them for an autograph – getting an audience with the Pope would be easier.

The website of the Entertainment Industry Development Corporation (www.eidc.com) provides the Shoot Sheet, a list of production companies and production titles shooting on location in LA over the next two weeks, with dates, times and location addresses. But note: it doesn't list directors and actors, and working titles may be uninformative. If you go to pick up a hard copy of the Shoot Sheet from the EIDC office (7083 Hollywood Boulevard, at Sycamore Avenue, 1-323 957 1000), you'll pay $10 for the privilege.

actually operates, you have to go to Paramount or Warner Brothers. Both promise to try to get you on to sound stages, so you can actually see a film shooting. Don't expect to shake hands with the stars, though: at best, you'll see a few vaguely familiar faces being whisked around on the golf carts that serve as transport on the lots.

Paramount Studios

5555 Melrose Avenue, at Gower Street, Hollywood (1-323 956 1777/http://store.paramount.com/ studio_tour.html). Bus 10, 11/US 101, exit Gower Street south. **Tours** 9am-2pm Mon-Fri (tours every hr); closed Sat, Sun. **Tickets** $15. **No credit cards**. **Map** p307 B2/3.

The two-hour walking tour of Paramount is good value, spinning you round the oldest and most attractive studio in LA, and also the only one still in Hollywood: it has been in the same place, give or take a few hundred metres, since 1915. Tickets are available on a first come, first served basis. No under-tens are allowed.

Warner Brothers Studios

4000 Warner Boulevard, at Hollywood Way & Olive Avenue, Burbank (1-818 954 1744/http://wbsf. warnerbros.com/cmp/addition.htm). Bus 96, 152, 163/ Hwy 134, exit Pass Avenue south. **Tours** *June-Sept* 9am-4pm Mon-Fri (tours every ½hr); closed Sat, Sun. *Oct-May* 9am-3pm Mon-Fri (tours every hr); closed Sat, Sun. **Tickets** $32. **Credit** AmEx, MC, V.

The Warner's tour is double the price of Paramount's for the same amount of time, and its lot doesn't have as much historical resonance. It is, however, the shooting location of most prime-time US television shows, including *Friends* and *ER*. No under-eights are allowed.

TV tapings

Televsion sitcoms often come with the pronouncement 'Filmed live before a studio audience', and if you want to see it happen, Los Angeles is the place. Tickets are free – but be warned, tapings can take over three hours. Unfortunately, dramas are made on closed sets, so there's no chance of watching a *Star Trek* or *ER* studio shoot.

Audiences Unlimited

100 Universal Plaza, Building 153, Universal City, CA 91608 (1-818 753 3470 ext 810/www.tvtickets. com).

This agency provides studio audiences for about 40 sitcoms, including *Third Rock from the Sun* and *Friends*. The easiest way to get a ticket is via its website, any time from 60 to two days before a show date. Or write (preferably at least a month in advance), saying which days you'll be in Los Angeles and which shows you'd like to see. Schedules for the next seven to ten days are also available by phone.

Galleries

LA's art gallery scene is small but lively – and spreading fast.

There were art dealerships in Los Angeles before World War II, and during the 1960s there was a lively gallery scene along La Cienega Boulevard. But LA came of cultural age only in the 1980s. The scene is still changing and expanding, as the hippest dealers and most advanced work move into areas where galleries would have been unthinkable only a few months before. Those spaces sometimes have short lives, but at least the gallery scene can finally boast an overall stability. LA has long attracted artists, but now it also has the critical mass of collectors (and curators and critics) that allows the artists to make a living.

It is also possible to enjoy some of LA's artistic riches without leaving your car. Murals dot the landscape, from the East LA barrios to Venice Beach, and there are also a number of outdoor sculptures to drive by – and some more (especially in Downtown) to walk by. For more information and tours of murals, contact the **Mural Conservancy of Los Angeles** (1-818 487 0416/www.lamurals.org) and **SPARC** (1-310 822 9560/www.sparcmurals.com).

Two monthly directories, *Art Scene* and *Art Now Gallery Guide* (available at all the galleries they list), provide a comprehensive briefing on LA's spaces. The *LA Weekly* and the *LA Times*'s Sunday Calendar section also provide extensive listings.

Most galleries are open from around 11am to 6pm from Tuesday to Saturday. Venues and phone numbers change often, so it's a good idea to ring first to save a wasted trip.

Santa Monica

Most of the galleries are found in the oceanside enclave of Santa Monica, mainly in the 'art malls'. The most prominent of these by far is **Bergamot Station** (*see below*), a sprawling former tram terminal. Other galleries can be found elsewhere in Santa Monica's industrial east side, including the cutting-edge **Blum & Poe** (1-310 453 8311), **Christopher Grimes** (1-310 587 3373) and the **18th Street Arts Complex** (1-310 453 3711) with its artist-run exhibition, performance and media spaces. **Angles** (1-310 396 5019), on the Main Street shopping thoroughfare near the water, has a cool aesthetic and an international roster of shows. Further south in Venice, the redoubtable

LA Louver (1-310 821 4955) specialises in LA's contemporary masters and younger artists from New York, Italy and Britain.

Bergamot Station
2525 Michigan Avenue, at Cloverfield Boulevard (1-310 829 5854). Bus Santa Monica 9/I-10, exit Clovefield Boulevard east. **Open** 10am-5pm Tue-Fri; 11am-5pm Sat; closed Mon; some galleries open Sun.
Some 30 galleries, plus several art-related outlets and the Santa Monica Museum of Art (*see p119*) occupy a complex of large sheds ringing a capacious parking area. Leading galleries include **Track 16**, with its irreverent and often museum-scaled shows; **Shoshana Wayne** and **Patrick Painter**, for the international avant-garde; **Rosamund Felsen**, devoted to local experimentalists; **Richard Heller**, devoted to local and international emerging talents; **Patricia Faure** and **Mark Moore**, devoted to all the above; **Frank Lloyd**, LA's one gallery committed exclusively to serious ceramics; photo galleries **Luisotti**, **Peter Fetterman**, **Craig Krull** and the **Gallery for Contemporary Photography**; and the unpredictable **Robert Berman Gallery**.

Other areas

A clutch of beyond-cool galleries – **ACME** (1-323 857 5942), **Marc Foxx** (1-323 857 5571), **Works on Paper** (1-323 964 9675), **Karyn Lovegrove** (1-323 525 1755), **1301 Projects** (1-323 938 5822), **Roberts & Tilton** (1-323 549 0223), **Daniel Weinberg** (1-323 954 8425) and **Chicago Projects** (1-323 931 1783) – have established a warren of spaces around Miracle Mile, across from the Los Angeles County Museum of Art (*see page 117*).

La Brea Avenue, between Santa Monica Boulevard and Third Street, is dotted with galleries of all kinds, most specialising in photography, including **Couturier** (1-323 933 5557), **Jan Kesner** (1-323 938 6834), **Apex** (1-323 634 7887), **Fahey/Klein** (1-323 934 2250)

Bergamot Station: number one for art.

and **Paul Kopeikin** (1-323 937 0765) – but don't miss non-photography galleries **Jan Baum** (1-323 932 0170) and **Jack Rutberg** (1-323 938 5222). Beverly Boulevard to the west sports more photographic (**Stephen Cohen**, 1-323 937 5525) and historic (**Tobey Moss**, 1-323 933 5523) galleries.

In artsy West Hollywood, a cluster of galleries has taken root along Melrose Avenue, Robertson Boulevard and Almont Street. **Kohn Turner** (1-310 854 5400), **Koplin** (1-310 657 9843) and print gallery **Remba** (1-310 657 1101) hold down Robertson. **Margo Leavin** (1-310 273 0603) perhaps the premier gallery for LA artists, is at the top of Robertson, across Santa Monica Boulevard, and nearby sits the hip **Kantor Gallery** (1-310 659 2124). On Melrose are contemporary galleries **Tasende** (1-310 276 8686), **Chac-Mool** (1-310 550 6792), **Louis Stern** (1-310 276 0147), **Herbert Palmer** (1-310 278 6407 and **O'Melveny** (1-310 273 7868).

Several galleries are devoted to pre-war California painting, among them **George Stern** (1-310 276 2600), **Edenhurst** (1-310 247 8151) and **William Karges** (1-310 276 8551). **Manny Silverman** on Almont (1-310 659 8256) specialises in American Abstract Expressionism and, up the block, **Regen Projects** (1-310 276 5424) shows local and national *ne plus ultra*.

Many artists still live in the SoHo-wannabe warehouse district east of Downtown; there are few commercial galleries left in that area, though the ones still extant are some of the city's best. The area around City Hall is beginning to attract non-profit spaces such as **Side Street Projects** (on South Main Street, 1-213 620 8895). Several artist-run galleries have also sprung up in the **Brewery Complex** (at North Main Street and Avenue 21) just north of Downtown – logically enough, as the Brewery is (or, at least, bills itself as) the largest artist live-work complex in the world.

There was some hope that a gallery scene would coalesce around the relocation of one of LA's most important alternative spaces, **Los Angeles Contemporary Exhibitions** (LACE, 1-323 957 1777), to 6522 Hollywood Boulevard, as part of the Hollywood redevelopment project. No such luck. Instead, the second and third generations of LA's cutting-edge, fly-by-night galleries have emerged in Tinseltown's true bohemia, Silver Lake and Echo Park. These are shoestring operations, often just gritty shopfronts and sometimes literally nothing more than gallerists' living rooms. In Hollywood proper can be found only **Newspace** (1-323 469 9353), ever the place to see Los Angeles's older and newer talent.

Art in Chinatown

Neither slick nor scruffy, the galleries that have appeared in the past couple of years amid the social clubs, souvenir shops and abandoned shopfronts at Chinatown's north end – especially along the pedestrianised Chung King Road – are devoted to new art, especially local but also international. The bottom end of the road is where the nominally hipper galleries cluster, including **China Art Objects** (the pioneer, 1-213 613 0384), **Goldman Tevis** (1-213 617 8217), and **dianepreuss**. At the top end, a more eclectic attitude prevails at the **Black Dragon Society**, which has rather restricted hours, if a lively exhibition schedule, and at **Inmo** (1-213 626 4225), where shows by local curators have alternated with exhibitions of prominent architects such as Eric Owen Moss. More galleries are expected to pop up along Chung King Road, and the scene has already spilled around the corner, on to vehicular Bernard Street, where **Acuna-Hansen** (1-323 441 1624) has been showing strange and wonderful stuff by regional talents.

Anyone who knew the New York art world in the 1980s will find a distant echo of the East Village in this small cluster of lively low-profile galleries appearing willy-nilly in a distinctly un-arty neighborhood, though there isn't the same frisson of danger as the druggy East Village, and the galleries themselves are multiplying a lot more slowly. Also, the after-gallery snack isn't pierogi but dim sum, and, at the time of writing, the Chinatown galleries aren't keeping Sunday hours (alas). But keep an eye cocked, as the excitement is mounting, slowly and subtly.

Arts & Entertainment

Gay & Lesbian

The gay life is the good life in LA. And the epicentre of it all – for men and women – is the city of West Hollywood.

LA is perhaps one of the nicest places on earth to be gay; its lack of an overriding character, its relaxed attitude to relationships and formal structures, and its strange mix of friendliness and anonymity make it the perfect place to live your life as you want. Furthermore, gay people have always heavily populated the creative industries to which the city is uniquely wedded: film, music and TV. This makes LA a gayer city than most. Gay LA is concentrated in West Hollywood, Hollywood and Silver Lake, with a few interesting outposts in the Valley and the beaches, and, more recently, the desert. As in other cities, however, the gay and lesbian scenes are still quite distinct from each other.

Resources

The *Community Yellow Pages* (available from bookshop A Different Light) is LA's lesbian/gay phone book, listing everything from plumbers and pet care to nightlife. The **West Hollywood Convention & Visitors Bureau** (*see page 82*) is also a useful source of information.

For gay and lesbian theatre productions, try the **Celebration Theatre** (7051B Santa Monica Boulevard, 1-323 957 1884) in West Hollywood or **Highways Performance Space** (1651 18th Street, 1-310 453 1755) in Santa Monica. The latter is surprisingly edgy for LA, and also has art exhibits and workshops.

The **Metropolitan Community Church** in West Hollywood (8714 Santa Monica Boulevard, 1-310 854 9110/www.mccla.org) offers multi-denominational services and is popular with both gays and lesbians.

A Different Light Bookstore

8853 Santa Monica Boulevard, at San Vicente Boulevard, West Hollywood (1-310 854 6601/ www.adlbooks.com/wh.html). Bus 4, 105, 304, DASH West Hollywood/I-10, exit La Cienega Boulevard north. **Open** 10am-midnight daily. **Credit** AmEx, MC, V. **Map** p306 A2.
Lesbian and gay books, mags, cards and videos, with super-friendly service and special activities almost nightly. Check out the bulletin board for events, rooms to rent, massages and whatnots.

LA Gay & Lesbian Center

1625 N Schrader Boulevard, at Hollywood Boulevard, Hollywood (1-323 993 7400/www.laglc. org). Metro Hollywood-Highland or Hollywood-Vine/

bus 180, 181, 217/US 101, exit Highland Avenue south. **Open** 9.30am-8pm Mon-Fri; 9.30am-1.30pm Sat; closed Sun. **Map** p307 A1.
When in trouble or doubt, this is the place to go: it's the largest gay and lesbian community centre in the world, offering legal, medical, outreach and education services, among many others.

The Village at Ed Gould Plaza

1125 N McCadden Place, between Lexington Avenue & Santa Monica Boulevard, Hollywood (1-323 461 2633). Bus 4, 304/US 101, exit Santa Monica Boulevard west. **Open** 9am-10pm Mon-Sat; 9am-9pm Sun. **Map** p307 A2.
The latest addition to the Gay & Lesbian Center, the Village has a beautiful courtyard, a coffeeshop and a theatre, and offers workshops, meeting rooms, a cybercentre and many helpful organisations. It also organises moonlit horse rides.

Gay

It's no great surprise that gay men visit Los Angeles in their thousands: the attractions of sun, sea, surf and endless pop culture make it a natural destination for guys from all over the world, for whom the Californian surfer-jock is also the ultimate desire-object. Much of what informs gay lifestyle in European cities draws its inspiration from LA; the current fashion for hairless, glistening, muscled bodies ('ripped' in the current parlance) is essentially an LA thing.

There's a less positive way of looking at this, too; a city supposedly built on narcissism and superficiality in human relationships does indeed sometimes seem like your average urban gay scene writ large. There's certainly far less diversity in the required look here: the youth obsession is overwhelming, body fascism is rampant, steroid use is common and drugs of all sorts have a massive foothold. Most worryingly, the return of unsafe sex, particularly among the young, in a city already ravaged by AIDS, has led, at the time of writing, to a syphilis outbreak, with possibly huge implications for future HIV infections.

But LA has a big plus: perhaps nowhere else in the world is there such a sense of gay success and achievement at the highest levels. Whether or not the Hollywood 'velvet mafia' really exists, there is no question that, with figures such as out film mogul David Geffen at the very top of the tree, the role models for gay men are world-class. There is a sense of an institutionalised, established gay society, and something approaching a gay hierarchy. And nowhere else can boast its own unofficial gay city – West Hollywood.

On a day-to-day level, gay visitors might actually find LA rather mundane; the lack of walking takes away that all-important street-eye contact, which is such a part of your average guy's cruising. And visibly gay centres are confined to certain parts of the city. But don't despair: in most of the 'fashionable' parts of LA there's a 50 per cent chance that almost every guy you meet will be gay. For the proud and partying types, the big gay events are spread throughout the year: there's **Mardi Gras** in spring (details from the West Hollywood visitors bureau), **Gay & Lesbian Pride** weekend in June and a chance to pull out the stops and dress to the nines at **Hallowe'en** in October (for both, *see chapter* **By Season**).

And outside LA, the desert resort of **Palm Springs** has become increasingly fashionable in recent years, and has a strong gay scene – *see chapter* **Trips Out of Town**.

INFORMATION

Pick up a copy of *Circuit Noise* (1-818 769 9390/www.circuitnoise.com), *Odyssey* (1-323 874 8788), *Frontiers* (1-323 848 2222/www.frontiers web.com), Latino-oriented *qvMagazine* (1-818 766 0023/www.qvmagazine.com) or *Edge* (1-323 962 6994): they're free and have all the latest what's what. You'll find them in bars, cafés, bookshops and other shops throughout West Hollywood. Website **www.westhollywood. com** is a useful guide for news and events.

Website **www.gay.com** has hundreds of chatrooms in which you can meet and make useful contacts, new friends or even line up some sex partners before your arrival in LA. The site has eight chatrooms alone devoted to LA, plus two for Long Beach and two for Orange County. For gay-related health issues, *see page 282* **Health & medical**.

West Hollywood

As Joan Rivers joked on her TV show: 'What separates the men from the boys? In West Hollywood, that's a crowbar.' WeHo (as it's known to locals) is without doubt the epicentre of LA gay life and the best place for gay visitors to be based if they want to immerse themselves quickly into the scene. The main drag, Santa Monica Boulevard, runs right through West Hollywood and acts as a sort of gay version of the parallel Sunset Strip (be warned: the whole

street is undergoing massive and unsightly road repairs, which won't be completed until autumn 2001). There are hundreds of gay businesses serving WeHo, and the established, residental tone of the area gives it a more laid-back, less predatory feel than other city centres.

One of the few places in Los Angeles where you don't feel weird walking, the city has a distinct character that is derived from its tanned, affluent and, some would say, hopelessly self-absorbed residents. The WeHo gay is ripped to within an inch of his life, has a jeep, a dog (for cruising purposes in the canyon parks), a boyfriend (until the Bigger Better Deal comes along), cares about his spiritual needs and treats his body like a temple – at which others should worship regularly. And if he works in the 'industry', his dream is to join the A-list ('Hi-Fags') up in the Hollywood Hills ('Swish Alps').

Accommodation

Gay-friendly hotels include **Le Montrose** (*see page 54*) and the **Ramada** (*see page 55*).

The San Vicente Inn-Resort

845 N San Vicente Boulevard, between Cynthia Street & Santa Monica Boulevard (1-310 854 6915/ 8944/fax 1-310 289 5929/www.gayresort.com). Bus 105, DASH West Hollywood/I-10, exit La Cienega Boulevard north. **Rates** $69-$259. **Credit** AmEx, DC, Disc, MC, V. **Map** p306 A2.
The Westside's only gay guesthouse, the San Vicente features free breakfast, a fabulous pool and jacuzzi, a tropical garden, nude sunbathing, proximity to local attractions and a high sexual temperature.

Bars & clubs

Micky's bar (8857 Santa Monica Boulevard, 1-310 657 1176/www.mickys.com), in the middle of West Hollywood's main drag, is always busy.

The Factory

652 N La Peer Drive, at Robertson Boulevard (1-310 659 4551). Bus 4, 105, 304, DASH West Hollywood/ I-10, exit Robertson Boulevard north. **Open** 9pm-2am Wed-Sat; 6pm-midnight alt Sun. **Admission** $3-$15. **Credit** *Bar only* AmEx, MC, V. **Map** p306 A2.
One of the newest and hippest gay clubs, which holds a tea dance every other Sunday (6pm-midnight) and a popular 1980s night every Wednesday.

Motherlode

8944 Santa Monica Boulevard, at San Vicente Boulevard (1-310 659 9700). Bus 4, 105, 304, DASH West Hollywood/I-10, exit La Cienega Boulevard north. **Open** noon-2am daily. **Admission** free. **No credit cards**. **Map** p306 A2.
Everyone's favourite beer bust on Sunday afternoons, Motherlode offers friendly guys playing pool and making small talk.

Arts & Entertainment

Rage

8911 Santa Monica Boulevard, between Larrabee Street & San Vicente Boulevard (1-310 652 7055). Bus 4, 105, 304, DASH West Hollywood/I-10, exit La Cienega Boulevard north. **Open** 1.30pm-2am Mon-Fri; 2pm-2am Sat, Sun. **Admission** $8-$10. **Credit** *Bar only* AmEx, MC, V. **Map** p306 A2.

There's dancing nightly in this quintessential West Hollywood gay club.

Revolver

8851 Santa Monica Boulevard, at Larrabee Street (1-310 659 8851). Bus 4, 105, 304, DASH West Hollywood/I-10, exit La Cienega Boulevard north. **Open** 4pm-2am Mon-Fri; 2pm-2am Sat, Sun. **Admission** free-$10. **No credit cards.** **Map** p306 A2.

At this entertaining video bar, you'll find plenty of guys having a good time watching each other have a good time.

Coffeehouses & restaurants

Gay dining in West Hollywood is excellent and varied. Among the newer establishments is **Mark's** restaurant (861 North La Cienega Boulevard, 1-310 652 5252), which has a very popular early-evening cocktail hour and jazz on Sunday nights. It attracts a smart, good-looking crowd. Also new and just along the street is **Blue Palms** (No. 829, 1-310 652 9007), which is slightly more intimate and a little less self-conscious. The food at both is first class. Two more established and still thriving favourites are **Basix Café** (8833 Santa Monica

Boulevard, 1-323 848 2460), which has a pavement terrace (all the better to ogle the passing view), and, literally next door, **Marix** (1108 North Flores Avenue, 1-323 656 8800), a very attractive and bustling place that serves good Tex-Mex food. Sunday nights at Marix are quite an institution. The **Cobalt Cantina** (*see page 226*) is also a very good bet. If you just want to chill with a grande latte in hand, then **Starbucks** on Santa Monica Boulevard (bang opposite the 24-Hour Fitness gym) is more or less totally gay.

The Abbey

692 N Robertson Boulevard, at Santa Monica Boulevard (1-310 289 8410). Bus 105, 220, DASH West Hollywood/I-10, exit Robertson Boulevard north. **Open** 7am-2am Mon-Thur; 7am-3am Fri; 8am-3am Sat; 8am-2am Sun. **Credit** AmEx, MC, V. **Map** p306 A2.

Formerly just a coffeehouse, the Abbey has expanded and now has a cocktail bar, with another one on the way. Extremely – and deservedly – popular, it serves superb and inexpensive food in one of the most pleasant of settings: a large outdoor patio complete with statues and fairy lights. And unlike the rest of WeHo's stereotypically 'whitebread' scene, it attracts an ethnically mixed crowd.

French Quarter

French Market Place, 7985 Santa Monica Boulevard, at Laurel Avenue (1-323 654 0898). Bus 4, 304, DASH West Hollywood/I-10, exit Fairfax Avenue north. **Open** 7am-midnight Mon-Thur, Sun; 7am-3.30pm Fri, Sat. **Credit** AmEx, MC, V. **Map** p306 B1.

Gorgeous guys and classy cocktails at the **Abbey** in West Hollywood.

Arts & Entertainment

Enclosed in a 'gay' shopping mall with tacky white fencing around it, this neighbourhood staple has an eclectic menu and an eclectic crowd. There's a terrace for outside dining. Expect to wait for a table.

Koo Koo Roo
8520 Santa Monica Boulevard, between La Cienega Boulevard & W Knoll Drive (1-310 473 5858/ www.kookooroo.com). Bus 4, 105, 304/I-10, exit La Cienega Boulevard north. **Open** 11am-10pm daily. **Credit** AmEx, MC, V. **Map** p306 A2.
Part of a chicken chain, this is where the muscle guys get their protein. It offers good, quickly served food: some liken it to the cast catering on a porn movie set. **Branches**: throughout the city.

Tango Grill
8807 Santa Monica Boulevard, at Hancock Avenue (1-310 659 3663). Bus 4, 304/I-10, exit La Cienega Boulevard north. **Open** 11.30am-11.30pm daily. **Credit** AmEx, MC, V. **Map** p306 A2.
Argentinian cuisine and grilled chicken are served at this friendly and efficient no-frills restaurant.

WeHo Lounge
8861 Santa Monica Boulevard, at San Vicente Boulevard (1-310 659 6180/events line 1-310 360 0430). Bus 4, 105, 304, DASH West Hollywood/ I-405, exit Santa Monica Boulevard east. **Open** noon-2am Mon-Sat; 11am-2am Sun. **Credit** MC, V. **Map** p306 A2.
Enjoy coffee and cakes in a laid-back setting, in the middle of the clubs and bars on the gay strip. Events include stand-up comedy and a gay dating game.

Gyms

LA is full of gyms: the following will pump you up and make you hard. **24-Hour Fitness** is a WeHo institution; it used to be the famous LA Sports Connection (nickname: Sports Erection). It has equipment on three floors and, unlike many other gyms, a great pool. The clientele is predominantly gay, so it's intensely cruisey. And don't miss the renowned **Gold's Gym**: the Cole Avenue branch promises a fantasy land of porn performers, prom queens and soap stars. For both, *see page 256.*

The Athletic Club
8560 Santa Monica Boulevard, at La Cienega Boulevard (1-310 659 6630). Bus 4, 105, 304/I-10, exit La Cienega Boulevard north. **Open** 5.30am-11pm Mon-Sat; 5.30am-9pm Sun. **Rates** $15 per day. **Credit** AmEx, Disc, MC, V. **Map** p306 A/B1.
Forget your shirt, bring your muscles.

Crunch
8000 Sunset Boulevard, at Laurel Avenue, West Hollywood (1-323 654 4550/www.crunch.com). Bus 2, 3, 302/I-10, exit Fairfax Avenue north. **Open** 5am-11pm Mon-Thur; 5am-9pm Fri; 8am-8pm Sat, Sun. **Rates** $20 per day. **Credit** AmEx, MC, V. **Map** p306 B1.

LA's gym of the moment boasts a great view of the Hollywood Hills from its windows, which competes with the Adonis factor inside. It's located in the Sunset Boulevard/Crescent Heights mall, itself a popular gay meeting place.

Hollywood

There's no real gay promenading to speak of in Hollywood and the general ambience is not as friendly as in West Hollywood, so there's little to entice the visitor. However, although most Hollywood bars are pretty divey, a number of well-established places remain hot and are worth a visit.

Bars & clubs

Gay nights at huge Hollywood club **Arena** (*see page 239*), a former ice factory, include Circus (9pm to 2am Tuesday and Thursday, 9pm to 4am Saturday) and Club 6655 (9pm to 2.30am Thursday). The security parking is a bonus. Dance club **Icon** runs an after-hours club at the Playroom (836 N Highland Avenue) and other one-off events at various venues; call 1-323 460 6630 for more information.

Spike
7746 Santa Monica Boulevard, at Genesee Avenue (1-323 656 9343). Bus 4, 304/I-10, exit Fairfax Avenue north. **Open** noon-2am Mon-Thur, Sun; noon-4am Fri, Sat. **Admission** $7; free 3-11pm Sun. **No credit cards. Map** p306 C1.
Spike is a Levi's/leather bar, with an always-interesting crowd: cruisey guys with sex on their minds. Officially, it's at the eastern end of West Hollywood, but in atmosphere it's more part of the Hollywood scene.

The Study
1723 Western Avenue, between Hollywood Boulevard & Russell Avenue (1-323 464 9551). Bus 180, 181, 207, 357/US 101, exit Hollywood Boulevard east. **Open** 11am-2am daily. **Admission** free Mon-Wed, Sat; $5 Thur, Fri, Sun. **No credit cards. Map** p307 C1.
A neighbourhood bar with a largely African-American crowd, this is a slight throwback to a 1970s gay pub, with none of the pretensions of its WeHo counterparts. It's also got a pool table.

Silver Lake

Silver Lake is the best-known gay area in LA after West Hollywood. Its character, however, is totally different; the crowd tends to be older, with less bare muscle in evidence, although there's certainly more leather and facial hair. If you feel happier, when in London, in Earl's Court rather than in Soho, then Silver Lake is the place for you.

Arts & Entertainment

Gay beaches

Southern California's beaches are a delight year round; these are particularly gay-friendly areas. For more information on LA's beaches, *see page 78.*

South Laguna Beach

It's a long drive down to Laguna from LA, but the water is clean and this beach is hot. It's on Pacific Coast Highway, just past the pier: look for the gay flag (easy to miss), park on the side of the road and take the stairs down to the beach. It's especially nice on a weekday. After the beach, check out the Boom Boom Room, which offers dancing, drink specials and plenty of tanned guys with their shirts off. Or grab a snack at Wahoo's Fish Tacos (1133 PCH, at Oak Street, 1-949 497 0033). If you want to stay over, try the Coast Inn (1401 PCH, at Mountain Road, 1-949 494 7588).

Venice Beach

Head for the stretch where Windward Avenue meets the beach, next to the wall, just down from Muscle Beach and in front of the heart of the famed Venice Boardwalk. Friendly neighbourhood bar the Roosterfish (1302 Abbot Kinney Boulevard, 1-310 392 2123), is a Venice Beach institution: no one should leave LA without a trip to 'the Fish'.

Will Rogers Beach

On PCH, north of the Santa Monica Pier, in front of the Beach Club. The beach is packed

Look for the rainbow flag at **Venice**.

on sunny weekends: it's fun, it's free, it's got tons of guys playing volleyball and it all lasts till sunset. Parking can be a drag, so it's best to pay to park in the lot. Patrick's Roadhouse across the street is always good for a laugh.

Bars & clubs

Tattoo, a popular bar attached to the **Cobalt** on Sunset Boulevard (*see page 226*), is a great place for Sunday brunch. Also try the monthly Dragstrip 66 at **Rudolfo's** (*see page 242*).

Cuffs

1941 Hyperion Avenue, between Fountain & Lyric Avenues (1-323 660 2649). Bus 175/US 101, exit Sunset Boulevard east. **Open** 4pm-2am Mon-Thur, Sun; 4pm-4am Fri, Sat. **Admisson** free. **No credit cards. Map** p308 B2.
This bar is quintessential Silver Lake.

Faultline

4216 Melrose Avenue, at N Vermont Avenue (1-323 660 0889/www.faultlinebar.com). Bus 10, 11, 204, 354, Community Connection 203/US 101, exit Vermont Avenue north. **Open** 4pm-2am Tue-Fri; 2pm-2am Sat, Sun; closed Mon. **Admission** varies (special events only). **No credit cards. Map** p308 A3.

The leather ethic is observed at this club; fortunately, there's a leather shop on the premises. The Sunday beer bust is always a kick in the rubber parts, and on Tuesday nights it's positively teeming.

Bathhouses & sex clubs

LA is also home to some good bathhouses and sex clubs. Take your own condoms.

Hollywood Spa

1650 Ivar Street, between Hollywood Boulevard & Selma Avenue, Hollywood (1-800 772 2582/1-323 464 0445). Bus 180, 181, 212, 217/US 101, exit Hollywood Boulevard west. **Open** 24hrs daily. **Admission** *per 8hrs* $30 room; $20 locker. **Credit** AmEx, MC, V. **Map** p307 B1.
Open 24 hours, this is the best-known bathhouse in the city. It has a pretty good gym – although patrons tend to get their training in before they visit – and a sweeping staircase to remind you of Busby Berkeley.

Arts & Entertainment

Prowl

*1064 Myra Avenue, at Santa Monica Boulevard,
Silver Lake (1-213 388 8040). Bus 4, 304/US 101,
exit Vermont Avenue north.* **Open** 9pm-4am Tue-
Sat; 3pm-4am Sun; closed Mon. **Admission** $15.
No credit cards. **Map** p308 B3.
Prowl by name…

Lesbian

LA is home to some of the most diverse ladies
around. Clubbers, career professionals and
carers; the single, the obsessed, the beloved and
the heartbroken: the City of Angels has them
all. And the look of the LA lesbian is all over
the map, too, from lipstick and thrift shops, to
chapstick and the Gap. So if you think you
won't blend in here, you may be surprised. West
Hollywood is known as Boys Town, but what
about the girls? Is there such a thing as Girls
Town? Well, in a way, yes, but it's not as
obvious. Ladies like to mingle in little pockets
in West Hollywood, Hollywood, Silver Lake
and the Valley. And the ladies in LA are
generally pretty friendly – as long as you're
not trying to steal their date!

Information & shops

Pick up free monthly mag *Lesbian News* (www.
lesbiannews.com) from local book or video
shops. Another free monthly, *Female FYI*, is a
good source for clubs, bars and other events,
but a little short on other reading matter.

August is **Lesbian Visibility Month**,
where the ladies are in the spotlight with dances,
comedy nights and social and educational
forums. Check listings magazines or www.
lesbianation.com for details. Another important
annual event is the **Outfest** gay and lesbian
film festival (*see page 216*).

Those with a spirit of adventure can hitch
up with women of all ages for camping, hiking,
dancing, theatre and other activities through
Women on a Roll (PO Box 4533, Oceanside,
CA 92052/1-888 469 6636/1-310 578 8888/
www. gowomen.org). And the ladies turn out
in droves to support their favourite basketball
team, the **LA Sparks** (*see page 252*
Basketball). Games sell out fast.

Women-run sex shop **The Pleasure Chest**
(*see page 195*) is a good places for erotic toys,
clothes and mags.

June L Mazer Archives

*626 N Robertson Boulvard, at Melrose Avenue, West
Hollywood (1-310 659 2478). Bus 105, 220, DASH
West Hollywood/I-10, exit Robertson Boulevard
north.* **Open** noon-3pm Tue, 1st Sun of the mth.
Map p306 A2.

The June L Mazer Archives houses a collection of
photos, films and books about lesbian life past and
present. Well worth visiting.

Midnight Special

*1318 Third Street Promenade, between Arizona
Avenue & Santa Monica Boulevard, Santa Monica
(1-310 393 2923/www.msbooks.com). Bus 4, Santa
Monica 1, 8/I-10, exit Fourth-Fifth Street north.*
Open 10.30am-11pm Mon-Thur, Sun; 10.30am-
11.30pm Fri, Sat. **Credit** AmEx, MC, V. **Map** p304 A2.
This popular bookshop specialises in politics and
culture, although there's a good selection of general
literature and a huge range of mags. Events include
open poetry evenings, author readings (with many
established lesbian writers) and documentary films.

Bars & clubs

It is rare for Los Angeles bars or clubs to devote
themselves to lesbians seven days a week.
What are being offered, though, are designated
nights for dykes. The best roving dance club
for women, **Fuel**, is held at a variety of venues
including the El Rey Theatre; call 1-310 394 6541
for information. On Thursdays, Culver City club
Fais Do-Do (*see page 233*) plays host to **Milk**:
cheap admission, beer only, cult movie watching
and live bands. **Salsa de Noche** is held on
the first Saturday of the month at **Rudolfo's**
Mexican restaurant in Silver Lake (*see page
242*), while, if you fancy a change from regular
clubbing, Sunday night is gay night at
Moonlight Rollerway (*see page 250*), where
you can skate to your favourite vinyl hits.

Benvenuto

*8512 Santa Monica Boulevard, at La Cienega
Boulevard, West Hollywood (1-310 659 8635). Bus
4, 105, 304/I-10, exit La Cienega Boulevard north.*
Open 5.30-10.30pm Mon-Thur, Sun; 5.30-11pm Fri,
Sat. **Admission** Free. **Credit** AmEx, Disc, MC, V.
Map p306 A/B1.
Gay gals, no cover charge, a full bar and DJ
Claudette on the decks. Oh, and there's food, too.

Girl Bar

*The Factory, 652 N La Peer Drive, at Robertson
Boulevard, West Hollywood (1-877 447 5252/
www.girlbar.com). Bus 4, 10, 11, 220, DASH West
Hollywood/I-10, exit Robertson Boulevard north.*
Open 9pm-2am Fri. **Admission** $6-$10. **Credit**
AmEx, MC, V. **Map** p306 A2.
Modelled to look like a trendy New York hotspot,
this is the place for twentysomething women to flock
and mingle. Call for info on special events.

Michelle's XXX Revue

*Club 7969, 7969 Santa Monica Boulevard, between
Fairfax Avenue & Crescent Heights Boulevard, West
Hollywood (1-323 654 0280). Bus 4, 304, DASH
West Hollywood/I-10, exit La Cienega Boulevard
north.* **Open** 9pm-2am Tue. **Admission** varies.
Credit MC, V. **Map** p306 B1.

Arts & Entertainment

Milk at Fais-Do-Do. *See p225.*

This legendary women's dance/strip club – on Tuesdays only – has reopened with go-go dancers all night long. Oh my!

Normandie Room

8737 Santa Monica Boulevard, between La Cienega & San Vicente Boulevards (1-310 659 6204). Bus 4, 105, 304, DASH West Hollywood/I-10, exit La Cienega Boulevard north. **Open** 5pm-2am daily. **Admission** free. **Credit** MC, V. **Map** p306 A2.

A popular neighbourhood bar with casual dress and eclectic lesbians every night of the week. The bar's motto reads: 'No homophobes, no heterophobes, no assholes'. Need we say more?

Oil Can Harry's

11502 Ventura Boulevard, between Tujunga Boulevard & Colfax Avenue, Studio City (1-818 760 9749). Bus 150, 240, 750/US 101, exit Tujunga Boulevard south. **Open** 9.15pm-12.30am Tue-Thur; 9pm-2am Fri; 8pm-2am Sat; closed Mon, Sun. **Admission** varies. **Credit** AmEx, MC, V.

Two-step and line dance with your best gal on your arm in a country twang. Whether you go solo or with a group, there's always someone to dance with, and the place has the nicest bar in town. Lessons are available on Tuesday and Thursday evenings (7.45-9.15pm).

The Palms

8572 Santa Monica Boulevard, at La Cienega Boulevard, West Hollywood (1-310 652 6188). Bus 4, 105, 304, DASH West Hollywood/I-10, exit La Cienega Boulevard north. **Open** 4pm-2am Mon-Fri; 2pm-2am Sat, Sun. **Admission** free. **Credit** AmEx, MC, V. **Map** p306 A/B1.

The oldest lesbian bar in Los Angeles, with dancing, a pool table and a patio. New ownership has meant a new coat of paint, and the place is generally cleaner (except for the bathrooms). The Sunday beer bust is very popular.

Puss N Boots

Jewel's Catch One, 4067 W Pico Boulevard, at Crenshaw Boulevard, Mid-City (1-323 734 8849). Bus 30, 31/I-10, exit Crenshaw Boulevard north. **Open** 9pm-2am Tue-Sun; closed Mon. **Admission** $5-$7. **Credit** MC, V.

An amazingly diverse group of women together in one room, plus a huge dancefloor and great beats to thump to. Get there early – it fills up fast.

Coffeehouses & restaurants

Gay venues that are also popular with lesbians include the **Abbey**, **French Quarter** and **Marix** (*see page 222* **Coffeehouses & restaurants**). If you're in Silver Lake, drop in on the delightful **Coffee Table** with its smoke-free patio (*see page 164*). Main courses at the places listed below cost $6 to $8.

Cobalt Cantina

Cobalt West, 616 N Robertson Boulevard, at Melrose Avenue, West Hollywood (1-310 659 8691). Bus 105, 220, DASH West Hollywood/I-10, exit Robertson Boulevard north. **Open** noon-3pm, 5-11pm Mon-Fri; noon-11pm Sat; 11am-10pm Sun. **Credit** AmEx, Disc, MC, V. **Map** p306 A2.

Fine food and great mood lighting. Sunday is ladies night, with drink specials.

Branch: Cobalt East, 4326 Sunset Boulevard, at Fountain Avenue, Silver Lake (1-213 953 9991).

Coffee Bean & Tea Leaf

8735 Santa Monica Boulevard, at Hancock Avenue, West Hollywood (1-310 659 8207). Bus 4, 105, 304, DASH West Hollywood/I-10, exit La Cienega Boulevard north. **Open** 8am-11pm Mon-Sat; 8am-9pm Sun. **Credit** AmEx, MC, V. **Map** p306 A2.

A lovely spot for a relaxing Sunday brunch. Very different, but just as much fun, are Thursday nights, when a variety of sub-television stars and drag queens host rock 'n' roll bingo.

Branches: throughout the city.

Highland Grounds

742 N Highland Avenue, at Melrose Avenue, Hollywood (1-323 466 1507). Bus 10, 11/US 101, exit Highland Avenue south. **Open** 9am-12.30am daily. **Credit** MC, V. **Map** p307 A3.

Cute staff, a patio and eye-opening coffee and tea. Things get crowded in the evenings, when there's live music and occasional open-mike nights.

Health

Lesbian Health Clinic

8240 Santa Monica Boulevard, at Harper Avenue, West Hollywood (1-323 650 1508). Bus 4, 304, DASH West Hollywood/I-10, exit La Cienega Boulevard north. **Open** 11am-6pm Mon-Fri; closed Sat, Sun. **Map** p306 B1.

Donor insemination, ob/gyn services, holistic care, HIV testing and a knowledgeable staff. A complete package for the healthy lesbian.

Women's Clinic

9911 W Pico Boulevard, suite 500, between Beverly Green & Roxbury Drives, Beverly Hills (1-310 203 8899). Bus Santa Monica 7, 13/I-10, exit Robertson Boulevard north. **Open** 11am-6pm Mon, Tue; 8am-3pm Wed, Thur, alternate Fri; closed Sat, Sun. **Map** p305 C3.

Health and counselling services. It's popular and appointments must often be made far in advance.

Arts & Entertainment

Music

Rock 'n' roll will never die in the music industry capital of the States – and the classical scene is thriving, too.

TICKETS & INFORMATION

Big-name concerts – both classical and rock – often sell out, so buy tickets in advance if you can. It's always worth checking with the box office on the day of the show, as the promoters sometimes release seats at that time. Whenever possible, try to get tickets directly from the venue – by phone, website or in person – to save on credit card booking charges. At smaller venues, you can usually pay on the door.

Alternatively, you can buy tickets through mega-service **Ticketmaster** (1-213 480 3232/ 1-714 740 2000/www.ticketmaster.com), whose many outlets can be found in Blockbuster Music, Tower Records, Robinsons-May and Ritmo Latino stores. Ticketmaster accepts credit cards (AmEx, Disc, MC, V), but the 'convenience' charges are fairly high. Tickets for selected shows are also available, without a service charge, at the Ticketmaster Box Office (6243 Hollywood Boulevard, between Vine and Gower Streets, open 10am-6pm Mon-Sat).

The most comprehensive music listings appear in the *LA Weekly*, while the *LA Times* Calendar section on Sundays is also a good source. For CD, tape and record shops, *see page 179*. For radio stations, *see page 286*.

Classical

Los Angeles Philharmonic

1-323 850 2000/www.laphil.org.
Established in 1919 by local multi-millionaire (and amateur musician) William Andrews Clarke, the Los Angeles Philharmonic has long served as civic proof that LA isn't the vast cultural wasteland the city's detractors make it out to be. However, it wasn't until the orchestra's 1964 move to the Dorothy Chandler Pavilion – and the concurrent tenure of Zubin 'Macho Maestro' Mehta as musical director – that the Phil began to attract international attention and praise. Since then, the world-class orchestra has expanded into a multi-tiered organisation responsible for most of the classical performances in LA. Most of these are staged in at the Chandler Pavilion (October to May; *see p228*) and at the Hollywood Bowl (June to September; *see p229*).

Thanks to the interests of its tenth and present music director, the youthful Finnish heart-throb Esa-Pekka Salonen, the Phil's programming consists of an unusually large contemporary repertoire, often side by side with the standard warhorses. Zubin

Mehta still has a strong relationship with the orchestra, as does Sir Simon Rattle, and both appear regularly. For more insight into its performances, the Philharmonic offers Upbeat Live!, a free pre-concert lecture in the Pavilion's Grand Hall starting one hour before each orchestra concert, and at noon before Friday matinées. Come 2003, the Phil is planning to leave the Chandler for the nearby Frank Gehry-designed Walt Disney Concert Hall – an exciting new venue for LA's musicians.

Los Angeles Opera

1-213 972 8001/www.laopera.org.
Debuting in late 1986 with an acclaimed production of Verdi's *Otello*, the LA Opera is one of the newest of the city's major arts companies – and currently one of the most fashionable. Now led by artistic director and legendary tenor Placido Domingo (whose arrival has pulled in massive donations), the company specialises in high-concept stagings of 'new productions, world premieres and infamous revivals'. Recent noteworthy productions have included Benjamin Britten's *Billy Budd*, starring Rodney Gilfry, and the world premiere of Tobias Picker's *Fantastic Mr Fox*. Performances are held at the Dorothy Chandler Pavilion (*see p228*).

Los Angeles Master Chorale

1-213 972 7282.
Described by Sir Simon Rattle as 'one of the finest choruses in the world', the 120-voice LA Master Chorale is the largest choir of its kind in the US. Founded in 1962 by conductor Roger Wagner – and led since 1991 by music director Paul Salamunovich – the Chorale regularly performs with the LA Philharmonic at the Chandler Pavilion and the Hollywood Bowl, and will move with the Phil into the new Disney Hall. The Chorale's extensive repertoire covers everything from Mozart and Bach to Cole Porter; its annual Christmas events – including a singalong presentation of Handel's *Messiah* – are especially popular.

Other orchestras

The **Los Angeles Chamber Orchestra** (1-213 622 7001/www.laco.org) is LA's foremost chamber ensemble, devoted to the entire repertoire from the 17th to the 20th centuries. It performs at UCLA's Royce Hall and the Mark Taper Forum (*see p257*). Tickets cost $12 to $48.

The **Da Camera Society's Chamber Music in Historic Sites** (1-310 440 1351) presents concerts by first-rate chamber ensembles and soloists in some of the city's more interesting buildings.

Tickets cost $24 to $68. The **Los Angeles Baroque Orchestra** (1-310 458 0425/www. labaroque.org) plays authentic, period instruments in various churches and small halls around town. Tickets cost $25 to $30.

The presence of other good-to-excellent ensembles in the region, such as the **Pasadena Symphony** (*see below* **Pasadena Civic Auditorium**) and the **Long Beach Symphony** (1-562 436 3203/ www.lbso.org), testifies to LA's demand for high-quality classical programming.

Venues

The Getty Courtyard at the **Getty Center** in Brentwood (*see chapter* **Museums**) presents the music of ancient Greece at 8pm on Saturdays and Sundays in summer.

Dorothy Chandler Pavilion

Performing Arts Center of Los Angeles County, 135 N Grand Avenue, between First & Temple Streets, Downtown (1-213 972 7211/www.performingarts centerla.org). Metro Civic Center-Tom Bradley/bus 78, 79, 96, 379, 427, DASH A, B/I-110, exit Fourth Street east. **Open** *Box office* 10am-6pm Mon-Sat; closed non-performance Sun. **Tickets** $8-$150. **Credit** AmEx, MC, V. **Map** p309 B2.

The grande dame of the city's concert scene and the largest hall in town devoted (almost) entirely to classical music, the Dorothy Chandler Pavilion is probably best known internationally for the one night every other year that it hosts the Academy Awards (though this is due to change in 2002, when the Oscars move to a new purpose-built home in Hollywood). Movie stars in tuxes aside, the home of the LA Opera, the LA Philharmonic and the LA Master Chorale is the place to go for an evening of high culture. The Pavilion's comfortably plush house seats 3,200 amid dark wood panelling, muted colours and iridescent crystal chandeliers. Sound quality, acceptable everywhere in the building, is best on the upper floors, though the view from the top balcony can be vertigo-inducing.

Built in the early 1960s after a fund drive by Dorothy 'Buff' Chandler, wife of the *LA Times*'s publisher Norman, the Pavilion sits at the south end of the LA County-operated Performing Arts Center (formerly the Music Center), a stone and marble edifice it shares with the Mark Taper Forum and the Ahmanson Theatre. Sandwiched between the Criminal Courts Building and the Department of Water and Power, it is an oasis in a rather empty corner of Downtown. Further south from the Pavilion is the future site of the Walt Disney Concert Hall.

Japan America Theater

244 S San Pedro Street, between E Second & E Third Streets, Downtown (1-213 680 3700). Bus 30, 31, 40, 42, 436, DASH A, D/I-110, exit Fourth Street east. **Open** *Box office* noon-5pm daily. **Tickets** $25-$50. **Credit** MC, V. **Map** p309 C2.

Modelled on a Japanese fan, this 840-seat venue in Little Tokyo hosts Japanese performing arts, from traditional Kabuki, Noh, Kageboschi (shadow-play) and Bunraku (puppet theatre) to contemporary music, comedy and dance.

Leo S Bing Theater

Los Angeles County Museum of Art, 5905 Wilshire Boulevard, between Fairfax & La Brea Avenues, Miracle Mile (information 1-323 857 6000/box office 1-323 857 6010/www.lacma.org). Bus 20, 21, 22, 436/I-10, exit Fairfax Avenue north. **Open** *Box office* noon-8pm Mon, Tue, Thur-Sun; closed Wed. **Credit** Amex, MC, V. **Map** p306 C3.

Located inside the LA County Museum of Art, the Bing presents Sundays Live (6pm, 1-323 485 6873), a series of free concerts featuring chamber ensembles and soloists, as well as evening concerts ($7-$15) on other days. Free courtyard jazz concerts take place on Fridays from 5.30pm to 8.30pm.

Pasadena Civic Auditorium

300 E Green Street, at Euclid Avenue, Pasadena (1-626 449 7360/Pasadena Symphony 1-626 793 7172/www.pasadena symphony.com). Bus 180, 181, 188, 256, Foothill Transit 187/I-110, exit Green Street east. **Open** *Box office* 10am-5pm Mon-Sat; closed Sun. **Tickets** $18-$60. **Credit** AmEx, Disc, MC, V.

The Pasadena Symphony shares this facility with several musicals a year and the Emmy Awards.

College venues

College venues include **Schoenberg Hall** and **Royce Hall** at UCLA (1-310 825 2101); **Norris Auditorium** at USC (1-213 740 7111); **Harriet & Charles Luckman Fine Arts Complex** at Cal State LA (*see page 260*); and the **Gindi Auditorium** at the University of Judaism (1-310 476 9777). Call the venues themselves for information on concerts and ticket prices.

Rock, roots & jazz

Los Angeles has reigned supreme as the music industry capital of the United States – and, by inference, the world – since the early 1970s, when local record companies such as Elektra and A&M racked up hit after hit, and prominent labels like Motown and Atlantic moved their operations west. But when it comes to establishing new trends or birthing ground-breaking bands, LA has pretty much been on the decline since the late-1980s, when hair metal ruled the Sunset Strip, rap avatars NWA came *Straight Outta Compton* and Jane's Addiction rocked the world on behalf of the city's freaked-out bohemian contingent.

Despite occasional notable exceptions, such as Snoop Dogg, No Doubt and Beck, 1990s LA produced a far greater percentage of

The Hollywood Bowl

A true LA landmark, the Hollywood Bowl is probably better known than Dodger Stadium, Staples Center and the Dorothy Chandler Pavilion put together. A perennial favourite with Angelenos and visitors, this world-famous jewel of an outdoor amphitheatre has been hosting concerts since its first LA Philharmonic performance on Easter morning 1921. Nestled in an aesthetically and acoustically blessed fold in the Bolton Canyon area of the Hollywood Hills, the 18,000-seat Bowl can bring out the romantic in even the terminally cynical.

The summer home of the LA Philharmonic (and, since 1991, conductor John Mauceri's pops-oriented Hollywood Bowl Orchestra), it has hosted performances by everyone from the Beatles to *Sesame Street*'s Big Bird, and regularly mixes classical concerts with appearances by rock, country, jazz and foreign pop performers. Some performances are followed by a fireworks display.

The Bowl is a country park and thus open to the public during the day. In the summer, orchestra rehearsals are held several mornings a week (9.30am-12.30pm). Evening events, which are closer to ritual than concert-going, start for most with an al fresco dinner eaten in the stands or one of the many picnic areas in the grounds. The Patio and Deck restaurants serve pre-concert meals and dinner picnic baskets can also be ordered.

The prized box seats at the front of the Bowl, sold by subscription for the classical and jazz series, are often handed down from generation to generation, making them virtually unobtainable. If budget isn't a limitation, check with the box office on the day of performance; these prime seats sometimes become available at short notice. But don't worry if you're a long way from the stage, as the sound system is updated virtually each year (though it's not so well suited to rock acts). The $1-$3 seats at the top, complete with enchanting vistas, are a great bargain.

The Bowl's bandshell (designed by Lloyd Wright in 1928, later updated by Frank Gehry and now being redesigned by Hodgetts + Fung) is currently the subject of a tug of war between the city's preservationists and music fans. The latter complain that the structure, however visually pleasing, is acoustically inferior, and that a world-class orchestra like the LA Phil deserves a better, bigger shell. The former insist that a bigger structure would seriously diminish the Bowl's charm. Stay tuned.

The Hollywood Bowl

2301 N Highland Avenue, at Odin Street, Hollywood (1-323 850 2000/restaurants 1-323 851 3588/www.hollywoodbowl.org). Bus Hollywood Bowl/US 101, exit Highland Avenue/ Hollywood Bowl. **Open** *June-Sept Box office* 10am-9pm Mon-Sat; noon-8pm Sun. **Closed** *Oct-May.* **Tickets** *Bench seats* $1-$24 Tue, Thur; $3-$26 Fri, Sat. *Box seats* $61-$75 Tue, Thur; $69-$90 Fri; $75-$95 Sat. *Other tickets vary.* **Credit** AmEx, Disc, MC, V. **Map** p307 A1.

Arts & Entertainment

commercial-minded clones than artists of original outlook or lasting value. As the new millennium dawns on an industry rocked by corporate mergers and the sudden proliferation of music-trading websites such as Napster (www.napster.com), local A&R types rarely even give the time of day to any act that doesn't have 'multi-platinum' stamped on its forehead. While this state of affairs might conceivably liberate LA's bands to forget about 'getting signed' and just get on with the business of making good music, it hasn't happened yet.

In the last half of the 1990s, the local media made much of Silver Lake's arty music scene (centered around venue Spaceland), as well as a citywide revival of 1960s-influenced pop sounds. Though they involved some extremely talented bands (including the Negro Problem, Wondermints and Baby Lemonade), neither scenes really managed to develop into something cohesive or influential. Despite the backlash engendered by the excessive media hype, much of the blame must be laid at the feet of the bands themselves, many of whom are still playing variations of set lists they performed five years ago.

This is not to say, however, that you won't find good music in Los Angeles. Although not a 'jazz town' like New York or a 'blues town' like Chicago, LA can hold its own when it comes to the quality and quantity of jazz and blues performances, and the city's role as a music-biz stronghold still makes it an important stop on any touring artist's itinerary. If anything, the sheer size and diversity of the city's populace ensure that all the world's musics are represented, for better or worse – though it is LA's lasting rock 'n' roll mythology that plays itself out every day in a very visible fashion, especially along the legendary Sunset Strip.

Although gangsta rap originated in neighbouring Compton and LA is home to such successful rap labels as Death Row (somewhat quiet at present while it deals with a multitude of lawsuits and owner Marion 'Suge' Knight does time) and Ruthless, don't count on seeing much of this urban African-American artform live in LA. Based on past history and the usual stereotypes – the fatal shooting of Biggie Smalls a few years back certainly didn't help – promoters and their liability insurers are hesitant to get involved. Paradoxically, but in keeping with their commitment to black music, the corporate-run House of Blues almost single-handedly continues to keep rap and hip hop in front of LA audiences.

One of the best ways to experience LA's diverse Latino culture is through its music. Well-known Latin pop stars appear frequently at mainstream venues such as the Universal

Visit **Al's Bar** for local bands. *See p232.*

Amphitheater, as well as more obscure locales such as the Pico Rivera Sports Arena (11003 Rooks Road, just off the I-605, 1-562 695 0509). Some weekends, merengue dances take place at the Hollywood Palladium. The salsa crowd does its thing at various venues, including the Conga Room, which specialises in star line-ups.

The Rock en Español movement (passionate guitar-heavy rock 'n' roll, sung in Spanish) has experienced a huge profile boost in recent years. Though the music's popularity isn't reflected in the playlists of Southern California's Spanish-language radio stations, it can be enjoyed live at the Palace in Hollywood and various smaller clubs. Local Rock en Español mainstays include Molotov, an appropriately explosive rap-metal combo with two bassists, and Pastilla, a talented quartet whose sublimely melodic brand of power-pop deserves a much wider audience.

More assimilated, a talented contingent of East LA-based bands play multi-faceted music all over town, most notably at the Conga Room and world music hangout LunaPark. Up-and-coming acts include Afro-Caribbean salseros Ricardo Lemvo and Makina Loca, and Ozomatli, whose nine-man line-up serves up a stimulating array of funky rhythms with jazzy flourishes and socially conscious lyrics.

Free shows of everything from roots to reggae to pop to world music take place in summer at the Santa Monica Pier and at California Plaza in Downtown. For year-round festival info, contact the City's Department of Cultural Affairs (1-213 485 2433).

Take photo ID to every music venue. This will not only enable you to drink (if you are 21 or older), but in many cases allow you through the door. Some shows are open to 18s and over, depending on the venue's alcohol licensing arrangement.

Major venues

The Summer Nights at the Ford series is the mainstay at the enchanting outdoor **John Anson Ford Amphitheatre**, which has presented everything from local dance troupes to alternative music acts, including French electronicists Air. The **Henry Fonda Theater** on Hollywood Boulevard presents occasional shows by adult-oriented acts such as Ray Davies. For both, *see chapter* **Theatre & Dance**.

Great Western Forum

3900 Manchester Boulevard, at Prairie Avenue, Inglewood (box office 1-310 673 1300). Bus 115, 211, 315, 442/I-405, exit Manchester Boulevard east. **Open** *Box office* 10am-6pm Mon-Fri; varies Sat, Sun. **Tickets** vary. **Credit** AmEx, MC, V.
No longer the city's premier 'enormo-dome,' thanks to the recent opening of Staples Center, the Forum occasionally serves as a venue for popular rap and foreign-language musical acts. An 18,000-seat arena built in the acoustically challenged 1970s style, and located in a fairly crummy part of town, the Forum probably isn't long for this world.

Greek Theater

2700 N Vermont Avenue, at Los Feliz Boulevard, Griffith Park (1-323 665 1927/www.nederlander. com/greek.html). Bus 204, Community Connection 203/US 101, exit Vermont Avenue north. **Open** *Box office* noon-6pm Mon-Fri; 10am-4pm Sat, Sun. **Closed** Nov-May. **Tickets** $15-$100. **Credit** AmEx,MC, V. **Map** p308 A1.
This bucolic, open-air, 6,000-seater in Griffith Park – immortalised in the annals of pop culture by Neil Diamond's *Hot August Night* LP – is a great place in the summer to catch pop and rock perennials such as John Fogerty, Santana or the Allman Brothers. One major drawback: the intractable stack parking.

Hollywood Palladium

6215 Sunset Boulevard, between Argyle & El Centro Avenues, Hollywood (1-323 962 7600/www. hollywoodpalladium.com). Metro Hollywood-Vine/ bus 2, 3, 210, 212/US 101, exit Vine Street south. **Open** *Box office & venue* from 7pm on performance days only. **Tickets** vary. **No credit cards**. **Map** p307 B2.
Mosh pits are common at this venue, which has the tightest door policy in town; even pens and chewing gum are banned. Recently refurbished (not that you can tell), the faded ballroom, once ruled by the sounds of Glenn Miller and Tommy Dorsey, has now been claimed by successful alterna-punk bands like Deftones, religious revival meetings and tapings for TV station KMEX.

The Palace

1735 N Vine Street, at Hollywood Boulevard, Hollywood (1-323 462 3000/www.hollywoodpalace. com). Metro Hollywood-Vine/bus 180, 181, 210, DASH Hollywood/US 101, exit Hollywood Boulevard west. **Open** *Box office* from 7pm on performance days only. **Tickets** vary. **No credit cards**. **Map** p307 B1.
In the heart of Hollywood, this 1927 theatre holds 1,200 fans for shows mainly of the alternative rock variety. The upstairs balcony provides an escape from the downstairs crush, but don't expect the sound to be clear anywhere; you've probably been in bomb shelters with better acoustics. At the end of the week, it turns into a club – *see p242*.

Pantages Theater

6233 Hollywood Boulevard, between Argyle Avenue & Vine Street, Hollywood (1-213 468 1770/www. nederlander.com/pantages.html). Metro Hollywood-Vine/bus 26, 163, 180, 181/US 101, exit Vine Street south. **Open** *Box office* 10am-6pm Mon; 10am-8pm Tue-Sat; 10am-6.30pm Sun. **Tickets** $15-$125. **Credit** AmEx, MC, V. **Map** p307 B1.
Another smallish (2,700-capacity) theatre with an art deco design, the venerable Pantages is a great place to see established acts and musical theatre productions such as *The Lion King*. Now that the Metro construction has been thankfully completed (and a new subway stop opened at Hollywood and Vine), the place is once again open for business on a regular basis.

Staples Center

1111 S Figueroa Street, between 11th & 12th Streets, Downtown (box office 1-213 742 7340/ www.staplescenter.com). Metro Pico/Bus 434, 436, 439, 442, 446, 460, DASH Downtown E/I-110, exit Ninth Street or Olympic Boulevard. **Open** *Box office* 10am-7pm Mon-Sat; 10am-5pm Sun (on event days only). **Tickets** $50-$150. **Credit** AmEx, Disc, MC, V. **Map** p309 A4.
Downtown new $375-million shrine to professional sports also occasionally plays host to high-ticket musical acts such as Bruce Springsteen and the Eagles. A plush and meticulously neat facility, the purple-seated, 20,000-capacity stadium possesses an

atmosphere that's a million miles from the old-school funkiness of the Great Western Forum, though most reports say that – $1.5-million sound system notwithstanding – it sounds just as terrible.

Universal Amphitheater

100 Universal City Plaza, Universal City (House of Blues concert line 1-818 777 3931/recorded information 1-818 622 4440/www.hob.com). Metro Universal City/bus 420/US 101, exit Universal Center Drive. **Open** *Universal Amphitheater box office* 1-9pm Mon, Thur-Sun; closed Tue, Wed. *CityWalk box office* 1-9pm Mon-Thur, Sun; 1-10.30pm Fri, Sat. **Tickets** vary. **Credit** AmEx, MC, V.

This slick, semicircular room for major pop, rock, R&B and Latin acts is probably not what God had in mind when he invented rock 'n' roll. But clean sightlines and good acoustics (except below the balcony) make this a popular spot for under-age Valley girls and other music lovers.

Veterans Wadsworth Theater

Veterans Administration Grounds, Wilshire & San Vincente Boulevards, Westwood (1-310 825 2101/ Jazz at the Wadsworth 1-310 825 5706). Bus 20, 320, Santa Monica 2, 3/I-405, exit Wilshire Boulevard west. **Open & tickets** vary; call for schedule. **Credit** AmEx, MC, V.

Located on the Veteran Administration's grounds and run by UCLA, the 1,400-seater Wadsworth presents many of the university's performing arts series programmes, ranging from classical recitals to ethnic dance performances to world music shows as well as the occasional pop concert.

Wiltern Theater

Wiltern Center, 3790 Wilshire Boulevard, at Western Avenue, Mid Wilshire (1-213 380 5005/www.avalon concerts.com/wiltern.asp). Metro Wilshire-Western/ bus 20, 21, 22, 207, 357/I-10, exit Western Avenue north. **Open** *Box office* from 3hrs before show. **Tickets** vary. **Credit** MC, V. **Map** p307 C4.

An art deco gem renovated and energised more than a decade ago by the late rock impresario Bill Graham, the Wiltern draws a mostly older crowd for the likes of Travis, Elvis Costello and the occasional dance troupe or musical. The venue's comfortable seating and human scale are a draw. The surrounding neighbourhood is crummy, but interesting – it's bang in the middle of Koreatown.

Rock

Al's Bar

305 S Hewitt Street, at Traction Avenue, Downtown (1-213 625 9703/www.alsbar.net). Bus 16, DASH A, Montebello 40/I-10, exit Alameda Street east. **Open** 6pm-2am Mon-Thur, Sat, Sun; 3pm-2am Fri. *Shows* 9pm daily. **Tickets** $5; free Tue, Wed. **No credit cards**.

Al's has been a favourite of loft-living bohemians and low-living alcoholics for years. Some might find the deep Downtown location and heavy vibe a tad scary, but many of LA's more compelling rock

Funky Hollywood rock club **Dragonfly**.

bands (including the Bell Rays, the Excessories and the Streetwalkin' Cheetahs) can be found sweating up a storm on its spartan stage. First-time visitors should definitely go in the company of someone who's been there before; the haphazard street layout can make finding Al's almost impossible if you're unfamiliar with the area. And leave your suede shoes at home, lest the overflowing toilets make you wish you had.

Dragonfly

6510 Santa Monica Boulevard, at Wilcox Avenue, Hollywood (1-323 466 6111/www.dragonfly.com). Bus 4, 420/I-10, exit La Brea Avenue north. **Open** 9pm-2am daily. **Tickets** (21s & over only) $5-$15. **Credit** AmEx, MC, V. **Map** p307 A2.

A Hollywood rock emporium masquerading as a Middle Eastern harem, Dragonfly plays host to a wide array of local bands. It's currently best known as the home of the Pretty Ugly Club, a Wednesday-night gathering of hair-metal throwbacks, hosted by former Faster Pussycat leader Taime Down. The sound is excellent, although the grab-bag booking policy – and the club's tendency to spin bad Euro disco or New Age music between sets, regardless of who's on the bill – can make for a somewhat excruciating experience. Escape from the music – and for a smoke – to the back patio.

El Rey Theatre

5515 Wilshire Boulevard, between Burnside & Dunsmuir Avenues, Miracle Mile (1-323 936 6400). Bus 20, 21, 22, DASH Fairfax/I-10, exit La Brea Avenue north. **Open & tickets** vary; call for schedule. **No credit cards**. **Map** p306 C3.

A gorgeous art deco relic in the heart of the Miracle Mile, the El Rey plays host to everyone from local DJs to old favourites like Tom Tom Club and Rickie Lee Jones. The sound and sightlines in this old ballroom are excellent, and there's usually plenty of elbow room. The El Rey also hosts one of LA's most happening club nights – *see p240* **Club Makeup**.

Fais Do-Do

*5257 W Adams Boulevard, at Cloverdale Avenue,
Culver City (1-323 954 8080/www.faisdodo.com).
Bus 37/I-10, exit La Brea Avenue south.* **Open** 7pm-
midnight Mon-Wed, Sun; 7pm-2am Thur-Sat.
Tickets $5-$8. **Credit** MC, V.

Once mostly the province of blues and zydeco acts,
Fais Do-Do (Cajun dialect for 'dance party') has
recently been co-opted by the local mod and indie-
rock scenes. Aside from great sightlines, the club
offers an impressive array of beers and fairly decent
Southern-style cooking. The opulent interior (the
pre-World War II building used to house a bank) and
the desolate-but-safe location only add to the club's
exotic, out-of-time vibe.

14 Below

*1348 14th Street, at Santa Monica Boulevard, Santa
Monica (1-310 451 5040/www.14below.com). Bus 4/
I-10, exit 26th Street north.* **Open** 3pm-2am Mon-Fri;
4pm-2am Sat; 7pm-2am Sun. **Tickets** (21s & over
only) $12-$30. **Credit** MC, V. **Map** p304 B2.

Grateful Dead tribute bands, washed-up 1980s acts
like Dave Wakeling and Gene Loves Jezebel and

local pop groups like Baby Lemonade and the
Andersons are some of the acts to appear regularly
at this popular Westside nightspot. The long, narrow
room (and incompetent sound engineers) can occasionally render the stage volume unbearable, but
you can save your ears by watching the show on
video monitors from the adjacent billiard rooms.

The Garage

*4519 Santa Monica Boulevard, at Virgil Avenue,
Silver Lake (1-323 683 3447/662 6802). Bus 4, 26,
304/US 101, exit Santa Monica Boulevard east.*
Open 5pm-3am Mon-Sat; from 6am Sun. **Tickets**
(21s & over only) $3-$8. **No credit cards**.
Map p308 A3.

Anything goes at this funky Silver Lake hangout,
which books everything from heavily pomaded
rockabilly bands (featured as part of Thursday's
regular Whorehouse club) to sci-fi metal psychos
Rebel Rebel. The beer's cheap, the mixed straight
and gay crowd is always friendly and in the mood
to party. If the sound system were halfway decent,
this would be the best club in Los Angeles. It also
runs a popular after-after-hours club; *see p241.*

Goldfingers

*6423 Yucca Street, between Wilcox Avenue &
Cahuenga Boulevard, Hollywood (1-323 962 2913).
Metro Hollywood-Vine/bus 1, 180, 210, 212/US 101,
exit Sunset Boulevard west.* **Open** 9pm-2am daily.
Tickets (21s & over only) $5. **Credit** AmEx, Disc,
MC, V. **Map** p307 A1.

Formerly the appropriately monikered Hell's Gate,
this tiny Hollywood club has been transformed into
a swinging playpen worthy of James Bond and Dean
Martin. The miniscule stage mostly accommodates
hip cabaret acts and lounge combos.

The Knitting Factory

*7021 Hollywood Boulevard, at Sycamore Avenue,
Hollywood (1-323 463 0204/www.knittingfactory.
com/KFLA). Metro Hollywood-Highland/bus 180,
181, 212/US 101, exit Hollywood Boulevard west.*
Open *Box office* 11am-9pm daily; *Club* varies; call
for schedule. **Tickets** $8-$10. **Credit** AmEx, MC, V.
Map p307 A1.

This West Coast sister of the famed NYC club
opened in summer 2000 after a series of embarrass-
ing delays – but the general consensus seems to be
that it was worth the wait. Located beneath the
Galaxy movie theatres, the place offers a variety of
cutting-edge touring acts on both a main stage and
in a more intimate 'lounge room'. There are also
'web booths' for the Internet music junkie, and a
restaurant serving 'eclectic fusion food' (but of
course!). *See also p241.*

Largo

*432 N Fairfax Avenue, between Oakwood &
Rosewood Avenues, Fairfax District (1-213 852
1073). Bus 14, 217, DASH Fairfax/I-10, exit
Fairfax Avenue north.* **Open** from 8pm Mon-Sat;
closed Sun. **Tickets** $10-$20. **Credit** AmEx, MC, V.
Map p306 B2.

Top five Rock venues

Whisky A Go-Go

No musical expedition to Los Angeles
would be complete without a pilgrimage to
this old landmark on Sunset Strip. Its
history, excellent sightlines and clear and
powerful sound system still render it a cut
above the rest. See page 237.

The Troubadour

Another old warhorse, in West Hollywood,
with great sound, good bands and a
comfortable vibe. They don't make 'em
like this anymore, but they sure oughta.
See page 234.

The Garage

The audience at this Silver Lake institution
raises even more hell than the acts
onstage. Bring an open mind and a thirst
for cheap beer. See page 233.

Wiltern Theater

You can't argue with this kind of art deco
splendour, especially when the sound is
so good and the seats are so comfy.
See page 232.

The Roxy

There isn't a bad seat (or standing room) in
the house at this Sunset standby, and the
sound system puts most other clubs to
shame. See page 237.

Arts & Entertainment

Located almost directly across from Canter's deli, the Largo is an intimate pub specialising in fairly decent food (call first for table reservations, or risk having to stand by the toilets) and high-quality acoustic music. A sizeable cult has developed around musical jack-of-all-trades Jon Brion, so obtaining entry to his regular Friday-night shows can be difficult – ditto for Aimee Mann and Michael Penn's performances. Robyn Hitchcock and Glen Tilbrook have been known to sit in with Brion when they're in town.

LunaPark

665 N Robertson Boulevard, at Santa Monica Boulevard, West Hollywood (1-310 652 0611). Bus 4, 10, 220, West Hollywood A, B, N/I-10, exit Robertson Boulevard north. **Open** *Club* 6.30pm-2am daily. *Restaurant* 6.30-11pm Tue-Thur, Sun; 6.30pm-midnight Fri, Sat; closed Mon. **Tickets** (21s & over only) $7-$12. **Credit** AmEx, MC, V. **Map** p306 A2.

Impresario Jean-Pierre Bocarra has for the past several years presented a wide array of music (in addition to comedy and performance art) to a mixed crowd in this comfortable club. Enter through the restaurant and either go downstairs to the low-ceilinged cabaret or make your way to the main room in the back.

Silverlake Lounge

2906 Sunset Boulevard, at Parkman Avenue, Silver Lake (1-323 666 2407/www.loop.com/~fold/). Bus 2, 3/US 101, exit Silver Lake Boulevard north. **Open** *For music* 8pm-2am Tue-Thur. **Tickets** (21s & over only) $5-$8. **No credit cards. Map** p308 B4.

Once a down-at-heel watering hole with a heavy transvestite population, the Silverlake Lounge has recently stepped into the fray as a much-needed addition to Silver Lake's music scene. The sound pretty much sucks, and the tiny room can get unbearably crowded at times, but it's a good place to go if you want to hear what locals like Ferdinand or Eagle are up to.

Spaceland

1717 Silver Lake Boulevard, at Effie Street, Silver Lake (1-213 833 2843/661 4380/www.club spaceland.com). Bus 201/US 101, exit Silver Lake Boulevard north. **Open** from 9pm daily. **Tickets** $7-$8. **Credit** AmEx, MC, V. **Map** p308 C3.

Still the most important club of the much-hyped Silver Lake scene, Spaceland presents cutting-edge touring acts, as well as popular local acts such as the Negro Problem and WACO. Beck used to be a regular, but the constant media and industry buzz surrounding the club has driven him elsewhere. The sightlines have been drastically improved, but the sound still leaves much to be desired. Still, the bartenders are friendly and the vibe generally convivial.

Temple Bar

1026 Wilshire Boulevard, between Tenth & 11th Streets, Santa Monica (1-310 393 6611/www.temple bar.com). Bus 20, 21, 22/I-10, exit Lincoln Boulevard

north. **Open** 6pm-2am Mon-Sat; 7pm-2am Sun. **Tickets** $3-$10. **Credit** *Bar only* AmEx, MC, V. **Map** p304 B2.

A much-needed addition to the Westside music scene, this candlelit lounge books local performers that tend to specialise in laid-back brands of hip hop and funk, though a little bit of rock and pop occasionally slips in through the cracks.

The Troubadour

9081 Santa Monica Boulevard, at Doheny Drive, West Hollywood (1-310 276 6168/www.troubadour. com). Bus 4, DASH A, West Hollywood/I-405, exit Santa Monica Boulevard east. **Open** 1.30pm-2am Mon-Fri; 3pm-2am Sat, Sun. **Tickets** $5-$12. **Credit** AmEx, MC, V. **Map** p306 A2.

Elton John made his US debut at the Troub in 1970 during the club's salad days, when it nurtured the careers of neo-folkies Jackson Browne, Linda Ronstadt and Warren Zevon. Resurrected from the depths of metaldom, the venue (which looks a bit like an Alpine ski lodge) once again hosts acts of taste and substance. Along with the Whisky and the Roxy (for both, *see p236* **Sunset Strip**), it has one of the best sound systems in town.

Vynyl

1650 N Schrader Boulevard, between Hollywood Boulevard & Selma Avenue, Hollywood (1-323 465 7449/recorded information 1-323 461 5889/ www.vynyl.com). Metro Hollywood-Vine/bus 1, 160, 180/US 101, exit Hollywood Boulevard west. **Open** 8pm-2am daily. **Tickets** free-$10. **Credit** *Bar only* AmEx, Disc, MC, V. **Map** p307 A1.

Formerly known as Moguls, Vynyl has been through several incarnations in the past decade – coffeehouse, independent film screening room and now a comfortable, spacious music venue. Bookings can be a mixed bag, depending on who's doing the promoting, so be sure to call in advance. Note that all shows have to end at midnight because of local zoning and curfew restrictions, which means that the music usually starts as early as 8pm. It's also a popular dance club; *see p243.*

Roots & blues

Country, folk and the music of Ireland can be heard at **Molly Malone's Irish Pub** (*see page 170*). Swing mecca the **Derby** in Los Feliz (*see page 241*), which has become almost unbearably hip in the wake of its appearance in the movie *Swingers*, offers regular swing lessons for beginners.

Babe & Ricky's Inn

4339 Leimert Boulevard, at 43rd Street, Leimert Park (1-323 295 9112). Bus 40, 105, 210, 310, DASH Crenshaw/I-10, exit Crenshaw Boulevard south. **Open** 10am-2am daily. **Tickets** (21s & over only) $4-$8. **Credit** AmEx, MC, V.

One of the oldest blues joints in LA, Babe & Ricky's may also be the only local blues club to actually reside in a predominantly black neighbourhood.

New to LA: the **Knitting Factory**. *See p233.*

The atmosphere is extremely friendly, the local blues acts more than respectable (don't miss the house band, Balls of Fire), and Mama Laura's fried chicken alone is worth the trip.

BB King's Blues Club

Universal CityWalk, 1000 Universal Center Drive, Universal City (1-818 622 5464). Metro Universal City/bus 420/US 101, exit Universal Center Drive. **Open** 5pm-1am Mon-Thur, Sun; 5pm-2am Fri, Sat. **Tickets** (21s & over only) $10-$15. **Credit** AmEx, DC, Disc, MC, V.
Local guitar slingers and the odd national R&B name ply their trade at the Los Angeles branch of blues master King's Memphis supper club. This is the most down-to-earth joint on Universal City's hideously commercial and plastic CityWalk.

The Conga Room

5364 Wilshire Boulevard, between Cloverdale Avenue & Detroit Street, Miracle Mile (1-213 938 1696/box office 1-323 549 9765/www.congaroom.com). Bus 20, 21, 22, 212/I-10, exit La Brea Avenue north. **Open** *Box office* 10am-6pm Tue-Sat. *Club* 6.30pm-1.30am Tue-Thur; 6pm-2am Fri, Sat. Closed Mon, Sun. **Tickets** (21s & over only) $12-$40. **Credit** AmEx, DC, Disc, MC, V. **Map** p307 A4.
Opened in 1998, this stylish, atmospheric club has been an extremely positive addition, both to LA's music scene and an otherwise drab part of Miracle Mile. Consistently booking some of the hemisphere's top Latin and Afro-Cuban acts, the Conga Room also offers dance lessons and some very fine 'nuevo latino' cuisine. It ain't cheap (drinks run in the $8 range, and tickets can cost three to four times as much), but if you've got a little salsa in your soul, make sure you put this place on your itinerary. *See also p240.*

Harvelle's

1432 Fourth Street, between Broadway & Santa Monica Boulevard, Santa Monica (1-310 395 1676). Bus 4, 304, Santa Monica 1, 2, 3, 7, 8/I-10, exit Fourth-Fifth Street north. **Open** 8pm-2am daily. **Tickets** (21s & over only) $3-$8; 2-drink minimum. **No credit cards. Map** p304 A2.
Santa Monica's self-styled 'home of the blues' is smokin' seven nights a week in a comfortable bar/lounge setting. The place is packed at weekends, so show up early to avoid any hassles.

McCabe's

3101 Pico Boulevard, at 31st Street, Santa Monica (1-310 828 4497/4403/www.mccabes guitar.com). Bus Santa Monica 7/I-10, exit Centinela Avenue south. **Open** 10am-10pm Mon-Thur; 10am-6pm Fri, Sat; 1-5pm Sun. **Tickets** $10-$20. **Credit** AmEx, DC, Disc, MC, V. **Map** p304 C3.
By day a guitar shop, by night (usually at the weekend – call first to check) McCabe's intimate (and draughty) back room is renowned for acoustic pickin' and singin' by country-folk-rock types such as Rosanne Cash and Jorma Kaukonen. No alcohol is served, but coffee and cookies are available.

The Mint

6010 W Pico Boulevard, at Crescent Heights Boulevard, Midtown (1-323 954 9630/www.themint hollywood.com). Bus Santa Monica 5, 7/I-10, exit La Cienega Boulevard north. **Open** (21s & over only) 8pm-2am daily. **Tickets** $5-$15. **Credit** AmEx, MC, V. **Map** p306 B4.
Reopened a couple of years ago with an enlarged capacity, the Mint's line-up of blues, jazz and roots satisfies those looking for good, honest, downhome jams. The food's pretty good, too.

Jazz

The Baked Potato

3787 N Cahuenga Boulevard, at Lankershim Boulevard, North Hollywood (1-818 980 1615/ www.thebakedpotato.com). Bus 96, 152, 420, 424,

Arts & Entertainment

Sunset Strip

If the LA music scene has a heart, it would have to be located on that West Hollywood stretch of Sunset Boulevard bordered by Doheny Drive to the west and Crescent Heights Boulevard to the east, better known colloquially as the 'Sunset Strip'. Then, as now, a glittering row of nightclubs, restaurants and pricey shops, the Strip got its nickname in the 1960s, when it became a magnet for Southern California teens. Acts ranging in hipness from the Byrds and Buffalo Springfield to Johnny Rivers and Trini Lopez performed at nightclubs such as Ciro's and the Whisky A Go-Go, but mostly, the Strip's teen contingent just came from the surrounding suburbs to hang out and meet other kids. Their presence didn't sit too well with the local shop owners, and in 1966 the police were called in to clear the sidewalks of the youthful loiterers. The ensuing confrontations (which also sprung from a protest over the closing of the popular club Pandora's Box) passed into legend as 'the riot on Sunset Strip', and briefly put an end to the area's reputation as a teen mecca.

The Sunset Strip nickname still sticks today, even though the past few decades have borne witness to several phases and incarnations, not all of them pretty. Briefly popular with the decadent glam-rock crowd in the early 1970s – when the Whisky and Rodney Bingenheimer's English Disco were *the* places to party – the Strip experienced something of a renaissance in the mid-1980s, when the local heavy metal scene began churning out such nationally known

acts as Ratt, Poison and Guns N Roses. The rise of grunge in the early 1990s sent most of the metal bands packing, but the onerous 'pay-to-play' policies of Sunset Strip club bookers have proved remarkably resilient. Though it certainly exhibits far less character than it once did, the Strip is still hopping; on a good night, the following clubs still provide a hint of that old Strip magic.

Coconut Teaszer

8117 Sunset Boulevard, at Crescent Heights Boulevard (1-323 654 4773). Bus 2, 3, 429/I-10, exit La Cienega Boulevard north. **Open** 6.30pm-2am daily. **Tickets** (18s & over only) Wed-Sun; (21s & over only) Mon-Tue; $10. **Credit** AmEx, MC, V. **Map** p306 B1.
Many bands that play the Teaszer would probably kill their own grandmothers for a record deal, which gives the place an air of desperation to accompany its painful decibel levels. Downstairs, the Crooked Bar showcases mostly talented unknowns playing acoustic sets.

425/US 101 north, exit Lankershim Boulevard south. **Open** 7pm-2am daily. *Shows* 9.30pm, 11.30pm daily. **Tickets** $10; 2-drink minimum. **Credit** AmEx, Disc, MC, V.
Musician and owner Don Randi's pint-sized room spawned the LA jazz fusion sound in the 1970s and is still the site of many a synth-driven romp, though local Latin jazz acts occasionally appear. Don't miss the menu full of – you got it – spuds.
Branch: 6266 Hollywood Boulevard, between Argyle Avenue & Vine Street, Hollywood (1-323 461 6400).

Catalina Bar & Grill

1640 N Cahuenga Boulevard, at Hollywood Boulevard, Hollywood (1-323 466 2210). Metro Hollywood-Vine/bus 1, 163, 180, 181, 212/ US 101, exit Cahuenga Boulevard south. **Open** 7pm-1am daily. *Shows* 8.30pm, 10.30pm daily.

Tickets $10-$20. **Credit** AmEx, Disc, MC, V. **Map** p307 B2.
Catalina Popescu consistently pulls jazz's heaviest hitters into her highly civilised, peach-shaded establishment. With the venue's bent toward be-bop, a residence here is de rigueur for old-guard names such as McCoy Tyner and Pharoah Sanders, as well as the new crop of jazz men typified by Branford Marsalis and Joshua Redman. Leave the cooking to the players, though: dining here isn't recommended.

Fifth Street Dick's Coffee Company

3347½ W 43rd Place, at Degnan Boulevard, Leimert Park (1-323 296 3970). Bus 40, 105, 210, 310, DASH Crenshaw/I-10, exit Crenshaw Boulevard south. **Open** 4pm-2am Mon-Thur; 4pm-5am Fri; 1pm-5am Sat; 1pm-2am Sun. *Shows* 9pm Mon-Thur; 9pm, 1am Fri, Sat; 5.30pm Sun. **Tickets** free-$5. **No credit cards.**

House of Blues
8430 Sunset Boulevard, at Olive Drive
(concert hotline 1-323 650 1451/box office
1-323 848 5100/www.hob.com). Bus 2, 3,
429/I-10, exit La Cienega Boulevard north.
Open Box office 10.30am-midnight daily.
Shows 8pm or 9pm daily. **Tickets** (usually
21s & over only) $10-$32. **Credit** AmEx, DC,
Disc, MC, V. **Map** p304 B1.
While most blues aficionados probably cringe
at the very sight of this club's faux-shack
exterior, it must be said that the HOB bookers
do a great job of mixing nationally known
blues, rap, country and rock acts. The poor
sightlines, cramped standing room, parking
problems and surly staff may give you your
own blues, but the food is excellent, and
the sound is pretty good if you don't stand
under the balcony.

Key Club
9039 Sunset Boulevard, at Doheny Drive
(1-310 274 5800/www.thekeyclub.net). Bus
2, 3, 429/ I-10, exit La Cienega Boulevard
north. **Open** Box office 10am-1am daily. Club
7pm-2am Wed, Fri, Sun. **Tickets** (usually 21s
& over only) $10-$22.50. **Credit** AmEx, MC,
V. **Map** p304 A1.
Formerly known as Billboard Live, this high-
tech, multi-level club (built on the foundations
of legendary metal stronghold Gazzari's) has
been only moderately successful in its
attempts to compete with the House of
Blues; if anything, the slick, 'futuristic' decor
is even nastier than the HOB's attempted
crossroads vibe.

The Roxy
9009 Sunset Boulevard, between San
Vincente Boulevard & Doheny Drive (1-310

276 2222/ www.theroxytheatre.com). Bus 2,
3, 429/I-10, exit La Cienega Boulevard north.
Open from 8pm daily. **Tickets** $10-$15.
Credit AmEx, DC, Disc, MC, V. **Map** p304 A1.
One of the Strip's few survivors from the
1970s, the Roxy has a history of career-
making performances by top names such
as Bob Marley, Neil Young and Bruce
Springsteen. Nowadays, most shows of note
are nouveau-punk and alternative bands
booked by promoter Goldenvoice. Unless
you're industry-connected, get there early to
snag a table or you'll be standing all night.
Still, the sound system is excellent and the
sightlines unencumbered.

Whisky A Go-Go
8901 Sunset Boulevard, at Clark Street
(recorded information 1-310 535 0579/office
1-310 652 4202/www.whiskyagogo.com).
Bus 2, 3, 429/I-10, exit La Cienega
Boulevard north. **Open** 8pm-2am daily. Shows
8.05pm daily. **Tickets** $10-$15. **Credit** AmEx,
DC, Disc, V. **Map** p304 A1.
Perhaps LA's most famous music venue,
the Whisky is still crazy after all these
years. The Doors were at one time the
house band – until the owner objected to
the lyrics of The End and banned the group
– and virtually all the significant pop acts of
the past three decades have played this
landmark club at one time or another. While
nationally known talent appears regularly,
most of the venue's fare is promising young
bands, many of whom can be heard for free
on Monday nights. For a true time-travel
experience, see if you can catch a Whisky
performance by Doors tribute band Wild
Child. Open to 18s and above.

The fate of this Leimert Park landmark was recently
in doubt, due to the death of much-loved proprietor
Richard Fulton, but traditional jazz workouts are
once again lasting into the wee hours in its upstairs
loft. Some of the city's most skilled practitioners
(including Dale Fielder and Ron Muldrow) hone their
chops here, usually for free. Dick's Sock-It-To-Me
cake alone is unmissable. Fifth Street Dick's is also
famous for the chess games that take place outside.

Jazz Bakery
3233 Helms Avenue, at Venice Boulevard, Culver
City (1-310 271 9039/www.jazzwest.com/jazz
bakery). Bus 33, 436, Culver City 1, 4/I-10, exit
La Cienega Boulevard south. **Open** Box office 1hr
before show. Shows 8.30pm Mon-Fri; 4pm, 8.30pm
Sat, Sun. **Tickets** $15-$35. **Credit** AmEx, MC, V.
You'll find mostly jazz of the straight-ahead variety
from members of the pantheon, such as Ahmad

Jamal and Dave Grusin. And the atmosphere is more
than slightly stuffy; this Culver City venue is for
serious jazz aficionados only.

The World Stage
4344 Degnan Boulevard, between 43rd Street &
43rd Place, Leimert Park (1-323 293 2451). Bus 42,
105, 305, DASH Crenshaw/I-10, exit Crenshaw
Boulevard north. **Open** varies; call for schedule.
Tickets $7-$10. **No credit cards**.
Strictly for the hardcore jazz fan (or player), this
space – founded by drummer Billy Higgins, who
conducts a drum workshop every Monday – is
where local cats come to blow, make connections
and hone their chops. No food, no booze, no dancefloor, just amazing sounds to spare. Big names occasionally sit in, but the young unknowns who
frequent the stage will usually knock you on your
ass by themselves.

Nightlife

At last, LA's dance scene has come of age and joined the international DJ circuit, while the city still retains its title as Comedy Central.

It's salsa night at **El Floridita**. *See p239.*

Dance clubs

Unlike New Yorkers, Angelenos once started the club circuit early and were home by 2.30am. That's all changed in the past few years as the world of dance music has gained a mainstream hold on Los Angeles. There are now clubs that stay open until 4am, after-hours clubs that open until 8am and even after-after-hours clubs that don't open until 9am and go on to the afternoon. The club scene is a happy, vibrant one, and people of different ethnic groups and sexual preferences mix easily.

LA is definitely a major date on all international DJs' tours. This is because several club promoters in other cities have set up shop here. Most notable among them is Dave Dean. Dean's club in Hollywood, Giant (*see page 240* **Big is beautiful**), has single-handedly spread to the masses the beats of such notables as Paul Oakenfold, Sasha and Digweed, Paul Van Dyk, Carl Cox and other mega-DJs of the house and trance worlds. Other DJs, such as DJ Carbo at the Viper Room (*see page 242*), have been plugging away for years and are still at the

forefront of LA's dance culture. But the reason Giant has been so successful is because the club is, well… so giant. The Viper Room holds several hundred, Giant several thousand.

Some clubs operate daily, others only once a month, and venues change regularly. Check out the *LA Weekly* for the latest on the club scene, and definitely visit electronic dance music shop Beat Non Stop (7262 Melrose Avenue, at Poinsettia Place, Hollywood, 1-323 930 2121). Also look for flyers at concert venues and available at some clothing stores on Melrose.

Los Angeles is also the capital of West Coast hip hop; pick up local fanzines *Ill Literature*, *Kronick* and *URB* for information on the scene. Good clubs are Boytrade on Fridays at El Rey Theatre (*see page 240* **Club Makeup**) and Chocolate Bar (call 1-323 860 8873 for location and time). For rap, try Valhalla at Opium Den (1605 North Ivar Avenue, at Selma Avenue, 1-323 466 7800). Also, pop into record store Fat Beats (*see page 180*) or tune in to Power 106 (KPWR, 105.9 FM) to hear the latest updates on shows.

Swing dancing, which became popular in LA in the 1930s, has also enjoyed a recent revival, and many Angelenos like to dress in 1950s-style clothes and go out each weekend to jive. The Derby (*see page 241*) is still the king of swing, but plenty of others have taken up the flag. Salsa dancing is a big craze, particularly at the tiny El Floridita in Hollywood (1253 North Vine Street, at Lexington Avenue, 1-323 871 8612) and the upmarket and celeb-filled Conga Room (*see page 240*). Many bars – such as Beauty Bar in Hollywood (1638 North Cahuenga Boulevard, at Hollywood Boulevard, 1-323 464 7676) and Lava Lounge (*see page 170*) – have their own DJs, even if they don't have a dancefloor.

Summer is the time for the big raves. Locations and times change often, so it is essential to pick up a local paper or flip through flyers. A couple – such as Coachella (1-213 480 3232/www.coachella.com) and Nocturnal Wonderland (1-323 871 8522/www. nocturnalwonderland.com) – are annual and held at the same location (Empire Polo Field, Indio, near Palm Springs), though dates vary. Also keep an eye out for promoters Ritual Events (www.ritual events.com), Moonshine (www.moonshine.com) and Insomniac (www.insomniacevents.com): they always put on a great event.

For clubs aimed specifically at gays and lesbians, *see chapter* **Gay & Lesbian**.

Top five — Dance clubs

Club Makeup
The best glitter and glam club in town. Shake your glitzy bon-bons all night. See page 240.

Giant
The best rave club with international DJs. Trance, house and techno until 4am. See page 240 **Big is beautiful**.

Knitting Factory
The best club to surf music sites while watching the fabulous avant-garde. See page 241.

Sugar
Best see-thru plastic bathrooms and shark tank. Check your inhibitions at the door. See page 242.

The Viper Room
The most famous club in Tinseltown is still cutting edge. Check out Tuesday night's Atmosphere. See page 242.

PRACTICAL INFORMATION
Transport is the biggest problem for Los Angeles clubgoers. You will need to either take a friend who promises to remain sober or be prepared to pay the exorbitant cab fares (forget using public transport). Cabs are also hard to find, and you can't just flag one down on the street, so don't leave your hotel without the number of a taxi company in your pocket. Some of the more upscale clubs operate a velvet rope policy. This basically means that the better you look, the more likely you will be to get in. Being female helps.

You have to be 21 or over to drink in California. Do not leave home without photo ID; all clubs 'card' people at the door. Once inside, you'll be given a wristband or a hand stamp, which will allow you to get served at the bar. There are a few clubs that admit people aged 18, and we've indicated them below. Very few clubs accept credit cards at the door, though they will at the bar. Admission usually costs from $5 to $15, but you can sometimes buy tickets in advance from a particular club's website or from Ticketmaster (1-213 480 3232/ www.ticketmaster.com).

Arena
6655 Santa Monica Boulevard, at Las Palmas Avenue, Hollywood (1-323 462 0714). Bus 4, 420/ US 101, exit Santa Monica Boulevard west. **Open** *Club* 9pm-2am Thur, Sun; 9pm-4am Fri, Sat. **Admission** Thur, Sat (18s & over) $10; Fri (all ages) $10. **No credit cards. Map** p307 A2.
At 22,000sq ft (2,050sq m), there's room for all your friends at Arena. Thursday and Friday are the prime nights here. Circus on Thursday nights attracts a mainly Asian crowd with techno, trance, jungle and drum 'n' bass; Friday attracts a mixed, all-ages crowd with deep house and old school beats. On Saturdays, the clubbers are gay and primarily Latino. The sound system BOOMS – but there is a patio where you can rest your eardrums, if not your body.

Blue
1642 N Las Palmas Avenue, between Hollywood Boulevard & Selma Avenue, Hollywood (1-323 468 3863/club information 1-323 462 7442). Metro Hollywood-Highland/bus 26, 163, 180, 181, DASH Hollywood/US 101, exit Hollywood Boulevard west. **Open** *Club* 10pm-2am Mon; 10pm-3am Wed; 10pm-6am Thur-Sat. **Admission** (18s & over) $5 Mon; $10 Wed-Sat. **Credit** *Bar & restaurant only* AmEx, MC, V. **Map** p307 A1.
With its outdoor smoking patio, floor-to-ceiling bar, two DJ rooms, ample space to sit and hang out, and prime location – slap bang in the middle of Hollywood – Blue has become a very popular venue. Monday nights are gothic, Wednesday is '80s night, Friday is techno and alternative club Stigmata is held on Saturdays.

Big is beautiful

Walk through the massive iron gate and up the red carpet, stop at the luminescent, oversized tent entrance and listen, because your ears are about to be assaulted with seamless mixes and global grooves from some of the world's best DJs. You are about to enter Giant, the mammoth Hollywood club that has single-handedly changed the face of the LA dance scene.

Promoter Dave Dean's mission was to 'align Los Angeles with other capitals of dance music, such as London, New York and Ibiza' – and he's certainly succeeded. Giant, which launched in January 2000 and is open only on Saturdays, is infamous for its long lines and for reaching capacity around 11pm. It also attracts a really varied crowd, something that's been lacking in the City of Angels. You'll see ravers mix with hipsters, industry types with club kids, straight with gay, drag queens with muscle men; it's a communal experience and it's all about the dancefloor. And what a dancefloor.

The main dance area has an elevated island stage where DJs, from international stars like Sasha, John Digweed, Paul Oakenfold and Paul Van Dyk to home-grown talent such as Jason Bentley and Sandra Collins, strutt their stuff, prominently reflected in the mirrors all around. When the body temperature gets too much, you can go up to the Loft or to the disco room, or outside to the huge patio watched over by a 100ft (30m) high balloon clown that nods and waves crazily to the beat.

With clubs in San Francisco and Las Vegas, Dean is spreading the Giant gospel and has plans for a massive New Year's party and various annual dance events around the US. And now, superstar DJ John Digweed has chosen LA for his next Global Underground album – a critically acclaimed series that spotlights the world's most happening dance scene cities. Proof positive that Dave Dean has created a renaissance in LA's clubbing world.

Giant

6655 Santa Monica Boulevard, at Las Palmas Avenue, Hollywood (1-323 464 7373/ www.giant club.com). Bus 4, 420/US 101, exit Santa Monica Boulevard west. **Open** *Club 9pm-4am Sat.* **Admission** *$15.* **No credit cards. Map** 307 A2.

Club Makeup

El Rey Theatre, 5515 Wilshire Boulevard, between Burnside & Dunsmuir Avenues, Miracle Mile (1-323 936 4790/769 5500/www.clubmakeup.net). Bus 20, 21, 22, DASH Fairfax/I-10, exit La Brea Avenue north. **Open** *Club 9pm-2am 1st Sat of the mth.* **Admission** $15. **No credit cards. Map** p306 C3.
The first Saturday of the month is host to Club Makeup, one of the most happening clubs in LA. It's flamboyant, daring and full of glitter and glam. The club also has a high celeb-factor, so get there early – the queues are l-o-n-g.

Conga Room

5364 Wilshire Boulevard, between Cloverdale Avenue & Detroit Street, Miracle Mile (1-323 938 1696/box office 1-323 549 9765/www.congaroom.com). Bus 20, 21, 22, 212/I-10, exit La Brea Avenue north. **Open** *Box office 10am-6pm Tue-Sat. Club 6.30pm-1.30am Tue-Thur; 6pm-2am Fri, Sat. Shows usually 10pm; days vary. Closed Mon, Sun.* **Admission** $12-$40. **Credit** AmEx, DC, Disc, MC, V. **Map** p306 C3.
Owned by Jimmy Smits and Jennifer Lopez, among others, this upscale club (and adjoining restaurants La Boca and El Comedor) has a high profile and is regularly visited by Latino celebrities. The crowd is always dressed up, even by Los Angeles standards, and there's plenty of salsa dancing to be had, with salsa classes held at 8pm on Thursdays. The Conga Room is also a popular and successful live music venue, often featuring top Latin and Afro-Cuban acts – *see p235*.

Coven 13

Information www.clubcoven13.net.
This is LA's premier goth club, and one of its longest running, which means honest-to-gosh vampires, dominatrixes in latex and the dedicated undead in black Victorian dress, clinging corsets and funeral veils. At time of writing, the club moves location frequently while it looks for a permanent home, so visit the website for the latest news.

Crush Bar

1743 N Cahuenga Boulevard, at Hollywood Boulevard, Hollywood (1-323 461 9017/www.crush bar.com). Metro Hollywood-Vine/bus 163, 180, 181, 212/US 101, exit Cahuenga Boulevard south. **Open** *Club 9pm-7.30am Fri, Sat.* **Admission** $10. **No credit cards. Map** p307 B1.

The premises aren't that attractive, but the Crush Bar scored in 2000 when it opened up after-hours clubs (from 2.30am) on Friday (Xtra Strength, 1-213 891 2775) and Saturday nights (Kaos, 1-213 891 2775). With plenty of seating, lots of clubbers from Giant and Blue move on to Crush to see the evening through to dawn. The rest of the time, it presents vintage Motown and soul.

The Derby

4500 Los Feliz Boulevard, at Hillhurst Avenue, Los Feliz (1-323 663 8979). Bus 180, 181/US 101, exit Sunset Boulevard east. **Admission** $5 Mon, Tue, Thur, Sun; $7 Wed, Fri, Sat. **Credit** *Bar only* AmEx, MC, V. **Map** p308 A1.

In a city smitten with swing dancing, sharp-dressed youth in the know can count on the Derby for floor-filling live music most nights of the week. Novices are welcome, and can join in a free swing lesson (8-9pm every night). Modern swing acts such as Royal Crown Revue and Big Bad Voodoo Daddy have played here. The Derby's circular bar in the middle of the ballroom with its 30ft (9m) high domed ceiling is the spot to be if you just want to watch. Dress nice or be sent packing.

Florentine Gardens

5951 Hollywood Boulevard, between Bronson Avenue & N Gower Street, Hollywood (1-323 464 0706). Metro Hollywood-Vine/bus 1, 180, 181, 217, 429/ US 101, exit Hollywood Boulevard west. **Open** *Club* 9pm-2am Thur-Sun. **Admission** (18s & over Thur-Sat; 21s & over Sun) $15 Thur; $12 Fri, Sat; free before 11pm, $8 after 11pm Sun. **Credit** *Bar only* AmEx, MC, V. **Map** p307 B1.

Where many hardened clubbers got their start, this cavernous danceteria is consistently packed with stylish kids (many of them Latino), who welcome the mix of funk, hip hop, disco and techno. Expect to queue to get in, and dress to impress to make sure that you do.

The Garage

4519 Santa Monica Boulevard, at Virgil Avenue, Silver Lake (1-323 683 3447/662 6802). Bus 4, 26, 304/US 101, exit Santa Monica Boulevard east. **Open** 5pm-3am Mon-Sat; from 6am Sun. **Admission** $3-$8. **No credit cards**. **Map** p308 A3.

The Garage, which was emblazoned with hell-spawned firepaint until complaining neighbours got it painted black, hosts a ton of hardcore punk acts. On Sunday mornings from 6am, it presents Last Man Standing, an after-after-hours club where Saturday-night clubsters can party right into Sunday afternoon. *See also p233.*

Goldfingers

6423 Yucca Street, between Wilcox Avenue & N Cahuenga Boulevard, Hollywood (1-323 962 2913). Metro Hollywood-Vine/bus 1, 180, 210, 212/US 101, exit Hollywood Boulevard west. **Open** 9pm-2am daily. **Admission** $5. **Credit** AmEx, Disc, MC, V. **Map** p307 A1.

With its velvet walls and go-go dancers, Goldfingers plays host to the popular Cadillac Club on Thursday nights. Expect classic rock 'n' roll with a multitude of bands performing and a good crowd dancing inside and smoking outside on the patio. This area of Hollywood has been cleaned up in the past couple of years; still, it makes sense to keep your wits about you. *See also p233.*

The Knitting Factory

7021 Hollywood Boulevard, at Sycamore Avenue, Hollywood (1-323 463 0204/www.knittingfactory. com/KFLA). Metro Hollywood-Highland/bus 180, 181, 212/US 101, exit Hollywood Boulevard west. **Open** 9pm-2am daily. **Admission** (18s & over) $8-$10. **Credit** AmEx, MC, V. **Map** p307 A1.

LA's newest club (it opened in summer 2000) comes straight from the Big Apple. Located in the Galaxy movie theatre building, it has a main stage for head-liners and a lounge area for more avant-garde performances. There's also an audio and video

Join the after-hours crush at the **Crush Bar**. *See p240.*

The Knitting Factory:
LA's newest club. *See p241.*

recording studio, and 'web booths' that allow patrons to surf music sites and check out its sister club in New York via a live link. *See also p233.*

The Palace

1735 N Vine Street, at Hollywood Boulevard, Hollywood (1-323 462 3000/www.hollywoodpalace. com). Metro Hollywood-Vine/bus 180, 181, 210, DASH Hollywood/US 101, exit Hollywood Boulevard west. **Open** *Club* 9pm-3am Fri, Sat. **Admission** (18s & over) $12 Fri; $15 Sat. **No credit cards.** **Map** p307 B1.

Located across the street from the landmark Capitol Records building, this cavernous blue edifice can – and does – hold a couple of thousand youngsters from all over the metropolitan area, who file in as the rock crowd leaves a gig. With a 20,000-watt (translation: really loud) sound system at full power and a laser show, the Palace is anything but intimate. An upstairs balcony provides a refuge for smoking and the odd grope. Music is provided by radio station DJs, so the fare is predictably commercial club cuts, new-wave classics and alternative floor-fillers. The rest of the week, the Palace hosts rock concerts – *see p231.*

Rudolfo's

2500 Riverside Drive, at Fletcher Drive, Silver Lake (1-323 669 1226/Dragstrip 66 1-323 969 2596/ www.dragstrip66.com). Bus 93, 96, 201, 603/US 101, exit Silver Lake Boulevard east. **Open** *Club* 9pm-2am Sat, Sun; *Dragstrip 66* 9pm-4am 2nd Sat of the mth.* **Admission** $10; $15 Dragstrip 66. **No credit cards.** **Map** p308 C2.

Featuring live bands and DJs, a large patio and blasting sound system, this Silver Lake Mexican restaurant plays host to various clubs, but it earns its true notoriety when Dragstrip 66 goes off once a month, when a gender-bending, glamour-loving crowd dances through themed nights such as 'Jesus, Mary – You're a Superstar'.

Sugar

814 Broadway, between Ninth Street & Lincoln Boulevard, Santa Monica (1-310 899 1989/ www.clubsugar.com). Bus 20, 21, 22, Santa Monica 3/I-10, exit Lincoln Boulevard north. **Open** *Club* 10pm-2am Thur-Sat. **Admission** $10. **Credit** *Bar only* AmEx, MC, V. **Map** p304 B2.

Sugar is like a grown-up's Disneyland, with an industrial-cum-whimsical feel. The restrooms are glass-encased (though there are stalls for privacy) and there is a cut-out between the men's and the ladies', just in case you can't bear to be parted from your other half. Elsewhere, a huge shark tank stretches across part of the club. The music is mixed; call for information.

The Viper Room

8852 Sunset Boulevard, at Larrabee Street, West Hollywood (1-310 358 1880/www.viperroom.com). Bus 2, 3, 105, 302, 429, DASH B/I-10, exit La Cienega Boulevard north. **Open** 9pm-2am daily. **Admission** $10-$15. **Credit** AmEx, MC, V. **Map** p306 A1.

Formerly dubbed Bugsy's after its previous owner, mobster Bugsy Siegel, and then owned by Johnny Depp (who sold the club but allows his name to be attached to it), the Viper Room will always be most famous for being the site of River Phoenix's death. It's an uninviting, low-ceilinged sweatbox that specialises in funk and disco favourites, while packing in Valley Girls and the guys who love them. Tuesday night is DJ Carbo's Atmosphere, a drum 'n' bass club that regularly grants guest slots to some great DJs. If you can deal with the collagen-enhanced crowd, this can be a wonderfully intimate spot to witness jam sessions by big-name artists.

Vynyl

1650 Schrader Boulevard, between Hollywood Boulevard & Selma Avenue, Hollywood (1-323 465 7449/recorded information 1-323 461 5889/ www.vynyl.com). Metro Hollywood-Highland or Hollywood-Vine/bus 1, 160, 180/US 101, exit Hollywood Boulevard west. **Open** 8pm-2am daily. **Admission** free-$15. **Credit** *Bar only* AmEx, Disc, MC, V. **Map** p307 A1.

Head back into the 1970s with this club, which opened in September 1999. The decor includes beautiful wallpaper and gold couches covered in clear plastic, and, weirdly, some of the floor is carpeted. But the sound system is phenomenal and the club has attracted some really big-name performers, such as Alanis Morrisette and Stone Temple Pilots. DJs peform at Spun on Saturday nights. *See also p234.*

The West End

1301 Fifth Street, at Arizona Avenue, Santa Monica (1-310 394 4647/club information 1-310 313 3293/ www.westendclubs.com). Bus 4, 304, Santa Monica 1, 2, 3, 8/I-10, exit Fifth Street north. **Open** 9pm-2am Tue-Fri, Sun; 4pm-2am Sat; closed Mon. **Admission** $10; $7 before 11pm Wed. **No credit cards. Map** p304 A2.

If you've spent the day on the Westside at the beach, and brought a change of clothes, this nearby club is a worthwhile bet. Rotating themed nights include reggae (Wed), R&B (Thur) and disco (Fri). Saturdays start at 4pm, when you can relive the 1980s all the way till 2am.

Comedy clubs

There are plenty of places to exercise your funny bone in Los Angeles. From improv comedy jams to talk shows, from spoof game shows to stand-up, the City of Angels has historically proven to be the place where comedic megastars are made. You'll find young comics hoping to be seen by a TV talent scout or you may be lucky to witness some unscheduled celebrity drop-ins. It's common practice for Hollywood's brightest stars, such as Jay Leno and Jerry Seinfeld, to try out gags on a more intimate club audience before going national with the new material. TV comedy writers also use this forum for sitcom ideas (and you can also join an audience for the taping of a TV sitcom – *see page 217*).

LunaPark in West Hollywood (*see page 234*) features alternative comedy regularly, as well as live music. Check the comedy section of the *LA Weekly* for up-to-date listings. Some clubs have age restrictions, so call first.

Acme Comedy Theater

135 N La Brea Avenue, between Beverly Boulevard & First Street, Hollywood (1-323 525 0202/ www.acmecomedy.com). Bus 14, 212/I-10, exit La Brea Avenue north. **Open** Box office from ½hr before show Wed, Fri-Sun. *Shows* 8pm Wed; 8.30pm, 10pm Fri; 8pm, 10.30pm Sat; 7.30pm Sun. Closed Mon, Tue, Thur. **Admission** $10-$15. **Credit** AmEx, MC, V. **Map** p306 C2/3.

Right next door to a good restaurant for easy pre-show dinners, Acme is a 99-seater with great sight-lines, comfy chairs and air-con. It also boasts alumni from Fox network's *Mad TV*. The skits run the gamut from current events to bathroom humour.

Comedy & Magic Club

1018 Hermosa Avenue, between 10th Street & Pier Avenue, Hermosa Beach (1-310 372 1193/www. comedyandmagicclub.com), exit Rosecrans Boulevard west. **Open** 12.30-9.30pm Tue-Sun. *Shows* 8pm Tue-Fri; 7.30pm, 10pm Sat; 7pm Sun. Closed Mon. **Admission** $10-$15; 2-drink minimum. **Credit** MC, V.

This club is classic vaudeville, with red velvet curtains and an intimate atmosphere. It has also hosted some of the finest comedians in the world. Jay Leno still cruises up on his Harley for Sunday-night gigs and Jerry Seinfeld has dropped by to try out new material. No shorts, tank tops, torn jeans or thongs. Reservations required.

The Comedy Store

8433 Sunset Boulevard, at La Cienega Boulevard, West Hollywood (1-323 656 6225/www.thecomedy store.com). Bus 2, 3, 429/I-10, exit La Cienega Boulevard north. **Open** 7.30pm-2am daily. *Shows* times vary. **Admission** $10-$15; 2-drink minimum. **Credit** AmEx, MC, V. **Map** p306 A/B1.

Owned by Mitzi Shore, mom of Pauly Shore, this warhorse of a comedy club, in the heart of Sunset Strip, has three rooms whose offerings run from A-list stand-up talent such as Roseanne and Paul Mooney to sketch and comedy fledglings. It has been the birthplace of such megastars as Robin Williams, David Letterman and Garry Shandling.

Groundlings Theater

7307 Melrose Avenue, at Poinsettia Place, Hollywood (1-323 934 9700/www.groundlings.com). Bus 2, 3, 429/I-10, exit Fairfax Avenue north. **Open** Box office 10am-8pm Thur-Sat; 10am-7.30pm Sun. *Shows* 8pm Thur; 8pm, 10pm Fri, Sat; 7.30pm Sun. Closed Mon-Wed. **Admission** $12-$18.50. **Credit** AmEx, MC, V. **Map** p306 C2.

Located on hip-and-happening Melrose Avenue, this sketch and improv company is an LA institution. The Groundlings have been around for more than 20 years and still produce sketch comedy that hits the mark time and again. *Saturday Night Live* consistently hires comedians from their ranks and the club has spawned top talents such as Julia Sweeney, Jon Lovitz and Pee Wee Herman. On the improv jam night Cookin' with Gas (8pm Thur), you might find celebrity guests riffing with the regulars. Booking advisable.

The Ice House

24 N Mentor Avenue, at Colorado Boulevard, Pasadena (1-626 577 1894/www.icehouseonline. com). Bus 181, 188, 256, 401/I-110, exit Colorado Boulevard east. **Open** *Box office* from 1hr before show Tue-Sun. *Shows* 8.30pm Tue-Thur; 8.30pm, 10.30pm Fri; 7pm, 9pm, 11pm Sat; 8pm Sun. Closed Mon. **Admission** $8.50-$12.50; 2-drink minimum. **Credit** AmEx, MC, V.

One of the oldest comedy venues in the Los Angeles area, this Pasadena club has two rooms; the Ice House (for stand-up) and the Ice House Annex (for sketch shows). The club has spawned comics of the stature of Robin Williams and Steve Martin, and many of these huge talents still come back to pay homage to the place where it all began.

The Improv

8162 Melrose Avenue, between Kilkea Drive & La Jolla Avenue, West Hollywood (1-323 651 2583/ www.improvclubs.com). Bus 10, 11, DASH Fairfax/ I-10, exit La Cienega Boulevard north. **Open** 6pm-2am daily. *Shows* 8pm Mon-Thur; 8.30pm, 10.30pm Fri, Sat; 8.30pm Sun. **Admission** $8-$11. **Credit** AmEx, MC, V. **Map** p306 B2.

A celebrity haunt and industry watering hole, the Improv is one of the highest rungs on the Hollywood comedy ladder. Deals – as well as drinks – are made at the bar ever night. It's a popular venue; booking is recommended.

LA Connection

13442 Ventura Boulevard, between Woodman & Coldwater Canyon Avenues, Sherman Oaks (1-818 784 1868/www.laconnectioncomedy.com). Bus 424, 522, DASH Sherman Oaks/US 101, exit Coldwater Canyon Avenue south. **Open** *Box office* 10am-6pm daily. *Shows* 9pm Thur; 8pm, 9pm, 10.30pm Fri; 7.30pm, 9pm, 10.30pm Sat; 3.30pm (improv for kids), 7pm, 8pm, 9pm Sun. Closed Mon-Wed. **Admission** $7-$12. **Credit** MC, V.

The long-running LA Connection is a company of comics best known for their live dubbing of B-movie classics. They offer numerous improv and sketch shows, which are funny but tend to be pretty predictable. Alumni include Matthew Perry and Kato Kaelin.

LA TheatreSports

The Bitter Truth Theater, 11050 Magnolia Boulevard, between Lankershim Boulevard & Vineland Avenue, North Hollywood (1-818 505 6406/www.theatresports.com). Metro North Hollywood/bus 156, 166, 183/Hwy 134, exit Lankershim Boulevard north. **Open** *Box office* from ½hr before show Fri-Sun. *Shows* 8pm, 10pm Fri, Sat; 7pm Sun. Closed Mon-Thur. **Admission** $10. **No credit cards.**

This critically acclaimed company is one hundred per cent improv. Having been located in the infamous B-movie director Ed Wood's old theatre in the heart of Hollywood for the past ten years, they've now moved to the Valley, but still offer unique improv formats and consistent, dangerous fun. Definitely worth a look.

Comedy Store: laughs nightly. *See p243.*

The Laugh Factory

8001 W Sunset Boulevard, at Crescent Heights Boulevard, West Hollywood (1-323 656 1336). Bus 26, 163, 212, 217/I-10, exit Fairfax Avenue north. **Open** from showtime daily. *Shows* 8pm Mon-Thur, Sun; 7.30pm, 10pm Fri, Sat. **Admission** $8-$10; 2-drink minimum. **Credit** MC, V. **Map** p306 B1.

Another premier stand-up club with plenty of industry connections and surprise appearances by big-time celebs. Many comics who appear on the *Tonight Show* perform here. Arrive early.

Cabaret & cigar bars

LA's cigar craze is definitely on the wane, but it still has its followers. For celebrities, nothing beats the **Grand Havana** in Beverly Hills (1-310 247 2900), but unless you're tight with Arnie (Schwarzenegger) or Jack (Nicholson) you'll need a miracle to get in.

Bloom's General Store

716 Traction Avenue, at Hewitt Street, Downtown (1-213 687 6571). Bus 16, DASH A, Montebello 14/ I-110, exit Fourth Street east. **Open** 8am-11pm Mon-Thur, Sun; 8am-11.30pm Fri, Sat. **No credit cards.**

Quite possibly the coolest place in LA to fire up a stogy, with more than three dozen brands of hand-rolled cigars in stock.

The Gardenia Club
7066 Santa Monica Boulevard, at La Brea Avenue, West Hollywood (1-323 467 7444). Bus 4, 212, West Hollywood A, B/I-10, exit La Brea Avenue north. **Open** *Dinner* from 7pm daily. *Shows* 9pm daily. **Admission** $10; 2-drink minimum. **Credit** AmEx, MC, V. **Map** p306 C1.
You're as likely to hear a Broadway veteran singing Cole Porter as you are to catch a Hollywood actress tackling Brian Wilson and Tom Waits. A no-frills, comfortable room, plus decent Italian food.

Masquers Cabaret & Dinner Theater
8334 W Third Street, between Kings Road & Orlando Avenue, West Hollywood (1-323 653 4848). Bus 14, 16, 105/I-10, exit La Cienega Boulevard north. **Open** *Dinner* from 6pm daily. *Shows* 7.30pm daily. **Admission** $5-$15. **Credit** MC, V. **Map** p306 B3.
With Moroccan and Italian food on the menu, loud art on the walls and a mirror ball spinning overhead, the entertainment here ranges from improvised lounge acts through musical comedy to stand-up.

Overstreets
9713 Little Santa Monica Boulevard, at Roxbury Drive, Beverly Hills (1-310 278 7322). Bus 4, 20, 21, 22, 27/I-405, exit Wilshire Boulevard east. **Open** 4pm-2am Mon-Fri; 6pm-2am Sat; closed Sun. **Credit** AmEx, MC, V. **Map** p305 B2.
A sartorial wine bar, where people come to schmooze, booze and cruise (and smoke some rather fine cigars). Check out the Raj room for live music. Plus multiple screen coverage of sports events.

San Gennaro Cigar Lounge
9543 Culver Boulevard, between Hughes Avenue & Robertson Boulevard, Culver City (1-310 836 0400). Bus 220, Commuter Express 438, Culver City 1, 4, 5/I-10, exit Robertson Boulevard south. **Open** 11am-10pm Mon-Thur; 11am-11pm Fri; 4-11pm Sat; 4-10pm Sun. *Shows* 8.45pm Fri, Sat. **Admission** $10; 2-drink minimum; free with dinner. **Credit** AmEx, MC, V.
Ol' Blue Eyes lives on at a twice-weekly tribute to Frank Sinatra (Fridays and Saturdays) with other Brat Pack crooners tacked on.

Strip clubs

The San Fernando Valley is, infamously, the capital of the porn industry, so you'll find strip joints of every hue from the sleazy to the reputable in LA. Most clubs have newspaper ads redeemable for discounted or free admission, and some have free lunch buffets. To find out which porn star is performing where, check the listings hidden at the back of the *LA Times* sports pages or at the back of the *LA Weekly*. You might even bump into a celeb; strip clubs have acquired

fashionable status in recent years, and some stars (Quentin Tarantino, Daryl Hannah) have even made movies or documentaries about them.

Body Shop
8250 Sunset Boulevard, at Harper Avenue, West Hollywood (1-323 656 1401/www.bodyshopclubla. com). Bus 2, 3/I-10, exit La Cienega Boulevard north. **Open** noon-3am Mon-Thur; noon-4am Fri, Sat; 5pm-3am Sun. **Admission** $10; 2-drink minimum. **No credit cards.** **Map** p306 B1.
This classy strip bar on the Sunset Strip attracts many tourists and is a venerable showgirl palace. Its late opening hours are a big draw.

Cheetahs
4600 Hollywood Boulevard, between Rodney Drive & Vermont Avenue, Los Feliz (1-323 660 6733). Bus 180, 181, 204, Community Connection 203, DASH Hollywood/US 101, exit Vermont Boulevard north. **Open** 12.30pm-2am Mon-Sat; 6pm-2am Sun. **Admission** free; 2-drink minimum. **No credit cards.** **Map** p308 A2.
A hangout for both men and women, this local strip joint has a neighbourhood bar feel.

Crazy Girls
1433 N La Brea Avenue, at Sunset Boulevard, Hollywood (1-323 969 0055). Bus 2, 3, 212/US 101, exit Highland Avenue south. **Open** noon-2am daily. **Admission** $5 after 6pm; 2-drink minimum. **Credit** AmEx, Disc, MC, V. **Map** p307 A2.
This strip club was used as a *Pulp Fiction* location and its VIP room, the Valentino Lounge, has hosted such eminent oglers as (if you believe everything you read) Julia Roberts, Geena Davis, Mick Jagger, Leonardo DiCaprio, Keanu Reeves, Kevin Spacey and the entire cast of *Friends*. You'll find private table dancing, pool tables and giant-screen televised sports.

Hollywood Tropicana
1250 N Western Avenue, at La Mirada Avenue, Hollywood (1-323 464 1653). Bus 207, DASH Western/US 101, exit Santa Monica Boulevard west. **Open** 7pm-midnight Mon-Fri; 7pm-2am Sat, Sun. **Admission** $10; 2-drink minimum. **No credit cards.** **Map** p307 C2.
Lingerie and mud wrestling are on the menu at this infamous strip club. A home-from-home to many of LA's rockers, it was made famous in the 1980s by Motley Crue's song 'Girls, Girls, Girls'.

Jumbo's Clown Room
5153 Hollywood Boulevard, between N Western & Normandie Avenues, Hollywood (1-323 666 1187/ www.jumbos.com). Metro Hollywood-Western/bus 180, 181, 206, 217/US 101, exit Hollywood Boulevard west. **Open** 2pm-2am daily. **Admission** free. **Credit** AmEx, Disc, MC, V. **Map** p307 C1.
Infamous as the place where Courtney Love once shook her bon-bons, Jumbo's has been in business for more than 20 years. It's entirely managed and operated by women, so the vibe is a little different, and it was the first strip joint to have live bands. Customers have included Mick Jagger and David Lynch.

Sport & Fitness

From baseball to *Baywatch*, skateboarding to scuba-diving, there's plenty of sporting fun in the sun.

Blessed with a climate that simply begs for outdoor activities, Southern Californians are legendary for indulging in everything under the gorgeous Californian sun when it comes to getting physical. Los Angeles is the birthplace of the 'tan, muscular bod' and the backdrop for television's *Baywatch*. Angelenos love to work out. Every day, thousands flock to the gym to work up a sweat and maybe even meet a mate. Whatever makes your heart race – surfing, cycling, golfing, horse riding, running, swimming, skateboarding, rollerblading – it's in play in LA.

For shops selling or renting sporting equipment, *see page 199*.

Participation sports

Aviation

Although introductory flights are mainly promotional ploys by small flying schools to get you to join, they're also a great chance to fly small aircraft without any previous experience. At Santa Monica Airport, try **American Flyers** (1-310 390 2099) or **Justice Aviation Services** (1-310 313 6792/www.justiceaviation.com). At Van Nuys Airport in the San Fernando Valley, the **Van Nuys Flight Center** 1-818 994 7300/www.kingaviation.com) offers introductory flights for $49 to $85.

Air Combat USA

230 N Dale Place, at Artesia Boulevard, Fullerton, Orange County (1-800 522 7590/www.aircombat usa.com). Bus Orange County Transit 25/I-5, exit Artesia Boulevard east. **Open** 7am-6pm daily. **Rates** $895-$1,495 (including video of your flight). **Credit** AmEx, Disc, MC, V.

This is not a flight simulator. Air Combat allows you to take control of an SF-260 Nato attack fighter and engage in a real-life dogfight. You leave from Fullerton Municipal Airport (about an hour's drive south from LA) and all dogfights take place over the channel between Catalina Island and the mainland.

Orbic Helicopters

16700 Roscoe Boulevard, between Balboa Boulevard & Woodley Avenue, Van Nuys (1-818 988 6532). Bus 152, 236, 418, exit Roscoe Boulevard west. **Open** 8am-6pm daily. **Rates** 25min demo flight $90-$110; other flights $85-$140 per hr. **Credit** AmEx, MC, V.

Baseball batting cages

More Major Leaguers hail from California than any other US state. Small wonder, then, that batting cages abound in LA. Whatever your skill level – whether you're ready to take a swing at a fastball or are striving to work on hitting the curve – there are plenty of batting cages with multi-speed automated pitching machines. Bats and helmets are provided.

The Batcade

220 N Victory Boulevard, between Magnolia Boulevard & Olive Avenue, Burbank (1-818 842 6455). Bus 96, 152, 183/US 134, exit Alameda Avenue north. **Open** 10am-midnight Mon-Thur, Sat; noon-midnight Fri; 10am-10pm Sun. **Rates** $7 per 15min; $22 per hr. **Credit** AmEx, MC, V.

A newish, high-tech place, with a fierce machine that pitches at 90mph (144kmph).

Batting Cages

620 E Colorado Street, at Glendale Avenue, Glendale (1-818 243 2363). Bus 90, 91, 183/US 134, exit Glendale Avenue south. **Open** 11.30am-10pm Mon-Fri; 9am-10pm Sat; 9am-9pm Sun. **Rates** $8.50 per 15min; $21 per hr. **No credit cards**.

Open since 1965, with each pitching machine named after a classic Dodgers pitcher (Sandy Koufax, Don Sutton, Don Drysdale et al).

Bowling

There is a multitude of bowling centres in the Los Angeles area. On-site professionals offer lessons, repair services and information.

Bay Shore Lanes

234 Pico Boulevard, between Fourth & Main Streets, Santa Monica (1-310 399 7731). Bus 33, 333, Santa Monica 2, 8/I-10, exit Fourth Street south. **Open** 9am-midnight Mon-Thur, Sun; 9am-1am Fri, Sat. **Rates** $3.50 per person; $2.50 shoe rental. **No credit cards. Map** p304 A3.

This 24-lane alley includes the swanky Red Carpet Lounge (*see p167*), home to twin bartenders the Trimbel sisters.

Hollywood Star Lanes

5227 Santa Monica Boulevard, between Hobart Boulevard & Kingsley Drive, Hollywood (1-323 665 4111). Bus 4, 304/US 101, exit Santa Monica Boulevard east. **Open** 24hrs daily. **Rates** $3 per person (including shoe rental). **Credit** MC, V. **Map** p307 C2.

The brand-new **Staples Center**. *See p253.*

An LA landmark for more than 40 years, this is where the Coen brothers filmed *The Big Lebowski*. It's a hotspot for swinging singles, with a cocktail lounge and a coffeeshop.

Cycling & mountain biking

It's easy to bike long distances in Los Angeles, so take plenty of water and some sunscreen. Riding off-road isn't actually legal, but there haven't been any efforts to stop the hundreds of cyclists that weave through the **Santa Monica Mountains**, home to the most popular and accessible MTBing areas: numerous fire trails jut off Mulholland Boulevard from Beverly Hills to Topanga and Malibu. You may have to squeeze under a gate or two, but keep pedalling until you reach the peaks. **Topanga State Park** in Topanga (1-310 455 2465) and **Malibu Creek State Park** in Calabasas (1-818 880

0350/ranger office 1-818 880 0367) may seem a little out of the way, but they're well worth it.

You can get a map of Santa Monica with marked bike trails from the Visitor's Information Center just north of Santa Monica Pier. Oceanfront stalls (there are many in Venice) rent beach bikes, usually with one gear and pedal brakes, so for anything more serious, visit a proper bicycle shop, such as these:

Bicycle Ambulance

707 Pico Boulevard, at Lincoln Boulevard, Santa Monica (1-310 395 5026). Bus Santa Monica 7, 11/I-10, exit Fourth-Fifth Street north. **Open** 9am-6pm daily. **Credit** AmEx, DC, Disc, MC, V. **Map** p304 B3.
Mountain bikes cost $15 a day if you're going to be riding around the beach; $25 if you're going off-road. Suspension costs an extra $5.

Spokes 'n' Stuff

1715 Ocean Front Walk, between Colorado Avenue & Pico Boulevard, Santa Monica (1-310 395 4748). Bus 33, 333, 434, Santa Monica 8/I-10, exit Ocean Avenue. **Open** 8.30am-5pm daily. **Credit** AmEx, DC, Disc, MC, V. **Map** p304 A3.
Located behind the Loews Hotel, mountain bikes cost from $5.50 an hour or $22 a day. There's also a branch in Griffith Park (1-213 662 6573), but it's only open on Saturday and Sunday.
Branches: 4175 Admiralty Way, at Via Marina, Marina del Rey (1-310 306 3332).

Bike paths

All bike paths except MTB routes are paved.
Griffith Park More than 14 miles (22km) of bike trails; can be hilly. Visit Woody's Bicycle World (3157 Los Feliz Boulevard, 1-323 661 6665) for information about the park, maps, rentals and friendly staff.
South Bay Bicycle Trail Extends 22 miles (35km) from Will Rogers State Beach south to Torrance.
Balboa Recreation Center 17015 Burbank Boulevard, at Woodley Avenue, Encino (1-818 756 9642). Flat bicycle paths for nine miles (14km). Best in winter.
Kenneth Hill Bikeway This five-mile (8km) path in Pasadena starts at Arroyo Boulevard and heads to Arroyo Seco and the Rose Bowl.

Fishing

Free public fishing is popular at the piers of many local beaches: try **Santa Monica Pier** (the nearest), **Seal Beach**, **Redondo Beach** or **Manhattan Beach**. For freshwater fishing, try the public park system's **Echo Park Lake** (1-213 250 3578) and **Lincoln Park Lake** in Lincoln Heights (1-213 237 1726). A much bigger lake is **Castaic Lake** in the Los Angeles National Forest north of LA. Fishing parties – fishing trips in someone else's boat – are a good way to get out and do some deep-sea fishing at a spot where the fish are biting.

Redondo Sport Fishing

233 N Harbor Drive, at Herondo Street, Redondo Beach (1-310 372 2111/www.redondosportfishing.com). Bus 130, 439, 215/I-405, exit Artesia Boulevard west. **Open** *Office* 5am-8pm daily. **Rates** **per person** *½-day trip* $25; $20 concessions; *¾-day trip* $36; $31 concessions. **Credit** AmEx, MC, V.

Call for fishing trip departure times. The company also hosts whale-watching trips running from the end of December.

Golf

Long before Tiger Woods emerged from the SoCal suburb of Orange County, golf enjoyed an immense following in LA among all ages and ethnic groups. With its ideal weather conditions and numerous public courses, this is the perfect city for the novice or pro. An LA City Recreation & Parks reservation card (available from any public course) allows you to book in advance. The rise of female pro Se Ri Pak mirrors the popularity of golf among LA's one million Koreans, and there are a number of multi-tiered driving ranges in Koreatown.

Griffith Park Golf Courses

4730 Crystal Springs Drive, Griffith Park (course 1-323 663 2555/shop 1-323 664 2255/www.golfersweb.com/golfla/griffith.htm). Bus 96/I-5, exit Crystal Springs Drive north. **Open** 6am-6pm daily. **Rates** $17.50-$25 per round; $14-$20 carts. **Credit** AmEx, MC, V.

There are two 18-hole championship courses and two nine-hole courses within Griffith Park. You can rent equipment at the pro shop.

Los Feliz Golf Course

3207 Los Feliz Boulevard, between I-5 & Garden Avenue, Los Feliz (1-323 663 7758). Bus 180, 181, 410, 418/I-5, exit Los Feliz Boulevard east. **Open** 7am-6pm or sunset daily. **Rates** $4.50 per round. **No credit cards.**

A public nine-hole course, meaning you only need your wedge and putter, leaving your other hand free to carry a six-pack. The LA River is one of the course boundaries. Tee time reservations are not necessary and there's an Eatz coffeeshop on site.

Rancho Park Golf Course

10460 W Pico Boulevard, between Motor & Patricia Avenues, Rancho Park (1-310 838 7373). Bus Santa Monica 7, Culver City 3/I-10, exit Overland Avenue north. **Open** 6am-6.30pm daily. **Rates** $20-$25 per round. **Credit** AmEx, MC, V.

Rancho Park (18-hole, par 71) claims to have more traffic than any other course in the world, which means that a) it's one of the nicest courses in LA, and b) it's one of the hardest to get on.

Sepulveda Golf Complex

Balboa & Encino courses: 16821 Burbank Boulevard, at Balboa Boulevard, Encino (1-818 995 1170). Bus 154, 236/US 101, exit Balboa Boulevard north.
Woodley Lakes course: 6331 Woodley Avenue, at Victory Boulevard, Van Nuys (1-818 780 6886). Bus 154/I-405, exit Burbank Boulevard west.
All **Open** 6.30am-7pm daily **Rates** $17-$22 per round. **Credit** AmEx, MC, V.

Three courses located in the same area. Balboa is an 18-hole, par 70 course, and both the Encino and Woodley courses are 18-hole, par 72. You can rent equipment and golf carts.

Griffith Park: great for golfers.

Hang-gliding

Windsports International

16145 Victory Boulevard, between Havenhurst &
Woodley Avenues, Van Nuys (1-818 988 0111/
www.windsports.com). Bus 236/I-405, exit Victory
Boulevard west. **Open** 10am-6pm Tue-Fri; 9am-noon
Sat; closed Mon, Sun. **Rates** introductory lesson
$59-$149. **Credit** AmEx, MC, V.
Locations vary, but you'll always launch from
sloping hills where the wind turbulence is more
predictable, not from cliffs.

Hiking

LA has some fantastic places to hike, from
Griffith Park and the Santa Monica Mountains
(including the Hollywood Hills) to the San
Gabriel Mountains – and all are quickly and
easily accessible (if you have a car). Useful
outfits include the venerable **Sierra Club** (LA
chapter: 1-213 387 4287/www.sierraclub.org),
which publishes a schedule of hikes and other
outdoor activities three times a year (available
in map and camping gear shops). Check the
website for details of organised hikes and
outings. For further suggestions, take a look
at Jerry Schad's *A foot & A field in Los Angeles*
County (Wilderness Press, updated in 1998)
or go to 'Trail finder' at www.gorp.com.

Horse riding

LA has a long tradition of horse riding. The
backdrop for dozens of Westerns, the area still
taps into the Old West archetype of the cowboy.
Rent-a-horse options are plentiful in these
stables and at **Sunset Ranch** (*see p89*) in
the Hollywood Hills.

Adventures on Horseback

2666 Triunfo Canyon Road, off Kanan Road,
Agoura Hills (1-818 706 0888/www.aohtrailhorses.
com). PCH, exit Kayan Dume Road east. **Open** 9am-
sunset Tue-Sun; closed Mon. **Rates** $25-$50 per hr.
Credit Disc, MC, V.
Rental, lessons and guided rides. Riding is in the
nearby Santa Monica Recreation Area, as well as on
private ranch trails and through vineyards.

Circle K Riding Stables

910 S Mariposa Street, at Riverside Drive, Burbank
(1-818 843 9890). Bus 96, 152/I-5, exit Alameda
Avenue west. **Open** 7.30am-7pm Mon-Fri; 7.30am-
6pm Sat, Sun. **Rates** $15 first hr; $10 each additional
hr; no under-7s. **No credit cards.**
Located next to the LAEC in Burbank.

Los Angeles Equestrian Center

480 Riverside Drive, at Main Street, Burbank (office
1-818 840 9066/stables 1-818 840 8401). Bus 96,
152/I-5, exit Alameda Avenue west. **Open** 8am-

5pm daily. **Rates** $15 1hr; $24 1½hrs; $28 2hrs;
no under-12s. **No credit cards.**
A public stables located on the northern edge of
Griffith Park, built for the 1984 Olympics, LAEC
rents horses for trail rides and also provides a map
of 54 miles of bridle paths within the park.

Ice hockey & ice-skating

Yes, ice hockey does exist under the sun. In fact,
this traditionally winter sport is very popular in
LA. The region is home to two National Hockey
League franchises, the Los Angeles Kings and
the Anaheim Mighty Ducks, which have a loyal
following. There are plenty of opportunities to
get in on a game at the local rink, and regular
ice-skating sessions also exist.

Culver City Ice Arena

4545 Sepulveda Boulevard, at Braddock Drive,
Culver City (1-310 398 5719/www.culvericearena.
com). Bus Culver CityBus 6, Santa Monica 12/I-405,
exit Sawtelle Boulevard south. **Open** 12.30-5pm
Mon-Fri; 11.30am-5pm, 8-10.30pm Sat; 1.30pm-5pm,
8-10.30pm Sun. **Rates** $6.25; $5.25 concessions;
$3.50 skate rental. **No credit cards.**
There are pick-up hockey games at noon on
Tuesdays, Thursdays and Fridays ($15).

Pool & billiards

You'll find a pool table in most bars and
bowling alleys. But if you want the freedom to
play as long as you like, try one of these:

Gotham Hall

1431 Third Street Promenade, between Broadway
& Santa Monica Boulevard, Santa Monica (1-310 394
8865/www.gothamhall.com). Bus 4, 304, Santa Monica
1, 2, 3, 7/I-10, exit Fourth Street north. **Open** 4pm-
2am Mon-Fri; 3pm-2am Sat, Sun. **Rates per table**
$7-$14 per hr. **Credit** AmEx, MC, V. **Map** p304 A2.
A very swanky establishment in Santa Monica's
popular, pedestrian-only shopping area. Dress up.

Hollywood Billiards

5750 Hollywood Boulevard, between Van Ness
Avenue & N Wilton Place, Hollywood (1-323 465
0115). Metro Hollywood-Western/bus 180, 181, 217/
US 101, exit Hollywood Boulevard east. **Open**
11am-3am Mon-Thur; 11am-6am Fri; 1pm-6am Sat;
1pm-3am Sun. **Rates per table** $6-$11 per hr.
Credit AmEx, MC, V. **Map** p307 B1.
A new location for Hollywood Billiards: the original
one burned down. It has a nice interior and a relaxed
atmosphere. Dress presentably.

Yankee Doodles

1410 Third Street Promenade, between Broadway &
Santa Monica Boulevard, Santa Monica (1-310 394
4632). Bus 4, 304, Santa Monica 1, 2, 7/I-10, exit
Fourth Street north. **Open** 11am-2am daily. **Rates**
per table $8-$10 per hr. **Credit** AmEx, Disc, MC, V.
Map p304 A2.

Horse around at the **Los Angeles Equestrian Center**. *See p249.*

Sports bar Yankee's has 30 pool tables and assorted arcade games, including foosball, air hockey and soft-tip darts. There are also 42 monitors and eight big-screen TVs showing satellite sports all day.

Rock climbing

One of the best outdoor climbing areas is at the south end of Point Dume at **Zuma Beach** (*see page 78*), while **Will Rogers State Historic Park** in Pacific Palisades (*see page 77*) includes the famed Inspiration Point, one of the highest peaks in the Santa Monica Mountains. Indoor walls, such as this one, are also popular:

Rocreation

11866 La Grange Avenue, at Bundy Drive, West LA (1-310 207 7199). Bus Santa Monica 10, 14/I-10, exit Bundy Drive north. **Open** 11am-10pm Mon, Wed; 6am-10pm Tue, Thur; 11am-8pm Fri; 9am-7pm Sat, Sun. **Rates** $15 per day; $5 gear hire. **Credit** AmEx, MC, V.
Three-hour classes are also available, for around $5.

Rollerhockey

Pick-up games can take place on open stretches of pavement virtually anywhere in LA. Good places to look include the **beach parking lot** just north of Ocean Park, in south Santa Monica, and at the **West Hollywood Park & Recreation Center** (647 North San Vicente Boulevard, between Melrose Avenue and Santa Monica Boulevard, 1-213 848 6534). For organised rollerhockey,

try the **Charles H Wilson Community Park** at Crenshaw Boulevard and Jefferson Street in Torrance (1-310 320 9529), which offer leagues as well as weekly pick-up games.

Rollerskating

What began as a disco-era novelty has evolved into an enduringly popular pastime that now thrives at LA's coolest roller rinks.

Moonlight Rollerway

5110 San Fernando Road, between Broadway & Colorado Avenues, Glendale (1-818 241 3630). Bus 94, 394/US 134, exit San Fernando Road south. **Open** 1.30-4pm, 8.30-10.30pm Mon; 1.30-4pm, 8-10.30pm Tue, Wed; 1.30-4pm Thur; 1.30-4pm, 7.30-11pm Fri; 7.30-11pm Sat; closed Sun. **Admission** $4.25-$6; $2 skate rental.
No credit cards.
Home to rollerdancing since the 1950s, Monday nights here (adults only) feature a young, hip, professional crowd. It's also the base of an organist who is one of the premier composers of roller rink music on the Rinx record label.

Scuba-diving

The best places to dive are off **Leo Carillo State Beach**, **Laguna Beach**, **Redondo Beach** and **Palos Verdes**, but if you're really serious, head to **Catalina Island** (*see chapter Trips*) or the **Channel Islands**. Most of the Los Angeles coastline consists of miles of sloping sand, but the coastal islands have rocky shores with plenty of kelp beds, fish and shipwrecks to explore. **Action Water Sports** in Marina del Rey (*see page 254* **Surf 'n' sand**) does beach dives and also runs scuba courses.

Splash/Dive

2490 Lincoln Boulevard, between Venice & Washington Boulevards, Venice (1-310 306 6733). Bus 33, 333, 436, Santa Monica 3/I-10, exit Lincoln Boulevard south. **Open** 10am-6pm Mon-Sat; 11am-5pm Sun. **Credit** AmEx, MC, V. **Map** p304 B5.
As well as offering gear rental (to certified divers), Splash runs a two-week certification course costing $400 ($25 discount if you don't have your own gear).

Skateboarding & rollerblading

Los Angeles has a vibrant street skating culture that has kept up with the changing times. For rollerbladers, there's simply no place like the **Strand**, an immaculate, paved path stretching 22 miles (35 kilometres) from Pacific Palisades south all the way to Manhattan Beach. Public parks along the beach also serve as gathering points for quality skaters who like to rehearse their tricks before an audience. Other tranquil settings for rollerblading include **Griffith Park**, **Ocean Front Walk** in Venice Beach and **Sepulveda Dam Recreation Center** in the San Fernando Valley.

Outside LA, **Vans Skate Park** (1-714 769 3800) offers a challenging array of bowls, ramps and ledges for skateboarding within the new Block shopping mall in Orange, in Orange County. Safety equipment is provided, but you'll have to bring your own board.

SkateLab Skate Park

4226 Valley Fair Street, off Capitol Street, Simi Valley (1-805 578 0040/www.skatelab.com). US 118, exit Stearns Street south. **Open** daily, times vary; call for details. **Admission** 5 day membership; per session $8 Mon-Thur; $10 Fri-Sun. **No credit cards**.
Travelling skaters should definitely check out this inexpensive park about a 50-minute drive from the city. Owned by former Dodger pitcher Scott Radinsky, a graduate of Simi Valley High, it's an awesome place, with two half-pipes and numerous smaller ramps and obstacles. Under-18s require a parent's signature on a release form; over-18s must bring photo ID. Check the website for a live webcam of the park.

Swimming

For the best beaches for swimming, *see page 78.* There are also a number of freshwater alternatives. At **Echo Park Lake Recreation Center** (1632 Bellevue Avenue, at Glendale Boulevard, 1-213 250 3578) there is an outdoor swimming pool at the lake and an indoor pool

just down the street at the recreation centre. The lake itself is for fishing, not swimming, though you can hire a paddle boat to explore its cool, lotus-filled environs. The city's YMCAs (*see p256*) also offer swimming pools.

Castaic Lake (1-805 257 4050), less than an hour north of LA on the I-5, is one of Southern California's nicest lakes. The cordoned-off swimming area is relatively small, but all power boats are confined to the upper lake, preserving the calm. $6 admits a car (and as many people and picnic items as you can pack inside) to the lake all day.

Tennis & racquetball

You can find tennis and racquetball courts at most gyms and recreation centres throughout LA; book a couple of days in advance.

Griffith Park has tennis courts ($6 per hour) at two sites: 12 lit ones at Griffith/Riverside (1-323 661 5318) and 12 unlit ones at Griffith/Vermont Canyon (1-323 664 3521). On weekdays before 6pm, they're available on a first come, first served basis; after 4pm you can book if you have a registration card (available to non-residents). Or try these tennis centres:

Marina Tennis Center

13199 Mindanao Way, at Glencoe Avenue, Marina del Rey (1-310 822 2255). Bus 108, 220/Hwy 90, exit Mindanao Way north. **Open** 8am-10pm Mon-Fri; 8am-10pm Sat, Sun. **Rates** $10 per hr. **Credit** MC, V.

Rustic Canyon Recreation Center

601 Latimer Road, between Brooktree & Hiltree Roads, Santa Monica (1-310 454 5734). Bus Santa Monica 9/I-405, exit Sunset Boulevard west. **Open** 9am-9.30pm Mon-Thur; 9am-5.30pm Fri; 9am-5pm Sat; 10am-5pm Sun. **Rates** free.

Tennis LA

2040 Avenue of the Stars, at Constellation Boulevard, Century City (1-310 282 0762). Bus 28, 328/I-405, exit Santa Monica Boulevard east. **Open** 7am-11pm daily. **Rates** $20 per hr. **Credit** MC, V. **Map** p305 B3.

Whale watching

Whale watching provides California's most extraordinary wildlife experience, and if you're in the area at the right time it's not to be missed. The annual season off Southern California's coastline is in winter (December to March), following the migratory habits of the gray and wright whales, the two most commonly seen species. In the Santa Barbara area north of LA, whale watching reaches its peak in summer, ending in mid-September. In recent years, a group of 800 humpback whales has been summering off Santa Barbara, and blue whales

Arts & Entertainment

are known to show there as well. Most marinas have numerous boats offering whale-watching trips and most operate on a 'sightings guaranteed' basis: if you don't see any whales, your money is refunded. Try these:

Catalina Cruises
320 Goldenshore Boulevard, at I-710, Long Beach (1-800 228 2546). Metro Pacific Transit Mall/bus 60, 232, Long Beach A, D/I-405, exit I-710 south. **Trips** *May-Nov* 10am-1pm Tue, Thur, Sat, Sun. *Apr-Dec* closed. **Rates** $15; $11-$12 concessions. **Credit** Disc, MC, V.

Sea Landing
Santa Barbara Harbor, off Harbor Way, Santa Barbara (1-805 963 3564/www.condorcruises.com). US 101, exit Cabrillo Way west. **Trips** *Feb-Apr* 9-11.30am, noon-2.30pm, 3-5.30pm daily; *July-Sept* 8am-5pm daily. No trips May, June, Oct-Jan. **Rates** *Feb-Apr* $27; $15 concessions; *July-Sept* $65; $35 concessions. **Credit** Disc, MC, V.

Board the *Condor* (with restaurant and full bar) to view the humpback whales feeding all summer off Santa Barbara. Expeditions are guided by naturalists from the Santa Barbara Museum of Natural History, and include a stop at the Painted Cave, the world's largest underwater sea cave.

Spectator sports

There are very few days each year when there isn't at least one professional sporting event taking place in LA, the site of two Olympics (1932 and 1984) and one soccer World Cup (1994 at the Rose Bowl in Pasadena). As the second-largest sports markets in the US (after New York), LA features an abundance of athletic franchises, all of which have a passionate following. The major change to LA's sporting scene has been the arrival of the sparkling new Staples Center in the heart of Downtown. Adjacent to the LA Convention Center, this state-of-the-art arena is used for everything from sporting events to concerts to political conventions. Most notably, the 20,000-seat arena is the new home for basketball's Lakers and Clippers, as well as ice hockey's Kings. Like most new stadiums, it has all the latest comforts, including 160 luxury suites, and has been an instant hit with SoCal's sports faithful.

INFORMATION & TICKETS
The *LA Times* has an award-winning sports section that lists the teams' games and broadcast schedules each day. *ESPN Magazine* and *Sports Illustrated* provide well-written and comprehensive general coverage of US sports.
    The best place to go for tickets are the teams' box offices. Ticket agencies charge booking fees, but sometimes it's the only way to get a ticket; try **Ticketmaster** (1-213 480 3232/1-714

740 2000/www.ticketmaster.com) and **Ticket Vision** (1-888 393 8425/www.ticketvision.com). You can often buy tickets from teams' websites, too. A riskier approach is to buy tickets from unauthorised touts (scalpers) who wait outside the venue before the event.

Baseball

Since moving from Brooklyn to LA in 1958, Major League Baseball's **LA Dodgers** (1-323 224 1448/www.dodgers.com) have won five World Series. In 1998, the team's longtime owners, the O'Malley family, sold the club to Rupert Murdoch's Fox Sports, which changed the roster dramatically, trading away star players like Mike Piazza and Hideo Nomo. One mainstay at the ballpark is organist Nancy Bea Hefley, whose musical selection adds an old-school flavour to the spectacle. The Dodgers haven't been baseball's champs since 1988, and it appears it will be some time before they accomplish the feat again as the team undergoes a rebuilding process. However, Dodger Stadium in lovely Chavez Ravine in the hills north of Downtown LA, is a must-see. Built in 1962, and recently renovated, it remains among the most immaculate ballparks in the US, and the famous foot-long 'Dodger dogs' are classic LA fare. Tickets cost $6 to $17.
    The **Anaheim Angels** (1-888 796 4256/ www.angelsbaseball.com) also play in the Major League, at Edison Field in Anaheim, Orange County. The Angels are owned by Disney, and their renovated ballpark is a few miles from Disneyland. Tickets cost $6 to $22.
    The baseball season runs from April to September. Play-offs and World Series games take place in October.

Dodger Stadium
1000 Elysian Park, at Stadium Way, Echo Park (1-323 224 1448). Bus 2, 3, 4, 302, 304/I-110, exit Dodger Stadium north. **Open** *Box office* 8.30am-5.30pm daily; longer on game days. **Credit** DC, MC, V.

Edison Field
2000 Gene Autry Way, between Katella & Orangewood Avenues, Anaheim, Orange County (information 1-714 634 2000). Bus Orange County Transit 50, 57/I-5, exit Katella Avenue east. **Open** *Box office* 9am-5.30pm Mon-Sat; longer on game days. **Credit** AmEx, MC, V.
You can only by tickets from the stadium in person; to pay by phone, call Ticketmaster (1-714 663 9000).

Basketball

After 12 years, Los Angeles can again lay claim to having a world-champion professional basketball team. The **LA Lakers** (1-213 742

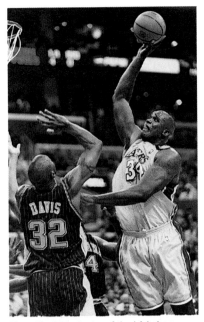

Shaquille O'Neal: star of the LA Lakers.

7333/www.lakers.com), in their first season in the sparkling new Staples Center, captured the National Basketball Association title in 2000. With the retirement of Michael Jordan, Laker centre Shaquille O'Neal reigns as the NBA's dominant player, while team mate Kobe Bryant has established himself as a star in his brief career. Longtime courtside supporters include actors Jack Nicholson and Dyan Cannon, and the crowd is usually sprinkled with a smattering of celebrities who never miss a rebound. Appropriately enough, the Lakers' fast-paced games are known to locals as 'showtime'. Tickets cost $21 to $160.

LA's other NBA team, the **Clippers** (1-213 742 7333/http://clippers.rivals.com), also play at Staples Center, but that's where the similarities between the teams end. The hapless Clippers are the league's worst team. Tickets start at $10. The season runs from October to the end of April, but count on the Lakers playing well into the play-offs, which extend until mid-June.

Come summertime, the fledgling Women's NBA takes over. The **Sparks** (1-310 330 2434/www. wnba.com/ sparks/), led by hometown heroine Lisa Leslie, are quickly emerging as one of the league's top teams. They are planning to move to Staples Center for the 2001 season. Tickets cost $7.50 to $35.

Staples Center

1111 S Figueroa Street, between 11th & 12th Streets, Downtown (box office 1-213 742 7340/ www.staplescenter.com). Metro Pico/Bus 434, 436, 439, 442, 446, 460, DASH Downtown E/I-110, exit Ninth Street or Olympic Boulevard. **Open** Box office 10am-7pm Mon-Sat; 10am-5pm Sun (on event days only). **Credit** AmEx, Disc, MC, V. **Map** p309 A4.

Football

Who says Los Angeles doesn't have football? The college game is alive and well, with UCLA and USC in town. UCLA's **Bruins** (1-310 825 2946/www.uclabruins.com) play at the Rose Bowl in Pasadena, while USC's **Trojans** (1-213 740 4672/www.usctrojans.com) play at the LA Memorial Coliseum in Downtown LA. Even though the Rams and Raiders of the National Football League have moved, the **Avengers** (1-310 473 7999/ www.laavengers. com) – of the fledgling Arena Football League, the upstart, indoor version of American football – routinely play to a full house at the Staples Center.

The college season runs from September to November, with the grand finale being the bevy of bowl games played across the country on New Year's Day, of which the most famous is at the Rose Bowl.

Tickets for UCLA and USC games cost around $25. The AFL season runs from April to August; tickets start at $7.

Los Angeles Memorial Coliseum

3911 S Figueroa Street, at Martin Luther King Jr Boulevard, Downtown (1-213 747 7111/748 6136/ www.stadianet.com/lacoliseum). Bus 40, 42, 81/ I-110, exit Martin Luther King Jr Boulevard west. **Open** Box office 10am-6pm Mon-Fri & event days. **Credit** AmEx, MC, V.

Rose Bowl

1001 Rose Bowl Drive, at Arroyo Boulevard, Pasadena (1-626 577 3100/www.rosebowlstadium. com). Bus 177/Hwy 134, exit Orange Grove Boulevard north. **Open** Box office 7.30am-5.30pm Mon-Thur & event days; closed Fri. **Credit** AmEx, MC, V.

Horse racing

There are three racetracks in the Los Angeles area. All feature flat racing and are closed for part of the year. Call for post times. Admission is around $5.

Hollywood Park Race Track & Casino

1050 S Prairie Avenue, between 90th Street & Century Boulevard, Inglewood (1-310 419 1500). Bus 211, 212/I-405, exit Manchester Boulevard east.

Arts & Entertainment

Sand 'n' surf

Those miles and miles of golden sand that make up Southern California's world-famous beaches are used for more than just sunbathing. A whole culture of beach life has grown up in which sport is as integral as sun and sea. If you really want to hook into the California lifestyle, you need to get on a surboard. But be warned: it's difficult. It can take weeks just to learn to sit on the board properly, let alone negotiate the whitewash. Windsurfing is even harder.

Most novice surfers opt for the easier-to-learn alternatives: boogie-boards (aka bodyboards), body surfing and skimboarding. If you're learning to surf, choose a wide-open beach break such as Zuma Beach, Will Rogers State Beach – the surfing is best where Sunset Boulevard meets the Pacific Coast Highway – Santa Monica Beach or El Porto, at Manhattan Beach. Intermediate surfers can find excellent beach breaks at Manhattan, Hermosa, Redondo and Huntington Beaches. Only experienced surfers should test their skill at the competitive, surfers-only point breaks, such as Topanga State Beach, near the intersection of PCH and

Topanga Canyon Road; Surfrider Beach (one of the most famous surf breaks in the world), by PCH and Cross Creek Road, just north of Malibu Pier (pictured); and the Wedge, a very dangerous break at the end of Balboa and Ocean Boulevards at the top of the Balboa Peninsula in Orange County.

There are plenty of places where you can hire surfboards. One of the best is **ZJ Boardinghouse** in Santa Monica (see page 199): surfboards cost $15 for six hours, $25 for 24 hours. They also rent wetsuits (which you'll need if you surf between October and May) and provide a daily surf report. **ET Surfboards** in Hermosa Beach (904 Aviation Boulevard, 1-310 379 7660) also stocks all kinds of boards.

If you want training with professional surfers, try **Paskowitz Surfing Camp** in San Clemente (164 West Avenida Ramona, 1-949 361 9283). The five-day surfing camp lets skilled surfers and beginners work on technique, relax by a campfire and sleep under the stars. The company also runs day camps, and surfing holidays with luxury accommodation in Mexico. Classes run from early June to mid September.

Los Alamitos Race Course

4961 Katella Avenue, at Walker Street, Los Alamitos, Orange County (1-714 236 4400). Bus Orange County Transit 50/I-5, exit Katella Avenue west.

Santa Anita Park

285 W Huntington Drive, between Baldwin & Santa Anita Avenues, Arcadia (1-626 574 7223). Bus 79, 188/I-210, exit Baldwin Avenue south.

Ice hockey

The **LA Kings** (1-888 546 4752/www.lakings. com) have slipped comfortably into their new home at Staples Center (*see page 253*), going as far as to don new uniforms. Former Kings forward Dave Taylor is now the team's general manager, and he's brought in high-scoring centre Jozef Stumpel as the Kings are once again contenders in the National Hockey League. Tickets cost $19.50 to $100.

The NHL's **Mighty Ducks** (1-714 704 2701/ www.mightyducks.com), another Disney-owned franchise, play at Arrowhead Pond in Anaheim and feature stars Paul Kariya and Teemu Selanne. Tickets start at $24. The **Long Beach Ice Dogs** (1-562 423 3647/http://icedogshockey. com) are one of the top teams in the second-tier

International Hockey League. The NHL season runs from early October to April. The Stanley Cup play-offs follow, and culminate in June.

Arrowhead Pond

2695 Katella Avenue, at Douglass Road, Anaheim, Orange County (1-714 704 2500). Bus Orange County Transit 203, 757/I-5, exit Katella Avenue east. **Open** Box office 10am-6pm Mon-Fri; 10am-4pm Sat; longer on game days. **Credit** AmEx, MC, V.

Motor racing

The annual glamour event is the Indy car **Long Beach Grand Prix**, which takes place on a street circuit in Long Beach in early April (*see page 204*). **California Speedway** in Fontana (tickets 1-909 428 9300), 90 minutes east of LA just off the I-10, hosts several Nascar events between April and September.

Irwindale Speedway

13300 E Live Oak Avenue, at I-605, Irwindale (1-626 358 1100/www.irwindalespeedway.com). Bus Foothill Transit 492/I-605 north, exit E Live Oak Avenue west. **Open** *Apr-Oct* from 5pm Sat only. Closed Nov-May. **Tickets** $15; $5 concessions. **Credit** MC, V.

The hottest new trend is kiteboarding – where a kite is attached to the board, allowing you to do acrobatics while surfing. **Action Water Sports** in Marina del Rey (4144 Lincoln Boulevard, 1-310 306 9539/ www.actionwater sports.com) provides lessons (from $75 for two hours, including all equipment).

Alternatively, you can take to the ocean on some kind of watercraft, either motorised (jet skis) or manual (sea kayaks). It's all about how much you want to pay, how much you want to exert yourself and how much you want to experience the water. Kayak rental is usually around $10 or $15 an hour (or around $40 a day) for a single-person kayak; doubles

are also available. Try **Malibu Ocean Sports**, next to Malibu Pier (22935 Pacific Coast Highway, 1-310 456 6302) or **Marin Boat Rentals** in Marina del Rey (Fisherman's Village, 13719 Fiji Way, 1-310 574 2822), which also rents electric boats. At **Jetski Fun** in Santa Monica (1753 Ninth Street, suite 201, 1-310 453 8754) you can rent wave runners and jet skis ($80 to $100 per hour) and also take tours.

If getting wet is not your thing, there's always that quintessential SoCal activity, beach volleyball. The best courts are on Manhattan Beach, Hermosa Beach and Santa Monica Beach, just south of the pier. Will Rogers State Beach also has courts south of the Santa Monica Canyon, near the parking lot, and Manhattan Beach hosts an annual Volleyball Open. A good resource is the **California Beach Volleyball Association** (1-800 350 2282).

For surfing and beach conditions, call **LA Surf & Weather** (1-310 578 0478) or check with the **Department of Beaches & Harbors** (1-310 305 9503) for the beach you're interested in. For a round-up of LA's best beaches, *see page 78* **Life's a beach**.

Opened in 1999 in the San Gabriel Valley, the half-mile paved oval is California's first short track built in 20 years. The 6,500-seat venue features a variety of stock car racing from April to October.

Soccer

Soccer is slowly and steadily catching on in LA as a spectator sport. The **LA Galaxy** (1-626 432 1540/www.lagalaxy.com), who play at the Rose Bowl in Pasadena (*see page 253*), has a solid fan base as it improves its stature in Major League Soccer, the five-year-old national men's professional league. Fans' favourites include Mexican goalkeeper Jorge Campos and Cobi Jones, the dreadlocked winger, who also plays for the US national side. Tickets cost $10 to $30. The Rose Bowl was also the site of the 1999 women's World Cup Finals, won by the US.

With a significant Latino population in LA, the thriving 'futbol' culture provides a base for millions of European-Americans living in LA to get their fix. There is a huge number of amateur teams and leagues, often organised by native country, which can be seen in action evenings and weekends at high schools, sports grounds

and public parks. Numerous bars and cafés around town show overseas matches on satellite TV; check the sports section of the Spanish newspaper *La Opinion* for Spanish-speaking coverage.

If you want to watch English premier league footie, plenty of bars, particularly in Santa Monica, broadcast games; try the **Cock & Bull** pub (2947 Lincoln Boulevard, at Pier Avenue, 1-310 399 9696) and **Ye Olde King's Head** (*see page 167*).

Fitness

Dance & fitness classes

Class times and fees can vary, so call ahead to check details.

Arthur Murray Studio

262 N Beverly Drive, between Dayton Way & Wilshire Boulevard, Beverly Hills (1-310 274 8867/ www.dancestudios.com). Bus 20, 21, 22, 720, DASH Beverly Hills/I-10, exit Robertson Boulevard north. **Open** 1-10pm daily; group classes 10am-2pm Sat. **Credit** AmEx, MC, V. **Map** p305 C2.

A conservative dance studio that will teach you just about any step from ballroom to swing.

Arts & Entertainment

Dove's Bodies

4010 Colfax Avenue, at Ventura Boulevard, Studio City (1-818 980 7866). Bus 150, 240, 750/US 101, exit Laurel Canyon Boulevard south. **Open** 9.30-11am, 6.30-7.30pm Mon-Thur; 9.30-11am Fri, Sat; 10-11.30am Sun. **No credit cards.**

An inspired, customised yet ever evolving circuit sculpting class that will melt fat, firm, tone and define.

Live Art Studios

1100 S Beverly Drive, suites 207 & 208, between Olympic & Pico Boulevards, Beverly Hills (1-310 277 9536). Bus 3/I-10, exit Robertson Boulevard north. **Open** 7am-7pm Mon-Fri; by appointment Sat; closed Sun. **Credit** AmEx, MC, V. **Map** p305 C3.

Angels, towers, erotica (exercises), transformers, magic circles and wands (equipment) make up Pilates, a low-impact form of exercise designed to lengthen as much as strengthen. Invented in the late 1920s, it has been practised for years by dancers.

Gyms

Gyms have sprouted in LA faster than Starbucks and Blockbuster combined; the following are open to non-members. YMCA often have gyms.

24-Hour Fitness

8612 Santa Monica Boulevard, at La Cienega Boulevard, West Hollywood (1-310 652 7440/ www.24hourfitness.com). Bus 4, 105, 304/I-10, exit La Cienega Boulevard north. **Open** 6am-11pm Mon-Fri; 6am-9.30pm Sat, Sun. **Rates** *Non-members* $15 per day. **Credit** AmEx, MC, V. **Map** p306 B2.

Right in the heart of West Hollywood, this branch offers a pool, sauna, weights, aerobics and even cardio kick-boxing. This gym is not open 24 hours, but the Santa Monica and Beverly Hills branches are. **Branches**: throughout the city.

Gold's Gym

360 Hampton Drive, at Rose Avenue, Venice (1-310 392 6004/www.goldsgym.com). Bus 33, 333, 436/ I-10, exit Lincoln Boulevard south. **Open** 4am-midnight Mon-Fri; 5am-11pm Sat, Sun. **Rates** *Non-members* $15 per day; $50 per week. **Credit** AmEx, Disc, MC, V. **Map** p304 A4.

'The mecca of bodybuilding' is how this truly impressive Temple of the Bod bills itself. **Branches**: throughout the city.

Hollywood Gym & Fitness Center

1551 N La Brea Avenue, between Hollywood & Sunset Boulevards, Hollywood (1-323 845 1420). Bus 2, 3, 212, 217/US 101, exit Highland Avenue south. **Open** 24hrs daily. **Rates** *Non-members* $12 per day; $25 per week; $75 per month. **Credit** AmEx, MC, V. **Map** p307 A1.

Yoga, Nautilus, free weights, aerobics, sauna and chiropractic facility. Kick-boxing is $15 a class.

Spectrum Club

2250 Park Place, at Douglas Avenue, Manhattan Beach (1-310 643 6878). Bus 126/I-405, exit Rosecrans Avenue west. **Open** 5am-11pm Mon-Thur; 5am-10pm Fri; 7am-7pm Sat, Sun. **Rates** *Non-members* $15 per day. **Credit** AmEx, MC, V.

The largest of ten Spectrum Clubs in the LA area, this place offers practically every kind of workout and level of instruction imaginable. Hours and rates vary among affiliates, so call for details. **Branches**: throughout the city.

YMCAs

For other locations, call 1-800 872 9622.

Santa Monica Family YMCA

1332 Sixth Street, between Santa Monica Boulevard & Arizona Avenue, Santa Monica (1-310 393 2721). Bus 20, 720, Santa Monica 2, 3/I-10, exit Fifth Street north. **Open** 6am-10pm Mon-Fri; 7am-7pm Sat; 11am-7pm Sun. **Rates** *Non-members* $10 per day. **Credit** AmEx, Disc, MC, V. **Map** p304 A2.

Racquetball and handball courts, free weights, boxing, aerobics, a lap pool, a spa, pick-up basketball and volleyball – and a running track on the roof.

Stuart M Ketchum Downtown YMCA

401 S Hope Street, at Fourth Street, Downtown (1-213 624 2348). Bus 76, 78, 378, 379/I-110, exit Ninth Street east. **Open** 5.30am-9.30pm Mon-Fri; 8am-4.30pm Sat; 9am-3.30pm Sun. **Rates** *Non-members* $10-$15 per day. **Credit** AmEx, Disc, MC, V. **Map** p309 B2.

Facilities include an indoor lap pool, running track, squash, racquetball and tennis courts.

Yoga

Currently something of a trend, particularly among professional women in their thirties and forties. Their role model may be Madonna, a recent devotee; her song *Shanti/Ashtangi* on the 1998 album *Ray of Light* is based on a Sanskrit chant. Also try the **BKS Iyengar Yoga Institute of LA** in West Hollywood (1-323 653 0357). Classes cost around £14.

Yoga Center West

1535 S Robertson Boulevard, at Cashio Street, Midtown (1-310 552 464). Bus 220/I-10, exit Robertson Boulevard north. **Open** 10am-8pm daily. **Credit** MC, V. **Map** p306 A4.

Classes in Kundalini yoga and stress reduction for all levels, from beginners to teachers-in-training. Choose from about 35 classes a week.

Yoga Works

1426 Montana Avenue, between 14th & 15th Streets, Santa Monica (1-310 393 5150). Bus Santa Monica 3/I-10, exit Lincoln Boulevard north. **Open** 6.30am-7.15pm Mon-Fri; 7.30am-5.30pm Sat; 8am-6.30pm Sun. **Credit** AmEx, MC, V. **Map** p304 B1.

There are two locations, both in Santa Monica, where Astanga and Iyengar yoga are taught. **Branch**: 2215 Main Street, between Ocean Park & Pico Boulevards, Santa Monica (1-310 393 5150).

Theatre & Dance

The performing arts may take second place to the silver screen, but LA's theatre scene, though small, is thriving.

Theatre

Los Angeles may be more associated with pop culture than any staged classical repertoire, but it's a little-known fact that the city had its own thriving Broadway theatre district back in the 1920s and 1930s. And theatre continues to flourish today – not despite the city's celluloid fixation but because of it. Many productions are tested on stage before they make it to your TV or local cinema, and many actors tread the boards, reading scripts and doing more experimental work to hone their skills. The sprawling city also has room for a huge variety of venues: from picnicking outdoors with Shakespeare in a rustic canyon, to watching a Broadway musical in a lavish art deco movie palace, to seeing a famous film star in a tiny 99-seat black box.

The best way to discover what's on is to pick up a copy of the *LA Times* or *LA Weekly*. For tickets and general information for most theatres, call Ticketmaster (1-323 480 3232/ www.ticketmaster.com) or Telecharge (1-800 233 3123/ www.telecharge.com) – note that you will have to pay a service charge. You can also buy half-price tickets for certain shows on the day of performance at www.theatrela.org/ WebTIX.htm. Other online booking agencies are www.tickets.com and www.ticketweb.com.

Major venues

Ahmanson Theatre & Mark Taper Forum
Performing Arts Center of Los Angeles County, 135 N Grand Avenue, between First & Temple Streets, Downtown (1-213 972 7211/Ahmanson Theatre & Mark Taper Forum 1-213 628 2772/ www.performingartscenterla.org). Metro Civic Center-Tom Bradley/bus 78, 79, 96, 379, 427, DASH A, B/ I-110, exit Fourth Street east. **Open** *Box office* noon-8pm Tue-Sun. *Shows* usually 8pm Tue-Fri; 2pm, 8pm Sat, Sun. Closed Mon. **Tickets** *Ahmanson Theatre* $25-$70; *Mark Taper Forum* $27-$47. **Credit** AmEx, Disc, MC, V. **Map** p309 B1.
Formerly known as the Music Center, LA's foremost performing arts complex houses two spaces – the Ahmanson Theatre and the Mark Taper Forum – as well as resident theatre company, the Center Theatre Group (1-213 972 0700). It's also the home of the Dorothy Chandler Pavilion (used by the LA Opera

and for other concerts – *see p228*), and is the site of the Disney Concert Hall, due for completion in 2003. The Ahmanson seats nearly 2,000, but there's not a bad chair in the house for huge Broadway musicals like *Martin Guerre, Les Miserables* and the *Scarlet Pimpernel*. The smaller Mark Taper Forum has 760 seats surrounding a thrust stage, so even if you're stuck in the back row you'll have a good view of such plays as August Wilson's *Jitney*, Neil Simon's *The Dinner Party* and Patrick Marber's *Closer*.

John Anson Ford Amphitheatre
2580 Cahuenga Boulevard E, just north of Cahuenga Terrace, Hollywood (1-323 461 3673/www.lacounty arts.org/ford.html). Bus 212, 420/US 101, exit Cahuenga Boulevard north. **Open** *Box office* May-Oct 10am-6pm daily; longer on performance days. *Nov-Apr* 10am-6pm Wed-Sun; longer on performance days; closed Mon, Tue. *Shows* usually 8pm Thur-Sat; 3pm, 8pm Sun. **Tickets** $7-$35. **Credit** AmEx, Disc, MC, V.
This intimate amphitheatre in the Hollywood Hills is just up the street from the more famous Hollywood Bowl and has been a landmark since the 1930s. A wonderful outdoor venue to see any show, it's part of an LA County regional park and so the stage is set against a rustic backdrop of chaparral and cypresses. From June to September, it's home to the Summer Nights at the Ford, when you can catch world music and dance, classical music, jazz, blues and theatre shows. The tiny, recently renovated indoor theatre, [Inside] the Ford, has theatre performances from November to April.

Pantages Theater
6233 Hollywood Boulevard, between Argyle Avenue & Vine Street, Hollywood (1-213 468 1770/www. nederlander.com/pantages.html). Metro Hollywood-Vine/bus 26, 163, 180, 181/US 101, exit Vine Street south. **Open** *Box office* 10am-6pm Mon; 10am-8pm Tue-Sat; 10am-6.30pm Sun. *Shows* times & days vary. **Tickets** $15-$125. **Credit** AmEx, MC, V. **Map** p307 B1.
Built in 1929, the Pantages' rich art deco style will have you staring in awe at its ceiling, and during the interval you'll have to tear yourself away from the beautiful lobby with its twin sweeping staircases. The 1950s saw it host the Academy Awards and the 1960s transformed it from a movie palace to a regular theatre. Legend has it that the ghost of eccentric millionaire Howard Hughes still roams the Pantages; he owned it for a few years in the early 1950s. Note that the Pantages box office does not sell tickets over the phone. *See also p231*.

Broadway musicals, such as *Swing!*, appear at the **Ahmanson Theatre**. *See p257.*

Shubert Theatre

2020 Avenue of Stars, at Constellation Boulevard,
Century City (1-800 233 3123). Bus 22, 27, 28, 316,
328, Santa Monica 5/I-405, exit Santa Monica
Boulevard east. **Open** *Box office* 10am-6pm Mon-Sat;
closed Sun. *Shows* times & days vary. **Tickets** vary.
Credit AmEx, DC, Disc, MC, V. **Map** p305 B3.
The Shubert, with its 2,000 seats, vies with the
Ahmanson for the larger touring productions. Long-
running shows have included *Beauty and the Beast*
and *Sunset Boulevard*. It also got *Ragtime* before it
was such a smash on Broadway. There's plenty of
underground parking.

Smaller venues

Coronet Theater

366 N La Cienega Boulevard, at Oakwood Avenue,
West Hollywood (1-310 657 7377/PKE 1-310 285
8148). Bus 10, 11, 105, 576, DASH Fairfax/I-10,
exit La Cienega Boulevard north. **Open** *Box office*
noon-6pm Mon; 10am-8pm Tue-Sat; noon-7pm Sun.
Shows 8pm Mon-Fri; 5pm, 8pm Sat; 3pm, 7pm Sun.
Tickets free PKE; $38-$45 others. **Credit** AmEx,
MC, V. **Map** p306 B2.
Monday nights are when the stars come out. This
272-seater in West Hollywood fills up quickly as
actors such as Gwyneth Paltrow, Frank Lagella,
Carol Burnett, Leonard Nimoy and Lily Tomlin read
scripts at 'PKE' – the Playwrights' Kitchen
Ensemble. Many of these scripts have gone on to TV
and film. It's free and there's always a buzz, so get
there early. There's a changing roster of productions, often comedies, on other nights.

Geffen Playhouse

10886 Le Conte Avenue, at Tiverton Avenue,
Westwood (1-310 208 6500/box office 1-310 208
5454/www.geffenplayhouse.com). Bus 2, 302, Santa
Monica 3, Culver City 6, CommuterExpress 573,
576/I-405, exit Wilshire Boulevard east. **Open**
Box office 9am-5.30pm Mon-Fri; noon-5pm Sat, Sun.
Shows 7.30pm Tue-Thur; 2pm Wed; 8pm Fri; 4pm,
8.30pm Sat; 2pm, 7pm Sun. **Tickets** $15-$43. **Credit**
AmEx, MC, V.

Lately, the Geffen has brought some great produc-
tions to LA, such as Pulitzer Prize-winner Donald
Margulies' *Dinner with Friends*, Martin McDonagh's
The Cripple of Inishmaan, Connor McPherson's *The*
Weir and works by David Mamet, John Patrick
Shanley and Doug Wright. It's a beautiful little
theatre with a gorgeous outdoor patio.

Henry Fonda Theater

6126 Hollywood Boulevard, at Gower Street,
Hollywood (1-323 468 1770/www.nederlander.com/
fonda.html). Metro Hollywood-Vine/bus 180, 181,
212, 217/US 101, exit Vine Street south. **Open**
Box office from 2pm on performance days only.
Shows times & days vary. **Tickets** $26-$36. **Credit**
AmEx, MC, V. **Map** p307 B1.
Even though it's just down the street from the
classy Pantages, this intimate, 800-capacity
Hollywood theatre suffers because those few blocks
take it into a more depressed neighbourhood.
Although it suffered earthquake damage in 1994
and hasn't been very busy since, it presents occasional touring shows, live musical performances and
stand-up comedy by the likes of Eddie Izzard.

Pasadena Playhouse

39 S El Molino Avenue, between Colorado Boulevard
& Green Street, Pasadena (1-626 356 7529). Bus
180, 181, 188, 256, 401, 402, Foothill Transit 187/
I-110 to Arroyo Parkway, exit Colorado Boulevard
east. **Open** *Box office* 10am-6pm daily. *Shows* 8pm
Fri; 4pm, 8pm Sat; 4pm, 7.30pm Sun. **Tickets** $15-
$42. **Credit** AmEx, MC,V.
A Pasadena landmark, the Playhouse opened in
1924, fell on hard times in the 1970s, was restored
and now stages many premieres and productions,
some of which have moved on to Broadway. It has
a cute outdoor patio, similar to the Geffen's, and a
good restaurant next door.

Will Geer Theatricum Botanicum

1419 N Topanga Canyon Boulevard, at Cheney
Drive, Topanga (1-310 455 3723/www.theatricum.
com). Bus 434/I-10, exit Pacific Coast Highway
north. **Open** *Box office* 9am-5pm Mon-Fri; longer on
performance days. *Shows* usually 8pm Fri; 4pm, 8pm

Arts & Entertainment

Sat; 4pm, 7.30pm Sun. **Tickets** $7-$17; free under-6s. **No credit cards.**
Bring a picnic: the Botanicum is an outdoor venue in the late Will Geer's backyard. Better known as Grandpa on *The Waltons*, Geer founded the theatre as a haven for blacklisted actors, artists and musicians in the 1950s. Although the company concentrates on Shakespeare, it has also produced such plays as *Harold and Maude* and *Our Town*. The season runs from June to October.

99-seat theatres

These small theatres are experimental, inventive and serve as creative hotbeds for actors, producers and writers. Under the 99-Seat Equity Waiver Agreement, theatres with fewer than 100 seats don't have to pay Equity (actors' union) wages. Therefore some of the bigger names in Los Angeles TV and film (who don't need the money) hone their skills in them and fringe productions (which don't have the money) flourish. In addition to the theatres listed below, the area known as Theater Row, in a run-down Hollywood neighbourhood, has several small spaces often used for short, one-off runs (which can be very hit-and-miss). Look out for productions at the **Attic Theatre Centre** (6562½ Santa Monica Boulevard, 1-310 659 3637) and the **Hudson** (6539 Santa Monica Boulevard, 1-323 856 4249). The Hudson is a group of four 99-seat theatres, all producing very different works: the Mainstage is primarily mainstream theatre; the Hudson Avenue is more eclectic; the Hudson Backstage presents works in progress; and the Hudson Guild presents classical pieces.

Actors' Gang Theatre

6209 Santa Monica Boulevard, at El Centro Avenue, Hollywood (1-323 465 0566/www.theactorsgang. com). Bus 4, 210, 310, 304,420, 426/US 101, exit Vine Street south. **Open** *Box office* 24hr recorded ticket line. *Shows* 8pm Tue-Fri, Sun; 8pm, 10.30pm Sat.* **Tickets** $10-$30. **Credit** AmEx, Disc, MC, V. **Map** p307 B2.
The Actors' Gang has become something of an institution under (former) artistic director Tim Robbins. Known for its strong political views, comic sensibilities, workshop productions and daring versions of classic plays, the group has won the LA Drama Critic's Circle award for excellence. Comfortable seats and good sightlines means the space is rented out to other companies, such as New York's Naked Angels and Chicago's Lookingglass Company.

The Evidence Room

2220 Beverly Boulevard, at N Alvarado Street, Silver Lake (1-213 381 7110). Bus 14, 200/US 101, exit Alvarado Street south. **Open** *Box office* 1hr before show. *Shows* times & days vary. **Tickets** $15-$25. **No credit cards.**

Started a few years ago in a run-down warehouse in Culver City by a bunch of college friends, the Evidence Room, now in a bigger, grander warehouse in Silver Lake, has established itself as one of LA's most provocative small theatre groups. Their repertoire ranges from adaptations of difficult German playrights to pulp thrillers to sci-fi – all performed with tremendous energy and inventiveness and invariably terrific sets. They also host great parties.

Met Theatre

1089 N Oxford Avenue, at Santa Monica Boulevard, Hollywood (1-323 957 1152/www.themettheatre. com). Bus 4, 175, 207, 304, 357, 420/I-10, exit Western Avenue north. **Open** *Box office* 24hr recorded ticket line; plus from 45mins before performance. *Shows* 8pm Tue-Sat; 7pm Sun. **Tickets** $20. **Credit** MC, V. **Map** p307 C2.
Founded by actors Amy Madigan, Ed Harris, Holly Hunter and Beth Henley, and aided by generous cheques from Bette Midler, Angelina Jolie, James Cameron, Rhea Perlman, Tom Cruise and Nicole Kidman, this company hosts actor/director/writer workshops with a high celeb factor.

Odyssey Theatre Ensemble

2055 S Sepulveda Boulevard, between Olympic & Santa Monica Boulevards, West LA (1-310 477 2055). Bus Culver City 6, Commuter Express 574/ I-405, exit Santa Monica Boulevard east. **Open** *Box office* 3-7pm Tue-Sat; noon-2pm Sun; closed Mon. *Shows* 8pm Wed-Sat; 7pm Sun. **Tickets** $20-$25. **Credit** AmEx, MC, V. **Map** p305 A5.
Nearly 30 years of productions have made this one of the most successful small theatres in LA. With its three under-100-seat houses, the Odyssey has been experimental and innovative in both the classical and original works it puts on. Past productions include Aristophanes' *The Frogs*, Odets's *Awake and Sing* and Mamet's *Speed the Plow*. There's also a great lobby to while away the intermission.

Tiffany Theater

8532 Sunset Boulevard, at La Cienega Boulevard, West Hollywood (1-310 289 2999). Bus 2, 3, 302, 429/I-10, exit La Cienega Boulevard north. **Open** *Box office* noon-5pm Tue, Wed; noon-6.30pm Thur-Sun; closed Mon. *Shows* times & days vary. **Tickets** $15-$25. **Credit** AmEx, MC, V. **Map** p306 A1.
Housing two 99-seat theatres, the Tiffany has presented quality dramas, though it now concentrates on lighter fare. Both theatres have wonderful sightlines, a large lobby and convenient parking.

Also recommended

Matrix Theater 7657 Melrose Avenue, West Hollywood (1-323 852 1445); **Canon Theatre** 205 N Canon Drive, Beverly Hills (1-310 859 2830); **Coast Playhouse** 8325 Santa Monica Boulevard, West Hollywood (1-323 650 8509); **Falcon Theatre** 4252 Riverside Drive, Burbank (1-818 955 8004); **A Noise Within** 234 S Brand Boulevard, Glendale (1-818 546 1924); **Santa Monica Playhouse** 1211 Fourth Street, Santa Monica (1-310 394 9779).

Outside LA

For those who are prepared to travel to see a show, beyond Los Angeles lie several legendary Tony Award-winning theatres: **La Jolla Playhouse** 2910 La Jolla Village Drive, La Jolla (1-858 812 3858); **Laguna Playhouse** 606 Laguna Canyon Road, Laguna Beach (1-949 497 2787); **Old Globe Theatre** 1363 Old Globe Way, San Diego (1-619 239 2255); and **South Coast Repertory** 655 Town Center Drive, Costa Mesa (1-714 708 5555).

Dance

Los Angeles is a cultural melting pot and nowhere is that more obvious than in its dance community. Although the city does not have a national dance group or ballet company, it more than makes up for that in the sheer multitude of choreographers and dancers from various ethnic groups, who re-create dances and music from around the world. From Kultura Philippine Folk Arts to Middle Eastern groups such as Avaz International Dance Theatre and Israeli folk dance troupe Keshet Chaim Dance Ensemble, the LA dance scene is a diverse one. There are also individuals to look out for such as Carla Luna, who keeps the flame of flamenco alive; Sophiline Cheam Shapiro, who showcases the traditions of her native Cambodia; and Hae Kyung Lee, who brings her Korean ancestry to LA with her group, the Seoul Contemporary Dance Company.

There are also more cutting-edge modern troupes, such as Diavolo Dance Theater, whose performers slam their bodies against solid objects in a dance form known as 'hyperdance'. Then there are companies that mesh different forms: Brockus Project Dance Company mixes jazz with modern dance, while the Jazz Tap Ensemble melds jazz with tap. Other groups are dedicated to certain choreographers, such as the American Repertory Dance Company, which focuses on the works of Martha Graham and Isadora Duncan.

To find out what's on during your visit, pick up a copy of the *LA Times* or *LA Weekly*.

Venues

The **Dorothy Chandler Pavilion** at the Performing Arts Center in Downtown LA (*see page 228*) is the place to catch some of the bigger touring dance companies, including the Bolshoi Ballet and American Ballet Theater. Many other smaller theatre venues often put on dance performances.

Harriet & Charles Luckman Fine Arts Complex at Cal State LA

5151 State University Drive, at the I-710 & I-10, Alhambra (box office 1-323 343 6600/www.cal statela.edu/univ/luckman/luckman.htm). Bus 256, 258/I-10, exit Eastern Avenue north. **Open** *Box office* 10am-6pm Mon, Wed-Fri; noon-6pm Tue; 10am-4pm Sat, Sun. *Shows* usually 8pm Fri, Sat. **Tickets** $20-$40. **Credit** AmEx, MC, V.

In the past few years, colleges have been putting on dance performances, with cutting-edge performers and choreographers. Cal State, with its state-of-the-art theatre, is no exception, presenting dance from around the globe.

UCLA Center for the Performing Arts

405 Hilgard Avenue, at Sunset Boulevard, Westwood (1-310 825 2101/www.performingarts.ucla.edu). Bus 2, 21, 429, 561, 576/I-405, exit Sunset Boulevard east. **Open** *Box office* 9am-5pm Mon-Fri; closed Sat, Sun. *Shows* usually 8pm; days vary. **Tickets** $10-$40. **Credit** AmEx, MC, V.

UCLA's elegant and refurbished Royce Hall now presents many international dance artists as part of its performing arts programme.

Regional venues

The **Cerritos Center for the Performing Arts**, 12700 Centre Court Drive, Cerritos (1-800 300 4345/1-562 916 8500/www.cerritos center.com) presents ballet and big-ticket performances. In Orange County, national touring groups, including Mark Morris and Canada's Cirque Eloize, appear at the **Irvine Barclay Theater** on the University of California-Irvine (1-949 854 4646/www.the barclay.org), while the **Orange County Performing Arts Center**, Segerstrom Hall, 600 Town Center Drive, Costa Mesa (1-714 556 2121/www.ocpac.org) offers touring ballet companies and Broadway musicals.

Summer presentations

Watercourt at California Plaza

350 S Grand Avenue, at W Third Street, Downtown (events line 1-213 687 2159/office 1-213 687 2190/ www.grandperformances.org). Metro Civic Center-Tom Bradley or Pershing Square/bus 30, 31, 40, 42, 436, 445, 466, DASH A, D/I-110, exit Fourth Street east. **Open** *Office* 9am-5.30pm Mon-Fri; closed Sat, Sun. *Shows* usually noon, 7pm; days vary. **Tickets** free. **Map** p309 B2.

Like the John Anson Ford Amphitheatre (*see p257*), the California Plaza in Downtown is a perfect place to see dance performances in the open air. A water fountain serves as a backdrop and some performers dally directly in the pond. Organised by Grand Performances, events take place from June to October – and are free.

Trips Out of Town

Trips Out of Town

Discover some of the American West's most striking landscapes and attractive towns, not to mention the surreal delights of Las Vegas.

The Los Angeles urban area has so many attractions that it's almost overwhelming, but don't forget that it is also the gateway to some stunning sights and scenery elsewhere in California and beyond. The coast beckons you to the cities of Santa Barbara and San Diego, while the deserts, mountains and lakes offer a respite from the cities. And don't forget surreal Las Vegas or exotic Mexico, all within a few hours' drive of America's second-largest city.

This being the land of the automobile, the easiest – sometimes the only – way to get to the places listed below is by car. On some trips, such as those up US 101 towards San Francisco or through the Mojave desert, the drive itself is the experience. All the destinations described below involve a drive of an hour and a half or more – sometimes much more. For information on car hire and tips on driving, *see page 279*. It is also possible to travel by plane, train and bus to larger destinations such as Palm Springs, Santa Barbara, Las Vegas and San Diego.

Tourist information

Accommodation

California Association of Bed & Breakfast Inns (CABBI) *2715 Porter Street, Soquel, CA 95073 (1-831 464 8159/www.cabbi.com)*.
California Hotel & Motel Association *PO Box 160405, Sacramento, CA 95816 (1-916 444 5780/1-800 678 2462/www.chma.com)*.

Camping & outdoors

California Department of Fish & Game *1416 Ninth Street, 12th floor, Sacramento, CA 95814 (1-916 653 7664/www.dfg.ca.gov)*.
California Department of Parks & Recreation *PO Box 94296-0001, Sacramento, CA 94296 (1-916 653 6995/www.cal-parks.ca.gov)*.
State Park campground reservations *1-800 444 7275/www.park-net.com*.
US Forest Service *630 Sansome Street, San Francisco, CA 94111 (1-707 562 8737/www.campingreservations.gov)*.

General information

California Trade & Commerce Agency Division Office of Tourism *801 K Street, suite 1600, Sacramento, CA 95814 (1-916 322 3424/1-800 862 2543/www.gocalif.ca.gov)*.
The website is a veritable mine of information, with detailed guides to different regions, maps, a hotel reservation service, and so on.

Mountains

You've no doubt heard that in Los Angeles you can ski in the morning and surf in the evening, and the resorts of **Lake Arrowhead** and **Big Bear**, less than two hours from the coast, prove it. The drive to the San Bernardino Mountains takes you east on the I-10 through Downtown and various uninteresting suburbs until you get to the other side of San Bernardino. There, to the north, the looming mountains transport you, in a winding uphill drive, from an arid and brush-covered landscape to alpine. Though near each other, the two resorts are different in character. Lake Arrowhead is prettier, affluent and more artsy, while the focus at Big Bear is on mountain sports.

If you want an Alpine climate and landscape without the skiing, an alternative destination is **Idyllwild**, a pleasant, artsy community at the crest of the San Jacinto Mountains above Palm Springs. For information on getting there via the Palm Springs Aerial Tramway, *see page 268* **Palm Springs**. If you're driving, come off the I-10 at the junction with Highway 243 and follow it south.

Lake Arrowhead & Big Bear

At an altitude of 5,000 feet (1,500 metres), Lake Arrowhead is another world – an artificial lake set among pine and oak forests and crystal-clear air, with the neo-Bavarian **Arrowhead Village** and various smaller tourist and residential communities tucked discreetly away in the woods. Snow-covered in winter and desert-hot in the summer, it is, like many such delightful places, overrun with tourists (best to go off-season or on a weekday).

This being the States, however, and not Bavaria, the tourists can't let go of the internal combustion engine; the lake is speedboat heaven and so not great for swimming (which is better accomplished at the nearby, smaller **Lake Gregory** – though that can also get pretty crowded). More pleasant is the hiking and fishing, or you could walk the three-mile (five-kilometre) circumference of Lake Arrowhead and tackle the gym apparatus en route. In winter, the focus is on cross-country

The striking, otherworldly desertscape of **Death Valley**. *See p265.*

skiing and skating – there's a big ice rink in Blue Jay Village, halfway around the lake from Arrowhead Village.

Big Bear is very inviting under the snow. It has a large lake and offers some of the best downhill and cross-country skiing close to LA. In summer, the mountains become the site for downhill mountain bike races, hiking and horse riding, while the lake is used for fishing, windsurfing, sailboarding, water-skiing and jetskiing. At the summer solstice, it's a prime spot for outdoor raves.

Where to stay & eat

There are numerous inns, hostelries and camping sites to choose from in Arrowhead. For details, contact the **Community Chamber of Commerce** (*see below*) located above Subway restaurant. The restaurant is nothing to write home about; your best bet is to buy picnic supplies at Jensen's Market in Blue Jay Village.

In Big Bear, try the following establishments: **Apples Bed & Breakfast Inn** (42430 Moonridge Road, Big Bear Lake, CA 92315, 1-909 866 0903, rates $130-$190); **Truffles Bed & Breakfast** (43591 Bow Canyon Road, Big Bear Lake, CA 92315, 1-909 585 2772, rates $138-$150) or **Windy Point Inn** (39015 North Shore Drive, Fawnskin, CA 92333, 1-909 866 2746, rates $125-$245).

Contact the **Big Bear Lake Resort Association** (*see below*) for details of camping sites and dining options.

Getting there

By car

For Lake Arrowhead, take the I-10 east to the I-215 north, then Hwy 30 east for one mile to Hwy 18 (Waterman Avenue exit). Follow Hwy 18 up the mountain and take the Lake Arrowhead turn-off. For Big Bear, continue on Hwy 18 and turn right across the dam to Big Bear Lake.

By train

Metrolink (1-800 371 5465/www.metrolinktrains.com) provides a regular service from Union Station to San Bernadino ($15 round trip, about 1½hrs). From there, Mountain Area Regional Rapid Transit Authority (MARTA, Big Bear 1-909 584 1111/Lake Arrowhead 1-909 338 1113) runs buses and a dial-a-ride service to Arrowhead and Big Bear.

By airport shuttle

You can get to Big Bear with Big Bear Shuttle (1-909 585 5514), which offers a door-to-door air service to Ontario and LAX airports and also a van service that can carry bikes, skis and snowboards. It costs $90 from Ontario airport; $180 from LAX.

Tourist information

Big Bear Lake Resort Association

630 Bartlett Road, Big Bear, CA 92315 (1-909 866 7000/www.bigbearinfo.com). **Open** 8am-6pm Mon-Fri; 9am-5pm Sat, Sun.

Lake Arrowhead Community Chamber of Commerce

PO Box 219, Lake Arrowhead, CA 92352 (accommodation 1-800 337 3716/1-909 337 3715/ marketing & tourism 1-909 336 1547/www.lake arrowhead.net). **Open** 9am-5pm Mon-Fri; 10am-3pm Sat; closed Sun.

Deserts

Though it may not seem so amid the greenery of Beverly Hills or Pasadena, Los Angeles is basically built on desert, sustaining itself with water pumped in from as far away as Northern California and the Colorado River. The forbidding dry moat encircling most of the city (and most of the Southwest, for that matter) is magnificent, humbling, weird – and not to be missed. The big cities of the Mojave desert – Palm Springs and Las Vegas (in Nevada) – are like other worlds transplanted into the surrounding desert. Otherwise, the desert

Desert safety

In the Los Angeles basin, the cold Pacific Ocean acts as a giant air-conditioner, but inland is like the Sahara (you're actually on the same latitude as North Africa). Summer temperatures regularly top 110°F (43°C); in winter, after dark, they can plummet below freezing. The best time to visit the desert is during temperate February and March, when most years it bursts briefly – but spectacularly – into spring bloom.

Sunstroke and heat exhaustion are two dangers to watch for in the desert. If you're visiting in the hot season – April to October – wear a hat and plenty of sunscreen, even if you're going outside for just a few moments. Hike early in the morning or late in the day, and never go hiking alone. Take plenty of water: a half-pint of Evian isn't going to cut it for a day out in Joshua Tree in July. A gallon a day per person is the recommended intake. In summer, high winds blow at 30-40mph (50-65kph), so lip salve is essential.

Make sure your vehicle is up to the trip, too. If it starts to overheat, turn the air-conditioning off, open the windows and turn the heating full on to let heat escape from the engine. If you park for any length of time, leave a window open a crack, and use care when getting back into your car – those door handles and steering wheels can get hot!

Promised Land. The trees also lend their name to **Joshua Tree National Park**, at the confluence of the Mojave and Sonora deserts. Enter from the south via the I-10 or from the north via Highway 62 and the small, uninteresting town of **Twentynine Palms** that services a Marine base nearby.

Admission is $10 per vehicle; there are two visitors' centres, one at each entrance (the main one is at 74485 National Park Drive in Twentynine Palms, 1-760 367 7511/www.nps.gov/jotr). The area also has spectacular rock formations that are very popular with climbers. Wildlife tends to be shy and nocturnal; early morning and evening are the best times to see coyotes or roadrunners.

North-west of the park, about five miles off Highway 62, is **Pioneertown**, originally a set for movies and TV (the *Cisco Kid* and *Gene Autry Show* were filmed here) and now a working, if tiny 'Main Street'. Pioneertown retains that Old West feel, and its dirt roads make you realise why so many cowboys were called 'Dusty'. It's anchored by **Pappy & Harriet's Pioneertown Palace** (1-760 365 5956/www.pioneertown.com), a getaway for the smart set and a hangout for locals, with big food and live country music. There are occasional gunfight demonstrations a few paces down the road near the old post office.

Nature lovers will be more inclined toward the **Pipes Canyon Preserve** outside of town, owned by a private conservation group and every bit as wild as a national park. Ask at the visitor centre (51010 Pipes Canyon Road, 1-760 369 7105) for information about cougars, bears and bobcats, petroglyphs and active springs. Admission to the preserve is free.

Where to stay

There are nine campgrounds in Joshua Tree National Park (but only two with water) and plenty of motels along Highway 62, but one place that really stands out in Twentynine Palms is the delightful, quirky **Twentynine Palms Inn** (73950 Inn Avenue, 1-760 367 3505/www.29palmsinn.com). It's been in the same family for four generations, and has individual cabins with period furnishings, a large vegetable garden, a swimming pool and a fine restaurant – and owner Jane Smith is a mine of local lore.

Also recommended in Twentynine Palms is **Homestead Inn** (74153 Two Mile Road, 1-760 367 0030/www.desertgold.com). This B&B owes its charms to its owner, Jerri Hagman, who has given every room in her ranch house its own personality, cooks up a breakfast worthy of the Famous Five and even provides

consists of mile upon mile of subtly hued, near-naked mountain ridges and plains, dotted with the vestiges of human habitation: dead mining towns, abandoned gas stations and diners on the old Route 66 and the ubiquitous US military, with its vast bases. The wilderness is inhabited by strange creatures of both the four- and the two-footed variety: coyotes and roadrunners, gun-toting rednecks and UFO believers – but you'll also find nature lovers, history buffs and the salt-of-the-earth types you'd imagine in rural America.

Joshua Tree National Park

To the north of Palm Springs, the desert valley gives way to massive granite monoliths, scrub and, as far as the eye can see, strange, jagged trees with spiky blooms. These are Joshua trees, actually a form of cactus, named after the prophet Joshua showing the way to the cassette tapes with directions to local sights. The B&B **Roughley Manor** (74744 Joe Davis Road, 1-760 367 3238) is anything but rough, with its Laura Ashley interior.

Death Valley National Park

As you bid LA farewell, heading up the 5 and 14 freeways through the Antelope Valley, the enormity of LA County's 4,000 square miles (10,360 square kilometres) is unmistakable. This is particularly true as you pass through **Lancaster**, a community that personifies the urban sprawl that has become a flashpoint in American politics in recent years, with picturesque street names such as Avenue M. In **Palmdale**, you can stop at **Edwards Air Force Base**, home of *The Right Stuff* and occasional site of space shuttle landings. There is a museum on the base, open five days a week, which has planes and memorabilia from over 50 years of flight testing. Once a year, usually in October, there is an open day when the public can see a display of the latest USAF technology in action (1-661 277 8050 for details).

Continue north on Highway 14 through the town of **Mojave** (a good place to get petrol) and join US 395, past the erosion-carved formations of **Red Rock Canyon State Park**, made famous in *Jurassic Park*. Turn east on to Highway 178 and head into **Death Valley**, one of the hottest places in the world.

Its stillness belies a varied terrain riddled with diverse plant and animal life, whose beauty lies in the subtle colours and geological formations of the undulating rock, dunes and dry salt lake bed – at 282 feet (86 metres) below sea level, it's the lowest point in the western hemisphere. Despite killer temperatures of 120°F (49°C) during the summer, and little water, humans have tried to inhabit Death Valley, leaving such landmarks as Scotty's Castle, a 1920s Spanish-Moorish mansion, and the Harmony Borax Works ruins. There are many dramatic vistas, but if you've seen Antonioni's sexy film *Zabriskie Point*, you won't want to miss that spot. Park admission is $10 per vehicle.

Where to stay & eat

There are several campgrounds (you can book at the Furnace Creek and Texas Spring group campgrounds on 1-800 365 2267), and three lodgings: the ultra-posh **Furnace Creek Inn**, the rustic-style **Furnace Creek Ranch** (both 1-800 236 7916/1-760 786 2345) and the inexpensive **Stovepipe Wells Village** (1-760 786 2387). They're less crowded in the summer – for obvious reasons.

Getting there

By car

Death Valley has several approach roads, leading from US 395 on the California side and US 95 from Nevada. The California approaches are probably the most breathtakingly scenic, particularly Hwy 190.

Tourist information

Death Valley Visitors Center

Death Valley National Park, Hwy 190, at Furnace Creek, Death Valley, CA 92328 (1-760 786 2331/ www.nps.gov./deva). **Open** 8am-4pm daily.

Las Vegas

The cluster of casinos at the state border is a brief desert bloom that signals your arrival in the gambling state of Nevada. When you finally enter the Las Vegas Valley, the city emerges from the nothingness like Shangri-La dipped in neon. You've arrived in the capital of kitsch: several mind-blowing miles of neon extravaganzas, over-the-top fantasy hotels, magic shows, sex shows, free drinks and all-you-can-eat buffets, all enticing you to part with your cash. It's horrendous and fabulous at the same time. The gambling never stops – which is exciting at night, depressing by day – and nor will you, until the adrenaline rush is over and you want to pass out or get out.

To get the biggest thrill out of Vegas, try to arrive at night and head straight for Las Vegas Boulevard (aka the Strip). Most of the action in Vegas takes place in the new themed casino-hotels that line the four-mile (6.5-kilometre) length of the Strip, and on Fremont Street in downtown. For the full story, you'll need the *Time Out Guide to Las Vegas*.

Main casinos

Apart from their deluxe suites and private gaming rooms, the hotel rooms and casinos are pretty generic. The difference is in the theming, the betting odds and stakes and the quality of the cheap food. So pick one, stay there and visit the rest. Casinos in Vegas change faster than the seasons – the latest one due for implosion is the Desert Inn, once owned by reclusive billionaire Howard Hughes – so by the time you read this, another kitsch colossus will have appeared. All major credit cards are accepted.

Bellagio

3600 Las Vegas Boulevard S, at W Flamingo Road, Las Vegas, NV 89109 (reservations 1-888 987 6667/ front desk 1-702 693 7444/fax 1-702 693 8546/ www.bellagiolasvegas.com). **Rates** $159-$759 room; $300-$1,600 suite.

Trips Out of Town

Built on the site of the famous Dunes hotel, this upmarket extravaganza, with its collection of fine art (Picasso, Cézanne, Degas), opened in 1998 to rave reviews. The $1.6-billion complex is modelled on an Italian village, surrounding a 12-acre (5ha) artificial lake – go there at night to see the truly amazing fountain display. Under-18s are not allowed on the property unless they're staying there.

Caesars Palace

3570 Las Vegas Boulevard S, at W Flamingo Road, Las Vegas, NV 89109 (reservations 1-800 634 6661/ 1-702 731 7110/fax 1-702 731 6636/www.caesars. com). **Rates** $100-$299 room; $250-$750 suite.

Caesars is the archetypal Vegas casino, with its low ceilings hung with crystal prisms, and staff clad in Roman costume. Check out the outsize version of Michelangelo's *David* – this one, unlike the original, is uncircumcised – and the surreal Caesars Forum Shops, a huge, enclosed, Rome-themed shopping mall complete with statues, a trompe l'oeil sky and programmed lighting that simulates a transition from dawn to dusk.

Mandalay Bay

3950 Las Vegas Boulevard S, between W Tropicana Avenue & Russell Road, Las Vegas, NV 89109 (reservations 1-877 632 7000/front desk 1-702 632 7777/fax 1-702 632 7011/www.mandalaybay.com). **Rates** $89-$500 room; $189-$1,000 suite.

The garish Y-shaped gold tower at the bottom of the Strip marks out this tropical-themed luxury playground. It's brighter and more spacious than many of the other casinos, with a cluster of good restaurants and a fabulous water park, complete with a wide sandy beach and wave machine.

The Mirage

3400 Las Vegas Boulevard S, between W Flamingo & Spring Mountain Roads, Las Vegas, NV 89109 (reservations 1-800 627 6667/1-702 791 7444/fax 1-702 791 7446/www.themirage.com). **Rates** $79-$400 room; $175-$1,025 suite.

Created by local casino tycoon Steve Wynn, this was the first of the massive themed casinos, opened in 1989. It draws the crowds with its elaborate Polynesian theming, an erupting volcano on the street and its hugely successful (and expensive) show by bizarre illusionists Siegfried and Roy and their white tigers.

New York-New York

3790 Las Vegas Boulevard S, at W Tropicana Avenue, Las Vegas, NV 89109 (reservations 1-800 675 3267/front desk 1-702 740 6822/fax 1-702 740 6700/www.nynyhotelcasino.com). **Rates** $54-$300 room; $100-$500 suite.

This is Vegas theming at its most extreme, with its one-third real-size New York skyline, including the Empire State building, Chrysler building, the Statue of Liberty and a miniature Brooklyn Bridge. Above them all, the Manhattan Express rollercoaster twists, turns and rolls, with a 144ft (44m) dive past the valet entrance.

Viva **Las Vegas**!

Paris

3655 Las Vegas Boulevard S, between Harmon Avenue & E Flamingo Road, Las Vegas, NV 89109 (reservations 1-888 266 5687/front desk 1-702 946 4222/fax 1-702 946 3830/www.paris-lv.com). **Rates** $49-$400 room; $350-$1,210 suite.

Ooh la la! Take the lift up the half-size facsimile of the Eiffel Tower for stunning views over the city (and Bellagio's lake on the opposite side of the Strip). Paris – which opened in 1999, along with the Venetian and Mandalay Bay – also offers a small and lively casino area and good French pastries.

Venetian

3355 Las Vegas Boulevard S, south of Sands Avenue, Las Vegas, NV 89109 (reservations 1-888 283 6423/front desk 1-702 414 1000/fax 1-702 414 2122/www.venetian.com). **Rates** $109-$599 single; $309-$1,000 suite.

Welcome to Venice, with a copy of the Doges' Palace, canals full of real water, authentic gondolas, ceiling frescos – oh, and they managed to squeeze in a casino and a shopping mall, too. The Venetian's world-class restaurants are proof of Vegas's new-found status as a gourmet dining destination.

Other casinos

Next door to the Mirage is **Treasure Island** (3300 Las Vegas Boulevard South, 1-800 944 7444/www.treasureislandlasvegas.com), which provides the best free spectacle along the Strip. Join thousands of other pedestrians to watch pirates and the British navy duke it out on Bucanneer Bay, amid much pyrotechnic cannonballing until a full-scale frigate disappears underwater.

At **Excalibur** (No.3850, 1-800 937 7777/ www.excaliburcasino.com), Wagner meets King Arthur and a flaming dragon in a confused medieval-themed cartoon castle. A 70-foot (21-metre) high bronze lion presides over the entrance of the gargantuan **MGM Grand** (No.3799, 1-800 929 1111/www.mgmgrand.com), the largest hotel in the world with more than 5,000 rooms. Families should check out **Circus Circus** (No. 2880, 1-800 634 3450/ www.circuscircus.com), where acrobats turn somersaults above the slot machines.

There's also the Egyptian-themed **Luxor** at the south end of the Strip (No.3900, 1-800 288 1000/www.luxor.com), complete with a 30-storey, sleek black glass pyramid and night-time lighting display. The newly rebuilt **Aladdin** (No. 3667, 1-877 333 9474/1-702 736 0111/www.aladdincasino.com) has Far Eastern theming, a 1,000-room tower and, of course, a massive shopping mall.

Off the Strip, you can join locals at the popular **Rio** (3700 W Flamingo Road, 1-888 746 7482/1-702 252 7777/www.playrio.com) for gaudy Latin-American theming and waitresses in teeny thongs, or mingle with the young and hip at the guitar-heavy and surprisingly sophisticated **Hard Rock Hotel** (4455 Paradise Road, 1-800 473 7625/1-702 693 5000/ www.hardrock.com).

Fremont Street

If you're starting to get annoyed that your gambling dollars are funding all these extravagant spectacles, take yourself to **El Cortez** (600 Fremont Street, 1-800 634 6703/ 1-702 385 5200). The nicotine-stained walls, smoke-filled, jammed gaming room and sour, ageing cocktail waitresses are a welcome relief after all the razzmatazz of the Strip. It also has single-deck and $2 blackjack tables and claims to have the 'loosest' slots in Vegas.

El Cortez is one of the few remaining outposts of seediness on Fremont Street – formerly Vegas's tawdry 'Glitter Gulch', now the **Fremont Street Experience**. Four street blocks have been enclosed in a huge barrel vault holding thousands of lightbulbs, which

provide stunning, computer-programmed light and sound shows, on the hour. Don't miss it.

You can play high-stakes poker at **Binion's Horseshoe** (128 Fremont Street, 1-800 237 6537/1-702 382 1600/www.horseshoe.com), host of the annual World Series of Poker, and have a good meal at the **Golden Nugget** (129 Fremont Street, 1-702 385 7111), the snazziest casino-hotel on Fremont.

Getting there

By car

Take the I-10 east to the I-15 north until you reach Las Vegas. It's 286 miles (458km). The drive takes around 5-6hrs.

By air

From LAX on American Eagle (1-800 433 7300/ www. aa.com), Southwest (1-800 435 9792/ www.southwestairline.com), United Express (1-800 241 6522/www.united.com) or America West (1-800 235 292/www.americawest.com). Round-trip flights start at around $75; about 1hr 15mins.

By train

Amtrak (1-800 872 7245/www.amtrak.com) has tentative plans to run one train a day from LA to Las Vegas, starting in spring 2001. Fares are not set.

By bus

Greyhound (1-800 229 9424/www.greyhound.com) has 19 buses a day. The journey time is 5½ hrs. Fare: $60 round trip.

Tourist information

Las Vegas Convention & Visitors Authority

3150 Paradise Road, Las Vegas, NV 89109 (1-702 892 0711/www.lasvegas24hours.com). **Open** 8am-5pm daily.

Heading North

The Pacific Coast Highway (Highway 1) starts in Santa Monica and wends its way through the hilly coastline of Malibu and to the agricultural flatlands of the small towns of **Oxnard** and **Ventura**. They serve as a jumping-off point for the **Channel Islands National Park**, a wildlife sanctuary on an archipelago of five islands: take a boat or plane from Oxnard's **Channel Islands Harbor** or **Ventura Harbor** (contact the Ventura Visitors & Convention Bureau on 1-805 648 2075/www. ventura-usa.com). If you want to bypass this portion of the trip, take US 101 through the San Fernando Valley where it meets up with the PCH just before Ventura.

Palm Springs

Permanently blue skies and a mercury level that never drops below 70°F (21°C) made this desert town an obvious winter playground for Hollywood movers and shakers in the 1920s and '30s and then again for the Rat Pack in the '60s. But after years of recession it became as tired as its blue-rinsed, surgically enhanced, golf cart-careening retirees. Now, with the resurgence of Martini-drinking, swing-dancing hipsters and modernist devotees, what was deemed retro and tacky is once again in vogue.

The town consists simply of a commercial spine – North Palm Canyon Drive (where most of the drinking and eating locales are clustered) leading into East Palm Canyon Drive. You can still find gems of modernist architecture by the likes of William Cody, Richard Neutra, John Lautner and Albert Frey (get the 'Palm Springs Brief History & Architectural Guide' at the visitors centre). Frey's classic 1965 Gas Tramway Station, a Jetsonian structure at the town entrance that came near to demolition, is now the **Montana St Martin Gallery** (2901 North Palm Canyon Drive, at Tramway Road, 1-760 323 7183). It's usually open noon to 7pm, Thursday to Monday.

A sojourn in Palm Springs usually consists of idling around the pool, but if you want the authentic desert, you can head south on South Palm Canyon Drive into the Indian Canyons for good hiking. For a total change of ecosystem, take the **Palm Springs Aerial Tramway** (1-760 325 1391, $17, $11 children, open 10am-8pm Mon-Fri; 8am-8pm Sat, Sun) to the crest of San Jacinto. From this alpine spot you can walk a mile to Idyllwild, a mountain retreat housing a small artsy community and school. And don't miss the 3,000 varieties of desert plants at the eccentric **Moorten Botanical Garden** (1701 South Palm Canyon Drive, 1-760 327 6555).

Palm Springs also has a well-established gay scene. The most popular bars are off East Palm Canyon Drive. Every year, for a whole weekend in March, the town plays host to the huge White Party, perhaps the most famous and lavish event of the Circuit.

Where to eat

For Cal-eclectic food, try **Johannes** (196 South Indian Canyon Drive, 1-760 778 0017), while

Montana St Martin Gallery.

Le Vallauris (385 West Tahquitz Canyon Way, 1-888 525 5852/1-760 325 5059) serves upscale French cuisine in a romantic setting. Other option are **Livreri's Italian Restaurant** 350 South Indian Canyon Drive, 1-760 327 1419); Continental cuisine at the **St James at the Vineyard** (265 South Palm Canyon Drive, 1-760 320 8041); and the 1950s-style **Muriel's Supper Club** (210 S Palm Canyon Drive, 1-760 416 6876), where the chef's 'tasting experience' ($75 per person without drink) is the most popular way to dine.

Where to stay

Many of the ever-increasing number of gay hotels are based around the area known as Warm Sands. Try the **East Canyon Hotel & Spa** (1-877 324 6835/1-760 320 1928), the small and pretty **La Posada** (1-888 411 4949/1-760 323 1402/www.laposada.com) or the wonderfully named **Inndulge**, (1-800 833 5675/1-760 327 1408/ www.inndulge.com) where they boast that clothing is forever optional.

Ballantines

1420 N Indian Canyon Drive, Palm Springs, CA 92262 (1 800 780 3464/1-760 320 1178/ www.ballantineshotels.com). **Rates** $169-$265. **Credit** AmEx, MC, V.
Scottish entrepreneur Fraser Robertson and his English artist girlfriend, Sarah Robarts, have transformed an unremarkable 1950s motel into a groovy sensual haven. Electric blue Astroturf pops around the pool and jacuzzi area, and the 14 rooms have theme monikers that promise divinely kitsch interiors, and don't for a moment disappoint. The Marilyn Monroe Room is painted in a fiendishly girlie pink with a classic 'atomic' sofa in pink vinyl, pink Formica counters, a pink-painted TV, black 1950s radio (which takes a minimum of five minutes to warm up) and a pink-and-black checked vinyl floor.

Korakia

257 S Patencio Road, Palm Springs,
CA 92262 (1 760 864 6411/fax 760 864
4147). **Rates** $119-$279. **No credit cards**.
Behind ornate, Moroccan-style doors lies a
cobblestone courtyard dotted with oleander,
date and olive trees, mosaic-encrusted
fountains and a teardrop-shaped pool.
Welcome to Korakia, originally built in 1924
by Scottish artist Gordon Coutts to remind him
of his beloved Tangiers. Restored by urban
archeologist Doug Smith, it's now a sensual
bohemian paradise; regular guests include
Annie Leibovitz and Tom Ford. Korakia's new
addition on the opposite side of the street is
a Mediterranean villa with guest houses, built
for early screen star J Carol Nash.

L'Horizon Garden Hotel

1050 E Palm Canyon Drive, Palm Springs,
CA 92262 (1-800 377 7855/1-760 323
1858/www.lhorizonhotel.com). **Rates** room
$125-$165; house $650. **Credit** AmEx, DC,
Disc, MC, V.
Modernist architect William Cody's white,
single-storey, flat-roofed bungalows,
scattered around the obligatory turquoise
pool and smooth manicured lawns, fill you
with the kind of optimism that is signature
Palm Springs circa the 1950s. The 21 rooms
have low-beamed wooden ceilings, pastel-
coloured walls and kingsize beds to give a
casual at-home feeling, while floor-to-ceiling
plantation shutters provide privacy. Perks
include a complimentary breakfast and
newspaper and use of bicycles.

Miracle Manor

12589 Reposo Way, Desert Hot Springs,
CA 92240 (1-760 329 6641/www.miracle
manor.com). **Rates** $80-$155. **Credit** MC, V.
Miracle Manor is located ten miles north-east
of Palm Springs in the sleepier, downmarket
Desert Hot Springs. From the outside it still
looks like a divey 1950s motel, but inside it's
now a chic, bare-bones monastery of style –
thanks to new owners, avant-garde designer
April Greiman and her partner architect,
Michael Rotundi. There are six modestly sized
rooms with adjoining bathrooms. Enjoy the
rock and cactus garden, soak in the
boomerang-shaped pool filled with mineral-
rich spring water or indulge in one of the
myriad massage or beauty treatments. There
are no phones or TVs.

The Willows Historic Palm Springs Inn

412 W Tahquitz Canyon, Palm Springs, CA
92262 (1-800 966 9597/1-760 320 0771/
fax 760 320 0780/www.thewillowspalm
springs.com). **Rates** $275-$525. **Credit**
AmEx, DC, Disc, MC, V.
Staying at the Willows, nestled on a hillside
a pillow throw from the San Jacinto
Mountains, is like staying in a posh friend's
Mediterranean villa. Built in 1927 for a
politician, past visitors have included Carole
Lombard and Clark Gable on their
honeymoon, Marion Davies (lifetime mistress
of newspaper magnate William Randolph
Hearst) and even Albert Einstein. It has eight
rooms – each evoking Hollywood's golden
era – and lush gardens dripping with scarlet
bougainvillea and towering palms.

Getting there

By car

Take the I-10 east and then Highway 111 into
the town itself. Just over 100 miles (160km);
about 2hrs. Watch out for the whirring wind
farms as you approach Palm Springs.

By air

From LAX on American Eagle (1-800 433
7300/www.aa.com) or United Express (1-800
241 6522/www.united.com). Round trip from
$150. The flight is about 50mins.

By bus

Greyhound (1-800 229 9424/
www.greyhound.com) operates ten buses a
day. Cost is $30 round trip; 2-4hrs.

Tourist information

Palm Springs Visitor Information Center

2781 N Palm Canyon Drive, CA 92262
(1-800 347 7746/1-760 778 8418/
www.palm-springs.org). **Open** 9am-5pm daily.

Korakia.

Trips Out of Town

After Ventura, it's well worth taking a detour inland on Highway 33 to idyllic **Ojai** (say 'Oh-hi'), a small community in a semi-arid valley of oaks and orange groves nestled at the foot of the imposing Topa Topa Mountains. The town is charming, a wealthy combination of leftover hippiedom and a provincial arts community that has spawned such treats as the annual and much-respected **Ojai Music Festival** in early summer, and **Barts Books** (302 West Matilija Road, 1-805 646 3755), an open-air, second-hand bookshop with shelves on the exterior walls.

Ojai is stuffed with great restaurants serving a range of cuisines. One not to be missed for dinner is the **Ranch House** (South Lomita Avenue; 1-805 646 2360), an old farmhouse with an idyllic herb garden from where much of your dinner may come. If you've never eaten fresh lemon verbena or tiny wild strawberries, you're in for a treat. For more information on the town, contact the **Ojai Valley Chamber of Commerce** (1-805 646 8126).

After Ojai, you can head west along Highway 150 – through staggering mountains – and rejoin US 101 for a pleasant drive past sparkling, south-facing coastline towards Santa Barbara. Many beaches here are hidden by coastal cliffs, including several at which anti-nudity laws receive only slack enforcement.

Santa Barbara

Santa Barbara is California's Riviera, 90 miles (145 kilometres) north of LA, next to the sparkling ocean (marred only by offshore oil rigs, causing occasional tar globs on bare feet) in a fertile valley framed by the lush Santa Ynez Mountains. The affluent inhabit the hillside communities of Montecito and Summerland south of town, but the region is also known for its great surf and a laid-back beach community feel. It was once home to the Spanish, who left a firm imprint in the shape of **Mission Santa Barbara** (*see page 272* **On a mission**) and some of the best Mission-style architecture in this region. There's only one tall edifice, the El Encanto Hotel; the rest are white-stucco, red-tiled buildings. There are also some historic adobe structures.

Park in any of the municipal parking lots (first 90 minutes free) and take a walk through the 12 blocks of downtown up busy **State Street**, lined with cafés and pleasant shops, from Gutierrez Street to Victoria Street and back down Anacapa Street. The 1920s El Paseo was California's first shopping mall – making it a landmark if there ever was one – and the **Santa Barbara Museum of Art** (1130 State Street, 1-805 963 4364) has recently mounted

some excellent, high-profile shows. The nearby Moorish **Santa Barbara Courthouse** is a marvel. You can drive the official **Scenic Route** for a climb through the surrounding hill communities, a stop at the mission and, from Alameda Padre Serra Road, a spectacular view over town and ocean. The Botanical Gardens and Hot and Cold Springs Trails are among many natural standouts.

Where to eat

Santa Barbara has many restaurants on a par with those of Los Angeles, but the city's best-regarded dining experience is to be had for under $10 at **La Super Rica Taqueria** (622 Milpas Street, 1-805 963 2840). It's renowned as the favourite Mexican restaurant of celebrity chef (and Santa Barbarian) Julia Child. You can also try **Brophy Bros Clam Bar & Restaurant** (119 Harbor Way, 1-805 966 4418), a casual spot with a harbour view and great seafood.

Where to stay

If you can afford it, stay at the luxurious **Biltmore Hotel** in Montecito (1260 Channel Drive, Santa Barbara, CA 93108, 1-800 332 3442). Otherwise, there are numerous B&Bs, including the **Cheshire Cat** (36 West Valerio Street, Santa Barbara, CA 93101, 1-805 569 1610). **Sycamore Cottage** (646 N Hope Avenue, Santa Barbara, CA 93110, 1-805 687 7055), run by Saral, a massage therapist and minister, and David, a screenwriter, is a secluded, woodsy retreat with only one (large) room. Otherwise, contact the **Hot Spots Passport Reservation Service** (1-800 793 7666/1-805 965 0430).

Getting there

By car

For the scenic route, head north on Hwy 1 (Pacific Coast Highway) and join the US 101, which goes direct to Santa Barbara. Distance is 96 miles (110km), and it takes about 2hrs.

By air

From LAX on American Eagle (1-800 433 7300/www.aa.com) or United Express (1-800 241 6522/www.united.com). $128-$284 round trip; about 40mins.

By train

Amtrak (1-800 872 7245/www.amtrak.com) schedules five trains a day. Round trip tickets cost $32-$48. The journey takes 2½-3hrs.

By bus

Greyhound (1-800 229 9424/www.greyhound.com) has 11 buses daily for a 2-4hr journey. $24 round trip.

Affluent and pretty **Santa Barbara**, a two-hour drive from LA. *See p270.*

Tourist information

Santa Barbara Visitor Information Center

1 Garden Street, Santa Barbara, CA 93101 (1-805 965 3021/www.santabarbara.com). **Open** *July, Aug* 9am-6pm Mon-Sat; 10am-5pm Sun; *Mar-June, Sept-Oct* 9am-5pm Mon-Sat; 10am-5pm Sun; *Nov-Feb* 9am-4pm Mon-Sat; 10am-4pm Sun.

Further up the coast

North from Santa Barbara on Highway 154 is the **Santa Ynez Valley**, heart of the burgeoning Central Coast wine growing region; much of it feels like Napa or Sonoma 20 years ago. The largest town is touristy **Solvang**, which claims the largest ethnic Danish population of any town in America and is home to the **Mission Santa Ines** (*see page 272* **On a mission**). Continue on Highway 1 to **San Luis Obispo**, a laid-back little town with a historic shopping area, another Spanish mission and the **Sycamore Mineral Springs** (*see page 274* **Spas & hot springs**). Don't miss the **Madonna Inn** (100 Madonna Road, San Luis Obispo, CA 93405, 1-800 543 9666), built in 1958 by road builder Alex Madonna and his wife Phyllis. Its 110 rooms are all different – elaborate fantasies based on a palette of blue, green and, predominantly, pink, pink, pink.

Other sights further north include the completely over-the-top **Hearst Castle** in San Simeon. Designed in the 1920s by celebrated California architect Julia Morgan for newspaper tycoon William Randolph Hearst, it was the model for Xanadu in *Citizen Kane*. It can be visited only by guided tour; details on 1-800 444 4445/www.hearstcastle.org. Then there's

spectacular **Big Sur**, a stunning stretch of coastline, with fog-swathed redwood forests and winding cliffs that drop sharply down to windy beaches; **Carmel** – a well-preserved, pretty town best known for its one-time mayor, Clint Eastwood; the **Monterey Peninsula** and touristy **Monterey** itself.

From here it is another 100 miles (160 kilometres) or so, via the surfing town of **Santa Cruz**, to **San Francisco** and its environs; that's most definitely another story, covered in the *Time Out San Francisco Guide*.

Heading South

Catalina Island

It's hard to imagine anywhere in Southern California where the golf cart could replace the automobile as the preferred mode of street transport, but this is the case on Catalina. *The Prisoner* would have felt at home on this small, impossibly cute island, about 20 miles (32 kilometres) from San Pedro, with its clean beaches and clear water, undulating pastures, natural bay and twee town named Avalon. Most of the island is owned by the Santa Catalina Island Company (1-310 510 2000), which maintains strict limits on cars and growth.

In the early 1900s, Catalina was an offshore playground for movie stars. In 1919, it was purchased by William Wrigley Jr – heir to the chewing gum fortune – who built the impressive art deco Avalon Theater and Casino, now the **Santa Catalina Island Museum** (1 Casino Way, Avalon; 1-310 510 2414/www.catalinas.net/museum/html), dedicated to the

On a mission

'With the best theological intentions in the world,' argues late Los Angeles historian Carey McWilliams in his seminal book *Southern California: An Island on the Land*, 'the Franciscan padres eliminated Indians with the effectiveness of Nazis operating concentration camps'. During the Spanish conquest of California, the Spanish missionary monks, led by Father Junípero Serra, founded a string of 21 missions from San Diego in the south to Sonoma, north of San Francisco. The first, San Diego de Alcala, was established in 1769, the last, San Francisco Solano, in 1823, and by 1848 the mission system had come to an end.

The aim behind the missions was to convert the tribal peoples and establish self-sustaining communities. They succeeded in creating productive, wealthy farms and a reputation for hospitality. Meanwhile, the forced Native American converts died in their thousands from a combination of depression, disease and malnutrition. In the late 19th century, the Californian missions were reinvented as an icon of tradition, solid values and romance. For the zealous Spanish padres had also left a legacy of mission architecture: white, sometimes Moorish buildings, with bougainvillea-shaded quadrangles and simple, solid interiors with handcrafted furniture. This revised image spawned Mission-style architecture and decor, a popular and influential branch of Californian design.

It is possible to tour the missions, many of which have been renovated or reconstructed and now function as Catholic parishes. The 21 missions are all located near US 101, which loosely follows the old El Camino Real ('Royal Road'), named in honour of the Spanish monarchy that financed the colonising expeditions. (The stretch of the 101 from San Diego to LA is now the I-5.)

In San Diego you can see the first mission to be founded, **San Diego de Alcala** (10818 San Diego Mission Road, 1-619 281 8449), and – a few miles north, just east of Oceanside on Highway 76 – the 18th, **San Luis Rey de Francia** (4050 Mission Avenue, San Luis Rey, 1-760 757 3651). The remains of **San Juan Capistrano** (1-949 234 1300) lie at in San Juan Capistrano, about 40 miles (64 kilometres) south of Long Beach. Every year, on 19 March, it celebrates the return of the cliff swallows from Argentina.

Mission Santa Barbara

In LA County itself you can visit **San Gabriel** (428 S Mission Drive, San Gabriel, 1-626 457 3035), formerly one of the wealthiest missions, with a copper baptismal font from King Carlos III of Spain and priceless statues. **San Fernando Rey de España** (15151 San Fernando Mission Boulevard, Mission Hills, 1-818 361 0186) is the largest free-standing adobe structure in California. Just north of LA, in Ventura, is **San Buenaventura** (211 East Main Street, 1-805 643 4318).

If you tour the Central Coast, you can visit **Santa Barbara** (2201 Laguna Street, Santa Barbara, 1-805 682 4713), **Santa Ines** in Solvang (1760 Mission Drive, 1-805 688 4815) and **La Purisima Conception** in Lompoc (2295 Purisima Road, 1-805 733 3713). **San Luis de Obispo de Tolosa**, whose chapel was built of logs, is further north in San Luis Obispo (751 Palm Street, 1-805 543 6850); further north still is **San Miguel Archangel** (775 Mission Street, San Miguel, 1-805 467 3256); then **San Antonio de Padua** (Mission Creek Road, Jolon, 1-831 385 4478), followed by **Nuestra Señora de la Soledad** (36641 Fort Romie Road, Soledad, 1-831 678 2586). The Moorish **San Carlos Borromeo de Carmelo** is at 3080 Rio Road in Carmel (1-831 624 3600) and the last in the Central Coast region is **San Juan Bautista** (Second and Mariposa Streets, San Juan Bautista, 1-831 623 4234).

For more information on the missions, check out www.california.missions.com.

island's history. A herd of buffalo (aka American bison) were brought to the island in 1924 for the filming of Zane Grey's *The Vanishing American*. They are now the main attraction in Catalina nature preserve, which occupies 86 per cent of the island.

There are also pigs, goats, deer, native ground squirrels, quail, foxes, rattlesnakes, the reinstated bald eagle, swordfish, tuna and numerous other species of flora and fauna. You can examine cacti, succulents and local plants at the **Wrigley Memorial & Botanical Garden** (1400 Avalon Canyon Road, 1-310 510 2288), check out fine Arabian horses at **El Rancho Escondido** (1-310 510 0772) and kayak, snorkel, jetski, scuba-dive or fish at **Two Harbors**, a resort village on the north-west of the island, and at some of the other beaches.

The island's climate and topography are similar to that of LA – but the air is much fresher. Shopping, restaurants, hotels and other tourist attractions are mainly to be found in the picture-postcard, white stucco, bayside town of **Avalon**. With a population of about 3,000 (jumping in summer to 6,000 in the week and 10,000 at weekends), it is the largest residential community on Catalina.

You can tour the island on foot, by sightseeing bus or rented bicycle, horse or golf cart. To hike, you need a permit, available free from the **Catalina Island Conservancy** (125 Claressa Avenue, Avalon; 1-310 510 2595/ www.catalinaconservancy.org).

Getting there

By boat

Catalina Express (1-310 519 1212) runs a regular, one-hour, $40 round-trip service from Long Beach and San Pedro Harbors. Catalina Flyer (1-949 673 5245) is a 75-minute catamaran service from Newport Beach; $38 round trip.

By air

Island Express (1-310 510 2525) offers a 15-minute helicopter flight from San Pedro and Long Beach Harbors ($125.40 round trip). Super Shuttle (1-310 782 6600/www.supershuttle.com) and Best Shuttle (1-310 670 7080/www.xpressshuttle.com) run airport shuttle services from all LA airports to Catalina Island sea and air terminals.

Where to stay

You can camp on Catalina, though you must get a permit and book in advance. For the Hermit Gulch Campground in Avalon Canyon, call 1-310 510 8368; for other sites, contact Catalina Island Camping (1-310 510 0303/www.scico.com). For hotels, contact the Chamber of Commerce.

Tourist information

Catalina Island Chamber of Commerce & Visitors Bureau

1 Green Pleasure Pier, Avalon, Catalina Island, CA 90704 (1-310 510 1520/www.catalina.com). **Open** 8am-5pm Mon-Sat; 9am-3pm Sun.

San Diego

Now hear this: San Diego has come into its own. California's second-largest city (and America's sixth-largest), this once sleepy, provincial town best known for its naval presence, year-round temperate weather and zoo, has blossomed into a cheerful centre of high-tech businesses, bio-medicine and tourism. It has some world-class theatres and museums, and is a natural for visitors with children. And although you'd scarcely guess it while in this overwhelmingly Anglo city, it's a mere 25 miles (40 kilometres) from the Mexican border town of Tijuana, steps from the US yet worlds apart (*see page 276*).

The heart of the city is downtown, combining a sparkling high-rise business district and a commercial core that locals actually use. Start at **Horton Plaza**, a complex of shops and restaurants on six lavishly decorated open-air levels: this vibrant, highly coloured collage of buildings conceived by Los Angeles architect Jon Jerde is a forerunner of his more recent themed mall, CityWalk at Universal Studios (*see page 108*).

Surrounding Horton Plaza is the historic, 16-block **Gaslamp Quarter**, a 19th-century district that had fallen on hard times and has been transformed into San Diego's hottest place for shopping and eating. **Croce's** restaurant and jazz bar (Fifth Avenue at F Street, 1-619 233 4355/www.croces.com), is the place that started it all in the mid-1980s (founded by Ingrid Croce, widow of singer Jim). Along Downtown's waterfront, facing south, are the massive **San Diego Convention Center** and the maritime-themed **Seaport Village**, a tourist trap, to be sure, but a pleasant one.

You could also spend your entire visit in San Diego in **Balboa Park**. Like New York's Central Park, it occupies a prominent piece of real estate at the centre of town, but its open spaces and sweeping vistas are accompanied by some outstanding cultural institutions. At the **Visitor Centre** (1549 El Prado, 1-619 239 0512/www.balboapark.org), you can find out what's going on at the 16 nearby park museums. These include the **San Diego Museum of Art** (1-619 232 7931/www.sdmart. com), **Reuben H Fleet Science Center** (1875 El Prado, 1-619 238 1233/www.rhfleet.org),

Trips Out of Town

San Diego's **Hotel del Coronado**.

the **Museum of Photographic Arts**
(1-619 238 7559/www.mopa.org), which
reopened in March 2000 after a four-fold
expansion, and the **Mingei International
Museum** (1-619 239 0003/www.mingei.org)
with eye-catching folk crafts from around
the globe. Hint: buy a Passport to Balboa Park
at the visitor centre – $25 versus $70 for
tickets purchased separately – or visit on the
third Tuesday of each month, when entry to
most museums is free.

Also in the park is the **Old Globe Theatre**
(1363 Old Globe Way, 1-619 231 1941, tickets
1-619 239 2255/www.oldglobe.org), one of
America's great regional theatres, modelled
on the Shakespearean Globe and predating
London's own Globe Theatre by several
decades. Perhaps owing to its British roots,
the Old Globe is where another great British
entertainment – the stage version of *The Full
Monty* – made its American debut.

Balboa Park is also home to the world-
famous **San Diego Zoo** (their words and ours),
located at 2920 Zoo Drive (1-619 234 3153/
www.sandiegozoo.org). Cruise Gorilla Tropics,

Tiger River and the Polar Bear Plunge, and let's
not forget the pandas. You can see animals in a
more natural habitat in the zoo's Wild Animal
Park, 30 miles (48 kilometres) north of town
(get a pass and directions from the zoo).

More animals, this time of the trick-playing,
marine variety, can be seen at **Sea World
Adventure Park** (1720 South Shores Drive,
1-619 226 3901/www.seaworld.com). Sea World
is part of **Mission Bay Park**, a vast aquatic
resort with glistening beaches and all the usual
watersports. It is also home to **Belmont Park**,
which features the Plunge – reportedly the
largest indoor swimming pool in Southern
California – and the Giant Dipper, a restored
1925 wooden rollercoaster.

You can get a sense of the might of the
US Navy driving across the two-mile long
Coronado Bay Bridge (which swoops over the
harbour from downtown to the 'island' of
Coronado – actually a peninsula): it yields a
dramatic view of the cruisers, aircraft carriers,
destroyers and other vessels anchored in the
bay. Most of Coronado is military, but it's also
home to a comfortable downtown and the 1888
Victorian Hotel del Coronado (1500 Orange
Avenue, San Diego, CA 92118, reservations
1-800 468 3533/www.hoteldel.com) – scene of
shenanigans in *Some Like It Hot* and one of the
US's largest all-wood structures. Tours of the
building, renovated in 2000, are offered daily,
and the dining room and poolside are great
places for a dramatic, stylish meal.

Spas & hot springs

You won't have fully experienced the laid-
back Californian lifestyle until you have
soaked in a hot tub. Wallow in warm waters
or hot mud, in natural surroundings, enclosed
spas or redwood tubs; the sophistication
scale extends in both directions.

Greater Los Angeles

Glen Ivy Hot Springs Spa

25000 Glen Ivy Road, at Temescal Canyon
Road, Corona, CA 92883-5103 (1-909 277
3529/1-800 454 8772/www.glenivy.com).
I-15 south, exit Temescal Canyon Road west.
Open Aug-Oct 9.30am-6pm daily. Nov-Mar
9.30am-5pm daily. **Rates** $24 Mon-Thur;
$29 Fri-Sun. **Credit** AmEx, MC, V.
Otherwise known as Club Mud, this Riverside
County spa is a fave with those who want to
wallow in the ooze but on a budget. For a

mere $24 (weekdays), you can enjoy day-long
use of the mineral sulphur baths (don't worry,
the rotten egg smell soon disappears) and a
good lathering in soft red clay, as well as a
steam room. No under-16s.

Between LA & San Francisco

Sycamore Mineral Springs Resort

1215 Avila Beach Drive, at US 101, San Luis
Obispo, CA 93405 (1-800 234 5831/1-805
595 7302/www.sycamoresprings.com).
US 101, exit Avila Beach Drive west. **Open**
Spa 24hrs daily. Restaurants 7.30am-9pm
Mon-Thur, Sun; 7.30am-10pm Fri, Sat.
Rates Massages $45-$90; rooms $127-
$300. **Credit** AmEx, Disc, MC, V.
It's worth driving the 200 miles (320km) to
San Luis Obispo (make it a stop on your
coastal trip to San Francisco) to soak in a

San Diego offers a dose of its pre-Anglo history in the form of **Point Loma**, west of downtown, and **Mission Valley** and **Old Town** to the north. From the Cabrillo National Monument at the southern tip of Point Loma, you get a panoramic view of San Diego as seen by Portuguese explorer Juan Rodriguez Cabrillo when he 'discovered' the West Coast in 1542. The Mission San Diego de Alcalla that founded San Diego moved from here in 1774, but some of the remaining Spanish settlement is preserved in the six-block **Old Town State Historic Park**; the subsequent transition to US rule is recorded in the adjacent Heritage Park.

Get a taste of 1950s and '60s San Diego in the Fifth Avenue business district of the **Hillcrest** neighbourhood, where there's a bevy of vintage cafés and shops. Hillcrest is also the centre of San Diego's active gay scene. About a 15-minute drive north of Hillcrest, the **La Jolla** district (say 'La Hoy-a') is Beverly Hills by the sea. Society matrons rub elbows with surfers along busy Prospect Street and the Cliff Walk, and dramatic coastline vistas give way to some excellent dining. Adjacent to La Jolla is the **Torrey Pines** district, home to the **Stephen Birch Aquarium** (2300 Expedition Way, 1-858 534 3474/www.aquarium.ucsd.edu).

Nature lovers of a different kind can check out **Black's Beach**, one of California's best-loved clothing-optional locations, down the cliffs beneath Torrey Pines Glider Port. Those with small children may prefer **Legoland**

California (1 Lego Drive, 1-760 918 5346/www.legolandca.com) in Carlsbad. Entire rides are made out of the blocks, kids love the stage shows and there's a model Lego factory on site.

Last but not least, San Diego is a mecca for sports. Specialities include great surfing at **Ocean Beach**, sports fishing at **Point Loma**, hang-gliding at the **Torrey Pines Glider Port** (2800 Torrey Pines Scenic Drive, 1-858 452 9858/www.flytorrey.com) and golf at several well-known courses; call ticket broker M&M Tee Times (1-858 456 8366/www.torreypines. com) or try your luck at a public course.

You can watch horse racing at the **Del Mar Thoroughbred Club** (Jimmy Durante Boulevard, 1-858 755 1141) in the emerging Del Mar suburb in north San Diego, polo at the **San Diego Polo Club** (14555 El Camino Real, Rancho Santa Fe, 1-858 481 9217) and pro baseball and football at **Qualcomm Stadium** (9449 Friars Road, 1-619 280 2121).

Although, as is usual in Southern California, the car is the most efficient way to take it all in, you can also get around the metropolitan area on San Diego Transit Corporation buses or use the San Diego Trolley between downtown and Old Town to the north or Tijuana to the south.

Where to eat

As you might expect, there are myriad dining options in San Diego. **Chive** (558 Fourth Avenue, 1-619 232 4483) in the Gaslamp

secluded open-air redwood tub under a tree. Twenty such spas dot the sycamore- and oak-lined hillside at this 100-year-old resort; you can also stay overnight.

Desert

Deep Creek Hot Springs
Hesperia, CA.
Getting there: *Take the Hesperia exit off the I-15 between LA and Barstow, then follow Hesperia's Main Street until it veers right, when you make a smooth left turn. Continue until you come to a left turn with a 15mph sign; take that, then the first right. Follow signs for Bowen's Ranch, where the parking attendant will give you a hiking map.*
There is no phone and no good road to Deep Creek; instead, you will have a 45-minute drive over increasingly bad roads until you park your car at Bowen's Ranch, and then a steep 2.2-mile (4km) hike. But the soak is that much sweeter when you finally arrive at

the river at the base of the dramatic San Bernardino Forest Canyon, with its 'clothing optional' hot spring pools at different levels on the rock-face. The best time to visit is in the week (weekends can be hectic) in late spring after the rains, when the river is high and the weather mild.

Two Bunch Palms
67425 Two Bunch Palms Trail, Desert Hot Springs, CA 92240 (1-800 472 4334/1-760 329 8791/www.twobunchpalms.com). I-10, exit Palm Drive north. **Open** 8am-10pm Mon-Thur, Sat, Sun; 8am-11pm Fri. Closed 2wks Aug. **Rates** *Relaxation services* $50-$200; *rooms* $175-$625. **Credit** AmEx, MC, V.
The soak of choice for celebs; this is where Tim Robbins took a mud-bath in *The Player*. He could have chosen a herbal or salt steam, or a lounge in the steamy spa pool. If you can't afford the rates, many of the other (cheaper) hotels in the area have jacuzzis or pools that use natural mineral waters.

Trips Out of Town

Quarter is the restaurant of the moment, while the newest nightspot is **Sing Sing** (655 Fourth Street, 1-619 231 6700), where duelling pianos blast rock 'n' roll favourites, and you can get house-brewed beers and pub food.

In Hillcrest, try the retro 1950s-themed **Corvette Diner Bar & Grill** (3946 Fifth Avenue, 1-619 542 1001), where you can view a high-sheen 1954 Corvette and eat some classic diner food. Other noteworthy places are **Kemo Sabe** (3958 Fifth Avenue, 1-619 220 6802), where the Southwest meets South-east Asian, and **Parallel 33** (741 West Washington Street, 1-619 260 0033), combining foods from around the globe at that latitude – Portugal, Spain, Lebanon, India, China, Japan and, of course, San Diego.

On Prospect Street in La Jolla, **George's on the Cove** (No.1250, 1-858 454 4244) sets standards year after year for California cuisine; **Roppongi** (No.875, 1-858 551 5252) for pan-Asian favourites served like tapas; or, for elegant Italian food in a garden setting, try **Trattoria Acqua** (No.1298, 1-858 454 0709).

In Balboa Park, the **Prado** (1549 El Prado, 1-619 557 9441) in the House of Hospitality building is one of San Diego's most noted new restaurants, serving Latin-inflected American cuisine, and the **Sculpture Garden Café** (1-619 696 1990) in the Museum of Art serves smart salads and sandwiches.

Where to stay

There is a huge choice of accommodation in San Diego; contact the tourist offices or call **San Diego Hotel Reservations** (1-800 728 3227/www.savecash.com).

Getting there

By car

From Downtown LA, take the I-5 south. From West LA, take the I-405 south and then join the I-5. The built-up LA region seems to go on and on – as far as San Clemente. After this you'll be driving through rolling hills and inaccessible shoreline, much of which is taken up by the Camp Pendleton Marine base. Near the San Diego County line, you'll see road signs warning you of people running across the freeway: this area is notorious for illegal immigrants trying to do a runner from boats that have sailed from Mexico (although nobody we know has actually seen this in action).

From LA, it takes about 2hrs with no traffic – not as unusual as you might think.

By air

From LAX on American Eagle (1-800 433 7300/www.aa.com) or Shuttle by United (1-800 241 6522/www.united com). Both cost $146-$400 for a round trip. About 50 mins.

By train

Amtrak (1-800 872 7245/www.amtrak.com) runs about ten trains per day. $46 round trip; about 2hrs 40mins.

By bus

Greyhound (1-800 231 2222/www.greyhound.com) has 31 buses a day. Fare is $22 round trip; 2-3hrs.

Tourist information

Balboa Park Visitors Center

House of Hospitality, 1549 El Prado, San Diego, CA 92101 (1-619 239 0512/www.balboapark.org). **Open** 9am-4pm daily.

San Diego Convention & Visitors Bureau

11 Horton Plaza, San Diego, CA 92101 (1-619 236 1212/www.sandiego.org). **Open** 8.30am-5pm Mon-Sat; closed Sun.

The Transit Store

102 Broadway, San Diego, CA 92101 (1-619 234 1060/www.sdcommute.com). **Open** 8.30am-5.30pm Mon-Fri; noon-4pm Sat, Sun.
Public transport information, plus tokens, passes, timetables, maps and brochures. Alternatively, for bus route information, call 1-619 233 3004; for trolley info, call 1-619 231 8549.

Tijuana

After squeaky-clean San Diego, the Mexican border town of Tijuana smacks you in the face like a strong Margarita. It's loud, it's messy, it's gaudy – and it's great; a first, intoxicating taste of the vibrant yet impoverished land beyond the border. You can stay there without a visa for up to 72 hours, but, particularly for non-US or Canadian citizens, it's important to take a passport in case you're asked for proof of nationality on your return. The main attraction for the day visitor is the tourist-oriented Avenida Revolución, a pulsating strip of vividly decorated discos, bars, restaurants, shops and street vendors selling everything from religious kitsch, leather goods and Mexican pottery to cheap cigarettes and alcohol.

To get there, drive the I-5 or I-805 south from San Diego for 25 miles (40km) to the San Ysidro International Border. Park and walk, bus or taxi the short distance into Tijuana. You could drive in, but the traffic is chaotic, most US rental car agencies do not permit their vehicles to be driven in Mexico, and even if you take your own car you will need to have Mexican insurance (which must be purchased on the US side of the border). Alternatively, take the San Ysidro South Line trolley (1-619 233 3004/www.sdcommute.com) from downtown San Diego. It runs every 15 minutes from 5am to 1am and all night Saturday; $4 round trip.

Directory

Directory

Getting Around

Given the sheer size and sprawl of Los Angeles, it's hardly surprising that Angelenos have a special relationship with the car. Driving is simply the quickest and easiest way to get around the city and, once you get the hang of the freeway system, it can actually be fun.

But, if you don't have access to a car, it doesn't mean that you're condemned to staying within walking distance of your hotel. Los Angeles actually has a very efficient bus system that goes just about everywhere, as well as a number of Metro (subway train) lines that are slowly gaining in popularity as they extend across the city. Because of the distances involved, if you're using public transport to get around, be prepared to plan ahead and always allow plenty of time for your journey.

To & from LAX

Los Angeles International Airport (LAX)

1-310 646 5252/www.lawa.org.
LAX is situated on the Westside, practically on the sea, and has eight terminals; flights from Europe usually arrive at the Tom Bradley International Terminal. A touch-screen booth in the terminal provides free printouts on transport from the airport; the same information (for LAX and a host of other US airports) can be found on www.quickaid.com.

By shuttle

A fleet of shuttles flits between the airport and every neighbourhood in LA, 24 hours a day. Most will drop you at your hotel; fares start at $15. Pick them up immediately outside the arrival terminals: dispatchers will advise you on which one to take.

If you're flying out of LAX, various companies will pick you up and take you there. Book 24 hours in advance. Try the following: **Airport Express Shuttle** (1-310 645 8181/1-800 311 5466/www.superairport shuttle.com); **Golden West Express** (1-800 917 5666/www. goldenwestexpress.com); **Shuttle 2000** (1-800 977 7872) and **Super Shuttle** (1-323 775 6600/1-310 782 6600/www.supershuttle.com).

By taxi

Taxis can be found immediately outside the arrival terminals. If you're staying on the Westside, a taxi ride from LAX will cost around $20 plus tip. If you're heading to Hollywood or beyond, it'll be at least $40 plus tip. There's a flat rate of $24 between LAX and Downtown.

By bus

There's a free shuttle from LAX to the nearby MTA bus terminal at Vicksburg Avenue and 96th Street. From there, buses go all over the city. If you're arriving at night, it's safer to hop on a shuttle rather a bus.

To & from Burbank

Burbank-Glendale-Pasadena Airport

1-818 840 8847/www.bur.com.
If you're flying from a US airport, you may fly into Burbank rather than LAX. It's served by shuttles and taxis like LAX and several car hire agencies have offices there. A free shuttle will take you to the MTA bus stop at Hollywood Way and Thornton Avenue in Burbank.

Airlines

Major international airlines

Air New Zealand 1-800 262 1234/www.airnewzealand.com.
American Airlines 1-800 433 7300/www.im.aa.com.
British Airways 1-800 247 9297/www.british-airways.com.
Continental Airlines domestic 1-800 525 0280/international 1-800 231 0856/www.continental.com.
Delta Air Lines 1-800 221 1212/www.delta-air.com.
Lufthansa 1-800 645 3880/www.lufthansa.com.
Northwest Airlines domestic 1-800 225 2525/international 1-800 447 4747/www.nwa.com.
SwissAir 1-800 221 4750/www.swissair.com.
TWA domestic 1-800 221 2000/international 1-800 892 4141/www.twa.com.

United Airlines 1-800 241 6522/www.ual.com.
US Air 1-800 428 4322/www.usair.com.
Virgin Atlantic Airways 1-800 862 8621/www.fly.virgin.com/usa.

Airlines flying to Burbank

American and **United** (*see above*) also fly to Burbank.
Alaska 1-800 426 0333/www.alaska-air.com.
America West 1-800 235 9292/www.americawest.com.
SkyWest 1-800 453 9417/www.skywest.com.
Southwest 1-800 435 9792/www.iflyswa.com.

Public transport

LA's public transport system is run by the **Metropolitan Transportation Authority** (MTA). Its telephone information operators will plan your journey for you, including connections, if you tell them where you are and where you want to go, as well as giving information on bus and Metro subway timetables, fares and passes. Expect to wait on hold for a while, though. You can get the same information on its website – **www.mta.net**. For a copy of the MTA's *Self-Guided Tours*, write to Metro, 425 Main Street, LA, CA 90013-1393.

MTA information lines 1-800 266 6883/1-213 626 4455.
MTA information centres
515 S Flower Street, at Fifth Street, Downtown. Metro Seventh Street/Metro Center/bus 60, 434, 436, 466/I-110 north, exit Sixth Street east. **Open** 7.30am-3.30pm Mon-Fri; closed Sat, Sun. **Map** p309 B3.
6249 Hollywood Boulevard, at Vine Street, Hollywood. Metro Hollywood & Vine/bus 180, 181, 212, 217/Us 101, exit Hollywood Boulevard west. **Open** 10am-6pm Mon-Fri; closed Sat, Sun. **Map** p307 B1.

Buses

The main mode of public transport in Los Angeles are the more than 2,000 **MTA** buses, their white with orange and red trim paintwork often covered

Directory

in garish advertising (not to mention graffiti). They cover over 200 routes throughout the LA area.

The **DASH** (Downtown Area Short Hop) A, B, C, D and E are five express shuttles (running every 15-45 minutes) that service Downtown and most of its important sites and landmarks, including the Garment District, Convention Center, MOCA, City Hall, USC, Union Station, Little Tokyo, Exposition Park and the Performing Arts Center. Fares are only 25¢. DASH also provides express shuttle services to other areas, including Beverly Hills, Venice, Hollywood, West Hollywood, Pacific Palisades, Crenshaw and Van Nuys/Studio City.

Municipal bus services include **Santa Monica City Bus Lines** aka 'The Big Blue Bus' (50¢ fare), which serves Santa Monica, Malibu and Venice; **West Hollywood Cityline** (50¢ fare), a shuttle service covering 18 locations in West Hollywood; **Commuter Express** ($1.10-$2.70), essentially a commuter bus service from Downtown LA to, among other destinations, Glendale, Encino, Westwood, Brentwood, Culver City and the San Fernando Valley; **Foothill Transit** (90¢-$2.75), primarily serving the San Gabriel and Pomona Valleys; and **Culver CityBus** (60¢ fare), covering Culver City, Venice, Mar Vista, LAX and Westwood/UCLA.

On busy lines, buses run every 5-10 minutes during peak hours; at night, it's every half hour or so. On the main crosstown routes, the service is 24-hour, but there's only one bus an hour after 11pm. The buses stick to their schedules, more or less. Buses also provide an insight into a different side of LA – people only take the bus if they haven't got a car; consequently, they're mainly used by the poor, the old and recent immigrants. They are safe, however.

Commuter Express 1-800 266 6883.
Culver CityBus 1-310 253 6500/www.ci.culver-city.ca.us.
DASH 1-213 580 5444/www.ladottransit.com.
Foothill Transit 1-626 967 3147/www.foothilltransit.com.
Santa Monica City Bus Lines 1-310 451 5444/www.bigbluebus. com.
West Hollywood City Line 1-800 447 2189.

Fares & bus stops

One trip on an MTA bus costs $1.35; children under five travel free. You'll need the exact fare and the machines on the buses take notes. If you plan to change buses, ask the driver for a transfer (25¢), a ticket that you can use on a subsequent journey that day.

The MTA bus stop sign is a big orange 'M' on a white rectangle. In Santa Monica, it's a blue triangle on a light pole marked 'Big Blue Bus'. If you're going to use the buses a lot, you can buy tokens from local stores and supermarkets. A bag of ten costs $9 and it's one token per journey. Or you can get a monthly pass for $49. You can use the same tokens on the Metro system.

Outside LA

For long-distance buses, head to the main Greyhound terminal; there's no booking, so it's first come, first served for seats. It's in a distinctly dodgy neighbourhood, but the terminal itself is safe.

Greyhound Terminal 1716 E Seventh Street, between S Alameda & Decatur Streets, Downtown (1-800 231 2222/1-213 629 8400/www.greyhound.com). Bus 60, 362/I-10, exit Alameda Street north. **Open** 24hrs daily.

Trains

The concept of a **Metro** subway line is a new one for LA and public awareness of the three lines – Red, Blue and Green – has only recently begun to come around to this foreign (read: 'New York') concept. As a result, the trains are rarely crowded, but then they only cover certain areas of the city. The MTA is opening new stations as fast as they can be built, so by the time you read this there will probably have been a couple of additions to the network. One trip costs $1.35 and transfers (between lines and between buses and trains) are available. Trains run 5am to 11pm daily.

Metro Red Line

A genuine underground subway, this is the newest line (it opened in 1993) – and probably the most useful for visitors. It starts at Union Station in Downtown and runs through to Wilshire Boulevard and Western Avenue, then north to Hollywood (with three stops along Hollywood Boulevard), Universal City and North Hollywood.

Metro Blue Line

Starting at the Red Line station at Seventh Street and Figueroa Street in Downtown, the Blue Line heads south, above ground, through South Central, before ending up in Long Beach. The view along the way offers a glimpse of a part of LA not normally seen by visitors.

Metro Green Line

This overground route links the area around LAX (there is no station at

the airport) with South Central and then Norwalk to the east. It's unlikely you'll need to use this particular route.

Outside LA

Union Station (800 N Alameda Street, Downtown, 1-213 683 6987, www.wgn.net/~elson/larail) is the place to go for any train heading out of LA. The **Metrolink** (1-213 808 5465) suburban lines cover Orange County, Riverside County and San Bernardino County. **Amtrak** trains (1-800 872 7245, www.amtrak.com), to destinations in California and all over the US, all depart from here.

Taxis & limos

Because of LA's size, taxis are not a cheap way of getting around, but they do take credit cards. The basic fee is $1.90 and then $1.60 per additional mile. You can't hail them, although there are taxi ranks in certain areas. Bars, restaurants and supermarkets will often call cabs for you. Companies include the **Yellow Cab Co** (1-800 200 6693/www.yellowcab.com); **Independent Taxi Co** (1-800 521 8294); **Checker Cab Co** (1-800 300 5007/www.checkercab.com). All three are 24 hour.

The limo is the quintessential LA form of transport; you'll see more limos here than just about anywhere else in the world. The cost of hiring one starts at around $40 an hour and the driver will expect a decent tip. Companies include **Gold Coach Limo** (1-800 546 6232), the **Ultimate Limousine** (1-800 710 1498/www.palmspringslimos.com) and **A1-West Coast Limousine Service** (1-310 671 8720).

Driving

Driving in LA presents its own unique challenges. When they're not jammed, the five-lane freeways can seem like racetracks, with cars jockeying for position by overtaking on both sides and weaving in and out of lanes. But intimidating as it may initially seem, LA is far less terrifying for drivers than London, Paris or New York. You'll quickly get used to it and, when it's late at night and the freeways are less crowded, driving can be a positive pleasure.

Freeways are referred to by their numbers – the 10, 110, 405 and so on – and often by names as well. The I-10 (I stands for Interstate) west of Downtown, for example, is known as the Santa Monica Freeway (for more explanation of the names and numbers of the major freeways, see *p68* **Street talk**). There is a speed limit of 65mph on the freeways, but

Directory

you'll see many cars going much faster. Don't expect people to indicate when they change lanes. The outside lanes are the fast lanes (though it's perfectly normal to overtake on the inside): it's best to stay in the middle ones until you need to exit.

Freeways often have a car-pool lane, which only cars carrying at least two or three people (depending on the signs) can use. This is not a members-only scheme; if you fit the criterion, you can use the lane (but make sure you get out of it well before your exit).

Any road apart from a freeway is known as a surface street. When you merge on to a freeway from a surface street, it's important to accelerate to freeway speed; similarly, be prepared to brake sharply when exiting. Exits are marked by the name of the surface street you join. Remember that you may be exiting off either side of the freeway.

Always plan your route before you leave: the freeway system does not take you directly from A to B and it moves swiftly, so you must know your freeway entrance and exit and the direction you are going (north, south, east or west) before you start. Otherwise, you can easily find yourself being sucked off at the wrong exit and getting lost in an unknown area.

On the surface streets, driving is much the same as in any US city. You can turn right on a red light if your way is clear, and the speed limit is 35mph, though it's often flouted. At four-way crossings, 'courtesy driving' is expected: cars cross in the order that they arrive at the junction. Note that California law requires all occupants of a car to wear a seatbelt.

Large and potentially dangerous intersections, where you should take special care, include the following:
Sunset Boulevard at La Brea Avenue, Highland Avenue (Hollywood); Crescent Heights Boulevard, Harper Avenue, Gardner Avenue (West Hollywood).
Wilshire Boulevard at Westwood Avenue (Westwood); Santa Monica Boulevard (Beverly Hills).
Santa Monica Boulevard at Avenue of the Stars (Century City); Westwood Avenue (West LA).
Bundy Drive at Pico Boulevard (West LA).
Sepulveda Boulevard at National Avenue (West LA).
In **Downtown LA**, watch out at the intersections of Alvarado and Third Streets; Broadway and Seventh Street; Aliso and Los Angeles Streets; Hill Street and Jefferson Boulevard; Main and Second Streets.

For a cultural overview of LA's unique relationship with the automobile, *see chapter* **Car City**.

American Automobile Association

Automobile Club of Southern California, 2601 S Figueroa Street, at W Adams Boulevard, Downtown, LA, CA 90007 (1-213 741 3686/ www.aaa-calif.com). Bus 81, 442, 444, 445, 446, 447/I-110, exit W Adams Boulevard west. **Open** 9am-5pm Mon-Fri; closed Sat, Sun.
The fabulous Triple A provides excellent maps, guidebooks (with restaurant and accommodation listings) and campsite guides – and it won't cost you a penny if you're a member or belong to an affiliated club, such as the British AA. Many hotels offer discounts to AAA members.

Car rental

To rent a car in the States – almost always an automatic – you'll need a credit card and a driver's licence (British ones are valid). Most companies won't rent to anyone under 25 (or, if they do, will add on a hefty surcharge). There are dozens of car rental companies in LA and it obviously pays to shop around. The national companies, which tend to offer the best deals and the most reliable vehicles, all have free 1-800 numbers (*see below*); many companies require you to book on these rather than at the local office.

Rates seesaw wildly, depending on demand; it can be a good idea to make a reservation weeks in advance. You can put a hold on a car without committing yourself (and if they run out of a car in that class, the hire company will upgrade you – a frequent and pleasurable occurrence). As a rule, you will not be allowed to take a hired car into Mexico.

Insurance

Remember that the price quoted will not include state sales tax or any form of insurance, but also that you may qualify for a discount: AAA members do (as do member of affiliated foreign clubs, such as the AA in Britain), and you can sometimes wangle a corporate deal if you show your business card.

Insurance will almost double your bill, but it is essential – and you are unlikely to be covered by your domestic policy. You will be offered both liability insurance (for damage you cause to other cars and their occupants) and a collision damage waiver (CDW), both around the $9-a-day mark. We recommend that you take out both – even though it will make the insurance as costly as the rental itself. Unlike other states, in California the baseline fee for hiring the car gives you no insurance cover

at all. Bearing all this in mind, it is probably worth considering fly-drive deals, renting via your home travel agent or getting quotes from a local branch of an international company.

If you get towed

The LAPD (Los Angeles Police Department) suggests you keep the rental lease agreement with you at all times in case your car gets towed away or stolen (most people stick it in the glove compartment – bad idea). If you do get towed, call the nearest police precinct to find out which impound lot the car has ended up in (there are ten in the LA area). Precinct phone numbers are in the front of the phone book in the 'City Government' listings. To reclaim your car, you'll need your rental papers, your passport or driving licence (with picture ID) and a wad of cash to pay for the parking ticket, the cost of towing ($70) and a day's storage (usually $12). You'll also need to know the licence plate (registration) number – if you don't have the rental agreement to refer to, you should find it on the car keys.

Car rental companies

Alamo 1-800 327 9633/ www.goalamo.com.
Avis 1-800 331 1212/www.avis.com.
Budget 1-800 527 0700/ www.budget.com.
Dollar 1-800 421 6878/ www.dollarcar.com.
Enterprise 1-800 325 8007/ www.enterprise.com.
Hertz 1-800 654 3131/ www.hertz.com.
National Car Rental 1-800 328 4567/www.nationalcar.com.
Thrifty Car Rental 1-800 367 2277/www.thrifty.com.
Rent-A-Wreck 1-800 535 1391/ www.rent-a-wreck.com.

Highway information

To find out about local traffic conditions, call the toll-free **CalTrans information hotline** (1-800 427 7623). For distances, traffic incidents and weather conditions, go to www.dot.ca.gov/onroad.htm. Radio station KNX (1070 AM) has traffic reports every six minutes, although these are suspended when a sporting event is being broadcast. KFWB (980 AM) also gives traffic reports every ten minutes, 24 hours a day, seven days a week.

Parking

Los Angeles is a city of drivers, which means parking in popular areas can be frustrating and sometimes downright impossible. If you see numerous spaces in busy areas, beware: parking restrictions vary enormously from area to area and street to street, and the signs detailing them are far from straightforward. Remember that you must park in the same direction that the traffic is going. Don't block driveways or fire hydrants and pay particular attention to kerb markings: if they're red, don't park there or you could get towed. Then go and look at all the signs on your side of the block – they will tell you the local parking laws. Most streets have street-cleaning days when parking is illegal, while many allow permit parking only after 6pm and at weekends.

All parking tickets accrued while in a rented vehicle are your responsibility. And don't think the car hire company will never track you down once you're back home. They always do. Even worse, fines double if not paid within 30 days. Fortunately, parking meters and free or cheap car parks are plentiful. Most parking meters take quarters (25¢), dimes (10¢) and nickels (5¢). And, of course, you can often use valet parking: you'll need to tip the valet (usually $1-$2) but it's much cheaper than paying a parking fine.

If you do get nabbed (and it can happen to anybody) there's a quick way to pay if you have a credit card; just call the LA parking information line on 1-800 464 1333, which lets users pay their tickets over the phone 24 hours a day, seven days a week. Just enter your violation and Visa or Mastercard number using the phone keypad and the voice-activated services will do the rest.

Roadside service

There are around 5,000 yellow public call boxes on the sides of all the major freeways and some roads in LA County. Spaced every quarter of a mile along the freeway, the yellow boxes are a free service to the public; drivers can use them to summon emergency roadside assistance. Special keypads allow the hard of hearing to access the line and service offers multilingual operators to way-out-of towners.

Members of the **American Automobile Association** (*see p280*) can call its emergency roadside service on 1-800 222 4357. There is also a service called **Freeway Service Patrol (FSP)**, which sends out roving tow trucks during the heavy rush hour periods (6-10am, 3-7pm Mon-Fri), with an all-day and weekend service to Downtown LA (6am-7pm daily). The FSP will change your flat tyre, jump-start your car, refuel your radiator, put a gallon of fuel in your petrol tank and tow you to designated 'drop' locations. The service is also, mercifully, free. More information can be found on its website: www.chp.net/fsp.

Motorbike rental

If you want to cruise the streets on a Harley, then try **Eagle Rider Motorcycle Rental**, located a couple of miles south of LAX (11860 S La Cienega Boulevard, between Imperial Highway & El Segundo Boulevard, 1-800 501 8687/1-310 536 6777/www.eaglerider.com). They're open 9am to 5pm daily, and you need to be over 21 and have a credit card and motorbike licence.

Cycling

You can cycle the bike paths that head down the coast through Santa Monica and Venice, and mountain bike in Griffith Park and Topanga Canyon, but otherwise the volume of traffic and distances involved make cycling difficult in LA. For more information on bike paths and rentals, *see p247*.

On foot

Perversely, certain sections of LA are best covered on foot. In particular, Downtown, central Hollywood, parts of West Hollywood, and the Santa Monica and Venice beachfronts are best explored by walking. Jaywalking – crossing the street anywhere except at a designated pedestrian crossing – can get you a $100 ticket. Seriously.

Resources A-Z

Attitude & attire

The people you will come across in LA will be perfectly, almost surreally, polite, chatty even (unless they're in their cars, of course, where they suffer from the usual pumped-up motormania). Be polite back and communication is unlikely to be a problem. However, it is not how you drive or talk, but how you look, and you definitely don't want to look like a tourist if you can help it, which means no fanny packs (bumbags), sandals with socks, nothing with the word 'California' on it.

Angelenos tend to dress with a deceptive, and usually expensive, casualness: for men, an open-necked, button-down shirt (Armani), blue jeans (French), tennis shoes (imported from Spain), sunglasses ($500 and up). Women have it a bit better (or worse, depending on your perspective): almost without exception they dress better than the men. If you want to dress to impress, remember that beige, cream, black, taupe, olive, grey and pale peach are considered the 'power' colours, whereas Hawaiian shirts or any sign of gold or white will peg you as a tourist as quickly as a camera around your neck or those black socks with sandals on your feet.

Business

In general, doing business in Los Angeles is, in some form or another, related to the film, entertainment, and multimedia industry: the city's schedule has been somewhat dictated by the need of the 'industry' to start shooting as soon as it is light and finish when the light fades. Partly because of this, many Angelenos start and finish work early and, because everyone has to drive, few drink at lunch or dinner (and don't believe the popular myth that West Coasters are lazier than East Coasters).

Don't worry if your business meeting is postponed several times before you actually get to the table; this is normal. The common LA affliction of 'flaking' (making and then rescheduling appointments) occurs in business as well as socially; it's nothing personal. Once you finally get to meet, the bargaining is as ruthless as anywhere else.

Because LA is so vast, you will probably need a car, a good street map and an advance plan to get to that business meeting on time. A mobile (cell) phone helps, too; no serious business person in this town is without one. And don't be afraid to sell your wares: Americans love the sound of success, and the louder and longer you can trumpet yours, the better. Don't be shy about celebrity name-dropping – if you have those kind of contacts, that is.

And don't be ashamed to talk about money. You may not want to show all your proverbial cards at the beginning of your meeting, but anything left unspoken, especially money, will only leave you stiffed later. As California is a sue-happy state, make sure you always get everything in writing.

Directory

Information centres

Los Angeles Area Chamber of Commerce

350 S Bixel Street, LA, CA 90017 (1-213 580 7500/fax 1-213 580 7511/www.lachamber.org). **Open** 8.30am-5pm Mon-Fri; closed Sat, Sun. Provides a wide range of information and referral services for the business community.

Couriers

DHL Worldwide Express

1-800 225 5345/www.dhlworld wide.com. **Open** usually 8am-8pm Mon-Fri; closed Sat, Sun. **Credit** AmEx, Disc, MC, V.
Air courier service with overnight delivery in the US. Pick-up at your location or a local DHL office; call for details. Like most courier services, there is no pick-up service after about 4pm, depending on office location.

Express Connection

1-310 447 8000/www.express connection.com. **Open** 24hrs daily. **Credit** AmEx, Disc, MC, V.
One of the fastest and most reliable courier services, Express will phone to tell you when your package was delivered. It can deliver anywhere in the US and has a 24-hour pick-up service. There are branches throughout LA.

Federal Express

1-800 463 3339/www.fedex.com. **Open** 9am-6pm Mon-Sat; closed Sun. **Credit** AmEx, DC, Disc, MC, V.
One of the largest couriers, with drop-off locations all over the city and pick-up available. Worldwide.

UPS

1-800 742 5877/www.ups.com. **Open** 24hrs daily. **Credit** air courier service only AmEx, MC, V.
No drop-off facilities, but pick-up and delivery (in those famous brown vans) is guaranteed. Worldwide.

Office services

For other copy shops, consult the *Yellow Pages*.

Kinko's

7630 Sunset Boulevard, at Stanley Avenue, Hollywood (1-213 845 4501/ www.kinkos.com). Bus 2, 3, 429/ I-10, exit Fairfax Avenue north. **Open** 24hrs daily. **Credit** AmEx, Disc, MC, V. **Map** p306 C1.
Kinko's light, bright and efficient copy houses offer everything you need from faxing and computing

to photocopying and even video-conferencing. Computers have Internet access and AOL email. **Branches**: throughout the city; ring 1-800 254 6567 for details.

Consulates

For problems with passports and other emergencies, call your consulate office. Only the countries listed below have offices in Los Angeles; nationals of other countries should call their consulate in Washington (to find the number, call directory assistance for Washington on 1-202 555 1212).

Australia 1-310 229 4800.
Canada 1-213 346 2700.
France 1-310 235 3200.
Germany 1-323 930 2703.
Italy 1-310 820 0622.
The Netherlands 1-310 268 1598.
New Zealand 1-310 207 1605.
Republic of Ireland (in San Francisco) 1-415 392 4214.
Spain 1-323 938 0158.
United Kingdom 1-310 477 3322/ 24hr emergency number 1-213 856 3755.

Consumer advice

Department of Consumer Affairs

Hotline 1-800 344 9940/deaf callers 1-916 322 1700/www.dca.ca.gov.
Investigates complaints and gives information/referrals for more than 42 state agencies on what actions and rights are available to consumers.

Better Business Bureau of the Southland

1-909 825 7280/fax 1-909 825 6246/ www.bbbsouthland.org.
Good for filing complaints against businesses. Also provides info on reliable businesses in your area.

Disabled

Since 1982, California's strict state building codes have ensured easy and equal disabled access to all city facilities, businesses, parking lots, restaurants, hotels and other public places. Consequently, newer facilities will be more accommodating than older ones, which, in many cases, have been retrofitted to comply with the barest requirements of the codes. To locate areas with handicapped facilities or access, look for the blue and white symbol of a wheelchair.

The MTA has special reduced fares and specific 'lift' buses with fixed times and schedules. For more

public transport information, phone its **Disabled Riders Information** line on 1-800 621 7828.

Dial-A-Ride

1-800 431 7882.
Refers mobility-impaired people and senior citizens to door-to-door transportation services.

Mayor's Office for Handicapped People

1-213 485 6334.
Information, resources and employment referral. Also has a copy of the Junior League's now-defunct 'Around Town with Ease' booklet: if you ask, staff will photocopy sections and send them to you.

Society for the Advancement of Travel for the Handicapped

1-212 447 7284/fax 1-212 725 8253.
Offers advice and referrals for disabled travellers planning trips to all parts of the US.

Electricity

Rather than the standard 220-240V, 50-cycle AC used in Europe, the US uses a 110-120V, 60-cycle AC voltage. Except for dual-voltage, flat-pin plug shavers, you will need to run any appliances you bring with you via an adaptor, available at airport shops.

Health & medical

It is rumoured that if you have no medical insurance, some Los Angeles hospitals – emergency rooms, in particular – may turn you away. This is, in fact, illegal: ERs are allowed to turn you away only if your injury is not considered an emergency, though they will do all they can to make you pay up. Taking out full medical cover is still imperative, ideally with a large and reputable company that will pay upfront rather than reimburse you later. Treatment for a broken finger, for example, in the tourist-inhabited parts of Los Angeles might set you back $5,000, a broken leg $25,000. A visit to an emergency room to treat an allergic reaction may cost as much as $1,000.

If your medical problem is not an emergency and you do not have health insurance, try the LA Free Clinic, but don't expect an immediate appointment.

For complementary and alternative medicine, *see p196*.

LA Free Clinic

8405 Beverly Boulevard, at Orlando Avenue, West Hollywood (1-323 653 1990/www.lafreeclinic.org). Bus 14/

I-10, exit La Cienega Boulevard north. **Open** 9am-7.45pm Mon-Thur; 9am-4.45pm Fri; closed Sat, Sun. **Map** p306 B2. Free medical and dental care. Call first to book an appointment.

Abortion & contraception

Family Planning Associates Medical Group

12304 Santa Monica Boulevard, between Bundy Drive & Centinela Avenue, West LA (1-310 820 8084). Bus 4, Santa Monica 1, 10, 14/ I-405, exit Santa Monica Boulevard west. **Open** 8am-5pm Mon-Fri; 8am-2pm Sat; closed Sun. **Branch**: 6000 W San Vincente Boulevard, at Fairfax Avenue & Olympic Boulevard, West Hollywood (1-213 937 1390).

AIDS & HIV

AIDS Clinic for Women

3860 W Martin Luther King Jr Boulevard, between Marlton Avenue & Buckingham Road, Crenshaw (1-323 295 6571). Bus 105, 608/ I-10, exit Crenshaw Boulevard south. **Open** 8.30am-5pm Mon-Fri; closed Sat, Sun.

AIDS Healthcare Foundation Clinic

West Hollywood Cedars-Sinai Medical Office Towers, 8631 W Third Street, suite 740-E, West Hollywood (24hr hotline 1-800 797 1717/1-310 657 9353). Bus 16, 27, 44, 105/I-10, exit Robertson Boulevard north. **Open** 8.30am-5.30pm Mon-Fri; closed Sat, Sun. **Map** p306 A3. HIV/AIDS medical provider offering quality care regardless of the patient's ability to pay. Next to the Beverly Center mall.

AIDS Project Los Angeles

1313 N Vine Street, at Fountain Avenue, Hollywood (1-323 993 1600/ 24hr hotline in English 1-800 922 2437/24-hour multilingual hotline 1-800 922 2438/www.apla.org). Bus 210, 310, 426, DASH Hollywood/ US 101, exit Sunset Boulevard west. **Open** 8am-9pm Mon-Fri; closed Sat, Sun. **Map** p307 B2. An outreach organisation for people with AIDS/HIV.

CDC National STD & AIDS Hotline

1-800 342 2437. **Open** 24hrs daily.

Emergencies

All are open 24 hours daily, except the Child Abuse Hotline.

Police, fire, ambulance
911 *(free from payphones)*.

American Red Cross
1-213 739 5200.

Child Abuse Hotline
1-800 540 4000. **Open** 9am-5pm Mon-Fri.

Coast Guard
1-310 215 2112.
Search and rescue emergencies.

LA County Department of Mental Health
1-800 854 7771.
Information and referral for psychiatric emergencies.

LA Suicide Prevention Hotline
1-213 381 5111.

Poison Information Center
1-800 876 4766.

Jeffrey Goodman Special Care Clinic

1625 Schrader Boulevard, at Hollywood Boulevard, Hollywood (1-323 993 7500). Metro Hollywood-Highland or Hollywood-Vine/bus 163, 180, 181, 212, 217/US 101, exit Cahuenga Boulevard south. **Open** 9am-6pm Mon-Fri; 9.30am-1.30pm Sat; closed Sun. **Map** p307 A1. This Hollywood clinic offers free, anonymous AIDS testing.

Alcohol abuse

Alcoholics Anonymous

1-323 936 4343.
Open 24hrs daily.

Dentists

LA Dental Society

1-213 380 7669/www.ladental society.com. **Open** 8.30am-5pm Mon-Thur; 8.30am-4.30pm Fri; closed Sat, Sun.
Referrals to approved practices.

Western LA Dental Society

1-310 641 5561. **Open** 10am-5pm Mon-Fri; closed Sat, Sun.
A phone referral service providing addresses and phone numbers of dentists who keep emergency hours.

Hospitals

The hospitals listed below all have emergency rooms.

Cedars-Sinai Medical Center

8700 Beverly Boulevard, at George Burns Road, West Hollywood (1-310 423 3277/www.csmc.edu). Bus 14, 16, 27, 83, 40/I-10, exit La Cienega Boulevard north. **Open** 24hrs daily. **Map** p306 A3.
Cedars-Sinai is the hospital of the rich and famous, and may cost you an arm and a leg. It is, however, conveniently located for West Hollywood and Beverly Hills.

Century City Hospital

2080 Century Park E, between Constellation & Olympic Boulevards, Century City (1-310 553 6211/ www.centurycityhospital.com). Bus 28, 328, 573, Commuter Express 534, Culver City 3/I-405, exit Santa Monica Boulevard east. **Open** 24hrs daily. **Map** p305 B3.

Children's Hospital of Los Angeles

4650 W Sunset Boulevard, at Vermont Avenue, Los Feliz (1-323 660 2450/www.chla.org). Bus 2, 3, 204/US 101, exit Vermont Avenue north. **Open** 24hrs daily. **Map** p308 A2.

St John's Health Center

1328 22nd Street, at Santa Monica Boulevard, Santa Monica (1-310 829 5511/www.stjohns.org). Bus 4, Santa Monica 1/I-10, exit 26th Street north. **Open** 24hrs daily. **Map** p304 B2.

St Joseph's Medical Center

501 S Buena Vista Street, at Alameda Avenue, Burbank (1-818 843 5111). Bus 96, 152/Hwy 134, exit Buena Vista Street north. **Open** 24hrs daily.

Rape & assault

LA Commission on Assaults Against Women Rape Hotline

Central LA 1-213 626 3393/ LA County 1-310 392 8381. **Open** 24hrs daily.

Shelter for Victims of Domestic Violence

1-800 548 2722/1-323 268 7564. **Open** 24hrs daily.

24-hour pharmacy

Rite-Aid Drugs

300 N Canon Drive, at Brighton Way, Beverly Hills (1-310 273 7293). Bus 3, 4, 14, 576/I-405, exit Wilshire Boulevard east. **Open** 24hrs daily. **Credit** AmEx, MC, V. **Map** p305 C2. Everything from pet food, beer and stationery to cosmetics, prescriptions and first-aid supplies. **Branches**: throughout the city.

Before you even hit the ground, your flight attendant will give you two forms to fill out: one for immigration and one for Customs. When you land, expect the Customs/immigration process to take about an hour. Customs officials are a charmless bunch, so smiling a lot and looking cute won't get you through any faster. And if they decide you might outstay your tourist visa, they'll ask some fairly personal questions about why, where and with whom you're staying. Don't take offence, just accept your entry permit and move on.

Current US Customs regulations allow foreign visitors to import the following duty-free: 200 cigarettes or 50 cigars (not Cuban, over-18s only), or 2kg of smoking tobacco; one litre of wine or spirits (over-21s only); and up to $100 in gifts ($400 for returning Americans). You can take up to $10,000 in cash, travellers cheques or endorsed bank drafts in or out of the country tax-free, and goods worth up to $1,000 (you pay a flat tax rate of 10% on any excess).

For more information, contact the US Customs Service at Los Angeles International Airport (LAX) on 1-310 215 2414 or go to www.customs.com.

If you already have an account with a global Internet Service Provider (ISP) such as AOL or CompuServe, you can use it in Los Angeles – all you have to do is change the dial-up access number (though you may have to pay a surcharge on top of your current plan). Alternatively, you can set up a temporary account with a reliable nationwide or local ISP, such as Earthlink. If you're travelling without a computer, the best places to log online are the Central Library (*see below*), mainstream office copy shops such as Kinko's (*see p282*) or one of LA's cybercafés (*see chapter* **Coffeehouses**).

AOL *1-800 827 6364/national dial-up number 1-800 716 0023/ www.aol.com.*
To find a list of dial-up access numbers in California from your existing AOL account before you leave for LA, go to the 'Keyword' button and type 'access numbers'. Alternatively, try http://access.web. aol.com/cgi/search.pl. You will have to pay a surcharge of £2.50 per hour online.
CompuServe *1-800 848 8990/ www.compuserve.com.*
To find a list of dial-up access numbers in California, go to www. compuserve.com/content/phone/ phone.asp.
Earthlink *1-800 327 8454/ www.earthlink.net.*
Earthlink is only available in the US, but it provides reliable, unlimited Internet access from over 2,300 local phone numbers nationwide for $19.95 per month. 'EarthLink 800' gets you toll-free access from anywhere within the continental US; call 1-800 395 8425 for details. To find local dial-up numbers, call 1-800 890 5128 and enter the area code you're staying in or go to http://www.earthlink.net/ home/access/numbers.html.

Other recommended local ISPs are:
www.labridge.com
www.lainternet.com/index.htm
www.usinter.net
www.val.net
www.vividnet.com
www.wman.com/index2.shtml
http://home.loop.com

Baggage, trip-cancellation and medical insurance should be taken care of before you leave home. The US is renowned for its superb healthcare facilities; the catch is that the cost will most likely put you back in the hospital. Most medical centres require details of your insurance company and policy number before you get treatment (unless it's an emergency).

LAX has storage lockers, but Union Station doesn't. If you want to store something for more than a week or so, call **Public Storage** on 1-800 447 8673 for your nearest location. The company has storage facilities all over Los Angeles. Minimum charges are for one month.

Los Angeles is a sue-happy city and however frivolous or unlikely you may think it, being sued is common. If you bump into someone's car at 15mph, they may try to sue you for thousands of dollars. So, if in doubt, consult an attorney: there are hundreds listed in the *Yellow Pages*.

If you think you have a claim against someone else, also consult an attorney. Although legal fees are high, most attorneys will work for a percentage of any settlement – usually one-third. If you are arrested and held in custody, call your insurer's emergency number for legal advice. Uninsured Brits can call the UK consulate's 24-hour emergency number (*see p282*).

Central Library

630 W Fifth Street, between Grand Avenue & Flower Street, Downtown (1-213 228 7000/www.lapl.org). Bus 16, 18, 78, 79, 96, Foothill 492, DASH E/I-110 north, exit Sixth Street east. **Open** 10am-8pm Mon-Thur; 10am-6pm Fri, Sat; 1-5pm Sun. **Map** p309 B3.
The most comprehensive library in the city, with excellent facilities and a very knowledgeable reference staff.

LA County Law Library

301 W First Street, at Broadway, Downtown (1-213 629 3531/ http://lalaw.lib.ca.us). Metro Civic Center/bus 4, 96, 420, 424/US 101, exit Broadway south. **Open** 8.30am-10pm Mon-Thur; 8.30am-6pm Fri; 9am-5pm Sat; closed Sun. **Map** p309 B2.

The third largest law library in the US, offering services for law research on any topic you can think of, both national and international.

Southwestern University Law Library

3050 Wilshire Boulevard, between Shatto Place & Westmoreland Drive, Mid Wilshire (1-213 738 5771/ www.swlaw.edu). Metro Wilshire-Vermont/bus 20, 21, 22/I-10 exit Vermont Avenue north. **Open** 8am-midnight Mon-Thur; 8am-9pm Fri; 9am-9pm Sat; 10am-9pm Sun. **Map** p308 A5.

This revitalised art deco structure, which used to be the historic Bullocks Wilshire department store, is a good place to do law research.

Liquor laws

Bars, dance clubs, restaurants, liquor stores and supermarkets that sell liquor can do so between the hours of 6am and 2am. Strip or burlesque clubs are not allowed to serve alcohol at all. The legal age for purchase and consumption of alcoholic beverages is 21. Picture ID, whether a driver's licence (state or foreign) or a passport, is strictly required for all who wish to imbibe. *See also* chapter **Bars**.

Lost property

Los Angeles is not the world's most honest city, but if you really think an honest soul may have handed in your beloved lost property, the best place is the local police department (listed at the front of the phone book under 'City Government').

If you've lost something at LAX airport, first try your airline, then the general lost property number (1-310 417 0440).

Media

Newspapers & magazines

The *Los Angeles Times* (35¢) has been the only major newspaper in town for the better part of the past decade. While certainly extensive (and occasionally excellent) in its coverage of local and worldwide events, this centrist publication's lack of estimable competition manifests itself in sloppy editing and an unforgivably lazy approach to fact-checking. The paper's Sunday Calendar section devotes plenty of space to the arts, with a predictable emphasis on Hollywood films and locally produced TV shows.

The *Wall Street Journal* (75¢) and *New York Times* ($1) are both widely available, but the *Washington Post* ($1.85) can be harder to track down. For British newspapers and magazines, head for the newsstand on Santa Monica's Third Street Promenade, at Arizona Avenue. Myriad foreign-language dailies – including *La Opinion* (25¢), published in LA and the largest Spanish-language newspaper in the country – are also available at newsstands and drop-boxes throughout the city.

To find out what's actually going on in LA at any given moment, the city's free weeklies are your best bet. Most widely read is the *LA Weekly*. While its features can range from the highly readable to the utterly impenetrable, it has wonderfully detailed arts listings. Newer and less influential is the *New Times*, one in a nationwide network of 'alternative' weeklies published by the New Times Corporation based in Phoenix, Arizona.

Of the many tabloids, the *Star* ($1.29) is probably the best bet, with the vastly improved *National Enquirer* ($1.29) running a close second. Both offer plenty of juicy gossip and fairly reliable reportage.

Though the venerable monthly magazine *Los Angeles* ($2.95) has tried to fashion itself as the West Coast's answer to *Vanity Fair* and the *New Yorker* rolled into one, it's definitely lighter and shallower than either. More interesting but harder to find is *Glue* ($3), a bi-monthly mag published out of Silver Lake.

The *Hollywood Reporter* and *Daily Variety* (both dailies, costing $1.50) are Hollywood's twin bibles, providing the latest scoops on industry manoeuvrings and projects in production. *Billboard* (weekly, $5.50) is the music biz's equivalent.

The best newsstand in the city is **World Book & News** (1652 N Cahuenga Boulevard, at Hollywood Boulevard, Hollywood, 1-323 465 4352). Nearly a full city block in length, it matches its overwhelming selection of international periodicals with an almost-as-impressive array of paperback books, which range from travel guides to the entire published oeuvre of influential ghetto novelist Iceberg Slim.

Television

If you've seen American television before, LA television isn't exactly going to blow your mind. One thing that is unique about LA is that it's possible to watch a show being made, either as part of a live studio audience (both *Friends* and *Third Rock from the Sun* are shot here) or at a location shoot. For info on both,

see p217. For comprehensive information about what's on the box, pick up the ever-popular *TV Guide* ($1.19), which has a handy table telling you which channel each cable station can be found on.

The networks

Like most US cities, Los Angeles has affiliates of the three major networks: CBS (KCBS, channel 2), NBC (KNBC, channel 4) and ABC (KABC, channel 7). The big three continue to be given a serious run for their money by Fox TV (KTTV, channel 11) the Warner Brothers network (KTLA, channel 5), and UPN (KCOP, channel 13). KWHY (channel 22), KMEX (channel 34) and KVEA (channel 52) serve the city's ever-increasing Latino population, while KSCI (channel 18) and KDOC (channel 56) offer a mix of Japanese, Korean, Chinese and Armenian programming, interspersed with infomercials. For local TV at its absolute worst, check out *Good Day LA* (KTTV, 7am Mon-Fri), a witless news and chat show featuring anchor bimbo Jillian Barberie.

Cable & public TV

Although cable TV requires a monthly fee, many Angelenos subscribe in order to improve both reception and choice of programmes. At present, there are more than 60 cable channels available, including ESPN and Fox Sports West (sports); CNN (24-hour international news); the Discovery Channel (nature and anthropological documentaries); the self-explanatory Food Network; and QVC and the Home Shopping Channel, both of which allow you to buy ugly jewellery and useless appliances from the privacy of your own home. Public access cable features anything and everything from Christian Science puppet shows to instruction in Kundalini yoga. The subscription-only HBO has made an impressive comeback in the past few years, thanks to the massive success of shows such as *The Sopranos* and *Sex and the City*.

The unfortunate thing is that, due to a lack of regulation, different cable companies provide different services to different neighbourhoods. Some networks, such as E! Entertainment Television (celebrity news and pop-culture documentaries) and Comedy Central (24-hour comedy) are limited to half-day programming or are unavailable in various parts of the city, and each cable company has a different monthly schedule.

KCET (channel 28) is LA's local Public Broadcasting Service affiliate, providing all the ponderous, self-important programming we've come to expect from public TV, though it also imports some of the best from the BBC.

Directory

Radio

It's hard to believe that a city that's been such a major player in the history of American music would be such a hotbed of unimaginative commercial radio programming, but, unfortunately, that's the case with LA radio. A great many Angelenos seem to listen to the radio solely for traffic reports, which you can hear at regular intervals on almost every station during morning and evening rush hours. That said, radio has a very important place in LA life, if only because most people drive rather than take public transport.

Talk radio

LA's AM band has become almost entirely the home of talk radio. KFI (640 AM) boasts two of the heaviest hitters in this department: ultra-conservative political pundit Rush Limbaugh (9am-noon Mon-Fri) and ultra-controversial pop psychologist Dr Laura Schlessinger (noon-3pm Mon-Fri). Lovers of the truly weird should check out Phil Hendrie's show (4-7pm Mon-Fri). More moderate is Larry Elder (3-7pm Mon-Fri) on KABC (790 AM), the self-described 'Sage of South Central'. The more liberal, pipe-smoking contingent has the gracious Warren Olney, whose 'Which Way LA?' (1-2 pm Mon-Fri, re-broadcast 7-8pm) on KCRW (89.9 FM) is probably the best issues-forum radio programme in California, though Larry Mantle's 'Air Talk' (9-11am, KPCC, 89.3 FM) comes close. KCRW's 'All Things Considered' (4-6.30pm Mon-Fri) is informative and listenable.

If you really want to wallow in the outrage and perversity of American 'shock' radio, Howard Stern (6-10am Mon-Fri, KLSX, 97.1 FM) is your man. Mark & Brian (5-10am Mon-Fri, 6-10am Sat, KLOS, 95.5 FM) and Rick Dees (5-10am Mon-Fri, KIIS, 102.7 FM) do their best to bring the yuks, but they're still several rungs below Stern on the hilarity scale.

For straight news, KNX (1070 AM), KFWB (980 AM), KNNS (1260 AM) and KNNZ (540 AM) all offer 24-hour, up-to-the-minute coverage.

Music

LA's two major dance and hip hop stations are the Beat (KKBT, 100.3 FM and Power 106 (KPWR, 105.9 FM. Power 106 plays harder, more hip hop oriented material, while the Beat steers more towards smoother, 'urban contemporary' sounds. Both stations have extremely popular morning hosts – comedian Steve Harvey mans the microphone for the Beat (6-10am Mon-Fri), while the 400lb Big Boy (whose corpulent form can be spied on hilarious billboards

throughout LA) handles the 6-10am weekday shift for Power 106.

KCMG (92.3 FM) serves up plenty of 'old-school' R&B from the 1960s and '70s. Don't miss soul icon Smokey Robinson's show (8-10pm Mon-Thur), which features an enchanting array of slow-jams for your dancing and romancing pleasure. Once the most influential alternative rock station in America, KROQ (106.7 FM) has seemed a little lost of late. KLOS (95.5 FM) mixes grunge hits of the early 1990s with older hard rockers, while Arrow 93 (KCBS, 93.1 FM) serves up classic rock and pop from the late 1960s and early '70s. Hal Lifson's 'Radio A Go-Go!' (7-9pm Sat, 10pm-1am Sun, KRLA, 1110 AM), plays a terrific array of 1960s hits.

'Jazz on the Latin Side', hosted by Jose Rizo (7-11pm, KLON, 88.1 FM) will have you sambaing in your seat. Tune in to KLON again on Sundays for John Clayton's 'Inside America's Music' (7-10pm), which always features an intriguing mix of jazz classics, rarities and new releases. Classical music fans should tune into KUSC (91.5 FM), KCSN (88.5 FM) or KKGO (105.1 FM).

Spanish & foreign language radio

The biggest change in LA radio over the past few years has been the proliferation of Spanish language talk and music stations. At least three popular English language stations have switched over since 1999, while established outlets such as Radio Amor (KLVE, 107.5 FM) continue to rack up massive ratings. Unfortunately, Spanish musical programming in LA is just about as uninspired as the stuff the gringo stations serve up. For a broader array of Latino sounds, check out 'Travel Tips for Aztlan' (10pm-midnight Sat) on KPFK (90.7 FM), when host Mark Torres spins the best in Latin ska and Rock En Español. On Saturdays and Sundays from 6am to 6pm, Alma del Barrio (KXLU, 88.9 FM) serves up a veritable salsa marathon.

While no other nationality can claim even close to the market share that the Spanish language stations currently boast, it's probably just a matter of time until Asian stations become more common. For now, there are two Vietnamese stations – KALI (106.3 FM) and KVNR (1480 AM) – two Korean – KYPA (1230 AM) and KFOX (1650 AM) – and three Chinese – KAZN (1300 AM), KWRM (1370 AM) and KMNY (1600 AM). There's also KIRM (670 AM), better known as Radio Iran, which broadcasts Persian music and news around the clock.

Public & college radio

Loyola Marymount college's KXLU (88.9 FM) provides noisy and nice indie sounds, although its weak signal can make it difficult to find. USC's KUSC (91.5 FM) features heavy doses of classical and talk, while public stations KCRW (89.9 FM), KPFK (90.7 FM) and KPCC (89.3 FM) deliver the usual eclectic mix of talk shows, news, world music, alt rock, jazz and classical.

KCRW, supported by a dedicated subscriber base, is the standout public radio station in town, with excellent news programmes and original (and often quite influential) music shows. English host Nic Harcourt presents new music and insightful interviews on 'Morning Becomes Eclectic' (9am-noon Mon-Fri), while Jason Bentley's 'Metropolis' (8-10pm Wed-Fri) and Garth Trinidad's 'Chocolate City' (10pm-midnight Wed-Fri) serve up the best in modern electronica and funk, respectively.

Money

As they say in Los Angeles: 'Cash talks; bullshit walks'…

The US dollar ($) is divisible into 100 cents (¢). Coin denominations run from the copper penny (1¢, with a relief of Abraham Lincoln); the silver nickel (5¢, Thomas Jefferson); dime (10¢, Franklin Delano Roosevelt); quarter (25¢, George Washington); and the less common half-dollar (50¢, John F Kennedy). Notes ('greenbacks'), all the same size, come in $1 (George Washington); $5 (Abraham Lincoln); $10 (Alexander Hamilton); $20 (Andrew Jackson); $50 (Ulysses S Grant); and $100 (Benjamin Franklin) denominations. Should you find yourself with the Susan B Anthony silver $1 coin, or the Thomas Jefferson $2 bill, don't spend them; they are collectors' items.

The design of US bills has recently been altered in order to discourage counterfeiting; the old design is still in circulation and is still valid. The new ones still have pictures of the above-mentioned American potentates (but now, apparently, on steroids). Be warned that because of widespread counterfeiting, especially of $50 and $100 bills, some small shops may not accept them; they also tend not to carry much change in fear of robbery.

ATMs

Automated Teller Machines are as numerous as cars in LA, found inside and outside banks, in some of the bigger shopping malls and in stores such as 7-Eleven.

There are many different card networks, including Star and Interlink, but the main ones are **Cirrus** (1-800 424 7787 for locations) and **Plus** (1-800 843 7587). Banks worldwide link into these two systems; if you have the appropriate symbol on your cash card you will be able to get money out using your usual PIN, though you might incur a $1.50-$2 surcharge for withdrawal. Most ATMs will also dispense cash advances from MasterCard and Visa and some will also take American Express. There is an interest charge for cash advances on credit or charge cards and sometimes a 'handling' charge, too. The maximum daily withdrawal ranges from $200 to $300.

Try to get to an ATM before the sun goes down, and in somebody else's company, as robbing ATM customers is a popular sport in Los Angeles – though it doesn't happen so very often. Panhandlers will often hang out by them as well, to provide that maximum guilt factor.

Banks

Most major banks can raise cash on a credit card. They also offer competitive currency exchange rates, along with international banking services, including cable transfers, foreign drafts on overseas banks and import/export financing. Banks are usually open 10am to 4.30pm Monday to Thursday; until 6pm on Friday; and from 9am or 10am to 2pm or 3pm on Saturday. They are closed on Sunday.

Bank of America 1-800 944 0404.
Home Savings of America
1-800 933 3000.
Great Western 1-800 492 7587.
Wells Fargo 1-800 869 3557.

Credit cards

Don't even think of coming to LA without at least one major credit card. The two accepted just about everywhere in the US are **MasterCard** (1-800 826 2181/www.mastercard.com) and **Visa** (1-800 336 8472/www.visa.com). **American Express** (1-800 528 4800/www.americanexpress.com) is also a prominent card, although some establishments will not accept it because of the high costs that AmEx charges merchants. Other, less common, cards are **Carte Blanche** (1-800 234 6377/www.citibank.com/dinersus/blanche), **Diner's Club** (1-800 234 6377), **Discover** (1-800 347 2683/www.discovercard.com) and **JCB** (1-800 366 4522). These are more likely to be accepted at higher-end places.

Lost or stolen credit cards

American Express 1-800 992 3404.
Diner's Club 1-800 234 6377.
Discover 1-800 347 2683.
MasterCard/Visa 1-800 556 5678.

Travellers' cheques & bureaux de change

Obtain travellers' cheques – in US dollars and from a well-known company – before your trip. Almost all shops, restaurants and so on will accept them with a passport or other identification, save for the occasional establishment that requires a minimum purchase. If you need to buy travellers' cheques in Los Angeles, many commercial banks sell them for face value plus one to three per cent.

Most currency exchange can be taken care of at LAX, where both **Lenlyn Limited** (open 7.30am-11.45pm daily, 1-310 417 0366) and **Traveler's Exchange** (open 6.30am-11pm daily, 1-310 649 1656) have offices in Terminals 2 and 5 and the Tom Bradley International Terminal. The *Wall Street Journal* and the *LA Times'* business section publish exchange rates daily.

If you need money wired to you, then **American Express MoneyGram** (1-800 926 9400 for locations) or **Western Union** (1-800 325 6000) can receive funds from anywhere in the world, although their high commission (usually around 10%) underscores their 'emergency only' status. The centrally located AmEx offices also offer this facility.

American Express Travel Services

327 N Beverly Drive, between Brighton & Dayton Ways, Beverly Hills (1-310 274 8277/lost & stolen cheques 1-800 221 7282/http://travel.americanexpress.com). Bus 4, 20, 27, DASH Beverly Hills/I-10, exit Robertson Boulevard north. **Open** 10am-6pm Mon-Fri; 10am-5pm Sat; closed Sun. **Map** p305 C2.
Branch: 8493 W Third Street, at La Cienega Boulevard, West Hollywood (1-310 659 1682).

Associated Foreign Exchange

433 N Beverly Drive, between Brighton Way & Little Santa Monica Boulevard, Beverly Hills (1-310 274 7610/www.afex.com). Bus 4, 20, 21, 22, 320/I-10, exit Robertson Boulevard north. **Open** 9am-5pm Mon-Fri; 10am-3pm Sat; closed Sun. **Map** p305 C2.

Thomas Cook Foreign Exchange Service

452 N Bedford Drive, between Brighton Way & Little Santa Monica Boulevard, Beverly Hills (any location 1-800 287 7362/lost & stolen cheques 1-800 223 7373/www.usthomas cook.com). **Open** May-Sept 9am-5pm Mon-Fri; 10am-4pm Sat; closed Sun. *Oct-Apr* 9am-5pm Mon-Fri; closed Sat, Sun. **Map** p305 B2.
Branches: 735 S Figueroa Street, Downtown; 8901 Santa Monica Boulevard, West Hollywood; 401 Wilshire Boulevard, Santa Monica.

Opening times

Although many establishments – such as city, state or government agencies, museums and coffeeshops – open at 8am or 9am, in LA, the magic hour is 10am. Most places open at 10am and close at 5pm. Many shops, boutiques and museums will have one or two days during the week when they are open until 8pm or 9pm; and many stay open on Sunday from noon until 5pm or later.

Postal services

Post offices are usually open 9am to 5pm, but often have last collections at 6pm. Many are open on Saturdays from 9am to 1pm or 2pm. There are often stamp vending machines and scales in the lobby, open out of hours. For general postal information and locations, check the front of any Pacific Bell LA Metropolitan phone book, or dial 1-800 275 8777.

US mailboxes are red, white and blue with the US Mail bald eagle logo printed clearly on the front and side. Pull the handle down and put your post (no packages) in the slot. Pick-up times are listed on the inside of the mailbox slot. Post offices in the central areas of LA include:

Beverly Hills

325 N Maple Drive, at Third Street. Bus 27, 316, 576/I-10, exit Robertson Boulevard north. **Open** 8.30am-5pm Mon-Fri; closed Sat, Sun. **Map** p305 C2.

Brentwood

200 S Barrington Avenue, at Sunset Boulevard. Bus 2, 302, 576/I-405, exit Sunset Boulevard west. **Open** 7.30am-5pm Mon-Fri; 7.30am-2pm Sat; closed Sun.

Santa Monica

1248 Fifth Street, at Arizona Avenue. Bus 4, 304, Santa Monica 1, 10/I-10, exit Fourth-Fifth Street north. **Open** 9am-6pm Mon-Fri; 9am-1pm Sat; closed Sun. **Map** p304 A2.

Directory

West Hollywood

1125 N Fairfax Avenue, at Santa Monica Boulevard. Bus 217, 218/ I-10, exit Fairfax Avenue north. **Open** 8.30am-5pm daily. **Map** p306 B1.

Poste restante

If you need to receive mail but don't know what your address will be, have it sent to: General Delivery, [your name], Los Angeles, CA 90086/9999, USA. You can then pick it up at the main Downtown post office at 760 N Main Street.

Private mail services

Mail Boxes Etc

1-800 789 4623. **Open** 9am-6.30pm Mon-Fri; 10am-5pm Sat; closed Sun. **Credit** AmEx, Disc, MC, V.
One of the numerous mail receiving and forwarding services in the city, with 90 locations in LA. Also offers shipping and business services.

Religion

Whether established religion or cult, if it exists, then it's here. Recruiting can take place in the unlikeliest setting, so beware of eager young things with invitations to 'special guest events': many cults are more interested in your wallet than your spiritual wellbeing.

For more on LA's religious tendencies, *see p16* **Let's get spiritual**.

Places of worship

Aatzei Chaim Synagogue

8018 W Third Street, between Crescent Heights Boulevard & Fairfax Avenue, West Hollywood (1-323 852 9104). Bus 16, 218, 316/ I-10, exit La Cienega Boulevard north. **Map** p306 B3.

All Saints Episcopal Church

504 N Camden Drive, at Santa Monica Boulevard, Beverly Hills (1-310 275 0123). Bus 3, 14, 316, 576/I-10, exit Robertson Boulevard north. **Map** p305 B2.

Beverly Hills Presbyterian Church

505 N Rodeo Drive, at Santa Monica Boulevard, Beverly Hills (1-310 271 5194/www.asec.org). Bus 3, 14, 316, 576/I-10, exit Robertson Boulevard north. **Map** p305 B/C2.

Buddhist Universal Association

2007 Wilshire Boulevard, at S Alvarado Street, Westlake (1-310 484 6500). Metro Westlake-MacArthur Park/bus 20, 21, 22/I-10, Hoover Street north. **Map** p308 B5.

Congregation Beth Israel Synagogue

8056 Beverly Boulevard, at Crescent Heights Boulevard, West Hollywood (1-323 651 4022). Bus 14, 316/ I-10, exit La Cienega Boulevard north. **Map** p306 B2.

First Baptist Church of Hollywood

6682 Selma Avenue, at Las Palmas Avenue, Hollywood (1-323 464 7343). Metro Hollywood-Vine/bus 180, 181, 212, 217/US 101, exit Hollywood Boulevard west. **Map** p307 A1.

First Southern Baptist Church of Hollywood

1528 N Wilton Place, at Sunset Boulevard, Hollywood (1-323 466 9631). Bus 2, 3, 302/US 101, exit Sunset Boulevard east. **Map** p307 B2.

Hope Lutheran Church of Hollywood

6720 Melrose Avenue, at Mansfield Avenue, Hollywood (1-323 938 9135). Bus 10, 11/I-10, exit La Brea Avenue north. **Map** p307 A2.

Islamic Cultural Centre

434 S Vermont Avenue, between Fourth & Fifth Streets, Mid Wilshire (1-213 382 9200). Metro Wilshire-Vermont/bus 201, 204, 354/I-10, exit Vermont Avenue north.

St Mary of the Angels Anglican Church

4510 Finley Avenue, between Hillhurst Avenue & Rodney Drive, Los Feliz (1-323 660 2700). Bus 26, 180, 181/I-5, exit Los Feliz Boulevard east. **Map** p308 A2.

St Monica's Roman Catholic Church

725 California Avenue, at Lincoln Boulevard, Santa Monica (1-310 393 9287). Bus 20, 720, Santa Monica 2/I-10, exit Lincoln Boulevard north. **Map** p304 B2.

Westwood United Methodist Church

10497 Wilshire Boulevard, at Warner Avenue, Westwood (1-310 474 4511/http://westwoodumc.org). Bus 20, 21, 720/I-405, Wilshire Boulevard east. **Map** p305 A3.

Safety

Unlikely as it may sound, the place that invented the terms 'car-jacking' and 'drive-by shooting' is actually a safer place for visitors than, say, Florida. However, it still makes sense to be cautious: don't fumble with your wallet or a map in public; always plan where you're going; avoid walking alone at night; keep your car doors locked while driving; avoid parking in questionable areas (when in doubt, use valet parking); and always lock your car.

As a pedestrian, walk with brisk confidence and people will most likely stay out of your way. As a motorist, avoid coming off the freeway in unfamiliar areas, never cut anyone off in traffic or yell epithets at other drivers, never drive too slowly or too quickly (65mph/104kph is a good median speed on the freeways), and always take a map with you. If you can afford it, rent a mobile phone.

A few areas that you should be careful about travelling to or through after dark include parts of Silver Lake, Hollywood, Koreatown, Compton, Echo Park, Highland Parks, Downtown and Venice.

Smoking

California has some of the most stringent anti-smoking laws in the world – as of 1 January 1998, it became the first state in the US to ban smoking in all enclosed public areas. This includes not only obvious places such as shops, restaurants, cinemas, theatres, libraries, museums and art galleries, but also waiting areas and ticket lines for trains and cruise ships, airports, bus depots, city buses, elevators, public toilets and bathhouses and also some 35,000 bars and casinos across the state. Most hotels also prohibit smoking, except in designated rooms.

There are few exceptions to this edict: the statute does not apply to casinos on Native American land, establishments that are owner-operated or have no employees, tobacco retailers or establishments 'that are not enclosed by four walls or a ceiling.' Some bars and bartenders also ignore smokers; *see* chapter **Bars** for more information. Those who ignore the ban can be fined up to $100 for a first offence, $200 for a second and $500 for a third.

Study

Los Angeles's numerous colleges and universities offer world-class instruction, both public (that is, state-funded) and private. This distinction is rarely noticeable in the quality of instruction, and only in tuition costs if you're a legal resident of California (residents pay considerably lower fees at public schools than non-residents). However, California's enduring fiscal crisis has left public institutions (such as UCLA) short on facility and equipment upgrades and with a high student-to-instructor ratio.

If you want to study in Los Angeles, expect to pay $10,000 to $25,000 (including tuition and basic living expenses) for a year of full-time study. Financial aid for foreign students – usually in the form of scholarships or 'work-study' (working for the school) – varies among institutions, so investigate the options early with their Financial Aid Officers to learn how to qualify.

FILM SCHOOLS

There's no better place to study the technical, creative, commercial and critical aspects of the movies than Los Angeles. It has the US's first film school, **USC's School of Cinema-TV** (1-213 740 2235), whose generous alumni, among them George Lucas, have helped to keep the equipment state of the art and the teaching supreme. **UCLA's Department of Theater, Film and Television** (1-310 825 5761) also has some of the best directing and producing courses in the country. The **American Film Institute** (2021 North Western Avenue, LA, CA 90027, 1-323 856 7628), the **Art Center College of Design** (*see below*) and the burgeoning graduate programme at **Chapman University's School of Film & Television** (333 North Glassell Avenue, Orange, CA 92866, 1-714 997 6765) are also smart choices for prospective film students.

LA is also well-endowed with libraries and research facilities for the student of film. **UCLA's Archive Research & Study Center** (1-310 206 5388) and **USC's Warner Brothers Archives** (1-213 748 7747) are important resources for film scholars, but a more beautiful facility and holder of many rare, film-related materials is the **Margaret Herrick Library** at the Academy of Motion Picture Arts & Sciences (333 South La Cienega Boulevard, Beverly Hills, 1-310 247 3000).It also has a phone reference service (1-310 247 3020), where operators research the answer to your most vexing movie trivia question.

The **Museum of Television & Radio** (*see chapter* **Museums**) has a large collection of TV shows and news footage on video which you can view. The **Central Library** also holds films and recordings. **Southwestern University** (1-213 738 5771) now has its law library in

an art deco landmark, the former Bullocks Wilshire department store (for both libraries, *see p284*).

Where to study

Art Center College of Design

1700 Lida Street, Pasadena, CA 91103 (1-626 396 2200/admissions 1-626 396 2373/fax 1-626 795 0578/ www.artcenter.edu).
The private and very stylish Art Center focuses on art and commercial and industrial design. It also has a site in La Tour-de-Peilz, Switzerland.

California Institute of Technology

1201 E California Boulevard, Pasadena, CA 91125 (1-626 395 6811/admissions 1-626 395 6341/fax 1-626 683 3026/www.caltech.edu).
This private college (known as CalTech) counts more than 20 Nobel laureates among its alumni and past and present faculty. This is where the local news turns for information on California earthquake activity.

Loyola Marymount University

7101 W 80th Street, LA, CA 90045 (1-310 338 2700/admissions 1-310 338 2750/fax 1-323 338 2797/ http://lmuweb.lmu.edu).
Founded by Jesuits, the private Loyola Marymount is primarily an undergraduate institution but also offers advanced degrees in law, education and business administration. The library holds extensive materials on early LA.

Occidental College

1600 Campus Road, LA, CA 90041 (1-323 259 2500/admissions 1-323 259 2700/fax 1-323 341 4875/ www.oxy.edu).

You'll get a glimpse of 'Oxy' on *Beverly Hills 90210*, whenever those perky TV teens hang out at 'California University'. It is a fine liberal arts college, small (about 1,600 students), private and conservative, with a large number of students from ethnic minorities.

Santa Monica College

1900 Pico Boulevard, Santa Monica, CA 90405 (1-310 450 5150/ admissions 1-310 452 9381/fax 1-310 399 1730/www.smc.edu).
A community college (state-funded and providing students with the first two years of the four-year bachelor's degree), SMC was founded in 1929 and ranks first among 107 California community colleges in the number of transfers to the esteemed University of California system. The college radio station, KCRW, is the leading public station in Southern California.

Southern California Institute of Architecture

5454 Beethoven Street, LA, CA 90066 (1-310 574 1123/admissions 1-310 574 3625/fax 1-310 574 3801/ www.sciarc.edu).
'SCI-Arc' may look like a modest warehouse from the outside, but it has been one of the leading architecture schools in the country since its establishment in 1972. Urban theorist Mike Davis (author of bestsellers *City of Quartz* and *Ecology of Fear*) is among this private school's distinguished faculty. The school also has a terrific public lecture series.

University of California – Los Angeles

405 Hilgard Avenue, LA, CA 90095 (1-310 825 4321/admissions 1-310 825 3101/fax 1-310 206 1206/ www.ucla.com).

Tip talk

Bartender 10%-15% (50¢ minimum)
Chambermaid 50¢-$1 per night
Cloakroom attendant $1 per item
Doorman $1-$2 (more for special services)
Hairdresser/barber 15%-20%
Porter $1-$4 for unloading, $1 per bag (including supermarket bag packers if they help you to your car)
Taxi driver 15%
Valet parking attendant $1-$2
Waiter 15% (20% for superb service, or if the place is very fancy and expensive, or if you're drunk). Some of the snazzier establishments will include the tip in the final tally

Directory

Tourist information

The main tourist bureau for the City of LA has two offices, one in Downtown and one in Hollywood. For local tourist offices, see the relevant sections of **Sightseeing**.

Los Angeles Convention & Visitors Bureau

685 S Figueroa Street, between Seventh Street & Wilshire Boulevard, Downtown (1-213 689 8822/fax 1-213 236 2395/www.lacvb.com). Metro Seventh Street-Metro Center/bus 26, 60, 427, 434, 460, Commuter Express 437, 448, Foothill Transit 495, DASH A/I-110, exit Ninth Street east. **Open** *8am-5pm Mon-Fri; 8.30am-3pm Sat; closed Sun.* **Map** *p309 A3.*
British visitors can also get information by calling the UK arm of the LACVB on 020 7318 9555.

Hollywood Tourist Bureau

The Janes House, 6541 Hollywood Boulevard, at Hudson Avenue, Hollywood (1-213 236 2331/www.lacvb. com). Bus 180, 210, 212/US 101, exit Hollywood Boulevard west. **Open** *9am-5pm Mon-Sat; closed Sun.* **Map** *p307 A1.*
The Janes House, built in 1903, is the last survivor of the Victorian houses that once lined Hollywood Boulevard.

UCLA is a public research university highly regarded for its undergraduate and graduate courses in the liberal and fine arts, as well as the sciences (biology is the most popular major). It has one of the largest library collections in the world and its athletic programme consistently cultivates championship sports teams.

University of Southern California

University Park, LA, CA 90089 (1-213 740 2311/admissions 1-213 740 8899/fax 1-213 740 6364/ www.usc. edu).
USC is the largest private, non-denominational university on the West Coast. Undergrads live amid a huge fraternity 'scene' where sports matter almost more than life itself (OJ Simpson went here). USC's best-known undergraduate fields are in journalism, business, theatre, architecture and communications. Also celebrated is the School of Cinema-TV's film production course.

Telephones

The local *Pacific Bell Yellow Pages' Customer Guide* is a valuable resource guide that gives essential emergency numbers, instructions on how to use public phones and information on call rates. Voicemail is inescapable in LA; note that the 'pound' key is marked # and the 'star' key is marked *.

Dialling & codes

Emergency Dial **911** for police, fire and medical emergency services.
Operator Dial **0**.
International operator Dial **00**.
Directory enquiries: local
For enquiries about numbers within your area code district, dial **411**.
Directory enquiries: national
Dial **1 + area code + 555 1212** (if you don't know the area code, dial the operator).
Toll-free numbers These are prefaced by 1-800, 1-888 or 1-877. For help on these numbers, dial 1-800 555 1212. Many are accessible from the UK, but then are not free of charge.

Area codes

The districts covered by some of the most common codes are:
213 Downtown
310 Santa Monica, Beverly Hills, Culver City, West LA, Inglewood
323 Hollywood, Eagle Rock, parts of Pasadena, parts of West Hollywood
562 Long Beach
626 Glendale, Monterey Park, parts of Pasadena
818 parts of San Fernando Valley
949 Laguna & Newport Beaches

Long-distance codes

702 Las Vegas
714 Orange County
805 Santa Barbara
619 San Diego
415 San Francisco

Making a call

Direct dial calls

If you're calling a number with the same area code as the phone you're calling from, dial the (seven-digit) number without the area code. If you're calling a different area code, dial **1 + three-digit area code + seven-digit number**.

International calls

Dial **011** followed by the country code (UK **44**; New Zealand **64**; Australia **61**; Germany **49**; Japan **81** – see the phone book for others). If you need operator assistance with international calls, dial **00**.

Collect calls

Also known as reverse charge calls; dial **0 + area code + number**.

Public & hotel phones

On a hotel phone, you may have to dial **0** or **9** before dialling the number (hotels put the dialling and billing instructions on the phone). You will also pay a surcharge: ask how much it is before you phone, as quite often using a phonecard, credit card or pay phone will work out cheaper, especially on long-distance or international calls. Smaller hotels and motels often will not allow you to call long-distance unless you call collect or use a credit card.
Public pay phones are plentiful in Los Angeles. Although they vary in appearance, they all work the same way: simply pick up the receiver, listen for a dialling tone and feed it change. Operator and directory calls are free. Local calls cost 35¢, with the cost increasing with the distance (a recorded voice will tell you to feed in more quarters). Make sure you have plenty of change as pay phones only take nickels, dimes and quarters.
It's nigh on impossible to make international calls using cash, but you can use your MasterCard credit card with **AT&T** (1-800 225 5288) or **MCI** (1-800 950 5555). Or buy a phonecard ($4-$50) – which gives you a fixed amount of time anywhere in the US, less time internationally – from large stores such as Rite-Aid, Sav-On and Payless Drug.

Mobile phones

Whereas in Europe mobile (cellular) phones work on the GSM network at either 900 or 1800mHz, the US does not have a standard mobile phone network that covers the whole country – which means that visitors from other parts of the US will have to check with their service provider that they can use their phone in LA. However, LA does offer access to the GMS network at 1900mHz, so European visitors – with 'tri-band' handsets that work in the US – should contact their service provider a few days before they leave to set up international roaming. Also check the price of calls before you go: rates will be hefty and you will probably be charged for receiving as well as making calls. So it might be cheaper to rent a mobile phone while you're in town – try the dealer below, or check the *Yellow Pages* – or even buy one with a prepaid amount of time on it. (If you are taking your mobile to LA, don't forget to pack your charger, and any adaptor you might need.)

Shared Cellular Technology

1-800 933 3836. **Open** 24hrs daily. **Credit** AmEx, DC, Disc, MC, V. Daily, weekly and monthly rentals of mobiles. The phones themselves are free; you pay for the air time ($1.95 per metered minute, including domestic long-distance calls and calls outside your own area code).

Time & dates

California operates on **Pacific Standard Time**, which is eight hours behind Greenwich Mean Time (London), three hours behind Eastern Standard Time (New York), two hours behind Central Time (Chicago) and one hour behind Mountain Time (Denver). Clocks go forward by an hour on the last Sunday in April, and back again on the last Sunday in October.

In the US, dates are written in the order of month, day, year; therefore 2.5.01 is the fifth of February 2001, not the second of May.

Toilets/restrooms

There is a dearth of public restrooms in LA. Big shopping malls have them, as do cinema complexes. Santa Monica and Venice beaches have plenty, though they're functional at best, squalid at worst. You may find yourself having to buy a coffee or a drink simply to use a restroom.

Visas

Under the Visa Waiver Scheme, citizens of Japan, the UK and all other West European countries (except Ireland, Portugal, Greece and the Vatican City) do not need a visa for stays of less than 90 days for business or pleasure, as long as they have a passport that is valid for the full 90-day period and a return or onward journey ticket (an open standby ticket is acceptable). Some restrictions apply – for example, if you have previously been turned down for a visa. For British citizens, the US embassy in London provides a reasonably comprehensive (though expensive) recorded message for all general visa enquiries (0898 200290).

Canadians and Mexicans do not need visas, but they may be asked for proof of their citizenship. All other travellers, including those from Australia and New Zealand, must have a visa – contact your nearest US embassy or consulate for more information.

When to go

Climate

With an annual average of 300 clear days, LA offers sun, blue skies, white clouds, palm trees and near-perfect 70°F/21°C to 75°F/24°C weather. It's the smog (which refracts the desert sun) combined with the heat (especially in the San Fernando Valley), often around 102°F/39°C in midsummer, that can be nightmarish.

The best times to visit are between September and November or March and May, since these periods offer mid-range temperatures (between 61°F/16°C and 82°F/28°C) and consistently beautiful days. In June and July, the coastal cities are swathed for most of the day in sea mist, referred to as 'June gloom'. January's cooler temperatures (between 45°F/7°C and 65°F/19°C) and frequent rainfall take the edge off the smog and heat – and the Santa Ana winds in July/August and October/November bring it back with a vengeance.

To check the weather, call **LA Weather Information** (1-213 554 1212). For 24-hour smog and air-quality checks, call **Southcoast Air Quality Management District** (1-800 288 7664). For online weather forecasts, try www.nswla.gov or www.weather. com. For more on LA's idiosyncratic climate patterns, *see chapter* **Geography & Climate**.

Public holidays

New Year's Day (1 Jan); Martin Luther King Jr Day (3rd Mon in Jan); President's Day (3rd Mon in Feb); Memorial Day (last Mon in May); Independence Day (4 July); Labor Day (1st Mon in Sept); Columbus Day (2nd Mon in Oct); Election Day (1st Tue in Nov); Veterans' Day (11 Nov); Thanksgiving Day (4th Thur in Nov); Christmas Day (25 Dec).

Working in LA

Fancy staying on a little longer and getting a job to boost your holiday spending money? Unless you're a US citizen or hold a Green Card or work visa, forget it. Labour laws are incredibly strict, with any company hiring illegal aliens facing hefty fines. A few years ago, it was occasionally possible to work for 'tips only'. Those days are long gone. If you wish to consult an excellent immigration attorney, however, call the **Law Offices of Ralph Ehrenpreis** (1801 Century Park East, suite 450, Century City, LA 90067, 1-310 553 6600).

Average temperatures

Month	Max (°F/°C)	Min (°F/°C)	Rainfall (in/cm)	Dry days
Jan	65/18	46/8	2.9/7.3	25
Feb	66/19	48/9	3.1/7.8	22
Mar	67/19	50/10	2.6/6.6	25
Apr	70/21	52/11	1/2.5	26
May	72/22	55/13	0.2/0.5	29
June	76/24	58/14	0	29
July	81/27	61/16	0	31
Aug	82/28	60/15	0	31
Sept	81/27	58/14	0.5/1.3	29
Oct	76/24	54/12	0.3/0.7	29
Nov	73/23	50/10	2/5	27
Dec	67/19	47/8	2/5	25

Humidity averages 65-77%.
Rainfall source: National Climatic Data Center

Directory

Further Reference

Books

Non-fiction

Richard Alleman: *The Movielover's Guide to Hollywood* Famous sites and tales.

Alternative Press of America: *Inside the LA Riots* Compendium of opinions on the 1992 riots.

Kenneth Anger: *Hollywood Babylon* The dark side of the Tinseltown myth.

Reyner Banham: *Los Angeles: The Architecture of Four Ecologies* Architectural history and paean to life in the fast lanes.

Leon Bing: *Do or Die* History of LA gang culture.

Al Clark: *Raymond Chandler in Hollywood* Biography of the author who made 'noir' and 'LA' synonymous.

Carolyn Cole & Kathy Kobayashi: *Shades of LA: Pictures from Ethnic Family Albums* Beautifully rendered scrapbook of the ethnic family in LA.

Mike Davis: *City of Quartz.* Exhilarating Marxist critique of LA's city 'planning'. *Ecology of Fear* More apocalyptic LA-bashing by Davis, this time focusing on LA's precarious ecology. *Magical Urbanism: Latinos Reinvent the US City* Davies's latest treatise.

David Gebhard & Robert Winter: *Los Angeles – An Architectural Guide* Walking tour through some well-known (and not so well-known) architectural landmarks.

William A Gordon (editor): *The Ultimate Hollywood Tour Guide* A walking/driving tour of Hollywood past.

Steve Harvey: *The Best of Only in LA* Collection of absurdities from popular *LA Times* columnist.

Barney Hoskyns: *Waiting for the Sun: Strange Days, Weird Scenes, and the Sound of LA* The music scene in LA from the 1960s to now.

Norman Klein: *The History of Forgetting* Part factual, part fictional analysis of LA's myth creation by eccentric cultural critic.

Anthony R Lovett & Matt Maranian: *LA Bizarro* Hilarious, off-the-wall guide to 'the obscure, the absurd and the perverse in LA'.

Carey McWilliams: *Southern California: An Island on the Land* A history of LA's sinfulness and its scandals – yeah! *North From Mexico: The Spanish-Speaking People of Los Angeles* Pioneering celebration of the Mexican heritage in the Southwest (written in 1948).

Leonard Michaels, David Reid, Raquel Scher (editors): *West of the West* Superb collection of essays on LA and California by Joan Didion, Amy Tan, Rudyard Kipling, Jack Kerouac, Aldous Huxley, Octavio Paz et al.

David Reid (editor): *Sex, Death & God in LA* Wonderful, navel-gazing essays from writers such as Eve Babitz, Ruben Martinez, Mike Davis and David Thomson.

Brian Roberts & Richard Schwadel: *LA Shortcuts: A Guidebook for Those Who Hate to Wait* Exactly what it sounds like.

Luis J Rodriguez: *Always Running* Autobiography of a Latino gang member.

Richard Romo: *East Los Angeles* A fascinating, scholarly history of the Barrio from the turn of the century to the Depression.

Paul Theroux: *Translating LA* Around the neighbourhoods with the great traveller.

Jeffery Toobin: *The Run of His Life: The People v OJ Simpson* Solid overview of the Trial of the Century.

Alexander Vertikoff & Robin Winter: *Hidden LA* LA's lesser-known landmarks, from the International Banana Museum to the Tower of Wooden Pallets.

Michael Webb: *Architecture + Design LA* Slim but comprehensive guide to the city's architectural highlights, plus a useful list of design stores.

Fiction

T Coraghessan Boyle: *The Tortilla Curtain* Post-Proposition-187 drama about prejudice, immigration and cultural barriers.

Charles Bukowski: *Hollywood* The legendarily drunk poet's musings on making a movie in Tinseltown.

James M Cain: *Double Indemnity, Mildred Pierce* Classic 1930s/'40s noir.

Raymond Chandler: *The Big Sleep, The Long Goodbye* Philip Marlowe in the classic hard-boiled detective novels.

Bret Easton Ellis: *Less Than Zero* 1980s coke-spoon-chic novel about being young and fast on both coasts.

James Ellroy: *The Black Dahlia, The Big Nowhere, LA Confidential, White Jazz* Ellroy's LA Quartet is a masterpiece of contemporary noir, while the black and utterly compelling *My Dark Places* recounts his search for his mother's killer.

John Fante: *Ask the Dust* Depression-era Los Angeles as seen by an Italian emigré.

Mick Farren: *Jim Morrison's Adventures in the Afterlife* Doc Holliday and Aimee Semple McPherson join Jim Morrison in a crazed and very funny romp through heaven and hell.

David Fine (editor): *Los Angeles in Fiction.* Anthology including work by Walter Mosely, Norman Mailer, Thomas Pynchon and James M Cain.

F Scott Fitzgerald: *The Pat Hobby Stories* Short stories about living and working in Hollywood from a Great American Writer who died there.

Dennis Hensley: *Misadventures in the 213* A laugh-out-loud romp through gay Hollywood.

Elmore Leonard: *Get Shorty* Miami loan shark turns movie producer in gutsy thriller.

John Miller (editor): *Los Angeles Stories* Fiction and essays by Henry Miller, F Scott Fitzgerald, Raymond Chandler, et al.

Walter Mosely: *The Easy Rawlins Mystery Series* The heir apparent to Philip Marlowe, Mosely's Easy Rawlins is an African-American PI in post-war LA. Also *Always Outnumbered, Always Outgunned* – from new series, with an ex-con named Socrates Fowler.

Budd Schulberg: *What Makes Sammy Run?* Furious attack on the studio system by one of its employees.

Bruce Wagner: *I'm Losing You*
Biting Hollywood satire.

Nathaniel West: *The Day of the Locust*
Classic, apocalyptic raspberry blown at the movie industry.

Evelyn Waugh: *The Loved One*
Hilarious and accurate satire on the American way of death.

Film

Blade Runner (1982)
The Bradbury Building makes a guest appearance in this classic sci-fi, where cop Harrison Ford hunts mutinous androids in 2019 LA.

Boogie Nights (1997)
The 1970s and '80s San Fernando Valley porn industry uncovered in all its amateurish, sleazy glory.

Boyz N the Hood (1991)
Can a right-thinking father stop his son falling prey to the culture of gang violence in South Central LA?

Bulworth (1998)
Hilarious political satire starring and co-scripted by Warren Beaty, who plays a rapping Democrat senator.

Chinatown (1974)
Roman Polanski's dark portrait of corruption – political and moral – in the boom time of 1940s LA. See also the 1990 sequel, **The Two Jakes**.

City of Angels (1998)
The urban and natural landscapes of LA have never looked more dreamily beautiful than in this remake of Wim Wenders' *Wings of Desire*.

Clueless (1995)
Satirical portrait of LA rich kids and their unarduous lives at Beverly Hills High, with a star performance by Alicia Silverstone.

Colors (1988)
Gritty locations, plausibly inarticulate dialogue and a welcome lack of sensationalism in Dennis Hopper's take on cops versus LA's murderous gangs.

Double Indemnity (1944)
Billy Wilder's sexy, sweaty, classic film noir, adapted from a novel by James M Cain, with dialogue by Raymond Chandler.

Earth Girls are Easy (1988)
The complexities of being a Valley Girl, explored through the eyes of three aliens.

El Norte (1983)
Life as part of the LA underbelly of illegal immigrants searching for a better life in the north.

The End of Violence (1997)
The Griffith Observatory has a starring role in Wim Wenders' love-hate letter to Hollywood.

Falling Down (1992)
Michael Douglas turns vigilante terrorist in a hellish LA of rude drivers, traffic jams, gangs and overpriced corner shops.

Get Shorty (1995)
John Travolta as a Miami loan shark who ends up in Hollywood, from the thriller by Elmore Leonard.

Heat (1995)
Sprawling crime drama, starring Pacino and De Niro, which captures the cold, steely glamour of the modern LA landscape.

Jackie Brown (1997)
Quentin Tarantino's mature adaptation of Elmore Leonard's *Rum Punch*: Pam Grier in sterling form.

LA Confidential (1997)
Film version of James Ellroy's novel: sleaze, violence, police corruption and sex scandals underlying the glamour of 1950s Tinseltown.

LA Story (1991)
Steve Martin's love letter to Los Angeles: a sentimental but sweet and quirky look at the relationships of a group of affluent Angelenos.

The Long Goodbye (1973)
Robert Altman's superb homage to Chandler, with Elliott Gould playing Philip Marlowe as a laid-back shambling slob.

The People vs Larry Flynt (1996)
Engaging portrayal of LA's very own porn king, the idiosyncratic and wheelchair-bound Flynt.

Pulp Fiction (1994)
Tarantino's witty, vivid, violent interweaving of three LA stories. A star-studded cast and bestselling soundtrack.

Short Cuts (1993)
More Altman, this time a epic and sprawling series of interconnected lives, adapted from stories by Raymond Carver.

Strange Days (1995)
Kathryn Bigelow's dystopian view of Los Angeles on the eve of 2000, with a sleazy Ralph Fiennes peddling hard-core VR clips.

Sunset Boulevard (1950)
Gloria Swanson and William Holden star in this classic but still relevant tale of faded fame, creative ambition and ego in the Hollywood system.

Swingers (1996)
An out-of-work actor and his pals trawl the Angeleno hotspots looking for honeys.

Terminator 2: Judgement Day (1991)
Fabulous special effects, Arnie as a caring cyborg and a dramatic motorbike/truck chase along the concrete bed of the LA River.

Music

Beach Boys: 'Surfin' USA'
Bran Van 2000: 'Drinking in LA'
Sheryl Crow: 'All I Wanna Do'
The Doors: 'LA Woman'
Ice T: 'Body Count', 'Colors'
Lightning Hopkins: 'Los Angeles Blues', 'Los Angeles Boogie'
Lyle Lovett: 'LA County'
Randy Newman: 'I Love LA'
NWA: 'Compton's N Tha House', 'Straight Outta Compton'
Tom Petty & the Heartbreakers: 'Century City'
Patti Smith: 'Redondo Beach'
Bob Seeger: 'Hollywood Nights'
Michelle Shocked: 'Come a Long Way'.
Tupac Shakur: 'To Live and Die in LA'
Donna Summer: 'MacArthur Park'
Frank Zappa: 'Valley Girl'

Websites

@LA
www.at-la.com
Boulevards Guide
www.losangeles.com
LA Source
http://members.tripod.com/~rshurtz/la.html
Vast compendia of links, which will connect you to a bewildering variety of LA-related sites. Includes arts and entertainment listings and reviews, weather forecasts, surf conditions, maps, sports listings, restaurant and accommodation reviews.

City of Los Angeles
www.ci.la.ca.us
The City of Los Angeles government home page: everything from 'AIDS Walk Los Angeles' to 'Economic & Demographic Info'.

Digital City Los Angeles
http://losangeles.digitalcity.com
Log on to the 'Citywise' section, where 'Best of LA' contains Angelenos' own choices for their favourite bar, burrito, snogging place, frozen yogurt and much more.

Driving information
www.mapquest.com
www.lainsider.com
www.smartraveler.com
The first is a route planner; the others provide updates on traffic.

Hollywood gossip sites
www.aint-it-cool-news.com
www.mrcranky.com
www.ZENtertainment.com
Three of the hottest websites for insiders' Hollywood scuttlebutt and pre-reviews of upcoming movies.

Surflink
www.surflink.com
Info on the day's surfing conditions, with online video images.

Directory

Index

Advertisers' Index

Please refer to the relevant sections for
addresses/telephone numbers

Place of interest and/or entertainment	
Railway station	
Parks or forests	
College/hospital	
Area name	**WEST LA**
Metro stop	Ⓜ Ⓜ
US interstate	75
US federal	41
State and provincial	64

Maps

LA Overview

RONALD REAGAN FREEWAY

118

FERNANDO

210

NORTHRIDGE

5

405

San
Fernando
Valley

170

Burbank-Glendale-
Pasadena Airport

VAN
NUYS

NORTH
HOLLYWOOD

101

STUDIO
CITY

134

AGOURA
HILLS

VENTURA FREEWAY

101

CALABASAS

27

p 307

p 306

HOLLYWOOD

BEL AIR

p 305

SANTA MONICA BLVD

WEST
HOLLYWOOD

Santa Monica Mountains

BRENTWOOD

PACIFIC
PALISADES

SUNSET BLVD

SAN DIEGO FREEWAY

SANTA MONICA BLVD

BEVERLY
HILLS

CENTURY
CITY

p 304

MALIBU

MALIBU
BEACH

PACIFIC COAST HIGHWAY

1

SANTA
MONICA

SANTA MONICA FREEWAY

WEST LA

10

CRENSHAW

VENICE

LINCOLN BLVD

CULVER
CITY

MARINA
DEL REY

405

INGLEWOOD

PLAYA
DEL REY

P a c i f i c

Los Angeles
International
Airport

EL SEGUNDO

HAWTHORNE

O c e a n

1

MANHATTAN
BEACH

HERMOSA
BEACH

REDONDO
BEACH

107

PALOS VERDES
ESTATES

0   6 miles
0   10 km

© Copyright Time Out Group 2000

RANCHO
PALOS VERDES

Santa Monica & Venice

Beverly Hills

0.75 mile

1 km

© Copyright Time Out Group 2000

A

B

C

Greystone Park

SUNSET BLVD

N DOHENY DR

ELEVADO AVE

BEVERLY HILLS

FOOTHILL RD

Beverly Hills Hotel

BENEDICT CANYON DR

SUNSET BLVD

BEVERLY GLEN BLVD

1

SANTA MONICA BLVD

N BEVERLY BLVD

W 3RD ST

BURTON WAY

Los Angeles Country Club

ELEVADO AVE

N CANON DR

N BEVERLY DR

Museum of TV and Radio

DAYTON WAY

CLIFTON WAY

2

Spadena House

WILSHIRE BLVD

WILSHIRE BLVD

CHARLEVILLE BLVD

S BEVERLY DR

S DOHENY DR

LITTLE SANTA MONICA BLVD

OLYMPIC BLVD

Century City Shopping Center

CENTURY PARK E

Roxbury Park

WHITWORTH ST

3

SANTA MONICA BLVD

AVE OF THE STARS

CENTURY CITY

PICO BLVD

ALCOTT ST

Armand Hammer Museum

CENTURY PARK W

BEVERLY GLEN BLVD

20th Century Fox Studios

Museum of Tolerance

BEVERWIL DR

OVERLAND AVE

OLYMPIC BLVD

Hillcrest Country Club

MOTOR AVE

4

WESTWOOD BLVD

VETERAN AVE

RANCHO PARK

Rancho Park Golf Course

WEST LA

Westside Pavilion

CHEVIOT HILLS

CASTLE HEIGHTS AVE

CATTARAUGUS AVE

PICO BLVD

MANNING AVE

MOTOR AVE

NATIONAL BLVD

SEPULVEDA BLVD

SANTA MONICA FREEWAY

NATIONAL PL

NATIONAL BLVD

5

SAN DIEGO FWY

SAWTELLE BLVD

VENICE BLVD

Time Out Los Angeles Guide **305**

Hollywood & Midtown

LOS FELIZ

Hollywood Bowl

A

B

BEACH-

WOOD DR

C

101 HOLLYWOOD FREEWAY

1

HOLLYWOOD HILLS

FRANKLIN AVE

Mann's Chinese Theater

Visitors Centre

HOLLYWOOD BLVD

YUCCA ST

VISTA DEL MAR

FRANKLIN AVE

N VAN NESS AVE

RUSSELL AVE

HOLLYWOOD BLVD

SELMA AVE

HAWTHORN AVE

SYCAMORE AVE

WHITLEY AVE

HUDSON AVE

SCHRADER BLVD

WILCOX AVE

N CAHUENGA BLVD

YUCCA ST

Pantages Theater

N ARGYLE AVE

ST ANDREWS PL

SUNSET BLVD

WINONA BLVD

SUNSET BLVD

LELAND WAY

HOLLYWOOD

N HIGHLAND AVE

N CHEROKEE AVE

N LAS PALMAS AVE

N MCCADDEN PLACE

FOUNTAIN AVE

LEXINGTON AVE

IVAR AVE

N GOWER ST

N BRONSON AVE

FOUNTAIN AVE

LA MIRADA AVE

N NORMANDIE AVE

N MARIPOSA AVE

N ALEXANDRIA AVE

N KENMORE AVE

2

N LA BREA AVE

ORANGE DR

N SYCAMORE AVE

SANTA MONICA BLVD

MANSFIELD AVE

CITRUS AVE

WILLOUGHBY AVE

WARING AVE

SEWARD ST

N CAHUENGA BLVD

VINE ST

EL CENTRO AVE

Hollywood Forever Cemetery

Paramount Studios

N WILTON PL

N WESTERN AVE

SANTA MONICA BL

KINGSLEY DR

HOBART BLVD

101 HOLLYWOOD FREEWAY

2

FORMOSA AVE

MELROSE AVE

CLINTON ST

N LARCHMONT BLVD

N BEACHWOOD DR

N VAN NESS AVE

MELROSE AVE

N HOBART AVE

N OXFORD AVE

N ARDMORE AVE

3

DAKWOOD AVE

Wilshire Country Club

BEVERLY BLVD

BEVERLY BLVD

W 1ST ST

W 1ST ST

W 2ND ST

W 2ND ST

S ROSSMORE AVE

W 3RD ST

W 3RD ST

4

W 3RD ST

HANCOCK PARK

S HIGHLAND AVE

N ORANGE DR

N SYCAMORE AVE

W 6TH ST

S LUCERNE BLVD

S WINDSOR BLVD

W 4TH ST

W 5TH ST

W 6TH ST

S NORMANDIE AVE

S ALEXANDRIA AVE

S MARIPOSA AVE

WILSHIRE BLVD

WILSHIRE BLVD

S LA BREA AVE

W 9TH ST

Wiltern Theater

HOBART BLVD

S WESTERN AVE

W 8TH ST

IROLO ST

OLYMPIC BLVD

S WILTON PL

W 9TH ST

KOREATOWN

5

W 12TH ST

CRENSHAW BLVD

0   0.75 mile

0   1 km

OLYMPIC BLVD

W 12TH ST

PICO BLVD

VENICE BLVD

PICO BLVD

© Copyright Time Out Group 2000

Time Out Los Angeles Guide **307**

timeout.com

The World's Living Guide

Metro Rail System

SAN FERNANDO
VALLEY

North Hollywood

Universal City

Hollywood / Western

Hollywood / Highland
Hollywood / Vine

Vermont / Sunset

Vermont / Santa Monica / LA City College

Vermont / Beverly

WILSHIRE
CENTER

Wilshire / Vermont

Wilshire / Western

Wilshire / Normandie

Westlake /
MacArthur

Grand

San Pedro

DOWNTOWN
LA

Union Station/
Gateway Transit Center

Civic Center / Tom Bradley

Pershing Square

7th Street / Metro Center

Pico (LA Convention Center / Staples Center)

Washington

Vernon

Slauson

Florence

Firestone

103rd Street / Kenneth Hahn

NORWALK

✈ LAX

Aviation
(Shuttle to LAX)

Mariposa / Nash
El Segundo / Nash
Douglas / Rosecrans
Marine / Redondo

Hawthorne

Crenshaw

Harbor Freeway

Vermont   Avalon

Long Beach

Imperial/
Wilmington/
Rosa Parks

I-605 / I-105

Lakewood

Compton

REDONDO
BEACH

Artesia

Del Amo

Wardlow

Willow

Pacific Coast Highway

1-800-COMMUTE
www.mta.net

Anaheim

Pacific

Transit Mall

5th Street

1st Street

LONG BEACH

N

METRO BLUE LINE
Downtown Los Angeles ◊ Long Beach

METRO GREEN LINE
Norwalk ◊ Redondo Beach

METRO RED LINE
Downtown Los Angeles ◊ San Fernando Valley
Downtown Los Angeles ◊ Wilshire Center

● Transfer Station
○ Station

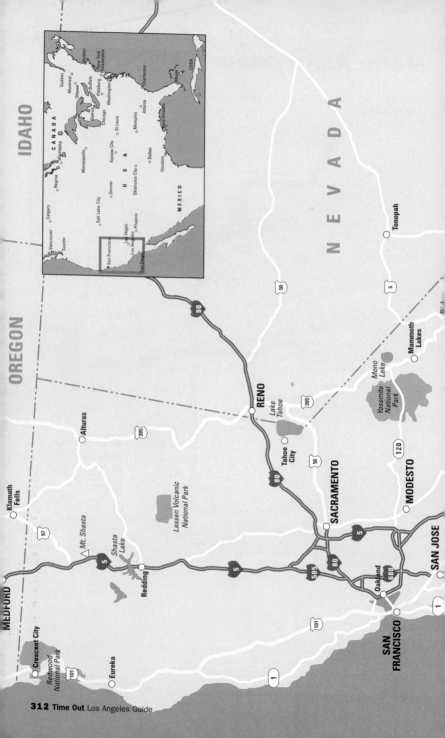

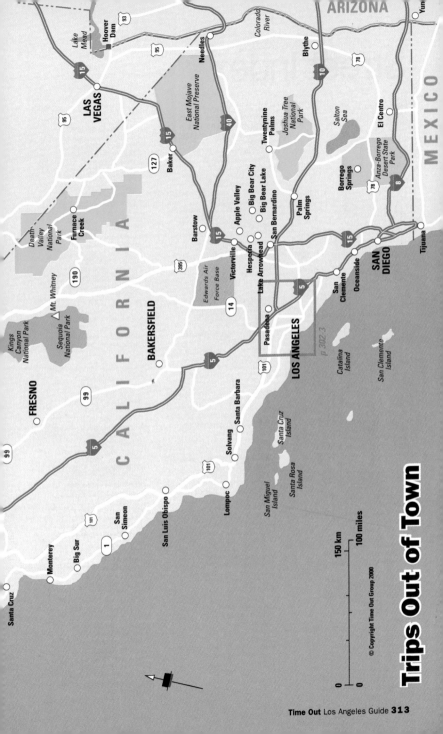

Trips Out of Town

Street Index